A-Z NOTTINGHAMSHIRE

C000280473

CONTENTS

Key to Map Pages	2-5
Large Scale Nottingham City Centre	6-7
Map Pages	8-143
Road Map Pages	
Index to Streets	
Index to Hospitals & Hospices	216

REFERENCE

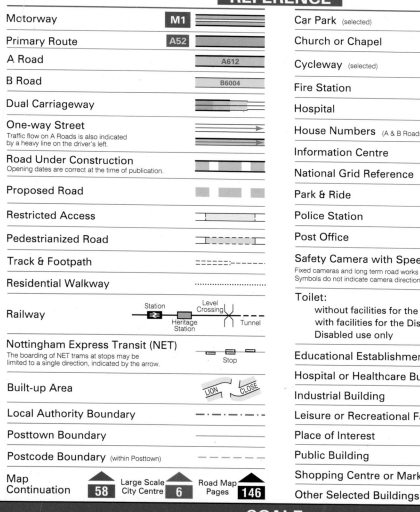

Motorway	**M1**
Primary Route	**A52**
A Road	A612
B Road	B6004
Dual Carriageway	
One-way Street Traffic flow on A Roads is also indicated by a heavy line on the driver's left.	→
Road Under Construction Opening dates are correct at the time of publication.	
Proposed Road	
Restricted Access	
Pedestrianized Road	
Track & Footpath	
Residential Walkway	
Railway Station / Level Crossing / Heritage Station / Tunnel	
Nottingham Express Transit (NET) The boarding of NET trams at stops may be limited to a single direction, indicated by the arrow. Stop	
Built-up Area LION CLOSE	
Local Authority Boundary	— · — · —
Posttown Boundary	
Postcode Boundary (within Posttown)	
Map Continuation 58	Large Scale City Centre **6**	Road Map Pages **146**

Car Park (selected)	P
Church or Chapel	†
Cycleway (selected)	🚲
Fire Station	■
Hospital	H
House Numbers (A & B Roads only)	13 8
Information Centre	i
National Grid Reference	⁴50
Park & Ride	Queen's Drive P+R
Police Station	▲
Post Office	★
Safety Camera with Speed Limit Fixed cameras and long term road works cameras. Symbols do not indicate camera direction.	(30)
Toilet: without facilities for the Disabled	▽
with facilities for the Disabled	▽
Disabled use only	▽
Educational Establishment	▢
Hospital or Healthcare Building	▢
Industrial Building	▢
Leisure or Recreational Facility	▢
Place of Interest	▢
Public Building	▢
Shopping Centre or Market	▢
Other Selected Buildings	▢

SCALE

Map Pages 8-143
1:16,896 3¾ inches (9.53 cm) to 1 mile 5.9cm to 1km

Large Scale City Centre Pages 6-7
1:8,448 7½ inches (19.05 cm) to 1 mile 11.8cm to 1km

0	¼	½ Mile
0   250   500   750   1 km

0	⅛	¼ Mile
0   125   250   375   500m

Copyright of Geographers' A-Z Map Company Limited

Fairfield Road, Borough Green, Sevenoaks, Kent TN15 8PP
Telephone: 01732 781000 (Enquiries & Trade Sales)
01732 783422 (Retail Sales)

www.az.co.uk
Copyright © Geographers' A-Z Map Co. Ltd.
Edition 3 2013

OS Ordnance Survey® This product includes mapping data licensed from Ordnance Survey® with the permission of the Controller of Her Majesty's Stationery Office.

Every possible care has been taken to ensure that, to the best of our knowledge, the information contained in this atlas is accurate at the date of publication. However, we cannot warrant that our work is entirely error free and whilst we would be grateful to learn of any inaccuracies, we do not accept any responsibility for loss or damage resulting from reliance on information contained within this publication.

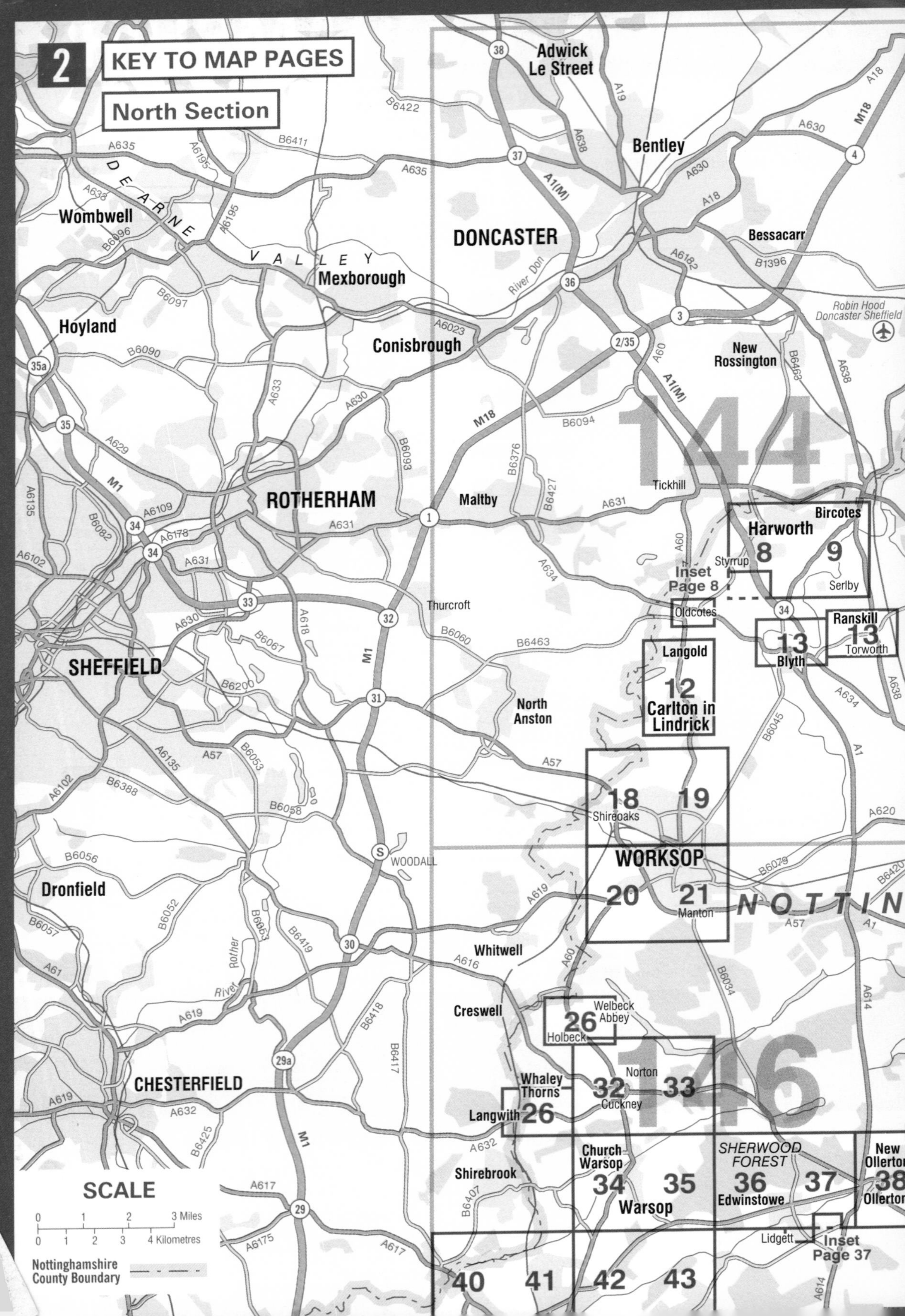
2
KEY TO MAP PAGES
North Section
Adwick Le Street
Bentley
DONCASTER
Bessacarr
Wombwell
DEARNE VALLEY
Mexborough
Hoyland
Conisbrough
New Rossington
Robin Hood Doncaster Sheffield
ROTHERHAM
Maltby
Tickhill
Harworth
Bircotes
Styrrup
Serlby
Inset Page 8
Oldcotes
Thurcroft
Ranskill
Torworth
Blyth
Langold
Carlton in Lindrick
SHEFFIELD
North Anston
Shireoaks
WORKSOP
Manton
NOTTIN
WOODALL
Dronfield
Whitwell
Creswell
Welbeck Abbey
Holbeck
Norton
Cuckney
Whaley Thorns
Langwith
CHESTERFIELD
Shirebrook
Church Warsop
Warsop
SHERWOOD FOREST
Edwinstowe
New Ollerton
Ollerton
Lidgett
Inset Page 37
SCALE
0 1 2 3 Miles
0 1 2 3 4 Kilometres
Nottinghamshire County Boundary
144
146
8
9
12
13
18
19
20
21
26
32
33
34
35
36
37
38
40
41
42
43

SCUNTHORPE

Bottesford

Burringham

M180

Messingham

Scotter

ISLE OF AXHOLME

Epworth

Kirton in Lindsey

Finningley

Haxey

Blyton

10 Misson

Misterton

145

Gainsborough

11

Walkeringham

Everton
10

Gringley
on the Hill **16**

Beckingham
16

Mattersey
thorpe **15**

Mattersey

Clayworth
15

Ingham

Lound
14
Sutton
cum Lound

North
Wheatley
17 South
Wheatley

Hayton
17
Clarborough

Sturton
le Steeple
24
Habblesthorpe

Marton

North Leverton

Sturton
by Stow

Babworth
22 **RETFORD**
23

Ordsall

South
Leverton
25
Treswell

Rampton

G H A M S H I R E

Woodbeck
Inset
Page 25

Church
Laneham
Laneham
29
Dunham-
on-Trent

Saxilby

27
Elkesley

East
Markham
28
Tuxford

147

North
Clifton
30

High
Marnham

South
Clifton

Thorney
31

LINCOLN

Walesby
27

Kirton
Boughton
39
Wellow

Normanton
on-Trent
125
Weston

Harby
31
Wigsley

Egmanton
124
Laxton

Sutton
on Trent
128

Girton
125
Besthorpe

Waddington

KEY TO MAP PAGES

South Section

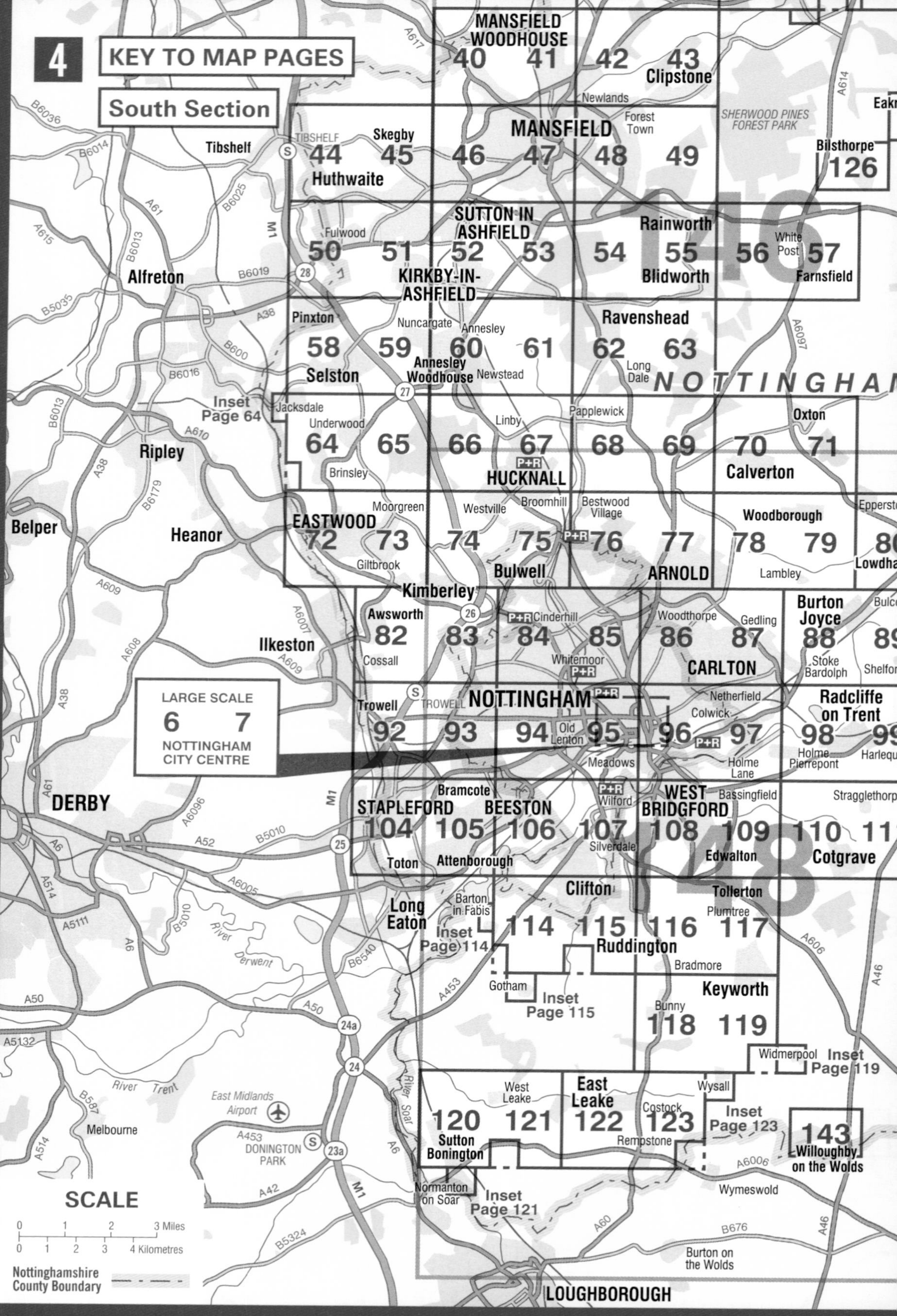

MANSFIELD WOODHOUSE
40 41 42 43
Clipstone
Newlands
MANSFIELD
Forest Town
SHERWOOD PINES FOREST PARK
Tibshelf
TIBSHELF
Skegby
44 45 46 47 48 49
Huthwaite
Bilsthorpe
126
SUTTON IN ASHFIELD
Rainworth
Fulwood
50 51 52 53 54 55 56 57
White Post
KIRKBY-IN-ASHFIELD
Blidworth
Farnsfield
146
Alfreton
Pinxton
Nuncargate
Annesley
Ravenshead
58 59 60 61 62 63
Selston
Annesley Woodhouse
Newstead
Long Dale
NOTTINGHAM
Inset Page 64
Jacksdale
Underwood
Papplewick
Oxton
Linby
Ripley
64 65 66 67 68 69 70 71
P+R
HUCKNALL
Brinsley
Calverton
Moorgreen
Westville
Broomhill
Bestwood Village
Woodborough
Belper
Heanor
EASTWOOD
72 73 74 75 76 77 78 79 80
Giltbrook
Bulwell
ARNOLD
Lambley
Lowdham
Kimberley
Awsworth
Cinderhill
Woodthorpe
Gedling
Burton Joyce
82 83 84 85 86 87 88 89
Ilkeston
Cossall
Whitemoor
CARLTON
Stoke Bardolph
Shelford
LARGE SCALE
6 7
NOTTINGHAM CITY CENTRE
Trowell
TROWELL
NOTTINGHAM
Netherfield
Colwick
Radcliffe on Trent
92 93 94 95 96 97 98 99
Old Lenton
Meadows
Holme Lane
Holme Pierrepont
DERBY
Bramcote
Wilford
WEST BRIDGFORD
Bassingfield
Stragglethorpe
STAPLEFORD
BEESTON
104 105 106 107 108 109 110
Toton
Attenborough
Silverdale
Edwalton
Cotgrave
148
Clifton
Tollerton
Long Eaton
Barton in Fabis
Plumtree
Inset Page 114
114 115 116 117
Ruddington
Bradmore
River Derwent
Gotham
Inset Page 115
Keyworth
Bunny
118 119
Widmerpool
Inset Page 119
River Trent
East Midlands Airport
River Soar
West Leake
East Leake
Wysall
Costock
Inset Page 123
120 121 122 123
143
Melbourne
DONINGTON PARK
Sutton Bonington
Rempstone
Willoughby on the Wolds
Normanton on Soar
Inset Page 121
Wymeswold
Burton on the Wolds
LOUGHBOROUGH
SCALE
0 1 2 3 Miles
0 1 2 3 4 Kilometres
Nottinghamshire County Boundary

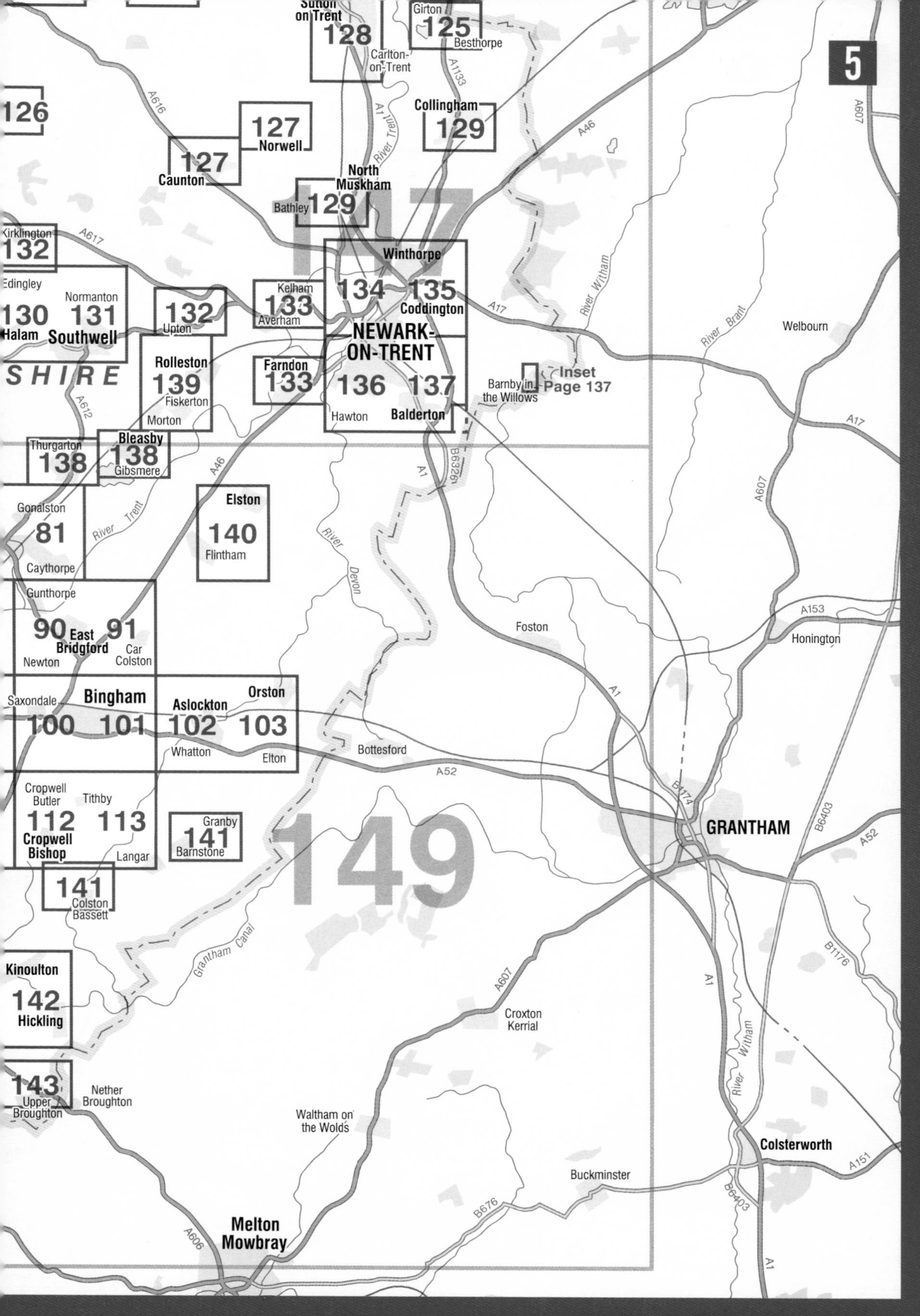

Sutton on Trent
128
Girton
125
Besthorpe
Carlton-on-Trent
A1133
126
A616
127
Norwell
127
Caunton
Collingham
129
A46
North Muskham
Bathley
129
147
Kirklington
132
A617
Winthorpe
Edingley
130
Normanton
131
Halam
Southwell
132
Upton
Kelham
133
Averham
134
135
Coddington
A17
River Witham
River Brant
Welbourn
NEWARK-ON-TRENT
SHIRE
Rolleston
139
Fiskerton
Morton
Farndon
133
136
137
Hawton
Balderton
Barnby in the Willows
Inset Page 137
A612
A17
Thurgarton
138
Bleasby
138
Gibsmere
A46
A1
B6326
A607
Gonalston
81
Caythorpe
River Trent
Elston
140
Flintham
River Devon
Gunthorpe
90
East Bridgford
91
Car Colston
Newton
Foston
A153
Honington
A1
Saxondale
Bingham
100
101
Aslockton
102
Orston
103
Whatton
Elton
Bottesford
A52
B1174
Cropwell Butler
Tithby
112
113
Cropwell Bishop
Langar
Granby
141
Barnstone
149
GRANTHAM
B6403
A52
141
Colston Bassett
B1176
Grantham Canal
Kinoulton
142
Hickling
A607
Croxton Kerrial
A1
River Witham
143
Upper Broughton
Nether Broughton
Waltham on the Wolds
Colsterworth
A151
Buckminster
B6403
B676
Melton Mowbray
A606
A1

6
A
B
C
D
E
1
2
3
4
5
6
7
95
FOREST RECREATION GROUND
Site of Goose Fair
Church Cemetery
Hollygrit School
MANSFIELD ROAD
HUNTINGDON ST.
MOUNT HOOTON ROAD
FOREST ROAD WEST
Mount Hooton
Nottingham High School
High School
Nottingham Girls' High School
Arboretum
ARBORETUM STREET
WAVERLEY ST.
Lovell Ho. (Nott. High Inf. Sch.)
Bowling Green
Derwent Ct.
WATERLOO PROM.
WATERLOO CRESCENT
HARDY STREET
LAWSON STREET
BURNS STREET
GEDLING STREET
TENNYSON ST.
GOODWIN ST.
ALL SAINTS STREET
Comm. Cen.
PRU
AYR STREET
RUSSELL STREET
Royal Victoria Ct.
Provident Works
ALFRETON ROAD
A610
A60
CROMWELL STREET
PORTLAND ROAD
General Cemetery
Runnymede Ct.
Raleigh Sq.
Portland Sq.
Canning Terrace
Canning Circus
ILKESTON ROAD
A609
DERBY ROAD
A6200
DERBY (BRIAN CLOUGH WAY)
WOLLATON STREET
TALBOT STREET
Regent Mews
Nottingham Trent University
Halls of Residence
SHAKESPEARE STREET
The Bonington Gall.
Dryden Cen.
Nottingham Trent University (City Campus)
Trent Uni.
CHAUCER STREET
New Coll. Nott.
Clarendon Chambers
Clarendon Ho.
Rock City
Royal Concert Hall
Royal Cen.
Theatre Royal
Cineworld
Nottingham
Bluecoat House
YMCA
Coun. Offs.
Guildhall
BURTON ST.
A6008
UP. PARLIAMENT ST.
NHS Walk-in Cen.
MAID MARIAN WAY
Albert Hall
Playhouse
RC Cathedral
The Convent
Ropewalk Ct.
NG7
The Park
TATTERSHALL DRIVE
NEWCASTLE DRIVE
Tennis Mews
Tennis Cts.
Bowling Green
Cavendish Ct.
Cavendish Mews
LINCOLN CIRCUS
NEWCASTLE CIRCUS
CLUMBER ROAD
CAVENDISH CRESCENT
Bowling Green
Pelham Cottages
New Lenton
LENTON AVENUE
PERVERIL DRIVE
Kenilworth Ct.
Cavendish Pl.
Park Heights
Hamilton Ct.
Standard Hill
Robin Hood Statue
Castle Museum & Art Gallery
Nottingham Castle
Nottingham Castle Caves
Museum of Nottingham Life
Bandstand Yard
BREWHOUSE YARD
City Point
Chapel Quarter
Gallery
Old Mkt. Sq.
NOTTINGHAM
South Nottingham College
Radio Trent
Eldon Chambers
BOULEVARD
CASTLE BOULEVARD
A6005
A453
WILFORD RD.
WILFORD ST.
County Archives
Government Offices
Dukes Wharf
Park Wharf
Tinkers Leen
CANAL
NOTTINGHAM CANAL
Superstore
CASTLE MEADOW RETAIL PARK
The Quays
Canalside Walk
FISHPOND DR.
The Gallery

7
F
G
H
J
K
58
96
1
2
3
4
5
6
7
St. Ann's Well Academy
St. Ann's
Sycamore Academy
Huntingdon Academy
Playing Field
Adventure Playground
Blue Bell Hill Primary School
Rosehill School
NG3
NG1
NG2
Stonebridge City Farm
Victoria Park
Robin Hood Ind. Est.
King Edward Park
Sneinton
Sneinton St. Stephen's C of E Prim. Sch.
Green's Windmill & Science Cen.
George's Green
William Booth Prim. Sch.
Bus Depot
Manvers Court
Nottingham Business Park
Warehouses
Works
Virgin Active
South Nottingham College (London Road Centre)
Meadow Trading Estate
Nottingham Station
NOTTINGHAM
Nottingham Magistrates Court
Nottingham Crown & County Court
Broad Marsh Bus Station
Broad Marsh Shopping Centre
City of Caves
Contemporary
Shire Hall & Galleries of Justice Mus.
Lace Market
Lace Market Theatre
St. Mary's Church
Capital FM Arena
The National Ice Centre
BBC East Midlands
NHS Walk-in Centre
Offices
Trent Ho.
Loxley Ho.
Victoria Centre
Victoria Market
LivingWell Health Club
Nott. Trent Univ.
H2 Fitness
Bus Station
Islamic Cen.
Gala Bingo
St. Mary's Rest Garden
New College Nottingham City (Bath Street)
Victoria Leisure Cen.
Broadway Cin.
Arts Theatre
Quasar Elite
Hockley
A60
A612
A6008
A6019
B684
B686
Mansfield Road
Woodborough Road
Glasshouse Street
Huntingdon Street
Lower Parliament Street
Parliament Street
London Road
Manvers Street
Carlton Road
Bath Street
Stonebridge Road
Queens Rd.
Canal Street
Station Street
Sneinton Road
Sneinton Hermitage
St. Ann's Well Road
Hungerhill Road
Peas Hill Road
Shelton Street
Bluebell Hill Road
Windmill Lane
Robin Hood Chase

8
A
B
C
D
E
1
2
3
4
5
6
7
61
62
92
91
59
460
388
144
INSET
HARWORTH
BAWTRY
A631
BLYTH RD.
TICKHILL ROAD
B6463
Fernlea
Swinno
GT. BLACK LA.
Goole Dike or River Torne
DONCASTER
BASSETLAW
Harworth Sewage Dike
Sewage Works
Doreen Villa
COMMON LA.
Rose Cottage
LOW COMMON
THORNE CL.
THORNHILL
BRACKEN WAY
BRIAR GRO.
HOLLY CT.
BRAMBLE WY.
Grey Gables
CHURCH WK.
CHURCH LA.
GREGORY CRES.
MAIN ST.
THE GREEN
STYRRUP HALL GOLF COURSE
A1(M) MOTORWAY
A1(M)
Crow Wood
Club Ho.
Driving Range
Play. Fld.
Hall
STYRRUP STREET
STYRRUP CARR
SERLBY RD.
PINFOLD LANE
OAKLANDS DR.
YEWS FM. CT.
STYRRUP
MAIN STREET
STYRRUP LA.
STYRRUP RD.
PAGDIN DR.
PINFOLD LA.
DN11
BLYTH ROAD
BAULK LANE
MOOR TOP RD.
MEADOW WY.
SHERWOOD R.
GRANGE RD.
RUTLAND CRES.
HAWKINS CL.
WELBECK RD.
BEECH
WHITBY ROAD
LINDSEY ROAD
Rec. Grd.
Pav.
SANDROCK ROAD
OXFORD DR.
Play. Fld.
THOMPSON AV.
SMITH SQ.
GREENWOOD AV.
RUTLAND DR.
ELMS AV.
WINDERMERE AV.
AMANDA
DORSET DR.
CAMBRIDGE RD.
DEVONSHIRE RD.
Cemetery
BAWTRY CL.
SAXON WY.
MAYFAIR CL.
RUSSELL AV.
Sch.
MELBOURNE GRO.
FIR DR.
WATER
HILL TOP
CT.
Well Hill Plantation
SCROOBY CL.
SCROOBY RD.
HILL ROAD
SCROOBY ROAD
GRANGE DR.
VIEW
BUCKINGHAM CT.
SAND RIDGE CT.
PLUMTREE CARAVAN PARK
THORESBY
ARUNDEL
Playing Field
Bircotes Leisure Centre
St. Patrick's Catholic Prim. Sch.
Snipe Park Wood
STRATHMORE CT.
WINDSOR CT.
HARDWICK CT.
CHATSWORTH CT.
HAREWOOD CT.
DORCHESTER
WEST
EAST STREET
FESTIVAL AV.
YORK RD.
BEVERLEY
SANDY MOUNT
HOLDERNESS
HERRIOT
GROVE
RAYTON CT.
ALEXANDRA ROAD
GROSVENOR ROAD
BROOKSIDE
WOODSIDE VW.
SNIPE PARK RD.
CREWE RD.
GILBERT
Schs.
Lib.
SHREWSBURY
TALBOT RD.
Hall
COLLIERY RD.
Cricket Grd.
Pav.
HARWORTH COLLIERY
Doncaster
Watersh Plantat
FARADAY CL.
SNAPE LANE
BRITISH COAL ENTERPRISE PARK
BRUNEL CL.
BRUNEL PARK INDUSTRIAL ESTATE
BRUNEL GA.
BRUNEL CLOSE
HAWORTH INDUSTRIAL ESTATE
BRYANS CL.
Lords Wood
Layla Planta
Triangle
HARWORTH PARK INDUSTRIAL ESTATE
Steer Bank Farm
Nook Flatt Wood
Sunny Nook
Elm Cottage
HARWORTH ROAD
Kirk View
A614
HARWORTH AV.
BAWTRY RD.
THE WOODLANDS
Deep Well Cottage
The Mound
Worksop S81
A60
DONCASTER HILL
OLDCOTES
A634
MALTBY RD.
BLYTH ROAD
WYNLEA DR.
ELMS
MERE DR.
Manor Farm
STYRRUP RD.
Burntout Wood
WEIRSYDE
MAIN STREET
East Lodge
Nursery House Farm
Olde Mill
West Lodge
Weir
Oldcotes Dyke
Fishpond Plantation
LAMB LANE
Hermeston Hall
Meadow Plantation
Worksop S81
DONCASTER RD.
Goldthorpe Farm
Goldthorpe Farm Cottage

9
63
64
465
BLYTH ROAD
GAINSBOROUGH RD.
A631
A614
A638
GREAT NORTH RD.
GREAT NORTH ROAD
PLUMTREE FARM INDUSTRIAL ESTATE
PLUMTREE ROAD
Plumtree Farm
BIRCOTES
Serlby Park Senior Sch.
The Old Vicarage
Hall
WHITE HOUSE RD.
WHITE HOUSE CT.
WINCHESTER M.
GALWAY GRO.
GALWAY AV.
GALWAY DR.
ESSEX RD.
ESSEX DR.
SUFFOLK ROAD
SUFFOLK GRO.
SUFFOLK AV.
NORFOLK DR.
NORFOLK GRO.
NORFOLK AV.
WHITEHOUSE DR.
CUMBERLAND CL.
CUMBERLAND HO.
WESTMORLAND HO.
MILNE AV.
MILNE GRO.
MILNE ROAD
MILNE DR.
DROVERSDALE RD.
MONCKTON RD.
CHURCH CRESCENT
HOWARD RD.
THE CRESCENT
White House Plantation
Droversdale Wood
Football Grd.
Sports Grd.
Ruins Plantation
Coronation Clump
WEST WOOD ESTATE
WESTWOOD RD.
BINBROOK CT.
LEEMING CT.
Sports Field
BAWTRY
Fish Pond
Fish Pond Wood
COCK HILL LA.
CHURCH ST.
COCK HILL CL.
PASTURES
STH. PDE.
Sports Grd.
Reservoir
LADY'S HOLT LANE
Nursery
GIBBET HILL LA.
FIVE ACRES PARK HOME ESTATE
Gibbet Hill
MILL LANE
Riverside Fishery
South Carr
Sowcarr
South Carr Farm
River Ryton
VICARAGE LANE
Penny Acre
LOW LANE
CHAPEL LA.
DOG LA.
HOLMFIELD CFT.
MANOR RD.
Manor House Farm
Ings Bank
SCROOBY
CH. LA.
STATION RD.
CH. VW.
MAYFLOWER AV.
SARACENS LANE
144
92
91
90
89
Bawtry Lodge
Broom Hill
The Holt
DN10
Neale's Covert
Harworth Lodge
Round Holt
Kennel Cottage
LANE
Ryton
River
Lodges
Meadowside Cottages
Serlby
The Woodlands
Serlby Hall
East Garden
Home Farm
The Laurels
SERLBY PARK
Golf Cottage
Club House
GREEN LANE
ROMAN BANK
Black Cat Plantation
SERLBY PARK GOLF COURSE
Hollins Holt
Lodge Farm
Scrooby Top Ho.
F
G
H
J
K
1
2
3
4
5
6
7

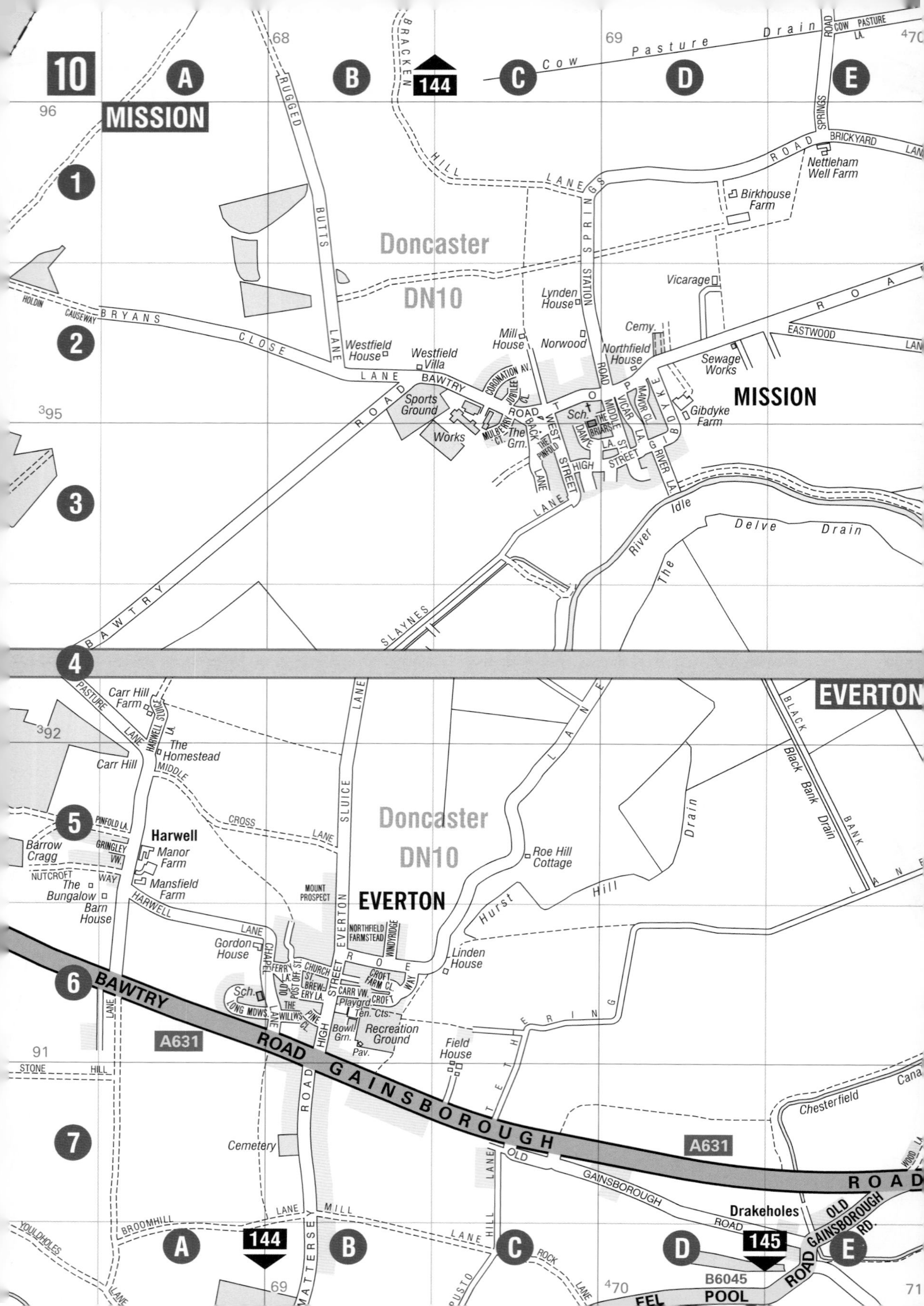
10
MISSION
Doncaster
DN10
MISSION
Bawtry Road
Bryans Close Lane
Rugged Butts Lane
Springs Road
Station Road
Westfield House
Westfield Villa
Sports Ground
Works
Mill House
Norwood
Lynden House
Northfield House
Cemy.
Vicarage
Sewage Works
Gibdyke Farm
Nettleham Well Farm
Birkhouse Farm
Brickyard Lane
Eastwood Lane
Cow Pasture Drain
River Idle
The Delve Drain
Slaynes Lane
Sch.
High Street
West Street
EVERTON
Doncaster
DN10
EVERTON
Harwell
Carr Hill Farm
The Homestead
Carr Hill
Barrow Cragg
Manor Farm
Mansfield Farm
The Bungalow
Barn House
Gordon House
Linden House
Roe Hill Cottage
Field House
Recreation Ground
Cemetery
Drakeholes
Hurst Hill
Black Bank Drain
Chesterfield Canal
Bawtry Road
Gainsborough Road
A631
B6045
144
145
Sluice Lane
Harwell Lane
Cross Lane
Pasture Lane
Mattersey Road
Broomhill Lane
Mill Lane
Stone Hill
Youldholes Lane

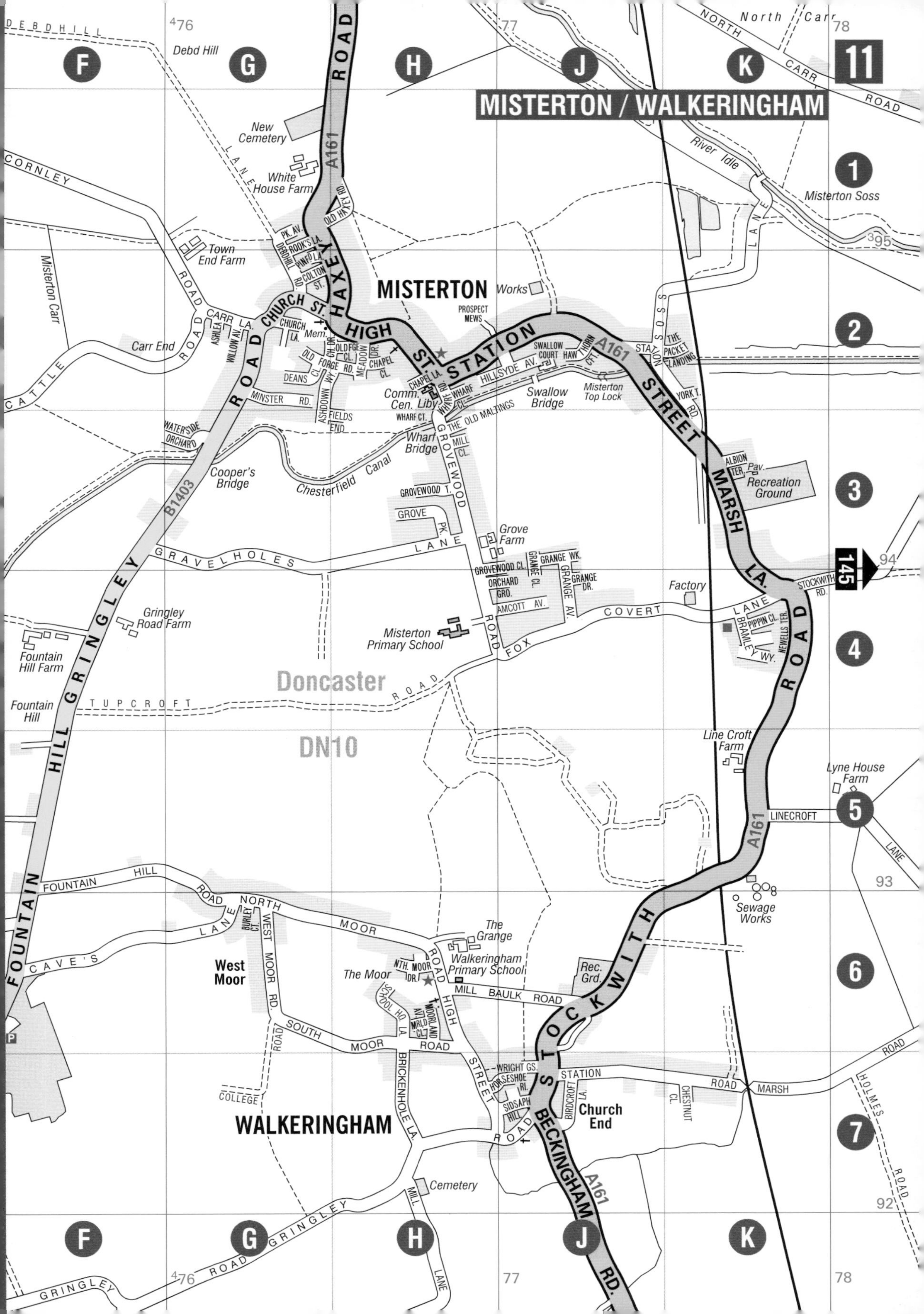
MISTERTON / WALKERINGHAM
MISTERTON
WALKERINGHAM
Doncaster
DN10
HAXEY ROAD
HIGH ST.
STATION STREET
MARSH LA.
STOCKWITH ROAD
STOCKWITH ROAD
BECKINGHAM RD.
A161
B1403
CHURCH ST.
FOUNTAIN HILL GRINGLEY ROAD
GRAVELHOLES LANE
FOX COVERT LANE
NORTH MOOR ROAD
SOUTH MOOR ROAD
MILL BAULK ROAD
STATION ROAD
MARSH ROAD
HOLMES ROAD
GRINGLEY ROAD
TUPCROFT ROAD
CAVE'S LANE
FOUNTAIN HILL ROAD
WEST MOOR RD.
BRICKENHOLE LA.
COLLEGE ROAD
NORTH CARR ROAD
CORNLEY ROAD
CATTLE ROAD
CARR LA.
MINSTER RD.
GROVEWOOD ROAD
LINECROFT LANE
MILL LANE
SOSS LANE
Chesterfield Canal
River Idle
New Cemetery
White House Farm
Town End Farm
Carr End
Misterton Carr
Debd Hill
Works
Comm. Cen. Liby.
Swallow Bridge
Misterton Top Lock
Wharf Bridge
Cooper's Bridge
Recreation Ground
Grove Farm
Factory
Misterton Primary School
Gringley Road Farm
Fountain Hill Farm
Fountain Hill
Line Croft Farm
Lyne House Farm
Misterton Soss
Sewage Works
The Grange
Walkeringham Primary School
The Moor
West Moor
Rec. Grd.
Church End
Cemetery
North Carr
145

CARLTON IN LINDRICK / LANGOLD

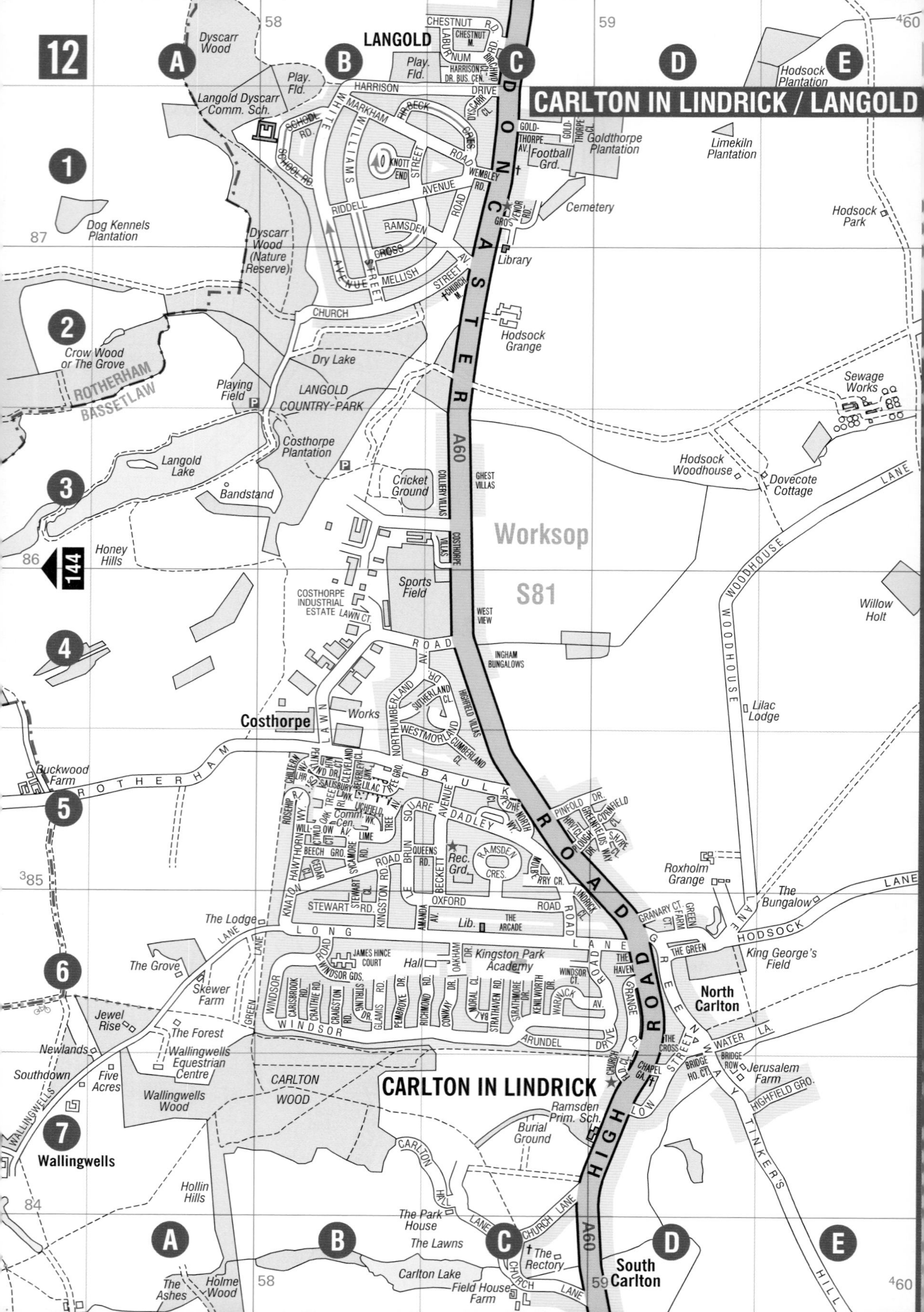

LANGOLD
CARLTON IN LINDRICK
Costhorpe
North Carlton
South Carlton
Wallingwells
Worksop
S81
Dyscarr Wood
Langold Dyscarr Comm. Sch.
Dog Kennels Plantation
Dyscarr Wood (Nature Reserve)
Crow Wood or The Grove
ROTHERHAM
BASSETLAW
Langold Lake
Bandstand
LANGOLD COUNTRY PARK
Dry Lake
Costhorpe Plantation
Cricket Ground
Sports Field
COSTHORPE INDUSTRIAL ESTATE
Honey Hills
Hodsock Plantation
Goldthorpe Plantation
Limekiln Plantation
Cemetery
Library
Hodsock Grange
Hodsock Park
Sewage Works
Hodsock Woodhouse
Dovecote Cottage
Willow Holt
Lilac Lodge
Roxholm Grange
The Bungalow
King George's Field
Jerusalem Farm
Buckwood Farm
The Lodge
The Grove
Skewer Farm
Jewel Rise
The Forest
Wallingwells Equestrian Centre
Newlands
Southdown
Five Acres
Wallingwells Wood
CARLTON WOOD
Kingston Park Academy
Ramsden Prim. Sch.
Burial Ground
Hollin Hills
The Park House
The Lawns
Carlton Lake
The Rectory
Field House Farm
The Ashes
Holme Wood
DONCASTER ROAD
A60
HIGH ROAD

144

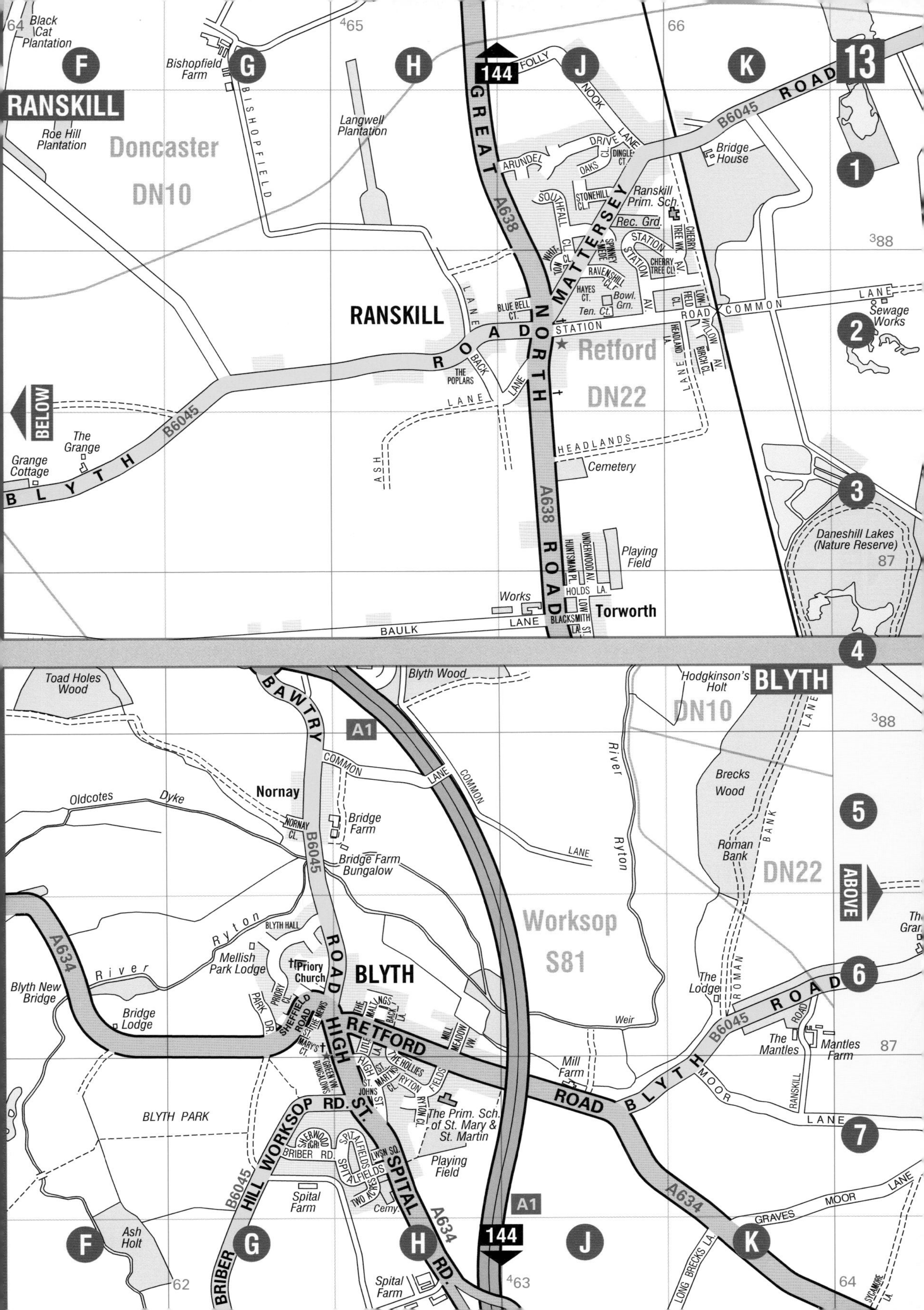
RANSKILL
Doncaster
DN10
Black Cat Plantation
Bishopfield Farm
Roe Hill Plantation
Langwell Plantation
BISHOPFIELD
GREAT NORTH ROAD
A638
FOLLY NOOK LANE
B6045 ROAD
Bridge House
Ranskill Prim. Sch.
Rec. Grd.
MATTERSEY
ARUNDEL
DRIVE
OAKS CL.
DINGLE CT.
SOUTHFALL CL.
STONEHILL CL.
STATION
CHERRY TREE WK.
CHERRY TREE CL.
RAVENSHILL CL.
SPINNEY
WEDE
WHITTON CL.
HAYES CT.
Bowl. Grn.
Ten. Ct.
BLUE BELL CT.
STATION ROAD
COMMON LANE
Sewage Works
LOWFIELD CL.
WILLOW AV.
HEADLAND LA.
BIRCH CL.
Retford
DN22
RANSKILL
ROAD
BACK LANE
THE POPLARS
LANE
ASH LANE
BLYTH
B6045
The Grange
Grange Cottage
HEADLANDS
Cemetery
Daneshill Lakes (Nature Reserve)
Playing Field
HUNTSMAN PL.
UNDERWOOD AV.
HOLDS LA.
LOW ST.
BLACKSMITH LA.
Works
Torworth
BAULK LANE
BELOW
ABOVE
144
Toad Holes Wood
Blyth Wood
Hodgkinson's Holt
BLYTH
DN10
BAWTRY
A1
COMMON LANE
COMMON
Nornay
NORNAY CL.
Bridge Farm
Bridge Farm Bungalow
Oldcotes Dyke
B6045
River Ryton
LANE
Brecks Wood
BANK LANE
Roman Bank
DN22
ROMAN
Worksop
S81
BLYTH HALL
Mellish Park Lodge
Priory Church
BLYTH
A634
Blyth New Bridge
Bridge Lodge
PARK DR.
PRIORY CL.
SHEFFIELD ROAD
THE MEWS
HIGH ROAD
THE MALTINGS
BACK LA.
RETFORD ROAD
MILL MEADOW VW.
ST. MARY'S CT.
GREEN VW. BUNGALOWS
LITTLE LA.
THE HOLLIES
HIGH ST.
ST. MARTINS CL.
ST. JOHNS CL.
RYTON FIELDS
RYTON CL.
Weir
Mill Farm
The Lodge
B6045 ROAD
The Mantles
Mantles Farm
RANSKILL ROAD
BLYTH ROAD
MOOR LANE
BLYTH PARK
WORKSOP RD.
ST.
The Prim. Sch. of St. Mary & St. Martin
SHERWOOD CR.
SPITALFIELDS
BRIBER RD.
LWSN SQ.
TWO ACRES
Playing Field
Spital Farm
Cemy.
SPITAL RD.
A634
BRIBER HILL
B6045
Ash Holt
GRAVES MOOR LANE
LONG BRECKS LA.
SYCAMORE LA.
The Gran

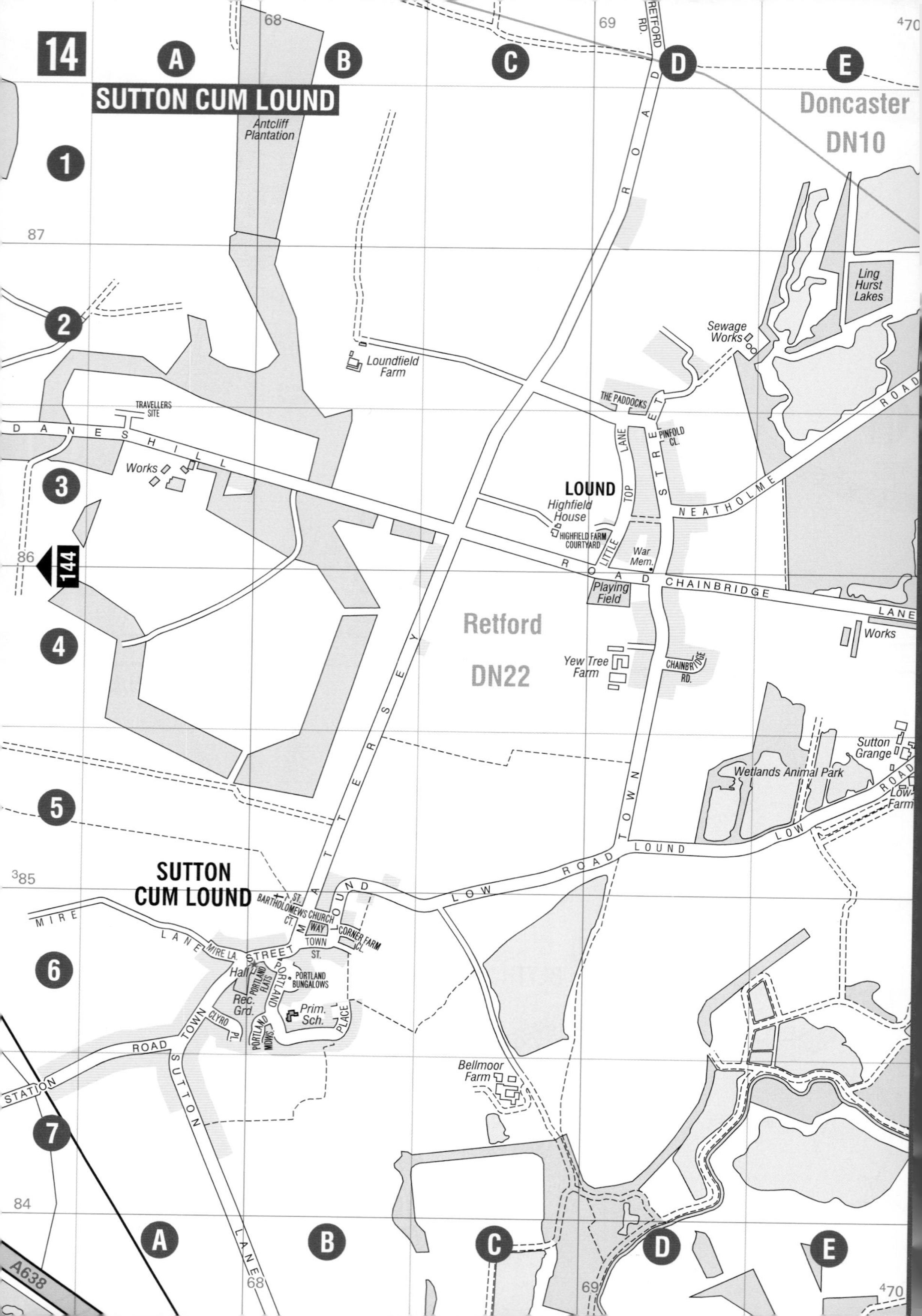
SUTTON CUM LOUND
Antcliff Plantation
Doncaster
DN10
Ling Hurst Lakes
Sewage Works
Loundfield Farm
THE PADDOCKS
PINFOLD CL.
TRAVELLERS SITE
DANES HILL
Works
LOUND
Highfield House
HIGHFIELD FARM COURTYARD
War Mem.
LITTLE TOP LANE
STREET
NEATHOLME ROAD
ROAD
CHAINBRIDGE LANE
Playing Field
Retford
DN22
Works
Yew Tree Farm
CHAINBRIDGE RD.
RETFORD RD.
ROAD
MATTERSEY ROAD
TOWN STREET
Sutton Grange
Wetlands Animal Park
Low Farm
LOW ROAD
LOUND LOW ROAD
SUTTON CUM LOUND
MIRE LANE
MIRE LA.
ST. BARTHOLOMEWS CT.
CHURCH WAY
CORNER FARM CL.
LOUND
TOWN ST.
STREET
Hall
PORTLAND FLATS
PORTLAND
PORTLAND BUNGALOWS
Rec. Grd.
Prim. Sch.
PLACE
CLYRO PL.
PORTLAND MEWS
STATION ROAD
TOWN
SUTTON LANE
Bellmoor Farm
A638
144
A B C D E
1 2 3 4 5 6 7
68 69 470
87 86 385 84

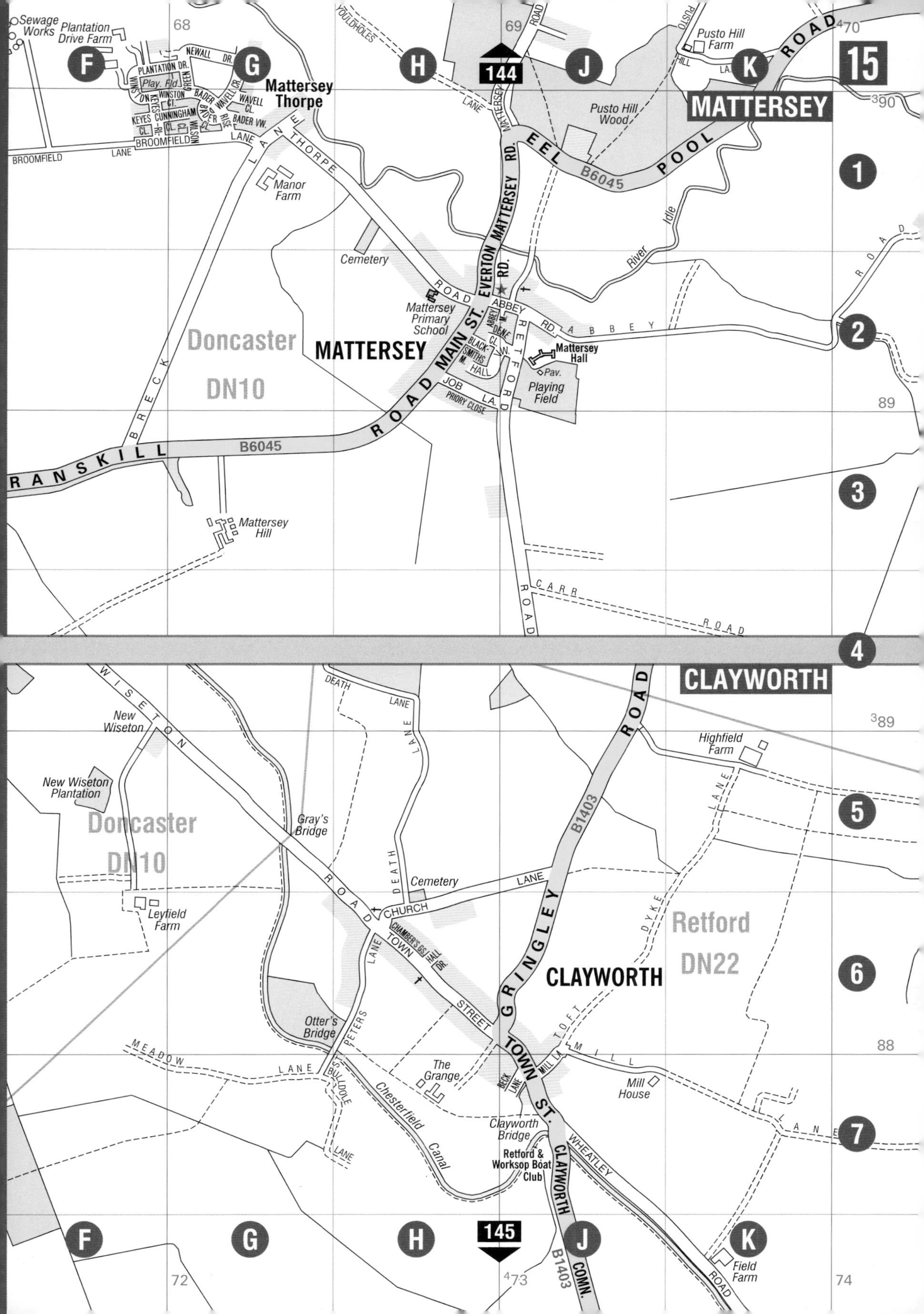

15
MATTERSEY
Mattersey Thorpe
Sewage Works
Plantation Drive Farm
Pusto Hill Farm
Pusto Hill Wood
Manor Farm
Cemetery
Mattersey Primary School
Mattersey Hall
Playing Field
Mattersey Hill
Doncaster
DN10
EEL POOL ROAD
B6045
RANSKILL ROAD
MAIN ST.
EVERTON RD.
MATTERSEY RD.
ABBEY RD.
RETFORD ROAD
CARR ROAD
THORPE ROAD
BRECK LANE
BROOMFIELD LANE
River Idle
144
CLAYWORTH
New Wiseton
New Wiseton Plantation
Gray's Bridge
Cemetery
Leyfield Farm
Highfield Farm
Otter's Bridge
The Grange
Mill House
Clayworth Bridge
Retford & Worksop Boat Club
Chesterfield Canal
Field Farm
Retford
DN22
WISETON ROAD
DEATH LANE
CHURCH LANE
GRINGLEY ROAD
B1403
TOWN STREET
TOWN ST.
PETERS LANE
MEADOW LANE
BULLDOLE LANE
TOFT DYKE LANE
MILL LANE
WHEATLEY ROAD
CLAYWORTH COMMON
145
F G H J K
1 2 3 4 5 6 7
68 69 470 72 473 74
390 89 389 88

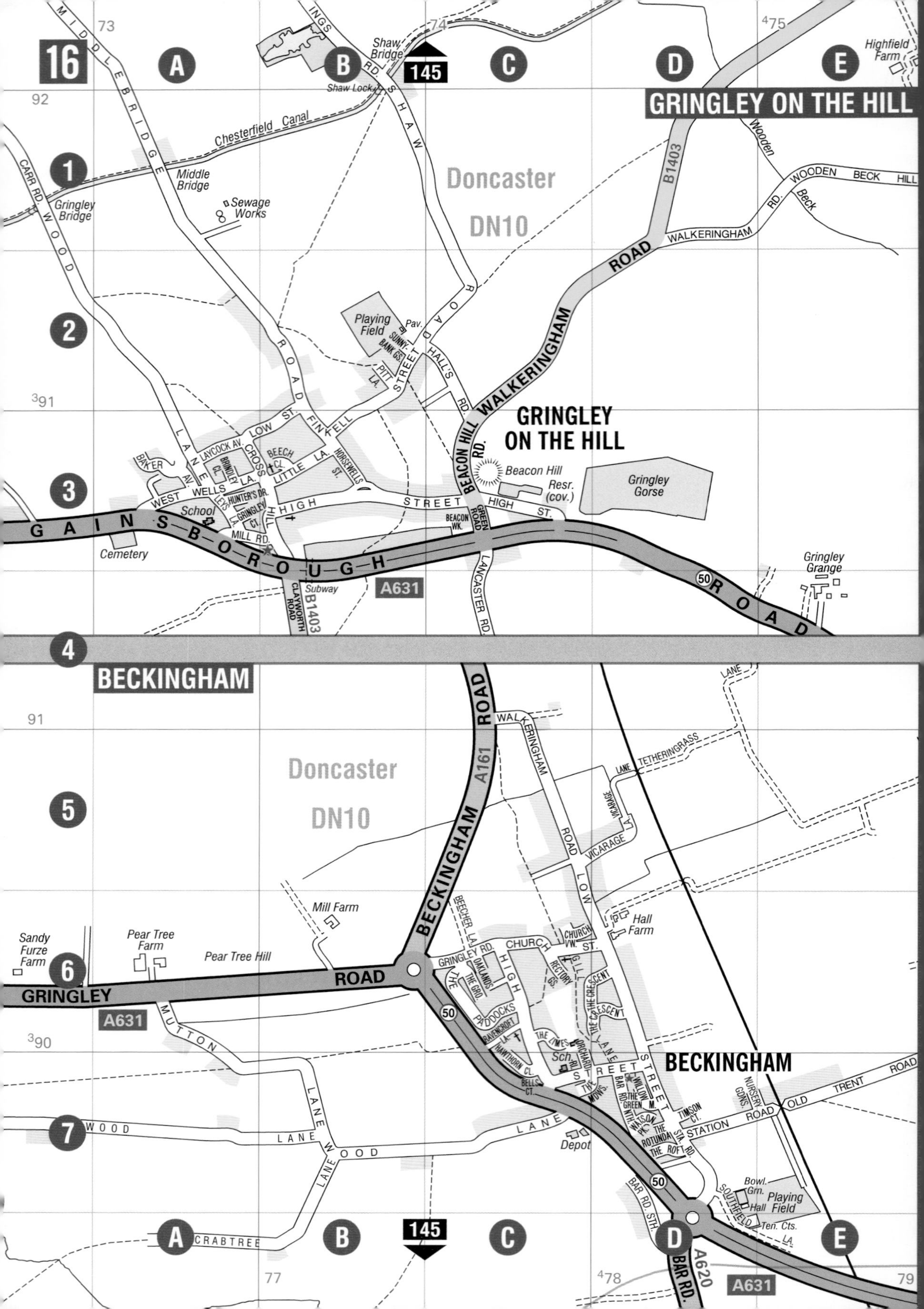
GRINGLEY ON THE HILL
BECKINGHAM
Doncaster
DN10
Doncaster
DN10
145
145
A B C D E
1 2 3 4 5 6 7
Highfield Farm
Shaw Bridge
Shaw Lock
Chesterfield Canal
Middle Bridge
Gringley Bridge
Sewage Works
Playing Field
Pav.
GRINGLEY ON THE HILL
Beacon Hill
Resr. (cov.)
Gringley Gorse
School
Cemetery
Subway
Gringley Grange
GAINSBOROUGH ROAD
A631
B1403
WALKERINGHAM ROAD
WOODEN BECK HILL
Wooden Beck
Mill Farm
Sandy Furze Farm
Pear Tree Farm
Pear Tree Hill
GRINGLEY ROAD
BECKINGHAM ROAD
A161
Hall Farm
BECKINGHAM
Depot
Bowl. Grn.
Playing Field
Hall
Ten. Cts.
OLD TRENT ROAD
STATION ROAD
A620
BAR RD.
WOOD LANE
MUTTON LANE
CRABTREE
TETHERINGRASS LANE
VICARAGE LA.
LOW ROAD
CHURCH ST.
HIGH STREET

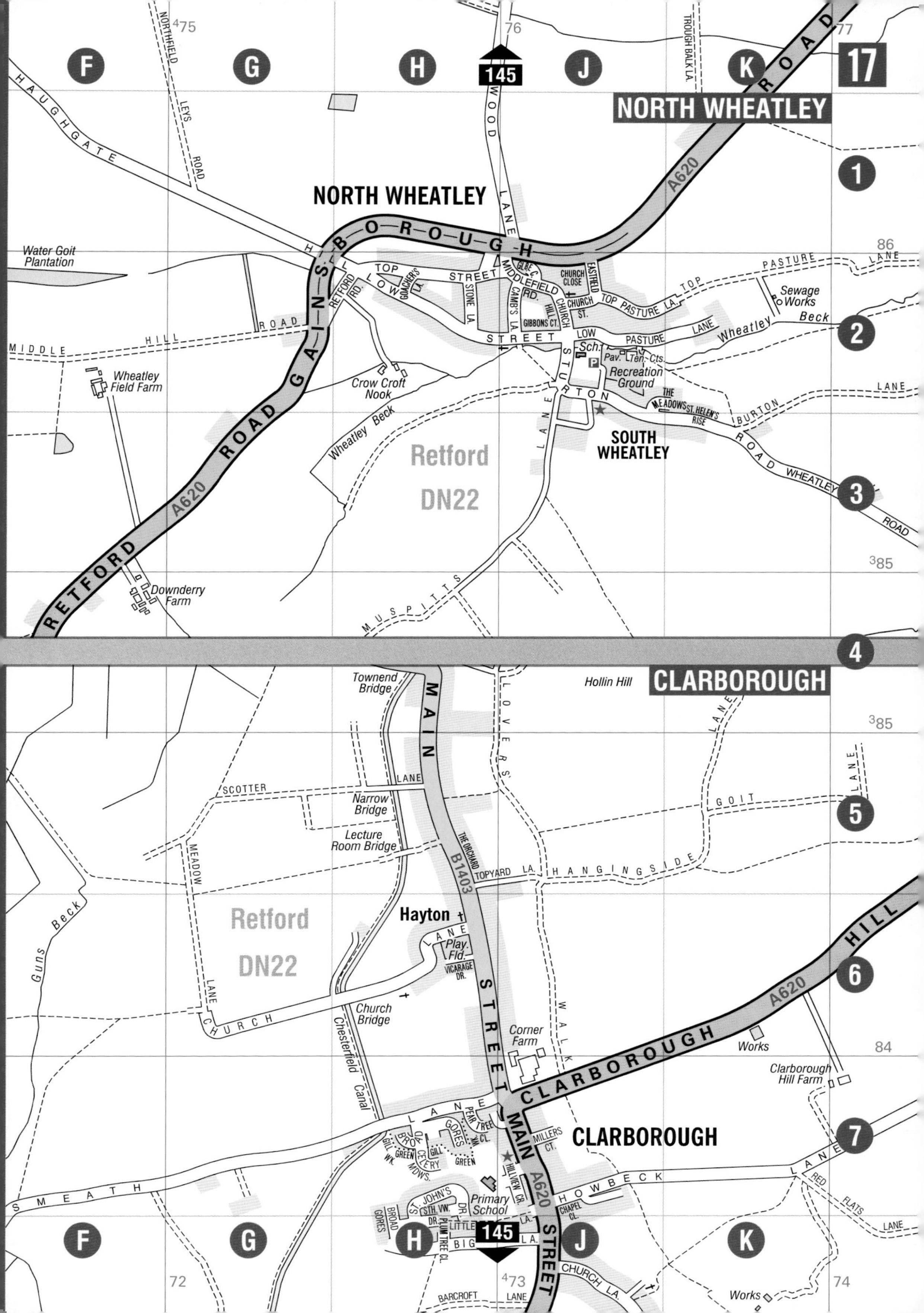
NORTH WHEATLEY
CLARBOROUGH
145
NORTH WHEATLEY
SOUTH WHEATLEY
Retford
DN22
Hayton
CLARBOROUGH
Water Goit Plantation
Wheatley Field Farm
Downderry Farm
Crow Croft Nook
Sewage Works
Recreation Ground
Townend Bridge
Hollin Hill
Narrow Bridge
Lecture Room Bridge
Church Bridge
Corner Farm
Works
Clarborough Hill Farm
Primary School
GAINSBOROUGH ROAD
RETFORD ROAD
A620
CLARBOROUGH HILL
MAIN STREET
B1403
HAUGHGATE HILL
NORTHFIELD
LEYS ROAD
WOOD LANE
TROUGH BALK LA.
MIDDLE HILL ROAD
TOP STREET
LOW STREET
TOP PASTURE LA.
LOW PASTURE LANE
PASTURE LANE
STURTON LANE
BURTON LANE
WHEATLEY ROAD
MUSPITTS
SCOTTER LANE
MEADOW LANE
CHURCH LANE
SMEATH LANE
TOPYARD LA.
HANGINGSIDE
GOIT LANE
LOVERS' WALK
HOWBECK LANE
RED FLATS LANE
CHURCH LA.
BARCROFT LANE
Chesterfield Canal
Wheatley Beck
Guns Beck
Play. Fld.
Sch.
Pav.
Ten. Cts.
THE ORCHARD
VICARAGE DR.
PEAR TREE CL.
MILLERS CT.
HILLVIEW CR.
CHAPEL CL.
ST. JOHN'S DR.
STH. VW.
BROAD GORES
LITTLE LA.
BIG LA.
PLUM TREE CL.
GILL WK.
GILL GREEN
CEMETERY
GORES
THE MEADOWS
ST. HELEN'S RISE
GIBBONS CT.
CHURCH CLOSE
EASTFIELD
GLEBE C.
MIDDLEFIELD RD.
CAMB'S LA.
STONE LA.
GOACHER'S LA.
RETFORD RD.
HILL CHURCH
CHURCH ST.
F G H J K
1 2 3 4 5 6 7
475 76 77 86 385 84 72 473 74

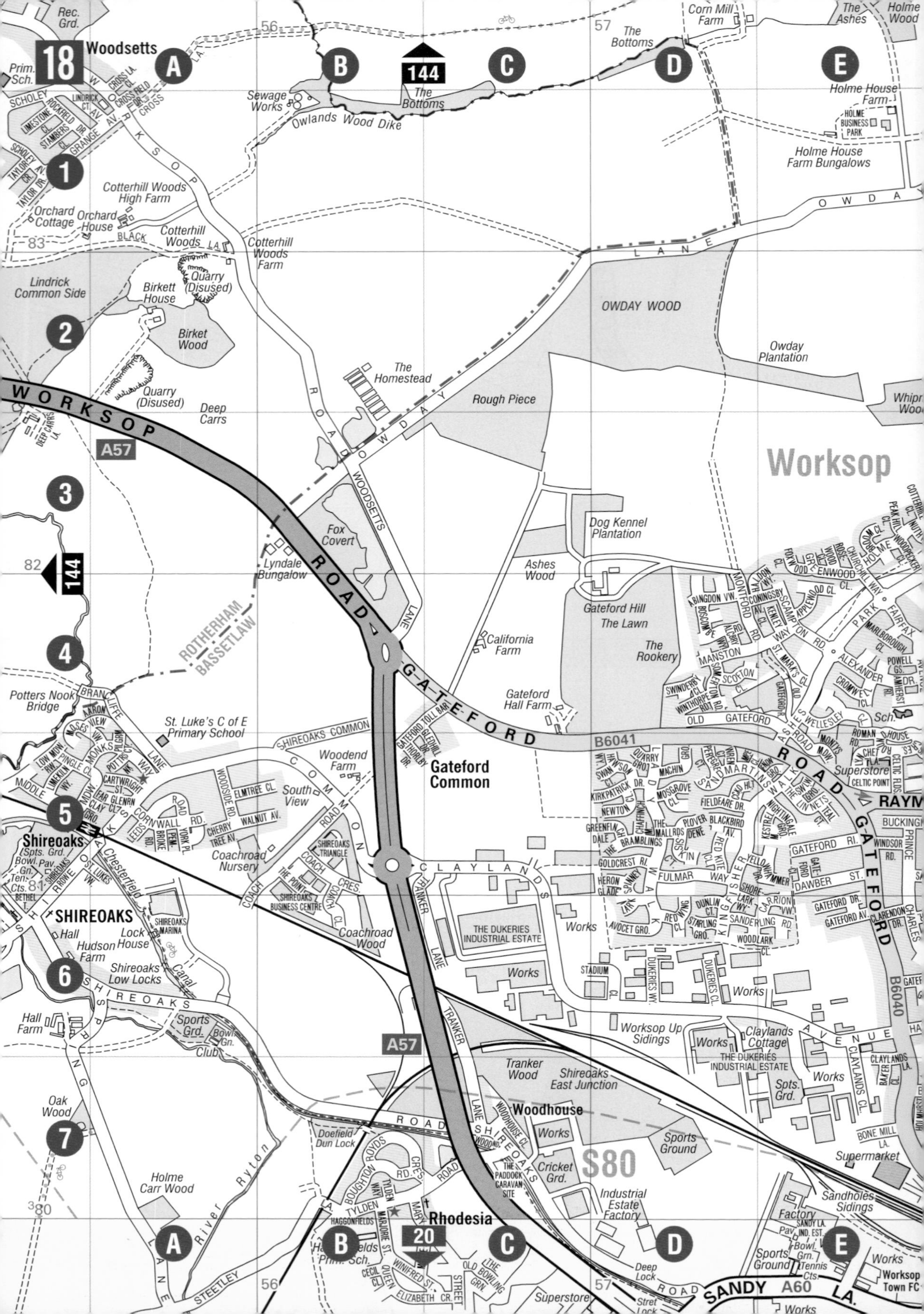

18
Woodsetts
Shireoaks
Rhodesia
Woodhouse
Worksop
Gateford Common
WORKSOP ROAD
A57
GATEFORD ROAD
B6041
B6040
SANDY LA.
A60
S80
Owday Wood
Owday Plantation
Rough Piece
Fox Covert
Dog Kennel Plantation
Ashes Wood
Gateford Hill The Lawn
The Rookery
California Farm
Gateford Hall Farm
Lyndale Bungalow
The Homestead
Birket Wood
Birkett House
Quarry (Disused)
Lindrick Common Side
Cotterhill Woods High Farm
Cotterhill Woods Farm
Orchard Cottage
Orchard House
The Bottoms
Owlands Wood Dike
Sewage Works
Corn Mill Farm
The Ashes
Holme Wood
Holme House Farm
Holme Business Park
Holme House Farm Bungalows
Deep Carrs
Potters Nook Bridge
St. Luke's C of E Primary School
Woodend Farm
South View
Coachroad Nursery
Coachroad Wood
The Dukeries Industrial Estate
Works
Stadium
Worksop Up Sidings
Claylands Cottage
Tranker Wood
Shireoaks East Junction
Sports Ground
Cricket Grd.
Industrial Estate Factory
The Paddock Caravan Site
Doefield Dun Lock
Haggonfields Prim. Sch.
Deep Lock
Superstore
Supermarket
Sandholes Sidings
Worksop Town FC
Oak Wood
Holme Carr Wood
River Ryton
Hall Farm
Hudson Farm
Shireoaks Low Locks
Shireoaks Marina
Lock House
Chesterfield Canal
Rotherham
Bassetlaw
144
20

19
144
144
21
South Carlton
Wigthorpe
Wigthorpe Hill
Field House Farm
Kegham End Plantation
Owday Lodge
Wigthorpe Farm
Wigthorpe Cottage
Wigthorpe House
Hardwick Ashes
Toll Bar Cottage
Forest Bungalow
Broom Covert
Council Depot
Keepers Ashes
Roundwood House
Broom Farm
Broom Cottage
Round Wood
Little Broom Wood
Nab's Ashes Wood
Black Wood
Breck House
Equestrian Centre
Silverdale
Glebe House
Kenwood
Lyn Dor
Sand Hill Plantation
Peaks Hill
Carlton Forest Fm. Cotts.
Black Screed
Freshfields
Peaks Hill Farm
Woodland Grove Farm
Carlton Forest Farm
Eddison Plantation
Long Plantation
Gateford Hill
Thievesdale House
S81
Gateford
Playing Field
St. John's C of E Prim. Sch.
Recreation Ground
Lib.
Jun. & Inf. Schs.
Play. Fld.
Bowl. Grn.
Champion's Plantation
Club House
Valley Sch.
Resrs. (covered)
Greenacre Cen.
Worksop Leisure Centre
New Worksop Play. Fld.
Post 16 Cen.
Sunnyside
KILTON FOREST GOLF COURSE
Hockey Pitch
Ten. Cts.
Football Pitch
Play. Fld.
BASSETLAW HOSPITAL
Mr Straw's House
Coll.
Wks.
Play. Fld.
School
College
Playground
WORKSOP
Worksop
Kilton
St. Augustine's Jun. & Inf. Schs.
Prim. Sch.
A60
CARLTON ROAD
B6045
B6041
THIEVESDALE LANE
LIQUORICE LANE
WIGTHORPE LA.
CHURCH LA.
TINKER'S HILL
CROSSLEY HILL LANE
HUNDRED ACRE LANE
RED LANE
THIEVESDALE LA.
FARMERS BRANCH
KILTON HILL
BLYTH ROAD
TURNER RD.
ANSTON AVENUE
VALLEY ROAD
PLANTATION
F
G
H
J
K
1
2
3
4
5
6
7
58
59
460
83
82
81
380

Rhodesia
WORKSOP
Worksop
Darfoulds
Haggonfields Prim. Sch.
Lady Lee Quarry Nature Reserve
Lady Lea
Lady Lea Farm
Holme Carr
Darfoulds Dike
Manor Lodge
Lodge Farm
Meadowholme Farm
Superstore
Industrial Estate
Cricket Grd.
Sports Ground
Supermarket
Sandy Lane Industrial Estate
Worksop Town FC
Rugby Grd.
Menagerie Cottage
Menagerie Wood
Manor Park House
West Wood
Worksop Manor
Manor Park
The Croft
Hill Top Cottage
Nursery
Darfoulds Farm
Harness Grove
Steetley Corner
Works
Ratcliffe Grange Farm
Hawk's Nest
Hawk's Nest Screed
S80
Pudding Hill Wood
Castle Farm
Oak Wood
Round Spinney
New Farm
Ox Pastures Farm
Wallingbrook Wood
MANSFIELD ROAD
CHESTERFIELD RD.
SANDY LANE
STEETLEY LANE
SPRING LANE
BROAD LANE
CASTLE FARM
RATCLIFFE LANE
FEATHERBED LANE
A57
A60
A619
18
146

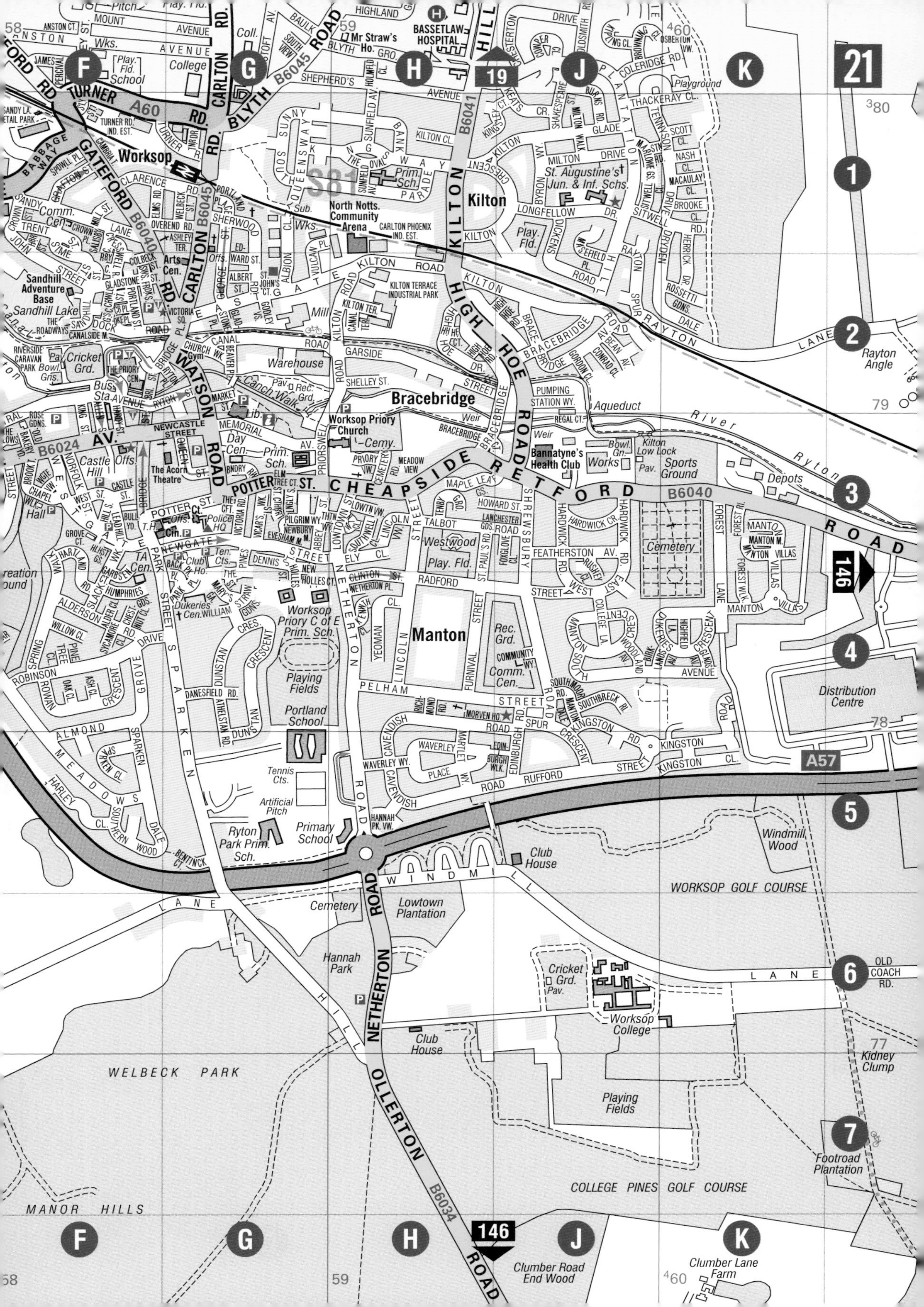

Worksop
Kilton
Bracebridge
Manton
S81
A60
A57
B6045
B6040
B6041
B6024
B6034
Bassetlaw Hospital
Mr Straw's Ho.
St. Augustine's Jun. & Inf. Schs.
North Notts. Community Arena
Carlton Phoenix Ind. Est.
Kilton Terrace Industrial Park
Sandhill Adventure Base
Sandhill Lake
Arts Cen.
Worksop Priory Church
Bannatyne's Health Club
The Acorn Theatre
Police HQ
Sports Ground
Cemetery
Westwood Play. Fld.
Rec. Grd.
Comm. Cen.
Worksop Priory C of E Prim. Sch.
Playing Fields
Portland School
Tennis Cts.
Artificial Pitch
Ryton Park Prim. Sch.
Primary School
Distribution Centre
Rayton Angle
Aqueduct
River Ryton
Depots
Kilton Low Lock
Windmill Wood
Worksop Golf Course
Club House
Lowtown Plantation
Hannah Park
Cricket Grd.
Worksop College
Welbeck Park
Manor Hills
Kidney Clump
Footroad Plantation
College Pines Golf Course
Clumber Road End Wood
Clumber Lane Farm
Carlton Road
Watson Road
Gateford Road
Turner Rd.
Blyth Road
High Hoe Road
Kilton Road
Retford Road
Cheapside
Potter St.
Netherton Road
Ollerton Road
Sparken Hill
Windmill Lane
Old Coach Rd.
Rayton Spur
Radford Street
Pelham Street
Rufford Road
Kingston Street
146
19

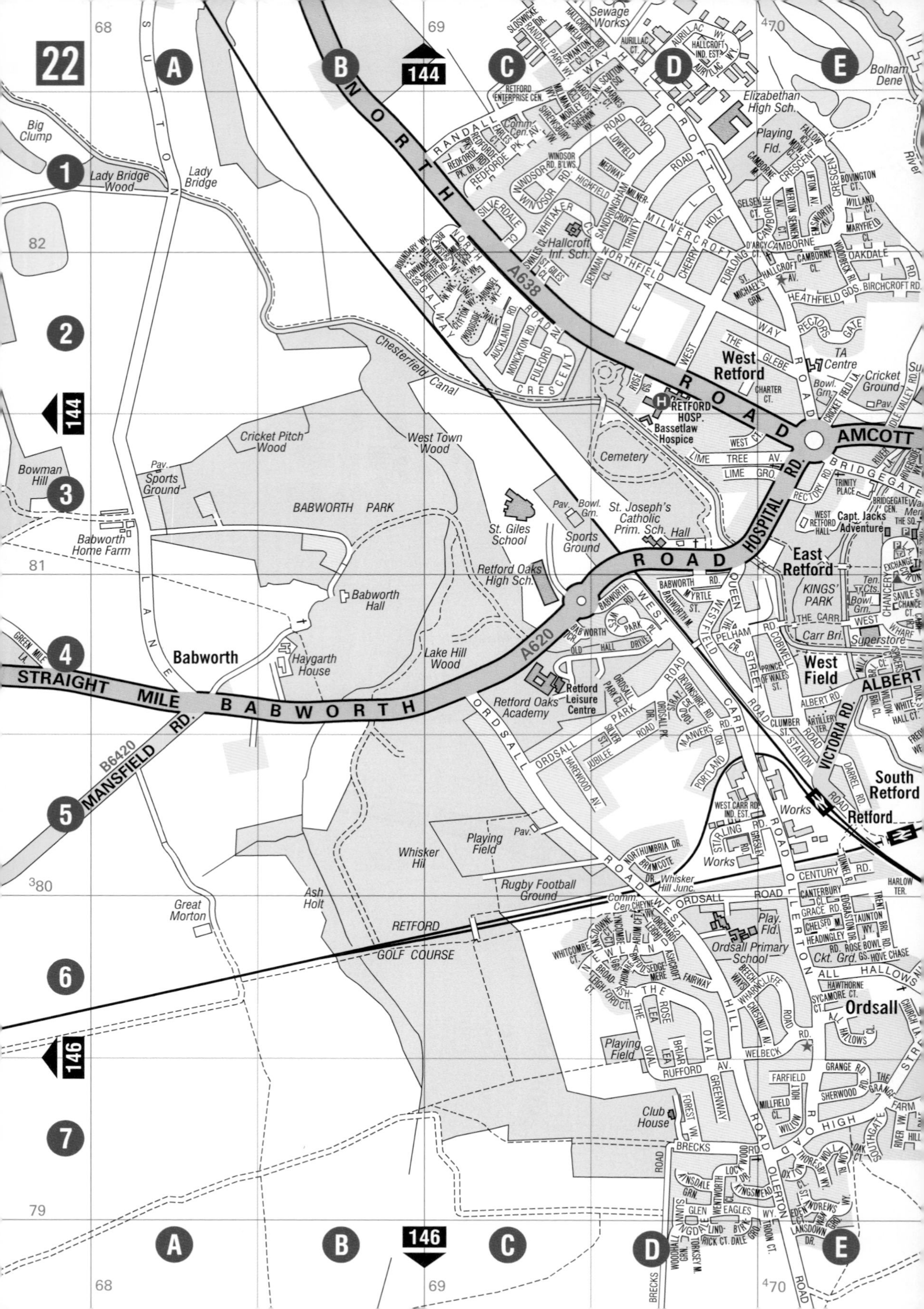

Big Clump
Lady Bridge Wood
Lady Bridge
Sutton Lane
Bowman Hill
Sports Ground
Babworth Home Farm
Babworth
Straight Mile
Babworth Road
A620
Mansfield Rd.
B6420
Great Morton
North Road
A638
Chesterfield Canal
Cricket Pitch Wood
West Town Wood
Babworth Park
St. Giles School
Babworth Hall
Haygarth House
Lake Hill Wood
Retford Oaks High Sch.
Retford Oaks Academy
Retford Leisure Centre
Whisker Hill
Ash Holt
Playing Field
Rugby Football Ground
Retford Golf Course
Club House
Sewage Works
Elizabethan High Sch.
Bolham Dene
Retford Enterprise Cen.
Hallcroft Inf. Sch.
West Retford
Retford Hosp.
Bassetlaw Hospice
Cemetery
St. Joseph's Catholic Prim. Sch.
TA Centre
Cricket Ground
Amcott
Hospital Rd.
Bridgegate
East Retford
Kings' Park
Carr Bri.
Superstore
West Field
Albert
Victoria Rd.
South Retford
Retford
Works
West Carr Rd. Ind. Est.
Whisker Hill Junc.
Ordsall Road
Ordsall Primary School
Ordsall
Ollerton Road
Welbeck Rd.
Brecks Road
High Road
Babworth Road
Ordsall Road
Carr Road
West Hill

144
146

Bolham
Bolham Manor
Moorgate Farm
Longholme Farm
Clarborough Hall
Welham
Whitsunday Pie Lock
Carr Hill Prim. Sch.
Chesterfield Canal
Welham Hall
THE GARDEN (CARAVAN PARK)
Recreation Ground
Balk Field
Works
RETFORD
The Meadows
Playing Field
Bracken Lodge Farm
Newton Farm
Newtown
Retford
DN22
Oaklands Track
Sports Ground
Thrumpton
Bracken Lane Prim. Sch.
Bracken Lane Farm
Walmoor
Fairfield
Morgan's Plantation
Top Lodge Plantation
Swindell Spring Wood
Bowling Grn.
Play. Field
Play. Fld.
White Houses
GROVE PARK
The Rookery
Kennels Plantation
MOORGATE
WELHAM ROAD
A620
ARLINGTON WAY
LONDON ROAD
A638
LEVERTON ROAD
GROVE LANE
BRACKEN LANE
GROVE COACH ROAD
GROVE ROAD
PINFOLD LANE
LITTLE GRINGLEY LANE
SHADY LANE
BLACKSTOPE LANE
WHINNEY MOOR LA.
GOOSEMOOR LA.
WHITEHOUSES RD.
River Idle
B6044 RD.
145
147
23
F G H J K
1 2 3 4 5 6 7
71 72 73
79 80 81 82

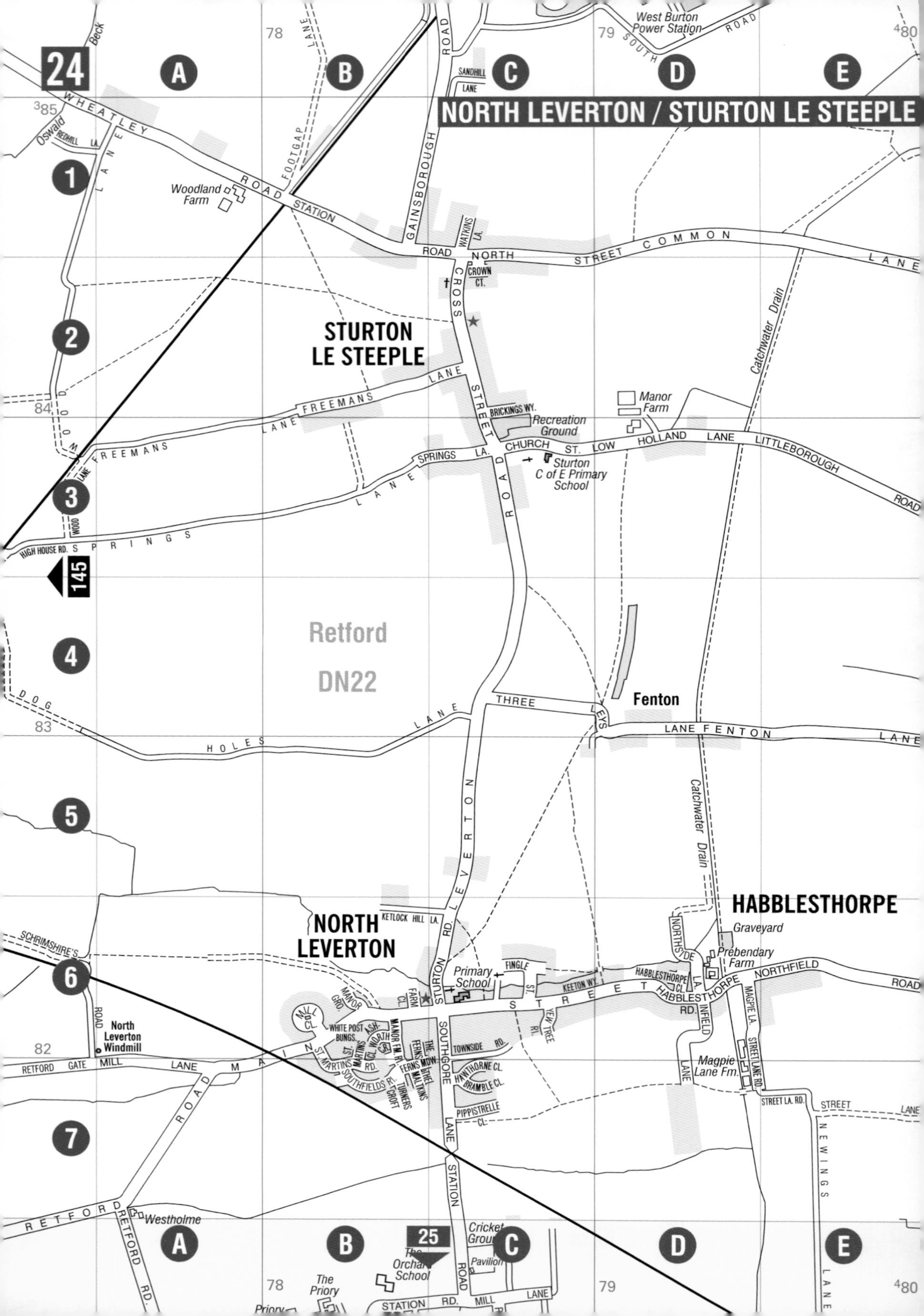

West Burton
Power Station

Beck

Wheatley

Oswald
REDHILL LA.

Woodland
Farm

ROAD STATION

FOOTGAP LANE

SANDHILL
LANE

GAINSBOROUGH ROAD

ROAD

WATKINS LA.

NORTH STREET COMMON LANE

CROWN
CT.

Catchwater Drain

**STURTON
LE STEEPLE**

CROSS STREET

LANE

FREEMANS LANE

FREEMANS LANE

WOOD LANE

SPRINGS LA.

BRICKINGS WY.

Recreation
Ground

Manor
Farm

CHURCH ST. LOW HOLLAND LANE LITTLEBOROUGH ROAD

Sturton
C of E Primary
School

HIGH HOUSE RD. S P R I N G S

▼**145**

Retford

DN22

D O G

HOLES LANE

THREE LEYS

Fenton

LANE FENTON LANE

Catchwater Drain

LEVERTON ROAD

HABBLESTHORPE

SCHRIMSHIRE'S

KETLOCK HILL LA.

Graveyard

NORTHSIDE

Prebendary
Farm

**NORTH
LEVERTON**

Primary
School

FINGLE ST.

HABBLESTHORPE CL.

HABBLESTHORPE RD.

INFIELD

NORTHFIELD ROAD

MAGPIE LA.

STREET LANE RD.

ROAD

North
Leverton
Windmill

MILL CL.

MANOR GRO.

FARM

WHITE POST
BUNGS.

ASH CL.

WORTH

SOUTHGORE LANE

KEETON WY.

STREET

YEW TREE RI.

Magpie
Lane Fm.

STREET LA. RD.

STREET LANE

NEWINGS LANE

RETFORD GATE MILL LANE MAIN ROAD

ST. MARTINS CL.

FERNS MDW.

WATKINS

TOWNSIDE RD.

HAWTHORNE CL.

SOUTHFIELDS RI.

TINKERS CROFT

BRAMBLE CL.

PIPPISTRELLE CL.

RETFORD ROAD

RETFORD RD.

Westholme

STATION ROAD

25
The
Orchard
School

Cricket
Ground

Pavilion

The
Priory

Priory

STATION RD. MILL LANE

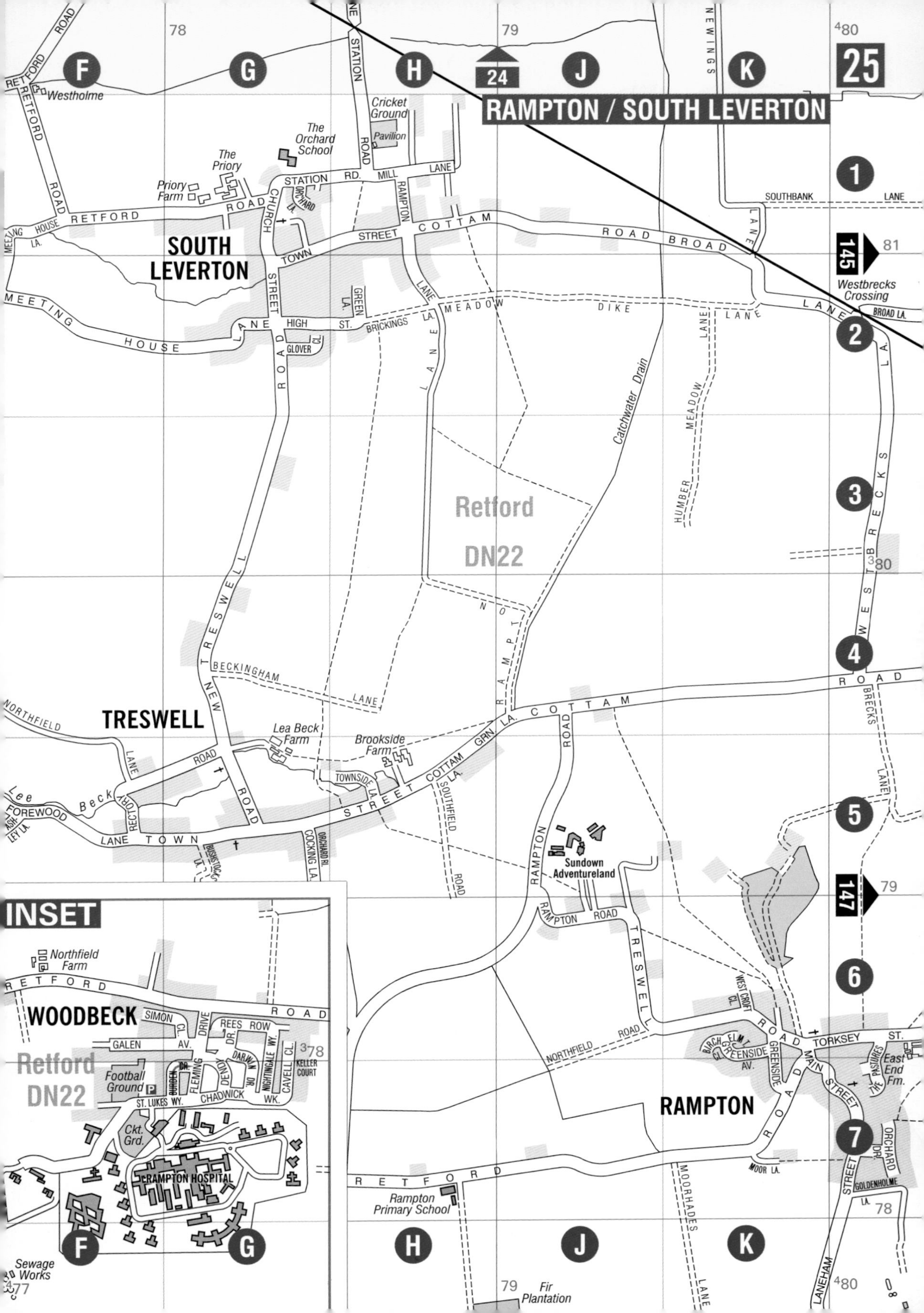
SOUTH LEVERTON
TRESWELL
RAMPTON
WOODBECK
INSET
Retford DN22
Westholme
Cricket Ground
Pavilion
The Orchard School
The Priory
Priory Farm
Westbrecks Crossing
Catchwater Drain
Lea Beck Farm
Brookside Farm
Sundown Adventureland
Rampton Primary School
Fir Plantation
East End Fm.
Northfield Farm
Football Ground
Ckt. Grd.
RAMPTON HOSPITAL
Sewage Works
RETFORD ROAD
STATION ROAD
STATION RD.
MILL LANE
RAMPTON LANE
COTTAM ROAD
BROAD LANE
SOUTHBANK LANE
NEWINGS
TOWN STREET
CHURCH STREET
MEETING HOUSE LA.
MEETING HOUSE LANE
HIGH ST.
GREEN LA.
GLOVER CL.
BRICKINGS LA.
MEADOW DIKE LANE
MEADOW LANE
HUMBER MEADOW LANE
WESTBRECKS LA.
TRESWELL ROAD
BECKINGHAM LANE
NEW ROAD
NORTHFIELD
LANE
RAMPTON LA.
COTTAM GRN. LA.
TOWNSIDE LA.
COTTAM STREET
SOUTHFIELD ROAD
TOWN LANE
RECTORY
FOREWOOD
ASH LEY LA.
Lee Beck
BISHOPS LA.
COCKING LA.
ORCHARD RI.
BRECKS LANE
RAMPTON ROAD
TRESWELL ROAD
NORTHFIELD ROAD
WEST CROFT CL.
TORKSEY ST.
BIRCH CL.
ELM T.
GREENSIDE AV.
GREENSIDE
MAIN STREET
THE PASTURES
ORCHARD DR.
GOLDENHOLME LA.
MOOR LA.
MOORHADES LANE
LANEHAM STREET
SIMON CL.
DRIVE
REES ROW
GALEN AV.
DR.
DARWIN DR.
NIGHTINGALE WY.
CAVELL CL.
KELLER COURT
BURDEN CR.
FLEMING
DENBY
CHADWICK WK.
ST. LUKES WY.
F G H J K
1 2 3 4 5 6 7
24
145
147
78 79 480 81 380 79 378 77

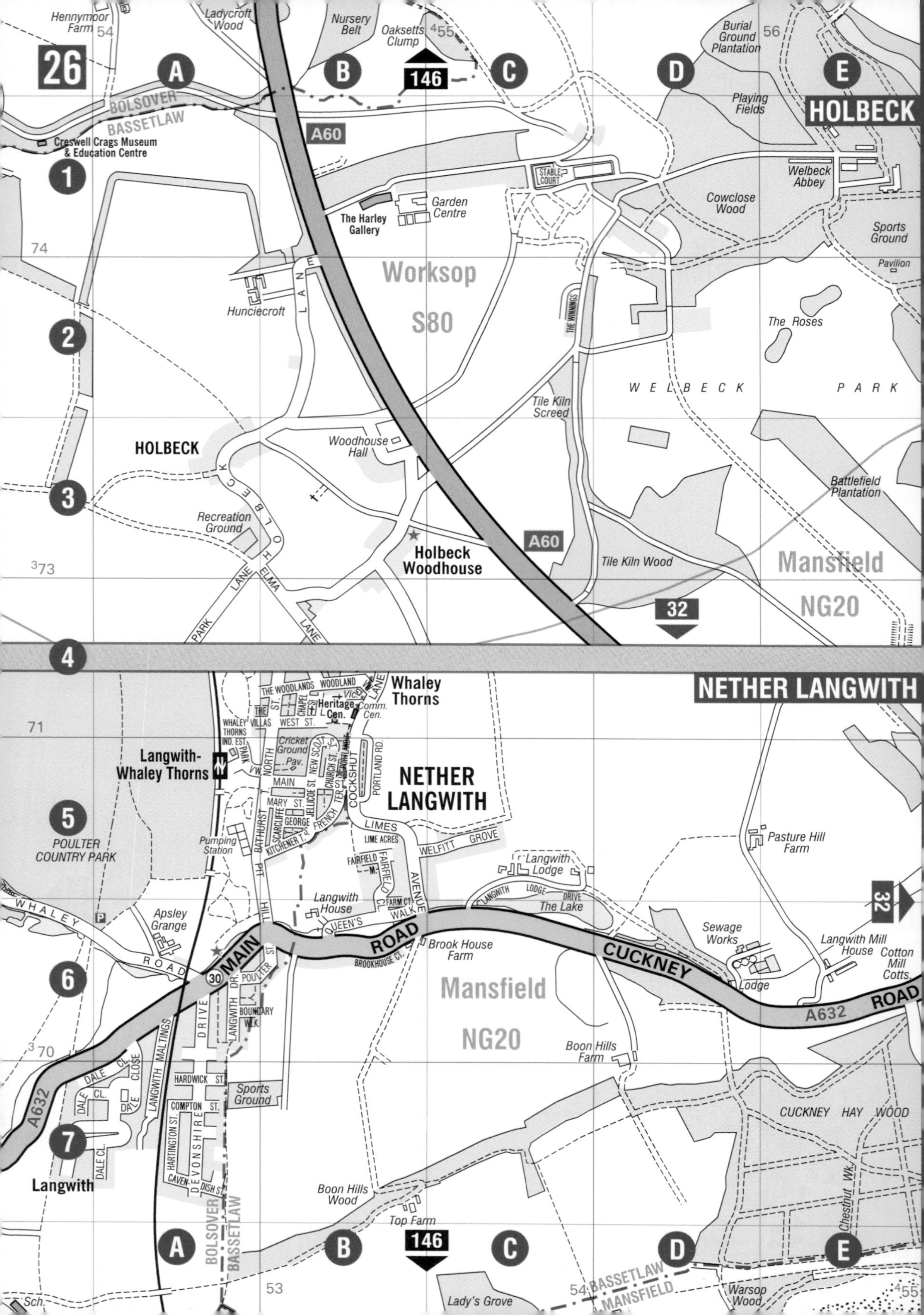

HOLBECK
NETHER LANGWITH
Hennymoor Farm
Ladycroft Wood
Nursery Belt
Oaksetts Clump
Burial Ground Plantation
146
BOLSOVER
BASSETLAW
A60
Creswell Crags Museum & Education Centre
Playing Fields
Stable Court
Welbeck Abbey
Garden Centre
The Harley Gallery
Cowclose Wood
Sports Ground
Pavilion
Worksop S80
Hunciecroft
Lane
The Winnings
The Roses
Welbeck Park
Tile Kiln Screed
Holbeck
Woodhouse Hall
Battlefield Plantation
Recreation Ground
Holbeck Woodhouse
Tile Kiln Wood
Mansfield NG20
32
Park Lane
Elma Lane
Whaley Thorns
Heritage Cen.
Comm. Cen.
Langwith-Whaley Thorns
Whaley Thorns Ind. Est.
Cricket Ground
Pav.
Cockshut Lane
Portland Rd.
Poulter Country Park
Pumping Station
Limes Avenue
Lime Acres
Welfitt Grove
Fairfield
Langwith Lodge
Langwith House
Queen's Walk
Farm Ct.
Langwith Lodge Drive
The Lake
Pasture Hill Farm
Whaley Road
Apsley Grange
Main Road
Cuckney Road
Brook House Farm
Brookhouse Ct.
Sewage Works
Langwith Mill House
Cotton Mill Cotts.
Lodge
A632
Pit Hill
Poulter St.
Langwith Dr.
Boundary Wlk.
Langwith Maltings
Dale Cl.
Dale Close
Hardwick St.
Compton St.
Hartington St.
Devonshire Drive
Cavendish St.
Sports Ground
Boon Hills Farm
Cuckney Hay Wood
Chestnut Wk.
Langwith
Boon Hills Wood
Top Farm
Lady's Grove
Warsop Wood
Sch.
Mansfield

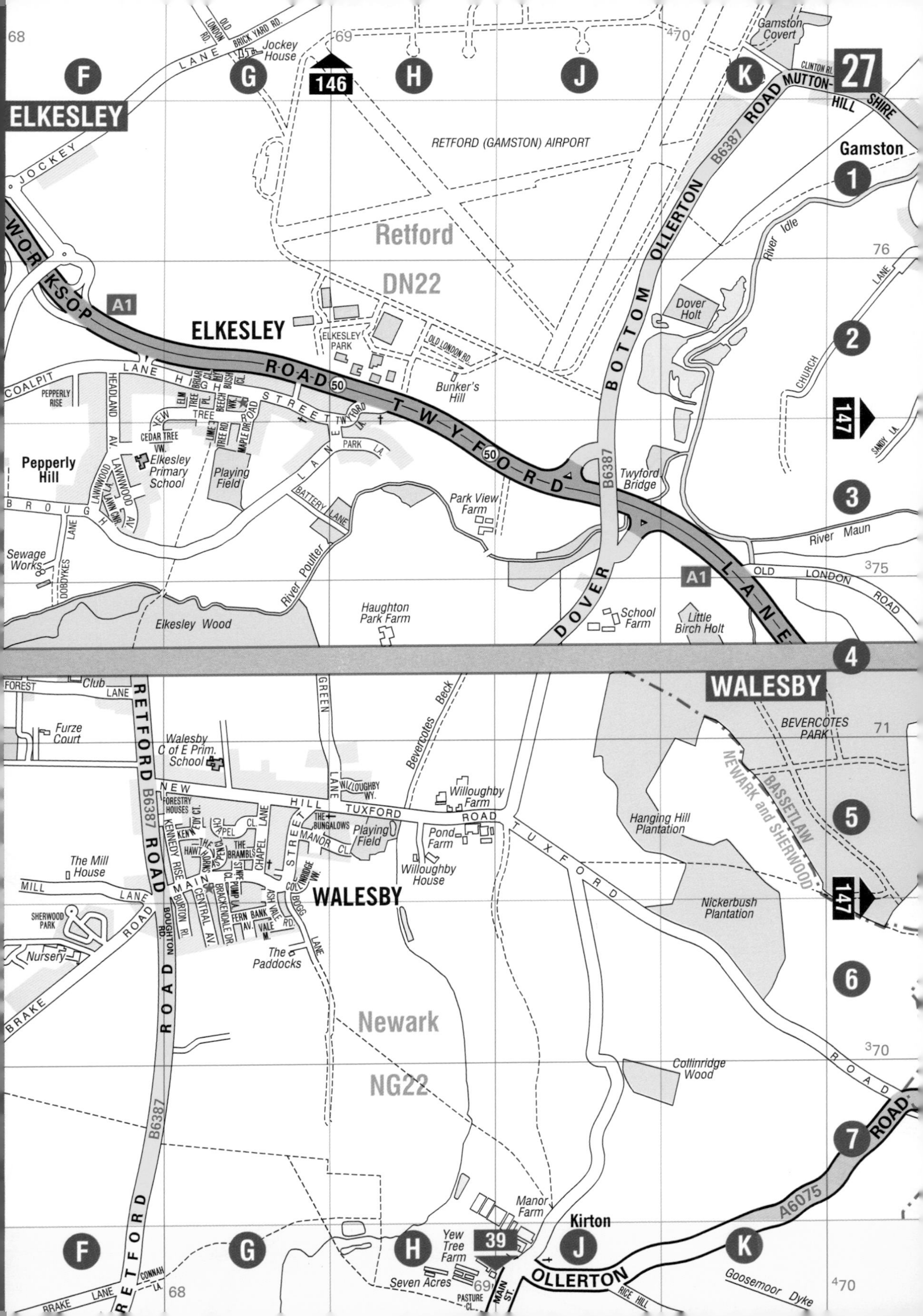
ELKESLEY
WALESBY
RETFORD (GAMSTON) AIRPORT
Retford
DN22
ELKESLEY
Pepperly Hill
Elkesley Primary School
Playing Field
Sewage Works
Elkesley Wood
Haughton Park Farm
Park View Farm
Bunker's Hill
Twyford Bridge
School Farm
Little Birch Holt
Dover Holt
Gamston
Gamston Covert
Jockey House
River Idle
River Maun
River Poulter
TWYFORD ROAD
BOTTOM OLLERTON ROAD
DOVER LANE
WORKSOP ROAD
WALESBY
Walesby C of E Prim. School
Furze Court
The Mill House
Sherwood Park
Nursery
The Paddocks
Willoughby Farm
Pond Farm
Willoughby House
Playing Field
Hanging Hill Plantation
Nickerbush Plantation
BEVERCOTES PARK
NEWARK and SHERWOOD
BASSETLAW
Newark
NG22
Collinridge Wood
Manor Farm
Kirton
Yew Tree Farm
Seven Acres
OLLERTON
Goosemoor Dyke
RETFORD ROAD
TUXFORD ROAD
BRAKE LANE

146
147
147
39

EAST MARKHAM / TUXFORD
Retford DN22
Newark
NG22
EAST MARKHAM
TUXFORD
West Markham
147
Sibthorpe
Beacon Hill
Cleveland Hill Farm
Sibthorpe Kennels
East Markham Primary School
Markham Hall
Manor Farm
Broad Gate Farm
Tuxford Windmill
South Hills Farm
Walks of Life Heritage Centre
Tuxford School
Playing Fld.
Artificial Pitch
Tennis Cts.
Cemetery
GREENACRES CARAVAN PARK
EASTFIELD PARK
LODGE LANE INDUSTRIAL EST.
A57
A1
B1164
A6075
CLIFF GATE
HIGH STREET
GREAT LANE
HAROLD LANE
FINNEY LANE
ASKHAM ROAD
TOP CART GAPS
BROAD GATE
LINCOLN STREET
PLANTATION ROAD
PLANTATION AV.
CROSSWAYS
TRINITY CRES.
KIRKE CL.
TRINITY CR.
BACK LANE
BACK LA.
NOOKIN
QUAKEFIELD
CHURCH STREET
HALL LANE
LOW STREET
YORK STREET
YORK PADDOCK
FARM LA.
OLD HALL LA.
STOCKS FOLD
COLLEGE CT.
QUEENS CL.
THE HALL CL.
BECKLAND HILL
MARK LANE
EAST VIEW
TUXFORD ROAD
MARKHAM ROAD
PRIESTGATE
CLEVELAND HILL
GT. NORTH ROAD
PARSON LA.
MAIN ST.
RETFORD ROAD
ELDON ST.
ELDON GRN.
AMERICA GS.
BURLEIGH RI.
BEVERCOTES LANE
LINCOLN ROAD
DARLTON RD.
MARNHAM ROAD
HILLSIDE
HILLSIDE CL.
ASHVALE
FARADAY AV.
GILBERT AV.
WELBECK PL.
LANDIA GRO.
MACHIN CL.
FLEMING AV.
NICHOLAS PL.
CHARTER PL.
WOODHOUSE PL.
HAYNES CL.
CAPPS PL.
MAYFAIR PL.
AVENUE
LINDEN AV.
MAPLE CL.
ASPEN CL.
ASPEN CT.
CHESTNUT WY.
BIRCH CT.
THE BEECHES
NEWARK RD.
MKT. PL.
BLUE BELL YD.
THE PASTURES
LANE
Prim. Sch.
Lib. Comm. Cen.
PEEL AV.
ORCHARD CR.
CLARK LA.
Play. Fld.
NEWCASTLE ST.
NEWCASTLE CT.
LEXINGTON GS.
LEXINGTON CT.
EGMANTON RD.
OLLERTON ROAD
LONG LANE
BRITISH FIELDS
LODGE LANE
GREAT NORTH RD.
MOORGATE
OLD
Hall
Wks.
Depot
Works
30
1
2
3
4
5
6
7
A
B
C
D
E
73
74
475
374
72
71

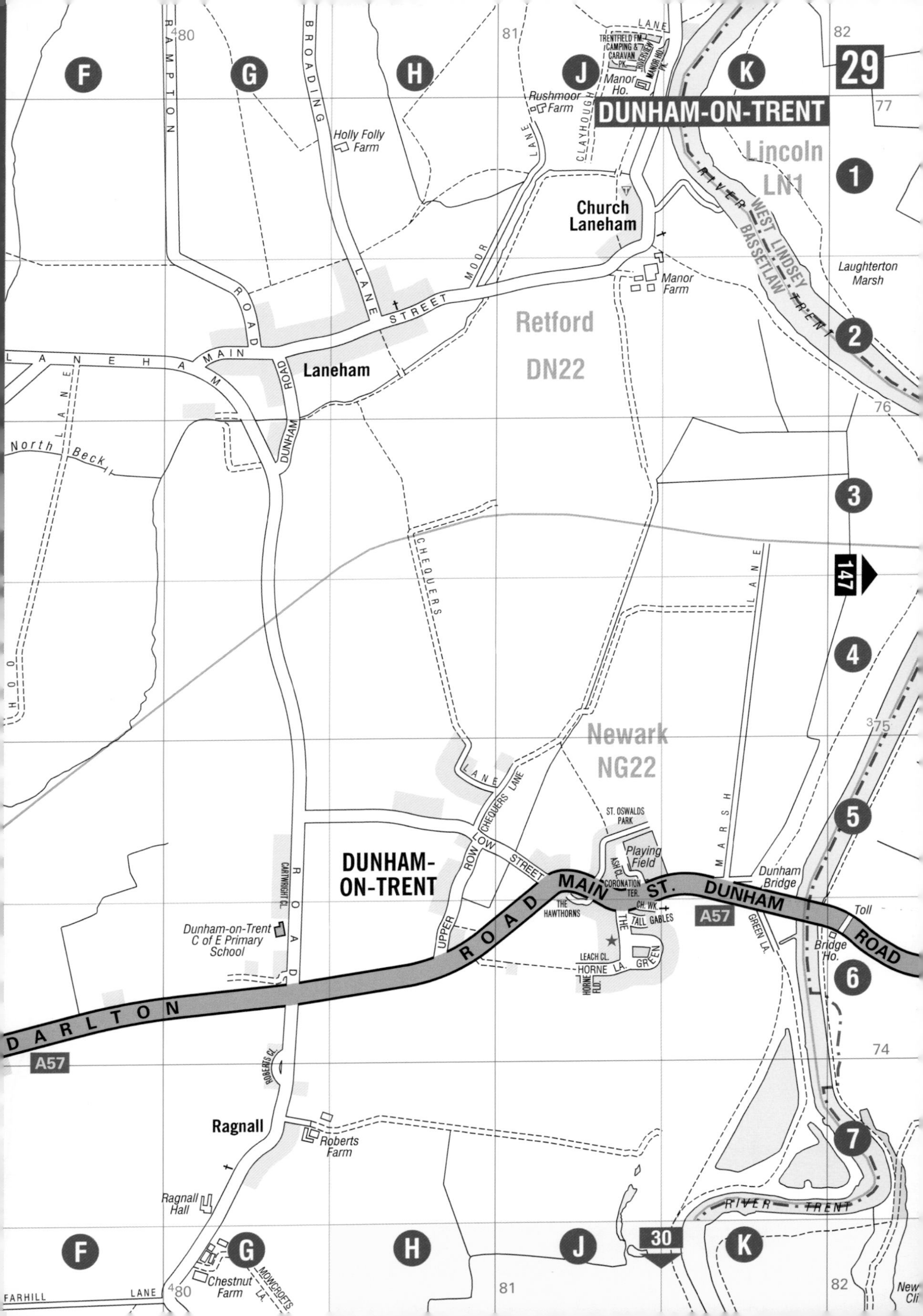
29
DUNHAM-ON-TRENT
Lincoln
LN1
Retford
DN22
Newark
NG22
Church
Laneham
Laneham
DUNHAM-
ON-TRENT
Ragnall
Rushmoor
Farm
Holly Folly
Farm
Manor
Ho.
Manor
Farm
Laughterton
Marsh
Dunham
Bridge
Toll
Bridge
Ho.
Playing
Field
Dunham-on-Trent
C of E Primary
School
Roberts
Farm
Ragnall
Hall
Chestnut
Farm
North Beck
RIVER TRENT
WEST LINDSEY
BASSETLAW
DARLTON ROAD
ROAD MAIN ST.
DUNHAM ROAD
A57
LOW STREET
CHEQUERS LANE
UPPER ROW
MARSH LANE
GREEN LA.
HORNE LA.
THE GREEN
LEACH CL.
THE HAWTHORNS
CORONATION TER.
CH. WK.
THE TALL GABLES
ST. OSWALDS PARK
CARTWRIGHT CL.
ROBERTS CL.
MOWCROFTS LA.
FARHILL LANE
TRENTFIELD FM. CAMPING & CARAVAN PK.
RIVERVIEW
MANOR HO. PK.
CLAYHOUGH LANE
MOOR LANE
STREET LANE
BROADING LANE
RAMPTON ROAD
MAIN ROAD
LANEHAM
DUNHAM ROAD
147
30

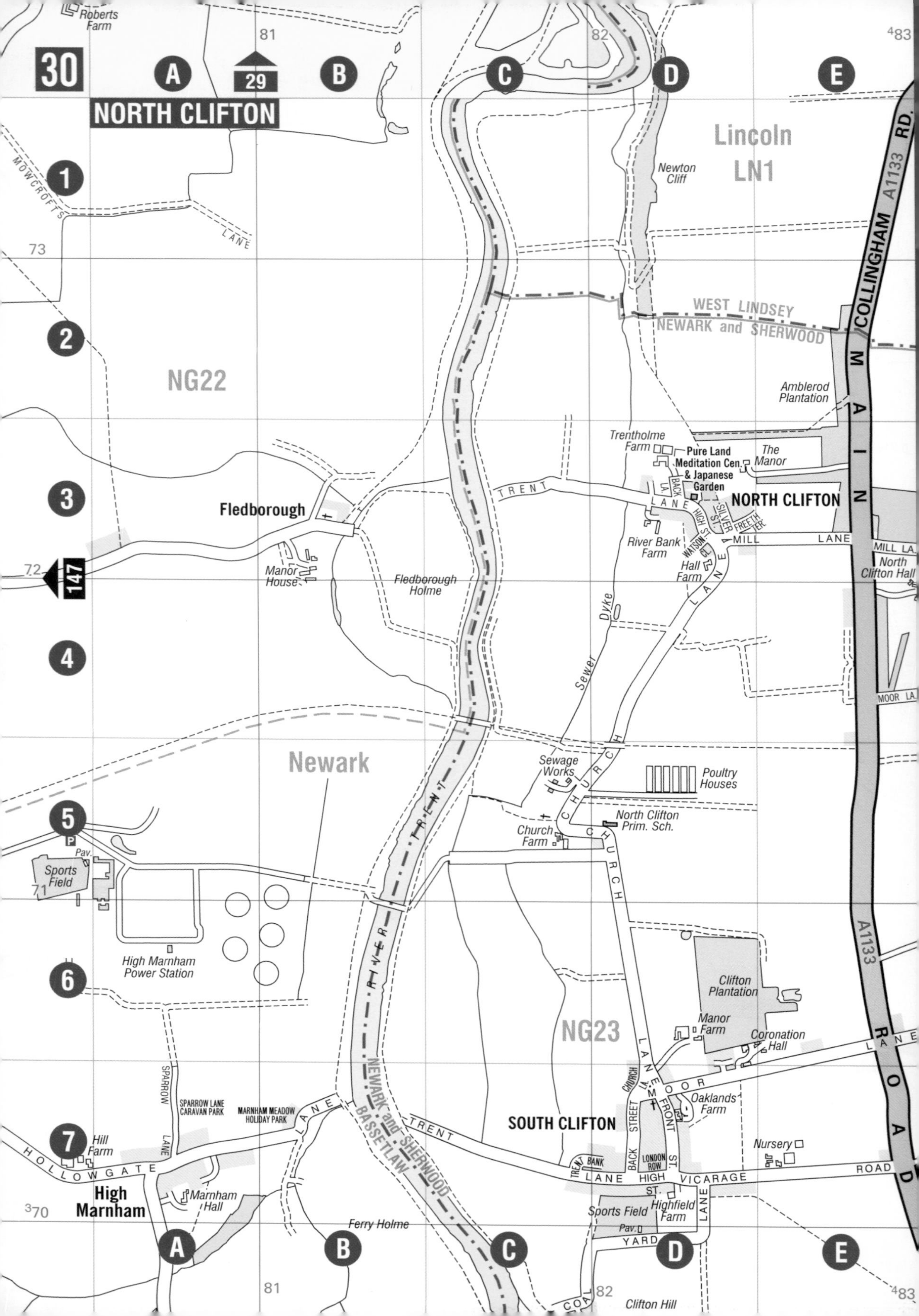

NORTH CLIFTON
29
147
A
B
C
D
E
1
2
3
4
5
6
7
81
82
483
73
72
71
370
Roberts Farm
MOWCROFTS LANE
Lincoln LN1
Newton Cliff
COLLINGHAM RD. A1133
WEST LINDSEY
NEWARK and SHERWOOD
NG22
Amblerod Plantation
Trentholme Farm
Pure Land Meditation Cen. & Japanese Garden
The Manor
BACK LA.
TRENT LANE
HIGH ST.
SILVER ST.
FREETH TER.
WATSON CL.
NORTH CLIFTON
MAIN
Fledborough
River Bank Farm
MILL LANE
MILL LA.
North Clifton Hall
Hall Farm
Manor House
Fledborough Holme
Sewer Dyke
MOOR LA.
Newark
Sewage Works
CHURCH LANE
Poultry Houses
North Clifton Prim. Sch.
Church Farm
RIVER TRENT
P
Pav.
Sports Field
High Marnham Power Station
Clifton Plantation
NG23
Manor Farm
Coronation Hall
MOOR LANE
SPARROW LANE
SPARROW LANE CARAVAN PARK
MARNHAM MEADOW HOLIDAY PARK
TRENT LANE
NEWARK and SHERWOOD
BASSETLAW
CHURCH LA.
FRONT ST.
Oaklands Farm
Hill Farm
HOLLOWGATE LANE
SOUTH CLIFTON
BACK STREET
LONDON ROW
TRENT BANK
Nursery
HIGH ST.
VICARAGE ROAD
ROAD
High Marnham
Marnham Hall
Sports Field
Highfield Farm
Pav.
LANE
YARD
Ferry Holme
COAL
Clifton Hill

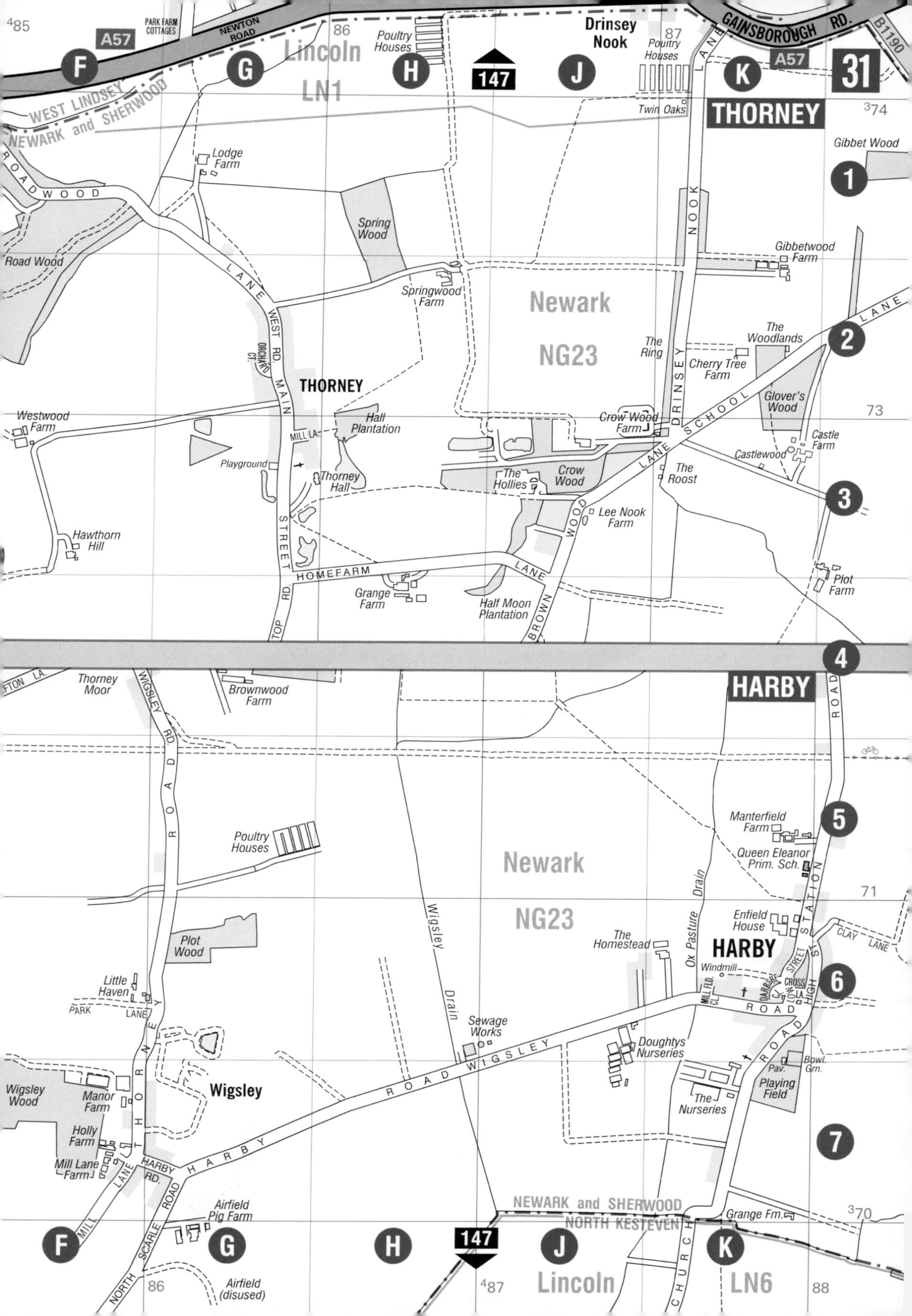

31
A57
PARK FARM COTTAGES
NEWTON ROAD
Lincoln
LN1
Poultry Houses
147
Drinsey Nook
Poultry Houses
GAINSBOROUGH RD.
B1190
THORNEY
Twin Oaks
WEST LINDSEY
NEWARK and SHERWOOD
Gibbet Wood
Lodge Farm
WOOD ROAD
Road Wood
Spring Wood
NOOK
Gibbetwood Farm
LANE
WEST RD.
MAIN
Springwood Farm
Newark
NG23
The Ring
The Woodlands
Cherry Tree Farm
ORCHARD CT.
THORNEY
DRINSEY
SCHOOL
Glover's Wood
Westwood Farm
Hall Plantation
Crow Wood Farm
MILL LA.
Castle Farm
Castlewood
Playground
The Hollies
Crow Wood
The Roost
Thorney Hall
STREET
Lee Nook Farm
WOOD
Hawthorn Hill
HOMEFARM
LANE
Plot Farm
TOP RD.
Grange Farm
Half Moon Plantation
BROWN
HARBY
Thorney Moor
WIGSLEY RD.
Brownwood Farm
ROAD
Manterfield Farm
Poultry Houses
Newark
Queen Eleanor Prim. Sch.
STATION
Wigsley
NG23
Enfield House
Plot Wood
The Homestead
Drain
Ox Pasture
HARBY
CLAY LANE
Windmill
Little Haven
PARK
LANE
MILL FLD. CL.
DARBASE CL.
LOW ST.
CROSS LA.
HIGH ST.
Sewage Works
Doughtys Nurseries
THORNEY
Wigsley Wood
Manor Farm
Wigsley
ROAD WIGSLEY
Pav.
Bowl. Grn.
Playing Field
The Nurseries
Holly Farm
Mill Lane Farm
HARBY RD.
HARBY
ROAD
Airfield Pig Farm
NEWARK and SHERWOOD
NORTH KESTEVEN
Grange Fm.
MILL
NORTH SCARLE
147
CHURCH
Airfield (disused)
Lincoln
LN6

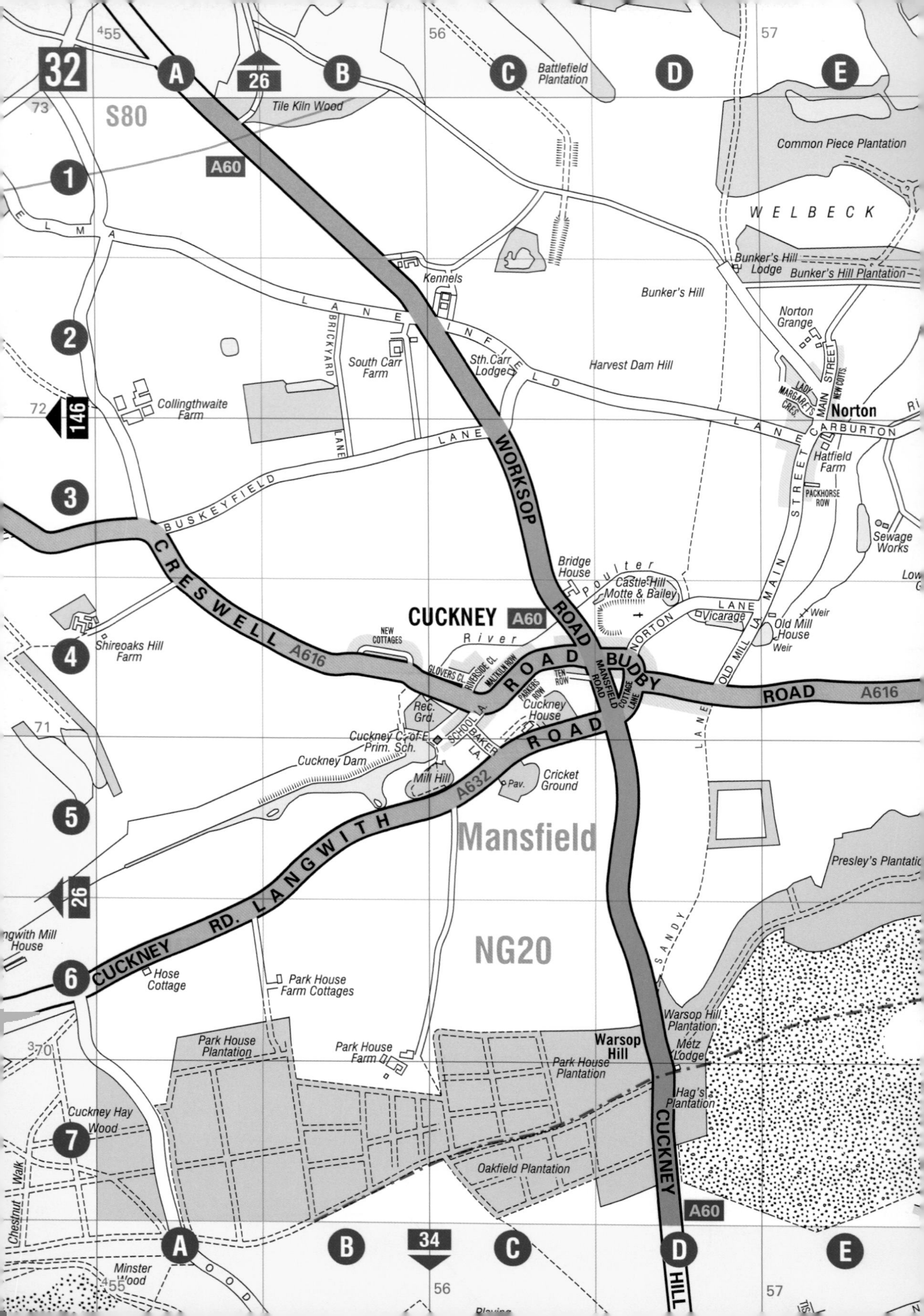

26
Battlefield Plantation
Tile Kiln Wood
S80
A60
Common Piece Plantation
WELBECK
ELMA
Bunker's Hill Lodge
Bunker's Hill Plantation
Kennels
Bunker's Hill
LANE INFIELD
BRICKYARD LANE
South Carr Farm
Sth.Carr Lodge
Harvest Dam Hill
Norton Grange
146
Collingthwaite Farm
LADY MARGARETS CRES.
MAIN STREET
NEW COTTS.
Norton
CARBURTON LANE
Hatfield Farm
PACKHORSE ROW
BUSKEYFIELD LANE
WORKSOP ROAD
Sewage Works
Bridge House
Poulter
Castle Hill Motte & Bailey
CUCKNEY
A60
NORTON LANE
Vicarage
Weir
Old Mill House
CRESWELL ROAD
A616
Shireoaks Hill Farm
NEW COTTAGES
River
GLOVERS CL.
RIVERSIDE CL.
MALTKILN ROW
TEN ROW
MANSFIELD ROAD
COTTAGE LANE
BUDBY ROAD
OLD MILL LA.
Rec. Grd.
PARKERS ROW
Cuckney House
SCHOOL LA.
BAKER LA.
Cuckney C. of E. Prim. Sch.
Cuckney Dam
Mill Hill
Pav.
Cricket Ground
A632
Mansfield
Presley's Plantation
26
Langwith Mill House
CUCKNEY RD. LANGWITH
SANDY LANE
NG20
Hose Cottage
Park House Farm Cottages
Warsop Hill Plantation
Métz Lodge
Park House Plantation
Park House Farm
Warsop Hill
Park House Plantation
Hag's Plantation
Cuckney Hay Wood
CUCKNEY HILL
Oakfield Plantation
Chestnut Walk
A60
34
Minster Wood
WOOD

F Moss Hall Plantation

G Tichfield Hill

H

J Pitiful Clump

Fox Hill Plantation

Pitiful Hill Plantation

K Youngrough Breck

Mellish's Plantation

1

73

GREAT LAKE

Kennel Plantation

Fox Covert Plantation

Cat Hills Plantation

Fasque Plantation

Fasque Screed

Nightingale Plantation

Worksop

Meadow Lodge

River Poulter

2

P A R K

Weir

Milnthorpe Lodge

Carburton Forge Dam

Carburton Dam

L I M E T R E E

Forge Lodge

Weir

Works

S80

Gibraltar Lodge

72

A V E N U E

Poulter

LANE

Corunna Lodge

Corunna Hill Plantation

Gibraltar Plantation

3

Bentinck Lodge

Battarain Plantation

Burn's Breck

Lord Woodstock's Plantation

Hazel Gap Wood

Hazel Gap

Hazel Gap Farm

146 ▶

Kingsland Lodge

atfield ge

A616

B U D B Y

4

71

High Hatfield

Sedan Lodge

Gleadthorpe Breck Plantation

D R.

5

Hatfield Plantation

BASSETLAW MANSFIELD

Gleadthorpe Screed

Gleadthorpe Plantation

Gleadthorpe Lodge

L A N E

6

37

Elkesley Hill

Football Ground

Cricket Ground

Sports Ground

BUDBY

ELKESLEY PL.

CRANBERRY PK.

MARION CL.

CRESCENT

PORTLAND CR. AV.

RUFFORD AV.

BUDBY CRES.

PREST AV.

HATFIELD

JACKSON TER.

Gleadthorpe Experimental Husbandry Farm

Gleadthorpe Grange

River Meden

H A N G E R

70

HILL

ROAD

EASTLAND DR.

EASTLANDS TER.

Gleadthorpe Cottage

7

Holborn Hill Plantation

EGMANTON

CARBURTON AV.

HAUGHTON

NORTON

OSSINGTON

MANBY

WISTON

LAXTON DR.

MELVILLE

PERLETHORPE CT.

KNEESALL

TUXFORD AV.

THORESBY

ROAD

Eastlands Jun. Sch.

Netherfield Inf. Sch.

NETHERFIELD

LANE

NETHERFIELD CL.

MEDEN SIDE

Play. Fld.

Meden Vale

P

Assarts Farm

EGMANTON

ETHERFIELD

F

G

H **35** ▽

J

K Boundary Plantation

The Bottoms

58

59

⁴60

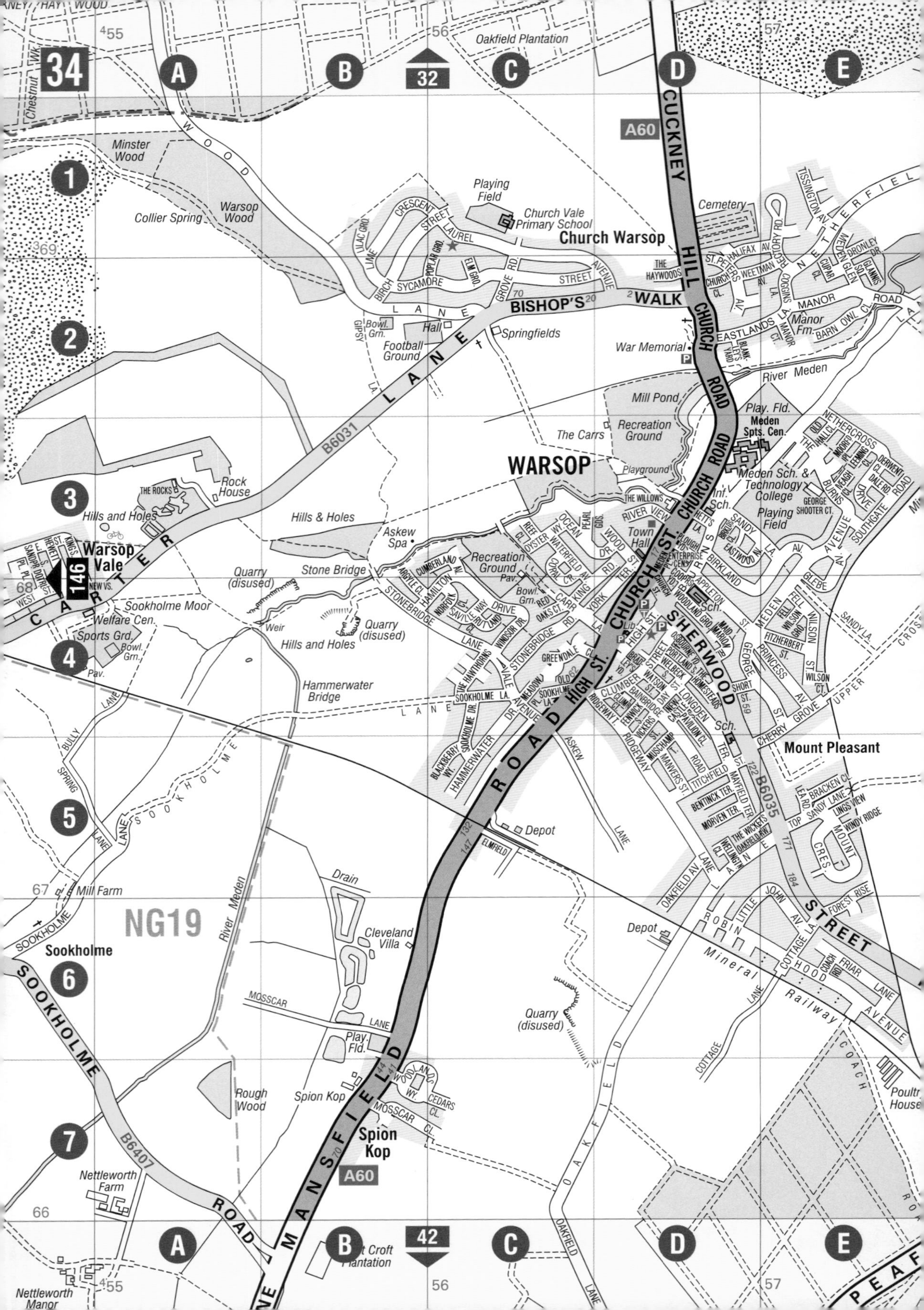

Oakfield Plantation
32
Minster Wood
Warsop Wood
Collier Spring
Playing Field
Church Vale Primary School
Church Warsop
CUCKNEY HILL
CHURCH ROAD
A60
Cemetery
BISHOP'S WALK
LANE
B6031
Bowl. Grn.
Hall
Football Ground
Springfields
War Memorial
River Meden
Mill Pond
Recreation Ground
The Carrs
Play. Fld.
Meden Spts. Cen.
WARSOP
Playground
Meden Sch. & Technology College
Playing Field
Rock House
THE ROCKS
Hills and Holes
Hills & Holes
Askew Spa
Town Hall
Warsop Vale
146
Quarry (disused)
Stone Bridge
Recreation Ground
CARTER
Sookholme Moor
Welfare Cen.
Sports Grd.
Bowl. Grn.
Pav.
Weir
Hills and Holes
Quarry (disused)
Hammerwater Bridge
SHERWOOD
HIGH ST.
CHURCH ST.
Mount Pleasant
B6035
Depot
ELMFIELD
MANSFIELD ROAD
Mill Farm
NG19
River Meden
Sookholme
SOOKHOLME
Drain
Cleveland Villa
Depot
STREET
Mineral Railway
MOSSCAR LANE
Play. Fld.
Quarry (disused)
Rough Wood
Spion Kop
Spion Kop
A60
OAKFIELD LANE
COTTAGE LANE
Poultry House
Nettleworth Farm
B6407
SOOKHOLME ROAD
42
Nettleworth Manor
Croft Plantation

F G H J K

33

35

1

2

3

36

4

5

6

7

F G H J K

43

Meden Vale

The Bottoms

Burns Farm

Netherfield Inf. Sch.

Eastlands Jun. Sch.

Play. Fld.

Assarts Farm

Assarts Hill Plantation

Sewage Works

Mansfield

NG20

Sod Wall Plantation

Jerusalem Plantation

Ling Plantation

THE LINGS

Warsop Quarter

Turner's Plantation

Bottom Vals Hill

Norman's Plantation

Top Vals Hill

Cabin Plantation

Black Pool

Blakeley Hill

Blakeley Hill Plantation

Meden Farm

Rough Piece

The Sarts

NG21

Bradmer Hill

Welbeck Colliery Junction

Towermill (disused)

Depots

Windmill Plantation

B6035

ROAD

LANE

A6075

A6075

Broomhill Grange

Gorseybrecks

Broomhill Gorse

Gleadthorpe New Plantation

Boundary Plantation

Holborn Hill Plantation

Hang

Hanger Hill

Fox Den Planta

Blackp Planta

Clips

Park

Gorsethorpe

FIELD A6075

Mansfield & Sherwood

NEWARK & SHERWOOD

CLIPSTONE

HANGER

HILL

DRIVE

DRIVE

CLIPSTONE

GREEN

DRIVE

DRIVE

FOREST

LANE

LING

BLAKELEY

Broomhill

Railway

59

369

68

67

66

460

58

59

60

33

36

37

38

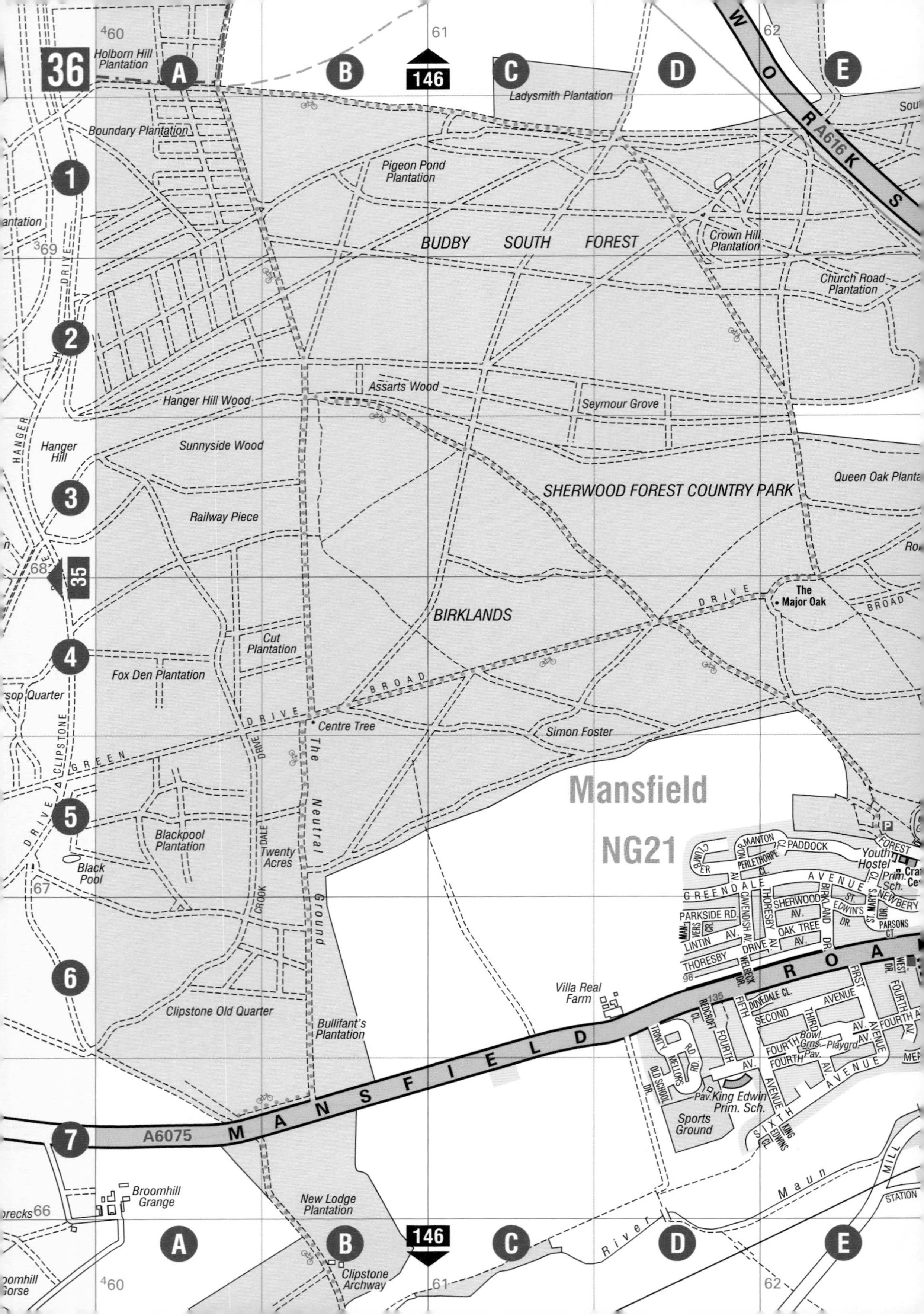
Holborn Hill Plantation
Ladysmith Plantation
Boundary Plantation
Pigeon Pond Plantation
BUDBY SOUTH FOREST
Crown Hill Plantation
Church Road Plantation
WORKSOP ROAD
A616
Assarts Wood
Hanger Hill Wood
Seymour Grove
Hanger Hill
HANGER HILL DRIVE
Sunnyside Wood
SHERWOOD FOREST COUNTRY PARK
Queen Oak Plantation
Railway Piece
The Major Oak
BIRKLANDS
BROAD DRIVE
Cut Plantation
Fox Den Plantation
Centre Tree
Simon Foster
GREEN DRIVE
CLIPSTONE DRIVE
CROOK DALE DRIVE
The Neutral Ground
Mansfield
NG21
Blackpool Plantation
Black Pool
Twenty Acres
Clipstone Old Quarter
Bullifant's Plantation
Villa Real Farm
MANSFIELD ROAD
A6075
Broomhill Grange
New Lodge Plantation
Clipstone Archway
River Maun
Sports Ground
King Edwin Prim. Sch.
Youth Hostel
Prim. Sch.
PADDOCK
FOREST
GREENDALE AVENUE
PARKSIDE RD.
LINTIN AV.
THORESBY DRIVE
SHERWOOD AV.
OAK TREE AV.
BIRKLAND DR.
PERLETHORPE CL.
MANTON
CLUMBER AV.
EDWIN'S DR.
ST. MARY'S
NEWBERY
PARSONS CT.
WELBECK DR.
REDCROFT CL.
FIFTH
DOVEDALE CL.
SECOND
THIRD
FOURTH AV.
FIRST AVENUE
FOURTH AVENUE
SIXTH AVENUE
TRINITY
NELLORS RD.
OLD SCHOOL DR.
Bowl. Grns. Pav.
Playgrd.
STATION
MILL
EDWINS
KING
4 60
61
62
3 69
68
67
66
146
35
A
B
C
D
E
1
2
3
4
5
6
7

Ceres Lodge
Grove
Smiths Hill
Vincent Grove
Charles Wood
Works
CHESTNUT AVENUE
146
Old Oaks
Old Buck Gates
Proteus Camp
Clay Pits
THORESBY PARK
Postmans Wicket
Ollerton Corner
Ollerton Assarts Plantation
Stilehollow Plantation
Hawk Clump
BILHAUGH
Shooting Range
B6034
BEECH AVENUE
BLYTH ROAD
38
Sherwood Forest Visitors Centre
A616 ROAD
Burstheart Hill
Sherwood Heath Nature Reserve
THORESBURY COLLIERY
MANSFIELD RD.
NEWARK ROAD
Weirs
Hamlyn Lodge
Cockglode Cottages
A6075
OLLERTON ROAD
River Maun
EDWINSTOWE
MAYTHORN GRO.
THE WHEELWRIGHTS
CHURCH ST.
SWINECOTE ROAD
COLLIERY VILLAS
MAID MARION DR.
GREENWOOD AV.
LYNDS CL.
LANSBURY
EAST LANE
HIGH ST.
Black Hills Plantation
Black Hills Farm
Carr Brecks Farm
Newark
Sewage Works
NG22
Rainworth Water
OLD RUFFORD ROAD
A614
STATION RD.
KINGS DR.
Ollerton Station Farm
Edwinstowe House
Weir
HIGH STREET
CHAPEL CT.
FRIEND LA.
DUKERIES CRES.
WOODHEAD CL.
BOY LANE
OLD STATION YARD
OCCUPATION LA.
RUFFORD ROAD
B6034
HENTON RD.
ABBEY RD.
CARVER CL.
BEARDSLEY RD.
GAITSKILL CRES.
ROBIN HOOD AV.
SANDY LA.
INSET
Lidgett
Mansfield
NG21
MERRYWEATHER CL.
SANDY LA.
GREENFIELD CL.
BROCKLEHURST DR.
HAWTHORNE WAY
OAKWOOD GRO.
PORTLAND ROW
PINEWOOD AV.
Sth. Forest Leisure Cen.
CLIPSTONE RD.
B6030
Holly Farm
Ollerton Hills
SHERWOOD CASTLE HOLIDAY FOREST

38
A
B
C
D
E
1
2
3
4
5
6
7
146
37
A614
A616
A6075
B6461
B6387
BLYTH ROAD
WORKSOP RD.
MANSFIELD RD.
OLLERTON RD.
MAIN ST.
BACK LA.
FOREST RD.
TUXFORD ROAD
WELLOW ROAD
NEWARK ROAD
RUFFORD ROAD
STATION RD.
BESCAR LANE
WHINNEY LANE
BRAKE LA.
Boughton Brake
Boughton Pumping Sta.
New Zealand Cottage
Ollerton Corner
River Maun
Works
Sports Ground
Maun Inf. Sch.
Forest View Jun. Sch.
Weir
Ollerton Hall
War Mem.
Ollerton Watermill
Weirs
Hamlyn Lodge
Ollerton
Superstore
Cemy.
Lib.
Sherwood Energy Village
Red Ho.
Sherwood Network Cen.
NEW OLLERTON
Depot
Newark
NG22
The Dukeries College
Dukeries Leisure Cen.
Playing Fields
Ollerton Prim. Sch.
Running Track
Bowling Greens
Games Cts.
Playing Field
Comm. Cen.
St. Josephs Catholic Prim. School
Sherwood Forest Crematorium
Fairholme Park Homes
Fairfield Park
Ollerton Station Farm
Poultry Houses
Wellow Dam
Crkt. Grd.
Pav.
Park Farm
Wellow
Wellow House School
Scotts Farm
Pinfold
Gorge Dyke
Brick Yard Farm
Brickyard Cottages
Caravan Site
Wellow Lodge
Ollerton Hills
Sherwood Castle Holiday Forest

F
G
H
J
K
27
146
147
Kirton
Boughton
Manor Farm
Yew Tree Farm
Seven Acres
Hall Farm
Glebe Farm
OLLERTON ROAD
A6075
STREET
MAIN
STATION RD.
RICE HILL
Goosemoor Dyke
GOLDEN HILL LA.
Gate House Farm
RETFORD ROAD
B6387
LANE
CONNAH LA.
BARONS DR.
Doncaster Farm
Playing Field
Doncaster Farm Cottages
Manor Farm
CHURCH ROAD
CHURCH RD.
MANOR CL.
PICKINS RW.
FAIRWEATHER CL.
The Willows
Pump House
Boughton Dyke
BOUGHTON INDUSTRIAL ESTATE (NORTH)
KIRTON PK.
THE FURZE
PRIMROSE LA.
PRIMROSE LANE
West View Farm
HARROW LA.
HARROW LANE CARAVAN SITE
Cocking Hill Farm
TRENT ROAD
MAUN WAY
LEEN CT.
BOUGHTON WY.
MEDEN RD.
MEDEN CT.
BOUGHTON INDUSTRIAL ESTATE (SOUTH)
Sewage Works
Works
Sports Ground
COCKING HILL ACRE EDGE ROAD
Norton Wood
Golden Hill
Reservoirs (covered)
Laxton Common
Beth Shalom Holocaust Centre
Westwood Farm
WELLOW PARK
Cocking Moor
Kennels Farm
Jordan Castle Lodge Farm
Jordan Castle
Jordan Castle Farm
MOOR LANE
COOKING
Gallow Hole Dyke
LANE
SHORTWOOD
A616
Endeavour
Wood Close Farm

40
146
46
New Houghton
Works
Lodge Farm
Pleasleypark Farm
Moorgate Hollow
Windyridge
Red House
PLEASLEY PARK
Mill
Mill Pond
PLEASLEY VALE BUSINESS PARK
Activity Centre
River
Pleasley Vale
The Coppice
Roman Villa (Site of)
Wren Hill Farm
Lower Radmanthwaite
Radmanthwaite Cottage
Mansfield
West Sidings
Playing Field
NG19
Pleasley Pit Country Park
PLEASLEY
Colliery (disused)
Cricket Ground
Pleasleyhill Farm
Pleasleyhill
Cemetery
Farmilo Primary School
Radmanthwaite
Upper Pleasley
Bungalow Farm
Pump House
River Meden
Moorhaigh Cottage
Sampson's Lane Farm
Moorhaigh Farm
Moorhaigh
Penniment Bungalow Farm
Cotton Plantation
Bull Farm
Nursing Home
Comm. Cen.
Rec. Grd.
Crescent Prim. Sch.
MILLENNIUM BUSINESS PARK
A617
A6191
B6407
B6417
CHESTERFIELD ROAD
COMMON LANE
NORTH ROAD
ABBOT RD.
Football Grd.
Play. Fld.
Sch.
Cemy.
Rec. Grd.

41
146
42
47
F
G
H
J
K
1
2
3
4
5
6
7
53
54
55
66
65
64
63
Warsop Park Farm
Ox Pasture Wood
Nettleworth Farm
Spring Wood
Hop Yard
Nettleworth Manor
River Meden
The Shrubbery
Hind Car Wood
Hind Car
Home Farm
Park Hall
Fish Pond
Littlewood
BOLSOVER
MANSFIELD
Little Matlock
Northfield Plantation
Meden
Works
TOP ROW
Meden Bank
Cricket Grd.
Stone Quarry
Garden Plantation
Quarry (Disused)
Quarry Plantation
MANSFIELD WOODHOUSE GOLF COURSE
Club House
The Birches
Park Hall Farm
Warehouse
The Bungalow
Stone Quarry
The Bungalow
Sunnydale
Sunnydale Farm
North Lodge
North Lodge Cottage
Northfield Prim. Sch.
Comm. Cen.
Bath House Farm
Manor Park Sports Complex
Games Ct.
Playing Field
Tennis Ct.
Bowl. Grns.
The Manor School
Playing Field
Tennis Courts
Schools
Fernlea
NORTHFIELD LANE
AVENUE
LITTLEWOOD
COMMON
FELTON AVENUE
THE FAIRWAYS
NORTH
LEEMING LANE
PEAFIELD LA.
MARPLES
Hornby Plantation
Playgrd.
Comm. Cen.
Rec. Grd.
Prim. Sch.
Works
OXCLOSE
Mansfield Woodhouse
Burial Grd.
A60
WELBECK RD.
WARSOP RD.
SOUTH
PRIORY RD.
LANE
A6075
DEBDALE
Sports Ground
Debdale Hall
Debdale Hall Farm
Debdale Hall Cottage
Cemetery
MANSFIELD WOODHOUSE
Maun Valley Park
FOREST PARK MOBILE HOMES
TALL TREES PARK HOMES
Hillcrest
OLD MILL LANE
A6117
B6032
MANSFIELD RD.
Yeoman Hill Park
Paddling Pool
Bandstand
SHERWOOD RISE
Queen Elizabeth Endowed School
Tennis Courts
Playing Fields
Swimming Cen.
CHESTERFIELD RD. STH.
Maun View
Works
OLD MILL LANE INDUSTRIAL ESTATE
Hallam's Grave
Sewage Treatment Works
Games

42
34
41
48
A
B
C
D
E
1
2
3
4
5
6
7
Spion Kop
Nettleworth Farm
Nettleworth Manor
The Bottoms
West Croft Plantation
Westfield House Farm
Forest Hill Plantation
Redbrick House
REDBRICK HO. CAMPSITE
Gravelhill Plantation
Old Churn Oak
SOOKHOLME ROAD
B6407
MANSFIELD RD.
LEEMING LANE
NORTH LEEMING
A60
LITTLEWOOD LA.
MANSFIELD WOODHOUSE GOLF COURSE
Club House
Fish Pond
THE FAIRWAYS
OAKFIELD LANE
PACKMAN'S ROAD
MANSFIELD NEWARK and SHERWOOD
Crimea Farm
Peafield Plantation
PEAFIELD NEW PLANTATION
Mansfield
Peafield Farm
Peafield Cottages
Small Dale
PEAFIELD
A6075
GREEN LANE
SPA LANE
Gorse Covert
Weir
Snake Hill
Whinney Hill
Hornby Plantation
River Maun
Weirs
Warren Cottages
Warren Farm
Community Centre
Peafield La. Prim. Sch.
Meadow Cottage
NG19
Spa Ponds
Garibaldi Plantation
Recreation Ground
MANSFIELD WOODHOUSE
NEW MILL LANE
Maun Valley Park
Candlemas Cliff
FOREST PARK MOBILE HOMES
TALL TREES PARK HOMES
Hillcrest
OLD MILL LANE
A6117
Superstore
Comm. Cen.
Prim. Sch.
CLIPSTONE RD. WEST
B6030
Newlands
CLIPSTONE
Forest

43
35
49
146
NG20
NG21
CLIPSTONE
Kings Clipstone
Parliament Oak
Gorseybrecks
Broomhill Gorse
GORSETHORPE COTTAGES
Lamb Pens Farm
SHERWOOD FOREST CARAVAN PARK
Cavendish Lodge
Lawn Hills
Cavendish Wood
River Maun
Chestnut Screed
Mast
Intake Wood
Waterfield Farm
High Rocks
Badger Hill
Cemetery
Baulker Farm
Works
Newlands Junior School
Playing Field
John T. Rice Inf. Sch.
Sports Ground
Football Grd.
Garibaldi College Playing Field
Vicar Pond
Vicar Water Visitor Cen.
VICAR WATER COUNTRY PARK
Bridleways Camping & Caravan Pk.
Newlands Farm
Clipstone Colliery Junction
CLIPSTONE FOREST
Vicar Water
EAST MANSFIELD ROAD
B6030
A6075

M1 MOTORWAY
M1
Stanley
Stanley House Farm
Stanley Farm
Stanley Grange
Dale Farm
Poultry Farm
Hillingdon
STANLEY LANE
SILVERHILL LANE
SHEPHERD'S LANE
ASHFIELD
BOLSOVER
The Hurst
Shepherd's Lane Farm
Dunsil Farm
Fackley
SILVERHILL COTTAGES
TEVERSAL CAMPING & CARAVAN SITE
Hare Plantation
Tibshelf Wharf Farm
WHARF LANE
The Cottage
Silverhill Farm
THE PARK
TIBSHELF ROAD
B6014
MANSFIELD RD.
WILD HILL
Overmoor Farm
SAW PIT LANE
Works
SAW PIT INDUSTRIAL ESTATE
TIBSHELF BUSINESS PK.
Shepherd's Lane Plantation
Whiteboro Cottages
CHESTERFIELD LANE
South Bank
Orchard Farm
City of Whiteborough Farm
Sewage Works
Marlpits Farm
Reservoirs (Covered)
Whiteborough Farm
River Meden
WHARF
Tibshelf Service Area
Newtonwood Lodge Farm
NEWTONWOOD LANE
Alfreton
Recreation Ground
Herrod's Hill
BRIERLEY FOREST GOLF COURSE
Woodend Cottage
Woodland Cottage
Rec. Grd.
SPANG LANE
Recreation Ground
DE55
Smallholding
WOODLAND AV.
STRAWBERRY BANK
PENNINE
CLEGG HILL DR.
PORTLAND HGTS.
Ten. Cts.
Play. Fld.
John Davies Prim. Sch.
Club Ho.
Hilltop Fm.
BARKER ST.
WENHAM LA.
ROWAN CROFT
BACK LANE
Holly House Farm
Playing Field
Brierley Forest Park Visitor Centre
JOHN DAVIES WORKSHOP
ROOLEY
Factory
NORTH ST.
Leisure Cen.
NEWCASTLE ST.
SAMPSONS YD.
SWANN YD.
HAWKINS AV.
SHERWOOD ST.
SUMMERHILL CT.
BOOTS YD.
MKT. ST.
MKT. PL.
NEWFALL ST.
FALL ST.
PARKSIDE
SKEGBY RD.
PARK GDNS.
HIGH ST.
Red Barn Farm
RED BARN LANE
Trotting Track
Longside Farm
Longside Cottage Farm
HUTHWAITE
SUTTON ROAD
Lib.
Bowl. Grns.
Pav.
MILL CL.
MILL LA.
War Mem.
LIME AV.
BEECH AV.
ELMHURST DR.
Cemy.
Ten Cts.
Huthwaite Welfare Grd.
CORNER CROFT AV.
Factory
TOWN LA.
Spring Farm
Sunnyside Farm
Factory
OAKLAND CFT.
CHURCH SIDE
FARNSWORTH GRO.
COLUMBIA ST.
COMMON RD.
CHURCH MEAD
Inf. Sch.
BLACKWELL ROAD
B6026
LA.
Yew Tree Farm
HUTHWAITE
50
BOWSER DR.
BLENHEIM PL.
LITTLE LANE
WAY
THE COUNTY ESTATE
WHITEGATES
LITTLE LA.
SUDBURY
CALKE DR.
ORDBURY
STAINSBY GRO.
YEW TREE DR.
ROSE COTTAGE DR.
OAKLAND AV.
SPRINGWELL ST.
GREENWOOD AV.
HIGH HALLES DR.
STREET
MERCIA CT.
CROSS
LANE
Greenwood

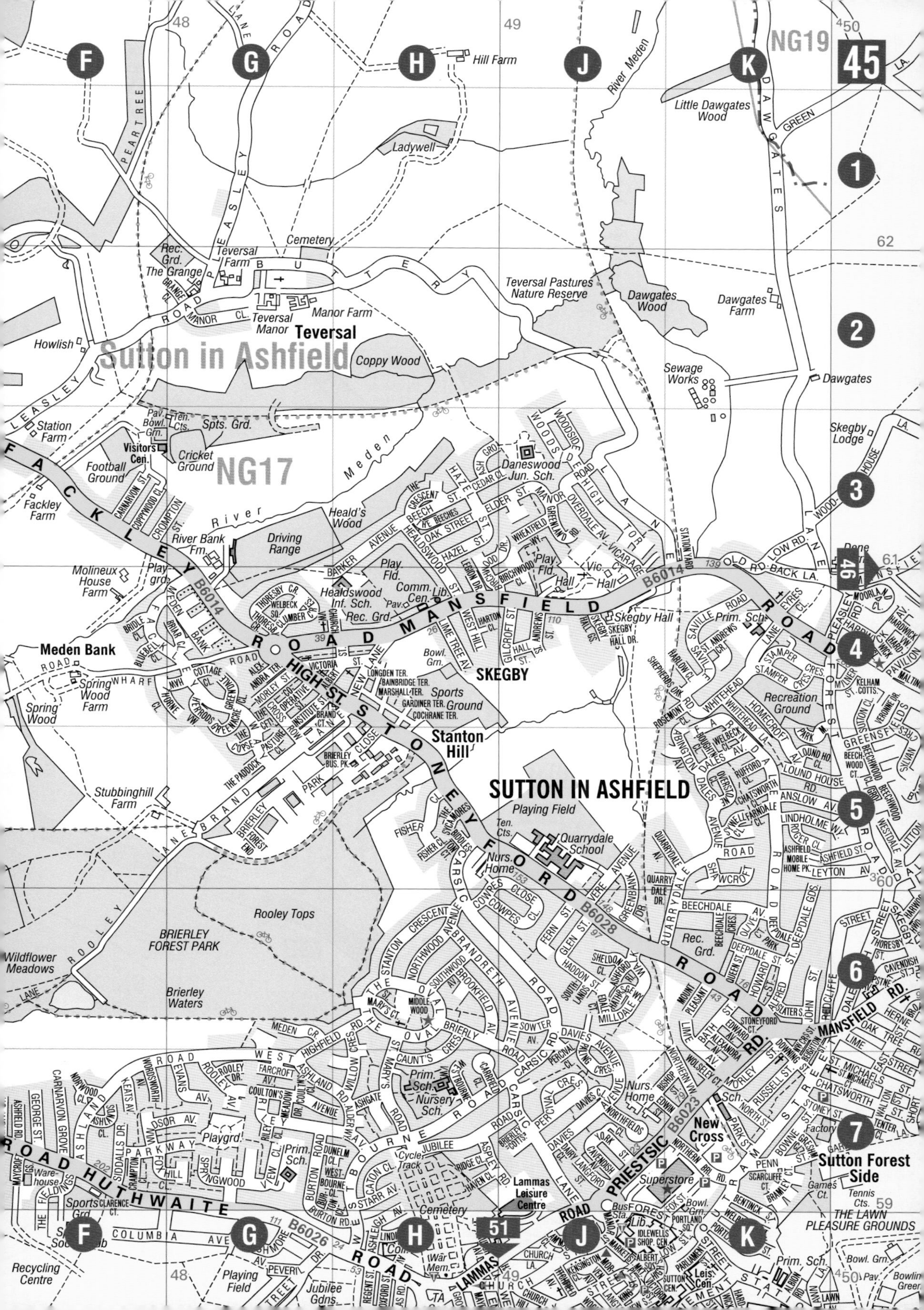
NG19
Hill Farm
River Meden
Little Dawgates Wood
Ladywell
Cemetery
Teversal Farm
Rec. Grd.
The Grange
Teversal Manor
Manor Farm
Teversal
Teversal Pastures Nature Reserve
Dawgates Wood
Dawgates Farm
Howlish
Sutton in Ashfield
Coppy Wood
Sewage Works
Dawgates
Station Farm
Spts. Grd.
Visitors Cen.
Cricket Ground
Football Ground
NG17
Daneswood Jun. Sch.
Skegby Lodge
Fackley Farm
River Bank Fm.
Driving Range
Heald's Wood
Molineux House Farm
Healdswood Inf. Sch.
Comm. Cen.
Rec. Grd.
Skegby Hall
Meden Bank
Spring Wood Farm
Spring Wood
SKEGBY
Recreation Ground
Sports Ground
Stanton Hill
SUTTON IN ASHFIELD
Stubbinghill Farm
Playing Field
Quarrydale School
Nurs. Home
Rooley Tops
BRIERLEY FOREST PARK
Wildflower Meadows
Brierley Waters
Prim. Sch.
Nursery Sch.
Playgrd.
Nurs. Home
New Cross
Sutton Forest Side
Superstore
Lammas Leisure Centre
Cemetery
Recycling Centre
Playing Field
Jubilee Gdns.
THE LAWN PLEASURE GROUNDS
FACKLEY ROAD
MANSFIELD ROAD
HIGH ST.
STONEYFORD ROAD
HUTHWAITE ROAD
PRIESTSIC ROAD
B6014
B6028
B6026
B6023
46
51

A
B
C
D
E
1
2
3
4
5
6
7
40
45
52
Bull Farm
Cotts Plantation
Water Lane Farm
Penniment Lodge Farm
Penniment House Farm
Penniment Farm
Penniment Cottage
A617
A6075
NG19
Dawgates
Skegby Lodge
Dene Farm
Nursery
Fields Farm
Hill Top
Fishpond Hill
Ashland Farm
Ashlands House
Dalestorth House
Reservoirs (Covered)
Road Safety Training Cen.
Playing Field
Playing Fields
Rosebrook Primary Sch.
Redgate Sch.
Ladybrook
Recreation Ground
B6014
SKEGBY ROAD
ABBOTT ROAD
BECK LANE
KINGS MILL ROAD EAST
MANSFIELD ROAD
Dalestorth
SUTTON IN ASHFIELD
Millbrook Unit
KING'S MILL HOSPITAL
KING'S TREATMENT CENTRE
Hospice
Day Cen.
Superstore
The Dukeries Cen.
Byron Ho.
Prim. School
Rec. Grd.
Comm. Cen.
Sutton in Ashfield
NG17
B6023
A38
KINGSMILL RESERVOIR
Sailing Club
The Mill Adventure Base
Viaduct
River Maun
STOKES TRADING EST.
ABBEY IND. PK.
ABBEY TRADE PK.
Works
Sewage Works
Sports Ground
Sutton Forest Side
Games Court
Tennis Cts.
THE LAWN PLEASURE GROUNDS
Playground
Factory
Hamilton Hill
Hamilton Hill Farm
MAUN VALLEY INDUSTRIAL PARK
Depot
Wks.
Bowling Green
Bowl. Grn.
Prim. Sch.
All Saints RC Sch.
Rec. Grd.

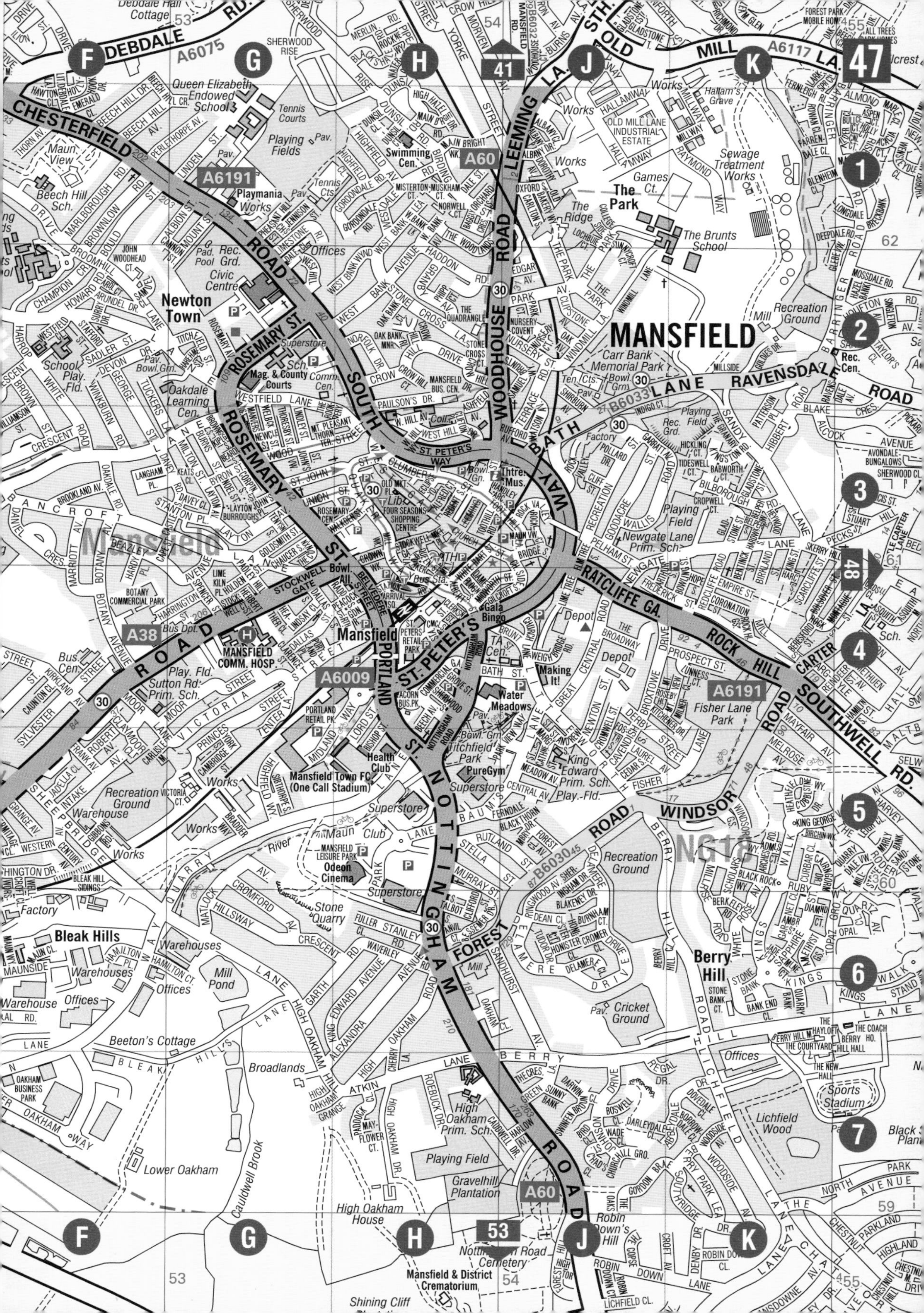
47
MANSFIELD
Mansfield
NG18
F
G
H
J
K
1
2
3
4
5
6
7
41
48
53
54
55
59
60
61
62
DEBDALE RD.
Debdale Hall Cottage
A6075
CHESTERFIELD ROAD
A6191
A60
A38
A6009
A6117
B6033
B6030
MILL LA.
OLD MILL LANE INDUSTRIAL ESTATE
Sewage Treatment Works
The Park
The Brunts School
Queen Elizabeth Endowed School
Playing Fields
Tennis Courts
Swimming Cen.
Playmania
Beech Hill Sch.
Maun View
Newton Town
Civic Centre
Rec. Grd.
Pad. Pool
Offices
Superstore
Mag. & County Courts
Oakdale Learning Cen.
ROSEMARY ST.
SOUTH
WOODHOUSE ROAD
LEEMING LA.
Carr Bank Memorial Park
MANSFIELD BUS. CEN.
RAVENSDALE ROAD
BATH LANE
ST. PETER'S WAY
Thtre. Mus.
FOUR SEASONS SHOPPING CENTRE
Lib.
Bus Sta.
Gala Bingo
Mansfield
STOCKWELL GATE
ROAD
MANSFIELD COMM. HOSP.
Bus Dpt.
Sutton Rd. Prim. Sch.
Play. Fld.
Bus Cen.
BOTANY COMMERCIAL PARK
RATCLIFFE GA.
ROCK HILL
SOUTHWELL RD.
CARTER LANE
Newgate Lane Prim. Sch.
Playing Field
Recreation Ground
Rec. Cen.
Depot
PORTLAND ST.
PORTLAND RETAIL PK.
ST. PETERS RETAIL PARK
Water Meadows
Making It!
Fisher Lane Park
WINDSOR ROAD
NOTTINGHAM ROAD
Titchfield Park
PureGym
Health Club
Mansfield Town FC (One Call Stadium)
King Edward Prim. Sch.
Recreation Ground
Warehouse
Works
River Maun
Odeon Cinema
MANSFIELD LEISURE PARK
QUARRY LANE
Stone Quarry
Bleak Hills
Warehouses
Mill Pond
Offices
Beeton's Cottage
Broadlands
OAKHAM BUSINESS PARK
Lower Oakham
Cauldwell Brook
High Oakham House
High Oakham Prim. Sch.
Playing Field
Gravelhill Plantation
Nottingham Road Cemetery
Mansfield & District Crematorium
Shining Cliff
Robin Hood's Hill
Berry Hill
Cricket Ground
Sports Stadium
Lichfield Wood
Offices
BERRY HILL LANE
LICHFIELD LANE
FOREST ROAD
Black Plant
NORTH PARK AVENUE
ROBIN DOWN LANE

48
A
B
C
D
E
1
2
3
4
5
6
7
42
47
54
CLIPSTONE
OLD MILL LANE
A6117
WEST ROAD
Superstore
Comm. Cen.
Holly Prim. Sch.
Forest Town Prim. Sch.
B6030
Hall
Bowling Green
Queensway Park
Forest Town
Heatherley Prim. Sch.
Valeclose Plantation
CLIPSTONE RD.
PUMP HOLLOW RD.
Sports Ground
NG19
Factory
Recreation Gd.
Rec. Cen.
Samworth Church Academy
RAVENSDALE ROAD
B6033
Play. Fld.
Samworth Church Academy Sec. Sch.
Tennis Courts
Playing Fields
Ravensdale
VIOLET HILL
OAK TREE LANE
CROWN FARM WAY
CROWN FARM IND. PARK
FLETCHERS WAY
BADGER WY.
Coun. Offs.
EAKRING ROAD
Mansfield
Rugby Football Ground
Abbey Primary Sch.
SHERWOOD HALL RD.
Old Racecourse
Pav.
Bowling Green
Tennis Courts
Racecourse Recreation Ground
A6117
St. Patricks Catholic School
Driving Range Club House
NG18
Wynndale Prim. Sch.
Central Nottinghamshire Healthcare Trust HQ
Oak Tree Lane Leisure Cen.
Superstore
SOUTHWELL ROAD WEST
A6191
Bannatyne's Health Club
Thompson's Grave
RATCHER HILL
Ratcher Hill Quarry
Oak House
Cedar House
Ransom Hill
BERRY HILL LANE
Reservoir (Covered)
Res. (Cov.)
OAK TREE BUSINESS PARK
ADAMSWAY
Berry Hill Prim. & Nursery Sch.
Sports Stadium
Lichfield Wood
Pavilions
Black Scotch Plantation
King George V Playing Field
BLACK SCOTCH LANE
BELLAMY RD. IND. ESTATE
ANGLIA WAY INDUSTRIAL ESTATE
RANSOM WOOD BUS. PK.
SHERWOOD OAKS BUSINESS PARK
NORTH PARK
THE AVENUE
CHATSWORTH DRIVE
OLD NEWARK RD.
Comm. Cen.
A617
55
56
57
59
60
61
62

ROAD
Bridleways Camping & Caravan Pk.
NEWLANDS
Newlands Farm
NEWLANDS ROAD
Vicar Water
Vicar Water Visitor Cen.
VICAR WATER COUNTRY PARK
Clipstone Colliery Junction
Long Plantation
SHERWOOD FOREST GOLF COURSE
MANSFIELD NEWARK and SHERWOOD
Club House
RING ROAD
NG21
MANSFIELD GOLF COURSE
CLIPSTONE FOREST
Strawberry Hill
Slurry Pond
Ransom Hall (North Nottingham Health HQ)
RANSOM WOOD BUSINESS PARK
RAINWORTH BY-PASS
A617
Red Oaks Day Cen.
Dawn House School
The Sherwood Village Settlement
Sports Pitch
Heathlands Prim. Sch.
RANSOM ROAD
Works
Spring Hill
Rainworth Nursery
Nursery Cott.
Filter Beds
Sewage Works
Rainworth Water
B6020
SOUTHWELL ROAD EAST
Three Thorn Hollow
HELMSLEY
THE CLOSE
NURSERY GDNS.
LEEWAY CL.
LEEWAY RD.
BIRCHWOOD PARK HOMES
WOODLANDS PARK HOMES
Rainworth

43
146
55

HUTHWAITE
Alfreton
DE55
Hilcote
Commonside
NG16
Kirkstead
Junction 28
M1 MOTORWAY
MANSFIELD ROAD
ALFRETON ROAD
BLACKWELL LANE
HUTHWAITE LANE
NEW LANE
BERRISTOW LANE
HILCOTE LANE
HIGH VIEW ROAD
COMMON ROAD
PINXTON LANE
KIRKBY LANE
BROOKHILL LANE
TOWN END
Recreation Ground
Fish Farm
Sewage Works
Works
Industrial Estate
Factory
Wincobank Farm
Berristow Farm
Normanton Lodge
EAST MIDLANDS DESIGNER OUTLET
Castle Wood
Range Farm
Terrace Wood
Brookhill Hall Farm
Brookhill Hall
Halfmoon Pond
Kirkby Cliff Farm
Shire Carr Farm
Crow Trees Farm
Grange Farm
CASTLEWOOD BUSINESS PARK
The Kurburgring (Karting)
FULWOOD INDUSTRIAL ESTATE
Freight Terminal
Cutting Farm
Greenwood Falls Farm
Twinyards Farm
Yew Tree Farm
Spring Farm
Pipes Fm.
Huthwaite Welfare Grd.
Frederick Gent School
Playing Field
Hotel
Cliff Farm
The Dumbles
Maghole Brook
ASHFIELD
BOLSOVER
B6026
B6406
B6027
B6019
A38
44
58

51
45
52
59
F
G
H
J
K
1
2
3
4
5
6
7
48
49
50
56
57
58
59
SUTTON IN ASHFIELD
Sutton in Ashfield
KIRKBY-IN-ASHFIELD
Kirkby-in-Ashfield
Nottingham
NG17
Fulwood
Bentinck Town
Castle Hill
Sutton Forest Side
HUTHWAITE ROAD
KINGS MILL ROAD W.
KINGS MILL ROAD
KINGS MILL ROAD EAST
ALFRETON ROAD
SUTTON ROAD
CHURCH HILL
CHURCH ST.
PINXTON LANE
PINXTON RD.
CHAPEL ST.
THE HILL
VICTORIA ROAD
PENNY EMMA WAY
LAMMAS RD.
PRIESTSIC RD.
OUTRAM STREET
STATION ROAD
LOW ST.
HIGH PAVEMENT
KIRKBY ROAD
SUTTON MIDDLE LA.
SOUTHWELL LANE
DIVISION ROAD
WILLOWBRIDGE LA.
BROOK ST.
CHURCH ST.
HIGH ST.
LEAMINGTON DR.
HARDWICK LANE
MITCHELL ST.
COLUMBIA AVENUE
CHARNWOOD ST.
FREDERICK ST.
HENNING LANE
CALLADINE LA.
ORCHARD WAY
WENTWORTH ROAD
COPELAND RD.
WILLOW AV.
BANKS AVENUE
BERRY AVENUE
HIGHFIELD AV.
LAWRENCE AV.
COW PASTURE LANE
ORCHARD WK.
HOCKLEY VALLEY
LIME TREE
CHESTNUT AVENUE
CEDAR AVENUE
BANNERMAN RD.
VERNON RD.
HARTLEY ROAD
OCCUPATION LA.
ELM TREE RD.
LOWMOOR RD.
A38
B6023
B6026
B6018
B6019
B6020
B6021
Lammas Leisure Centre
Superstore
Bus Sta.
Lib.
IDLEWELLS SHOP. CEN.
Leis. Cen.
Coll.
War Mem.
Cemetery
Jubilee Gdns.
Recreation Ground
Play. Fld.
Sports Grd.
Sports & Social Club
Recycling Centre
Mapplewells Prim. Sch.
Pasture Farm
Works
Factories
Playing Field
Leamington Prim. Sch.
Rec. Grd.
THE LAWN PLEASURE GROUNDS
Ashfield Skills Centre
Running Track
Ashfield Sch. & Technology College
Birchwood Grange
Bloomer Wood
The Dumbles Bungalow
Mowlands Farm
Boar Hill
Franderground Farm
Greenwood Prim. Sch.
Orchard Prim. Sch.
Tichfield Park
Springfield Cottage
Depot
Cemetery
Fish Ponds
Jeffries Sch.
Studfold Farm
Studfold Wood
River Erewash
The Stables
Rec. Grd.
Portland
SOUTHWELL LANE IND. ESTATE

52
Sutton Forest Side
SUTTON IN ASHFIELD
THE LAWN PLEASURE GROUNDS
MILL ROAD
A38
46
EAST
COXMOOR ROAD
A617
Hamilton Hill
Hamilton Hill Farm
CAULDWELL
Nursery
Sutton in Ashfield
STATION ROAD
B6022
NEWARK ROAD
KIRKBY FOLLY RD.
MAUN VALLEY INDUSTRIAL PARK
Willow Wood Cen.
Round Hill
Roundhill Farm
Redhouse Farm
NG17
B6139
Fairway
Bellever
The Cedars
Sherwood Observatory
Hacienda
High Close
COXMOOR
La Vista
Windmill Hill
KINGS
PENNY EMMA WAY
B6021
Sutton Parkway
Kirkby Hardwick
51
LOWMOOR RD. IND. EST.
PROSPECT UNITS
LOWMOOR BUSINESS PARK
BYRON AVENUE
Nottingham
DAVID STREET
MARY STREET
SIDINGS ROAD
EDWARD STREET
LOWMOOR ROAD
NG17
KIRKBY-IN-ASHFIELD
Coxmoor Lodge
Coxmoor Farm
Coxmoor Plantation
SOUTHWELL LANE
Nursing Home
ALEXANDRA
Factory
Playing Field
Football Ground
ASHFIELD HEALTH VILLAGE
MILTON STREET
POPLAR AVENUE
Cox Moor
Kirkby-in-Ashfield
Council Offs.
VICTORIA ROAD
URBAN RD.
STATION ST.
Abbey Hill Prim. Sch.
Bracken Hill Sch.
DIAMOND AVENUE
B6020
BLIDWORTH
DERBY ROAD
A611
Heaths Cottages
Forest
KINGSWAY
Kingsway Park
Reservoirs (covered)
Studfold Farm
Studfold Wood
Cemetery
60
Pearl Farm
Kingsway Prim. Sch.
Vernon Farm
Halfmoon
Portland

53
Lower Oakham
High Oakham House
Playing Field
Prim. Sch.
Nottingham Road Cemetery
Mansfield & District Crematorium
Shining Cliff Plantation
Cauldwell Wood
Cauldwell Dam
CAULDWELL ROAD
Robin Down's Hill
ROBIN DOWN LANE
LICHFIELD LANE
DORCHESTER DRIVE
NEWARK ROAD
W. Notts. Coll. (Derby Rd. Site)
Tennis Cts.
OLD ROAD
A611
A60
A617
Rushey Cottage
Rushley Farm
NG18
Stonehills Plantation
Stonehills Farm
MANSFIELD
ASHFIELD
Rushley Pumping Station
Thieves' Wood
Thieves Wood Visitor Centre
Forest House
THIEVES WOOD LANE
GOLF COURSE
Club House
Two Oaks Farm
THIEVES' WOOD
Portland College
Fountaindale School
Mansfield
COXMOOR ROAD
B6139
NOMANSHILL WOOD
Rainworth Water
NG21
GEDLING
Little Nomanshill Wood
Forest Cottage
B6020
KIRKBY ROAD
NG15
Campfield Farm
LITTLE RICKET LANE
Table Tree
Blue Eaves
MANSFIELD RD.
Hallams Farm
Sheppar Stone
47
54
61
53

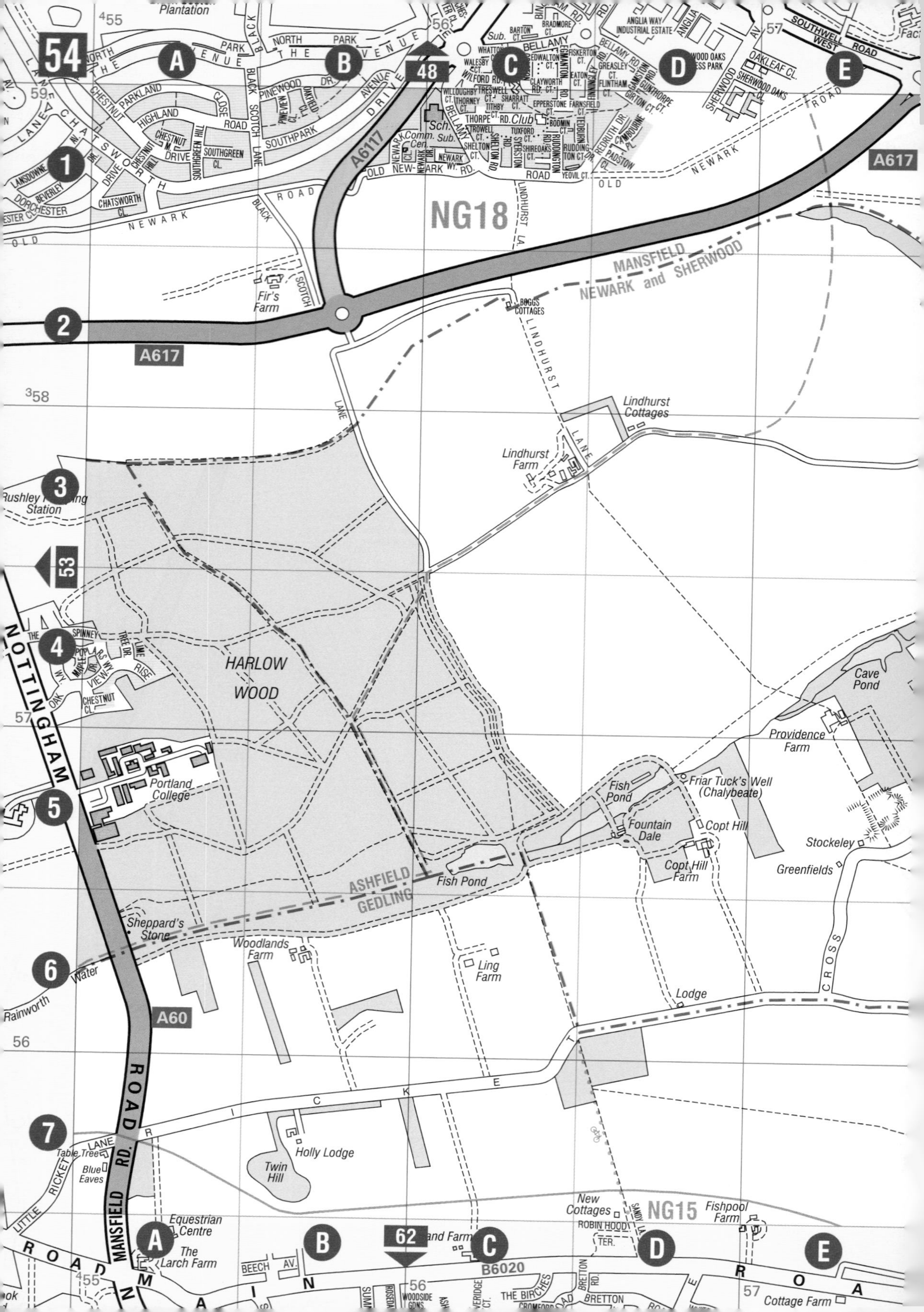

Plantation
NORTH PARK
THE AVENUE
PARKLAND
CHESTNUT
HIGHLAND
CLOSE ROAD
BLACK SCOTCH LANE
PINEWOOD DR.
SOUTHPARK AVENUE DRIVE
SOUTHGREEN HILL
SOUTHGREEN CL.
CHATSWORTH
LANSDOWNE
BEVERLEY
DORCHESTER
CHATSWORTH CL.
OLD NEWARK ROAD
A6117
48
BELLAMY
Sch.
Comm. Cen.
Sub.
THORPE RD.
Club
ANGLIA WAY INDUSTRIAL ESTATE
SHERWOOD OAKS BUSINESS PARK
OAKLEAF CL.
SHERWOOD OAKS CL.
SOUTHWELL ROAD WEST
A617
NG18
LINDHURST LA.
MANSFIELD
NEWARK and SHERWOOD
Fir's Farm
BOGGS COTTAGES
LINDHURST LANE
Lindhurst Cottages
Lindhurst Farm
Rushley Pumping Station
53
HARLOW WOOD
THE SPINNEY
POPLARS WY.
MAPLE DR.
LIME TREE DR.
RISE VIEW
OAK WY.
CHESTNUT CL.
NOTTINGHAM
Portland College
Cave Pond
Providence Farm
Fish Pond
Friar Tuck's Well (Chalybeate)
Fountain Dale
Copt Hill
Copt Hill Farm
Stockeley
Greenfields
ASHFIELD
GEDLING
Fish Pond
Sheppard's Stone
Woodlands Farm
Ling Farm
Rainworth Water
A60
Lodge
CROSS
RICKET
ROAD
Table Tree
Blue Eaves
LITTLE RICKET LANE
Holly Lodge
Twin Hill
MANSFIELD RD.
New Cottages
SANDY LA.
NG15
Fishpool Farm
ROBIN HOOD TER.
Equestrian Centre
The Larch Farm
62
Larch Farm
BEECH AV.
B6020
MAIN ROAD
WOODSIDE GDNS.
THE BIRCHES
BRETTON RD.
Cottage Farm
455
56
57
359
358
57
56

Three Thorn Hollow
The Sherwood Village Settlement
Heathlands Prim. Sch.
SOUTHWELL ROAD
B6020
Rainworth Nursery
RAINWORTH BY-PASS
A617
Rainworth Water
Bishopshill Plantation
Foulevil Brook
EAST LANE
KIRKLINGTON ROAD
Sports Ground
RAINWORTH
Python Hill Prim. Sch.
Lake View Prim. Sch.
Rainworth Leisure Cen.
Joseph Whitaker School
Playing Fields
Nature Reserve
Rainworth Lodge
Mansfield
WARSOP LANE
MANSFIELD LANE
Hill View
Hillcrest
Lyncroft
New Farm
Cottage Farm
Saw Mill
High Park
High Lease
CROSS LANE
NEW LANE
Norwood Hill Close
Norwood Hill
Brick and Pond Farm
Brick Kiln Hill
Boundary Wood
BURMA RD. IND. EST.
BLIDWORTH IND. PK.
NG21
BLIDWORTH
Leisure Cen.
Blidworth Oaks Prim. Sch.
The Hawthornes
Norwood Hill Farm
Redgate Farm
MANSFIELD ROAD
MAIN STREET
Hilltop Fm.
Blidworth Towermill
Rock Farm
The Ranch
FISHPOOL ROAD
B6020
Church Farm
Vicarage
Cornerways
OAKS LANE
GEDLING
NEWARK and SHERWOOD
49
56
63

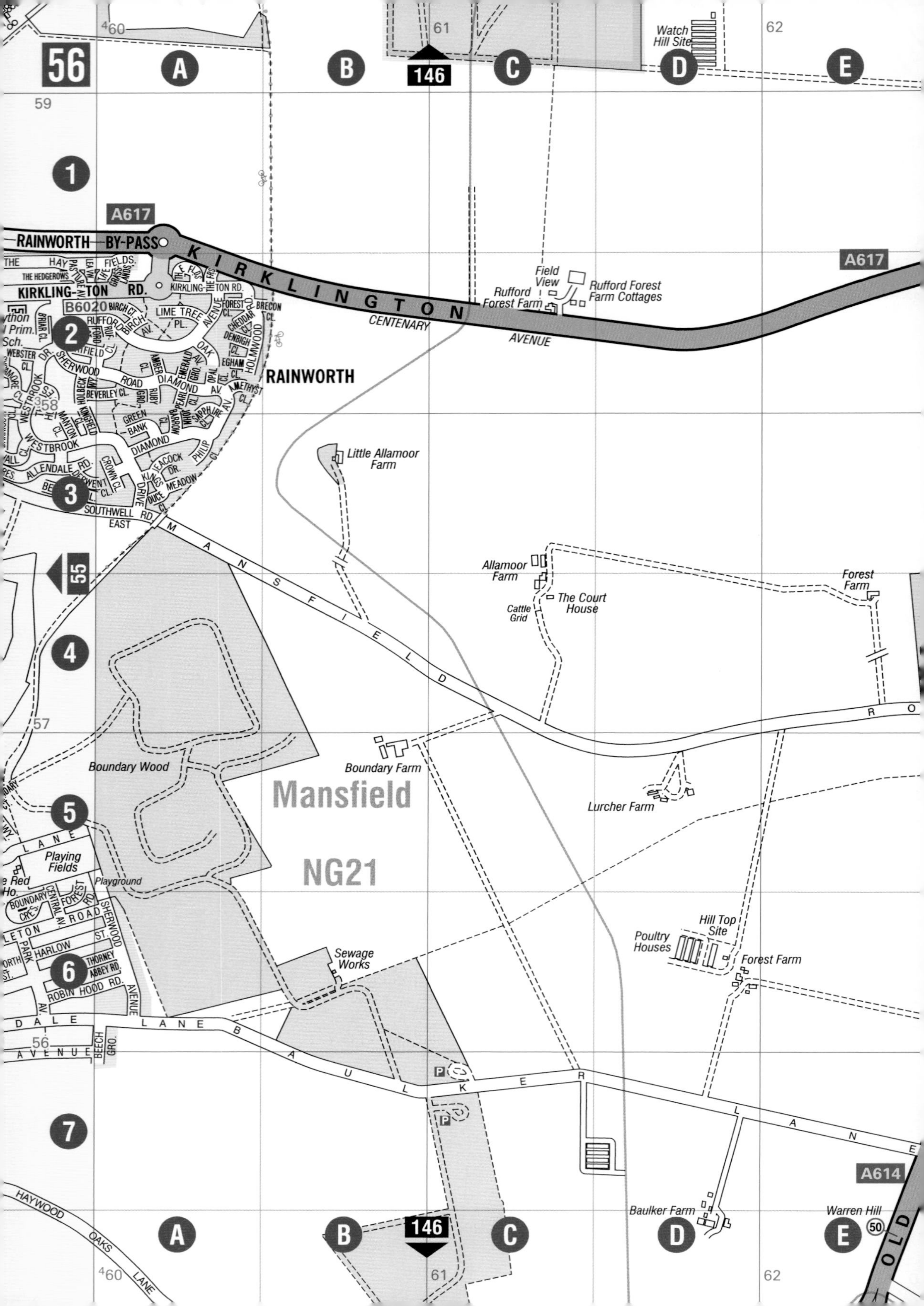
A
B
C
D
E
146
Watch Hill Site
1
2
3
4
5
6
7
A617
RAINWORTH BY-PASS
KIRKLINGTON
KIRKLING-TON RD.
B6020
CENTENARY
AVENUE
Field View
Rufford Forest Farm
Rufford Forest Farm Cottages
RAINWORTH
Little Allamoor Farm
SOUTHWELL RD. EAST
MANSFIELD
55
Allamoor Farm
The Court House
Cattle Grid
Forest Farm
Boundary Wood
Boundary Farm
Mansfield
NG21
Lurcher Farm
Playing Fields
Playground
Sewage Works
Hill Top Site
Poultry Houses
Forest Farm
BAULKER LANE
Baulker Farm
Warren Hill
A614
HAYWOOD OAKS LANE
OLD
146

F
G
H
J
K
63
64
465
59
358
57
56
1
2
3
4
5
6
7
146
A614
A617
50
OLD RUFFORD ROAD
KIRKLINGTON ROAD
RUFFORD ROAD
COCKETT LANE
FARNSFIELD ROAD
Lockwell House Farm
Lockwell Hill Wood
Lockwell Hill
Lockwell Hill Farm
Cottage Farm
HEXGREAVE PARK
Cockett Barn Farm
Hexgreave Park
Cockett Farm
BROOMFIELD LANE
Farnsfield House
Forest Farm
Newark
White Post Farm
Wheelgate Adventure Park
Mill Farm
Ash Farm
MANSFIELD ROAD
White Post
NG22
STATION LANE
Cricket Ground
Pav.
Merrins Farm
FARNSFIELD
Hill House Farm
St. Michael's C of E Prim. Sch.
Ten.Ct.
Bowl.Grn.
Play. Fld.
Lib.
VICARAGE LA.
MAIN STREET
BLIDWORTH RD.
BECK LANE
HALL CL.
BRICKYARD LA.
SOUTHWELL RD.
Playgrd.
QUAKER LANE
COTTON MILL LA.
Carr Banks Farm
Football Ground
Cricket Ground
Pav.
New Farm
LONGLAND LANE
Longland Farm
BLANCHBECK LANE
COMBS LA.
COMBS
Memorial
Riddings Hill Farm

Kirkstead
PINXTON
Pinxton Wharf
Hall Green
Commonside
Rosemaryhill
NG16
DE55
SELSTON
Selston Green
Dove Green
Allen's Green
Handstubbin
Alma
Toadhole
Barrows Green
New Westwood
Selston Common
Woodnook
KIRKBY
M1 MOTORWAY
BROOKHILL INDUSTRIAL ESTATE
Recreation Ground
Playing Field
Selston Leisure Centre
Selston High Sch.
SELSTON (PAR 3) GOLF COURSE
Langton Siding
Langton Hall Farm
Kirkby Park's Farm
The Dumble
Hobsic Farm
Selston Hall
Hall Farm
Broom Close Farm
Hall Green Farm
Hillbank Farm
Pastures Farm
The Gables Riding School
Pinfold Farm
Pingle Hill
Pye Hill
Toadhole Farm
Ashes Farm
Home Farm
Lea Farm
Melbourne House Farm
Woodnook Nursing Home
Holly Hill Nursing Home
Railway Cottages
Sewage Works
Lady's Well
BOLSOVER
ASHFIELD
ALFRETON ROAD
NOTTINGHAM ROAD
MANSFIELD ROAD
PARK LANE
KIRKBY LANE
SELSTON ROAD
LANGTON HOLLOW
STONEY LANE
COMMONSIDE
STATION ROAD
CHURCH LANE
BARROWS HILL LANE
WAGSTAFF LANE
ROAD
Middlebeck Bridge

50
64

59
51
60
65
PINXTON LANE
B6019
Bentinck Town
PINXTON RD.
CHURCH HILL
LANE
B6018
Rec. Grd.
Meadow Farm
Sewage Works
Lower Portland
Portland Fields House
Works
Wks.
BENTINCK WORKSHOPS
PARK LANE BUSINESS PARK
The Stables
LABURNUM AV.
Cemetery
Depot
River Erewash
Studfold Wood
Portland Park
Grives Wood
The Bungalow
Portland Park Visitors Cen.
The Nook
Grives Farm
Old Mill Pond
Weir
NG17
High Cliff
The Hollies
PARK
Kirkby Woodhouse
Prospect Fm.
HARDSTAFF CL.
SHERWOOD
Prim. Sch.
Play. Fld.
NUNCARGATE
Rise Hill
Cricket Ground
Pav.
MAIN ROAD
Rec. Grd.
Cemetery
The Gables
Croft Cottage
Bleak Hall Farm
Sycamore Farm
Lib.
Reservoir (covered)
Salmon Farm
Salmon House
Southfields Farm
ANNESLEY WOODHOUSE
FOREST ROAD
Bryngwyn
Annesley Woodhouse Quarry Nature Reserve
Butler Wood
Nottingham
Suvla Bay
SALMON LANE
Kirkby Park's Farm
Two Dale Farm
Toll Bar Farm
Annesley Lane End
Skegness
Damstead
Works
LITTLE OAK DRIVE
Sherwood Park
Fish Ponds
Davis's Bottom
LAKE VIEW DRIVE
SHERWOOD BUSINESS PARK
Works
WILLOW DRIVE
SENTINEL
Old Park Hi
Frank's Plantation
Icehouse Wood
NG15
M1
M1 MOTORWAY
Junction 27
MANSFIELD ROAD
A608
MANSFIELD RD.
Middlebrook Farm
Brook
Millington Springs
Middle
Depot
Home Farm
William Wood Spinney
ROAD
F
G
H
J
K
1
2
3
4
5
6
7
48
49
450
355
54
53
52

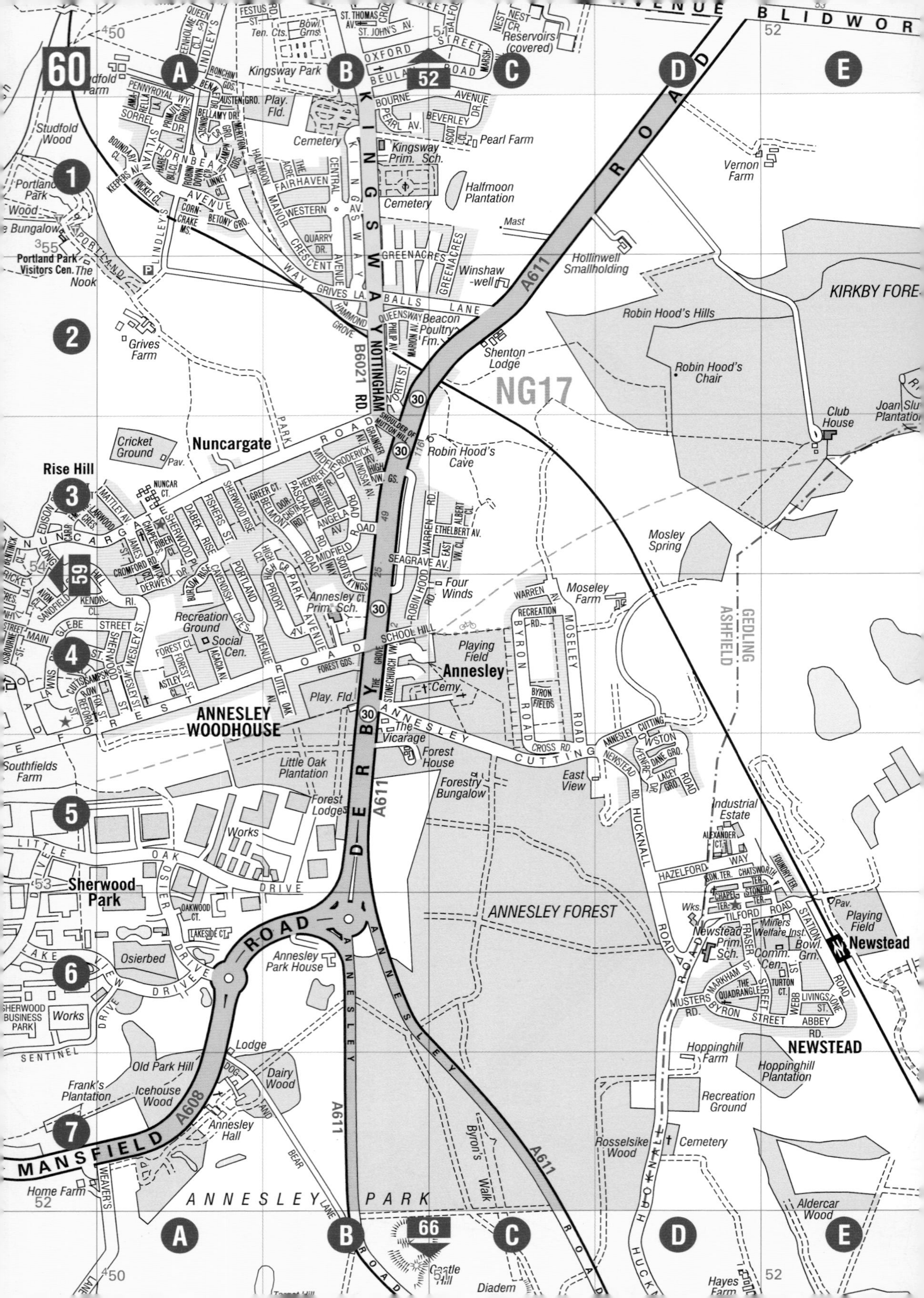
Kingsway Park
Studfold Farm
Studfold Wood
Portland Park Wood
Portland Park Visitors Cen.
The Nook
Grives Farm
Cemetery
Kingsway Prim. Sch.
Pearl Farm
Halfmoon Plantation
Reservoirs (covered)
Vernon Farm
Hollinwell Smallholding
Winshaw-well
Beacon Poultry Fm.
Shenton Lodge
KIRKBY FOREST
Robin Hood's Hills
Robin Hood's Chair
NG17
Club House
Joan Sluice Plantation
Cricket Ground
Nuncargate
Rise Hill
Robin Hood's Cave
Mosley Spring
Four Winds
Moseley Farm
Annesley Ct. Prim. Sch.
Recreation Ground
Social Cen.
Playing Field
Annesley
Cemy.
GEDLING
ASHFIELD
ANNESLEY WOODHOUSE
Play. Fld.
The Vicarage
Forest House
Southfields Farm
Little Oak Plantation
Forestry Bungalow
East View
Forest Lodge
Industrial Estate
Works
Sherwood Park
ANNESLEY FOREST
Newstead Prim. Sch.
Miners Welfare Inst.
Comm. Cen.
Bowl. Grn.
Playing Field
Newstead
Osierbed
Annesley Park House
SHERWOOD BUSINESS PARK
NEWSTEAD
Hoppinghill Farm
Hoppinghill Plantation
Lodge
Old Park Hill
Dairy Wood
Frank's Plantation
Icehouse Wood
Annesley Hall
Recreation Ground
Rosselsike Wood
Cemetery
Byron's Walk
Home Farm
ANNESLEY PARK
Aldercar Wood
Castle Hill
Diadem
Hayes Farm
MANSFIELD ROAD
DERBY ROAD
NOTTINGHAM RD.
KINGSWAY
ANNESLEY ROAD
HUCKNALL ROAD
BLIDWORTH
A611
A608
B6021
52
66
59

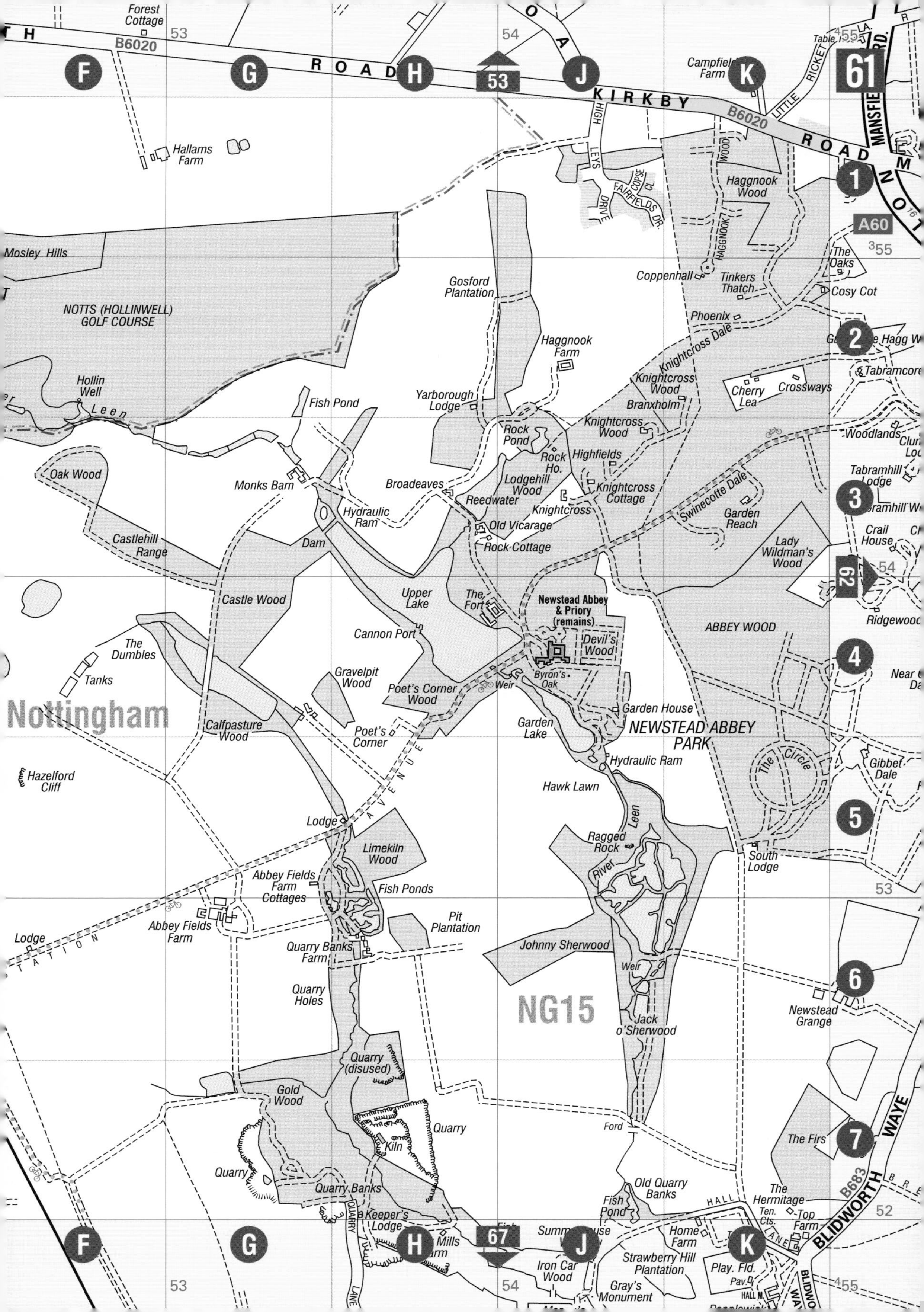
KIRKBY ROAD
B6020
Forest Cottage
Hallams Farm
Campfield Farm
Haggnook Wood
Mosley Hills
NOTTS (HOLLINWELL) GOLF COURSE
Hollin Well
Leen
Fish Pond
Gosford Plantation
Haggnook Farm
Yarborough Lodge
Coppenhall
Tinkers Thatch
The Oaks
Cosy Cot
Phoenix
Knightcross Dale
Knightcross Wood
Branxholm
Cherry Lea
Crossways
Tabramcore
Oak Wood
Monks Barn
Broadeaves
Rock Pond
Rock Ho.
Highfields
Lodgehill Wood
Knightcross Cottage
Reedwater
Knightcross
Swinecotte Dale
Garden Reach
Woodlands
Tabramhill Lodge
Hydraulic Ram
Castlehill Range
Dam
Old Vicarage
Rock Cottage
Lady Wildman's Wood
Crail House
Ridgewood
Castle Wood
Upper Lake
The Fort
Newstead Abbey & Priory (remains)
Devil's Wood
ABBEY WOOD
The Dumbles
Tanks
Cannon Port
Gravelpit Wood
Poet's Corner Wood
Weir
Byron's Oak
Garden House
Nottingham
Calfpasture Wood
Poet's Corner
Garden Lake
NEWSTEAD ABBEY PARK
Hydraulic Ram
The Circle
Gibbet Dale
Hazelford Cliff
Hawk Lawn
AVENUE
Lodge
Limekiln Wood
Ragged Rock
River Leen
South Lodge
Abbey Fields Farm Cottages
Fish Ponds
Abbey Fields Farm
Lodge
STATION
Pit Plantation
Quarry Banks Farm
Johnny Sherwood
Weir
Newstead Grange
Quarry Holes
NG15
Jack o'Sherwood
Quarry (disused)
Gold Wood
Quarry
Kiln
The Firs
Ford
Quarry
Quarry Banks
Old Quarry Banks
Fish Pond
The Hermitage
Top Farm
BLIDWORTH WAYE
B683
Keeper's Lodge
Mills Farm
Home Farm
Strawberry Hill Plantation
Iron Car Wood
Gray's Monument
Play. Fld.
Pav.
HALL M.
HALL LANE
QUARRY LANE
MANSFIELD RD.
LITTLE RICKET LA.
HIGH LEYS DRIVE
FAIRFIELDS DR.
COPSE CL.
HAGGNOOK WOOD
A60
53
54
55
52
62
67

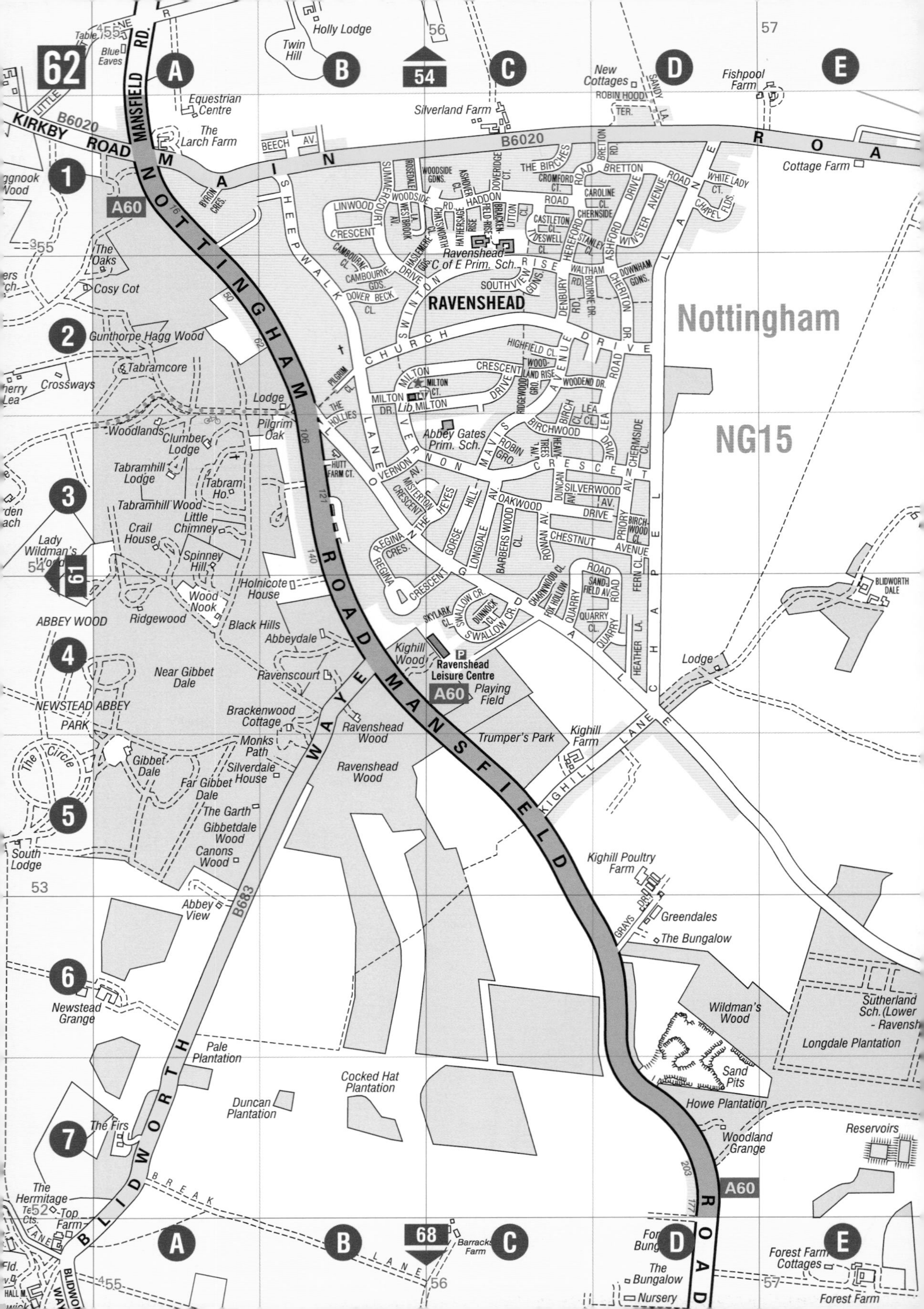
54
68
61
A
B
C
D
E
1
2
3
4
5
6
7
55
56
57
54
53
52
RAVENSHEAD
Nottingham
NG15
A60
B6020
B683
MANSFIELD RD.
KIRKBY ROAD
MAIN ROAD
NOTTINGHAM ROAD
MANSFIELD ROAD
WAYE
BLIDWORTH WAYE
BREAK LANE
KIGHILL LANE
CHAPEL LANE
SHEEPWALK LANE
CHURCH DRIVE
VERNON CRESCENT
LONGDALE LANE
SANDY LA.
Holly Lodge
Twin Hill
Equestrian Centre
The Larch Farm
Silverland Farm
New Cottages
ROBIN HOOD TER.
Fishpool Farm
Cottage Farm
Table
Blue Eaves
LITTLE
Crow Wood
BEECH AV.
BYRON CRES.
SUMMERCOURT
ROSEDALE
WOODSIDE GDNS.
ASHOVER CL.
DOVERIDGE CT.
THE BIRCHES
BRETTON RD.
CROMFORD CT.
WHITE LADY CT.
CHAPEL FLDS.
LINWOOD CRESCENT
WOODSIDE RD.
WESTBROOK AV.
CHATSWORTH CL.
HATHERSAGE RISE
HADDON
BRACKENFIELD RISE
LITTON CL.
CASTLETON CT.
TIDESWELL CL.
CAROLINE CL.
CHERNSIDE
HEREFORD
STANLEY CL.
ASHFORD DRIVE
WINSTER AVENUE
CAMBOURNE CL.
CAMBOURNE GDNS.
HASLEMERE GDS.
Ravenshead C of E Prim. Sch.
SWINTON RISE
SOUTHVIEW GDNS.
WALTHAM
BOURNE DR.
DOWNHAM GDNS.
CHERITON DR.
DENBURY RD.
DOVER BECK CL.
HIGHFIELD CL.
WOODLAND RISE
WOODEND DR.
PILGRIM CL.
MILTON CRESCENT
MILTON CT.
MILTON DR.
Lib.
THE HOLLIES
RIDGEWOOD GRO.
BIRCH LEA
BIRCHWOOD
Abbey Gates Prim. Sch.
ROBIN GRO.
MAVIS AV.
TREES
HEAVEN
CHERMSIDE CL.
LEA DRIVE
HUTT FARM CT.
VERNON AV.
MISTERTON CRESCENT
THE HEYES
GORSE HILL
DUNCAN AV.
SILVERWOOD AV.
OAKWOOD DRIVE
PRIORY AV.
BIRCHWOOD CL.
BARBERS WOOD CL.
ROWAN AV.
CHESTNUT AVENUE
REGINA CRES.
REGINA CRESCENT
SWALLOW CR.
SKYLARK CL.
DUNNOCK CL.
CHARNWOOD CL.
FOX HOLLOW
QUARRY ROAD
SAND FIELD AV.
QUARRY CL.
FERN CL.
HEATHER LA.
Kighill Wood
Ravenshead Leisure Centre
Playing Field
Trumper's Park
Kighill Farm
Ravenshead Wood
The Oaks
Cosy Cot
Gunthorpe Hagg Wood
Tabramcore
Crossways
Lodge
Pilgrim Oak
Woodlands
Clumber Lodge
Tabramhill Lodge
Tabram Ho.
Tabramhill Wood
Little Chimney
Crail House
Spinney Hill
Lady Wildman's Wood
Holnicote House
Wood Nook
Ridgewood
ABBEY WOOD
Black Hills
Abbeydale
Near Gibbet Dale
Ravenscourt
NEWSTEAD ABBEY PARK
Brackenwood Cottage
Monks Path
Silverdale House
The Circle
Gibbet Dale
Far Gibbet Dale
The Garth
Gibbetdale Wood
Canons Wood
South Lodge
Abbey View
Newstead Grange
Pale Plantation
Cocked Hat Plantation
Duncan Plantation
The Firs
The Hermitage
Top Farm
Barracks Farm
The Bungalow
Nursery
Kighill Poultry Farm
GRAYS DR.
Greendales
The Bungalow
Wildman's Wood
Sand Pits
Howe Plantation
Woodland Grange
Longdale Plantation
Sutherland Sch.(Lower - Ravensh
Reservoirs
BLIDWORTH DALE
Lodge
Forest Farm Cottages
Forest Farm

63

F 58 **G** 460 **K**

The Ranch
Rock Farm
ROCK TER.
B6020
CLAYBANK VILLAS
FOREST TW.
ASHWELL TER.
BUTLER
MILL
SCARLET
BECK
SOU...
CRES
ANDREW
FARR W.
GRE...
HAYWOOD
OAKS

MAIN **ST.**
FIELD
Cornerways
59
FARR
DRIVE
LANE

Church Farm
Vicara...
55

BLIDWORTH

1

Haywood Oaks
355

FISHPOOL

RD.

NEWARK and SHERWOOD

GEDLING

Bottom Farm

Blidworth Bottoms

2

Jackson's Hill

CALVERTON RD.
TOP
Rose Cottage Farm

BECK

BLIDWORTH

Kirkfield

Mansfield

Green Park

3

Sykebreck Farm
Long Wood

NG21

se Cottage

GORSE COVERT

LANE

146 54

Appleton Dale House

Appleton Dale

4

Forestry Tower

5

Blidworth Lodge

R
G

53

GORSE COVERT

ong Dale

Sand Holes

6

Longdale Craft Centre
ool

L
A
N
E

Forestry Bungalows

Big Tithe Farm

50

OLD
RUFFORD
RD.

LONGDALE

LANE

7

WHINBUSH

Papplewick Pumping Station

Forestry Houses

NG14

A614

69

Pea Plantation

50
RUFFORD

F 58 **G** 59 **H** **69** **J** 460 **K**

52

64
58
72
A
B
C
D
E
1
2
3
4
5
6
7
JACKSDALE
New Westwood
Westwood
Recreation Ground
Westwood Inf. Sch.
Oak Tree Farm
Westwood Farm
Yewtree Farm
Nursery
Wansley Hall
Wansley Hall Farm
Manor Cottage
White Cottage
Kill Dogs
Manor Farm
Mexborough House
Brookside Farm
Bagthorpe
Nottingham
Bagthorpe Common
Football Grd.
Lea Farm
Home Farm
Alma
Underwood Hill Farm
Underwood Hill
Poole Farm
Rec. Grd.
Underwood Green
Hill Farm
Plain Spot Farm
Plain Spot
Cherry Tree Farm
Underwood C of E Prim. Sch.
Cricket Grd.
Cornfield Rise
Pollington House
New Brinsley
Oaktree Farm
Works
Depot
Willeylane End
Willeylane Plantation
NG16
Hobsic
Gin Farm
Gin House
Allandale Farm
Sewage Pumping Station
Brinsley Gin
Brinsley Prim. Sch.
Rec. Grd.
Bowl. Grn.
Tennis Ct.
Football Ground
Nursing Home
Saints Coppice Farm
Saints Coppice
Willey Wood Farm
Hunt's Hill
Clinton Cottage
BRINSLEY
Manor Farm
Cocker House Farm
Coneygrey Plantation
Coneygrey Farm
Grange Fields
CORDY LANE
ALFRETON
CHURCH LANE
A608
MANSFIELD ROAD
B600
Pye Hill
SELSTON RD.
B6016
PYE HILL RD.
Jacksdale Prim. Sch.
Nursery
Jacksdale Nature Reserve
Cromford Canal (Disused)
Bagthorpe Brook
INSET

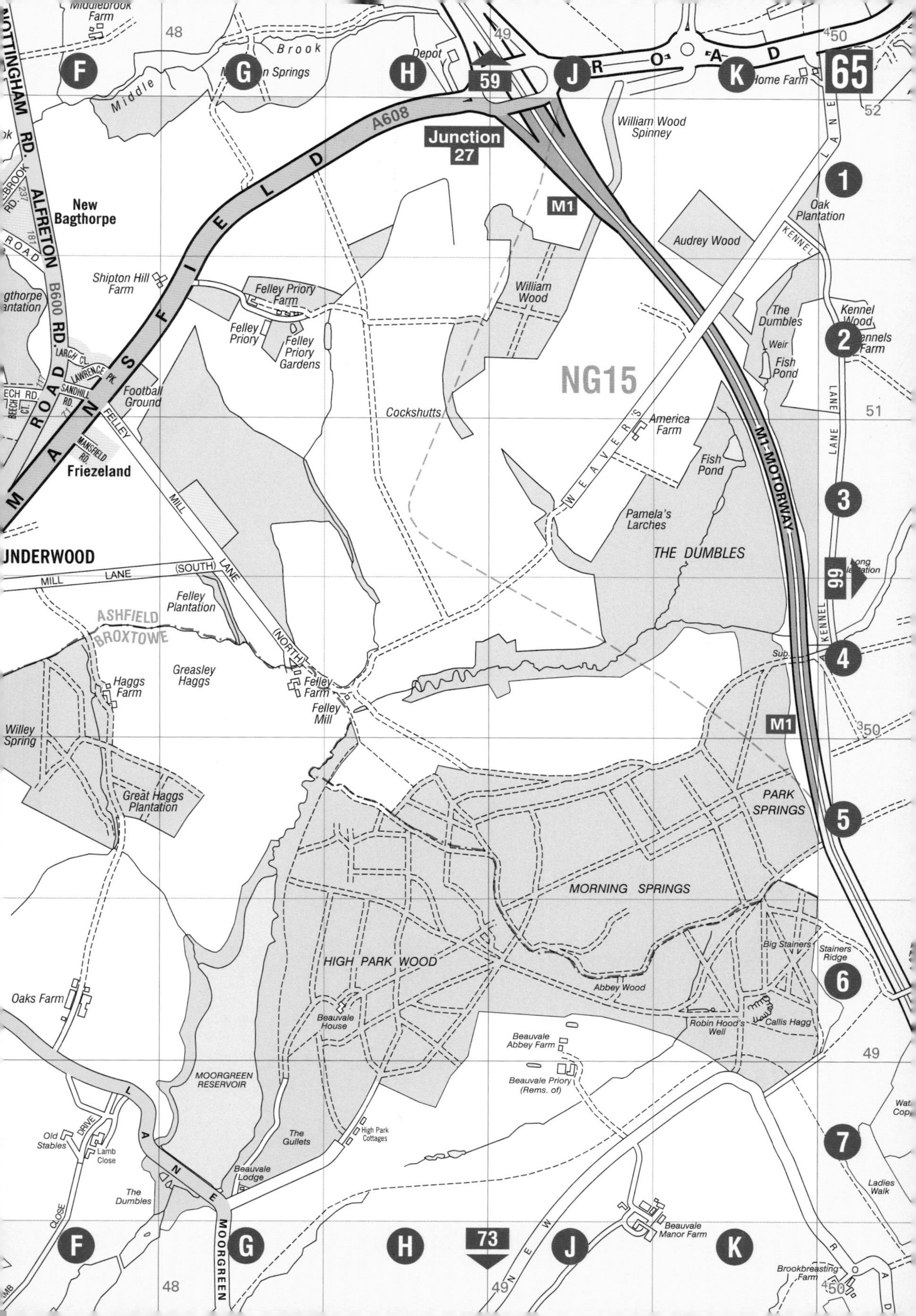

Middlebrook Farm
Brook
Middle
Depot
59
Junction 27
A608
MANSFIELD ROAD
William Wood Spinney
Home Farm
New Bagthorpe
ALFRETON RD.
B600 RD.
NOTTINGHAM RD.
M1
Oak Plantation
Audrey Wood
KENNEL
Shipton Hill Farm
Felley Priory Farm
William Wood
Felley Priory
Felley Priory Gardens
The Dumbles
Weir
Fish Pond
Kennel Wood
Kennels Farm
LARCH CL.
LAWRENCE PK.
SANDHILL RD.
Football Ground
NG15
FELLEY
MANSFIELD RD.
Friezeland
Cockshutts
WEAVERS
America Farm
LANE
51
Fish Pond
M1-MOTORWAY
Pamela's Larches
MILL
THE DUMBLES
UNDERWOOD
MILL LANE (SOUTH)
99
Felley Plantation
ASHFIELD
BROXTOWE
(NORTH)
Greasley Haggs
Haggs Farm
Felley Farm
Felley Mill
Sub.
Willey Spring
M1
50
Great Haggs Plantation
PARK SPRINGS
MORNING SPRINGS
HIGH PARK WOOD
Big Stainers
Stainers Ridge
Abbey Wood
Oaks Farm
Beauvale House
Robin Hood's Well
Callis Hagg
Beauvale Abbey Farm
49
MOORGREEN RESERVOIR
Beauvale Priory (Rems. of)
The Gullets
High Park Cottages
Old Stables
DRIVE
Lamb Close
Beauvale Lodge
The Dumbles
CLOSE
MOORGREEN
73
NEW
Beauvale Manor Farm
Ladies Walk
Brookbreasting Farm
48
49
50

66
60
65
74
M1
A B C D E
1 2 3 4 5 6 7
52
51
350
49
450
ANNESLEY
PARK
Annesley Hall
A608
DOG AND BEAR LANE
Byron's Walk
ANNESLEY
A611
Rosselsike Wood
Cemetery
HUCKNALL ROAD
Aldercar Wood
Castle Hill
Diadem Hill
Target Hill
Hayes Farm
Oak Plantation
WEAVER'S
KENNEL LANE
Heatherdale Pond
Joe's Wood
The Dumbles
Kennel Wood
Kennels Farm
Fish Pond
Big Pond
ANNESLEY ROAD
Top Wigha Farm
GEDLING
ASHFIELD
Wighay Wood
Balaklava Wood
PARK FOREST
GIPSY LANE
Thurland Hall Farm
Long Plantation
NOTTINGHAM INT. CLOTHING CEN
BY-PASS
WASHDYKE LANE
New Farm
Whyburn House
Nottingham
Whyburn Cottages
PARK SPRINGS
A611
HUCKNALL
M1 MOTORWAY
MISK HILL
Poultry Farm
Nursery
Big Stainers
Stainers Ridge
Misk Farm
Reservoir (covered)
Silo Farm
WHYBURN LANE
Reservoirs (covered)
Callis Hagg
Reservoir (covered)
WOOD LANE
LONG ACRE
Long Hill
Reservoir (Cov.)
Fox Covert
Brier Plantation
Beacon Hill
PRIORY RD.
BEAUVALE ROAD
NG16
Beauvale
Watnall Coppice
Beacon Hill Farm
Beacon Hill House
Leiver's Hill
ASHFIELD
BROXTOWE
Bottom Plantation
THE COMMON
NABBS LANE
Running Track
Watnall Coppice
Ladies Walk
Coppice Farm
BABBACOMBE WAY
Playing Field
The Holgate School
NEW ROAD
Brookbreasting Farm
BOLINGEY WAY
Ruffs
Playground

61
75
68
NG15
LINBY
PAPPLEWICK
Wighay
HUCKNALL
Hucknall
Butler's Hill
F
G
H
J
K
1
2
3
4
5
6
7
53
54
55
52
51
50
49
Quarry
Quarry Banks
Kiln
Keeper's Lodge
Weir Mills Farm
Fish Pond
Summerhouse Wood
Old Quarry Banks
Iron Car Wood
Strawberry Hill Plantation
Gray's Monument
Mason's Monument
Home Farm
The Hermitage
Top Farm
The Firs
Play. Fld.
Pav.
Papplewick Hall
Weir
Mill Pond Plantation
The Lodge
Mortons Farm
Church Plantation
Linby-cum-Papplewick C of E Prim. Sch.
School Plantation
Sherwood House
Hall Farm
West View Court
West View Farm
The Poplars
Castle Mill Farm
Dam Banks
Playgrd.
Colliery Farm
Linby Ho.
Cricket Ground
Station House
Pump House
Moor Pond Wood
The Mill House
Papplewick Moor
Grange Cottages
Grange Farm
Congel Hill
Great Northern Cotts.
The National C of E Academy
Nursing Home
Recreation Ground
Prim. Sch.
Leen Mills Prim. Sch.
Primary School
Hucknall Leis. Cen.
Rec. Grd.
Playing Field
Club House
Driving Range
HUCKNALL GOLF COURSE
Superstore
Byron Bingo
Beardall St. Prim. Sch.
Nurs. Home
Bus Sta.
ASHGATE RETAIL PK.
Works
IMEX ENTERPRISE PARK
Annie Holgate Jun. & Inf. Schs.
Bowl. Grn.
Tennis Cts.
Titchfield Park
Cemetery
Rec. Ground
Household Waste Cen.
LEEN VALLEY COUNTRY PARK
Hucknall Town FC
River Leen
MAIN STREET
B683
BLIDWORTH WAYE
B6011
LINBY LANE
FOREST LANE
MOOR ROAD
MAIN ST. LINBY ROAD
WIGHAY ROAD
ANNESLEY ROAD
QUARRY LANE
CHURCH LANE
HAYDEN LANE
WATERLOO ROAD
PAPPLEWICK LANE
WIGWAM LANE
BAKER STREET
HIGH STREET
WATNALL ROAD
BY-PASS
BESTWOOD ROAD
DERBYSHIRE LANE
OGLE STREET
WEST STREET
BEARDALL STREET
STATION ROAD
ST. MARYS WAY

68
62
76
67
A
B
C
D
E
1
2
3
4
5
6
7
PAPPLEWICK
NG15
NG6
Nottingham
MANSFIELD ROAD
A60
B6011
B683
FOREST LANE
BREAK LANE
GOOSEDALE LANE
MAIN STREET
MOOR ROAD
BLIDWORTH WAYE
The Firs
Woodland Grange
Barracks Farm
Forest Bungalow
The Bungalow
Nursery
Forest Farm Cottages
Forest Farm
King Edward's Plantation
The Lodge
Mortons Farm
West View Farm
West View Court
BLACKSMITHS CT.
New Plantation
Vincent Plantation
The Woodlands
Vincent Lodge
Barracks Farm Cottage
Keeper's Cottage
Seven Mile Wood
Warren Plantation
Forest Lodge
Seven Mile House
Seven Mile Plantation
North Lodge
BURNTSTUMP
SHERWOOD
Moor Pond Wood
Papplewick Moor
Stanker Hill Farm
Grange Farm
PAPPLEWICK GRANGE
GRANGE MOOR
Congel Hill
Fox Covert
The Duck Ponds
River Leen
ASHFIELD
GEDLING
Sports Ground
Pav.
Goosedale Farm
Weir
Raceground Hill
Round Hill Plantation
HUCKNALL GOLF COURSE
Sunnyside Poultry Farm
Gordon's Farm
Two Acres
Twelve Acre Farm
Six Ways Pig Farm
Hundred Acres Farm
Killarney Park
Coronation Strip
AVENUE
SUNRISE
DRIVE
CHAPMANS WK.
SMITHY VW.
LEWIS
Cobbler's Hill Farm
LEEN VALLEY COUNTRY PARK
Mushroom Farm
CRIMEA PLANTATION
Westhouse Farm
455
56
57
52
51
350
49
203
115
63

Papplewick Pumping Station
Forestry Houses
63
Pea Plantation
A614
OLD RUFFORD ROAD
SANSOM WOOD
Sansom Wood Farm
Sansom Wood Gorse
ASH LANE
Great Burntstump Plantation
Sawpit Plantation
Watchwood Plantation
Richmond's Farm
Lagoon
Oak Wood
Burntstump Plantation
Ckt. Grd.
Burntstump Country Park
The Nursery
Beech Wood
Spts. Gd.
THE PARK BMI HOSPITAL
Burntstump Country Park Woodland Walks
Arnold Seely C of E Prim. Sch.
Foxcovert Plantation
GRAVELLY HOLLOW
70
NG14
Cockliff Wood
Sports Ground
Cockliffe Hill Farm
Cockliffe House
Dairy Farm
The Warren
The Knoll
Round Plantation
Sports Ground
Patchings Art Centre
MAIN STREET
NG5
Cottage Wood
OLLERTON ROAD
Turnpike Plantation
RAMSDALE PARK GOLF CENTRE
B6386
Jubilee Plantation
Ramsdale Cottages
Robin Hood Farm
The Rowans
Greenwood Bonsai Studio
Driving Range
Club Ho.
East Hill Plantation
OXTON ROAD
HOLLINWOOD
Ramsdale House
Hollinwood House
Ramper Covert
Fox Covert
Forest Farm
Bottomhouse Farm
Leila's Plantation
A60
RAMSDALE PARK
North Peacock
The Belt
Calverton Hill
Ramsdale Park
Ramsdale Hill
77
GEORGE'S LANE
Reservoirs

A
B
C
D
E
1
2
3
4
5
6
7
146
69
78
460
61
62
52
51
350
49
A614
A6097
OLD RUFFORD ROAD
50
Salterford Cottages
Salterford Dam
SALTERFORD
WHINBUSH
LANE
WHINBUSH LANE
Lagoon
Lagoon
Lagoon
OXTON BOGS
Gorse Covert
Foulds Plantation
Beanford Farm
BEANFORD LANE
ROAD
Lodge Farm
Thorndale Plantation
Whitehaven Farm
FLATTS LANE
Nottingham
NG14
OXTON
B6386
HOLLINWOOD LA.
LANE
Broom House
Carrington Farm
CARRINGTON LANE
MANSFIELD LA.
CALVERTON BUS. PK.
HILL CREST PARK
JAMES DR.
PATON CT.
HOYLE RD.
WILLIAMS DR.
Works
Recreation Ground
Tennis Court
Bowling Green
Pav.
Sports Ground
Pav.
NORTH GRN.
HOLLINWOOD
COLLYER
PARK ROAD
SEELY
NEWMAN RD.
LABRAY
LANE
FOREST ROAD
Rec. Grd.
RAMSDALE AV.
SHERWOOD AV.
PEPPER
AVENUE
ROAD
ROAD
SHERBROOKE CL.
Calverton Leisure Centre
Cemy.
Colonel Frank Seely Sch.
Sir John Sherbrooke Jun. Sch.
Manor Park Inf. Sch.
FLATTS
MANSFIELD
RAMSDALE PARK GOLF CENTRE
RILEY GDNS.
BOAR GS.
Rec. Ground
MARSHALL
RED CL.
GATES
JCT.
THE PASTURES
WEST
END
LONG WEST CFT.
STREET
MAIN
ROAD
CHERRY TREE CL.
CLOSE
LANE
Nabarro Ct.
CASTLE
TOWER CL.
CALVERTON
MEWS
OLD HALL CL.
MANOR RD.
HIGH HURST
BUCK LEE DR.
THE NOOK
ROAD
MANSFIELD LA.
TITHE LA.
WATCHWOOD GRO.
WALNUT GRO.
FORGE AV.
HOLT GRO.
WOOD GRO.
SALTERFORD AV.
SHERWOOD GRO.
BECK AV.
BROADFIELD
ROAD
FOXWOOD GRO.
MERE AV.
MERE CL.
THORNDALE
BROOM CL.
BROOM
RICHMOND AV.
GRIMESMOOR RD.
THE BAINBR.
PARK RD. EAST
CLOVER FIELDS
THE HOLLINS
EAST
LANE
CROOKDOLE LANE
CROOKDOLE
DUNELM DR.
MOOR
PARK RD.
DOVER BECK CL.
SPRGWD CL.
ROES LA.
ROAD
EAST
Windles Square
CLOSE
ORCHARD
THE GROVE
DR.
OAK GRO.
PADDOCK
LAND GRO.
LESLIE
St. Wilfrid's Square
Lib.
P
LONGUE DR.
ROWAN CL.
JUMELLES DR.
ELMTREE RD.
LITTLE LA.
DOVEYS ORCHARD
LONGUE
MAPLE CL.
GORSE CL.
DRIVE
LANE
LAMP WOOD CL.
James Seely Play. Fld.
Cricket Ground
Pav.
WOODS LA.
SMITHY VW.
Springwater Lodge
Riding Sch.
St. Wilfrid's C of E Prim. Sch.
LANE
WAY
STREET
BONNER
AVENUE
THE POOL
BURNOR RD.
PLUM TREE GDS.
NEVILLE
CHURCH MDW.
HILL
RENALS
BRICKENELL RD.
STRIPES VW.
SPINDLE VW.
DARK
Borrowside Farm
Bonner Hill
BONNER LANE
FOXWOOD LANE
LANE
Hollinwood House
Fox Covert
Spring Cottages
Lamp Wood
GEORGE'S
ROAD
SPINDLE
LANE
SPINDLE
Fox Wood
High Trees
Foxwood House

F
G
H
J
K
1
2
3
4
5
6
7
63
64
465
52
51
350
49
Windmill Hill
Far Leys
Oxton Hill Farm
SOUTHWELL RD.
Birkhouse
Marsett House
Deer Leap
HILL
B6386
ROAD OXTON
Ridge House
Reservoirs (covered)
Birkhouse Wood
Oxton Dumble
LANE
HONEYKNAB
WINDMILL
CHAPEL LA.
BLIND
ORCHARD CT.
THE ORCHARDS
Pav.
Cricket Ground
Sports Ground
OXTON
STREET
Fish Pond
MANOR CL.
CHURCH VW.
ELMCROFT
NEW RD.
SANDY LA.
SCHOOL GDNS.
MAIN
WATER
NOTTINGHAM RD.
Meadow View
EPPERSTONE ROAD
SOUTHWELL
Holly Lodge
Southwell
NG25
NETHER FIELD
Rossellewood Farm
Rosselle Wood
Norwood Farm
146
Park Farm
Order
OXTON
Mill Farm
Dover
A6097
50
EPPERSTONE PARK
Crifton Mill
CRIFTIN ENTERPRISE CENTRE
NEWARK and SHERWOOD
GEDLING
Beck
Cottage Farm
Greenacres
Slaughter House
Kennels
Camping & Caravan Park.
Grimestone Dyke
LANE
Spring Hill Farm
Works
MOOR LANE
LAKELAND ROAD
Moor Farm Holiday & Home Park
Club Ho.
Driving Range
Grimesmoor Dyke
Experimental Fish Farm
SPRINGWATER GOLF COURSE
148
Hill House
Chapel Farm
CHAPEL LANE
CHURCH LA.
Plantation Cotts.
EPPERSTONE
MAIN STREET
WEST PK.
MANOR
PK. LA.
Epperstone Manor (Notts. Constabulary HQ)
Bowl. Grn.
Pav.
Sports Ground
BLAND LA.
TOAD LA.
PARK LA.
HILL
EPPERSTONE BY-PASS
Grimesmoor
ROE HILL
79
Shelt Hill Farm
Fox Covert
Cemetery
ROE
SHELT

72
64
A
B
C
D
E
1
2
3
4
5
6
7
Manor Farm
Stoney Paddock
STONEY LANE
Cocker House Farm
MANSFIELD ROAD
A608
Coneygrey Plantation
Coneygrey Farm
Grange Fields Farm Cottage
Weir
River Erewash
LANGLEY MILL BY-PASS
A610
Hall Farm
Lodge
COCKERHOUSE RD.
EASTWOOD HALL
Nether Green
Brinsley Brook
Ber Mar Anda Residential Mobile Home Pk.
Lanky Bills Fun Shack
CROMFORD ROAD IND. EST.
HALL ROAD
Langley Mill
Foundry
LANGLEY PARK
Playgrd.
Rec. Grd.
QUEEN ST.
DEAN STREET
BRIDGE ST.
VICTORIA ST.
Superstore
WESLEY ST.
JOSHUA BUS. PK.
CHRYSALIS WAY
Nether Green Hall Pk. Brook
Pavilion
Mushroom Farm Ct.
MEADOWBANK
Works
Playing Fields
Eastwood Comm. Sports Centre
Eastwood Comp. Sch.
D H Lawrence Heritage Cen.
Rec. Ground
HALL PARK DR.
GREENHILLS ROAD
Beauvale Brook
Cricket Ground
COACH DRIVE
ROBEY DRIVE
THORPE RD.
MEADOW CL.
LAMB CLOSE
LOWER BEAUVALE
D H Lawrence 'Sons & Lovers' Cottage
Lynncroft Prim. Sch.
Playing Field
Tennis Cts.
Langley Mill
Tom Norman Meml. Gdns.
ROAD DERBY ROAD
STATION ROAD
ELNOR STREET
ACCESS 26 BUS. PK.
ENTERPRISE
NEW DERBY ROAD
OLD DERBY RD.
DERBY ROAD
A608
Superstore
NOTTINGHAM ROAD
LANGLEY BUS. PK.
Bowling Green
MILNHAY
Works
Depot
ANCHOR ROAD
Pine Tree Wk.
BLACKTHORN
The Rectory
CHURCH STREET
Tennis Courts
IVY LANE
DEVONSHIRE DR.
RATCLIFFE ST.
HOGGS FLD.
Argyle M.
Liby.
Offs.
WALKER STREET
THREE TUNS ROAD
EDWARD ROAD
Bowl. Grn.
Eastwood Town FC (Coronation Pk.)
Coronation Park
Brookhill Leys Prim. Sch.
AMBER DR.
Brook Ct.
TOWSON AV.
LIME AV.
BROOKVALE RD.
Rec. Grd.
Depot
KIMBERLEY EASTWOOD BY-PASS
Bailey Grove
Erewash
Sewage Works
Prim. Sch.
MIDLAND RD.
PLUMPTRE WAY
The Island
KIRKSTONE
BROOKFIELD
Langley
LACEYFIELDS RD.
Playground
KEW CR.
Bailey Brook
EASTWOOD
A610
Playing Field
Works
Pavilion
Cemetery
Playgrd. Rec. Grd.
Cemy.
CRESCENT
CHEWTON AV.
PHILIP AV.
ROCKLEY AV.
Brickyard Cotts.
TINSLEY ROAD
BROOKHILL LEYS RD.
NEWMANLEYS ROAD
HEWTON
NEW THORPE
DAWSON CLOSE
New Eastwood
Works
Factory
Lacey Fields Farm
Heanor DE75
Nottingham Canal
Swing-Bridge
Eastwood Lock
(Disused)
AMBER VALLEY
BROXTOWE
NEWMANLEYS ROAD (STH.)
COMMONS CL.
HALLS LANE
Erewash
Weir
Shipley Lock
Shipley Gate
Boat Inn Farm
LONG LANE
BIRCH PARK
KIMBERLEY-EASTWOOD
Sports Ground
Pavilion
HASSOCK LANE NORTH
A6007
Algrave Hall Farm
Purdy House Farm
Bentley's Plantation
Poplars Farm
The Bungalow
AMBER VALLEY EREWASH
DE7
Cornanhay Wood
SHIPLEY
THE FIELD
CANAL
445
46
47
348
345

73
65
74
82
Nottingham
NG16
Lower Beauvale
Beauvale
Hill Top
Moorgreen
Greasley
Bogend
Newthorpe
Newthorpe Common
Giltbrook
Watnall Chaworth
Watnall Cantelupe
KIMBERLEY
Colliers Wood
Watnall Wood
Sledder Wood
Quarry Wood
Beauvale Manor Farm
Brookbreasting Farm
Crowhill Farm
Hall Farm
Greasley Castle Fm.
GREASLEY CASTLE (Rems.of)
Opencast Workings
GILTBROOK RETAIL PARK
Superstores
A610
B600
B6010
A6096

74
66
73
83
A
B
C
D
E
1
2
3
4
5
6
7
450
51
52
48
47
46
345
Ladies Walk
Coppice Farm
Watnall Coppice
Plantation
Brookbreasting Farm
NEW ROAD
ROAD
LANE
ARROW
M1
M1 MOTORWAY
Crowhill Farm
Starthwood Farm
Watson's Wood
Hollybush Farm
Littlefields Farm
Sledder Wood
Quarry Wood
Hall Farm
B6009
LONG LANE
WATNALL LANE
Eel Hole Farm
Stubbing Wood Farm
Starth Wood
Eelhole Wood
Leisure Cen.
Lib.
Sch.
Westville
Ruffs
Recreation Ground
The Holgate School
Playing Field
Running Track
HUCKNALL
HUCKNALL AERODROME
THE AERODROME
Sports Ground
Works
Bulwell Woodhall Farm
Woodhall Farm Cottages
Fish Pond
BLENHEIM
BLENHEIM CT.
BROXTOWE
ASHFIELD
BULWELL WOOD
NG16
CENTURION BUSINESS PARK
DABELL
PARK ROAD
Watnall Chaworth
MAIN ROAD
Common Farm
New Farm Cottage
New Farm
FERNWOOD COMMERCIAL WORKSHOPS
Driving Test Centre
Meteorological Station
WATNALL
COMMON LA.
B600
Bakery
NEW FARM WOOD
SELLER'S WOOD Nature Reserve
Redfield House Farm
Cemy
New Nuthall
High Wood Cemetery
WATNALL ROAD
Kimberley Leisure Centre
Games Courts
Cricket Grd.
Graphic Ho.
Playing Field
Springfield Paddocks
CHILTON DRIVE
NEWDIGATE
CORBIERE AVENUE
Railway Cotts.
Cider Orchard

75
Butler's Hill
Broomhill
Hazelgrove
Farleys
Nottingham
NG15
NG6
Blenheim
BULWELL
Bulwell Forest
MILL LAKES COUNTRY PARK
LEEN VALLEY COUNTRY PARK
NOTTINGHAM CITY GOLF COURSE
BULWELL FOREST GOLF COURSE
HUCKNALL INDUSTRIAL PARK
HUCKNALL BY-PASS
BESTWOOD BUSINESS PARK
NORTHERN CEMETERY
67
76
84

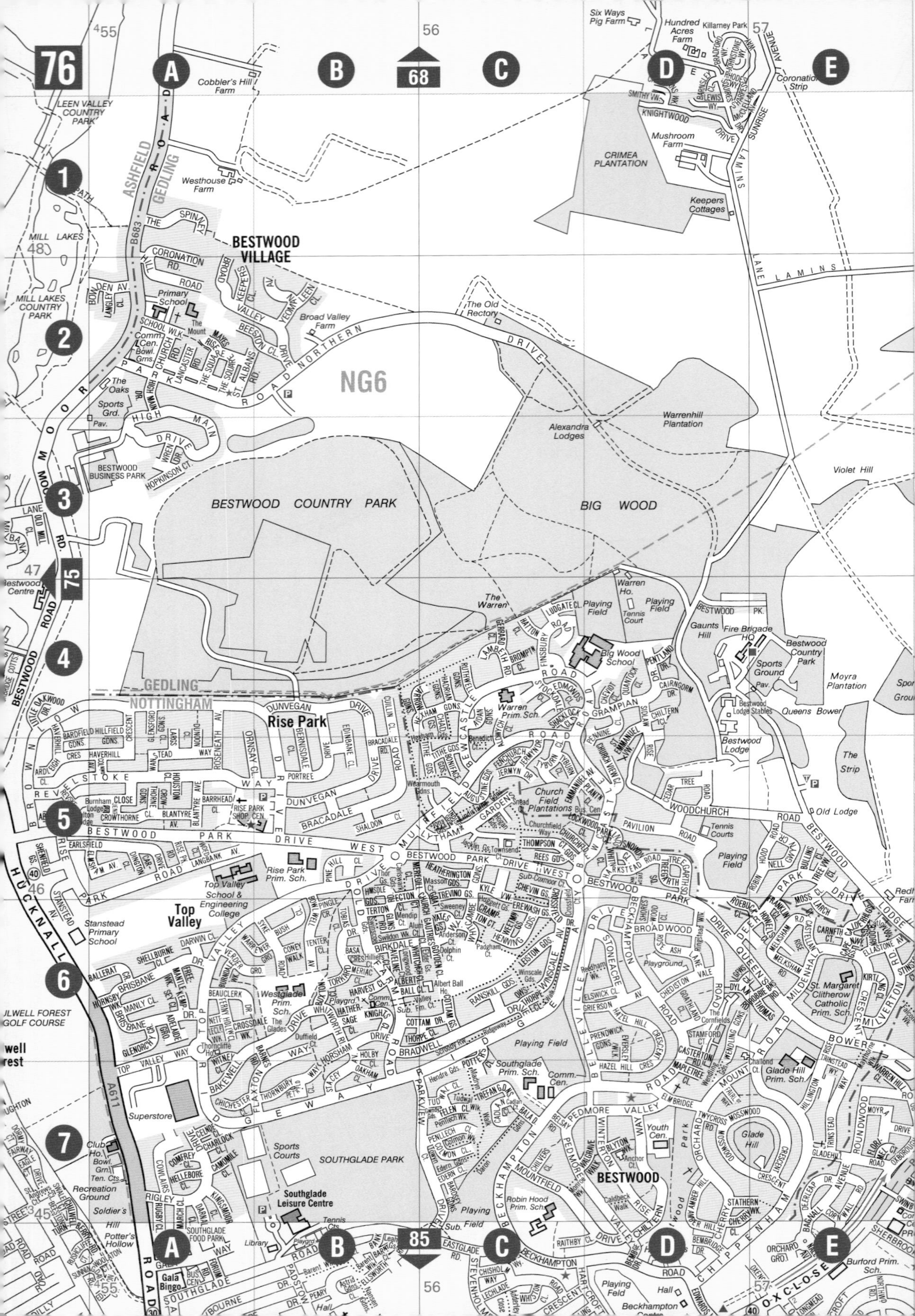
A
B
68
C
D
E
56
57
455
Six Ways Pig Farm
Hundred Acres Farm
Killarney Park
Coronation Strip
Cobbler's Hill Farm
LEEN VALLEY COUNTRY PARK
1
2
3
4
5
6
7
ASHFIELD
GEDLING
ROAD
B683
Westhouse Farm
MILL LAKES
48
MILL LAKES COUNTRY PARK
THE SPINNEY
BESTWOOD VILLAGE
CORONATION RD.
Primary School
The Mount
Broad Valley Farm
The Old Rectory
NORTHERN DRIVE
NORTHERN ROAD
NG6
CRIMEA PLANTATION
Mushroom Farm
KNIGHTWOOD DRIVE
SUNRISE AVENUE
LAMINS LANE
Keepers Cottages
The Oaks
Sports Grd.
HIGH MAIN DRIVE
BESTWOOD BUSINESS PARK
HOPKINSON CT.
MOOR ROAD
Alexandra Lodges
Warrenhill Plantation
Violet Hill
BESTWOOD COUNTRY PARK
BIG WOOD
47
75
BESTWOOD ROAD
Bestwood Centre
The Warren
Warren Ho.
Playing Field
Tennis Court
Big Wood School
Gaunts Hill
Fire Brigade HQ
Bestwood Country Park
Sports Ground
Moyra Plantation
Bestwood Lodge Stables
Queens Bower
Bestwood Lodge
The Strip
Old Lodge
GEDLING
NOTTINGHAM
Rise Park
DUNVEGAN DRIVE
Warren Prim. Sch.
BEWCASTLE ROAD
GRAMPIAN
Church Field Plantations
WOODCHURCH ROAD
PAVILION ROAD
Tennis Courts
Playing Field
BESTWOOD PARK DRIVE WEST
BESTWOOD PARK DRIVE
RISE PARK SHOP. CEN.
Rise Park Prim. Sch.
Top Valley School & Engineering College
Top Valley
Stanstead Primary School
46
HUCKNALL ROAD
BESTWOOD PARK DRIVE WEST
Westglade Prim.
St. Margaret Clitherow Catholic Prim. Sch.
Glade Hill Prim. Sch.
Glade Hill
Playing Field
Southglade Prim. Sch.
Comm. Cen.
BULWELL FOREST GOLF COURSE
TOP VALLEY WAY
A611
Superstore
Club Ho.
Recreation Ground
Soldier's Hill
Potter's Hollow
45
Sports Courts
SOUTHGLADE PARK
Southglade Leisure Centre
SOUTHGLADE FOOD PARK
Library
Youth Cen.
BESTWOOD
Robin Hood Prim. Sch.
Playing Field
85
Gala Bingo
SOUTHGLADE ROAD
BECKHAMPTON ROAD
Playing Field
Hall
Beckhampton Centre
Burford Prim. Sch.
CHIPPENHAM ROAD
FOX CLOSE
30
40

Ramsdale Park
North Peacock
69
Calverton Hill
Ramsdale Park
Ramsdale Hill
The Belt
South Peacock
A60
A614
Woodlands
Reservoirs (covered)
Tophouse Farm
LITTLE LIME LA.
Limelane House
MANSFIELD ROAD
OLLERTON ROAD
LIME LANE
GEORGE'S LANE
CALVERTON ROAD
Wood Farm
NG14
B684
Dorket Head Farm
Leapool
Brick Works
WOODBOROUGH LANE
Dorket Head
Japanese Plantations
Stockings Farm
Red Hill
Ten. Court
Cherry Holt
Reservoir (Covered)
New Farm
78
Works
Nottingham
KILLISICK LANE
Redhill
Redhill Academy
Leisure Centre
Derrymount Sch.
Richard Bonington Prim. Sch.
Recreation Ground
Playing Field
Family Cen.
Comm. Centre
Pinewood Inf. Sch.
Killisick Jun. Sch.
Cemetery
Arnold Mill Prim Sch.
Recreation Ground
NG5
Robert Mellors Prim. Sch.
Coppice Farm Prim. Sch.
Christ The King Catholic School
ARNOLD
Arnold View Prim. Sch.
Daybrook
Superstore
86
Arnold Hill School & Technology College
(Main Site)
(Lower Site)
ARNOT HILL PARK
MANSFIELD ROAD
NOTTINGHAM ROAD

78
70
77
87
A
B
C
D
E
1
2
3
4
5
6
7
60
61
62
48
47
46
45
Lamp Wood
LANE
GEORGE'S
SPINDLE
LANE
ROAD
BONNER LANE
Bonner Hill
FOXWOOD
Fox Wood
High Trees
Foxwood House
Thorne
Wynhill
LANE
WESTFIELD LA.
Wood Farm
Woodborough Park
Southwood
Bank Farm
Bank Hill Cottage
The Bank
WOOD-BOROUGH LANE
B684
BANK ROAD
Arnold Lodge
NG3
NOTTINGHAM
Wood Barn Farm
Lambley House
HUNGERHILL LANE
Nottingham
PLAINS
Barn Farm
Howbeck Clo.
Mellish Rugby Football Club
Fox Covert
NG5
CATFOOT LANE
Foxhill Farm
Cottage Farm
Nursery
Play Area
NG4
Highclere House
Coppice Farm
Mapperley Plains
MAPPERLEY
DRIVE
ORCHARD
ROAD
Middlebeck Farm
Coppice Farm Prim. Sch.
Lambley Dumble
SPRING LANE
Springlane Farm
Chicken Farm
RNOLD
Playing Field
Site)

SPRINGWATER GOLF COURSE
ROE HILL
Grimesmoor
71
MAIN
Chapel Farm
Plantation Cotts.
EPPERSTONE BY-PASS
A6097
Epperstone Manor (Notts. Constabulary HQ)
Bowl. Grn.
Pav.
Sports Ground
EPPERSTONE
PARK LA.
BLAND LA.
TOAD LA.
Dover Beck
Shelt Hill Farm
Fox Covert
Daybreak
Cemetery
PRIVATE ROAD
ASH GRO.
BIRCH RISE
SUNNINGDALE DRIVE
DOVERBECK DR.
OLDACRES
PLOUGHMAN AV.
ALDENE WAY
HAWTHORN CL.
CROFT
WHITES
THE MEADOWS
BROAD CL.
FIELD LA.
NEW ROW
TAYLORS CFT.
ROE LANE
MAIN STREET
Woodborough Hall
PARK AV.
Rec. Grd.
CHURCH WK.
PINFOLD CL.
PINFOLD CR.
BUCKLAND DR.
SMALL'S CROFT
CHARNWOOD WY.
HOLME CL.
OLD MANOR CL.
LOWDHAM LANE
Nursery
Woodlands
WOODBOROUGH
Wood's Foundation C of E Prim. Sch.
Vicarage
Hall
Play. Field
SMITHY CL.
Fox Covert
NG14
Lowdham Grange
GRANGE FM. COTTS.
80
47
PLOUGHMAN WOOD
HMP LOWDHAM GRANGE
LONG MEADOW HILL
THE GREEN
SYKE
ROCKLEYS VIEW
LINGWOOD LANE
Well Cottage
GREEN LANE
Hunters Hill
Jericho Farm
Lil-Yan Poultry Farm
NEWARK and SHERWOOD
GEDLING
46
Lowinds Farm
Hywinds Farm
LAMBLEY ROAD
Park Lane Nurseries
Bateman House
Harlow Wood Farm
PARK LANE
The Poplars
DUMBLES
CHURCH STREET
Cocker Beck
LAMBLEY
ORCHARD
STEELES WY.
TRINITY CR.
MILL LA.
CHAPEL LA.
WILLOW CR.
RISE
COCKER BECK
GRANGE CL.
ROSS LA.
Works
Lambley Prim. Sch.
Rec. Grd.
MAIN STREET
Cemetery
Cornwall's Hill
Broughton Park
Bulcote Wood
NG14
FLAMSTEAD AV.
CROMWELL CRES.
NEGUS CT.
Works
Stockhill Farm
88
345
SPRING
Road
LAMBLEY BRIDLE ROAD
Bulcote Lodge Fram
63
64
465
F G H J K
1 2 3 4 5 6 7

A
B
C
D
E
148
66
67
465
Chapel Farm
CHURCH LA.
CHAPEL
NEEPS CFT.
LANE
HAGG
MAIN
STREET
PADDOCK
FARM COTTS.
Bentley Wood
erstone Manor
. Constabulary HQ)
Bowl. Grn.
Pav.
Sports Ground
MANOR PK. LA.
BLAND LA.
TOAD LA.
PARK LA.
EPPERSTONE
The Old House
Elm Park
Rifle Range
Netherfield Farm
Village Hall
Pav.
Epperstone Playing Field
Beck
Order
ROAD
GONALSTON
48
Dover
LOWDHAM
Wash Bridge
Netherfield Farm House
EPPERSTONE
A6097
50
Beck
LOWDHAM LA.
OLD
GEDLING
NEWARK and SHERWOOD
Nursery
Woodlands
The Old Mill House
Car Holt Farm
EPPERSTONE
Furleys Cotts.
ROAD
Lowdham Mill
Weir
Car Holt
Nottingham
Nurseries
Eliment Hill Farm
West End Villas
The Old Vicarage
Dover
GRANGE FM. COTTS.
The Hut
Orchard Nurseries
KINGFISHER CT.
Brookfield
47
79
EPPERSTONE RD.
THE LEYS
MOUNT PLEASANT
Prim. Sch.
Cemetery
A6097
RIDGE HILL
Barker Hill
Hill House
THE
LONG MEADOW
HILL
GREEN
HILL SYKE
ROCKLEYS VIEW
CHURCH LA.
The Old Hall
Greenacres
Grove Farm
THE PRIORS
THE FORGE
NURSERY GS.
FRANCKLIN
St. Mary's CL.
FRANCKLIN RD.
BARKER HILL
ROGERS AV.
BLACK-THORN DR.
MAIN
ROAD
The Beck House
Nursery
Beck
STONEY BANK
TON LA.
THE OLD DAIRY
MANOR HOUSE CL.
Hall Rec. Grd.
LOWDHAM
SOUTHWELL
RED LA.
PLOUGH LA.
Elm Tree Farm
CRANLEIGH DR.
NEIGHBOURS
PROSPECT VS.
MAGNA
Charta Mews
OLD TANNERY DRIVE
Hunters Hill
Low Meadow
Worlds End
BROOKSIDE
Rec. Grd.
THE CORNER
Pav.
War Mem.
MORLEY'S CL.
WILLOW HOLT
MERE-VALE CL.
LIME TREE
NEWTON CL.
STATION RD.
NOTTM. RD.
NG14
BYPASS
LOWDHAM
46
Cocker
VICTORIA AV.
LONG-MOOR AV.
BLENHEIM
WORCESTER CL.
RUSSET
ROSS CL.
THE SIDINGS
BECK-SIDE
LAMBLEY
Lowinds Farm
Hywinds Farm
ROAD
A612
NOTTINGHAM
Brakes Farm
SKITHORNE RISE
Lowdham
GUNTHORPE RD.
PAVILION CT.
Lowdham Lodge
Marlock Bridge
ROAD
COTTAGE PASTURE LA.
Slurry Pond
Little Marlock
7
A612
Sunny Bank
Sibthorpe House
Mumby House
Beecroft Farm
Cocker
Beck
345
Hill Farm
89
ll Trees
urseries
465
66
67
MAIN
OLD
The Manor House
1
2
3
4
5
6

81
138
90
149
Thurgarton
Hoveringham
HOVERINGHAM
Gonalston
Caythorpe
NOTTINGHAM ROAD
A612
A6097
STATION ROAD
HOVERINGHAM LANE
THURGARTON LANE
GONALSTON LANE
THORPE LANE
MAIN STREET
BOAT LANE
BRADLEYS LANE
LANSIC LANE
BROOKFIELD DR.
HOMELEIGH LA.
POST OFFICE YD.
OLD HILL LANE
THE AVENUE
Car Dyke
Causeway Dyke
RIVER TRENT
Spital Wood
Spitalwood Dumble
The Dumble
Wood Barn
Springfield House
The Gorse
Spital Farm
Glebe Farm
The Hall
The Old Rectory
The Old Kennels
Holme Farm
The Almshouses
The Hermitage
Cliff Mill
Cliff Mill Farm
Norrisdene
Gonalston Crossing
Hoveringham Mill
Ford
Westfield House
Lansic House
Works
New Farm
Rose Cottage
Four Winds
Hall Farm
Flora Farm
Lindum Cotts.
Kneeton View
Cricket Grd.
Pav.
West Farm
Manor Farm
St. Michael's Farm
Church Farm
Ferry Farm
Lowdham Farm
Playing Field
Kennels
Springfield
Fernhill House
Brackenhill
Hillcrest
Clayton's Cottage
Caythorpe House
Watson's Piece
NG13
TRENT HILLS
Marlock Cottages
Marlock House Farm
Holly Farm
F G H J K
1 2 3 4 5 6 7
68 69 470
48 47 46 345

KIMBERLEY
AWSWORTH
NG16
Nottingham
Babbington
Cossall Marsh
Cossall
Ilkeston Junction
73
92
A610
A6096
KIMBERLEY BY-PASS
EASTWOOD ROAD
GIN CLOSE WAY
AWSWORTH & COSSALL BY-PASS
GILTBROOK RETAIL PARK
Superstores
Sewage Works
Gilt Brook
Gilt Briggs Farm
Crabcroft Farm
Recreation Ground
Central College (Church Hill Centre)
The Fives
Whisgills
Grasscroft Farm
Babbington Hall
Babbington House Farm
Reservoir (Covered)
Strelley Park Farm
Holly Copse Nature Reserve
SPRING WOOD
Turkey Fields Farm
Robbinetts Cottage
Moss Cottage
Grange Farm
GRANGE ESTATE
Manor Farm
Cedar Farm
Almshouses
The Hollies
Robbinetts Arm (Disused)
Brickyard Plantation Nature Reserve
OLDMOOR WOOD Nature Reserve
Oldmoor Pond
Cossall Common
Common Farm
Nursery
Foundry House
Gin Stables
Bridge Farm
Newton's Bri.
River Erewash
Nottingham Canal (Disused)
White House Fm.
The View
Bungalow Farm
Awsworth Prim. Sch.
Play. Fld.
COSSALL INDUSTRIAL ESTATE
CORONATION ROAD
MILLERSHIP WY.
Bakers Brothers Mobile Home Cvn. Site
Larklands Inf. Sch.
Small Holding
BROXTOWE
EREWASH
Factory
Hollywell Prim. Sch.
Brewery
Manor Farm
ROBINETTES LANE
WESTBY LANE
NEWTON'S LANE
MILL LANE
COSSALL ROAD
DEAD LANE
CHURCH LANE
AWSWORTH LANE

83
F
G
H
J
K
74
New Nuthall
High Wood Cemetery
Redfield House Farm
Bakery
Kimberley Leisure Centre
The Kimberley Sch.
Games Courts
Cricket Grd.
Playing Field
Graphic Ho.
Superstore
Cemetery
The Coppice
Knowle Wood
Larkfields
Larkfields Jun. & Inf. Schs.
Playing Fields
Springfield Paddocks
M1
M1 MOTORWAY
Low Wood
NG6
1
2
3
4
5
6
7
Nursery
Home Farm
Community Centre
NUTHALL
THE LAKE
Brackenhurst
A610
EASTWOOD
Knowlepark Farm
Kimberley Prim. Sch.
Swingate
Verge Wood
Junction 26
Subway
A610
A6002
Hempshill Barns
Hempshill Hall
84
Horsendale Prim. Sch.
Swingate Farm
Windmill Farm
Windmill Plantation
NOTTINGHAM
BROXTOWE
Bridlepath Cottage
Chilwell Dam Plantation
BROXTOWE COUNTRY PARK
NOTTINGHAM BUSINESS PARK
Lodge
Broad Oak Plantation
Seagrave Prim. Sch.
BROXTOWE PK. BUS. CEN.
Home Farm
Quarry House
Fish Pond
NG8
Strelley Hall
Stonepit Plantation
Old Rectory Farm
Moat
Broad Oak Farm
STRELLEY
Rec. Grd.
Comm. Cen.
Jubilee
Playgrd.
Superstore
Westbury School
Playing Fields
Brocklewood Jun. & Inf. Schs.
The Denewood Cen.
Playing Field
Melbury Prim. Sch.
Harvey Hadden Sports Complex
Harvey Hadden Stadium
Bilborough Park
Catstone Hill
Reservoir (covered)
93
Bilborough Coll.
Bilborough
Glenbrook Prim. Sch.
Tennis Courts
Bowling Grn.
WOODHOUSE ROAD
STRELLEY ROAD
MAIN ROAD
B6004
B600
NOTTINGHAM ROAD
MORNINGTON CRESCENT
GUNNERSBURY WAY
WOODFIELD ROAD
DENEWOOD
450
51
52
45
44
43
42

A
B
C
D
E
1
2
3
4
5
6
7
75
83
94
BULWELL
Bulwell
Highbury Vale
Hempshill Vale
Cinderhill
Broxtowe
Aspley
NG6
NG16
NG8
High Wood Cemetery
Low Wood
NORTHERN CEMETERY
Snape Wood Prim. Sch.
Bus Depot
Rec. Grd.
Bowling Grn.
Hempshill Hall Prim. Sch.
Crabtree Farm Prim. Sch.
Comm. Cen.
Highbury Hospital
Bulwell Academy
Mellish Sports Centre
Playing Fields
Hempshill Barns
Hempshill Hall
Offices
Phoenix Park
P+R
Play Cen.
Charles Way Bus. Park
Open Space
Mill Street Playing Field
Football Pitch
Games Ct.
New College Nottingham (Basford Hall)
Quarry Holes Plantation
Cinderhill Gym
Playground
Recreation Ground
Playing Field
Rosslyn Park Prim. Sch.
The Elms
BROXTOWE WOOD
BROXTOWE COUNTRY PARK
BROXTOWE NOTTINGHAM
Old Basford Prim. Sch.
Sikh Temple
Ellis Guilford Sch. & Sports College
Tennis Courts
BAR LANE INDUSTRIAL PARK
Whitemoor Prim. Sch.
Minver Cres. Sports Centre
Ambleside Prim. Sch.
Aspley Comm. & Training Centre
The Aspley Centre
Recreation Ground
Superstore
Bowling Grn.
King George V Playing Flds.
Brocklewood Jun. & Inf. Schs.
Highwood Player Jun. & Inf. Sch.
St. Teresa's Catholic Prim. Sch.
The Trinity Catholic Sch. (Lower)
The Trinity Catholic Sch. (Upper)
Beechdale Ho. (Nursing Home)
Aspley Rehabilitation Unit
Bluecoat Academy
Harvey Hadden Stadium
Harvey Hadden Sports Complex
Bilborough Park
Nottingham Indoor Bowls Centre
Robins Wood Ho.
New Aspley Gardens
David Lloyd Leisure
Hadden Park High Sch.
Glenbrook Prim. Sch.
A610
A6002
A6514
B682
B6004
B6008
B690
KIMBERLEY-EASTWOOD BY-PASS
NUTHALL ROAD
WESTERN BOULEVARD
VERNON ROAD
HIGHBURY ROAD
ASPLEY LANE
BROXTOWE LANE
BELLS LANE
CINDERHILL ROAD
STOCKHILL LANE
NOTTINGHAM ROAD
HIGHFIELD DRIVE
MILLENNIUM WAY WEST
MILLENNIUM WAY EAST
STRELLEY ROAD
BEECHDALE ROAD
ALLENDALE AVENUE
MINVER CRESCENT
HILCOT DRIVE
SHERBORNE ROAD
MELBOURNE ROAD
ASPLEY PARK DRIVE
DENEWOOD CRESCENT
HARVEY ROAD
LOW WOOD ROAD
HEMPSHILL LANE
CRABTREE ROAD
COVENTRY ROAD
MAIN ST.
BULWELL HIGH RD.
STOCK WELL
HENRIETTA STREET
PICCADILLY
LOGAN ST.
KERSALL DR.
WOODLAND AV.
HIGHBURY AV.
SAXONDALE DR.
GREENWICH AVENUE
LADBROOKE CRES.
BAR LANE
BASFORD ROAD
WHITEMOOR RD.
HASLEMERE RD.
LODGE CL.
PRESTWOOD DRIVE
TRENTHAM DR.

BESTWOOD
76
SOUTHGLADE PARK
Southglade Leisure Centre
SOUTHGLADE FOOD PARK
Gala Bingo
Henry Whipple Prim. Sch.
Playing Fields
Community Centre
Beckhampton Centre
Sunrise Hill
Bestwood Park Hawthorns
Burford Prim. Sch.
Community Centre
CITY HOSPITAL
Maternity
Children's Centre
Nurses Home
Hospice
Playing Field
St. Andrews Lodge
Old Basford
VERNON PARK
Nottingham
Sherwood
HMP NOTTINGHAM
Seely Jun. & Inf. Schs.
NG5
Severn Trent Water Authority
Bagthorpe Gardens
Carrington
Ellesmere Bus. Park
Basford
Whitemoor
Gas Holders
Depot
New Basford
Djanogly City Academy
NG7
Wilkinson St.
Shipstone St.
Hyson Green
Radford Rd.
Noel Street
Forest Fields
Sherwood Rise
The Open University
NG3
Mapperley Park
Sports Ground
Nottingham Health Auth. Admin. Dept.
FOREST RECREATION GROUND
Hyson Grn. Mkt.
New Art Exchange
95
98
HUCKNALL ROAD
HUCKNALL LANE
VALLEY ROAD
MANSFIELD ROAD
NOTTINGHAM ROAD
SHERWOOD RISE
ARNOLD ROAD
OXCLOSE LANE
BOULEVARD
GREGORY BLVD.
A611
A6514
B6004
B683
B682
A60
A6130
F
G
H
J
K
1
2
3
4
5
6
7
55
56
57
45
44
43
42

A
B
C
D
E
77
85
96
1
2
3
4
5
6
7
58
59
45
44
43
42
ARNOLD
Arnold Hill School & Technology College
(Main Site)
(Lower Site)
Playing Field
Daybrook
Daybrook Square
ARNOT HILL PARK
Borough Council Offs.
Burford Prim. Sch.
Community Centre
Day Brook Rec. Grd.
NG5
Arno Vale Jun. Sch.
Arnold Woodthorpe Inf. Sch.
Ernehale Jun. & Inf. Schs.
Woodthorpe
THACKERAY'S LANE
ARNO VALE ROAD
A6211
A60
A6514
B684
MANSFIELD ROAD
VALLEY ROAD
GEDLING ROAD
NOTTINGHAM WOODTHORPE HOSP.
Recreation Ground
Sunken Gdns.
Miniature Golf Course
WOODTHORPE GRANGE PARK
Mapperley
Mapperley Plains Prim. Sch.
Cricket Ground
Club House
MAPPERLEY
Nottingham
NG3
Porchester
Walter Halls Prim. Sch.
Duncan Macmillan House
Nottingham Academy (Ransom Road Site)
Playing Fields
Mapperley Sports Village
Springwood Day Cen.
Mapperley Park
Recreation Ground
Stonepit Coppice Gardens
Hungerhill Gardens
Alexandra Park
Hospice
Brendon Lawrence Sports Hall
Thorneywood
Thorneywood Unit
Hogarth Prim. Sch.
Standhill Inf. Sch.
Rec Ground
Rec Grd.

87
78
88
97
F
G
H
J
K
1
2
3
4
5
6
7
60
61
62
345
44
43
42
PLAINS
B684
Springlane Farm
Chicken Farm
Crimea Farm
Lambley Dumble
Lambley Prim. Sch.
Rec. Grd.
Wicketwood Hill
Grass Road
Wood Farm
Hill Top Nursery
SPRING LA.
Gedling Wood
Glebe Farm
Harvey's Plantation
Kennels
Gedling Farm
Chase Farm
GOLF COURSE
ARNOLD LANE
A6211
NG4
Scotgrave Farm
Household Waste and Recycling Centre
Gedling Wharf
Playing Field
Pavilion
Gedling
Rec. Ground
The Gedling School
Comm. Cen.
Lib.
Cemetery
Hardstaff Almshouses
Stanhope Prim. Sch.
St. Andrews House
Carlton Digby Sch.
Westdale Jun. & Inf. Schs.
WESTDALE LANE
WOLLATON
CHESTERFIELD
Willow Farm Prim. Sch.
Carlton le Willows Academy
Gedling Manor
Youth Cen.
MAIN RD.
SHEARING HILL
COLWICK LOOP ROAD
Phoenix Inf. Sch.
Priory Jun. Sch.
All Hallows Prim. Sch.
Haddon Prim. Sch.
Carlton Academy
Carlton Forum Leisure Cen.
Football Pitch
Braywood Gardens
Richard Herrod Cen.
Recreation Ground
Carlton Cemetery
CARLTON
TA Cen.
Central Inf. Sch.
Central Jun. Sch.
Council Offices
B686
BURTON ROAD
STATION
Carlton
Sacred Heart Catholic
Bowl. Grn. Rec. Ground
Football Ground
Pavilion

LAMBLEY
BURTON JOYCE
Nottingham
NG4
Stoke Bardolph
Gedling Wood
Barron's Plantation
Crock Dumble
Wicketwood Hill
Wood Farm
Hill Top Nursery
Burtonwood Farm
Stockhill Farm
Lodge Farm
Cemetery
Cornwall's Hill
Stock Farm
Bulcote Wood
Broughton Park
Bulcote Lodge Fram
The Mount
Fox Hill
Glebe Farm
Gedling Wood Farm
White Gates
Poultry Farm
Gedling House
Carlton le Willows Academy
Gedling Manor
Playing Field
New Plantation
Sewage Disposal Works
Works
Burton Joyce
The Poplar Sports Ground
Sports Ground
Stoke Farm
Cricket Field
Recreation Ground
Football Ground
NOTTINGHAM ROAD
BURTON ROAD
TRENT VALLEY ROAD
CHURCH ROAD
STOKE LANE
LAMBLEY LANE
LAMBLEY BRIDLE ROAD
SPRING LANE
GEDLING RUSHCLIFFE
A612
A6211
79
87
98
63
64

Bulcote
SHELFORD
NG14
NG12
BURTON MEADOWS
THE HAMS
RIVER TRENT
Hill Farm
Riding School
Bulcote Hill Plantation
Sibthorpe House
Mumby House
Sunny Bank
Beecroft Farm
Slurry Pond
Tall Trees Nurseries
The Manor House
The Lodge
The Cottage
Bulcote Crossing
Corporation Cottages
Bulcote Farm
NEWARK and SHERWOOD
GEDLING
Little Marlock
Grange Farm
The Cedars
The Park
LOWDHAM ROAD
Cocker Beck
Shelford Manor
Shelford Manor Cottages
The Holmes
Moor Close Plantation
Waterfurrows Plantation
The Old Vicarage
Play. Fld.
Holly Farm
Bosworth Farm
Ashdown
The Cottage
The Hill
Scarborough House
Shelford Nurseries Caravan Park
Mill Bridge
Swallow Plantation
The Dam
FERRY LANE
MANOR LANE
WATER LANE
WATERFURROWS LA.
SHELFORD HILL
SHELFORD ROAD
MAIN ROAD
OLD MAIN RD.
CHURCH ST.
WEST ST.
MAIN RD.
PINFOLD LA.
BOSWORTH CL.
FIELD LANE
A612
80
90
99

GUNTHORPE
EAST BRIDGFORD
NEWTON
NG14
NG12
LOWDHAM ROAD BY-PASS
A6097
A46
THE AVENUE
MAIN ST.
TRENTSIDE
TRENT LANE
RIVER TRENT
Gunthorpe Bridge
Gunthorpe Lock
Warehouse
Lock House
Weir
The Moorings
Bridgeford Court Caravan Park
Water Reclamation Works
NEWARK and SHERWOOD
RUSHCLIFFE
Little Marlock
Holly Farm
The Park
Parklands
Grange Farm
The Cedars
Lodge Farm
Caravan Site
Glebe Farm
Playing Field
Gunthorpe C of E Prim. Sch.
Riverdale Park
Manor Farm
Long Plantation
Foxhills Farm
Moor Close Plantation
Hill Farm
Cuttle Hill
East Bridgford Hill
School
Butt Close Playing Field
Sewage Pump. Station
KNEETON LANE
KIRK HILL
BRIDGFORD STREET
BRUNT'S LANE
SPRINGDALE LANE
MAIN STREET
BUTT STREET
CROSSWAYS DR.
COLLEGE ST.
Newton Fields
Mill Farm
Glebe Farm
Newton House Farm
Yew Tree Farm
White House
SHELFORD ROAD
MAIN STREET
EAST BRIDGEFORD ROAD
NEWTON AIRFIELD
TRENCHARD
FAIRWAY CRES.
FRIAR WLK.
Playgrd.
Tennis Cts.
ANSON RD.
HAMPDEN RD.
BATTLE CL.
CHIPMUNK
Nursery
Newton Spring
TRENT HILLS
OLD HILL

81
89
100

Nottingham

NG13

Car Colston

Little Green

Topfield Farm
Old Hill Farm
Bungalow Farm
Glebe Farm
Cape Farm
Lammas Farm
Fosse Fields Farm
Sandfield House
CLOSES
SIDE LANE
Arborfield
SPRINGDALE LANE
Ashclose Poultry Farm
Toll Bar Farm
Nursery
Woodside Farm
Bulwell House
Burrowsmoor Holt
Burrow Fields
Castle Hill
High Westing Farm
TENMAN LANE
Parrots Nest
Thoroughfare Holt
MICKLEMOOR LANE
Bottom Plantation
Moorfield Cottage
Pav.
Cricket Ground
The Hall
Hall Farm
Manor Farm
Wilmot CL
Hall
Bingham CT
CHURCH LA
Old Hall
Fosse Farm
Fosse Poultry Farm
Shackerdale Farm
Shackerdale Wood
Shacker Dale
Newfield
Red Lodge
Stoneydale Plantation
Barbara's Wood
Blagg's Covert
The Shacker
Brunsell Hall
Beech Close Farm
Nursery
Field House Farm
CAR LA.
SCHREVETON ROAD
KNEETON ROAD
OCCUPATION ROAD
FOSSE LANE
Fosse Way (Roman Road)
NEW ROAD
RED LODGE LANE
LANE
A46

Grid references (top): F 470 G 71 H J 72 K 91 345

Grid references (bottom): F 470 G 71 H 101 J 72 K

Right side markers: 1, 2, 44, 3, 149, 4, 43, 5, 6, 42, 7

Bottom markers: F G H 101 J K

82
104
A
B
C
D
E
1
2
3
4
5
6
7
48
49
41
40
39
38
ILKESTON
TROWELL
Trowell Service Area
Nottingham
NG9
Ilkeston
DE7
New Stapleford
Gallows Inn
Stanton Gate
M1
M1-MOTORWAY
A609
A6007
B6003
B6004
NOTTINGHAM RD.
ILKESTON ROAD
NOTTINGHAM ROAD
STAPLEFORD ROAD
TROWELL ROAD
ILKESTON ROAD
COSSALL ROAD
WATERLOO LANE
STONEY LANE
FURNACE ROAD
RIVER EREWASH
EREWASH
BROXTOWE
NOTTINGHAM CANAL (Dis
EREWASH CANAL
FIELDS ROAD
CROMPTON ROAD
MERLIN WAY
LOWS LANE
SEVEN OAKS ROAD
QUARRY HILL
GOLF CLUB ROAD
MOORBRIDGE LANE
STANTON GATE
STANTON ROAD
PASTURE ROAD
HICKINGS LANE
Small Holding
Warehouse
Wks.
Depot
Play Fld.
GALLOWS INN IND. ESTATE
Meadow Farm
Field House
Grange Wood
Mill
Gallows Inn Bridge
Gallows Inn Playing Field
Uplands Farm
Rectory
Trowell C of E Prim. Sch.
Trowell Junction
Shortwood Farm
Shortwood House
Waterloo Houses
Caravan Site
Trowell Hall
Factory
Works
Football Grd.
Sports Ground
Timber Yard
CROMPTON ROAD INDUSTRIAL ESTATE
Depots
Sewage Works
Swansea Bridge Cottages
Nursery
Swancar Farm
Stanton Works
Junction Lock
Field Farm
Stapleford Hill
LANGHAM PARK
Under-pass
EREWASH VALLEY GOLF COURSE
Club House
GOLF COURSE
Jubilee House Christian School
Playing Field
Club
Ind. Est.
Community Cen.
Albany Inf. Sch.
Albany Junior School
Hickings La. Rec.
Wadsworth Fields
Leicester Ho.

STRELLEY
83
Bilborough
Bilborough Sports Centre
Bilborough Coll.
Nottingham Univ. Samworth Academy
Harvey Hadden Sports Complex
Harvey Hadden Stadium
Bilborough Park Pav.
Miniature Golf Course
Westbury School
Melbury Prim. Sch.
Catstone Hill
Reservoir (covered)
Shaw's Plantation
Gables Farm
Spring Farm
Moor Farm
Trowell Moor
Tottle Brook
Portland Prim. Sch.
Bolsover Road Rec. Grd.
NG8
Glaisdale Park Industrial Estate
Old Park Farm Gardens
Martin's Pond Nature Reserve
Martin's Pond
Superstore
A609
TROWELL ROAD
RUSSELL DR.
94
BALLOON WOOD INDUSTRIAL ESTATE
Balloon Wood
Firbeck Prim. Sch.
Fernwood School
Playing Field
Fernwood Jun.& Inf. Schs.
Sports Ground
Potter's Plantation
Birchwood Nurseries
Coventry Lane Bridge
Hulks Farm
Bramcote Moor
Bramcote Crematorium
MOOR FARM INN LA.
Sand Pit
Bramcote Hills College
Deddington Plantation
WOLLATON
Thompson's Wood
Open Space
Bramcote Hills Prim. Sch.
The Bramcote School
Bramcote Hills Park
Foxwood Academy
Running Track
Crow Hill
Bramcote Leisure Centre
Bramcote Hills
A52
A6002
A6007
DERBY ROAD
(BRIAN CLOUGH WAY)
B6006
Recreation Ground
Cemetery
105
Beeston Fields Prim. Sch.
F
G
H
J
K
1
2
3
4
5
6
7
50
51
52
41
40
39
38

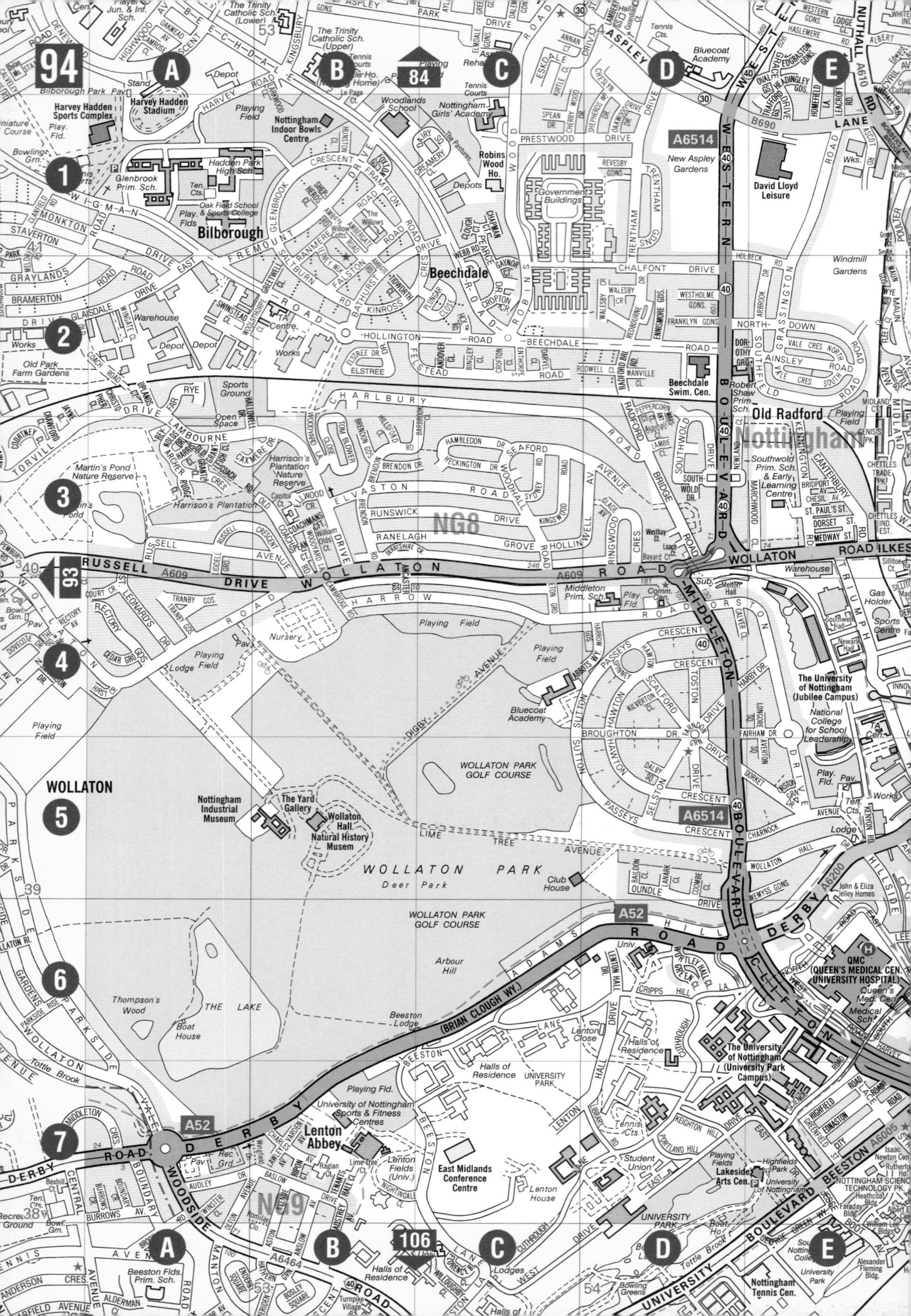

95
F
G
H
J
K
1
2
3
4
5
6
7
85
6
96
6
107
55
56
57
41
40
39
38
Hyson Green
Radford Rd.
Noel Street
Djanogly Comm. Leis. Cen.
Djanogly City Academy
BOULEVARD
A6130
FOREST RECREATION GROUND
The Forest
Site of Goose Fair
Games Ct.
Putting Green
Church Cemetery
A60
MANSFIELD
The Open University
NG5
NG1
NG7
NG2
ALFRETON
GREGORY
A610
RADFORD
BOULEVARD
Hyson Grn. Mkt
New Art Exchange
Superstore
Gala Bingo
Castle Retail Park
Radford
Leisure Cen.
Bloomsgrove Industrial Estate
ILKESTON ROAD
A609
LENTON
Recreation Ground
Nottingham High Sch.
Arboretum
Nottingham Trent Uni.
University
General Cemetery
Halls of Residence
HUNTINGDON
WOODBOROUGH
Victoria Mkt.
LivingWell Health Club
Victoria Cen.
Royal Cen.
Cineworld
WOLLATON
DERBY
Canning Circus
The Park
NEWCASTLE
(BRIAN CLOUGH WAY)
A6200
Standard Hill
Nottingham Castle Mus.
MAID MARIAN WAY
Old Mkt. Sq.
Lace Mkt.
Broad Marsh Shop. Cen.
Shire Hall
New Lenton
Old Lenton
Lenton Recreation Ground
Savoy Cin.
The Lenton Cen.
CASTLE BLVD.
A6005
County Archives
Nottingham Mag. Court
Station
NOTTINGHAM
QUEENS RD.
A6019
Government Offices
Castle Meadow Retail Park
Castle Marina Park
NOTTINGHAM
ABBEY BRIDGE
Superstore
Castlebridge Office Village
Lenton North Junction
ng2 Business Park
Stephenson College
NET Extension (Under Construction)
Meadows
WILFORD
A453
Riverside Prim. Sch.
QUEENS DRIVE
Wilford Bridge
RIVER TRENT
Queens Drive Industrial Estate
The University of Nottingham (King's Meadow Campus)
A52
BOULEVARD
Dunkirk
Showcase Cinema
Tenpin
Portland Leisure Cen.
Greenfields School
Recreation Ground
Tennis Courts
EMBANKMENT
VICTORIA

96
A
B
C
D
E
1
2
3
4
5
6
7
86
7
95
108
58
59
38
Alexandra Park
Hungerhill Gardens
Hungerhill Gardens
Sycamore Academy
St. Ann's
St. Ann's Well Academy
Primary Academy
Blue Bell Hill Prim. Sch.
Rosehill Sch.
Stonebridge City Farm
KK Sports & Leisure Cen.
South Nottingham College (Carlton Road Centre)
Hogarth Prim. Sch.
Standhill Inf. Sch.
NG3
Playing Field
Open Space
Nottingham
Nottingham Academy
Nottingham Wildcats Arena
Iona School
Edale Rise Prim. Sch.
Recreation Ground
COLWICK WOOD
Colwick Wood
Roughill Wood
Nottingham Academy (Greenwood Road Site 1)
Colwick Crossing
Nottingham Greyhound Stadium
Racecourse
Grandstand
Sports Ground
Paddock
Storage Tanks
Sneinton
Victoria Leis. Cen.
Victoria Park
Gala Bingo
Lace Mkt.
Capital FM Arena
The National Ice Cen.
Shire Hall
BBC East Midlands
NHS Walk-in Cen.
NOTTINGHAM
Nottingham Mag. Court
Station St.
Crown & County Ct.
South Nottingham College (London Road Centre)
Meadow Trading Estate
Cattle Market
Notts County FC & Nottingham RFC (Meadow La.)
Meadows
Portland Leisure Cen.
Nottingham Forest FC (City Ground)
Nottinghamshire Co. Cricket Club (Trent Bridge)
County Hall
Civic Cen.
Turners Quay
British Waterways Board
Timber Yard Depot
Park Yacht Club
NG2
NOTTINGHAM RUSHCLIFFE
TRENT FIELDS
Football Ground
Pavilion
Tennis Courts
Playing Field
Hawthorne Lodge
Carlight Gdns. Park Homes
Adbolton
Recreation Ground
Meml. Gdns.
A60
A612
A6019
A6011
A6520
B686
B684
WOODBOROUGH ROAD
CARLTON ROAD
DALESIDE ROAD
MANVERS STREET
LONDON ROAD
QUEENS ROAD
MEADOW LANE
LADY BAY BRIDGE
TRENT BRIDGE
RADCLIFFE ROAD
TRENT BOULEVARD
RIVER TRENT
VICTORIA EMBANKMENT

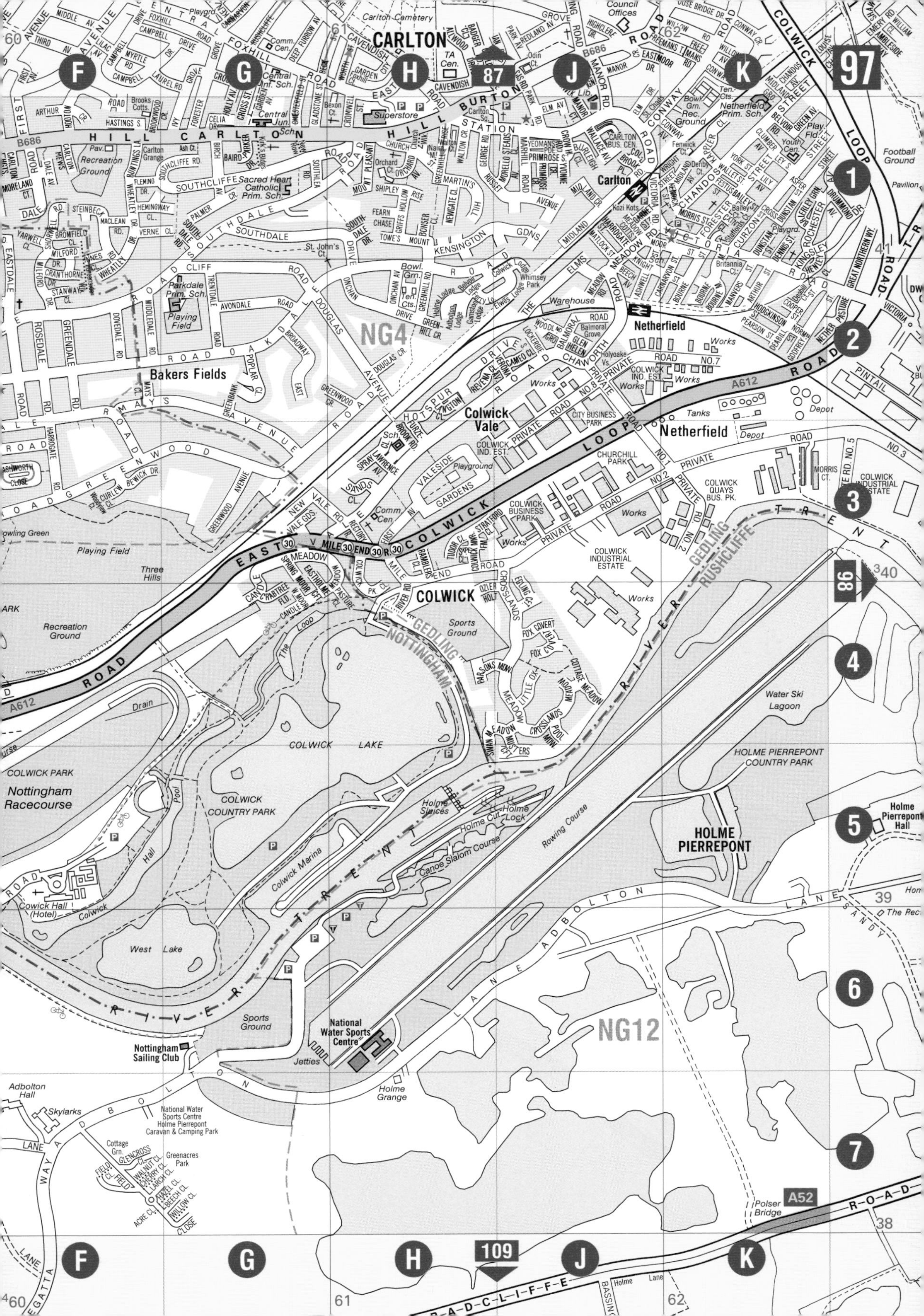

A
B
C
D
E
1
2
3
4
5
6
7
63
64
39
38
340
88
97
110
Stoke Farm
Works
Cricket Field
Stoke Bardolph
ST. LUKE WY.
STOKE
LANE
STANHOPE CR.
Top Row
NG14
Football Ground
Pavilion
COLWICK LOOP ROAD
TRENT VALLEY ROAD
A6211
A612
TEAL CLOSE
DW Fitness Club
Works
VICTORIA
PARK WAY
VICTORIA BUSINESS PARK
PINTAIL CLOSE
DRAKE RD.
MALLARD RD.
Depot
PRIVATE ROAD
MORRIS CT.
PRIVATE RD. NO. 5
COLWICK INDUSTRIAL ESTATE
NO. 3 PRIVATE ROAD NO. 4
Ouse Dyke
Nottingham
NG4
Stoke Lock
Hallow Well
GEDLING
RUSHCLIFFE
RIVER TRENT
Viaduct
Water Ski Lagoon
HOLME PIERREPONT COUNTRY PARK
Brook
Polser
ISLAND LANE
Recreation Grd.
Radcliffe Lodge
Radcliffe
BROOKFIELD
RADCLIFFE ON TRENT
The Chestnuts
Manor Ho.
Holme Pierrepont Hall
The Firs
HOLME LANE
HOLME PIERREPONT
Home Farm
ADBOLTON LA.
The Rectory
SANDY LANE
THE GREEN
MAIN ROAD
WHARF LANE
CLIFF LANE
THE AVENUE
GRANDFIELD CRES.
GRANDFIELD AV.
HAMILTON DR.
OAK TREE AV.
FERNWOOD DR.
ROCKLEY AV.
CLIFF WAY
CHESTNUT GRO.
LORNE GRO.
ROAD
BINGHAM ROAD
SHELFORD RD.
Comm. Cen.
Radcliffe-on-Trent Junior Sch.
Cemetery
WHITWORTH
ORFORD AV.
BAILEY LA.
VANCOUVER AV.
WATER LANE
SHADWELL GRO.
VICARAGE
CHURCH
PRINCE EDWARD CRES.
ST. LAWRENCE BOULEVARD
Bailey Ct.
PADDOCK CL.
KINGS WAY
DOUGLAS CL.
AVENUE
DRIVE
Lamcote Ms.
LAMCOTE GDNS.
YEW TREE CL.
RSPCA Animal Shelter
NOTTINGHAM
GRANTHAM RD.
A52
Cedar Lodge Caravan Park
Pav.
Sports Ground
LEES BARN ROAD
Lees Barn
Lamcote Field
Works
Holme House
STRAGGLETHORPE
RADCLIFFE RD.
Polser Bridge

Swallow Plantation
No Joke Plantation
Malkin Hill
Gibbet Hill
Shelford Lodge Farm
Crown Cottages
Shelford Road Farm
Spellow Hill
Spellow Farm
Depot
Lawson's Barn Farm
Jubilee Plantation
Hill Farm
Brickyard Plantation
NG12
Playing Field
Harlequin
Upper Saxondale
New House
Parr's Barn Farm
Radcliffe-on-Trent Infant School
South Nottinghamshire Academy
Dewberry Hill
Club House
RADCLIFFE ON TRENT GOLF COURSE
Sunpit Plantation
Radcliffe Barn Farm
Hall Farm
New Barn Farm
Cropwell Court
The Fields
Saxton's Lings
Lings Cottage
Cropwell Lings
Shelford Nurseries Caravan Park
The Hill
SHELFORD ROAD
SHELFORD HILL
OATFIELD LANE
HENSON LANE
SAXONDALE DRIVE
RIVER TRENT
A52
A46
89
100
111

A
B
C
D
E
90
NEWTON AIRFIELD
MAIN STREET
Newton Spring
Sewage Works
Ash Holt
NEWTON GARDENS
(Roman Road)
Foss Road Farm
Dawson's Plantation
Jubilee Plantation
A46
Nottingham
Sycamore Farmhouse
Lodge Farm
Saxondale
Manor Farm
Mount Pleasant
Manor Farm Cottages
A52
Saxondale Island
NOTTINGHAM
BINGHAM
Brickyard Plantation
Playing Field
Linear Park
Foss Farm
Lings Farm
Cropwell Lings
Lings Cottage
NG12
TOOT HILL
High Thorpe
Top Brackendale Farm
Cropwell Grove Farm
New Banks Farm
Lodge
HARDIGATE RD.
Newlands
Cropwell Court
112
99

F
G
H
J
K
91
113
102
1
2
3
4
5
6
7
470
71
72
41
40
39
38
High Westing Farm
Bottom Plantation
Car Dyke
Holme Farm
Moor Bridge
Parson's Hill
NG13
Sewage Works
MOOR
MOORBRIDGE
Works
Moorbridge Ct.
Playing Field
Tennis Ct.
Bingham
Pav.
BINGHAM INDUSTRIAL PARK
CARNARVON CL.
PLACE
KIRKHILL
GILLOTTS CL.
MOOR LA.
STATION ST.
LANGTRY GDS.
ST. MARYS
LANE
PRIORS CL.
BROWNES RD.
VICTORIA RD.
NURSERY RD.
CARR RD.
DOUGLAS RD.
BANES RD.
Robert Miles Jun. Sch.
CHURCH CL.
GROVE RD.
BUTT RD.
ABBEY ROAD
Playgrd.
Carnarvon Primary School
NEWGATE ST.
SCHOOL LA.
MARKET PL.
CHURCH ST.
HOLME ST.
FAIRFIELD ST.
CHESTERFIELD AV.
CARNARVON DRIVE
LONG ACRE
CROW CT.
COGLEY
RUTLAND RD.
FOSTERS LA.
MANOR RD.
CHERRY ST.
EAST ACRE
Oak Lodge
Beech Lodge
ASPEN CL.
HOLLY CL.
JUNIPER CL.
BLACKTHORN CL.
GDS.
WILLOW
RAYMOND DR.
WALKERS CL.
THE CROFTS
MELVYN DR.
BANKS CRES.
THE PADDOCK
FISHER LA.
BANKS PADDOCK
BEETHAM CL.
EBBS LA.
PINFOLD LA.
PERRY GRO.
DARK LA.
ROWAN CL.
ARCH CL.
POPLAR CL.
ASH CL.
MAPLE CL.
BEECH AV.
OAK AV.
CEDAR CL.
SYCAMORE
ELM AV.
HAZEL CL.
DERRY LA.
THE BANKS
GRANTHAM ROAD
Stanhope Wy.
Bingham Leisure Centre
Cemetery
BELVOIR VALE GRO.
DRIVE
MALLARD CL.
WADES WY.
GOLDCREST
NIGHTINGALE WAY
Toot Hill School
Playing Field
Tennis Courts
Games Court
Sports Arena
SANDPIPER CL.
KESTREL
OSPREY
WOODPECKER
DOVE CL.
SWALLOW CL.
SKYLARK CL.
AVOCET CL.
BINGHAM
Play. Fld.
LANGAR RD.
CHAPLEFIELD GRO.
STARNHILL WY.
TITHBY ROAD
GRANTHAM BY-PASS
A52
60
ROAD
Sub.
CHAPEL LANE
Reservoir
Starnhill Cottages
Starnhill Farm
Starnhill Plantation
SMITE
Spring Farm
Spring Farm Cotts.
Whitefield Farm
Tithby Grange Cottages
Tithby Grange
MICKLEMOOR LA.

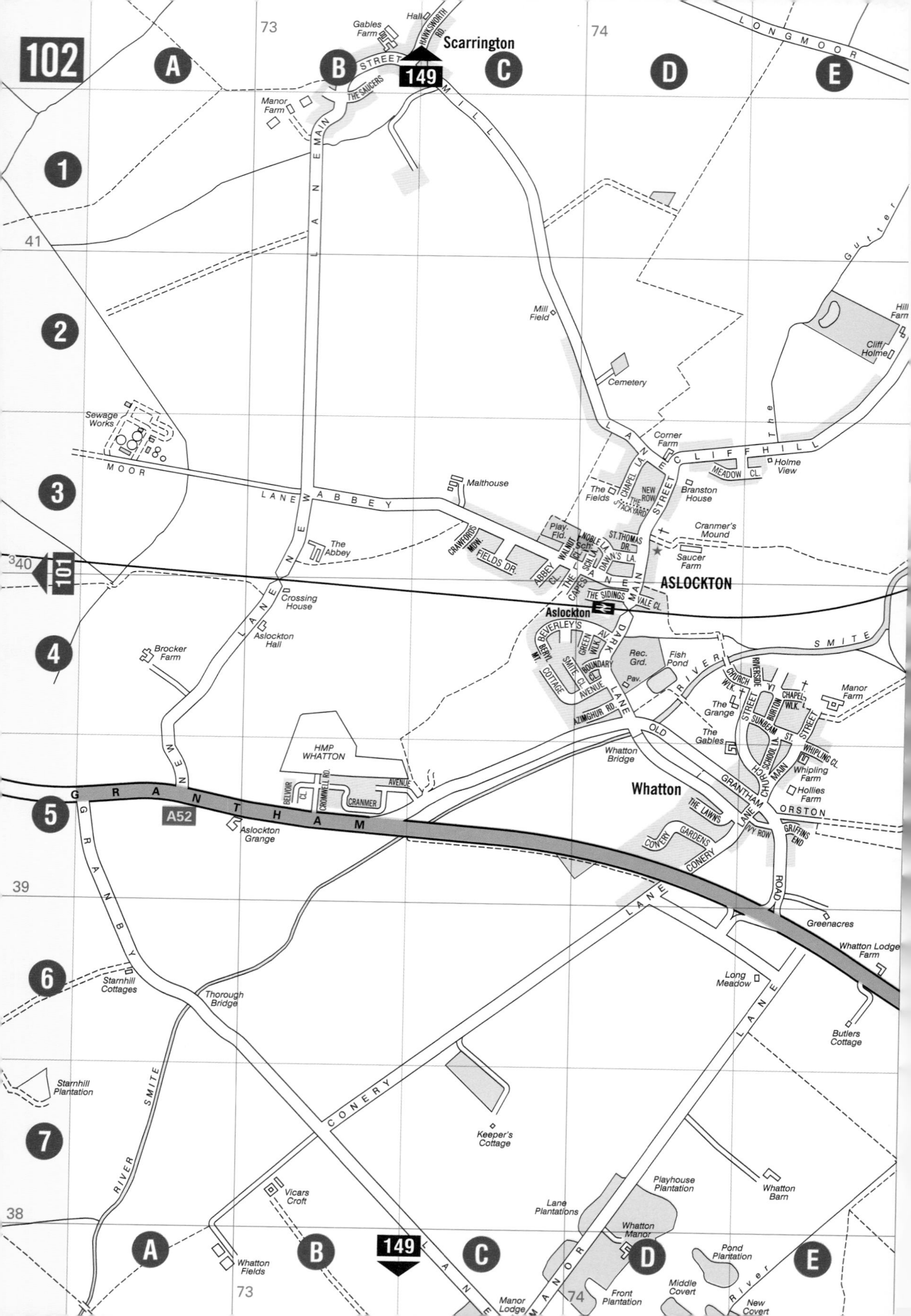
Scarrington
Hall
Gables Farm
HAWKSWORTH RD
STREET
THE SAUCERS
149
Manor Farm
MAIN
MILL
LANE
Mill Field
Cemetery
Hill Farm
Cliff Holme
The Gutter
Sewage Works
MOOR LANE
ABBEY
Malthouse
Corner Farm
CLIFF HILL
MEADOW CL.
Holme View
CHAPEL LA.
NEW ROW
THE STACKYARD
STREET
The Fields
Branston House
Cranmer's Mound
Play. Fld.
NOBLE LA.
ST. THOMAS DR.
Sch.
SCH. LA.
DAWN'S LA.
Saucer Farm
The Abbey
CRAWFORDS MDW.
FIELDS DR.
WALNUT CL.
ABBEY CL.
THE CAPES
ASLOCKTON
101
Crossing House
THE SIDINGS
VALE CL.
Aslockton
Aslockton Hall
BEVERLEY'S
GREEN WLK.
AVENUE
DARK LANE
Rec. Grd.
Pav.
Fish Pond
SMITE
RIVER
Brocker Farm
BERYL
MT. COTTAGE
SMITE CL.
BOUNDARY CL.
AZIMGHUR RD.
CHURCH WLK.
RIVERSIDE
LA.
CHAPEL WLK.
Manor Farm
The Grange
STREET
SUNBEAM
BURTON ST.
The Gables
OLD
Whatton Bridge
SCHOOL LA.
CHURCH
MAIN
WHIPLING CL.
Whipling Farm
Hollies Farm
HMP WHATTON
BELVOIR CL.
CROMWELL RD.
AVENUE
CRANMER
GRANTHAM
Whatton
THE LAWNS
GARDENS
COVERY
CONERY
IVY ROW
ORSTON
GRIFFINS END
ROAD
A52
Aslockton Grange
GRANBY
Greenacres
Whatton Lodge Farm
Long Meadow
Butlers Cottage
Starnhill Cottages
Thorough Bridge
Starnhill Plantation
RIVER SMITE
CONERY
Keeper's Cottage
Playhouse Plantation
Whatton Barn
Lane Plantations
Whatton Manor
Vicars Croft
Pond Plantation
Whatton Fields
Front Plantation
Middle Covert
River
Manor Lodge
MANOR
New Covert
A B C D E
1 2 3 4 5 6 7
73 74
41 40 39 38

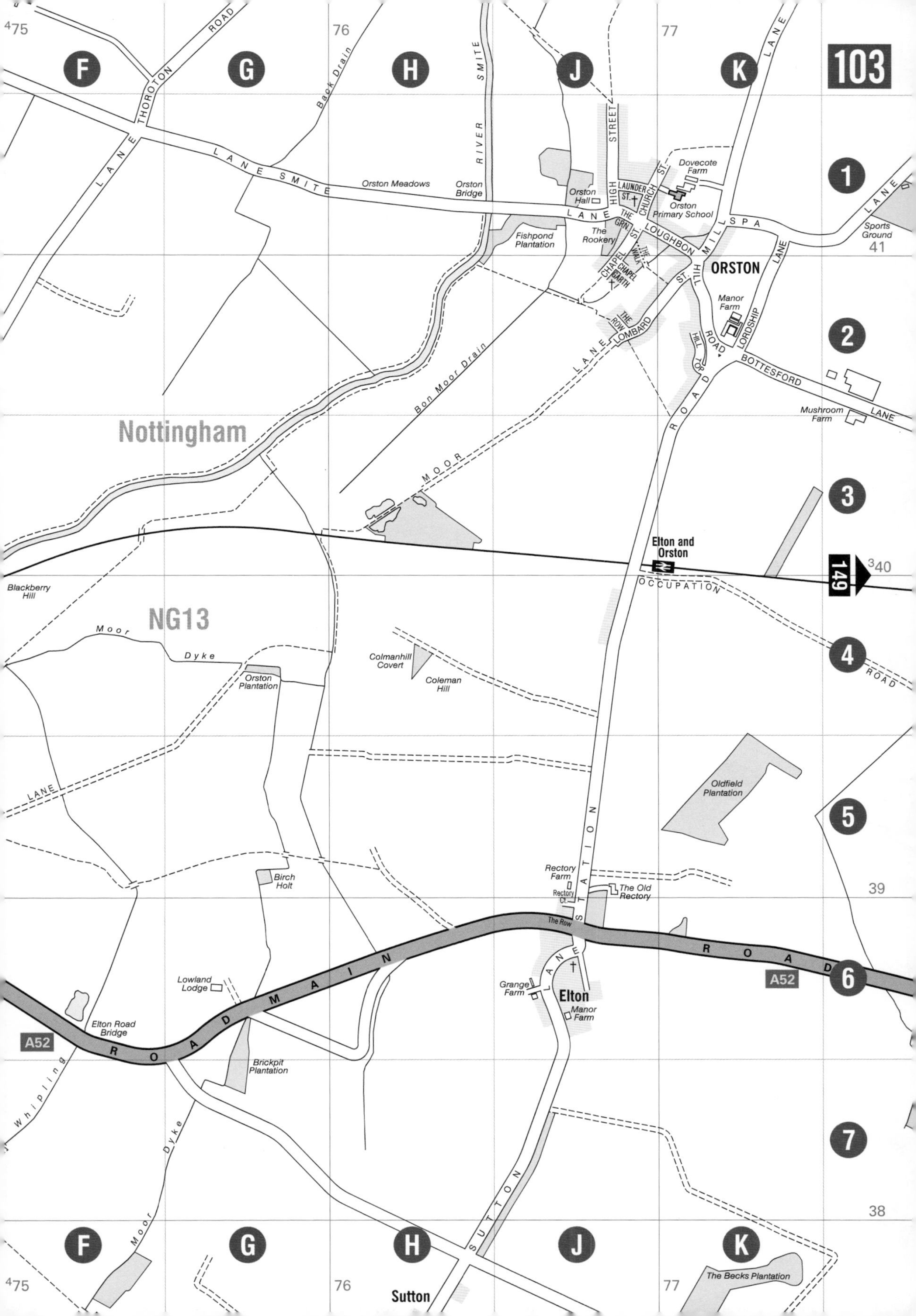
475
76
77
F
G
H
J
K
THOROTON
ROAD
LANE
LANE SMITE
Back Drain
RIVER SMITE
Orston Meadows
Orston Bridge
STREET
HIGH
Orston Hall
LAUNDER ST.
CHURCH ST.
Dovecote Farm
Orston Primary School
THE GRN
The Rookery
Fishpond Plantation
LOUGHBON
MILL
SPA LANE
Sports Ground
41
1
ORSTON
THE WALK
CHAPEL
CHAPEL GARTH
HILL ST.
Manor Farm
LORDSHIP LANE
THE ROW
LOMBARD
LANE
HILL TOP
ROAD
BOTTESFORD LANE
2
Mushroom Farm
Bon Moor Drain
Nottingham
MOOR
3
Elton and Orston
149
340
OCCUPATION
ROAD
Blackberry Hill
NG13
Moor Dyke
Orston Plantation
Colmanhill Covert
Coleman Hill
4
LANE
Oldfield Plantation
5
STATION
Rectory Farm
Rectory Ct.
The Old Rectory
39
Birch Holt
The Row
MAIN ROAD
A52
6
Lowland Lodge
Grange Farm
LANE
Elton
Manor Farm
Elton Road Bridge
A52
Brickpit Plantation
Whipling
Dyke
Moor
SUTTON
7
38
F
G
H
J
K
475
76
77
Sutton
The Becks Plantation

A
B
C
D
E
92
Stanton Gate
Ilkeston
GOLF COURSE
DE7
EREWASH VALLEY GOLF COURSE
M1 MOTORWAY
M1
Stony Clouds Local Nature Reserve
Cloudside
Pasture Lock
Stanton Gate New Sidings
Ind. Est.
Christian School
Playing Field
PASTURE ROAD
B6003
Albany Inf. Sch.
Albany Junior School
HICKINGS LANE
Hickings La. Rec. Grd.
B6004
Wadsworth Fields Primary School
Leicester Ho.
WADSWORTH
SHERWIN
CENTRAL AVENUE
B5010
St. John's C of E Primary School
Bob's Rock
Tennis Courts
STAPLEFORD
Cemetery
Cloud House
Church Farm
St. Giles Park
Mill
Halls
Cloudside Jun. Sch.
Play. Fld.
SANDIACRE
STANTON ROAD
RIVER EREWASH
EREWASH BROXTOWE
EREWASH CANAL
ORCHARD PK. IND. EST.
ASCOT PK. EST.
College
Lib.
CHURCH STREET
DERBY ROAD
TOTON
NOTTINGHAM ROAD
Windmill Hill
Hill Top Farm
Fairfield Prim. Sch.
Queen Elizabeth Park
Play Cen.
Warehouse
Cricket Grd.
Sports Ground
Recreation Ground
Inf. Sch.
Playing Field
SISLEY AVENUE
WESTERLANDS
STAPLEFORD BY-PASS
(BRIAN CLOUGH WAY)
A52
Archers Field Recreation Ground
George Spencer Academy & Tech. Coll.
George Spencer Academy & Tech. Coll. (Lower Site)
Toton Lane
Toton La. Park & Ride (Under Construction)
Sewage Works
Warehouses
Works
Weir
Sandiacre Lock
Bessell Lane Farm
Nursery
STATION RD.
DERBY RD. IND. EST.
Cricket Ground
Rec. Ground
LONGMOOR LANE
B6002
NG10
Junc. 25
Recreation Ground
Springfield Park
Longmoor Prim. Sch.
Sports Ground
Depot
Toton Sidings
Dockholm Lock
TOTON LA.
STAPLEFORD LANE
Toton Bispham Dr. Jun. Sch.
Banks Rd. Inf. Sch.
LONG EATON
Highfield Sch.
Mills
TRENT BUS. CENT.
Eaton Vale Cen.
English Martyrs' School
Wilsthorpe Sch.
Ten. Cts.
St. James Park
By Pass Channel
Playing Field
PETERSHAM ROAD
Rec. Grd.
LONG MOOR
Windermere Gdns.
48
49
38
37
36
35

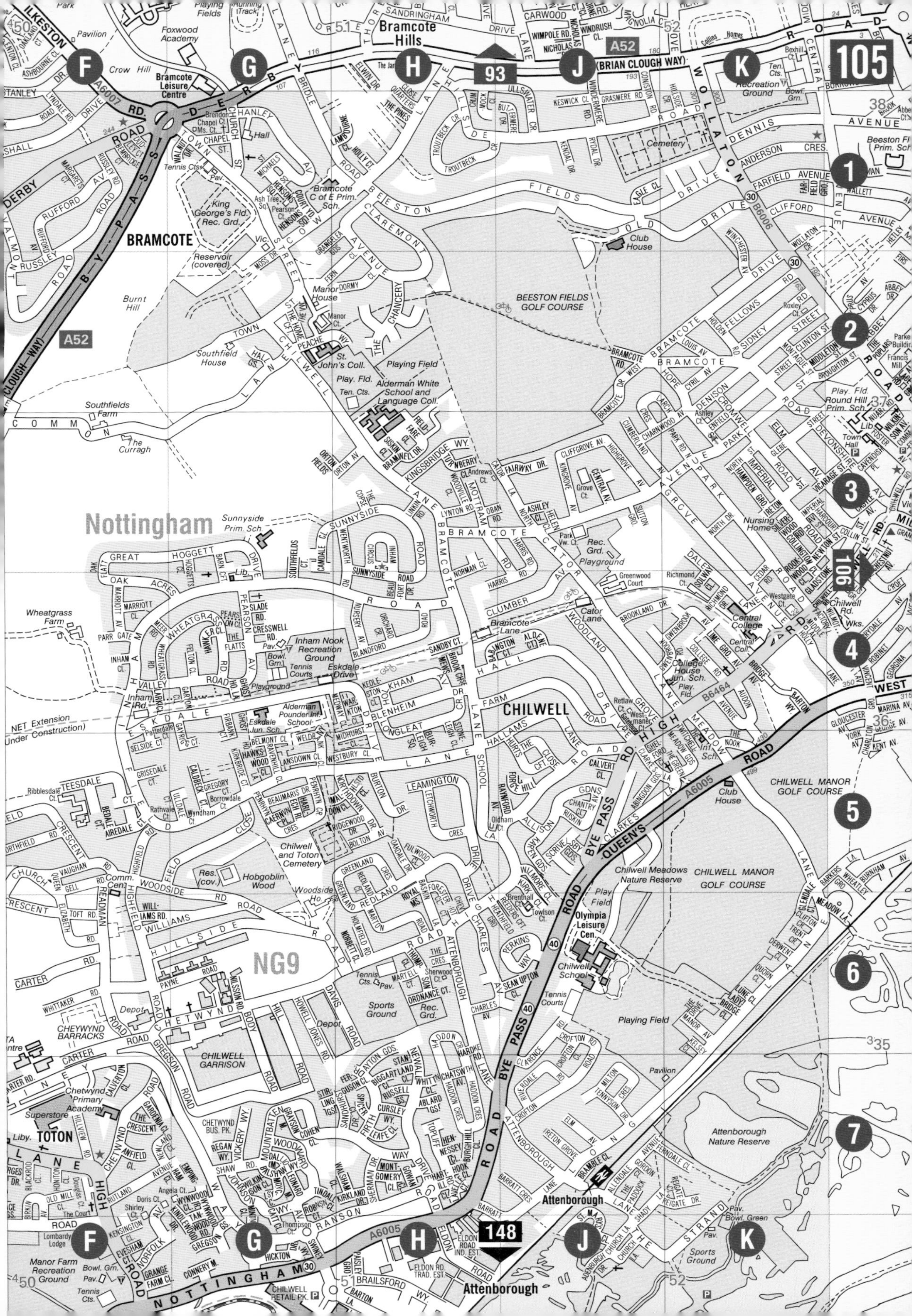
Bramcote Hills
93
A52
(BRIAN CLOUGH WAY)
DERBY ROAD
BRAMCOTE
Bramcote Leisure Centre
Foxwood Academy
Crow Hill
King George's Fld. Rec. Grd.
Burnt Hill
Southfield House
Southfields Farm
The Curragh
A52
BEESTON FIELDS GOLF COURSE
Club House
Cemetery
St. John's Coll.
Alderman White School and Language Coll.
Nottingham
Sunnyside Prim. Sch.
Wheatgrass Farm
Inham Nook Recreation Ground
Eskdale Drive
CHILWELL
NET Extension Under Construction
Alderman Pounder Inf. School
Eskdale Jun. Sch.
Hobgoblin Wood
Chilwell and Toton Cemetery
NG9
CHILWELL GARRISON
CHEYWYND BARRACKS
Chetwynd Primary Academy
Superstore
TOTON
Manor Farm Recreation Ground
Sports Ground
Central College
College House Jun. Sch.
QUEEN'S ROAD
A6005
CHILWELL MANOR GOLF COURSE
Chilwell Meadows Nature Reserve
Olympia Leisure Cen.
Chilwell School
Playing Field
Attenborough Nature Reserve
Attenborough
148
CHILWELL RETAIL PK.
ELDON ROAD IND. EST.
ELDON RD. TRAD. EST.
NOTTINGHAM ROAD
106
Round Hill Prim. Sch.
Beeston Fl Prim. Sch
Recreation Ground
Town Hall
Nursing Home
Chilwell Rd.
F G H J K
1 2 3 4 5 6 7

106
A
B
C
D
E
1
2
3
4
5
6
7
94
105
114
Lenton Abbey
East Midlands Conference Centre
THE UNIVERSITY OF NOTTINGHAM
Lakeside Arts Cen.
Student Union
UNIVERSITY PARK
Boating Lake
South Nottingham College
Nottingham Tennis Cen.
Halls of Residence
Sports Ground
Cricket Ground
Tennis Courts
Sorting Office
Nottingham
NG7
NG9
BEESTON
Beeston Flds. Prim. Sch.
Round Hill Prim. Sch.
Town Hall
Superstore
Beeston Town Cen.
John Clifford Prim. Sch.
Mecca Bingo
BOULEVARD IND. PK.
Chemical & Pharmaceutical Works
Sewage Works
Refuse Tip
Rylands
Rec. Ground
Factory
BEESTON BUSINESS PARK
BUSINESS CENTRE BEESTON
Beeston Rylands Jun. Sch.
Trent Vale Inf. Sch.
Sports Ground
Weir Field Recreation Ground
Pavilion
Rugby Ground
CHILWELL MANOR GOLF COURSE
Playing Field
Beeston Marina Mobile Home Park
Attenborough Nature Reserve
Beeston Sailing Club
Holme Pit (Fish Pond)
Clifton Wood
Clifton Hall
Home Farm
Stables
Lee Westwood Sports Centre
Nottingham Trent University (Clifton Campus)
Games Court
Glapton Prim. Sch.
BROXTOWE
NOTTINGHAM
WOODSIDE ROAD
UNIVERSITY BOULEVARD
QUEEN'S ROAD WEST
QUEEN'S RD. EAST
BEESTON CANAL
A6464
A6005
A453
B6006
53
54
35
36
37
38

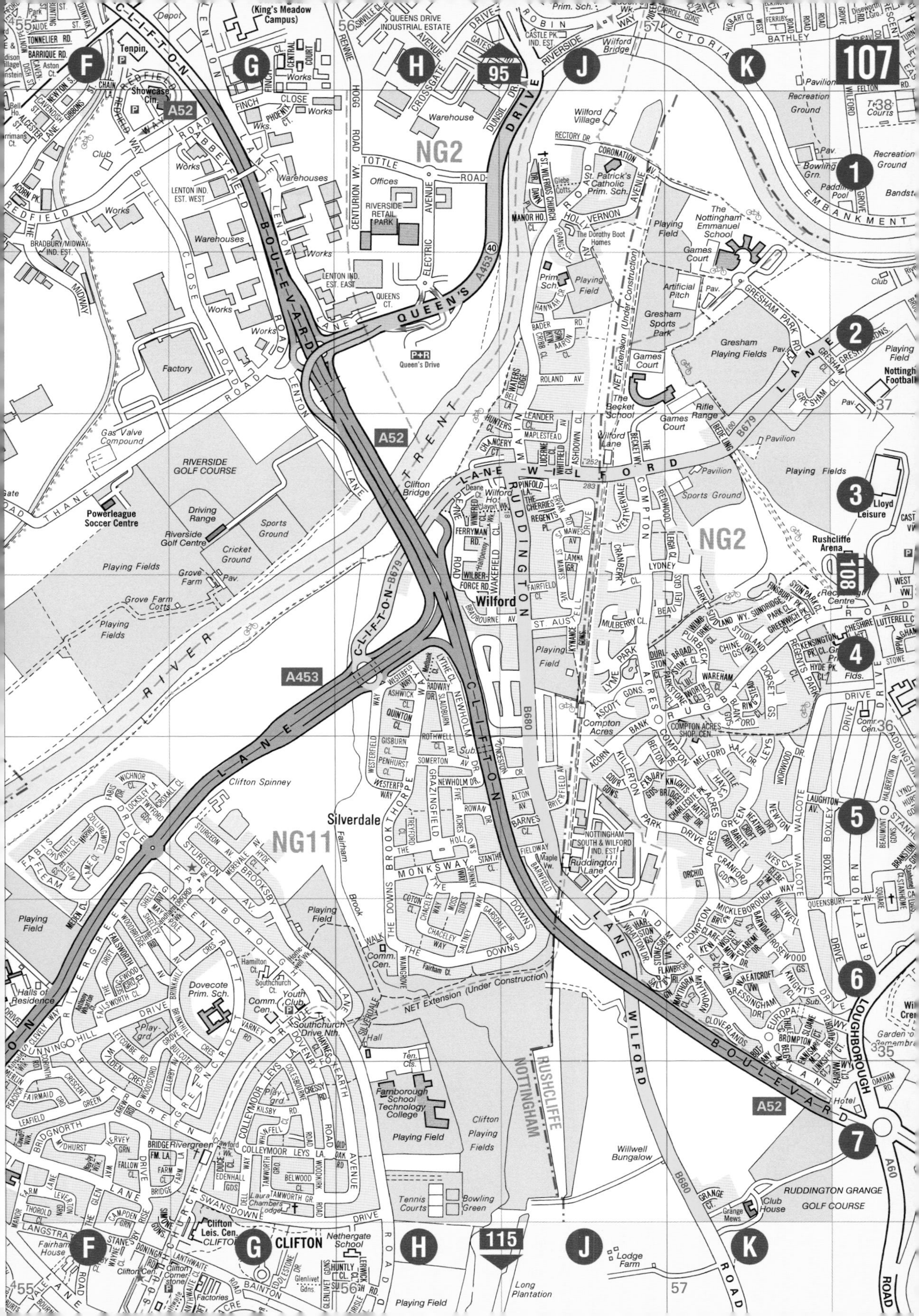

NG2
NG11
Wilford
Silverdale
CLIFTON
Compton Acres
RIVERSIDE GOLF COURSE
RIVERSIDE RETAIL PARK
QUEENS DRIVE INDUSTRIAL ESTATE
Gresham Sports Park
Gresham Playing Fields
RUDDINGTON GRANGE GOLF COURSE
Farnborough School Technology College
The Nottingham Emmanuel School
Rushcliffe Arena
Lloyd Leisure
Powerleague Soccer Centre
Clifton Bridge
Clifton Spinney
Clifton Playing Fields
NET Extension (Under Construction)
RUSHCLIFFE
NOTTINGHAM
A52
A453
A60
B679
B680
95
108
115

A
B
C
D
E
96
1
2
3
4
5
6
7
107
116
Nottinghamshire Co. Cricket Club (Trent Bridge)
County Hall
Recreation Ground
Tennis Courts
Meml. Gdns.
Paddling Pool
Bandstand
NOTTINGHAM
RUSHCLIFFE
RIVER TRENT
VICTORIA EMBANKMENT
Playing Field
The Hall Liby.
THE PARK
Grantham Canal (Dis.)
Gamston Bridge
Nottingham Forest Football Academy
West Park
Playing Fields
David Lloyd Leisure
Rushcliffe Arena
Superstore
Recycling Centre
NG2
Funky Pots
WEST BRIDGFORD
Nottingham
Depot
Public Open Space
Abbey Road Prim. Sch.
St. Edmund Campion Catholic Prim. Sch.
War Memorial Playing Fields
Greythorn Prim. Sch.
South Nottingham College
The West Bridgford School
Heymann Prim. Sch.
Hostel & Day Cen.
Jesse Gray Primary Sch.
Grosvenor Sch.
Rushcliffe School
Rushcliffe Leisure Centre
Playing Field
Sunny Crest
Lodge Farm
Southern Cemetery
Jewish Cemy.
Jewish Cemetery
Wilford Hill
Wilford Hill Crematorium
Reservoir (covered)
Garden of Remembrance
Sharphill Wood
Sharp Hill
Spinney Hill
Nursery
NG11
Edwalton Hall
Westwoods
Hill Farm House
EDWALTON GOLF COURSE
Landmere Farm
Mickleborough Hill
Garden Centre
Toll Bar House
RUDDINGTON GRANGE GOLF COURSE
LOUGHBOROUGH ROAD
MELTON ROAD
A60
A606
A52
A52
BOULEVARD
LANDMERE LANE
RADCLIFFE ROAD
58
59
38
37
36
35

97
110
117
RADCLIFFE ROAD
A52
A6011
Holme Lane
BASSINGFIELD LANE
NATHANS LANE
Landfill Waste Site
Polser Brook
Council Yard
GAMSTON LINGS BAR ROAD
Gamston
Bel-Air Residential Homes
Grange Fm.
Superstore
GAMSTON DISTRICT CEN.
Comm. Cen.
Prim. Sch.
LINGS BAR HOSP.
Holly Farm
Lea Farm
Manor Farm
The Elms Farm
Bassingfield
Cherry Tree Cottage
Smallholding
Grantham Canal (Disused)
Tollerton Bridge
TOLLERTON ROAD
Tollerton Park Caravan Park
Hill Farm
NOTTINGHAM AIRPORT
Hangar
Control Tower
NG12
Meadow Covert
Edwalton Primary Sch.
EDWALTON GOLF COURSE
EDWALTON
Club Ho.
LITTLE LANE
Homestead Farm
Jubilee Plantation
CHESTNUT M.
COTGRAVE LANE
Bassingfield House
Manor Farm
Glebe Farm
The Lake
Nursery
Tollerton Nurseries
Thurlbeck
Sewage Works
TOLLERTON
Hall Farm
The Decoy
Tollerton Wood
Tollerton Prim. Sch.
MEDINA DRIVE
SUNNINDALE DR.
FRANKLIN DR.
BURNSIDE
RUSSELL FARM CL.
LINGS BAR ROAD
EDWALTON LINGS LANE
Greenacres Park

110
98
109
148
RADCLIFFE ROAD
STRAGGLETHORPE
Holme House
Lamcote Field
Works
Landfill Waste Site
Thornton's Holt Camping Park
Shepherd's Houses
Cockedhat Plantation
North Farm
Polser Brook
MAIN ROAD
Driving Range
Cotgrave Place
Club House
THE NOTTINGHAMSHIRE GOLF COURSE
COTGRAVE COUNTRY PARK
Cotgrave Bridge
Grantham Canal (Disused)
Lock House
LANE
PEASHILL
Peashill Farm
Brown's Bridge
Weirs
Homefields
Gozen Lodge
Windmill Hill
Thurlbeck Dyke
WOODGATE
Sewage Works
COTGRAVE
BINGHAM RD.
Candleby Lane School
Ash Lea Sch.
Playing Field
Bowl. Grns.
Club
Prim. Sch.
Rectory
Cemy.
Lib.
Baker's Hollow
PLUMTREE ROAD
COTGRAVE LANE
Boot Pit
Clipston
Manor Farm
MILL LANE
The Brickyard
Brickyard Plantation
Scotton's Hill
Play. Fld.
A
B
C
D
E
1
2
3
4
5
6
7
38
37
36
35
63
64

Stragglethorpe
Nottingham
NG12
Hall Farm
Radcliffe Barn Farm
CROPWELL ROAD
New Barn Farm
Cropwell Court
Lodge
The Fields
RADCLIFFE RD.
A46
The Limes
Paddock Cottages
Brown's Cotts.
Foss Bridge
Berry Hill
Sports Ground
Pav.
COLLIERS WAY
COLLIERS BUSINESS PARK
LANE
Hollygate Farm
Mann's Bridge
NOTTINGHAM ROAD
MANVERS BUS. PK.
HOLLYGATE IND. PARK
Hollygate Bridge
Hollygate House
Works
Cropwell Bridge
The Bungalow
COLSTON GATE
Play. Fld.
Foss House
FOSSE
Cotgrave Leisure Centre
Playing Fld.
Foss Cottages
Reservoir (covered)
HILL
SKYLARK
Groundwells Farm
ROAD
Smith's Round Hill
Long Plantation
Cropwell Wolds Farm
Three Corner Plantation
Cotgrave Copse
Firdale Holt
Stone Pit Plantation
CROPWELL WOLDS
99
112
148

CROPWELL BUTLER
CROPWELL BISHOP
Tithby
NG12
A46
100
111
148
141
Hardigate
Newlands
The Grove
Radcliffe Road
The Limes
Barnsfield Farm
Cropwell Grange
Works
Grange Pk.
Main Road
Back Lane
The Court
Old School House Cl.
Carpenters Cl.
The Posts
Rookery Pk.
Meadow Court
Street
Tithby Road
Cemetery
Lych Gate
Butler Close
Rookery Cottages
Stratford House
Lower Brackendale Farm
Millfield Cottage
Millfield House
Manor Farm
Bingham Road
Dovecote La.
Holly Tree Farm
Meadow Lane
Hoe Road
Bishop Road
Cropwell Road
Hoe Hill
Barlows Cl.
Butler
Ethelden Cl.
Sewage Works
Hoe View Road
Parkin
Salvin Cl.
Hardys Cl.
Cooper Cl.
Thurlby Cl.
Squires Cl.
Newberry Cl.
Kendal
Hall Dr.
The Maltings
Springfield
Spring Hill
Brownhill Cl.
St. Giles Wy.
Rawlings Ct.
Spring Vw.
Cropwell Bishop Primary School
Marshall Rd.
Smiths Cl.
Church Street
Kerrs Wk.
Mercia Av.
Clarke
Old Lenton Cl.
Hoe Nook
Field La.
Barratt Cl.
Mill La.
Dobbin Cl.
Playing Field
Hall
Fern Road
Fern Hill
Fern Hill Cottage
Nottingham Road
Works
Cropwell Bridge
Richards Cl.
Home Farm
Manor Ct.
Pasture Lane
Mill Hill
Fern Hill Farm Cottages
Fern Hill Farm
Ash Holt
Hill
Skylark
Canalside Industrial Park
Kinoulton Road
Colston
Groundwell Farm
Swab's La.
Old Brickyard Plantation
Blue Hill
Colston La.
Bridlewood House
Reecy Plantation
Home Farm Cottages
New
New Banks Farm
38
37
36
35
68
69

Whitefield Farm
Cotts.
Tithby Grange Cottages
Tithby Grange
Crane's Covert
TITHBY ROAD
BINGHAM ROAD
ROAD
RIVER SMITE
Nottingham
Wiverton Hall Farm
Moat Covert
Wiverton Hall
New Plantation
NG13
Smite Hill Covert
Smite Hill Farm
Northfield Farm
Wiverton Smite Bridge
Langar Lane Covert
LANGAR LANE
ROAD
The Ferns
Covert Farm
Langar Lane Bridge
BARNSTONE ROAD
Works
Langar C of E Primary School
Langar Ho.
CHURCH LA.
BARNSTONE RD.
MUSTERS
BUTLERS FIELD
BELVOIR CR.
MAIN ST.
FAIR HOWE CRES.
WILLOW LA.
HARBY RD.
Langar C of E Primary School
Tennis Court
The Limes Farm
LANGAR
CROPWELL ROAD
LANGAR LA.
Edmondthorpe Lodge
Winifred Wood
101
149
141
F G H J K
1 2 3 4 5 6 7
470 71 72
38 37 36 35

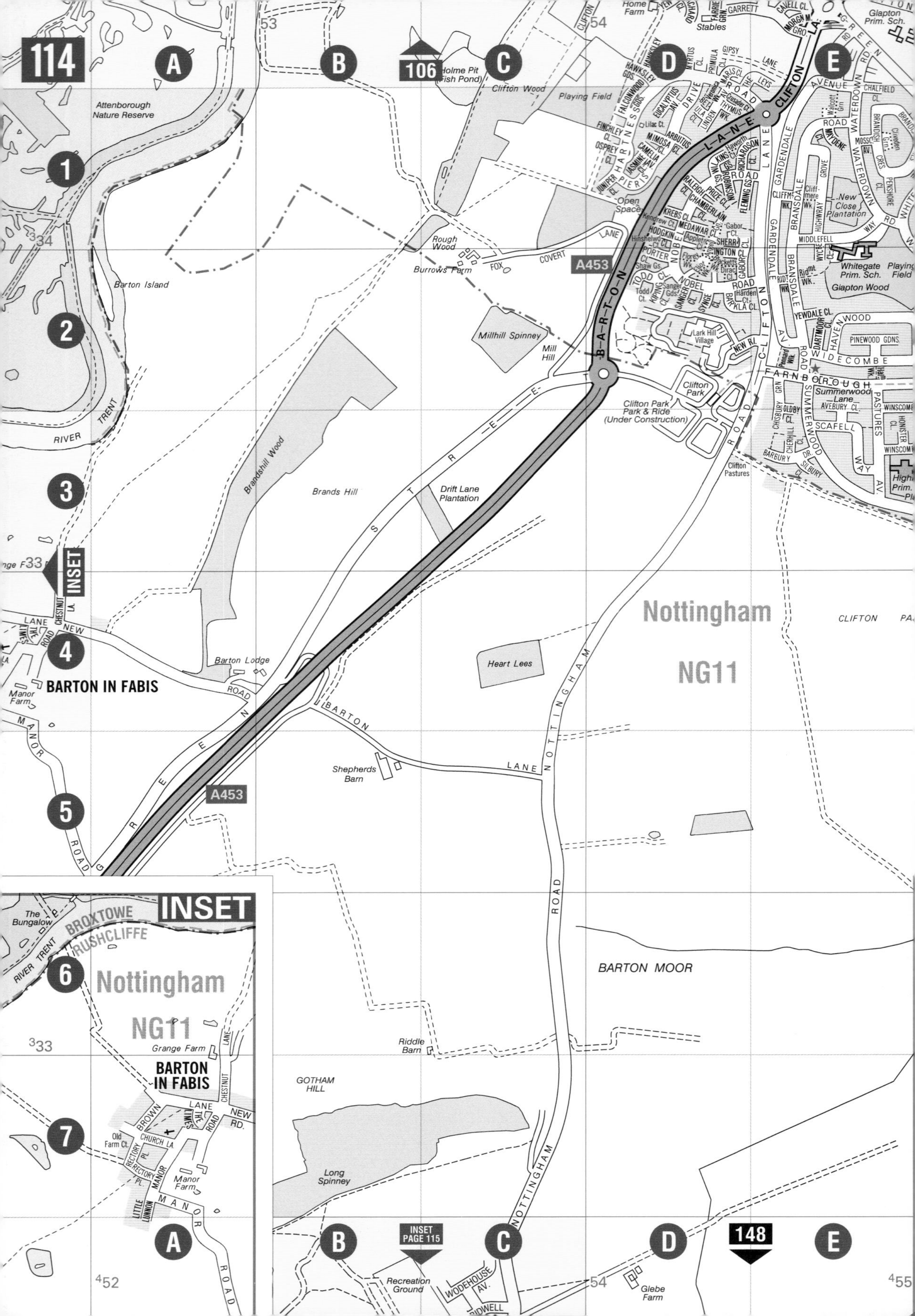
A
B
C
D
E
106
Holme Pit (Fish Pond)
Clifton Wood
Playing Field
Attenborough Nature Reserve
Barton Island
RIVER TRENT
Rough Wood
Burrows Farm
FOX COVERT LANE
A453
Millhill Spinney
Mill Hill
Open Space
Brandshill Wood
Brands Hill
Drift Lane Plantation
Clifton Park
Clifton Park Park & Ride (Under Construction)
Clifton Pastures
Lark Hill Village
Glapton Prim. Sch.
Whitegate Prim. Sch.
Playing Field
Glapton Wood
New Close Plantation
Summerwood Lane
BARTON LANE
CLIFTON LANE
CLIFTON LA.
FARNBOROUGH ROAD
WIDECOMBE
GARDENDALE
BRANSDALE
WATERDOWN
SUMMERWOOD
SCAFELL
PINEWOOD GDNS.
YEWDALE CL.
HAVEN WOOD
MIDDLEFELL
NOBEL ROAD
TODD CL.
SANGER CL.
SYNGE CL.
RICHARDSON
FLEMING GS.
CHAMBERLAIN
MEDAWAR CL.
HODGKIN
KREBS CL.
RALEIGH
PRIZE CL.
MIMOSA CL.
CAMELIA AV.
JASMINE CL.
ARBUTUS CL.
EUCALYPTUS AV.
FALCONWOOD GDS.
HAWKSLEY GDS.
FINCHLEY CL.
OSPREY CL.
JUNIPER CL.
PIERIS
HARTNESS RD.
MYRTUS CL.
PRIMULA CL.
GIPSY LANE
THE LEYS
GARRETT
Home Farm
Stables
CLIFTON
Nottingham
NG11
CLIFTON PA
Heart Lees
NOTTINGHAM ROAD
BARTON LANE
Barton Lodge
NEW ROAD
BARTON IN FABIS
Manor Farm
MANOR ROAD
GREEN STREET
CHESTNUT LA.
THE LIMES
Shepherds Barn
INSET
33
34
1
2
3
4
5
6
7
BARTON MOOR
Riddle Barn
GOTHAM HILL
Long Spinney
INSET PAGE 115
148
Recreation Ground
WODEHOUSE AV.
Glebe Farm
NOTTINGHAM
452
54
455
53
The Bungalow
BROXTOWE
RUSHCLIFFE
RIVER TRENT
Nottingham
NG11
333
Grange Farm
BARTON IN FABIS
BROWN LANE
THE LIMES
NEW RD.
CHESTNUT LANE
CHURCH LA.
Old Farm Ct.
RECTORY PL.
MANOR
Manor Farm
LITTLE LUNNON
MANOR ROAD

115
107
116
148
INSET
F
G
H
J
K
1
2
3
4
5
6
7
CLIFTON
Clifton Leisure Centre
CLIFTON PARK
Nethergate School
Playing Field
Playing Fields
Willwell Bungalow
Lodge Farm
Long Plantation
RUDDINGTON GRANGE GOLF COURSE
Club House
Grange Mews
South Nottingham College (Clifton Centre Charnwood)
Tennis Cts.
Football Ground
Fairham Bridge
Fairham Brook Nature Reserve
Factories
Milford Prim. Sch.
Academy
Holy Trinity
Brecks Plantation
Brook Hill
NOTTINGHAM
RUSHCLIFFE
Tall Trees Farm
Printing Works
James Peacock Infant School
Village Mus.
Cemetery
Youth & Comm. Cen.
Victoria Pk.
Rec. Grnd.
St. Peter's C of E Junior Sch.
Play. Fld.
Easthorpe Cotts.
RUDDINGTON
Nottingham Transport Heritage Centre
Ruddington Station
RUSHCLIFFE COUNTRY PARK
Leys Farm
West End
Fields Farm Cottages
Great Central Railway (Nottingham)
Ruddington Fields Farm
Moorend Farm Cottages
Moorend Farm
Moor Farm
RUDDINGTON MOOR
BRADMORE MOOR
B680
WILFORD ROAD
FARNBOROUGH ROAD
CLIFTON LANE
HIGH ST.
KIRK LA.
ASHER LANE
PASTURE LANE
BARLEYLANDS
MOOR LANE
SOUTHCHURCH DRIVE
SUMMERWOOD LANE
Nottingham
NG11
GOTHAM
Long Spinney
Round Spinney
Recreation Ground
Tennis Cts.
Liby. & Hall
Bowls Grn.
Factory
Home Farm
Gotham Prim. Sch.
Playing Fld.
The Rectory
Depot
Nursery
KEGWORTH ROAD
CURZON STREET
MOOR LANE
GYPSUM WAY
55
56
57
53
54
34
33
32
31
30

A
B
C
D
E
1
2
3
4
5
6
7
58
59
108
115
118
RUDDINGTON GRANGE
GOLF COURSE
Nursery
Sharp Hill
Hill Farm House
LANDMERE
LOUGHBOROUGH
OLD ROAD
Landmere Farm
Home Farm
Hall Farm
WAYTE CT.
Mickleborough Hill
Ruddington Hall
Lodge
Roberts Farm
Garden Centre
Toll Bar House
LANE
Landmere
LANDMERE LANE
A52
MELTON ROAD
A606
GAMSTON LINGS BAR ROAD
MELTON
Olgalans Lodge
St. Peter's C of E Junior School
A60
Playing Field
ASHWORTH
DEVON DR.
AVENUE
PAGET CRES.
WILFORD CRES
SAVAGES RD.
ST. MARYS
LWR. CANAAN
UPPER CANAAN
PACKMAN DR.
ABINGDON
SALCOMBE CRES.
Play. Fld.
RUFFORD
RUFFORD WLK.
CRES.
STREET
Easthorpe Farm
Works
Nottingham
EASTHORPE
HIGH ST.
ROAD
Easthorpe Cotts.
SYCAMORE CL.
SAXBY CT.
KIRK
B680
LANE
FLAWFORTH
FLAWFORTH AV.
Nursery
The Orchard
Hillcrest
Flawforth Lodge
Shire Farm
Flawford House Farm
Crockhill Wood
RUDDINGTON
ELMS
CLOSE
GDNS.
Youth & Comm. Cen.
Bowl. Grn.
Pav.
Elms Park (Rec. Grd.)
MOOR LANE
WESLEY WY
GREENWOOD GDS.
DICKSON DR.
STEVENSON GDS.
SHEEPFOLD
SELLARS AV.
PARK LA.
HARVEY
Playing Field
NG11
FIELDS AV.
WHEATLEY
Works
Nottingham Transport Heritage Centre
Ruddington Station
WAY
THE AVENUE
MERE WAY
RUDDINGTON FIELDS BUSINESS PARK
Barn Farm
LANE
MILL
Long Farm
FARMER
MANOR FM. CL
BLACKCLIFFE FARM M
DONKEY LA.
STREET
LITTLEMOOR LA.
FAR MAIN STREET
BRADMORE
Nursery
BRADMORE MOOR
MOOR LANE
POCK
Nursery
Rancliffe Wood
31
32
33
334

TOLLERTON

PLUMTREE

NORMANTON-ON-THE-WOLDS

KEYWORTH

Plumtree Park

NG12

Sewage Works

Play Field

Priory Circus

Nursery

109

The Lake

Tollerton Nurseries

COTGRAVE

Hall Farm

The Decoy

Tollerton Wood

Tollerton Prim. Sch.

MEDINA DRIVE

SUNNINDALE

FRANKLIN HALL

MEADOW

HIGH

HILL VW.

HOE FM.

GROVE RD.

PRIORY AVENUE

LENTON AV.

OTHIAN RD.

BURNSIDE

RUSSELL FARM CL.

STANSTEAD AV.

STELLA AV.

SEDGLEY

MUIR

STELLA GRO.

STELLA AV.

ORCHARD CL.

BENTWICK CT.

PENDOCK CT.

TOLLERTON LANE

MAIN ROAD

Ranch House

Hoehill Farm

3 34

Hoe Hill

Weir

Hoe Hill Cottages

CLIPSTON LANE

THE LEYS

WOLDS LANE

148

33

NORMANTON-ON-THE-WOLDS

Town End Cottages

Manor Farm

Hall Farm

Plumtree

SADDLERS YARD

CHURCH LA.

FELLOWS YD.

BRADLEYS YD.

THE POPLARS

Plumtree Sch.

PINFOLD LA.

OLD MELTON ROAD

MELTON

ROAD

PLUMTREE

Chapel Yard

The Lawns

Manor House

Normanton House

Avenue Farm

4

Flawford House

Cricket Grd. Pav.

STATION LANE

Chestnut Farm

A606

HACK LANE

5

Blackcliffe Hill

BRADMORE LANE

32

Playing Field

Pav.

Sheltons Houses

PLATT LANE

6

NORMANTON WOLDS

Crossdale Drive Prim. Sch.

PARK AV.

PARK

PARK

FERN

ROAD

GREEN CL.

Poplars Cl.

PARKSIDE

British Geological Survey

Plumtree Park

KNIPE CROSS

HILLCREST RD.

BEAUMONT

HIGHBURY

DEVILLE

RANCLIFFE AV.

HIGHFIELD RD.

ABBOT CL.

BISHOPS CL.

SIDMOUTH CL.

CROSSDALE

BEVERLEY

BR. CR.

BROOKDALE

GDNS.

ROSE

VILLA

GRO.

ROAD

FRANKLYN GDS.

FEIGNIES CT.

ADAMS HILL

CLIFTON GDNS.

LYNCOMBE GDNS.

NORMANTON LANE

LOWLANDS DR.

WOLDS RISE

COVERT RD.

MOUNT PLEASANT

DEBDALE LANE

CHESTNUT ROAD

THELDA

DALE

BARNT CL.

WYNBRECK DR.

ASHLEY CRES.

CLUMBER GDS.

WALTON DR.

CHERRY HILL

HIGH VIEW AV.

MEADOW DR.

THE RODINGS

SPINNEY CL.

HAYES RD.

PLANTATION

INTAKE RD.

CROFT

FARNHAM RD.

MANOR

ROAD

HILL

ROSE

CHURCH

RANNOCK GDS.

Walton Ct.

ASHLEY RD.

COMMOCK GDS.

DRIVE

BEECH AV.

MOUNT PLEASANT

Cotton's Plantation

NOTTINGHAM ROAD

PARK AV. WEST

PARK

EAST WOOD AV.

WEST CL.

CHARN. WOOD

KEYWORTH

Keyworth Prim. Sch.

South Wolds Comm. Acdmy.

Rec. Grd.

119

Keyworth Leis. Cen.

Keyworth Lib.

SELBY LA.

ELM

WINDMILL CL.

LAUREL

OLD LANE

METTHE AV.

MAPLE CL.

WILLOW BROOK

STANTON LANE

Firs Farm

Stanwolds Kennels

31

Woodfields

SUNNY

Green Fm.

Key VI Fitness

HAWTHORN RD.

COMMERCIAL RD.

BRADMORE
116
PENDOCK
Nursery
BRADMORE MOOR
MOOR
Rancliffe Wood
LANE
BUNNY
BRADMORE BUS. PK.
KEYWORTH
Long Plantation
VICTORIA RD.
ALBERT RD.
BUNNY MOOR
MOOR
LANE
A60
Walled Gdn.
Long Plantation
Bunny C of E Primary School
MOOR
Lodge Plantation
Long Plantation
Brookfield
MOOR VW.
The Paddock
CHURCH ST.
Bunny Hall
NG11
148
MAIN STREET
BUNNY
THOMAS PARKYN CL.
BUNNY HALL PARK
Football Ground
LOUGHBOROUGH
Wysall Road Farm
Fairham Brook
GOTHAM
LANE
Silver Seal Mine
Windmill Hill
Works
Works
Woodside Farm
HILL
New Wood
Chestnut Farm
OLD WOOD
BRADMOR
Bunny Hill
Bunny Hill Riding School
Woodlands
BUNNY HILL TOP
Bunny Hill Farm
Lodge Farm
Loughborough
ASH LANE
Greenfields Farm
BUNNY
LE12
Intake Wood
Rough Plantation
Highfields
NOTTINGHAM ROAD
123
Rookery Wood
Small Rough Plantation

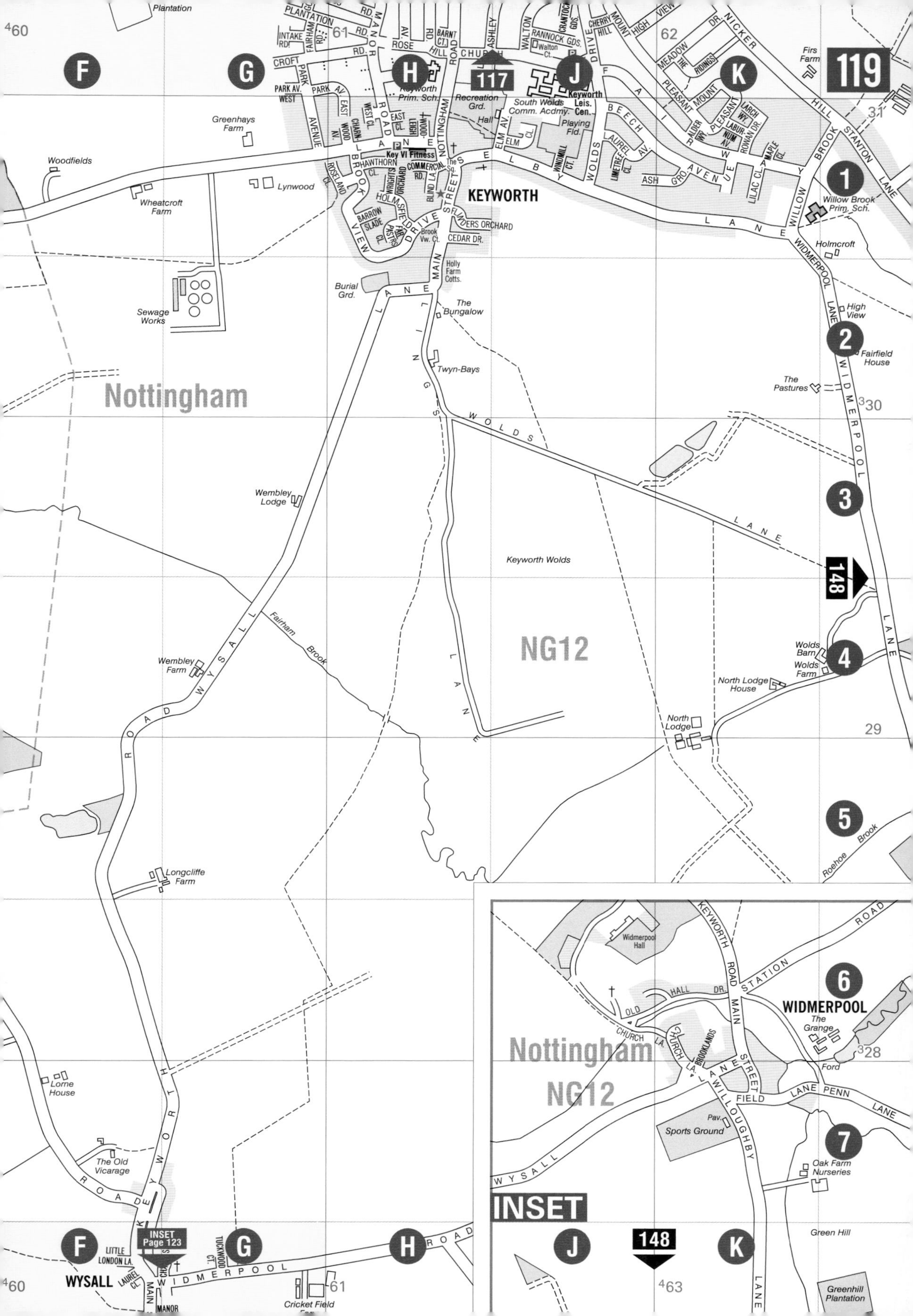

119
117
148
INSET
INSET Page 123
KEYWORTH
WYSALL
WIDMERPOOL
Nottingham
NG12
Keyworth Wolds
Plantation
Greenhays Farm
Woodfields
Wheatcroft Farm
Lynwood
Sewage Works
Burial Grd.
The Bungalow
Twyn-Bays
Holly Farm Cotts.
Wembley Lodge
Wembley Farm
Fairham Brook
Longcliffe Farm
Lorne House
The Old Vicarage
Cricket Field
Keyworth Prim. Sch.
Recreation Grd.
Hall
South Wolds Comm. Acdmy.
Keyworth Leis. Cen.
Playing Fld.
Key VI Fitness
Firs Farm
Willow Brook Prim. Sch.
Holmcroft
High View
Fairfield House
The Pastures
Wolds Barn
Wolds Farm
North Lodge House
North Lodge
Roehoe Brook
Widmerpool Hall
The Grange
Ford
Pav.
Sports Ground
Oak Farm Nurseries
Green Hill
Greenhill Plantation
WOLDS LANE
WIDMERPOOL LANE
WYSALL ROAD
KEYWORTH ROAD
WIDMERPOOL ROAD
NOTTINGHAM ROAD
MAIN STREET
SELBY LANE
BROOK VIEW DRIVE
STATION ROAD
HALL DR.
OLD CHURCH LA.
CHURCH LA.
BROOKLANDS
MAIN STREET
FIELD LANE
PENN LANE
WILLOUGHBY LANE
WILLOW BROOK
STANTON LANE
NICKER HILL

KINGSTON ON SOAR
KINGSTON PARK
Nottingham
NG11
Loughborough
LE12
Weir
The Pool
Sluice
Boat House
148
Station Plantation
Woodside
University of Nottingham (Sutton Bonington Campus Dairy Centre)
Scotland Farm
Scotland Plantation
Moulter Hill
Kingston Brook
Halls of Residence
Farm Buildings
Froghole Farm
Domleo's Spinney
Black Pool
Sewage Works
Playing Field
Nursery
Veterinary Laboratories Agency
University of Nottingham (Sutton Bonington Campus)
School of Biosciences Divisions
School of Veterinary Medicine & Science
Sports Centre
Gold Hill Farm
Tennis Courts
Cemetery
Glebe Farm
Works
Valley Farm
Bowl Grn.
St. Michaels House
Hall Farm Cottages
Hall Farm
The Hall
St.Anne's Manor
Lodge
Pavilion
Hall
SUTTON BONINGTON
Devil's Elbow
Sutton Bonington Primary School
Park Lane Farm
HATHERNWARE INDUSTRIAL ESTATE
County Council Depot
A6006
RIVER SOAR
INSET
MELTON ROAD
LANDCROFT LANE
HUNGARY LANE
TROWELL LANE
PITHOUSE LANE
WEST LEAKE LANE
STATION ROAD
COLLEGE ROAD
MARLE PIT HILL
MAIN STREET
PARK LANE
PASTURE LANE
SOAR LANE
LONG STATION ROAD
KEGWORTH RD.
GOTHAM RD.
OLD BULL FARM CL.
CHESTNUTS CL.
SUTTONFIELDS DR.
BOLLARD'S LA.
BUCK'S LA.
RECTORY CL.
ST. ANNE'S LA.
SWAN CT.
THE PADDOCKS
GABLE'S LEA
BARRINGTON CT.
PASTURE CL.
ORCHARD CL.
WILLOW CL.
POOLE LA.
SHEPHERD'S CL.
CHARNWOOD AV.
CHARNWOOD FIELDS
SUTTON CL.
A B C D E
1 2 3 4 5 6 7
450 51 52
27 26 25 24

121
148
122
F
G
H
J
K
1
2
3
4
5
6
7
53
54
55
51
452
24
325
323
26
27
Grange Farm
The Cottage
Crow Wood
Club Ho.
RUSHCLIFFE GOLF COURSE
Rushcliffe Halt
STOCKING LANE
GOTHAM ROAD
Rushcliffe Lodge
Ash Spinney
Fir Dale Plantation
Fox Hill
Foxhill Wood
Reservoir (covered)
Fox Hill Farm
THISTLE BANK
BROOKFIELDS
THE ARCHES
BROOK END
THE BURROWS
NORTHFIELD
HAREFIELD
HOLLIS MDW.
ROFFE
COSBY
Kingston Brook
West Leake
Hall
MAIN STREET
VILLAGE FARM CL.
LANE
West Leake Manor
Churchside Farm
Old Rectory
Sewage Works
Hall
WEST LEAKE ROAD
STATION ROAD
FIELD END CL.
BIRCH LEA
ROPEWALK
BATEMAN
EXETER CL.
BATEMAN RD.
YORK CL.
TRURO CL.
EAST LEAKE
SOUTHWELL CL.
WIN-MANOR
FARM
SCHOOL
SPRUCE CL.
TWENTYLANDS DR.
TWENTYLANDS ROAD
LEIVERS CLOSE
OLD RECTORY CL.
BURTON
SYCAMORE ROAD
MAPLE CL.
WILLOW CL.
OAK CR.
BROOKSIDE AV.
PINE CL.
YEW CL.
BEECH AV.
POPLAR AV.
ASH WK.
CEDAR AV.
ORCHARD CL.
BROOKS ROAD
KIRK LEY ROAD
RILEY AVENUE
REMPSTONE ROAD
BRICKYARD LANE
Manor Farm
Calke Hall Farm
California Farm
California Plantation
New Plantation
Cold Harbour Plantation
Woodgate Farm
Emsway
TRAVELL'S HILL
WOODGATE
Hills Farm
Brickyard Plantation
The Gorse
Gould's Barn
Sheep Spinney
Stackyard Spinney
Pit Hole
Whitehills Farm
Devil's Garden
REMPSTONE ROAD A6006 MELTON ROAD
Limekiln Farm
Limekiln Cotts.
Stanford Hills Farm
Trafalgar Wood
Shaw's Park Farm
The Plains
The Evergreens
Stanford Hills
The Belt
Kingsbrook Ct.
LEAKE LANE
INSET
PARK LANE
A6006
MOOR LANE
Loughborough
Playing Field
LE12
FAR LANE
MAIN STREET
Normanton House
Normanton on Soar
Normanton on Soar Prim. Sch.
STONEHURST LA.
BUTT LANE
SOAR LA.
VILLAGE RD.
RUSHCLIFFE
CHARNWOOD
RIVER SOAR
PASTURE LANE
Foot Ferry

EAST LEAKE
COSTOCK
Loughborough
LE12
Rushcliffe Halt
RUSHCLIFFE GOLF COURSE
Sports Ground
Sharpley Hill
Taft Leys
East Leake Academy
East Leake Leis. Cen.
Lantern La. Prim. Sch.
Brookfurlong Farm
Kingston Brook
Stone Bridge
Playing Field
Library
Brookside Prim. Sch.
Youth Club
Sports Field
Brooklyn
The Elms Farm
Mill Hill
Manor Farm & Woodland
Sheepwash Brook
Four Elms
Green Acres
Riseholme Farm
The Lings Farm
The Gorse
Gould's Barn
Home Farm Cottages
Home Farm
Beech Tree Lodge
Costock Hill
Stanford Hills Farm
Colonel's Covert
ASHBY ROAD
MELTON ROAD
A6006
EAST LEAKE (LOUGHBOROUGH ROAD)
REMPSTONE ROAD
Rempstone Hall Convent
Rempstone Hall Farm
Lings Farm
Ash Plantation
Lings Spinney
Football Ground
Cricket Field
STANFORD PARK
Nursery
Miniature Golf Course
Stanford Hall Estate
Tennis Courts
Stanford Hall
Theatre
Cherry Hill
Damhead Plantation
Elm Spinney
Black Firs
Floodgate Plantation
The Plains
The Belt
Stanford Hills
Kingsbrook Ct.
Dog Kennel Wood
148
121
55
56
57
27
26
25
24

F 58 **G** **H** 118 Intake Wood **J** Rough Plantation **K** **123**

Highfields

Rookery Wood

Wysall Rough Plantation

Grange Farm

Lough Rough Plantation

Nottingham

NG12

INSET 27

1

2

Field Farm

ROAD COSTOCK ROAD

Hall Farm

Scotland Hill Farm

Nouvelle Farm

Glebe Farm

THORPE LANE

3

148 26

Nursery

4

Canaan Farm

REMPSTONE LANE

Wolds Farm

5

Sheepwash Brook

Hill Farm

Oaklands Farm

INSET

LITTLE LONDON LA.

WIDMERPOOL ROAD

WYSALL

Cricket Field Farm

6

Burial Ground

MANOR HOUSE DR.

Bowl. Green

148 327

REMPSTONE

Grange Farm

Playing Field Pav.

LITTLE LINCOLN

Tennis Court

Nottingham

7

MAIN STREET WYMESWOLD ROAD A6006 ROAD

THE OLD ENGINE YARD

COSTOCK ROAD

Kingston

NG12

Sutcliffe Plantation

F **G** 148 **H** **J** Windyridge Farm **K** Brooklea Farm

Sutcliffe Hill 58 460 Thorpe in the Glebe 461

A **B** **C** **D** **E**

72 HOPYARD LANE 73 4 74

BASSETLAW
NEWARK and SHERWOOD

Goosemoor Dyke

TUXFORD ROAD

1

69

TOP LANE

LANE

GRAVEL LANE

NORTH FM.

Egmanton
Grange Farm

Manor
Farm

BIRNOR LANE RD.

2

KIRTON LANE

Bankside
Farm

TANYARD

MAIN ST.

WESTON
CHURCH VW.

GADDICK
VIEW

ROAD

EGMANTON

WOOD

LANE HOLME

Abbing
Moor Farm

3

HOLME

Hall
Farm

Woodlands
Court

MILL LANE

ROAD

WOOD

Newark

Egmanton Wood

³68

◄ **147**

NG22

Egmanton Hill
Farm

4

Motte &
Bailey

LAXTON

Egmanton Wood

East Park
Wood

Pav.

Cricket
Ground

Cross Hill

5

Town End
Farm

Home View
Farm

Smithy
Farm

Cross Hill
Farm

New Bar
Farm

TIMOTHY BRO.

LANE

Bar
Farm

Sports
Ground

THE BAR

STONY

BALK

67

TOWN END

HIGH

STREET

LAXTON

Laxton
Visitor
Cen.

P

MAIN STREET

ACRE EDGE RD.

TOAD LANE

EELS LANE

CHAPEL LA.

MOORHOUSE

Bottom
Farm

ROAD

6

Moorgate
Farm

ROAD

GREEN

LANE

Ide
Farm

7

Mill Field

Moorhouse Beck

Copthorne
Farm

66

South Field

A **B** **C** **D** **E**

KNEESALL 72 73 4 74

NORMANTON ON TRENT / WESTON

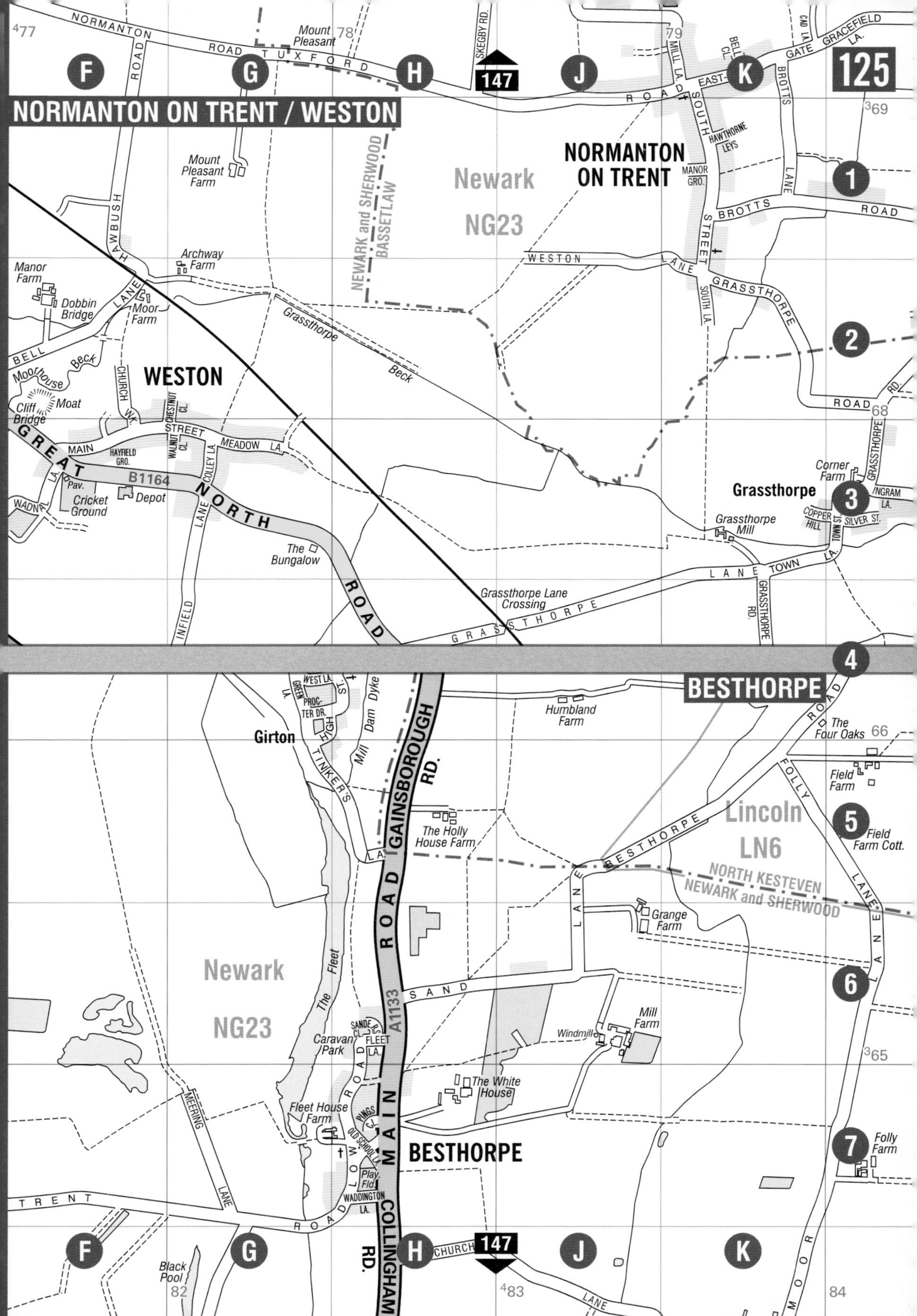
NORMANTON ON TRENT
Newark
NG23
WESTON
Grassthorpe
BESTHORPE
Girton
Lincoln
LN6
NORTH KESTEVEN
NEWARK and SHERWOOD
NEWARK and SHERWOOD
BASSETLAW
Newark
NG23
BESTHORPE
147
147

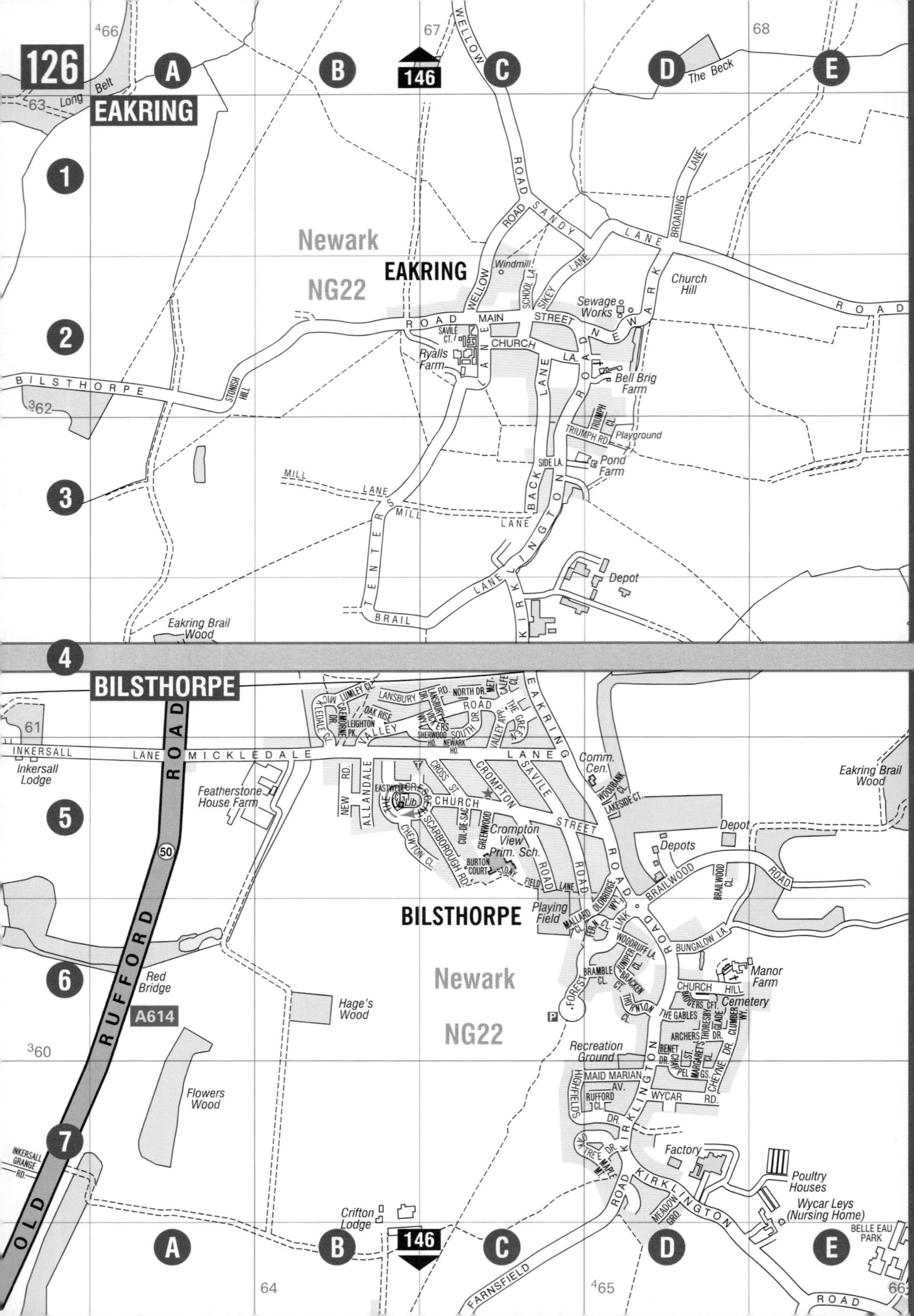
EAKRING
BILSTHORPE
Newark
NG22
Long Belt
The Beck
Windmill
Church Hill
Sewage Works
Ryalls Farm
Bell Brig Farm
Playground
Pond Farm
Depot
Eakring Brail Wood
MAIN STREET
CHURCH LA.
WELLOW ROAD
SANDY LANE
BILSTHORPE ROAD
MILL LANE
BRAIL LANE
KIRKLINGTON ROAD
BACK LANE
BROADING LANE
NEWARK ROAD
INKERSALL LANE
MICKLEDALE LANE
Inkersall Lodge
Featherstone House Farm
Crompton View Prim. Sch.
Comm. Cen.
Depots
Playing Field
Manor Farm
Cemetery
Recreation Ground
Factory
Poultry Houses
Wycar Leys (Nursing Home)
BELLE EAU PARK
Red Bridge
A614
RUFFORD ROAD
OLD RUFFORD ROAD
Hage's Wood
Flowers Wood
Crifton Lodge
FARNSFIELD ROAD
146

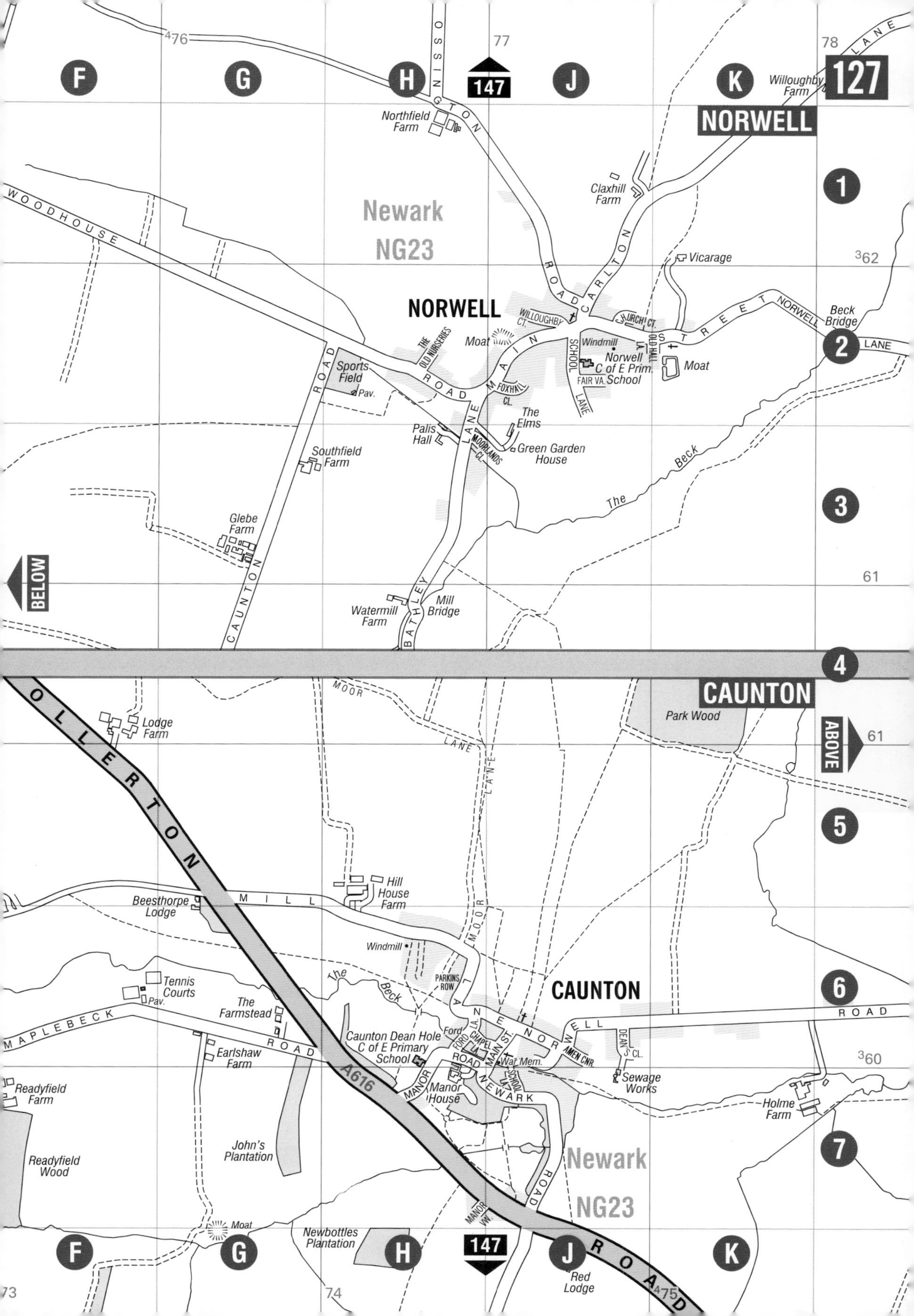

F   G   H   147   J   K

476   77   78

Willoughby Farm

1

Northfield Farm

Claxhill Farm

Newark NG23

Vicarage

362

NISSONGTON LANE

WOODHOUSE

ROAD

CARLTON

NORWELL

Beck Bridge

CHURCH CT.

STREET

NORWELL

2

LANE

WILLOUGHBY CT.

Moat

Windmill

Norwell C of E Prim. School

Moat

OLD HALL

Sports Field

Pav.

THE OLD NURSERIES

ROAD

MAIN

SCHOOL

FOXHALL CL.

FAIR VA.

The Elms

Green Garden House

The Beck

3

Southfield Farm

Palis Hall

MOORLANDS CL.

LANE

Glebe Farm

CAUNTON

61

BELOW

Watermill Farm

Mill Bridge

BATHLEY LANE

4

MOOR

Park Wood

ABOVE

61

Lodge Farm

LANE

5

OLLERTON

Hill House Farm

MILL

Beesthorpe Lodge

Windmill

MOOR LANE

PARKINS ROW

The Beck

CAUNTON

ROAD

6

360

Tennis Courts

Pav.

The Farmstead

ROAD

Earlshaw Farm

MAPLEBECK

A616

Caunton Dean Hole C of E Primary School

Ford

FORD LANE

CHAPEL LANE

MAIN ST.

War Mem.

NORWELL LANE

DEAN'S CL.

AMEN CNR.

Sewage Works

Holme Farm

Readyfield Farm

MANOR ROAD

Manor House

SCHOOL LANE

NEWARK ROAD

7

Readyfield Wood

John's Plantation

Moat

Newbottles Plantation

MANOR WY.

Newark NG23

Red Lodge

475D

F   G   H   147   J   ROAD   K

73   74

67

78 A   B   79   C   D   480   E   LANE

1   GREAT   Redroofs Farm
Weston Mill Farm
Lodge Plantation
B1164

Grange Farm
Dunstall Lodge
Sports Ground
Pav.
North Holme

2   A1   Red Holt
66
Works   Poplar Farm
PARRY BUSINESS PARK
Crow Park
AVENUE
SNELL CL.
The MEERINGS
STERN THORPE CL.
Rec. Grd.
STATION
BULHAM
ROAD
HIGH
Cemetery
Woodbine Farm
Play. Fld.
Prim. Sch.
SUTTON ON TRENT
First Holme
INGRAM
LANE
CHURCH ST.

3   OSSINGTON   Common Farm
BRAMBLEBECK LA.
LANE
NORTH
Crow Pk. Bridge
HEMPLANDS LA.
Hounsfield Wy.
Grasmere Farm
STREET
SERV.
FORGE CL.
OLD ENGINE GDNS.
The VINES
Lib.
MIDDLE HOLME LANE
Cuckstool Dyke

147   Lady Charlotte's Plantation
Barrel Hill
EAVES LA.
The Bungalow
Hillside
The Gatehouse
BARREL HILL
ASH LA.
WITCH LA.
WILLOW HOLT
POPLAR CL.
ROSE FARM
ROAD
PALMER
ROAD
The COCK STUDS.
FAR HOLME LA.
The Manor House

4   A1   Newark NG23
365
27
SHIRES WY.
FLORAL VS.
MAIN
Works
Landrace Farm

5   Stud Farm
CARLTON
B1164
59
Carlton Ho.
The Rhymes

6   OSSINGTON
LANE
CASTLE HILL
ROAD
Works
B1164
ROAD
Carlton Lake
Mill Farm
Windmill
RIVER
TRENT
CARLTON FERRY LA.

64   Whiteley Plantation
CARLTON
LANE
CARLTON MANOR CARAVAN PK.
FERRY
Long Walk
Carlton Hall
CHURCH LA.
MAIN
STREET
OLD BELL LA.

7   A1
CARLTON-ON-TRENT

Willoughby Farm

78 A   B   79   C   D   480   E
GREAT NORTH RD.

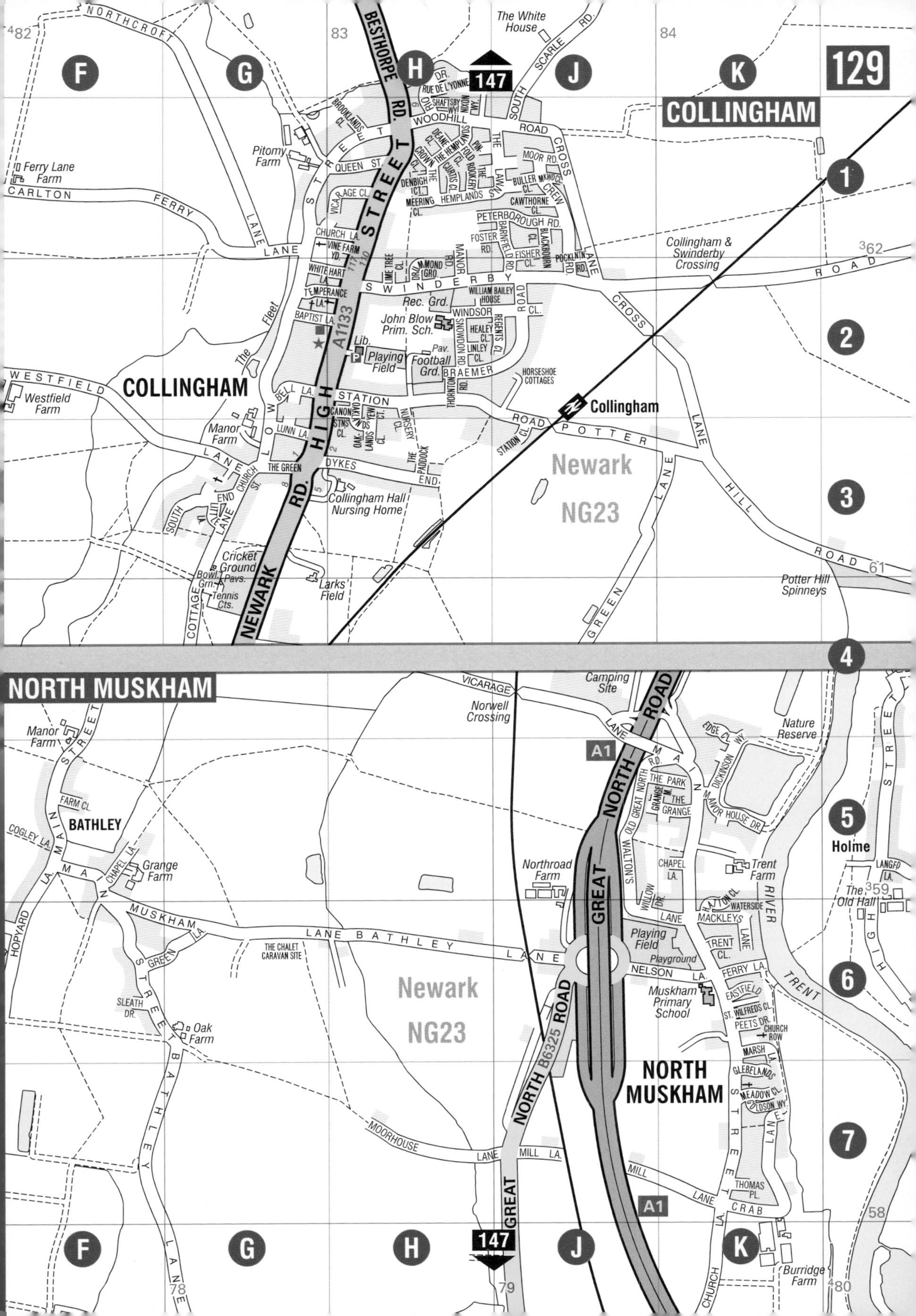

COLLINGHAM
NORTH MUSKHAM
147
147
F
G
H
J
K
1
2
3
4
5
6
7
Newark
NG23
Collingham
BATHLEY
Holme
NORTH MUSKHAM
Collingham & Swinderby Crossing
Norwell Crossing
Pitomy Farm
Ferry Lane Farm
Westfield Farm
Manor Farm
The White House
John Blow Prim. Sch.
Collingham Hall Nursing Home
Cricket Ground
Larks Field
Potter Hill Spinneys
Camping Site
Nature Reserve
Grange Farm
Oak Farm
Northroad Farm
Trent Farm
The Old Hall
Muskham Primary School
Burridge Farm
THE CHALET CARAVAN SITE
HIGH STREET
NEWARK RD.
BESTHORPE RD.
SWINDERBY ROAD
POTTER HILL ROAD
STATION ROAD
CARLTON FERRY LANE
WESTFIELD LANE
GREAT NORTH ROAD
NORTH ROAD
BATHLEY LANE
MUSKHAM LANE
BATHLEY STREET
MAIN STREET
RIVER TRENT

A
B
C
D
E
1
2
3
4
5
6
7
67
68
56
55
54
53
132
146
Station House
Cotton Mill Dyke
Edingley Beck
STATION ROAD
HOLME LANE
Moat
MAIN STREET
BELFIELDS YD.
CHAPEL CL.
STATION ROAD
Highfields Nursing Home
EDINGLEY
EDINGLEY HILL
Newark
NG22
Goldhill Farm
Diamond Cottage Farm
GREAVES LANE
LITTLE LA.
MANSFIELD LANE
Halam Beck
Halam Osier Beds Wood
Grange Farm
St. Helens Croft
Mill Farm
Halam Mill
MANSFIELD ROAD
THE LANE
LOW LANE
NORWOOD PARK GOLF COURSE
NEWHALL LANE
SAINT HELEN'S LANE
Ford
Strickland Farm
GRAY LANE
HALAM
Halam C of E Prim. Sch.
TURNPIKE LANE
SCHOOL LANE
New Plantation
Club House
NORWOOD PARK
Middlebeck Farm
BACK LANE
RADLEY R.
RADLEY TER.
HALAM HILL
ST. MICHAELS CL.
The Temple Wood
Machin's Farm
CHURCH LANE
MANOR FLDS
Farm Plantation
Norwood Park Farm
HALAM HILL
SAVERSICK LANE
COOKS LA.
Halam Beck
Lowbank Farm
CUTLERSFORTH
OXTON ROAD
Cricket Ground
Pav.
Cutlersforth Farm
THE PUMPING STATION
LEACHCROFT HILL
Westhorpe Hall
WESTHORPE
Westhorpe
THE HOLME
B6386
CUNDY HILL
RADLEY ROAD
Thorney Abbey Farm
BATH LANE
OXTON ROAD
New Radley Farm

KIRKLINGTON RD.
A617
HOCKERTON
Hockerton Grange
Manor Farm
Hockerton Dumble
THE PADDOCKS
CAUNTON RD.
GABLES DR.
Meadow Farm
Far Corkhill Farm
Cork Hill
Middle Corkhill Farm
Little Corkhill Farm
CORKHILL LANE
MAYTHORNE INDUSTRIAL ESTATE
THE OLD SILK MILL
MAYTHORNE LANE
Driving Range
Southwell
NG25
Chestnut Farm
Normanton
NORMANTON LANE
HOCKERTON ROAD
Recreation Ground
RIVER GREET
Ornamental Water Gardens
MILL PARK INDUSTRIAL ESTATE
Crow Wood
Lodge Plantation
KIRKLINGTON ROAD
KIRKLINGTON LANE
Rifle Range
Upton Field
GALLEY HILL ROAD
UPTON ROAD
A612
The Workhouse
Greet Bri.
STATION RD.
NEWARK ROAD
RIVERSIDE
Depot
War Mem.
Lib.
BURGAGE LANE
QUEEN ST.
KING ST.
MARKET SQ.
Lowe's Wong Jun. & Inf. Sch.
CHURCH STREET
EASTHORPE
Southwell Minster
WESTGATE
B6386
Sch.
Tanyard Farm
Westhorpe Dumble
Bowl. Grn. Ten. Cts.
War Mem. Rec. Grd. Pav.
Squire's Pond
Cemetery
Mon.
Potwell Dyke
The Minster School
Southwell Leisure Cen.
Games Court
Rugby Football Ground
Wilderness
Bracken Lodge
NOTTINGHAM ROAD
BRACKENHURST LANE
CREW LANE INDUSTRIAL ESTATE
CREW LANE
Depot
SOUTHWELL
Dale Farm
Brandreth
Park Farm
Smithfield Farm
FISKERTON RD.
SPRING HILL
FISKERTON
CRINK LANE
POLLARD'S LANE
Brinkley Hall Farm
Brinkley Hill Farm
147
F
G
H
J
K
1
2
3
4
5
6
7
69
470
71
56
355
54
53

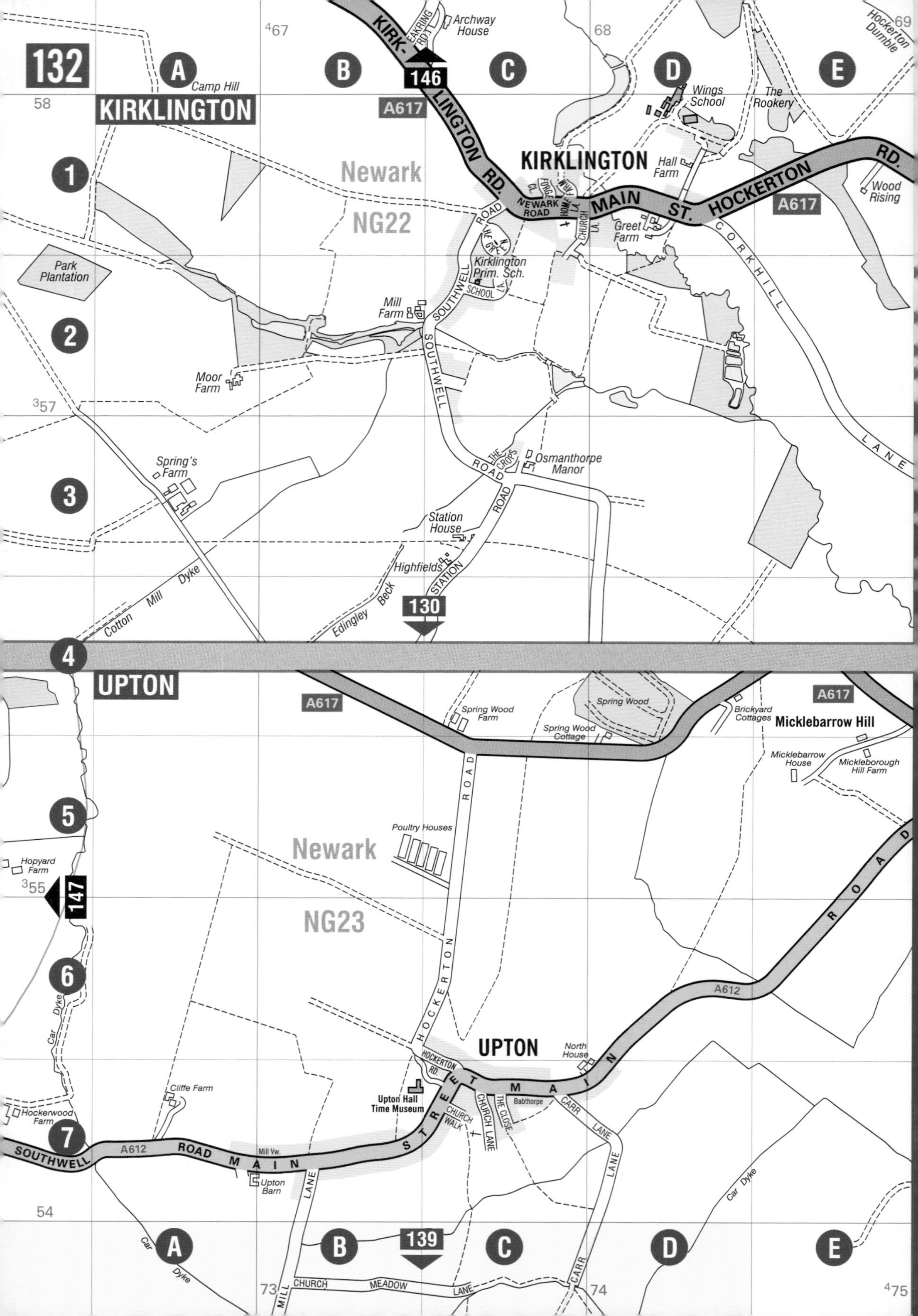
KIRKLINGTON
Camp Hill
Newark
NG22
KIRKLINGTON
Archway House
Wings School
The Rookery
Hockerton Dumble
Hall Farm
Greet Farm
Wood Rising
KIRKLINGTON RD.
MAIN ST.
HOCKERTON RD.
NEWARK ROAD
A617
Park Plantation
Kirklington Prim. Sch.
SCHOOL LA.
Mill Farm
SOUTHWELL ROAD
Moor Farm
Spring's Farm
Osmanthorpe Manor
THE CROPS
Station House
Highfields
STATION ROAD
Edingley Beck
Cotton Mill Dyke
CORKHILL LANE
146
130
UPTON
A617
Spring Wood Farm
Spring Wood
Spring Wood Cottage
Brickyard Cottages
Micklebarrow Hill
Micklebarrow House
Mickleborough Hill Farm
Poultry Houses
Newark
NG23
Hopyard Farm
147
HOCKERTON ROAD
UPTON
North House
Upton Hall Time Museum
Cliffe Farm
Hockerwood Farm
SOUTHWELL ROAD
A612
MAIN STREET
Mill Vw.
Upton Barn
CHURCH WALK
CHURCH LANE
THE CLOSE
Babthorpe
CARR LANE
MILL LANE
CHURCH MEADOW LANE
Car Dyke
139

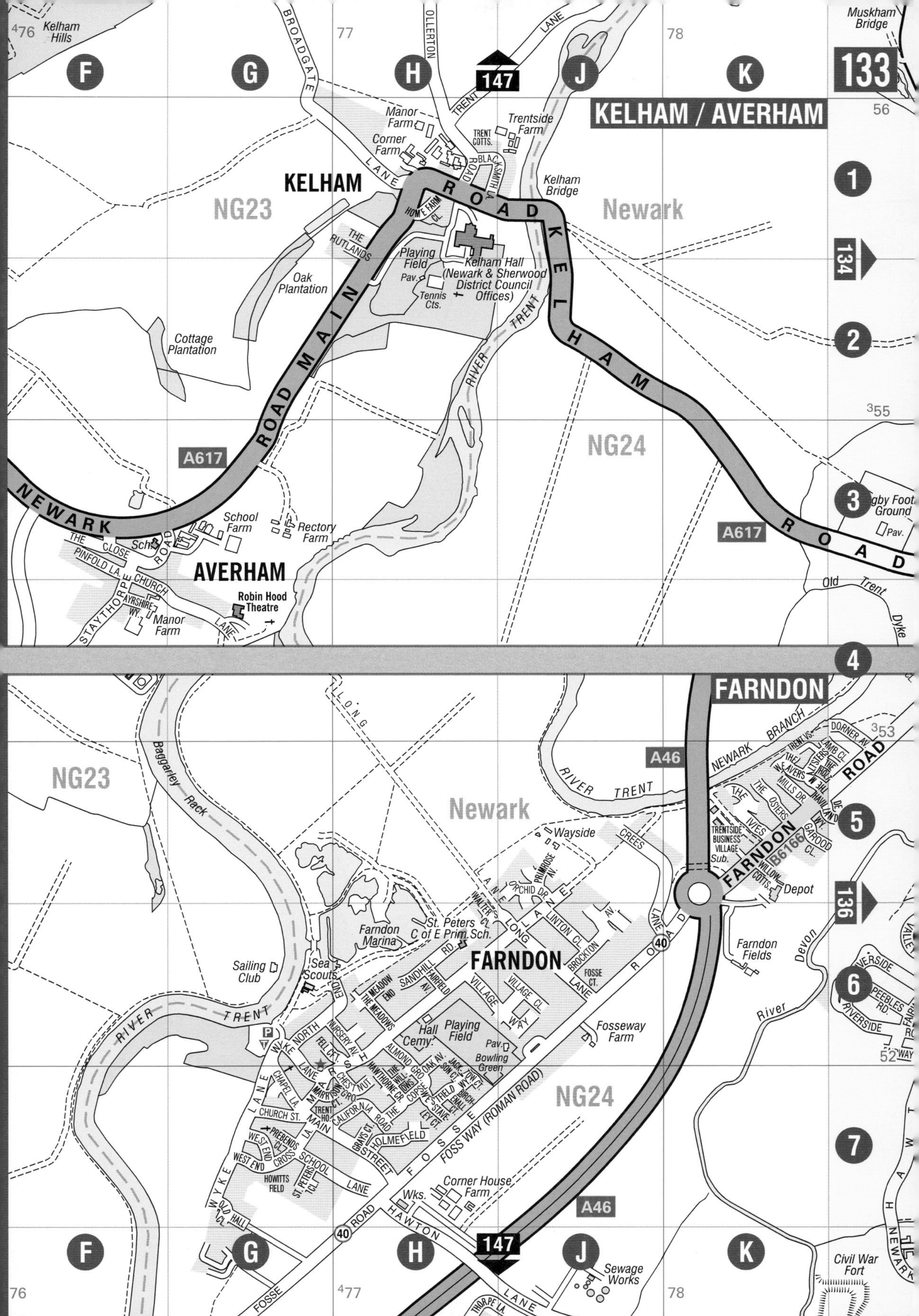
KELHAM
AVERHAM
FARNDON
Newark
NG23
NG24
Kelham Hills
Muskham Bridge
Manor Farm
Corner Farm
Trentside Farm
Trent Cotts.
Kelham Bridge
Kelham Hall (Newark & Sherwood District Council Offices)
Playing Field
Pav.
Tennis Cts.
Oak Plantation
Cottage Plantation
The Rutlands
Home Farm Cl.
Blacksmith La.
Broadgate
Ollerton
Trent Lane
Lane
Main Road
Kelham Road
Newark Road
A617
River Trent
School Farm
Rectory Farm
Sch.
The Close
Pinfold La.
Church
Staythorpe
Ayrshire Wy.
Manor Farm
Robin Hood Theatre
Lane
Old Trent Dyke
Rugby Football Ground
Pav.
147
134
136
Baggarley Rack
Long Lane
A46
Newark Branch
Road
Trent Vs.
Dorner Av.
Lamb Cl.
The Weavers
The Holt
The Osiers
Mills Dr.
The Ivies
Havilland Wy.
Garood Cl.
Trentside Business Village
Sub.
Farndon Road
B6166
Willow Cotts.
Depot
Wayside
Crees Lane
Primrose Av.
Orchid Dr.
Walter's Cl.
Linton Cl.
Brockton Av.
Fosse Ct.
Road
40
St. Peters C of E Prim. Sch.
Farndon Marina
Farndon Fields
Devon
River
Sailing Club
Sea Scouts
Marsh Lane
Nursery Av.
The Meadows
Meadow End
Sandhill Rd.
Fairfield Av.
Village Way
Village Cl.
Hall Cemy.
Playing Field
Pav.
Bowling Green
Fosseway Farm
North End
Wyke Lane
Fell Ct.
Almond Gro.
Oak Av.
Jackson Ct.
Zion Ct.
Chestnut Gro.
Hawthorne Cr.
The Willows
Copse
Theld Enall Wy.
Birch Ct.
Staves Ct.
Ley Ct.
Marrison Ct.
Trent Ho.
California Road
The Gro
Grays Ct.
Holmefield
Main Street
Chapel La.
Church St.
Prebends Cl.
West End
Cross Lane
School Lane
Howitts Field
St. Peters Cl.
Old Hall Cl.
Wyke Lane
Fosse Way (Roman Road)
Fosse Road
Hawton Lane
Wks.
Corner House Farm
Sewage Works
Thorpe La.
Civil War Fort
Riverside
Peebles Rd.
Valley
Hawton Road
Newark
Pav.
F G H J K
1 2 3 4 5 6 7
76 77 78
56 55 53 52

A
B
C
D
E
1
2
3
4
5
6
7
147
133
136
SOUTH MUSKHAM
Little Carlton
NG23
NEWARK-ON-TRENT
OLLERTON RD. A616
GREAT NORTH ROAD
B6325
A1
A46
A617
A616
B6326
B6166
KELHAM ROAD
ROBERT DUKESON AVENUE
RIVER TRENT
Winthorpe Lake
Winthorpe Bridge
Crankley Point
Muskham Bridge
The Grange
Sailing Club
Sewage Works
Newark Crossing
Nether Lock
Rugby Football Ground
Newark Cricket Ground
Kelham Road Dairy Farm
Valley Farm
Rectory Farm
Church Lane Crossing
Factory
Sports Ground
Tanks
Silos
The Kings Marina
Lorry Park
Cattle Market
Newark Castle
Newark Northgate
Northgate Retail Park
Jolly Jungle Playland
LA Fitness
Newbridge Works
Caravan Site
Theatre
Prim. Sch.
Playground
Comm. Cen.
Castlegate Cen.
Bus Sta.
Warwick Brewery
Friary Gds.
Beacon Hill Bri.
Brunel Bus. Pk.
Newark Bus. Pk.

F
G
H
J
K
147
A46
Hall Farm
Langford Hall
Winthorpe Crossing
Cricket Ground
Pav.
Winthorpe Prim. Sch.
Comm. Cen.
High Wood
Elk Racing Outdoor Karting Circuit
Airfield (disused)
Quarry Plantation
WINTHORPE
Newark
Nursing Home
Lingspot Farm
Newark Showground
Newark Golf Centre (Driving Range)
Bowling Green
Service Area
Newark Air Museum
A17
A1
Depot
Drove Cottage Farm
The Bungalow
Works
Playing Field
Factory
Beaconfield Farm
NG24
CODDINGTON
Black's Farm
Coddington C of E Primary School
Coddington House
Vale Farm
Moat
Beacon Hill Conservation Park
Cotswold
Reservoir (covered)
137
A1133
FOSS WAY (ROMAN ROAD)
DROVE LANE
BECKINGHAM ROAD
BRUNEL DRIVE
STEPHENSON WAY
JESSOP WAY
ENTERPRISE PARK
BRUNEL DR. WORKSHOPS
Play. Fld.
1
2
3
4
5
6
7
81
82
83
57
56
55
54

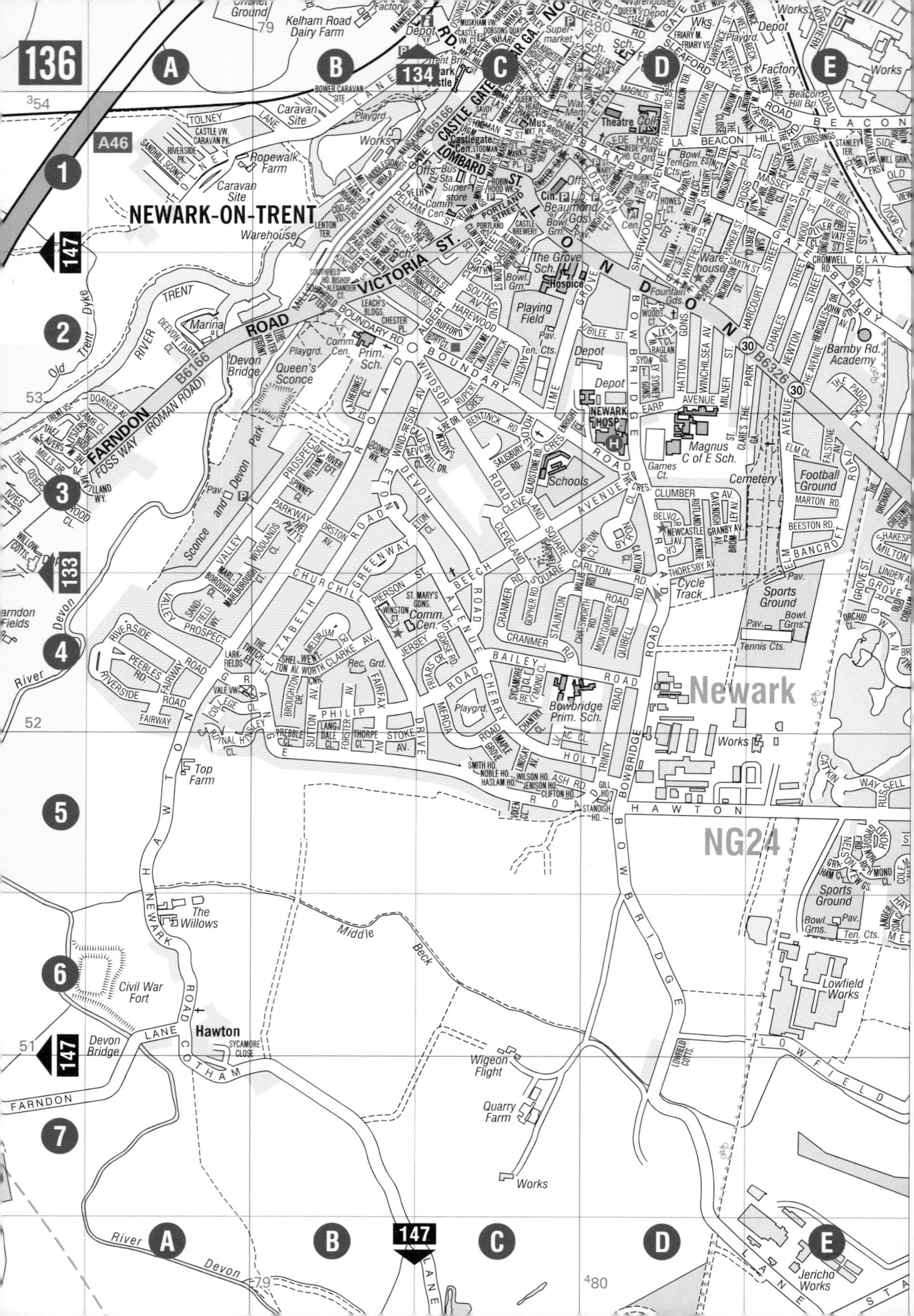

NEWARK-ON-TRENT
Newark
NG24
A46
B6166
B6326
134
147
133
A
B
C
D
E
1
2
3
4
5
6
7
Kelham Road Dairy Farm
Caravan Site
Ropewalk Farm
Warehouse
Marina
Devon Bridge
Queen's Sconce
Sconce and Devon Park
FARNDON ROAD
FOSS WAY (ROMAN ROAD)
VICTORIA ST.
LONDON ROAD
CASTLE GATE
LOMBARD ST.
PORTLAND STREET
BOUNDARY RD.
Theatre
Castlegate Cen.
Beaumond Gds.
The Grove Sch.
Hospice
Playing Field
Depot
NEWARK HOSP.
Schools
Magnus C of E Sch.
Cemetery
Football Ground
Barnby Rd. Academy
Cycle Track
Sports Ground
Tennis Cts.
Bowbridge Prim. Sch.
Works
Top Farm
The Willows
Middle Beck
Civil War Fort
Hawton
Devon Bridge
Wigeon Flight
Quarry Farm
Lowfield Works
Jericho Works
HAWTON ROAD
BOWBRIDGE ROAD
NEWARK ROAD
COTHAM LANE
FARNDON
LOWFIELD
River Devon
River Trent
Old Trent Dyke
79
480
354
53
52
51

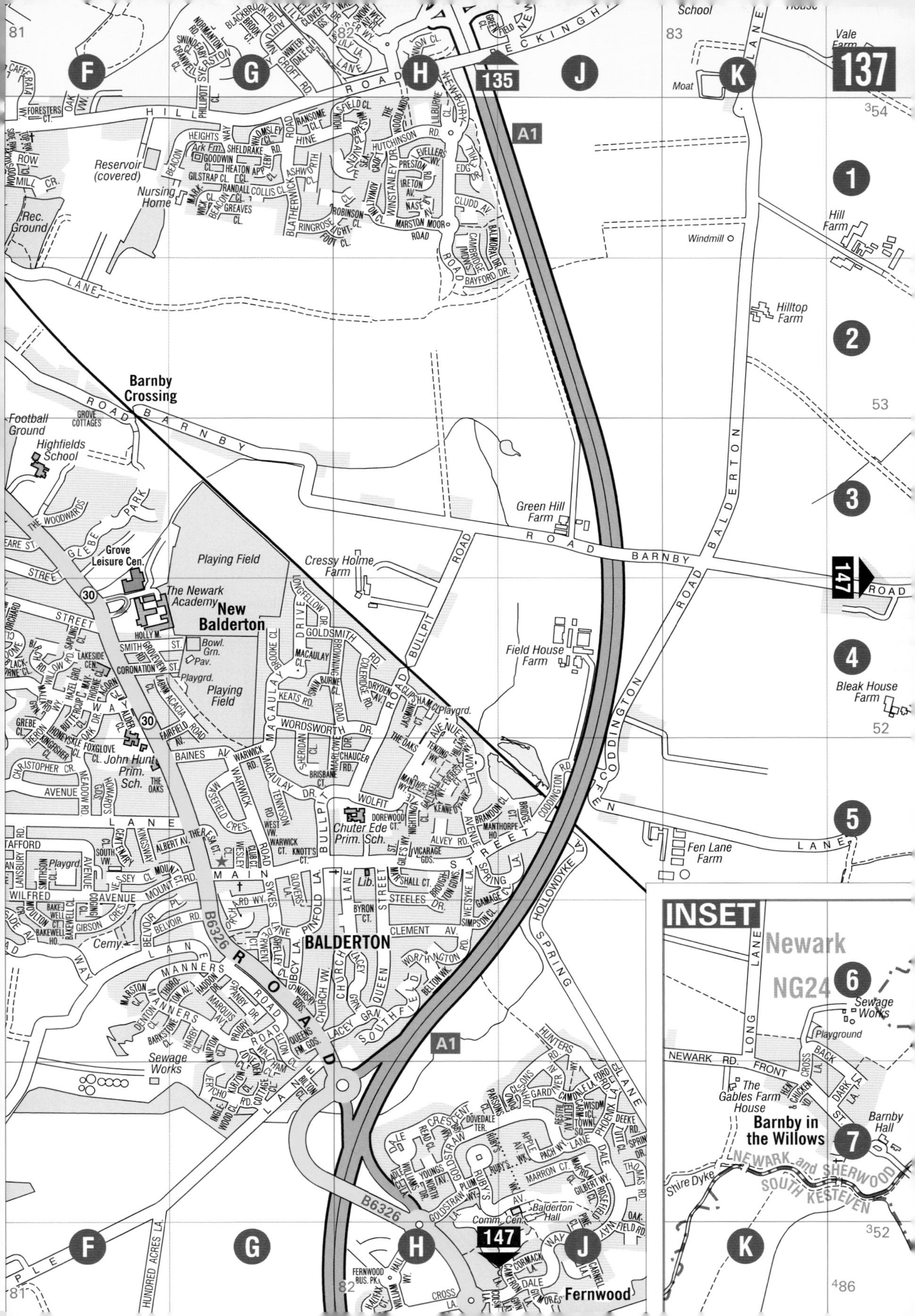
137
135
147
A1
B6326
New Balderton
Balderton
Barnby Crossing
Fernwood
Barnby in the Willows
INSET
Newark
NG24
NEWARK and SHERWOOD
SOUTH KESTEVEN
Shire Dyke
Reservoir (covered)
Nursing Home
Rec. Ground
Football Ground
Highfields School
Grove Leisure Cen.
The Newark Academy
Playing Field
Bowl. Grn.
Pav.
Playgrd.
John Hunt Prim. Sch.
Chuter Ede Prim. Sch.
Lib.
Cemy.
Sewage Works
Comm. Cen.
Balderton Hall
Fernwood Bus. Pk.
Cressy Holme Farm
Green Hill Farm
Field House Farm
Fen Lane Farm
Hilltop Farm
Hill Farm
Bleak House Farm
Vale Farm
Windmill
Moat
School
The Gables Farm House
Barnby Hall
Playground
Ark Fm.
BARNBY ROAD
BALDERTON ROAD
CODDINGTON ROAD
BULLPIT ROAD
MAIN STREET
HOLLOWDYKE LA.
SPRING LANE
FEN LANE
LONG LANE
HILL ROAD
BECKINGHAM
NEWARK RD.
FRONT ST.
BACK LA.
DARK LA.
HIGHFIELD LA.
HUNDRED ACRES LA.
WOLFIT AV.
WORDSWORTH DR.
MACAULAY DR.
GOLDSMITH RD.
MARSTON MOOR ROAD
BLATHERWICK RD.
F
G
H
J
K
1
2
3
4
5
6
7
81
82
83
354
53
52
352
486

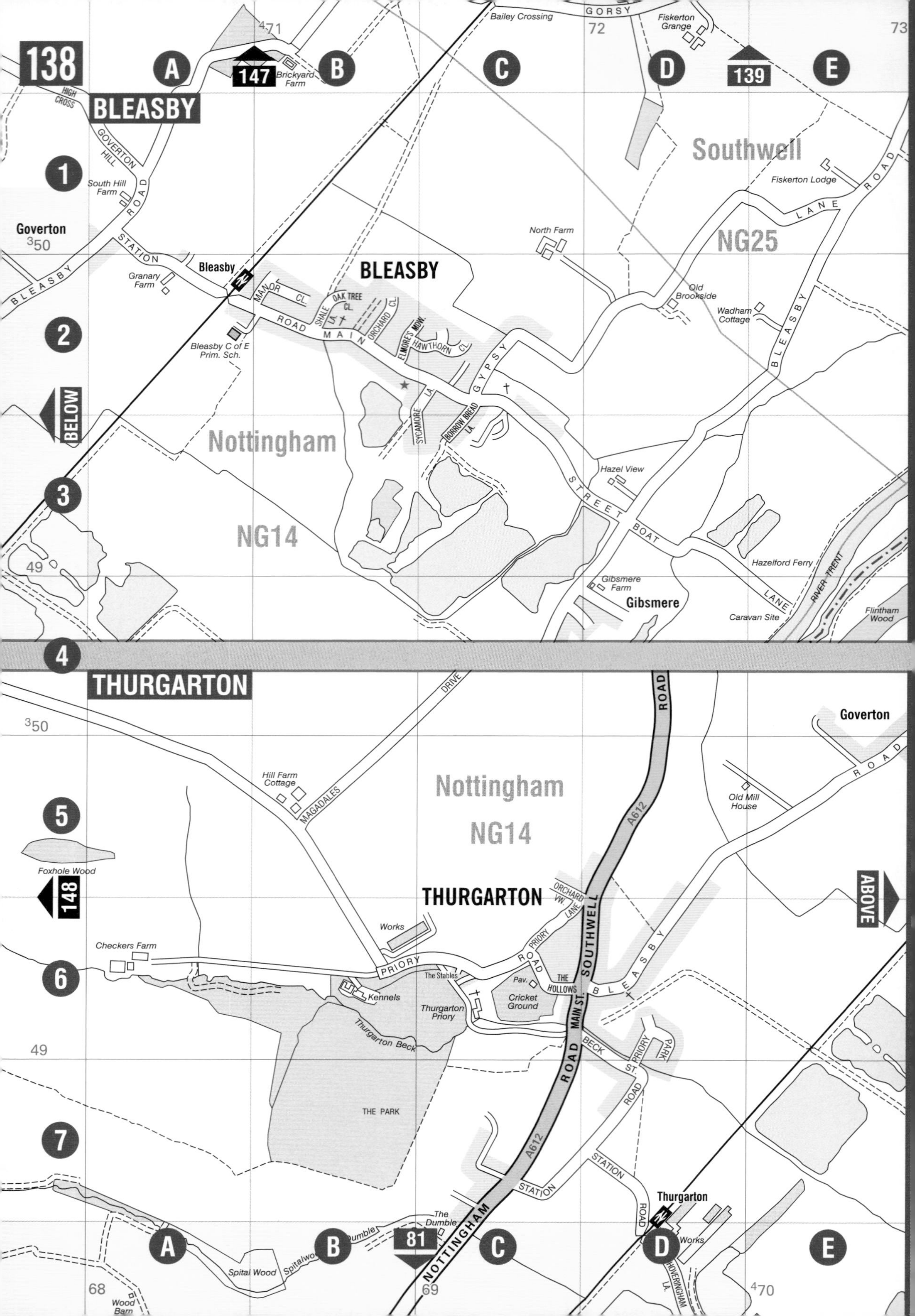

BLEASBY

A **B** **C** **D** **E**

147 Brickyard Farm · Bailey Crossing · GORSY · Fiskerton Grange · 139

471 · 72 · 73

HIGH CROSS

GOVERTON HILL

1 South Hill Farm · North Farm · **Southwell** · Fiskerton Lodge

Goverton ³50

STATION ROAD

BLEASBY ROAD

Granary Farm · Bleasby · **BLEASBY** · Old Brookside · Wadham Cottage · **NG25**

LANE

BLEASBY ROAD

2 MANOR CL. · SHALE LA · OAK TREE CL. · MAIN ROAD · ORCHARD CL. · ELMORE'S MDW. · HAWTHORN CL. · GYPSY · BLEASBY ROAD

Bleasby C of E Prim. Sch.

SYCAMORE LA.

BORROW BROAD LA.

◄ BELOW

Nottingham

Hazel View

STREET BOAT LANE

3 **NG14** · Hazelford Ferry · RIVER TRENT

Gibsmere Farm · **Gibsmere** · Caravan Site · Flintham Wood

49

4

THURGARTON

DRIVE

ROAD

A612

Goverton

³50

Hill Farm Cottage · MAGADALES · **Nottingham** · Old Mill House · ROAD

NG14

5

Foxhole Wood

THURGARTON

ORCHARD VW.

SOUTHWELL ROAD

BLEASBY ROAD

ABOVE ►

◄ 148

Checkers Farm · Works · PRIORY ROAD · The Stables · Pav. · THE HOLLOWS

6 Kennels · Thurgarton Priory · Cricket Ground

Thurgarton Beck

MAIN ST. · BECK · PRIORY ST. · PRIORY PARK

49

7 THE PARK

STATION ROAD

Thurgarton

Works

A **B** **C** **D** **E**

Spital Wood · Spitalwood · Dumble · The Dumble · 81 · NOTTINGHAM ROAD · STATION · HOVERINGHAM LA.

Wood Barn

68 · 69 · 470

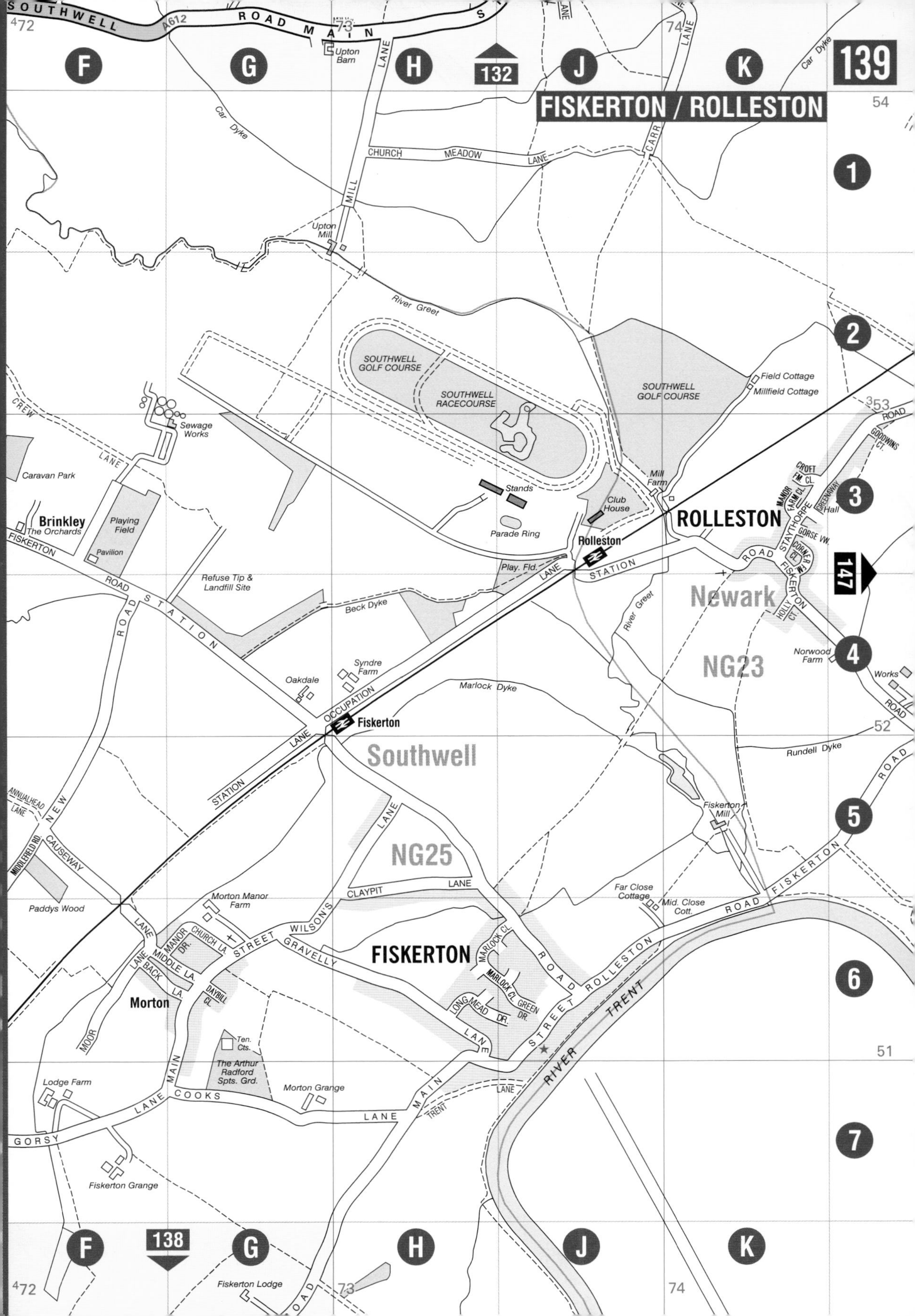

Upton Barn

CHURCH MEADOW LANE

MILL LANE

Upton Mill

River Greet

1

2

SOUTHWELL GOLF COURSE

SOUTHWELL RACECOURSE

SOUTHWELL GOLF COURSE

Field Cottage

Millfield Cottage

353 Road

GOODWINS CT.

CREW LANE

Sewage Works

Caravan Park

Stands

Parade Ring

Mill Farm

Club House

ROLLESTON

CROFT

M CL.

MANOR FARM CL.

STATION

GORSE VW.

HOPPE

CHOLLELY CL.

PINFOLD

Hall

SPEARHEAD

3

Brinkley
The Orchards

Playing Field

Pavilion

FISKERTON ROAD

STATION ROAD

Refuse Tip & Landfill Site

Beck Dyke

Rolleston

Play. Fld.

STATION LANE

River Greet

Newark

ROAD

FISKERTON

147

Syndre Farm

Oakdale

OCCUPATION LANE

Marlock Dyke

Fiskerton

Southwell

NG23

Norwood Farm

Works

ROAD

4

52

Rundell Dyke

Fiskerton Mill

ANNUALHEAD LANE

MIDDLEFIELD RD.

NEW LANE

CAUSEWAY

Paddys Wood

STATION LANE

CLAYPIT LANE

NG25

WILSONS STREET

GRAVELLY LANE

Far Close Cottage

Mid. Close Cott.

FISKERTON ROAD

ROLLESTON STREET

5

Morton Manor Farm

MANOR DR.

CHURCH LA.

MIDDLE LA.

BACK LA.

DAYBILL CL.

Morton

FISKERTON

MARLOCK CL.

MARLOCK CL. GREEN

LONG MEAD DR.

LANE

6

51

MOOR LANE

Lodge Farm

MAIN LANE

COOKS LANE

Ten. Cts.

The Arthur Radford Spts. Grd.

Morton Grange

MAIN LANE

TRENT LANE

RIVER TRENT

7

GORSY LANE

Fiskerton Grange

Fiskerton Lodge

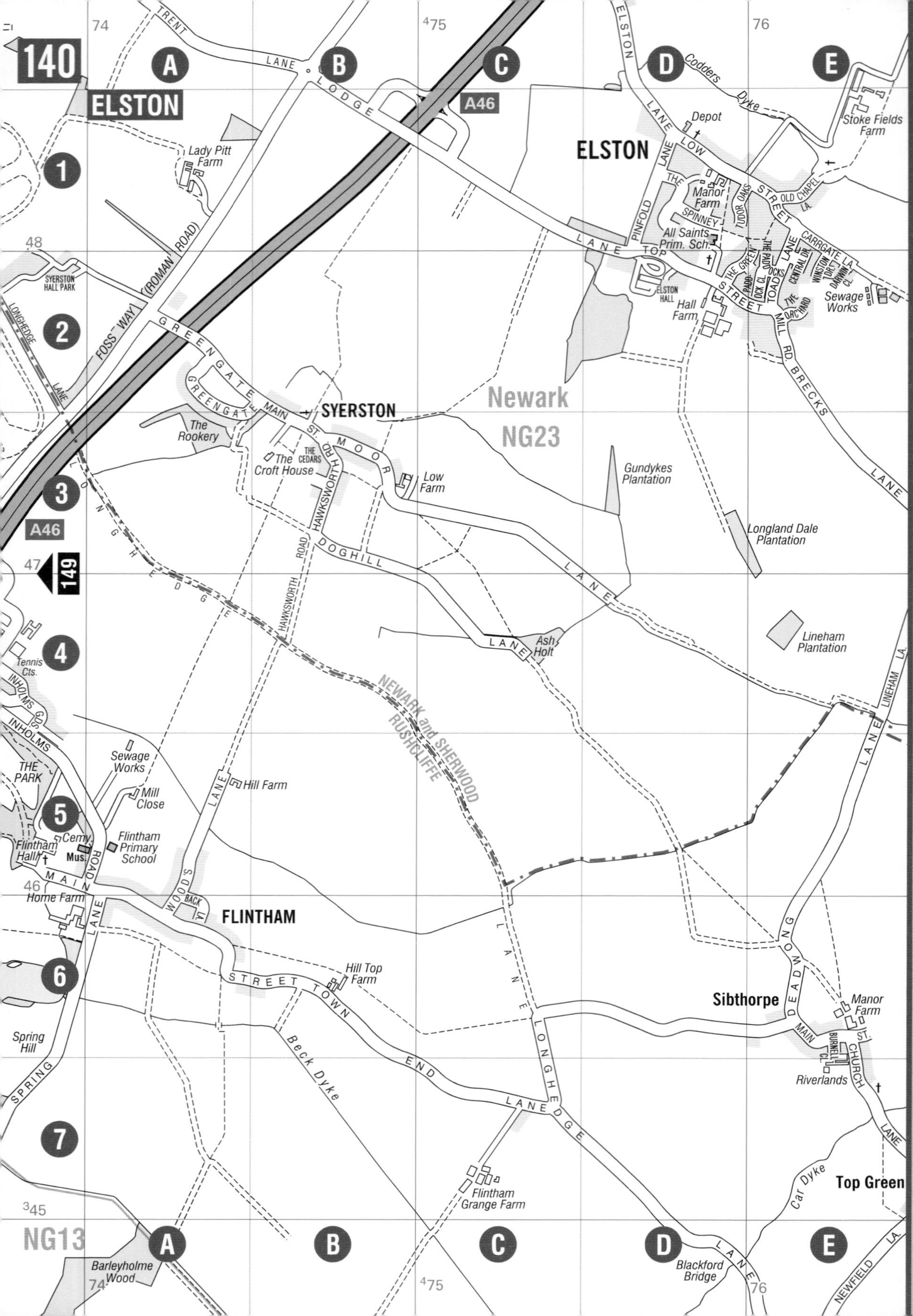
ELSTON
A
B
C
D
E
1
2
3
4
5
6
7
74
475
76
48
47
46
345
A46
TRENT LANE
LODGE LANE
Lady Pitt Farm
FOSS WAY (ROMAN ROAD)
SYERSTON HALL PARK
LONGHEDGE LANE
GREENGATE
MAIN ST.
SYERSTON
The Rookery
The Croft House
THE CEDARS
HAWKSWORTH RD.
MOOR LANE
Low Farm
DOGHILL LANE
Ash Holt
Newark
NG23
Gundykes Plantation
Longland Dale Plantation
Lineham Plantation
LINEHAM LA.
ELSTON LANE
Codders Dyke
Depot
Stoke Fields Farm
LOW STREET
OLD CHAPEL LA.
Manor Farm
THE SPINNEY
PINFOLD LANE
TUDOR OAKS
All Saints Prim. Sch.
TOP STREET
ELSTON HALL
Hall Farm
THE GREEN
PADDOCKS
CARRGATE LA.
CENTRAL DR.
WINSTON CT.
DARWIN CL.
THE ORCHARD
Sewage Works
MILL RD.
BRECKS LANE
NEWARK and SHERWOOD
RUSHCLIFFE
Tennis Cts.
INHOLMS GDNS.
INHOLMS
THE PARK
Sewage Works
Mill Close
Hill Farm
WOOD'S LANE
Flintham Hall
Cemy.
Mus.
Flintham Primary School
MAIN ROAD
Home Farm
BACK LA.
FLINTHAM
Hill Top Farm
TOWN STREET
END LANE
Beck Dyke
LONGHEDGE LANE
Spring Hill
SPRING LANE
Flintham Grange Farm
DEADWONG
Sibthorpe
Manor Farm
MAIN ST.
BURNELL CL.
CHURCH LANE
Riverlands
Top Green
Car Dyke
NEWFIELD LA.
Blackford Bridge
NG13
Barleyholme Wood

149

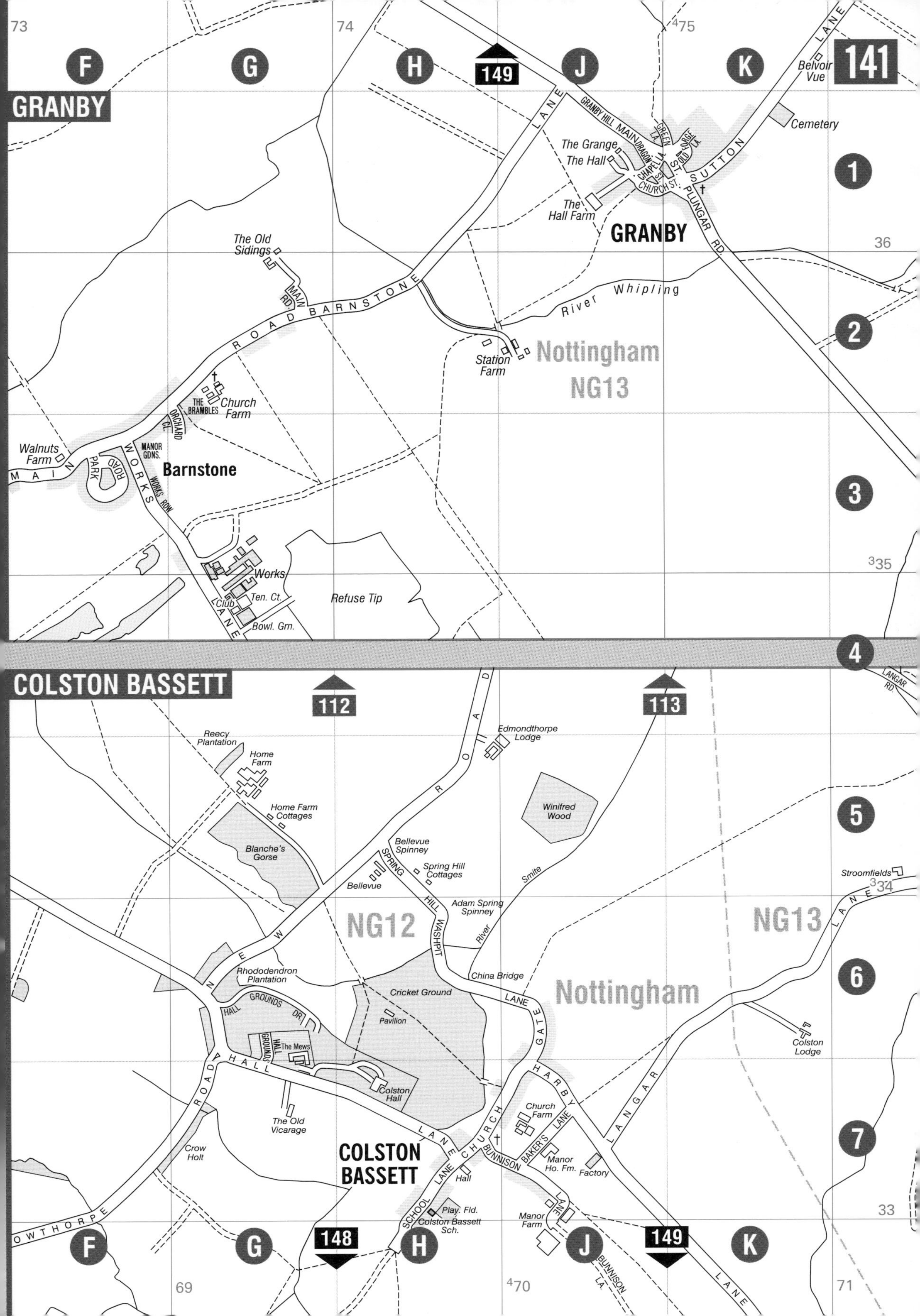
GRANBY
The Grange
The Hall
The Hall Farm
Belvoir Vue
Cemetery
The Old Sidings
Station Farm
River Whipling
Nottingham NG13
Church Farm
Walnuts Farm
Barnstone
Works
Refuse Tip
Ten. Ct.
Club
Bowl. Grn.
BARNSTONE ROAD
SUTTON LANE
PLUNGAR RD.
WORKS LANE
WORKS ROW
MAIN RD.
PARK ROAD
COLSTON BASSETT
Reecy Plantation
Home Farm
Home Farm Cottages
Edmondthorpe Lodge
Winifred Wood
Blanche's Gorse
Bellevue Spinney
Spring Hill Cottages
Bellevue
Adam Spring Spinney
NG12
NG13
Stroomfields
Rhododendron Plantation
Cricket Ground
Pavilion
China Bridge
Nottingham
Colston Lodge
The Mews
Colston Hall
The Old Vicarage
Crow Holt
Church Farm
Manor Ho. Fm.
Factory
Hall
Play. Fld.
Colston Bassett Sch.
Manor Farm
NEW ROAD
HALL ROAD
HALL LANE
HARBY LANE
LANGAR LANE
SCHOOL LANE
CHURCH LANE
BUNNISON LANE
OWTHORPE

149
112
113
148
149

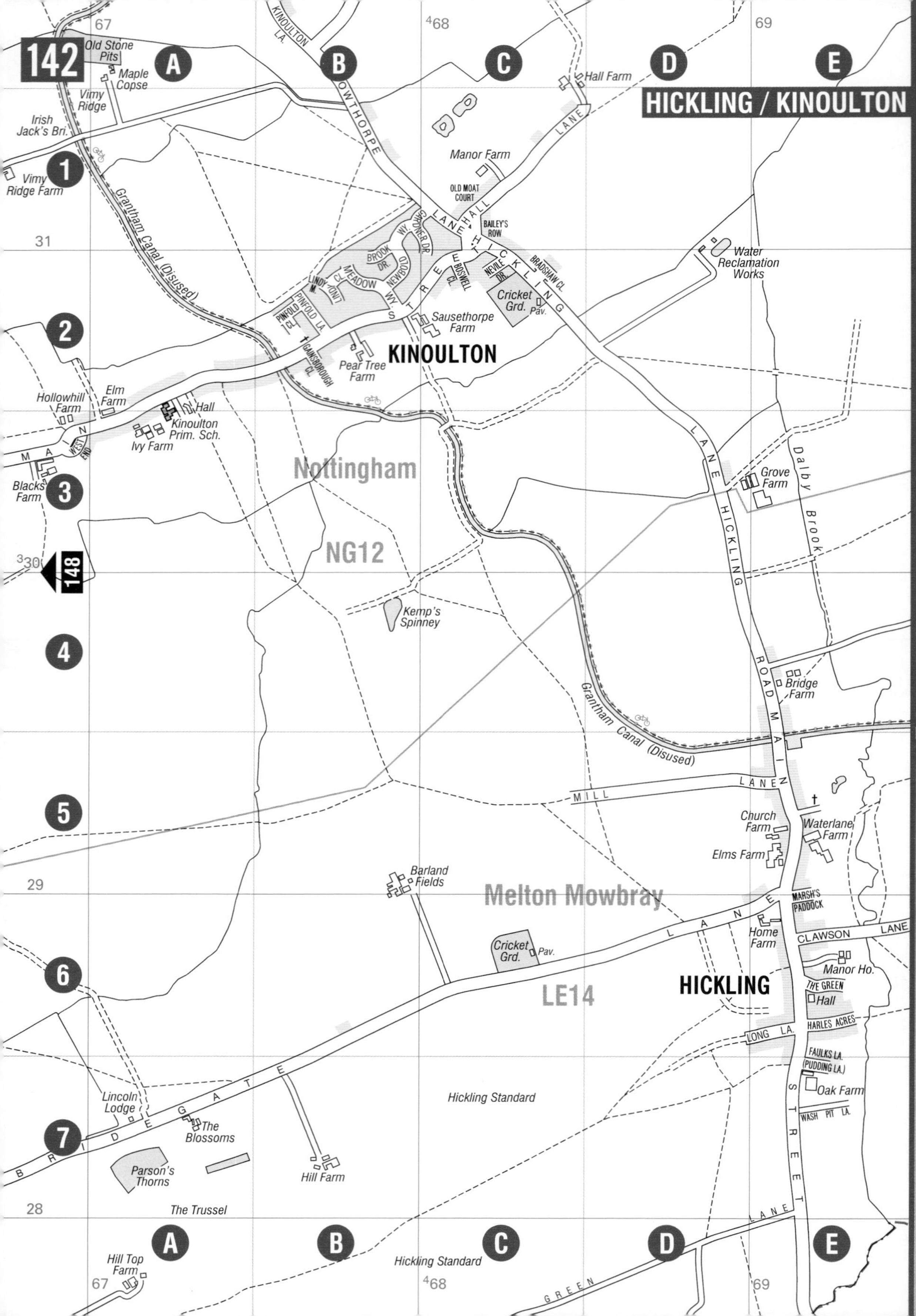

Old Stone Pits
Maple Copse
Vimy Ridge
Irish Jack's Bri.
Vimy Ridge Farm
Grantham Canal (Disused)

Hall Farm
Manor Farm
OLD MOAT COURT
BAILEY'S ROW
Water Reclamation Works

BROOK DR.
SPENCER DR.
NEWMAN CL.
MEADOW CT.
PINFOLD LA.
GAINSBOROUGH CL.
BOSWELL CL.
NEVILE DR.
BRADSHAW CL.
Cricket Grd.
Pav.

KINOULTON

Sausethorpe Farm
Pear Tree Farm
Hollowhill Farm
Elm Farm
Hall
Kinoulton Prim. Sch.
Ivy Farm
MAIN
Blacks Farm

Nottingham

NG12

148

Grove Farm
Dalby Brook

Kemp's Spinney

HICKLING LANE
ROAD MAIN

Grantham Canal (Disused)

Bridge Farm

MILL LANE

Church Farm
Waterlane Farm
Elms Farm

Barland Fields

Melton Mowbray

MARSH'S PADDOCK

LE14

Cricket Grd.
Pav.

Home Farm
CLAWSON LANE
Manor Ho.
THE GREEN
Hall
HARLES ACRES

HICKLING

LONG LA.
FAULKS LA.
(PUDDING LA.)
Oak Farm
WASH PIT LA.
STREET LANE

Hickling Standard

Lincoln Lodge
The Blossoms
BRIDEGATE

Parson's Thorns

Hill Farm

The Trussel

Hill Top Farm

Hickling Standard

GREEN

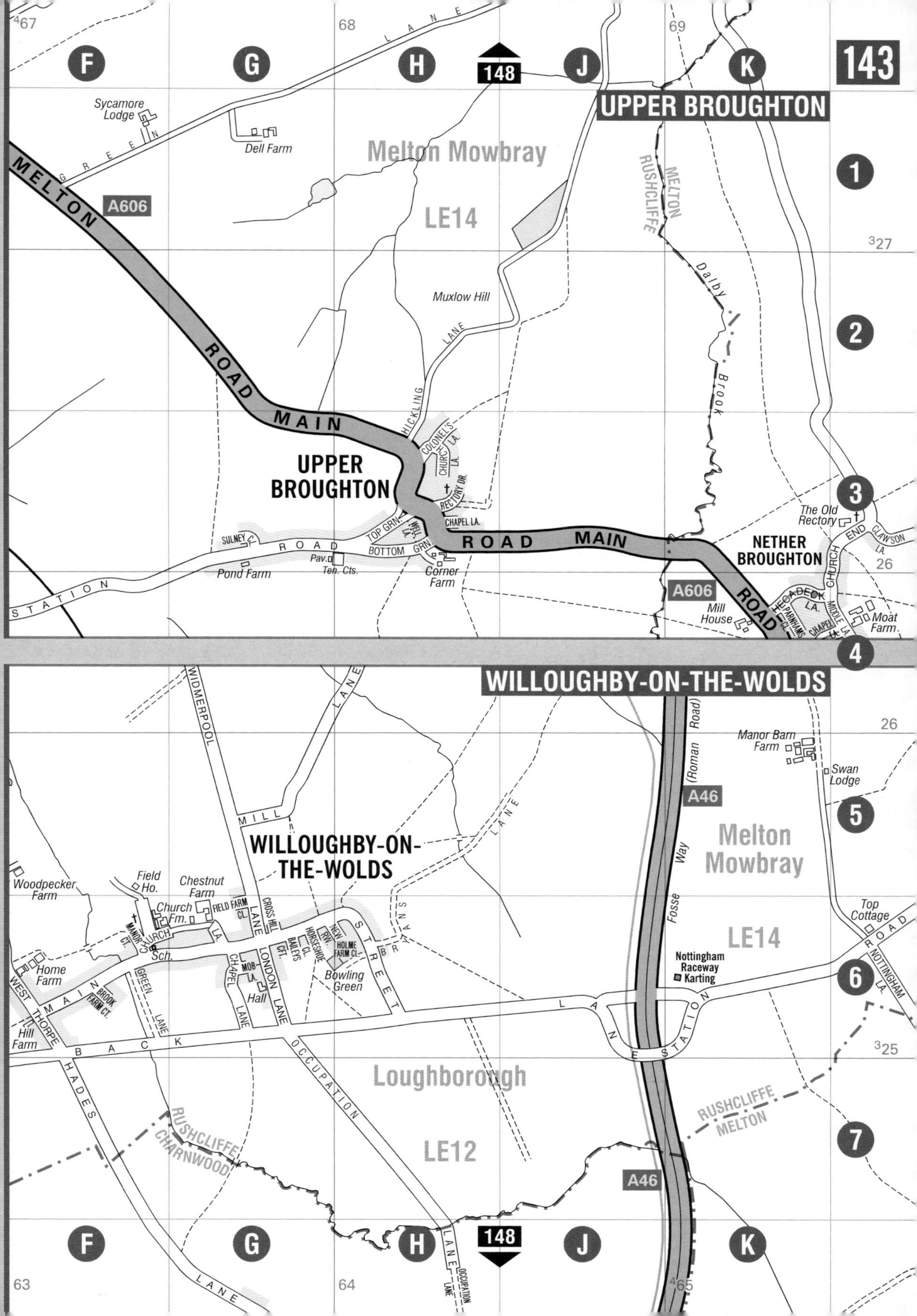

F **G** **H** [148] **J** **K**

UPPER BROUGHTON

1

2

3

4

Sycamore Lodge

Dell Farm

MELTON
A606

GREEN

Melton Mowbray

LE14

MELTON

RUSHCLIFFE

Dalby Brook

327

Muxlow Hill

ROAD MAIN

HICKLING LANE

COLONELS LA.
CHURCH LA.

UPPER
BROUGHTON

RECTORY DR.

CHAPEL LA.

The Old
Rectory

SULNEY CL.

TOP GRN.

WELL GRN.

ROAD MAIN

CHURCH END

CLAWSON LA.

26

Pond Farm

STATION

ROAD

BOTTOM GRN.

Pav.
Ten. Cts.

Corner
Farm

NETHER
BROUGHTON

MOORE LA.

A606

Mill
House

HECADECK LA.

PARNHAMS

CHAPEL LA.

Moat
Farm

ROAD

WILLOUGHBY-ON-THE-WOLDS

5

6

7

WIDMERPOOL LANE

MILL

LANE

LANE

(Roman Road)
A46

Manor Barn
Farm

Swan
Lodge

26

Woodpecker
Farm

Field
Ho.

Chestnut
Farm

**WILLOUGHBY-ON-
THE-WOLDS**

CROSS HILL

FIELD FARM CL.

FIELD FARM

CHURCH FM.

MANOR CFT.

Church

Sch.

LA.

NEW
FEN
CL.

HORSESHOE
CL.

BALEYS

HOLME
FARM CL.

BRIANS LANE

STREET

Fosse Way

Melton
Mowbray

LE14

Top
Cottage

ROAD

NOTTINGHAM LA.

Nottingham
Raceway
Karting

Home
Farm

WEST THORPE

BROOK
FARM CT.

GREEN LANE

MOB.
LA.

LONDON LANE

CHAPEL
LANE

Hall

Bowling
Green

325

Hill
Farm

MAIN

BACK

HADES LANE

RUSHCLIFFE
CHARNWOOD

OCCUPATION LANE

LANE

STATION

RUSHCLIFFE
MELTON

Loughborough

LE12

A46

LANE

OCCUPATION LANE

F **G** **H** [148] **J** **K**

467 68 69

63 64 65

144
DONCASTER
ROTHERHAM
MEXBOROUGH
CONISBROUGH
SWINTON
RAWMARSH
MALTBY
BENTLEY
ADWICK LE STREET
WORKSOP
146
Askern
Stainforth
Hatfield
Armthorpe
Bessacarr
Warmsworth
New Edlington
New Rossington
Bawtry
Harworth
Tickhill
Thurcroft
Dinnington
North Anston
Carlton in Lindrick
Aughton
Wales
Kiveton Park
Whitwell
Clowne
Barlborough
Sprotbrough
Goldthorpe
South Elmsall
South Kirkby
Carcroft
Skellow
DONCASTER NORTH
WOODALL
BLYTH
ROBIN HOOD DONCASTER SHEFFIELD
NOTTING

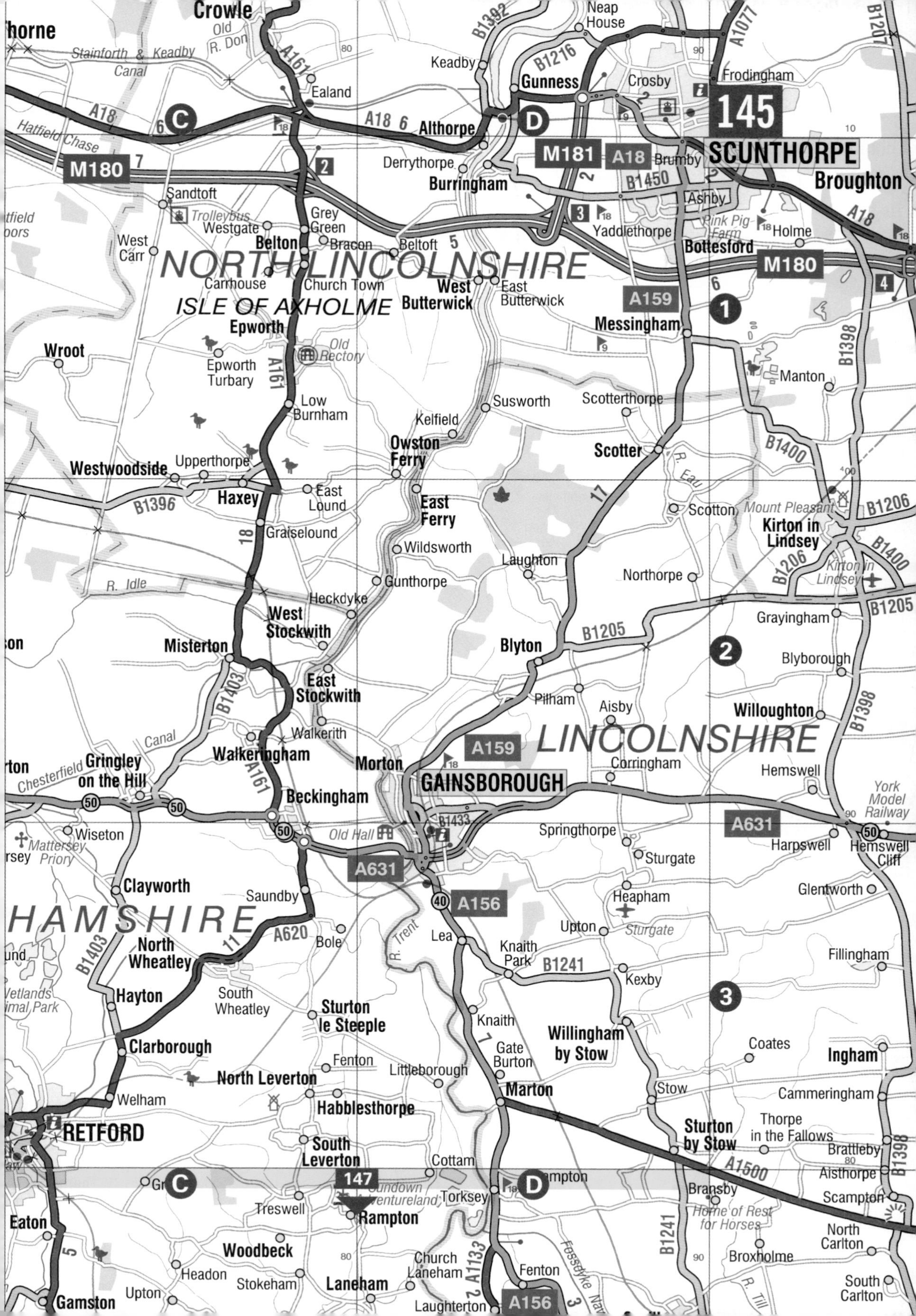

145
SCUNTHORPE
GAINSBOROUGH
RETFORD
NORTH LINCOLNSHIRE
ISLE OF AXHOLME
LINCOLNSHIRE
HAMSHIRE
Crowle
Old R. Don
Stainforth & Keadby Canal
Hatfield Chase
Keadby
Neap House
Gunness
Crosby
Frodingham
Ealand
Althorpe
Derrythorpe
Burringham
Brumby
Broughton
Ashby
Bottesford
Yaddlethorpe
Pink Pig Farm
Holme
Sandtoft
Trolleybus
Westgate
West Carr
Belton
Grey Green
Bracon
Beltoft
Carrhouse
Church Town
West Butterwick
East Butterwick
Epworth
Old Rectory
Epworth Turbary
Wroot
Messingham
Manton
Low Burnham
Susworth
Scotterthorpe
Kelfield
Owston Ferry
Scotter
Westwoodside
Upperthorpe
Haxey
East Lound
East Ferry
Scotton
Mount Pleasant
Kirton in Lindsey
Graiseland
Wildsworth
Laughton
Northorpe
R. Idle
Gunthorpe
Heckdyke
West Stockwith
Misterton
Blyton
Grayingham
Blyborough
East Stockwith
Pilham
Aisby
Willoughton
Walkerith
Walkeringham
Canal
Chesterfield
Gringley on the Hill
Morton
Corringham
Hemswell
York Model Railway
Beckingham
Wiseton
Mattersey Priory
Old Hall
Springthorpe
Sturgate
Harpswell
Hemswell Cliff
Clayworth
Saundby
Heapham
Glentworth
Upton
Bole
Lea
Knaith Park
R. Trent
North Wheatley
South Wheatley
Kexby
Fillingham
Hayton
Sturton le Steeple
Knaith
Willingham by Stow
Clarborough
Fenton
Littleborough
Gate Burton
Coates
Ingham
North Leverton
Marton
Welham
Habblesthorpe
Stow
Cammeringham
South Leverton
Sturton by Stow
Thorpe in the Fallows
Brattleby
Cottam
Aisthorpe
Sundown Adventureland
Torksey
Bransby
Scampton
Treswell
Rampton
Home of Rest for Horses
North Carlton
Eaton
Woodbeck
Church Laneham
Broxholme
Headon
Stokeham
Laneham
Fenton
South Carlton
Gamston
Upton
Laughterton
R. Till
M180
M181
A18
A159
A161
A631
A156
A620
A1500
A1133
A1077
B1392
B1216
B1207
B1450
B1396
B1398
B1400
B1206
B1205
B1403
B1433
B1241
147

146
144
148
A57
Beighton
Wales
Todwick
Woodsetts
Ryton
Bilby
M1
Kiveton Park
South Anston
A57
Chesterfield Canal
Holbrook
Norwood
Thorpe Salvin
Shireoaks
Rhodesia
Netherthorpe
Ranby
Babworth
Scofton
NT Mr Straw's House
A620
Killamarsh
WOODALL
WORKSOP
A1
Ordsall
Spinkhill
A619
Steetley Chapel
B6079
Renishaw
A618
Barlborough
Manton
A57
B6420
Clowne
Whitwell
A60
B6043
Hodthorpe
Belph
Clumber Park
Hardwick Village
A614
Gamston
Mastin Moor
Elkesley
A616
B6042
B6034
Chapel NT
R. Poulter
Woodthorpe
B6418
Creswell Crags
Harley Gallery
Stanfree
Elmton
Creswell
Holbeck
Bothamsall Castle
Poolsbrook
Shuttlewood
Holbeck Woodhouse
Great Lake
Carburton
Haughton
Bevercotes
DERBYSHIRE
THE DUKERIES
B6387
Whaley
Whaley Thorns
Norton
Perlethorpe
B6417
Gallery
Thoresby
Walesby
Cuckney
Bolsover
Langwith
Meden Vale
Nether Langwith
A632
Budby
Carr Vale
Hillstown
Scarcliffe
Upper Langwith
Willow Tree Farm
Church Warsop
Warsop Vale
B6037
Major Oak
New Ollerton
Boughton
Palterton
B6034
A616
Shirebrook
Warsop
Sherwood Forest
Edwinstowe
Heath
Stony Houghton
Ollerton
Bramley Vale
Glapwell
Sookholme
A6075
Lidgett
Wellow
Doe Lea
New Houghton
B6407
R. Meden
B6035
Kings Clipstone
R. Maun
Watermill
Rowthorne
A60
Rufford Abbey
Ault Hucknall
Pleasley
MANSFIELD WOODHOUSE
King John's Palace
Hardwick Hall NT
A617
Clipstone
Kneesall
Palace
NOTTINGH
A6191
Old Hall
Moorhaigh
Sherwood Pines
SHERWOOD PINES FOREST PARK
M1
Teversal
B6030
Forest Town
Eakring
A617
B6014
Skegby
A6075
A6117
A614
TIBSHELF
MANSFIELD
Bilsthorpe
Stanton Hill
Huthwaite
SUTTON IN ASHFIELD
Newton
A6191
Blackwell
B6026
Fulwood
B6023
B6020
Rainworth
Kirklington
A617
White Post Farm
A38
KIRKBY-IN-ASHFIELD
B6021
B6018
Blidworth
Farnsfield
B6139
A60
Wheelgate Adventure Park
Edingley
B6019
B6020
Pinxton
John King
Nuncargate
A611
Halam
The Workhouse NT
Ravenshead
Annesley Woodhouse
Annesley
A6097
Newstead Abbey
Longdale Craft Centre
B600
Selston
Newstead
R. Leen
B683
Oxton
B6386
Southwell
Halloughton
Bagthorpe
Jacksdale
Underwood
Pumping Station
Hall
Papplewick
A614
Friezeland
Linby
A608
B6011
New Brinsley
HUCKNALL
SHERWOOD FOREST
B6386
Beauvale Priory
Thurgarton
Brinsley
M1
Calverton
Folk
Epperstone
A610
B600
D.H. Lawrence
Westville
B683
Woodborough
Moorgreen
Beauvale
Newthorpe
B6009
Bestwood Village
Gonalston
Hucknall
A60
Lowdham
EASTWOOD
A612
Langley
Kimberley
Bulwell
Cocker Beck

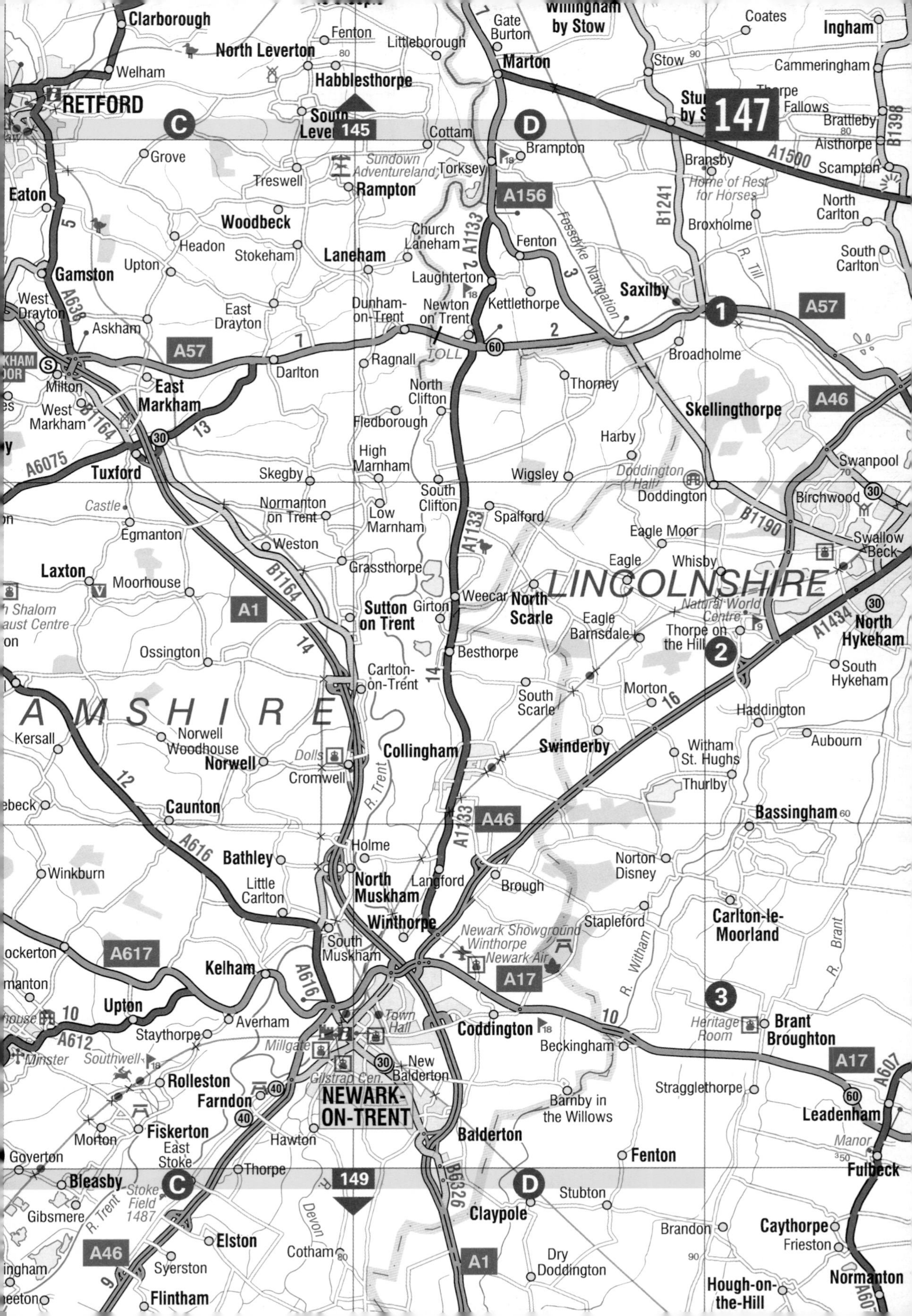

147
Clarborough
Fenton
Littleborough
Gate Burton
Willingham by Stow
Coates
Ingham
North Leverton
Welham
Habblesthorpe
Marton
Stow
Cammeringham
RETFORD
Thorpe in the Fallows
Brattleby
B1398
C
145
D
Cottam
Brampton
Aisthorpe
A1500
Grove
Sundown Adventureland
Torksey
Bransby
Scampton
Treswell
Rampton
A156
Home of Rest for Horses
Eaton
B1241
North Carlton
Woodbeck
Broxholme
Headon
Stokeham
Church Laneham
Laneham
A1133
Fenton
Fossdyke Navigation
R. Till
South Carlton
Upton
Gamston
Laughterton
Saxilby
West Drayton
A638
East Drayton
Dunham-on-Trent
Newton on Trent
Kettlethorpe
1
A57
Askham
TOLL
Broadholme
A57
Ragnall
Darlton
Milton
North Clifton
Thorney
East Markham
West Markham
B1164
Fledborough
Skellingthorpe
A46
Harby
A6075
Tuxford
High Marnham
Skegby
Wigsley
Doddington Hall
Doddington
Swanpool
Birchwood
Castle
Normanton on Trent
Low Marnham
South Clifton
Spalford
B1190
Egmanton
Weston
Eagle Moor
Swallow Beck
Laxton
Moorhouse
Grassthorpe
Eagle
Whisby
LINCOLNSHIRE
B1164
A1
Sutton on Trent
Girton
Weecar
North Scarle
Natural World Centre
Eagle Barnsdale
Thorpe on the Hill
2
A1434
North Hykeham
Ossington
Besthorpe
South Hykeham
Carlton-on-Trent
South Scarle
Morton
Haddington
Kersall
Norwell Woodhouse
Norwell
Dolls
Cromwell
Collingham
Swinderby
Witham St. Hughs
Aubourn
Thurlby
R. Trent
Caunton
A1133
A46
Bassingham
Holme
A616
Bathley
Norton Disney
Winkburn
Little Carlton
North Muskham
Langford
Brough
Winthorpe
Stapleford
Carlton-le-Moorland
Newark Showground
Winthorpe
Newark Air
R. Witham
R. Brant
A617
South Muskham
Kelham
A616
A17
3
Upton
Averham
Town Hall
Coddington
Heritage Room
Brant Broughton
A612
Staythorpe
Millgate
Beckingham
Minster
Southwell
New Balderton
A17
Rolleston
Gilstrap Cen.
Stragglethorpe
A607
Farndon
NEWARK-ON-TRENT
Barnby in the Willows
Leadenham
Morton
Fiskerton
Hawton
Balderton
Manor
East Stoke
Fenton
Fulbeck
Goverton
Thorpe
149
C
D
Bleasby
Stoke Field 1487
B6326
Stubton
Claypole
Gibsmere
R. Trent
R. Devon
Brandon
Caythorpe
Frieston
Elston
A46
Syerston
Cotham
Dry Doddington
A1
Normanton
Flintham
Hough-on-the-Hill

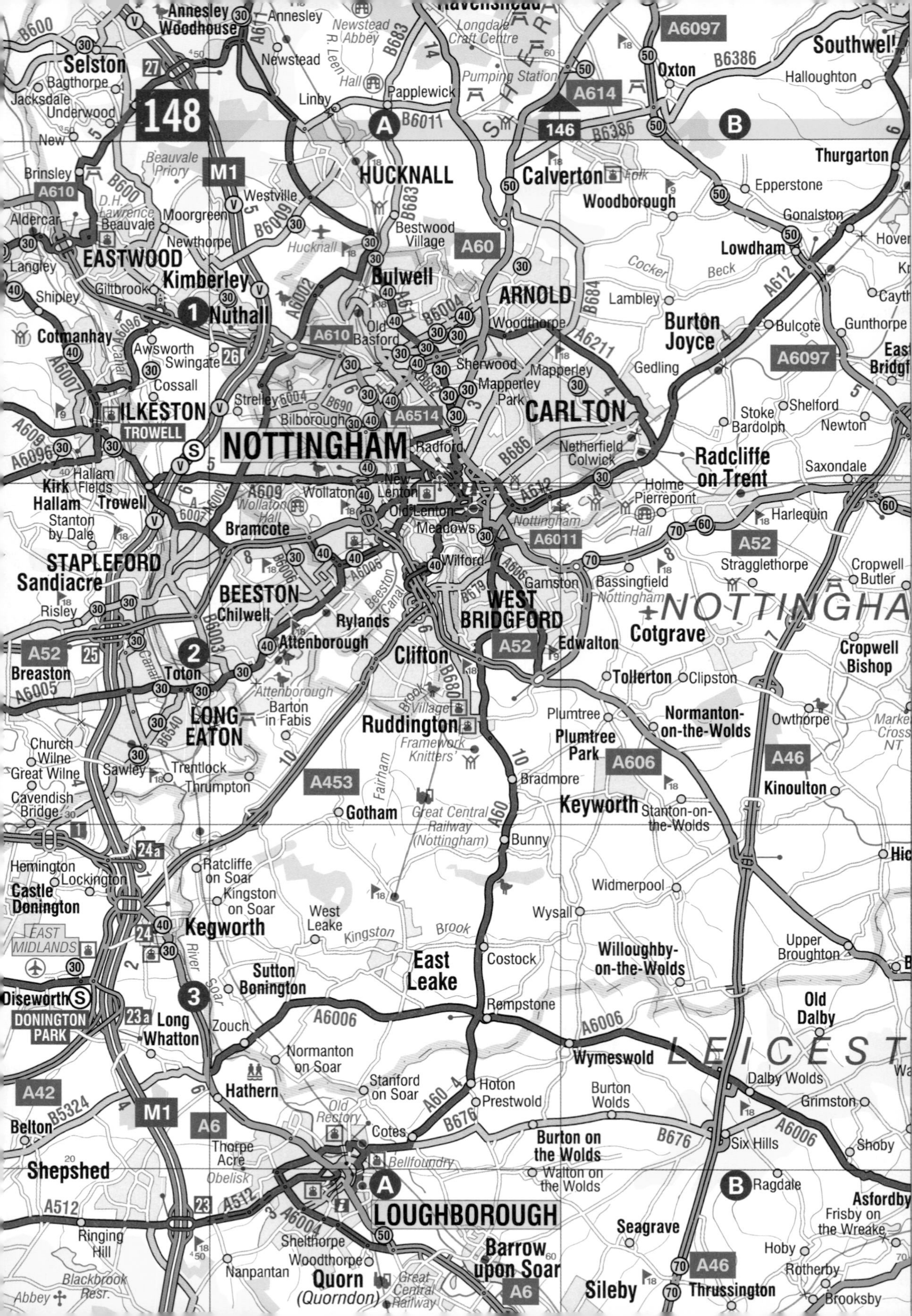

148
146
Annesley Woodhouse
Annesley
Newstead Abbey
Newstead
Ravenshead
Longdale Craft Centre
Pumping Station
Southwell
Oxton
Halloughton
Selston
Bagthorpe
Jacksdale
Underwood
New
Linby
Papplewick
Calverton
Thurgarton
Epperstone
Gonalston
Lowdham
Brinsley
Beauvale Priory
D.H. Lawrence
Aldercar
Beauvale
Moorgreen
Westville
Newthorpe
HUCKNALL
Hucknall
Bestwood Village
Woodborough
Langley
EASTWOOD
Kimberley
Giltbrook
Shipley
Nuthall
Bulwell
ARNOLD
Lambley
Cocker Beck
Burton Joyce
Bulcote
Gunthorpe
Caythorpe
Hoveringham
Cotmanhay
Awsworth
Swingate
Cossall
Old Basford
Woodthorpe
Sherwood
Mapperley
Mapperley Park
Gedling
East Bridgford
Strelley
Bilborough
ILKESTON
TROWELL
CARLTON
Stoke Bardolph
Shelford
Newton
NOTTINGHAM
Radford
Netherfield
Colwick
Radcliffe on Trent
Saxondale
Kirk Hallam
Hallam Fields
Trowell
Wollaton
Wollaton Hall
New Lenton
Old Lenton
Meadows
Nottingham
Holme Pierrepont
Hall
Harlequin
Stanton by Dale
Bramcote
Wilford
Gamston
Bassingfield
Stragglethorpe
Cropwell Butler
STAPLEFORD
Sandiacre
Risley
BEESTON
Chilwell
Beeston Canal
Rylands
Attenborough
WEST BRIDGFORD
Edwalton
Cotgrave
Cropwell Bishop
NOTTINGHAM
Breaston
Toton
Clifton
Tollerton
Clipston
LONG EATON
Barton in Fabis
Ruddington
Village
Framework Knitters'
Plumtree
Plumtree Park
Normanton-on-the-Wolds
Owthorpe
Church Wilne
Great Wilne
Sawley
Trentlock
Thrumpton
Cavendish Bridge
Bradmore
Kinoulton
Keyworth
Stanton-on-the-Wolds
Gotham
Fairham Brook
Great Central Railway (Nottingham)
Bunny
Hemington
Lockington
Castle Donington
Ratcliffe on Soar
Kingston on Soar
Widmerpool
West Leake
Kingston Brook
Wysall
EAST MIDLANDS
Kegworth
River Soar
East Leake
Costock
Willoughby-on-the-Wolds
Upper Broughton
Sutton Bonington
Diseworth
DONINGTON PARK
Long Whatton
Zouch
Rempstone
Old Dalby
Normanton on Soar
Wymeswold
LEICESTERSHIRE
Hathern
Hoton
Prestwold
Stanford on Soar
Burton Wolds
Dalby Wolds
Grimston
Belton
Old Rectory
Cotes
Burton on the Wolds
Six Hills
Shoby
Thorpe Acre
Shepshed
Bellfoundry
Obelisk
Walton on the Wolds
Ragdale
Asfordby
Frisby on the Wreake
LOUGHBOROUGH
Ringing Hill
Shelthorpe
Woodthorpe
Seagrave
Barrow upon Soar
Hoby
Nanpantan
Quorn (Quorndon)
Great Central Railway
Sileby
Thrussington
Rotherby
Brooksby
Blackbrook Resr.
Abbey
M1
A610
A60
A614
A6097
B6386
B6011
B683
A611
A6002
B6009
B600
A612
A6211
B684
B6004
A6514
B690
B686
A609
A6096
A6007
A609
A6011
A52
A606
A6005
B6003
B6540
B679
B680
A453
A46
A6006
A42
A6
B5324
B676
A512
A6004

A612
Staythorpe
Millgate
Room
Broughton
Minster
Southwell
A46
New Balderton
NEWARK-ON-TRENT
Beckingham
A17
A607
Rolleston
Farndon
Gilstrap Cen.
Barnby in the Willows
Stragglethorpe
Leadenham
Morton
Fiskerton
Hawton
Balderton
Manor
C
D
Fenton
149
Goverton
147
A1
Fulbeck
Bleasby
East Stoke
Thorpe
B6326
Stubton
Gibsmere
R. Trent
East Stoke 1487
R. Devon
Claypole
Brandon
Caythorpe
Frieston
Elston
Cotham
Dry Doddington
Syerston
Normanton
Hough-on-the-Hill
Flintham
Sibthorpe
Hougham
Carlton Scroop
Gelston
1
Shelton
Staunton in the Vale
Long Bennington
Westborough
A46
River Witham
Screveton
Hawksworth
Marston
Hall
A153
Honington
Flawborough
Kilvington
Foston
Thoroton
Car Colston
Alverton
Beck
Scarrington
LINCOLNSHIRE
Barkston
Orston
Syston
Bingham
Aslockton
Normanton
Allington
Castle
Foston
Belton
Belton House NT
B1174
A607
Bottesford
GRANTHAM NORTH
Great Gonerby
Whatton
Elton
Easthorpe
A52
Sedgebrook
Manthorpe
Sutton
Muston
Londonthorpe
Vale of Belvoir
Gonerby Hill Foot
R. Smite
Fithby
Barrowby
Grantham House NT
MSHIRE
Granby
Stenwith
Earlesfield
GRANTHAM
Barnstone
Barkestone-le-Vale
Redmile
Woolsthorpe By Belvoir
Langar
2
A1
A52
Naturescape
Denton Resr.
Colston Bassett
Plungar
Belvoir
B1174
Canal (dis.)
Denton
Harlaxton
Woodnook
B6403
Little Ponton
Grantham
Knipton
R. Devon
Harston
A607
Stathern
Harby
Knipton Resr.
Stroxton
Great Ponton
Hungerton
Hose
Branston
Wyville
Eastwell
Eaton
Croxton Kerrial
Witham
Water Spout
Long Clawson
Stoke Rochford
Easton
Walled
Bescaby
Saltby
Skillington
Nether Broughton
Goadby Marwood
Waltham on the Wolds
A606
Clawson Hill
Woolsthorpe-by-Colsterworth
3
Manor
Scalford
Stonesby
Sproxton
Colsterworth
A151
Chadwell
Holwell
ERSHIRE
Ab Kettleby
Stainby
Buckminster
COLSTERWORTH
A607
Potter Hill
B676
B6403
Coston
Twinlakes Theme Park
Saxelbye or Saxelby
Sewstern
Gunby
North Witham
R. Eye
Thorpe Arnold
Garthorpe
Asfordby Hill
Freeby
Saxby
South Witham
A6006
C
B676
D
Wyfordby
Wymondham
R. Wreake
MELTON MOWBRAY
Brentingby
Stapleford
Thistleton
A1
Kirby Bellars
A607
A606
B6047
Edmondthorpe
RUTLAND
Burton Lazars
Market Overton
Teigh

INDEX

Including Streets, Places & Areas, Industrial Estates,
Selected Flats & Walkways, Service Areas, Stations and Selected Places of Interest.

HOW TO USE THIS INDEX

1. Each street name is followed by its Postcode District and then by its Locality abbreviation(s) and then by its map reference;
   e.g. **Abbey Bri.** NG7: Lent . . . .6F **95** is in the NG7 Postcode District and the Lenton Locality and is to be found in square 6F on page **95**.
   The page number is shown in bold type.

2. A strict alphabetical order is followed in which Av., Rd., St., etc. (though abbreviated) are read in full and as part of the street name;
   e.g. **Ashcourt Gdns.** appears after **Ash Ct.** but before **Ash Cres.**

3. Streets and a selection of flats and walkways that cannot be shown on street map pages **6-143**, appear in the index with the thoroughfare to which they are connected shown in brackets; e.g. **Abbey Gro.** *S80: Work* . . . . 3G **21** (off Abbey St.)

4. Addresses that are in more than one part are referred to as not continuous.

5. Places and areas are shown in the index in **BLUE TYPE** and the map reference is to the actual map square in which the town centre or area is located and not to the place name shown on the map. Map references for entries that appear on street map pages **6-143** are shown first, with references to road map pages **144-149** shown in brackets;
   e.g. **ARNOLD** 7H **77** (1A **148**)

6. An example of a selected place of interest is **Bassetlaw Mus.** 3F **23**

7. An example of a station is **Aslockton Station (Rail)** . . . . 4D **102**. Included are Rail **(Rail)**, Nottingham Express Transit **(NET)** and **Park & Ride**.
   e.g. **Forest, The (Park & Ride) (Nottingham)** 1H **95**

8. Service Areas are shown in the index in **BOLD CAPITAL TYPE**; e.g. **TIBSHELF SERVICE AREA** 4A **44**

9. Map references for entries that appear on large scale pages **6** & **7** are shown first, with small scale map references shown in brackets;
   e.g. **Abbotsford Dr.** NG3: Nott 2G **7** (2A **96**)

GENERAL ABBREVIATIONS

All. : Alley	**Ent.** : Enterprise	**Pde.** : Parade
App. : Approach	**Est.** : Estate	**Pk.** : Park
Arc. : Arcade	**Fld.** : Field	**Pas.** : Passage
Av. : Avenue	**Flds.** : Fields	**Pl.** : Place
Bk. : Back	**Gdns.** : Gardens	**Pct.** : Precinct
Blvd. : Boulevard	**Gth.** : Garth	**Prom.** : Promenade
Bri. : Bridge	**Ga.** : Gate	**Res.** : Residential
Bldg. : Building	**Gt.** : Great	**Ri.** : Rise
Bldgs. : Buildings	**Grn.** : Green	**Rd.** : Road
Bungs. : Bungalows	**Gro.** : Grove	**Shop.** : Shopping
Bus. : Business	**Hgts.** : Heights	**Sth.** : South
C'way. : Causeway	**Ho.** : House	**Sq.** : Square
Cen. : Centre	**Ind.** : Industrial	**Sta.** : Station
Chu. : Church	**Info.** : Information	**St.** : Street
Circ. : Circle	**Intl.** : International	**Ter.** : Terrace
Cir. : Circus	**La.** : Lane	**Trad.** : Trading
Cl. : Close	**Lit.** : Little	**Up.** : Upper
Comn. : Common	**Lwr.** : Lower	**Va.** : Vale
Cnr. : Corner	**Mnr.** : Manor	**Vw.** : View
Cott. : Cottage	**Mkt.** : Market	**Vs.** : Villas
Cotts. : Cottages	**Mdw.** : Meadow	**Vis.** : Visitors
Ct. : Court	**Mdws.** : Meadows	**Wlk.** : Walk
Cres. : Crescent	**M.** : Mews	**W.** : West
Cft. : Croft	**Mt.** : Mount	**Yd.** : Yard
Dr. : Drive	**Mus.** : Museum	
E. : East	**Nth.** : North	
Emb. : Embankment	**No.** : Number	

LOCALITY ABBREVIATIONS

Ann : **Annesley**	Bunny : **Bunny**	East M : **East Markham**
Ann W : **Annesley Woodhouse**	Bur J : **Burton Joyce**	East S : **East Stoke**
Arn : **Arnold**	Calv : **Calverton**	Eastw : **Eastwood**
Aslo : **Aslockton**	Carb : **Carburton**	Eaton : **Eaton**
Aspl : **Aspley**	Car C : **Car Colston**	Edin : **Edingley**
Atten : **Attenborough**	Carl : **Carlton**	Edwal : **Edwalton**
Aver : **Averham**	Carl L : **Carlton in Lindrick**	Edwin : **Edwinstowe**
Aws : **Awsworth**	Carl T : **Carlton-on-Trent**	Egma : **Egmanton**
Babb : **Babbington**	Caun : **Caunton**	Elk : **Elkesley**
Babw : **Babworth**	Cayt : **Caythorpe**	Elston : **Elston**
Bagt : **Bagthorpe**	Chil : **Chilwell**	Elton : **Elton**
Bald : **Balderton**	Chu L : **Church Laneham**	Epp : **Epperstone**
Barn W : **Barnby in the Willows**	Chu W : **Church Warsop**	Eve : **Everton**
Barn M : **Barnby Moor**	Cin : **Cinderhill**	Farnd : **Farndon**
Barns : **Barnstone**	Clar : **Clarborough**	Farns : **Farnsfield**
Bart F : **Barton in Fabis**	Clay : **Clayworth**	Fen : **Fenton**
Basf : **Basford**	Clif : **Clifton**	Fir : **Firbeck**
Bath : **Bathley**	C'ton : **Clipston**	Fis : **Fiskerton**
Bawt : **Bawtry**	C'tone : **Clipstone**	Flin : **Flintham**
Beck : **Beckingham**	Codd : **Coddington**	Gam : **Gamston**
Bee : **Beeston**	Coll : **Collingham**	Gate : **Gateford**
Best : **Besthorpe**	Cols B : **Colston Bassett**	Ged : **Gedling**
Bestw : **Bestwood**	Colw : **Colwick**	Gilt : **Giltbrook**
Bestw V : **Bestwood Village**	Coss : **Cossall**	Girt : **Girton**
Bilb : **Bilborough**	Costh : **Costhorpe**	Gon : **Gonalston**
Bils : **Bilsthorpe**	Costo : **Costock**	Goth : **Gotham**
Bing : **Bingham**	Cotg : **Cotgrave**	Gran : **Granby**
Birc : **Bircotes**	Cott : **Cottam**	Grass : **Grassthorpe**
Blac : **Blackwell**	Crom : **Cromwell**	Grea : **Greasley**
Blea : **Bleasby**	Crop Bi : **Cropwell Bishop**	Gri H : **Gringley on the Hill**
Blid : **Blidworth**	Crop Bu : **Cropwell Butler**	Grove : **Grove**
Blyth : **Blyth**	Cuck : **Cuckney**	Gun : **Gunthorpe**
Bol : **Bolham**	Dane : **Danethorpe**	Habb : **Habblesthorpe**
Bou : **Boughton**	Darf : **Darfoulds**	Halam : **Halam**
Bram : **Bramcote**	Darl : **Darlton**	Harby : **Harby**
Brink : **Brinkley**	Drake : **Drakeholes**	Harwe : **Harwell**
Brins : **Brinsley**	Dri N : **Drisney Nook**	Harwo : **Harworth**
Brox : **Broxtowe**	Dun T : **Dunham-on-Trent**	Hath : **Hathern**
Bud : **Budby**	Eakr : **Eakring**	Haw : **Hawton**
Bulc : **Bulcote**	East B : **East Bridgford**	Hay : **Hayton**
Bulw : **Bulwell**	East L : **East Leake**	Hea : **Heanor**

Hick : **Hickling**
Hick P : **Hickling Pastures**
High M : **High Marnham**
Hilc : **Hilcote**
Hock : **Hockerton**
Hods : **Hodsock**
Hodt : **Hodthorpe**
Holb : **Holbeck**
Holb W : **Holbeck Woodhouse**
Hol : **Holme**
Hol P : **Holme Pierrepont**
Hove : **Hoveringham**
Huck : **Hucknall**
Huth : **Huthwaite**
H Grn : **Hyson Green**
Ilk : **Ilkeston**
Jack : **Jacksdale**
Kel : **Kelham**
Kett : **Kettlethorpe**
Key : **Keyworth**
Kimb : **Kimberley**
K Cli : **Kings Clipstone**
King : **Kingston on Soar**
Kin : **Kinoulton**
Kirk A : **Kirkby-in-Ashfield**
Kirk : **Kirklington**
Kirt : **Kirton**
Knee : **Kneeton**
Lamb : **Lambley**
Lane : **Laneham**
Lang : **Langar**
Lang M : **Langley Mill**
Lango : **Langold**
Langw : **Langwith**
Lax : **Laxton**
Lent : **Lenton**
Lent A : **Lenton Abbey**
Lin : **Linby**
Lit C : **Little Carlton**
Lit G : **Little Gringley**
Long E : **Long Eaton**
Lound : **Lound**
Lowd : **Lowdham**
Mans : **Mansfield**
Mans W : **Mansfield Woodhouse**
Mapp : **Mapperley**
Mapp P : **Mapperley Park**
Mkt W : **Market Warsop**
Matt : **Mattersey**
Matt T : **Mattersey Thorpe**
Mayt : **Maythorne**
Mede V : **Meden Vale**
Miss : **Misson**
Mist : **Misterton**
Moor : **Moorhouse**
Mort : **Morton**
Neth B : **Nether Broughton**
Neth : **Netherfield**
Neth L : **Nether Langwith**
New T : **Newark-on-Trent**
New B : **New Balderton**
New H : **New Houghton**
Newi : **Newington**
New O : **New Ollerton**
News : **Newstead**
Newth : **Newthorpe**
Newton : **Newton**

Newt T : **Newton on Trent**
Norm : **Normanton**
Norm S : **Normanton on Soar**
Norm W : **Normanton-on-the-Wolds**
Norm T : **Normanton on Trent**
Nth C : **North Clifton**
Nth L : **North Leverton**
Nth M : **North Muskham**
Nth S : **North Scarle**
Nth W : **North Wheatley**
Nort : **Norton**
Norw : **Norwell**
Norw W : **Norwell Woodhouse**
Nott : **Nottingham**
Nunc : **Nuncargate**
Nuth : **Nuthall**
Oldc : **Oldcotes**
Oll : **Ollerton**
Omp : **Ompton**
Ord : **Ordsall**
Ors : **Orston**
Owt : **Owthorpe**
Oxt : **Oxton**
Pap : **Papplewick**
Perl : **Perlethorpe**
Pinx : **Pinxton**
Plea : **Pleasley**
Plum : **Plumtree**
Pye B : **Pye Bridge**
Rad T : **Radcliffe on Trent**
Radf : **Radford**
Ragn : **Ragnall**
Rain : **Rainworth**
Ramp : **Rampton**
Rans : **Ranskill**
Rave : **Ravenshead**
Redh : **Redhill**
Remp : **Rempstone**
Retf : **Retford**
Rhod : **Rhodesia**
Rock : **Rockley**
Roll : **Rolleston**
Rudd : **Ruddington**
Ruff : **Rufford**
Sand : **Sandiacre**
Saun : **Saundby**
Sax : **Saxilby**
Saxon : **Saxondale**
Scaf : **Scaftworth**
Scar : **Scarrington**
Scre : **Screveton**
Scro : **Scrooby**
Sels : **Selston**
Serl : **Serlby**
Shel : **Shelford**
Sher : **Sherwood**
Ship : **Shipley**
Shire : **Shireoaks**
Sibt : **Sibthorpe**
Skeg : **Skegby**
Sook : **Sookholme**
Sth C : **South Clifton**
Sth L : **South Leverton**
Sth M : **South Muskham**
Sth N : **South Normanton**
Sth S : **South Scarle**
Sout : **Southwell**

Sth W : **South Wheatley**
Stanf S : **Stanford on Soar**
Stant D : **Stanton-by-Dale**
Stant H : **Stanton Hill**
Stant W : **Stanton-on-the-Wolds**
Stap : **Stapleford**
Stoke B : **Stoke Bardolph**
Stony H : **Stony Houghton**
Stre : **Strelley**
Stu S : **Sturton le Steeple**
Sty : **Styrrup**
Sut B : **Sutton Bonington**
Sut L : **Sutton cum Lound**
Sut A : **Sutton in Ashfield**
Sut T : **Sutton-on-Trent**
Swin : **Swinethorpe**
Syer : **Syerston**
Teve : **Teversal**
Thor : **Thorney**
Thru : **Thrumpton**
Thur : **Thurgarton**
Tibs : **Tibshelf**
Tick : **Tickhill**
Tith : **Tithby**
Toll : **Tollerton**
Top V : **Top Valley**
Torw : **Torworth**
Toton : **Toton**
Tres : **Treswell**
Trow : **Trowell**
Tuxf : **Tuxford**
Unde : **Underwood**
Upp B : **Upper Broughton**
Upton : **Upton**
Wale : **Walesby**
Walk : **Walkeringham**
Wall : **Wallingwells**
Wars : **Warsop Vale**
Want : **Watnall**
Welb : **Welbeck**
Welh : **Welham**
Well : **Wellow**
West Br : **West Bridgford**
West Bu : **West Burton**
West D : **West Drayton**
West L : **West Leake**
West M : **West Markham**
West S : **West Stockwith**
Weston : **Weston**
Westw : **Westwood**
Whal T : **Whaley Thorns**
What : **Whatton**
Widm : **Widmerpool**
Wigs : **Wigsley**
Wigt : **Wigthorpe**
Wilf : **Wilford**
Will W : **Willoughby on the Wolds**
Wint : **Winthorpe**
Wise : **Wiseton**
Woll : **Wollaton**
Woodbe : **Woodbeck**
Woodbo : **Woodborough**
Woods : **Woodsetts**
Woodt : **Woodthorpe**
Work : **Worksop**
Wym : **Wymeswold**
Wys : **Wysall**

A

Aaron Cl. NG11: Wilf 2J **107**
Abba Cl. NG16: Kimb 7K **73**
Abbey Bri. NG7: Lent .6F **95**
Abbey Cir. NG2: West Br 2D **108**
Abbey Cl. NG13: Aslo .3C **102**
  NG15: Huck 6E **66**
Abbey Ct. NG7: Lent .4G **95**
  NG9: Bee 1A **106**
  NG18: Mans 3B **48**
Abbeydale Dr. NG18: Mans 7K **47**
Abbey Dr. NG9: Bee .2A **106**
Abbeyfield Rd. NG7: Lent 1G **107**
Abbey Gro. NG3: Nott .1C **96**
  S80: Work 3G **21**
      (off Abbey St.)
Abbey Ind. Pk. NG18: Mans 6E **46**
Abbey La. NG13: Aslo .3B **102**
Abbey M. DN10: Matt .2H **15**
  NG25: Sout 5H **131**
Abbey Rd. DN10: Matt .2J **15**
  NG2: West Br 2D **108**
  NG9: Bee 1A **106**
  NG13: Bing 3H **101**
  NG15: News 6E **60**
  NG16: Eastw 4F **73**
  NG17: Kirk A 6C **52**
  NG18: Mans 3A **48**
  NG21: Blid 6K **55**
  NG21: Edwin 7F **37**
Abbey St. NG7: Lent .6F **95**
  S80: Work 3G **21**
Abbey Trade Pk. NG18: Mans 6E **46**
Abbot Cl. NG12: Key .6H **117**
Abbotsbury Cl. NG5: Top V 5K **75**

Abbots Cl. NG5: Arn 1A **86**
Abbots Dr. NG15: Huck 7E **66**
Abbotsford Dr. NG3: Nott 2G **7** (2A **96**)
Abbots Rd. NG15: Huck 7E **66**
Abbot St. NG16: Aws .3B **82**
Abbots Wlk. NG15: Huck 7E **66**
Abbots Way NG8: Woll 4C **94**
Abbott Cres. NG22: Farns 4K **57**
Abbott Lea NG19: Mans 2D **46**
Abbott Rd. NG19: Mans 3C **46**
Abbotts Cft. NG19: Mans 1E **46**
Abbott's Way NG24: New T 7E **134**
Abercarn Cl. NG6: Bulw 7H **75**
Abercarn M. NG6: Bulw 7H **75**
Aberconway St. NG21: Blid 6J **55**
Aberdeen St. NG3: Nott 4J **7** (3B **96**)
Aberford Av. NG8: Basf 7E **84**
Abingdon Dr. NG11: Rudd 2A **116**
Abingdon Gdns. NG5: Woodt 2D **86**
  NG9: Chil 5J **105**
Abingdon Rd. NG2: West Br 2D **108**
Abingdon Sq. NG8: Aspl 6C **84**
Abingdon Vw. S81: Gate 4D **18**
Abington Av. NG17: Skeg 5K **45**
AB KETTLEY 3C **149**
Ablard Gdns. NG9: Chil 7H **105**
Acacia Av. NG17: Ann W 4A **60**
Acacia Cl. NG15: Huck .1H **75**
  S80: Work 3D **20**
Acacia Ct. NG19: Mans W 1A **48**
Acacia Cres. NG4: Carl 7J **87**
Acacia Gdns. NG16: Want 6K **73**
Acacia Rd. NG24: New B 4G **137**
Acacia Wlk. NG9: Bee .3A **106**
Academy Cl. NG6: Basf 4F **85**
Acaster Cl. NG9: Bee .5C **106**
Access 26 Bus. Pk. NG16: Lang M 3A **72**

Acer Cl. NG16: Pinx 1A **58**
Ackford Dr. S80: Work 2E **20**
Acle Gdns. NG6: Bulw .5H **75**
Acorn Av. NG16: Gilt 6F **73**
Acorn Bank NG2: West Br 5J **107**
Acorn Bus. Pk. NG18: Mans 4H **47**
Acorn Cen. NG16: Lang M 3A **72**
Acorn Cl. NG24: New B 4F **137**
Acorn Dr. NG4: Ged 4K **87**
Acorn Pk. NG7: Lent .1F **107**
Acorn Theatre, The
  Worksop 3G **21**
Acorn Vw. NG17: Kirk A 5C **52**
Acorn Way NG18: Mans 6D **48**
Acre, The NG17: Kirk A 1B **60**
A'court St. NG7: H Grn .2G **95**
Acre Edge Rd. NG22: Lax . . . . .5J **39** & 6A **124**
Acton Av. NG6: Basf 3E **84**
Acton Rd. NG5: Arn 6F **77**
Adams Hill NG7: Nott .6C **94**
  NG12: Key 7J **117**
Adams Row NG25: Sout 5G **131**
Adam St. DE7: Ilk 2A **92**
Adams Wlk. NG1: Nott .5G **7**
Ada Pl. NG15: Huck 5G **67**
Adamsway NG18: Mans 7C **48**
Adbolton Av. NG4: Ged 6H **87**
Adbolton Gro. NG2: West Br 6E **96**
Adbolton La. NG2: West Br 7E **96**
  NG12: Hol P 6J **97**
Adbolton Lodge NG4: Carl 2H **97**
Adderley Cl. NG5: Bestw 1H **85**
Addington Ct. NG12: Rad T 4F **99**
Addington Rd. NG7: Radf 2G **95**
Addison Dr. NG15: Huck 5E **66**
Addison Rd. NG4: Carl .7E **86**

Addison St.—Antill St.

Addison St. NG1: Nott 1D 6 (1J 95)
Addison Vs. NG16: Eastw 5C 72
(not continuous)
Adelaide Cl. NG9: Stap 7E 92
Adelaide Gro. NG5: Top V 6A 76
Adel Dr. NG4: Ged 5H 87
Adenburgh Dr. NG9: Atten 7J 105
Adlington Cotts. NG17: Sut A 2B 52
Admirals Ct. NG18: Mans 5K 47
Adrians Cl. NG18: Mans 5A 48
Adrian's Wlk. DN22: Retf 6F 23
Adwalton Cl. NG24: New T 1H 137
ADWICK LE STREET 1A 144
ADWICK UPON DEARNE 1A 144
Aeneas Ct. NG5: Sher 7J 85
Aerial Way NG15: Huck 1F 75
Aerodrome, The NG15: Huck 3E 74
Agnes Vs. NG3: Mapp 5B 86
Aidan Gdns. NG5: Top V 4C 76
Ainsdale Cl. NG24: Bald 7H 137
Ainsdale Cres. NG8: Cin 4B 84
Ainsdale Grn. DN22: Ord 7D 22
Ainsley Rd. NG8: Aspl 2E 94
Ainsworth Dr. NG2: Nott 7J 95
Aintree Cl. NG16: Kimb 7J 73
Aira Cl. NG2: Gam 3G 109
Airedale S81: Work 5J 19
Airedale Ct. NG9: Chil 5F 105
Airedale Wlk. NG8: Woll 5H 93
AISBY 2D 145
AISTHORPE 3D 145
Aitchison Av. NG15: Huck 6F 67
Alandene Av. NG16: Want 7A 74
Albans Ct. NG19: Mans W 7E 42
Albany Cl. NG5: Arn 7G 77
NG15: Huck 1C 74
NG19: Mans W 1J 47
Albany Ct. NG9: Stap 7D 92
Albany Dr. NG19: Mans W 1J 47
Albany Pl. NG19: Mans W 1J 47
Albany Rd. NG7: Basf 7H 85
Albany St. DE7: Ilk 2A 92
Albemarle Rd. NG5: Woodt 3A 86
Alberta Av. NG16: Sels 5D 58
Alberta Ter. NG7: H Grn 7H 85
Albert Av. NG4: Carl 1E 96
NG8: Aspl 7E 84
NG9: Stap 2C 104
NG16: Jack 6A 64
NG16: Nuth 7C 74
NG24: Bald 5F 137
Albert Ball Cl. NG5: Top V 6B 76
Albert Ball Ho. NG5: Top V 6C 76
Albert Cl. NG17: Ann W 3C 60
Albert Einstein Cen. NG7: Nott 7E 94
Albert Gro. NG7: Lent, Radf 5A 6 (3G 95)
Albert Hall
Nottingham 5D 6 (4J 95)
Albert Mill NG7: Radf 2A 6 (2H 95)
Albert Rd. DN22: Retf 4E 22
NG2: West Br 1C 108
NG3: Nott 6A 86
NG7: Lent 5G 95
NG9: Bee 1B 106
NG10: Sand 3A 104
NG11: Bunny 2B 118
Albert Sq. NG7: Lent 5F 95
NG17: Sut A 1J 51
NG19: Mans W 5J 41
Albert St. NG1: Nott 6F 7 (4K 95)
NG4: Ged 6J 87
NG9: Stap 2C 104
NG12: Rad T 5E 98
NG15: Huck 6H 67
NG16: Eastw 3D 72
NG17: Stant H 4G 45
NG18: Mans 4H 47
NG19: Mans W 5J 41
NG24: New T 2C 136
S80: Work 2G 21
Albion Cl. S80: Work 2G 21
Albion Ri. NG5: Arn 5H 77
Albion Rd. NG17: Sut A 1K 51
Albion St. NG1: Nott 7E 6 (5K 95)
NG9: Bee 2A 106
NG19: Mans 1G 47
NG24: New T 1C 136
Albion Ter. DN10: Mist 3K 11
Albury Dr. NG8: Aspl 6C 84
Albury Sq. NG7: Nott 5A 6 (4H 95)
Alcester St. NG7: Lent 1F 107
Alcock Av. NG18: Mans 3K 47
Alconbury Way S81: Gate 4D 18
Aldene Ct. NG9: Chil 4J 105
Aldene Way NG14: Woodbo 2G 79
ALDERCAR 1A 148
Alder Cl. NG19: Mans W 1A 48
NG24: New B 4F 137
S80: Work 4F 21
Alder Ct. NG17: Sut A 5D 46
Alder Gdns. NG6: Bulw 7G 75
Alder Gro. NG19: Mans W 4H 41
NG22: New O 3D 38
Alderman Cl. NG9: Bee 1A 106
Aldermens Cl. NG2: Nott 6K 95
Alderney St. NG7: Lent 5G 95
Alderson Rd. S80: Work 4F 21
Alderton Rd. NG5: Bestw 1K 85
Alder Way NG12: Key 1K 119
NG17: Sut A 7H 45
Aldgate Cl. NG6: Bulw 6G 75
Aldridge Cl. NG9: Toton 7D 104
Aldrin Cl. NG6: Bulw 2A 84
Aldworth Cl. NG5: Bestw 1J 85
Aldwych Cl. NG5: Arn 5C 76
NG16: Nuth 5J 83
Alexander Av. NG16: Sels 5B 58
NG24: New T 4E 134
Alexander Cl. NG15: Huck 4H 67
Alexander Ct. NG15: News 5D 60
Alexander Dr. S81: Gate 4E 18
Alexander Fleming Bldg. NG7: Nott 1E 106
Alexander Rd. NG7: Nott 6A 6 (4H 95)
NG22: Farns 4J 57
Alexander Ter. NG16: Pinx 3A 58
Alexandra Av. NG17: Sut A 6K 45
NG18: Mans 6H 47
NG19: Mans W 5H 41
Alexandra Cres. NG9: Bee 3B 106
Alexandra Gdns. NG5: Sher 6J 85
Alexandra M. NG5: Sher 7J 85
ALEXANDRA PARK 7A 86
Alexandra Rd. DN11: Birc 2E 8
Alexandra St. NG5: Sher 7J 85
NG9: Stap 3C 104
NG16: Eastw 4D 72
NG17: Kirk A 5B 52
Alexandra Ter. NG17: Stant H 4G 45
Alford Cl. NG9: Bee 4B 106
Alford Rd. NG2: West Br 3E 108
NG12: Edwal 3E 108
Alfred Av. NG3: Mapp 5D 86
Alfred Cl. NG3: Nott 1F 7 (2K 95)
Alfred Ct. NG18: Mans 3H 47
Alfred St. NG16: Pinx 7A 50
NG17: Kirk A 7A 52
NG17: Sut A 6K 45
Alfred St. Central NG3: Nott 1F 7 (2K 95)
Alfred St. Nth. NG3: Nott 1E 6 (2K 95)
Alfred St. Sth. NG3: Nott 3J 7 (3B 96)
Alfreton Rd. DE55: Pye B 6A 58
NG7: H Grn, Radf, Nott 2A 6 (1F 95)
NG16: Pinx 7A 50
NG16: Sels 6A 58
NG16: Unde 1F 65
NG17: Sut A 4D 50
(not continuous)
Alison Av. NG15: Huck 4J 67
Alison Wlk. NG3: Nott 2G 7 (2A 96)
Allandale NG22: Bils 5B 126
Allcroft St. NG19: Mans W 5J 41
Allen Av. NG3: Mapp 6D 86
Allenby Rd. NG25: Sout 6F 131
Allendale Av. NG8: Aspl 6A 84
NG9: Atten 7J 105
Allendale Rd. NG21: Rain 3K 55
Allendale Way NG19: Mans W 1A 48
Allen Dr. NG18: Mans 5B 48
Allen Fld. Ct. NG7: Lent 7A 6 (5G 95)
ALLEN'S GREEN 6D 58
Allen's Grn. Av. NG16: Sels 6D 58
Allen St. NG15: Huck 5G 67
S80: Work 2F 21
Allen's Wlk. NG5: Arn 5H 77
All Hallows Cl. DN22: Ord 6E 22
All Hallows Dr. NG4: Ged 5J 87
All Hallows St. DN22: Ord 6E 22
All Hallows Vw. DN22: Ord 6E 22
Alliance St. NG24: New T 6D 134
ALLINGTON 1D 149
Allington Av. NG7: Lent 7A 6 (5G 95)
Allington Dr. NG19: Mans 3D 46
Allison Av. DN22: Retf 7H 23
Allison Gdns. NG9: Chil 5J 105
All Saints Ct. NG17: Huth 1E 50
All Saints St. NG7: Radf 2B 6 (2H 95)
All Saints Ter. NG7: Radf 2B 6 (2H 95)
Allsopp Dr. S81: Work 6G 19
Allwood Cl. NG18: Mans 2A 48
Allwood Dr. NG4: Carl 7H 87
Allwood Gdns. NG15: Huck 7H 67
ALMA 7D 58
Alma Cl. NG1: Nott 2E 6 (2K 95)
NG4: Ged 5K 87
Alma Hill NG16: Kimb 6J 73
Alma Rd. DN22: Retf 3G 23
NG3: Nott 2C 96
NG16: Sels 7D 58
Alma St. NG7: Basf 7H 85
ALMHOLME 1A 144
Almond Cl. NG15: Huck 1H 75
NG16: Kimb 7J 73
Almond Ct. NG2: Nott 6K 95
Almond Gro. NG17: Kirk A 5K 51
NG24: Farnd 6H 133
S80: Work 5F 21
Almond Ri. NG19: Mans W 1A 48
Almond Wlk. NG4: Ged 5K 87
Almond Way NG8: Bilb 1J 93
Alnwick Cl. NG6: Bulw 1E 84
Alpha Ter. NG1: Nott 1D 6 (2J 95)
Alpine Ct. S80: Work 3D 20
Alpine Cres. NG4: Carl 7H 87
Alpine St. NG6: Basf 5F 85
Alport Pl. NG18: Mans 3D 48
ALTHORPE 1D 145
Althorpe St. NG7: Radf 4A 6 (3H 95)
Alton Av. NG11: Wilf 5J 107
Alton Cl. NG2: West Br 6K 107
Alton Dr. NG16: Gilt 6F 73
Alum Ct. NG5: Top V 6B 76
Alverstone Rd. NG3: Mapp P 6K 85
ALVERTON 1C 149
Alvey Rd. NG24: Bald 5H 137
Alvey Ter. NG7: Radf 3F 95
Alwood Gro. NG11: Clif 6E 106
Alwyn Ct. NG9: Bee 4A 106
Alwyn Rd. NG8: Brox 5A 84
Alyth Ct. NG6: Basf 4G 85
Amanda Av. S81: Carl L 6C 12
Amanda Rd. DN11: Harwo 2C 8
Amarella La. NG17: Kirk A 1A 60
Amber Cl. NG21: Rain 2A 56
Amber Dr. NG16: Lang M 4A 72
Ambergate Rd. NG8: Bilb 1B 94
(not continuous)
Amber Gro. NG17: Sut A 3H 51
NG19: Mans W 7E 42
Amber Hill NG5: Bestw 7D 76
Amberley Ct. NG19: Mans W 7F 43
Amber Rd. NG9: Bee 6B 106
Amber St. NG18: Mans 6K 47
Amber Trad. Cen. NG16: Kimb 7H 73
Ambleside NG2: Gam 2F 109
NG22: New O 3C 38
Ambleside Dr. NG16: Eastw 3B 72
Ambleside Grange S81: Work 4G 19
Ambleside Rd. NG8: Aspl 6B 84
Ambleside Way NG4: Ged 7A 88
Amcott Av. DN10: Mist 4J 11
Amcott Way DN22: Retf 3E 22
Amelia Ct. DN22: Retf 1C 22
Amen Corner NG23: Caun 6J 127
America Gdns. NG22: Tuxf 5C 28
Amersham Ri. NG8: Aspl 6C 84
Amesbury Cir. NG8: Cin 4B 84
Amethyst Cl. NG21: Rain 2A 56
Amethyst Dr. NG17: Sut A 3H 51
Amethyst Gdns. NG18: Mans 6K 47
Amherst Ri. S81: Gate 4E 18
Ampthill Ri. NG5: Sher 3J 85
Ancaster Gdns. NG8: Woll 3B 94
Anchorage, The NG14: Bur J 3E 88
Anchor Cl. NG8: Aspl 5C 84
Anchor Ct. NG5: Bestw 7D 76
Anchor Rd. NG16: Eastw 3A 72
Anders Dr. NG6: Bulw 2A 84
Anderson Cl. NG24: Bald 6E 136
Anderson Ct. NG5: Top V 6C 76
Anderson Cres. NG9: Bee 1K 105
Andover Cl. NG8: Bilb 2C 94
Andover Rd. NG5: Bestw 1F 85
NG19: Mans 4D 46
Andrew Av. DE7: Ilk 1A 92
NG3: Mapp 5D 86
Andrew Dr. NG21: Blid 7J 55
Andrews Ct. NG9: Chil 3H 105
Anfield Cl. NG9: Toton 7F 105
Anford Cl. NG6: Bulw 2C 84
Angela Av. NG17: Nunc 3B 60
Angela Cl. NG5: Arn 4G 77
Angela Ct. NG9: Toton 7F 105
Angel All. NG1: Nott 5G 7 (4A 96)
Angelica Ct. NG13: Bing 4D 100
Angell Grn. NG11: Clif 2D 114
Angel Row NG1: Nott 5E 6 (4K 95)
Angletarn Cl. NG2: West Br 3F 109
Anglia Way NG18: Mans 7D 48
Anglia Way Ind. Est. NG18: Mans 7D 48
Angrave Cl. NG3: Nott 1K 7 (1B 96)
Angrave Rd. LE12: East L 1A 122
Angus Cl. NG5: Arn 5K 77
NG16: Kimb 2F 83
Anmer Cl. NG2: Nott 7J 95
Annan Ct. NG8: Aspl 7C 84
Anne's Cl. NG3: Mapp 5D 86
ANNESLEY 4B 60 (3A 146)
Annesley Cutting NG15: Ann 4B 60
Annesley Gro. NG1: Nott 1D 6 (2J 95)
Annesley La. NG16: Sels 6E 58
ANNESLEY LANE END 6F 59
Annesley Rd. NG2: West Br 2C 108
NG15: Ann, Huck 6B 60
(not continuous)
Annesley Way NG19: Mans 4D 46
ANNESLEY WOODHOUSE 4K 59 (3A 146)
Annesley Woodhouse Quarry Nature Reserve 5H 59
Annies Cl. NG15: Huck 1F 75
Annualhead La. NG25: Mort 5F 139
Anslow Av. NG9: Lent A 1B 106
NG17: Skeg 5K 45
Anson Cl. S81: Work 4F 19
Anson Rd. NG13: Newton 1C 100
Anstey Ri. NG3: Nott 3C 96
Anston Av. S81: Work 7F 19
Anston Ct. S81: Work 7F 19
Anthony Wharton Ct. NG11: Clif 6F 107
Antill St. NG9: Stap 3C 104

Anvil Ct. NG18: Mans 6H 47
Apollo Dr. NG6: Bulw 2A 84
Appin Rd. NG19: Mans 5D 46
Apple Av. NG24: Bald 7J 137
Appleby Cl. NG24: New T 1G 137
Appleby Ct. S81: Work 4G 19
Appleby Rd. NG19: New H 3A 40
Appledore Av. NG8: Woll 6J 93
Appledorne Way NG5: Arn 5G 77
Apple Fitness Gym
    Worksop 2G 21
Appleton Cl. NG11: Clif 1D 114
Appleton Ct. NG9: Bee 5C 106
Appleton Gdns. NG3: Mapp 2E 86
Appleton Ga. NG24: New T 1D 136
Appleton Rd. NG9: Bee 5C 106
    NG21: Blid 6K 55
Appleton St. NG20: Mkt W 4D 34
Apple Tree Cl. NG12: Edwal 5D 108
    NG24: New T 6D 134
Appletree Cl. NG25: Sout 5H 131
Appletree La. NG4: Ged 5J 87
Apple Wlk. NG3: Nott 7D 86
Applewood Cl. S81: Gate 4E 18
Applewood Gro. NG5: Sher 4A 86
Arboretum St. NG1: Nott 1C 6 (2J 95)
Arbrook Dr. NG8: Aspl 2E 94
Arbutus Cl. NG11: Clif 1D 114
Arcade, The NG24: New T 1C 136
    S81: Carl L 6C 12
Archdale Rd. NG5: Bestw 1K 85
Archer Cres. NG8: Woll 3A 94
Archer Rd. NG9: Stap 4D 104
Archers Dr. NG22: Bils 6D 126
Arches, The LE12: East L 2A 122
Arches Cl. NG16: Aws 2B 82
Arches Rd. NG18: Mans 5K 47
Arch Hill NG5: Redh 3G 77
Archway Cotts. NG25: Sout 6G 131
Archway Ct. NG7: Radf 2G 95
    (off Limpenny St.)
Arden Cl. NG9: Lent A 1B 106
    NG15: Huck 1J 75
Arden Gro. NG13: Bing 3D 100
Ardleigh Cl. NG5: Top V 5K 75
Ardmore Cl. NG2: Nott 7K 7 (5C 96)
Arena, The NG1: Nott 6D 6 (4J 95)
Argyle Cl. NG20: Mkt W 3B 34
Argyle Ct. NG7: Radf 3G 95
Argyle M. NG16: Eastw 4D 72
Argyle St. NG7: Radf 3A 6 (3G 95)
    NG16: Lang M 2A 72
    NG18: Mans 4K 47
Aria Ct. NG9: Stap 3C 104
Ariel Cl. NG6: Basf 2G 85
Arkers Cl. NG6: Basf 4E 84
Arklow Cl. NG8: Aspl 5B 84
ARKSEY 1A 144
Arkwright St. NG2: Nott 7A 96
Arkwright St. Nth. NG2: Nott 5K 95
Arkwright St. Sth. NG2: Nott 7A 96
Arkwright Wlk. NG2: Nott 6A 96
    (not continuous)
Arleston Dr. NG8: Woll 5J 93
Arlington Av. NG19: Mans W 6A 42
Arlington Cl. NG15: Huck 2G 75
Arlington Dr. NG3: Mapp P 6K 85
Arlington Way DN22: Retf 3F 23
Armadale Cl. NG5: Arn 6A 78
Armfield Rd. NG5: Arn 1F 87
Armstrong Rd. DN22: Retf 3F 23
    NG6: Bulw 2A 84
    NG19: Mans 3D 46
Armstrong Way NG7: Basf 6F 85
ARMTHORPE 1B 144
Arncliff Cl. NG8: Woll 4H 93
Arndale Rd. NG5: Sher 2K 85
Arne Ct. NG2: Nott 7K 95
Arnesby Rd. NG7: Lent 5E 94
Arno Av. NG7: H Grn 7J 85
ARNOLD 7H 77 (1A 148)
Arnold Av. DN22: Retf 7H 23
    NG25: Sout 5H 131
Arnold La. NG3: Ged, Mapp 2E 86
    NG4: Ged 4H 87
Arnold Leisure Cen. 6H 77
Arnold Rd. NG5: Bestw 3F 85
    NG6: Basf, Bestw 3F 85
Arnos Gro. NG16: Nuth 4J 83
Arnot Hill Pk. 1B 86
Arnot Hill Rd. NG5: Arn 1B 86
Arnot Ho. NG4: Carl 7H 87
    (off Foxhill Rd. E.)
Arno Vale Gdns. NG5: Woodt 2C 86
Arno Vale Rd. NG5: Woodt 2B 86
Arnside NG9: Stap 4D 104
Arnside Cl. NG5: Bestw 2J 85
Arnside Rd. NG5: Bestw 2H 85
A Road NG7: Nott 3D 106
Arran Cl. NG9: Stap 6D 92
Arran Sq. NG19: Mans 5D 46
Arrival Sq. NG18: Mans 4H 47
Arthur Av. NG7: Lent 4G 95
    NG9: Stap 1E 104
Arthur Cres. NG4: Carl 1F 97

Arthur Grn. Av. NG17: Ann W 3J 59
Arthur Mee Rd. NG9: Stap 4D 104
Arthur St. NG4: Neth 2K 97
    NG7: Radf 1B 6 (2H 95)
    NG16: Pinx 1B 58
    NG18: Mans 4J 47
Artic Way NG16: Kimb 7H 73
Artillery Ter. DN22: Retf 4E 22
Arum Cft. DN22: Ord 6D 22
Arun Dale NG19: Mans W 6K 41
Arundel Cl. NG10: Sand 5A 104
Arundel Ct. NG19: Mans 2F 47
Arundel Dr. DN22: Rans 1J 13
    NG9: Bram 6G 93
    NG19: Mans 2F 47
    S81: Carl L 6C 12
Arundel St. NG7: Lent 4A 6 (3H 95)
Arundel Wlk. DN11: Birc 1E 8
Arundel Way DN22: Retf 2C 22
Ascot Av. NG16: Kimb 7J 73
Ascot Cl. NG17: Kirk A 1C 60
Ascot Dr. NG5: Redh 6F 77
    NG15: Huck 1D 74
    NG18: Mans 3B 48
Ascot Pk. Est. NG10: Sand 2B 104
Ascot Rd. NG8: Aspl 1E 94
Ascott Gdns. NG2: West Br 4J 107
ASFORDBY 3C 149
ASFORDBY HILL 3C 149
Ashbourne Cl. NG9: Bram 7F 93
Ashbourne Ct. NG6: Bulw 1A 84
Ashbourne Rd. NG16: Unde 3E 64
Ashbourne St. NG7: Lent 4A 6 (3H 95)
Ashburnham Av. NG7: Lent 4G 95
ASHBY 1D 145
Ashby Av. NG19: Mans W 4K 41
Ashby Rd. LE12: Remp 6C 122
Ashchurch Dr. NG8: Woll 6J 93
Ash Cl. NG13: Bing 4H 101
    NG14: Bur J 3D 88
    NG14: Woodbo 2G 79
    NG15: Huck 1C 74
    NG16: Pinx 2B 58
    NG22: Dun T 5J 29
    S80: Work 4F 21
Ash Ct. NG4: Carl 1G 97
Ashcourt Gdns. NG17: Sut A 1G 60
Ash Cres. NG16: Nuth 1G 83
    NG17: Kirk A 5H 51
    NG19: Mans W 7A 42
Ashcroft DN22: Ord 6D 22
Ashdale Av. NG15: Huck 1G 75
Ashdale Rd. DE7: Ilk 2A 92
    NG3: Nott 2E 96
    NG5: Arn 6J 77
Ashdown Cl. NG11: Wilf 3J 107
Ashdown Gro. NG13: Bing 4E 100
Ashdown Way DN10: Mist 3G 11
Ashe Cl. NG5: Arn 7K 77
Asher La. NG11: Rudd 4K 115
Ashes Pk. Av. S81: Gate, Work .. .4E 18
Ashfield Av. NG9: Bee 4C 106
    NG18: Mans 2H 47
Ashfield Dr. NG17: Kirk A 6K 51
Ashfield Mobile Home Pk. NG17: Skeg .5K 45
Ashfield Rd. NG2: Nott 4C 96
    NG17: Huth 7F 45
Ashfield St. NG17: Skeg 5K 45
Ashford Ct. DN22: Ord 6D 22
Ashford Dr. NG15: Rave 1D 62
Ashford Ri. NG8: Woll 6J 93
Ashforth Av. NG17: Sut A 6J 45
Ashforth Bus. Cen. NG3: Nott 1G 7
Ashforth St. NG3: Nott 1G 7 (2A 96)
Ashgate NG17: Sut A 7H 45
Ashgate Retail Pk. NG15: Huck .. .6J 67
Ashgate Rd. NG15: Huck 6H 67
Ash Gro. NG9: Stap 4C 104
    NG10: Sand 2A 104
    NG12: Key 1J 119
    NG14: Woodbo 1G 79
    NG16: Brins 5B 64
    NG16: Sels 5D 58
    NG17: Skeg 3H 45
Ash Holt Dr. S81: Work 4G 19
Ashiana NG2: Nott 5J 7 (4B 96)
Ashington Dr. NG5: Arn 4H 77
Ashland Rd. NG17: Sut A 7G 45
Ashland Rd. W. NG17: Sut A 7F 45
Ashlands Cl. NG17: Sut A 7F 45
Ash La. DN22: Rans 3H 13
    LE12: Costo 7A 118
    NG15: Pap 3F 69
Ashlea DN10: Mist 2G 11
Ash Lea Cl. NG12: Cotg 7E 110
Ashleigh Av. NG17: Sut A 1H 51
Ashleigh Way NG19: Mans W 7C 42
Ashley Cl. NG9: Chil 3J 105
Ashley Ct. NG9: Bee 3K 105
    S81: Work 7G 19
Ashley Cres. NG12: Key 7J 117
Ashley Gro. NG15: Huck 6E 66
Ashley La. DN22: Tres 5F 25
Ashley Rd. NG12: Key 7H 117
    S81: Work 6F 19
Ashley St. NG3: Nott 4J 7 (3B 96)

Ashley Ter. S80: Work 1G 21
Ashling Cl. NG2: Nott 6B 96
Ashling St. NG2: Nott 6B 96
Ashmore Av. NG17: Sut A 1G 51
Ashness Cl. NG2: Gam 3F 109
Ashover Cl. NG3: Nott 7B 86
    NG15: Rave 1C 62
Ashridge Way NG12: Edwal 5F 109
Ash Rd. NG24: New T 5C 136
Ashton Av. NG5: Arn 4H 77
Ashton Ct. NG8: Bilb 1J 93
    NG17: Skeg 5A 46
Ash Tree Av. NG19: Mans W 4J 41
Ash Tree Cl. NG25: Sout 6G 131
Ash Tree Ct. NG8: Stre 4H 83
Ash Tree Sq. NG9: Bram 1G 105
Ashurst Gro. NG15: Huck 2E 74
Ashvale NG22: Tuxf 7D 28
Ash Va. Rd. NG22: Wale 5G 27
Ashvale Rd. NG22: Tuxf 6C 28
Ash Vw. NG7: Radf 2G 95
Ash Vs. NG5: Sher 6J 85
Ashville Cl. NG2: Nott 7H 95
Ash Wlk. LE12: East L 4K 121
Ashwater Dr. NG3: Mapp 1G 87
Ashwell Av. NG19: Mans W 4A 42
Ashwell Ct. NG5: Woodt 3B 86
Ashwell Gdns. NG7: H Grn 7F 85
Ashwell St. NG4: Neth 2J 97
Ashwell Ter. NG21: Blid 7H 55
Ashwick Cl. NG11: Wilf 4H 107
Ashwood Av. NG17: Kirk A 5C 52
Ashwood Cl. NG17: Sut A 2J 51
    NG19: Mans W 4A 42
Ashwood Gro. NG17: Sut A 2J 51
Ashwood Rd. S80: Work 3C 20
Ashworth Av. NG11: Rudd 2K 115
Ashworth Cl. NG3: Nott 3F 97
    NG24: New T 1G 137
Ashworth Cres. DN22: Nth L 6B 24
    NG3: Mapp 5E 86
Ashworth Dr. NG19: Mans W 5A 42
Askeby Dr. NG8: Stre 6J 83
ASKERN 1A 144
Askew La. NG20: Mkt W 5C 34
ASKHAM 1C 147
Askham Ct. NG2: Gam 2F 109
    (off Radcliffe Rd.)
Askham Rd. NG22: East M 2C 28
ASLOCKTON 3D 102 (1C 149)
Aslockton Dr. NG8: Aspl 5E 84
Aslockton Station (Rail) 4D 102
Aspect Bus. Pk. NG6: Bulw 6F 75
Aspen Cl. NG13: Bing 4H 101
    NG22: Tuxf 7D 28
    NG22: Wale 5G 27
Aspen Ct. NG19: Mans W 1A 48
    NG22: Tuxf 7D 28
Aspen Rd. NG6: Bulw 1A 84
Asper St. NG4: Neth 1K 97
Aspinall Ct. NG8: Woll 3D 94
ASPLEY 7C 84
Aspley La. NG8: Aspl, Bilb 6A 84
Aspley Pk. Dr. NG8: Bilb 7B 84
Aspley Pl. NG7: Radf 2G 95
Aspley Rd. NG17: Sut A 7H 45
Asquith M. NG18: Mans 4A 48
Asquith St. NG18: Mans 4A 48
Assarts Rd. NG16: Nuth 3K 83
Astbury Dr. NG21: Rain 1G 55
Aster Rd. NG3: Nott 1J 7 (1A 96)
Astle Ct. NG5: Arn 1F 87
Astley Cl. NG17: Ann W 4A 60
Astley Dr. NG3: Nott 6C 86
ASTON 3A 144
Aston Av. NG9: Lent A 1B 106
Aston Ct. NG7: Lent 7F 95
Aston Dr. NG6: Bulw 4J 75
Aston Grn. NG9: Toton 6D 104
Astral Dr. NG15: Huck 2E 74
Astral Gro. NG15: Huck 2D 74
Astrid Gdns. NG5: Bestw 1G 85
Astron Ct. NG15: Huck 2E 74
Astwood Cl. NG8: Bilb 1K 93
Athelstan Rd. S80: Work 4G 21
Atherfield Gdns. NG16: Eastw 3D 72
Atherton Ri. NG8: Cin 4C 84
Athorpe Gro. NG6: Basf 4F 85
Atkin La. NG18: Mans 7H 47
Atkinson Gdns. NG16: Nuth 2G 83
Atrium, The NG2: Nott 7H 7 (5A 96)
ATTENBOROUGH 7J 105 (2A 148)
Attenborough La. NG9: Atten, Chil .6H 105
    (not continuous)
Attenborough Nature Reserve 7K 105
Attenborough Station (Rail) 7J 105
Attercliffe Ter. NG2: Nott 7K 95
Attewell Rd. NG16: Aws 2A 82
Attlee Av. NG19: Mans W 1C 48
AUBOURN 2D 147
Aubrey Av. NG2: Nott 6K 7 (4B 96)
Aubrey Rd. NG5: Sher 5J 85
Auckland Cl. NG7: Radf 3F 95
Auckland Rd. DN22: Retf 2C 22
    NG15: Huck 1D 74
AUCKLEY 1B 144

Audley Dr. NG9: Lent A 7A 94
Audon Av. NG9: Chil 4K 105
Audrey Cres. NG19: Mans W 4H 41
AUGHTON 3A 144
Augustine Gdns. NG5: Top V 5C 76
AULT HUCKNALL 2A 146
Aurillac Ct. DN22: Retf 1D 22
Aurillac Way DN22: Retf 1D 22
Austen Av. NG7: H Grn 1H 95
Austen Gro. NG17: Kirk A 1A 60
AUSTERFIELD 2B 144
Austin Cl. NG18: Mans 2A 48
Austins Dr. NG10: Sand 5A 104
Austin St. NG6: Bulw 7J 75
Austrey Av. NG9: Lent A 1B 106
Autumn Ct. NG15: Huck 7G 67
Autumn Cft. Rd. NG24: New T 7G 135
Avalon Cl. NG6: Bulw 1F 85
Avebury Cl. NG11: Clif 2E 114
Aveline Cl. NG5: Top V 6B 76
Avenue, The NG11: Rudd 5A 116
  NG12: Rad T 4E 98
  NG14: Calv 6D 70
  NG14: Gun 1A 90
  NG17: Sut A 2H 51
  NG18: Mans 7K 47
  NG24: New T 2E 136
Avenue A NG1: Nott 5H 7 (4A 96)
Avenue B NG1: Nott 5H 7 (4A 96)
Avenue C NG1: Nott 5J 7 (4B 96)
Avenue D NG1: Nott 5J 7 (4B 96)
Avenue E NG1: Nott 4J 7 (3B 96)
Avenue DN22: Retf 5F 23
AVERHAM 3F 133 (3C 147)
Averham Cl. NG19: Mans 4D 46
Averton Sq. NG8: Woll 5E 94
Aviemore Cl. NG5: Arn 5K 77
Avocet Cl. NG13: Bing 5H 101
  NG15: Huck 4H 67
Avocet Gro. S81: Gate 6D 18
Avocet Wharf NG7: Lent 6H 95
Avon Av. NG15: Huck 3E 74
Avonbridge Cl. NG5: Arn 5A 78
Avon Cl. NG17: Nunc 4K 59
Avondale NG12: Cotg 6F 111
Avondale Bungs. NG18: Mans 3A 48
Avondale Rd. NG4: Carl 2G 97
Avon Gdns. NG2: West Br 2C 108
Avonlea Cl. DE7: Ilk 2A 92
Avon Pl. NG9: Bee 2B 106
Avon Rise DN22: Retf 3G 23
Avon Rd. NG3: Nott 3E 96
  NG4: Ged 5J 87
Avon Way NG18: Mans 5C 48
  S81: Work 5F 19
AWSWORTH 2B 82 (1A 148)
Awsworth & Cossall By-Pass NG16: Aws, Coss 3A 82
Awsworth La. NG16: Coss 5B 82
  NG16: Kimb 2C 82
Awsworth Rd. DE7: Ilk 4A 82
Axford Cl. NG4: Ged 5J 87
Axmouth Dr. NG3: Mapp 2G 87
Aylesbury Way NG19: Mans W 7A 42
Aylesham Av. NG5: Arn 1C 86
Aylestone Dr. NG8: Bilb 7C 84
Ayrshire Way NG23: Aver 4F 133
Ayr St. NG7: Radf 2A 6 (2H 95)
Ayscough Av. NG16: Nuth 1H 83
Ayton Cl. NG2: Nott 6J 95
Ayton Gdns. NG9: Chil 7H 105
Azalea Ct. NG16: Gilt 6G 73
Azimghur Rd. NG13: What 4D 102

B

Babbacombe Dr. NG5: Bestw 1J 85
Babbacombe Way NG15: Huck 7D 66
Babbage Way S80: Work 1F 21
BABBINGTON 3D 82
Babbington Cl. DE7: Ilk 2A 92
Babbington Cres. NG4: Ged 5H 87
Babbington Dr. NG6: Cin 3C 84
Babbington La. NG16: Kimb 3E 82
Babington Ct. NG9: Chil 4H 105
Babtthorpe NG23: Upton 7C 132
BABWORTH 4A 22 (3B 144)
Babworth Ct. NG18: Mans 3K 47
Babworth Cres. DN22: Retf 4C 22
Babworth Mews DN22: Retf 4D 22
Babworth Rd. DN22: Babw, Retf 4A 22
  (not continuous)
Back La. DN10: Miss 3C 10
  DN22: Rans 2H 13
  LE12: Will W 6F 143
  NG12: Crop Bu 2B 112
  NG12: Norm W 4K 117
  NG16: Nuth 1J 83
  NG17: Huth 7D 44
  NG17: Skeg 4K 45
  NG22: Eakr 3C 126
  NG22: East M 2D 28
  (not continuous)
  NG22: Halam 5C 130
  NG22: Oll 5B 38
  NG23: Flin 6A 140

Back La. NG23: Nth C 3D 30
  NG24: Barn W 6K 137
  NG25: Mort 6F 139
  S81: Blyth 6H 13
Back Pk. Pl. S80: Work 3G 21
Back St. NG23: Sth C 7D 30
Bacon Cl. NG16: Gilt 6E 72
Bacton Av. NG6: Bulw 6H 75
Bacton Gdns. NG6: Bulw 6H 75
Baden Powell Rd. NG2: Nott 4D 96
Bader Cl. DN10: Matt T 1G 15
Bader Ri. DN10: Matt T 1G 15
Bader Rd. NG11: Wilf 2J 107
Bader Vw. DN10: Matt T 1G 15
Badger Av. NG4: Carl 7H 87
  NG15: Huck 7C 66
Badgers Cft. NG22: Bils 6D 126
Badgers Chase DN22: Retf 1F 23
Badger Way NG19: Mans W 3E 48
Baggaley Cres. NG19: Mans 1H 47
Bagnall Av. NG5: Arn 1K 85
Bagnall Cotts. NG6: Bulw 2C 84
Bagnall Rd. NG6: Basf, Cin 3C 84
Bagshaw St. NG19: Plea 4B 40
BAGTHORPE 1D 64 (3A 146)
Bagthorpe Cl. NG5: Sher 4H 85
BAGTHORPE COMMON 2E 64
Baildon Cl. NG8: Woll 5D 94
Bailey Cl. NG5: Arn 7F 77
Bailey Ct. NG4: Neth 1K 97
  NG12: Rad T 6D 98
Bailey Cres. NG19: Mans 3E 46
Bailey Dr. NG3: Mapp 2E 86
BAILEY GROVE 4B 72
Bailey Gro. Rd. NG16: Eastw 4B 72
Bailey La. NG12: Rad T 6D 98
Bailey Rd. NG24: New T 4C 136
Baileys Cft. LE12: Will W 6G 143
Bailey's Row NG12: Kin 1C 142
Bailey St. NG4: Neth 1K 97
  NG6: Basf 5F 85
  NG9: Stap 3B 104
Bainbridge, The NG14: Calv 6E 70
Bainbridge Rd. NG20: Mkt W 4D 34
Bainbridge Ter. NG17: Huth 1D 50
  NG17: Stant H 4H 45
Baines Av. NG24: New B 5G 137
Bainton Gro. NG11: Clif 1G 115
Baird-Parker Dr. NG4: Carl 1G 97
Baker Av. DN10: Gri H 3A 16
  NG5: Arn 5J 77
Baker Brook Cl. NG15: Huck 7K 67
Baker Cl. S81: Work 7E 18
Bakerdale Rd. NG3: Nott 2E 96
Baker La. NG20: Cuck 5C 32
Baker Rd. NG16: Gilt, Newth 6G 73
  NG19: Mans W 3J 41
Bakers Brothers Mobile Home Caravan Site
  DE7: Ilk 6A 82
Bakers Cl. NG7: Radf 2F 95
  NG12: Cotg 6D 110
BAKERS FIELDS 2E 96
Baker's La. NG12: Cols B 7J 141
  NG15: Huck 6G 67
Baker St. NG1: Nott 1D 6 (1J 95)
  NG15: Huck 6G 67
Bakewell Av. NG4: Carl 6H 87
Bakewell Cl. NG24: New B 6F 137
Bakewell Dr. NG24: New B 6F 137
Bakewell Dr. NG5: Top V 7A 76
Bakewell Ho. NG24: Bald 6F 137
Bakewell La. NG15: Huck 2H 75
Bakewell Wlk. NG18: Mans 4E 48
Bala Dr. NG5: Bestw 7C 76
BALBY 1A 144
BALDERTON 5G 137 (3D 147)
Balderton Ct. NG18: Mans 3E 46
Balderton Ga. NG24: New T 1D 136
Balderton La. NG24: Codd 3K 137
Baldwin Cl. NG19: Mans W 7D 42
Baldwin Ct. NG7: Radf 4A 6 (3G 95)
Baldwin St. NG7: Radf 3A 6 (3H 95)
  NG16: Newth 5G 73
Balfour Rd. NG7: Lent, Radf 4A 6 (3G 95)
  NG9: Stap 3C 104
Balfour St. NG17: Kirk A 7C 52
Balfron Gdns. NG2: Nott 6J 95
Balisier Ct. NG3: Nott 1F 7 (2K 95)
BALK FIELD 3G 23
Ballantrae Cl. NG5: Arn 6K 77
Ballater Cl. NG19: Mans 7E 40
Ballerat Cres. NG5: Top V 6A 76
Ball Hill DE55: Sth N 5A 50
Balloon Wood Ind. Est.
  NG9: Bram 4F 93
Balls La. NG17: Kirk A 2B 60
Ball St. NG3: Nott 1C 96
Balmoral Av. NG2: West Br 1B 108
Balmoral Cl. NG10: Sand 6A 104
  NG19: Mans W 4A 42
  S81: Carl L 6C 12
Balmoral Ct. DN11: Birc 1E 8
  (off Dorchester Rd.)
Balmoral Cres. NG8: Woll 3H 93
Balmoral Dr. NG9: Bram 6G 93
  NG19: Mans 7E 40
  NG24: New T 1H 137

Balmoral Gro. NG4: Colw 2J 97
  NG15: Huck 5H 67
Balmoral Ho. NG5: Woodt 3A 86
Balmoral Lodge NG19: Mans 7E 40
Balmoral Rd. NG1: Nott 1C 6 (2J 95)
  NG4: Colw 2J 97
  NG13: Bing 4D 100
Balshaw Way NG9: Chil 7G 105
Bamburgh Cl. NG17: Kirk A 4J 51
Bamford Dr. NG18: Mans 4D 48
Bamkin Cl. NG15: Huck 7H 67
Bampton Ct. NG2: Gam 2F 109
Banbury Av. NG9: Toton 6E 104
Banchory Cl. NG19: Mans 7E 40
Banchory La. NG19: Mans 7E 40
Bancroft Ho. NG18: Mans 3G 47
  (off The Connexion)
Bancroft La. NG18: Mans 3F 47
Bancroft Rd. NG24: New T 3E 136
Bancroft St. NG6: Bulw 7J 75
Bandstand Yard 6D 6
Banes Rd. NG13: Bing 4J 101
Bangor Wlk. NG3: Nott 1F 7 (1K 95)
Bank Av. NG17: Sut A 2J 51
Bank End Cl. NG18: Mans 6K 47
Bankfield Dr. NG9: Bram 7H 93
Bank Hill NG14: Woodbo 3D 78
Bank Pl. NG1: Nott 5F 7 (4K 95)
Banks, The NG13: Bing 4F 101
Banks Av. NG17: Kirk A 5J 51
Banks Cl. NG5: Arn 1E 86
Banks Cres. NG13: Bing 4F 101
Bank Side DN22: Ord 7F 23
Banksman Cl. NG3: Nott 1C 96
Banks Paddock NG13: Bing 4G 101
Banks Rd. NG9: Toton 6D 104
Bank St. NG16: Lang M 2A 72
Banks Yd. NG6: Bulw 7H 75
  (off Main St.)
Bank Ter. DN22: Retf 2F 23
Bankwood Cl. NG8: Aspl 6B 84
Bannatyne's Health Club
  Mansfield 6B 48
  Worksop 3J 21
Bannerman Rd. NG6: Bulw 1D 84
  NG17: Kirk A 6K 51
Baptist La. NG23: Coll 2G 129
Bar, The NG22: Lax 5B 124
Barbara Sq. NG15: Huck 4F 67
Barber Av. NG16: Jack 6A 64
  NG17: Skeg 4H 45
Barber St. NG16: Eastw 4E 72
Barbers Wood Cl. NG15: Rave 3C 62
Barbrook Cl. NG8: Woll 3C 94
Barbury Dr. NG11: Clif 3E 114
Barcroft La. DN22: Clar 7H 17
Barden Rd. NG3: Mapp 2D 86
Bardfield Gdns. NG5: Top V 4K 75
Bardney Dr. NG6: Bulw 6G 75
Bardsey Gdns. NG5: Bestw 7C 76
Barent Cl. NG5: Bestw 1G 85
Barent Wlk. NG5: Bestw 1G 85
Bar Gate NG24: New T 7C 134
Barker Av. NG16: Jack 6A 64
  NG17: Skeg 4H 45
Barker Av. E. NG10: Sand 3A 104
Barker Av. Nth. NG10: Sand 3A 104
Barker Ga. NG1: Nott 5G 7 (4A 96)
  NG15: Huck 6F 67
Barker Hill NG14: Lowd 4D 80
Barkers La. NG9: Chil 5A 106
Barker St. NG17: Huth 6D 44
BARKESTONE-LE-VALE 2C 149
Barkla Cl. NG11: Clif 2D 114
BARKSTON 1D 149
Barkstone Cl. NG24: Bald 6F 137
Bar La. NG6: Basf 5D 84
  NG8: Aspl 5D 84
Bar La. Ind. Pk. NG6: Basf 5E 84
BARLBOROUGH 1A 146
Barley Cl. NG2: West Br 5K 107
Barleydale Dr. NG9: Trow 6C 92
Barleylands NG11: Rudd 4K 115
Barley M. NG19: Mans W 3A 42
Barley Way NG24: New T 4E 134
Barlock Rd. NG6: Basf 3F 85
Barlow Dr. Nth. NG16: Aws 3A 82
Barlow Dr. Sth. NG16: Aws 3A 82
Barlows Cl. NG12: Crop Bi 4C 112
Barlows Cotts. NG16: Aws 2B 82
Barlows Cotts. La. NG16: Aws 2B 82
BARNBURGH 1A 144
BARNBY CROSSING 3F 137
BARNBY DUN 1B 144
Barnby Ga. NG24: New T 1D 136
BARNBY IN THE WILLOWS 7K 137 (3D 147)
Barnby Moor 3B 144
Barnby Rd. NG24: Bald, Barn W, New T 2E 136
Barnby Wlk. NG5: Sher 2K 85
Barn Cl. NG6: Bulw 2A 84
  NG12: Cotg 7D 110
  NG18: Mans 5B 48
  S81: Work 5H 19
Barn Ct. NG17: Kirk A 6J 51
Barn Cft. NG9: Chil 3G 105
  NG18: Mans 4B 48
Barndale Cl. NG2: West Br 6K 107
Barnes Cl. NG11: Wilf 5J 107

Barnes Ct.—Belgrave M.

Barnes Ct. DN22: Retf . . . 1D 22
Barnes Cres. NG17: Sut A . . . 3J 51
Barnes Rd. NG5: Top V . . . 6B 76
Barnet Rd. NG3: Nott . . . 1E 96
Barnett Ct. NG12: Key . . . 7H 117
Barnfield NG11: Wilf . . . 5J 107
Barnfield Rd. NG23: Coll . . . 1J 129
Barn Owl Cl. NG20: Chu W . . . 2E 34
Barnsley Cl. NG6: Bestw V . . . 7D 68
Barnsley Ter. NG2: Nott . . . 7K 95
BARNSTONE . . . 3F 141 (2C 149)
Barnstone La. NG13: Barns, Gran . . . 2H 141
Barnstone Rd.
NG13: Barns, Lang . . . 7K 113
Barnston Rd. NG2: Nott . . . 3C 96
Barnum Cl. NG8: Woll . . . 3K 93
Barons Cl. NG4: Ged . . . 6H 87
Barons Dr. NG22: Bou . . . 2F 39
Barrack La. NG7: Nott . . . 5A 6 (4G 95)
Barra M. NG2: Nott . . . 6J 95
Barratt Cl. NG9: Atten . . . 7J 105
NG12: Crop Bi . . . 5B 112
Barratt Cres. NG9: Atten . . . 7J 105
Barratt La. NG9: Atten . . . 7H 105
Barrel Hill Rd. NG23: Sut T . . . 4C 128
Barrhead Cl. NG5: Top V . . . 5A 76
Barringer Rd. NG18: Mans . . . 2K 47
NG19: Mans W . . . 1K 47
Barrington Cl. NG12: Rad T . . . 6D 98
Barrington Ct. LE12: Sut B . . . 6B 120
Barrique Rd. NG7: Lent . . . 7F 95
Bar Rd. DN10: Beck, Saun . . . 7D 16
DN22: Saun . . . 7D 16
Bar Rd. Nth. DN10: Beck . . . 7D 16
Bar Rd. Sth. DN10: Beck . . . 7D 16
BARROWBY . . . 2D 149
Barrow Hill Wlk. *NG18: Mans . . . 4D 48*
(off Beeley Cl.)
Barrows Ga. NG24: New T . . . 5E 134
BARROWS GREEN . . . 7A 58
Barrows Hill La. NG16: Westw . . . 7B 58
Barrow Slade NG12: Key . . . 1H 119
BARROW UPON SOAR . . . 3A 148
Barrydale Av. NG9: Bee . . . 4A 106
Barry St. NG6: Bulw . . . 7H 75
Bars Hill LE12: Costo . . . 3E 122
Bartley Gdns. NG14: Calv . . . 5A 70
Bartlow Rd. NG8: Bilb . . . 1J 93
Barton Cl. NG11: Rudd . . . 4J 115
NG19: Mans W . . . 1D 48
Barton Ct. NG18: Mans . . . 7C 48
BARTON IN FABIS . . . 7A 114 (2A 148)
Barton La. NG9: Atten, Chil . . . 7H 105
NG11: Bart F . . . 4B 114
NG11: Clif . . . 2D 114
Bartons Cl. NG16: Newth . . . 4G 73
Barton St. NG9: Bee . . . 4B 106
Barton Way NG9: Chil . . . 4K 105
Barwell Dr. NG8: Stre . . . 6J 83
Basa Cres. NG5: Top V . . . 6B 76
Basford Rd. NG6: Basf . . . 6E 84
Basford Stop (NET) . . . 4F 85
Baskin La. NG9: Chil . . . 5H 105
Baslow Av. NG4: Carl . . . 6G 87
Baslow Dr. NG9: Lent A . . . 7B 94
Baslow Way NG18: Mans . . . 5D 48
Bassetlaw Mus. . . . 3F 23
Bassett Cl. NG16: Kimb . . . 7J 73
BASSINGFIELD . . . 2J 109 (2B 148)
Bassingfield La. NG2: Gam . . . 2G 109
(not continuous)
NG12: Rad T . . . 1J 109
BASSINGHAM . . . 3D 147
Bastion St. NG7: Radf . . . 3F 95
Bateman Gdns. NG7: H Grn . . . 1G 95
Bateman Rd. LE12: East L . . . 3K 121
Bateman's Yd. NG17: Kirk A . . . 7H 51
Bath La. NG18: Mans . . . 3J 47
NG25: Sout . . . 7E 130
BATHLEY . . . 5F 129 (3C 147)
Bathley La. NG23: Bath, Lit C . . . 7G 129
NG23: Norw . . . 4H 127
NG23: Nth M . . . 6H 129
Bathley St. NG2: Nott . . . 7K 95
Baths La. NG15: Huck . . . 6H 67
Bath St. NG1: Nott . . . 3G 7 (3A 96)
NG17: Sut A . . . 6K 45
NG18: Mans . . . 4H 47
Bathurst Dr. NG8: Bilb . . . 2B 94
Bathurst Ter. NG20: Whal T . . . 5A 26
Bathwood Dr. NG17: Sut A . . . 1A 52
NG18: Mans . . . 5E 46
Battery La. DN22: Elk . . . 3G 27
Battle Cl. NG13: Newton . . . 1C 100
Baulk, The S81: Work . . . 7G 19
Baulker La. NG21: Blid . . . 7B 56
NG21: C'tone . . . 5K 43
NG22: Farns . . . 7B 56
Baulk La. DN11: Harwo . . . 1C 8
DN22: Torw . . . 4H 13
NG9: Stap . . . 1E 104
S81: Work . . . 7F 19
(not continuous)
Baum's La. NG18: Mans . . . 5H 47
BAWTRY . . . 1J 9 (2B 144)
Bawtry Cl. DN11: Harwo . . . 2C 8
Bawtry Rd. DN10: Eve, Scaf . . . 6A 10
DN10: Miss, Newi . . . 4A 10
DN10: Serl . . . 7D 8
DN11: Birc, Harwo . . . 2C 8
DN11: Harwo, Tick . . . 1D 8
S81: Blyth, Serl . . . 7D 8 & 4G 13
Bawtry Wlk. NG3: Nott . . . 2C 96
Bayard Ct. NG8: Woll . . . 3D 94
Bayford Dr. NG24: New T . . . 2H 137
Bayliss Rd. NG4: Ged . . . 4G 87
Baysdale Dr. NG19: Mans W . . . 1B 48
Bayswater Rd. NG16: Kimb . . . 7K 73
Baythorn Rd. NG8: Bilb . . . 2J 93
Beacon Ct. NG22: New O . . . 5D 38
Beacon Dr. NG17: Kirk A . . . 5C 52
Beacon Flatts NG9: Bee . . . 3C 106
Beacon Hgts. NG24: New T . . . 1G 137
Beacon Hill Conservation Pk. . . . 7F 135
Beacon Hill Dr. NG15: Huck . . . 1C 74
Beacon Hill Ri.
NG3: Nott . . . 3J 7 (3B 96)
Beacon Hill Rd. DN10: Gri H . . . 3C 16
NG24: New T . . . 1D 136
Beacon Rd. NG9: Bee . . . 3C 106
Beaconsfield Dr. NG24: Codd . . . 6J 135
Beaconsfield Gro. NG24: Codd . . . 6J 135
Beaconsfield St. NG7: H Grn . . . 7G 85
Beaconsfield Street Stop (NET) . . . 7G 85
Beacon Ter. NG24: New T . . . 1D 136
Beacon Vw. NG22: New O . . . 5C 38
Beacon Wlk. DN10: Gri H . . . 3C 16
Beacon Way NG24: New T . . . 1G 137
Bean Av. S80: Work . . . 2J 21
Bean Cl. NG6: Bulw . . . 2A 84
Beanford La. NG14: Calv . . . 2C 70
NG25: Oxt . . . 2C 70
Beardall St. NG15: Huck . . . 6H 67
NG18: Mans . . . 3G 47
Beardsall Ho. *NG7: Lent . . . 4F 95*
(off Faraday Rd.)
Beardsall's Row DN22: Retf . . . 3F 23
Beardsley Gdns. NG2: Nott . . . 6J 95
Beardsley Rd. NG21: Edwin . . . 7G 37
Beardsmore Gro. NG15: Huck . . . 4F 67
Beast Mkt. Hill NG24: New T . . . 7C 134
Beastmarket Hill NG1: Nott . . . 5E 6 (4K 95)
Beauclerk Dr. NG5: Top V . . . 6A 76
Beaufit La. NG16: Pinx . . . 1C 58
Beaufort Ct. NG2: West Br . . . 6K 107
Beaufort Dr. NG9: Chil . . . 4H 105
Beaufort Way S81: Work . . . 4F 19
Beaulieu Gdns. NG2: West Br . . . 4K 107
Beauly Dr. NG19: Mans . . . 5D 46
Beaumaris Dr. NG4: Ged . . . 6A 88
NG9: Chil . . . 5G 105
Beaumont Av. NG18: Mans . . . 5B 48
NG25: Sout . . . 6F 131
Beaumont Cl. NG9: Stap . . . 7D 92
NG12: Key . . . 6H 117
Beaumont Gdns. NG2: West Br . . . 5A 108
Beaumont Ri. S80: Work . . . 2E 20
Beaumont Sq. NG8: Woll . . . 3G 93
Beaumont St. NG2: Nott . . . 6K 7 (4B 96)
Beaumont Wlk. NG24: New T . . . 6E 134
BEAUVALE
Nottingham, NG15 . . . 7E 66
Nottingham, NG16 . . . 3F 73 (1A 148)
Beauvale NG16: Newth . . . 4F 73
Beauvale Ct. NG15: Huck . . . 7E 66
Beauvale Cres. NG15: Huck . . . 7D 66
Beauvale Gdns. NG17: Ann W . . . 4J 59
Beauvale Ri. NG16: Eastw . . . 3F 73
Beauvale Rd. NG2: Nott . . . 7K 95
NG15: Huck . . . 7D 66
NG17: Ann W . . . 4J 59
Beaver Grn. NG2: West Br . . . 2A 108
Beaver Pl. S80: Work . . . 2G 21
Beazley Av. NG18: Mans . . . 3F 47
Beck Av. NG14: Calv . . . 5D 70
Beck Cl. NG19: New H . . . 2A 40
Beck Cres. NG19: Mans . . . 3E 46
NG21: Blid . . . 7J 55
Beckenham Rd. NG7: Radf . . . 2G 95
Beckett Av. NG19: Mans . . . 1E 46
S81: Carl L . . . 5C 12
Beckett Ct. NG4: Ged . . . 4G 87
Becket Way, The NG2: West Br . . . 3J 107
Beckford Rd. NG2: Nott . . . 5C 96
Beckhampton Rd. NG5: Bestw . . . 6D 76
BECKINGHAM
Doncaster . . . 6C 16 (2C 145)
Newark-on-Trent . . . 3D 147
Beckingham Ct. *NG18: Mans . . . 3E 46*
(off Kelham Rd.)
Beckingham La. DN22: Sth L . . . 4G 25
Beckingham Rd.
DN10: Beck, Walk . . . 7J 11 & 6C 16
NG24: Codd . . . 7J 135
Beckland Hill NG22: East M . . . 3C 28
Beck La. DN22: Clay . . . 7J 15
NG17: Skeg . . . 4B 46
NG21: Blid . . . 7J 55
NG22: Farns . . . 6J 57
Beckley Rd. NG8: Brox . . . 5A 84
Beckside NG2: West Br . . . 5F 109
NG14: Lowd . . . 5E 80
Beck St. NG1: Nott . . . 4G 7 (3A 96)
NG4: Carl . . . 7G 87
NG14: Thur . . . 6D 138
Bedale S81: Work . . . 4H 19
Bedale Ct. NG9: Chil . . . 5F 105
Bedale Rd. NG5: Sher . . . 2K 85
Bedarra Gro. NG7: Lent . . . 4F 95
Bedeham La. NG13: Car C . . . 4K 91
Bede Ho. Ct. NG24: New T . . . 1D 136
Bede Ho. La. NG24: New T . . . 1D 136
Bede Ling NG2: West Br . . . 3K 107
Bedford Av. NG18: Mans . . . 3A 48
Bedford Ct. NG7: H Grn . . . 7G 85
NG9: Stap . . . 7D 92
Bedford Gro. NG6: Bulw . . . 2E 84
Bedford Row NG1: Nott . . . 4H 7 (3A 96)
Bedlington Gdns. NG3: Mapp . . . 5B 86
Beecham Av. NG3: Nott . . . 2C 96
Beech Av. LE12: East L . . . 4K 121
NG3: Mapp . . . 3C 86
NG4: Neth . . . 2J 97
NG7: Basf . . . 7H 85
NG9: Bee . . . 4C 106
NG10: Sand . . . 2A 104
NG12: Key . . . 1J 119
NG13: Bing . . . 4H 101
NG15: Huck . . . 6G 67
NG15: Rave . . . 1B 62
NG16: Nuth . . . 1G 83
NG16: Pinx . . . 1C 58
NG17: Huth . . . 7E 44
NG17: Kirk A . . . 6J 51
NG18: Mans . . . 4H 47
NG22: New O . . . 4C 38
NG22: Oll . . . 3K 37
NG24: New T . . . 4C 136
S81: Work . . . 6G 19
Beech Cl. DN10: Gri H . . . 3B 16
NG2: West Br . . . 7G 97
NG6: Cin . . . 3D 84
NG12: Edwal . . . 5E 108
NG12: Rad T . . . 6E 98
Beech Ct. NG3: Mapp . . . 3D 86
NG16: Unde . . . 2F 65
NG19: Mans W . . . 4H 41
Beech Cres. NG19: Mans W . . . 7A 42
Beechcroft S81: Work . . . 6H 19
BEECHDALE . . . 2B 94
Beechdale Av. NG17: Sut A . . . 6K 45
Beechdale Cres. NG17: Sut A . . . 6K 45
Beechdale Rd. NG8: Aspl, Bilb . . . 7A 84
NG19: Mans W . . . 7C 42
Beechdale Swimming Cen. . . . 2D 94
Beecher La. DN10: Beck . . . 6C 16
Beeches, The NG3: Nott . . . 7D 86
NG17: Skeg . . . 3H 45
NG22: Tuxf . . . 7C 28
Beeches Wlk. NG25: Sout . . . 6H 131
Beech Gro. NG21: Blid . . . 6A 56
S81: Carl L . . . 5B 12
Beech Hill Av. NG19: Mans . . . 1F 47
Beech Hill Cres. NG19: Mans . . . 7F 41
Beech Hill Dr. NG19: Mans . . . 1F 47
Beech Lodge NG13: Bing . . . 4H 101
Beech Rd. DN11: Harwo . . . 1D 8
NG16: Unde . . . 2F 65
Beech St. NG17: Skeg . . . 3H 45
Beech Tree Av. NG19: Mans W . . . 4H 41
Beech Wlk. DN22: Elk . . . 2G 27
Beechways DN22: Ord . . . 6D 22
Beechwood Cl. NG17: Skeg . . . 5A 46
NG19: Mans W . . . 1C 48
Beechwood Ct. NG17: Skeg . . . 5A 46
Beechwood Gro. NG17: Skeg . . . 5A 46
Beechwood Rd. NG5: Arn . . . 6J 77
NG17: Kirk A . . . 4K 51
Beehive St. DN22: Retf . . . 4F 23
Beeley Av. NG17: Sut A . . . 2J 51
Beeley Cl. NG18: Mans . . . 4D 48
BEESTON . . . 2B 106 (2A 148)
Beeston Bus. Pk. NG9: Bee . . . 5B 106
Beeston Cl. NG6: Bestw V . . . 2A 76
Beeston Ct. NG6: Bulw . . . 7K 75
Beeston Flds. Dr. NG9: Bee, Bram . . . 1H 105
Beeston Fields Golf Course . . . 1J 105
Beeston La. NG7: Nott . . . 7C 94
Beeston Marina Mobile Home Pk.
NG9: Atten . . . 6B 106
Beeston Rd. NG7: Nott . . . 7E 94
NG24: New T . . . 3E 136
Beeston Sailing Club . . . 7B 106
Beeston Station (Rail) . . . 4B 106
Beetham Cl. NG13: Bing . . . 4G 101
Beggarlee Pk. NG16: Newth . . . 2F 73
BEIGHTON . . . 3A 144
Beighton Ct. NG18: Mans . . . 5D 48
Beighton St. NG17: Sut A . . . 7K 45
Bel-Air Res. Homes NG2: Gam . . . 2G 109
Belconnen Rd. NG5: Bestw . . . 2G 85
Beldover Ho. *NG7: Lent . . . 4F 95*
(off Faraday Rd.)
Belfields Yd. NG22: Edin . . . 2A 130
Belford Cl. NG6: Bulw . . . 6F 75
Belfry Cl. NG17: Kirk A . . . 4J 51
Belfry Way NG12: Edwal . . . 5F 109
Belgrave M. NG2: West Br . . . 6K 107

Belgrave Rd.—Birley St.

Belgrave Rd. NG6: Bulw 7G **75**
Belgrave Sq. NG1: Nott 4D **6** (3J **95**)
Belgravia Ct. S81: Work 5G **19**
Bellamy Dr. NG17: Kirk A 1A **60**
Bellamy Rd. NG18: Mans 7C **48**
Bellamy Rd. Ind. Est. NG18: Mans 7C **48**
Bellar Ga. NG1: Nott 5H **7** (4A **96**)
Bell Cl. NG23: Norm T 1K **125**
Belle Eau Pk. NG22: Bils 7E **126**
Belle Isle Rd. NG15: Huck 7G **67**
Belleville Dr. NG5: Bestw 7D **76**
Bellevue Ct. NG3: Nott 1J **7** (2B **96**)
Belle Vue La. NG21: Blid 6J **55**
Bell Ho. NG7: Nott 1F **107**
Bell La. NG11: Wilf 2J **107**
NG23: Coll 2G **129**
NG23: Weston 2F **125**
Bellmond Cl. NG24: New T 4C **136**
Bells Ct. DN10: Beck 7C **16**
Bells La. NG8: Cin 5B **84**
Bell St. NG4: Carl 7G **87**
Belmont Av. NG6: Bulw 7J **75**
Belmont Cl. NG9: Chil 5G **105**
NG15: Huck 2G **75**
NG19: Mans W 7C **42**
Belmont Rd. NG17: Nunc 3B **60**
Belmore Gdns. NG8: Bilb 3J **93**
Belper Av. NG4: Carl 6G **87**
Belper Cres. NG4: Carl 6G **87**
Belper Rd. NG7: H Grn 1A **6** (1G **95**)
Belper St. NG18: Mans 3K **47**
Belper Way NG18: Mans 3K **47**
BELPH 1A **146**
Belsay Rd. NG5: Bestw 7C **76**
Belsford Ct. NG16: Want 6A **74**
BELTOFT 1D **145**
BELTON
Grantham 2D **149**
Loughborough 3A **148**
Scunthorpe 1C **145**
Belton Cl. NG10: Sand 5A **104**
Belton Dr. NG2: West Br 5J **107**
Belton's Cotts. LE12: East L 1A **122**
Belton St. NG7: H Grn 7G **85**
Belvedere Av. NG7: H Grn 7G **85**
Belvedere Cl. NG12: Key 6H **117**
Belvedere Ho. *NG18: Mans* *3G* **47**
(off The Connexion)
Belvedere St. NG18: Mans 4H **47**
BELVOIR 2D **149**
Belvoir Cl. NG13: What 5B **102**
Belvoir Cres. NG13: Lang 7K **113**
NG24: New T 3D **136**
Belvoir Hill NG2: Nott 6K **7** (4C **96**)
Belvoir Lodge NG4: Carl 2H **97**
Belvoir Pl. NG24: Bald 6F **137**
Belvoir Rd. NG2: West Br 7D **96**
NG4: Neth 1K **97**
NG24: Bald 6F **137**
Belvoir St. NG3: Mapp 5C **86**
NG15: Huck 5F **67**
Belvoir Ter. NG2: Nott 6K **7** (4C **96**)
Belvoir Va. Gro. NG13: Bing 4G **101**
Belward St. NG1: Nott 5H **7** (4A **96**)
Belwood Cl. NG11: Clif 7G **107**
Bembridge S81: Work 6J **19**
Bembridge Ct. NG9: Bram 1F **105**
Bembridge Dr. NG5: Bestw 1J **85**
(not continuous)
Bencaunt Gro. NG15: Huck 5G **67**
Bendigo La. NG2: Nott 5D **96**
Benedict Ct. NG5: Top V 5C **76**
Benet Dr. NG22: Bils 6D **126**
Benington Dr. NG8: Woll 5H **93**
Ben Mayo Ct. NG7: Radf 2G **95**
Benner Av. DE7: Ilk 3A **92**
Bennerley Ct. NG6: Bulw 6F **75**
Bennerley Rd. NG6: Bulw 6F **75**
Bennet Dr. NG17: Kirk A 7A **52**
Bennett Av. NG18: Mans 4B **48**
Bennett Rd. NG3: Mapp 4D **86**
Bennett St. NG3: Mapp 5C **86**
NG10: Long E 6B **104**
NG10: Sand 4A **104**
Benneworth Cl. NG15: Huck 1F **75**
Bennington Wlk. NG19: Mans W 5A **42**
Ben St. NG7: Radf 2G **95**
Bentinck Av. NG12: Toll 1G **117**
Bentinck Chambers *NG18: Mans* *4H* **47**
(off Market St.)
Bentinck Cl. NG17: Nunc 3K **59**
NG22: Bou 2E **38**
Bentinck Ct. NG2: Nott 5J **7**
S80: Work 5G **21**
Bentinck Rd. NG4: Carl 5F **87**
NG7: H Grn, Radf 1A **6** (2G **95**)
NG24: New T 3C **136**
Bentinck St. NG15: Huck 5F **67**
NG17: Ann W 4K **59**
NG17: Sut A 7K **45**
NG18: Mans 4K **47**
Bentinck Ter. NG20: Mkt W 5D **34**
BENTINCK TOWN 1H **59**
Bentinck Workshops NG17: Kirk A 1H **59**
BENTLEY 1A **144**
Bentley Av. NG3: Nott 2D **96**
Bentwell Av. NG5: Arn 7J **77**
Beresford Rd. NG19: Mans W 3J **41**
Beresford St. NG7: Radf 3F **95**
NG18: Mans 4K **47**
Berkeley Av. NG3: Mapp P 7K **85**
Berkeley Ct. NG5: Sher 6K **85**
Berkeley Cres. NG12: Rad T 5J **99**
Berkeley Rd. NG18: Mans 6K **47**
Ber Mar Anda Res. Mobile Home Pk.
NG16: Lang M 2A **72**
Bernard Av. NG15: Huck 4H **67**
NG19: Mans W 4H **41**
Bernard Rd. NG19: Mans 2D **46**
Bernard St. NG5: Sher 6J **85**
Bernard Ter. NG5: Sher 6J **85**
Bernisdale Cl. NG5: Top V 5B **76**
Berridge Rd. NG7: H Grn 7H **85**
Berridge Rd. Central NG7: H Grn 7G **85**
Berridge Rd. W. NG7: H Grn 1F **95**
Berriedale Cl. NG5: Arn 5K **77**
Berristow Grange NG17: Sut A 2G **51**
Berristow La. DE55: Sth N 3A **50**
Berristow Pl. DE55: Sth N 4C **50**
Berry Av. NG17: Kirk A 5J **51**
Berrydown Cl. NG8: Aspl 6D **84**
BERRY HILL 5A **48**
Berry Hill Cl. NG18: Mans 6J **47**
Berry Hill Gdns. NG18: Mans 6B **48**
Berry Hill Gro. NG4: Ged 5H **87**
Berry Hill Hall NG18: Mans 6A **48**
Berry Hill La. NG18: Mans 7J **47**
Berry Hill M. NG18: Mans 6K **47**
Berry Hill Rd. NG18: Mans 5J **47**
Berry Pk. Lea NG18: Mans 7K **47**
Berwick Av. NG19: Mans 2D **46**
Berwick Cl. NG5: Bestw 1K **85**
Berwin Cl. NG10: Long E 7A **104**
Beryldene Av. NG16: Want 7A **74**
BESCABY 3D **149**
Bescar La. NG22: Oll 5A **38**
Bescoby St. DN22: Retf 4F **23**
Besecar Av. NG4: Ged 5H **87**
Besecar Cl. NG4: Ged 5H **87**
BESSACARR 1B **144**
Bessell La. NG9: Stap 4B **104**
Bessemer Dr. NG18: Mans 6H **47**
BESTHORPE 7H **125** (2D **147**)
Besthorpe Ct. NG18: Mans 3E **46**
Besthorpe Rd. LN6: Nth S 5J **125**
NG23: Best, Coll 1H **129**
BESTWOOD 7D **76**
Bestwood Av. NG5: Arn 6G **77**
Bestwood Bus. Pk. NG6: Bestw V 3A **76**
Bestwood Cl. NG5: Arn 6G **77**
Bestwood Country Pk. 3A **76**
Bestwood Footpath NG6: Bestw V 1K **75**
NG15: Bestw V, Huck 1K **75**
Bestwood Lodge Dr. NG5: Arn 5E **76**
Bestwood Lodge Stables NG5: Arn 4D **76**
Bestwood Pk. NG5: Arn 4D **76**
Bestwood Pk. Dr. NG5: Top V 5D **76**
Bestwood Pk. Dr. W. NG5: Top V 5K **75**
Bestwood Pk. Vw. NG5: Arn 5G **77**
Bestwood Rd. NG6: Bulw 6J **75**
NG15: Huck 1J **75**
NG16: Pinx 2C **58**
Bestwood Ter. NG6: Bulw 6K **75**
BESTWOOD VILLAGE 2A **76** (1A **148**)
Bethel Ct. NG19: Mans W 5J **41**
Bethel Gdns. NG15: Huck 1C **74**
Bethel Ter. S81: Shire 6A **18**
Bethnal Wlk. NG6: Bulw 7H **75**
Beth Shalom Holocaust Cen. 5K **39**
Betony Cl. NG13: Bing 4D **100**
Betony Gro. NG17: Kirk A 1A **60**
Bettison Ct. NG3: Mapp 3D **86**
Betts Av. NG15: Huck 2G **75**
Betula Cl. NG11: Clif 1D **114**
Beulah Rd. NG17: Kirk A 7B **52**
Bevan Cl. NG21: Rain 3K **55**
Bevel St. NG7: H Grn 1G **95**
BEVERCOTES 1C **147**
Bevercotes Cl. NG24: New T 3B **136**
Bevercotes La. NG22: Tuxf 6A **28**
Beverley Cl. NG8: Woll 4G **93**
NG21: Rain 2K **55**
Beverley Dr. NG16: Kimb 7J **73**
NG17: Kirk A 1C **60**
NG18: Mans 1K **53**
Beverley Gdns. NG4: Ged 6J **87**
Beverley Rd. DN11: Harwo 2D **8**
Beverley's Av. NG13: What 4C **102**
Beverley Sq. NG3: Nott 1J **7** (1B **96**)
Beverley Wlk. S81: Carl L 5B **12**
Bewcastle Rd. NG5: Arn, Top V 5C **76**
Bewick Dr. NG3: Nott 3F **97**
Bexhill Ct. NG9: Bee 7K **93**
Bexleigh Gdns. NG8: Bilb 7B **84**
Bexon Ct. NG4: Carl 1H **97**
Bexwell Cl. NG11: Clif 2F **115**
Biant Cl. NG8: Cin 4C **84**
Biddleston Ct. NG17: Sut A 5H **45**
Bideford Cl. NG3: Mapp 2G **87**
Bidford Rd. NG8: Brox 6A **84**
Bidwell Cres. NG11: Goth 6G **115**
Big Barn La. NG18: Mans 5B **48**
Biggart Cl. NG9: Chil 7H **105**
Big La. DN22: Clar 7H **17**
Bigsby Rd. DN22: Retf 2G **23**
Biko Sq. NG7: H Grn 7G **85**
Bilberry Wlk. NG3: Nott 1K **7** (2B **96**)
Bilbie Wlk. NG1: Nott 3D **6** (3J **95**)
BILBOROUGH 1K **93** (1A **148**)
Bilborough Rd. NG8: Bilb, Stre 3G **93**
NG18: Mans 3K **47**
Bilborough Sports Cen. 1H **93**
BILBY 3B **144**
Bilby Gdns. NG3: Nott 3C **96**
Billesdon Dr. NG5: Sher 3G **85**
Billingsley Av. NG16: Pinx 1A **58**
BILSTHORPE 5C **126** (2B **146**)
Bilsthorpe Rd. NG22: Eakr 2A **126**
Bilton Cl. NG24: Bald 7G **137**
Binbrook Ct. DN10: Bawt 1J **9**
Binding Cl. NG5: Sher 6J **85**
Binding Ho. NG5: Sher 6J **85**
BINGHAM 4F **101** (1C **149**)
Bingham Av. NG17: Skeg 5A **46**
Bingham By-Pass NG13: Bing 4C **100**
Bingham Ind. Pk. NG13: Bing 3F **101**
Bingham Leisure Cen. 4G **101**
Bingham Rd. NG5: Sher 5K **85**
NG12: Cotg 6E **110**
NG12: Rad T 5E **98**
NG13: Lang, Tith 3E **112**
NG18: Mans 7C **48**
Bingham Station (Rail) 3G **101**
Bingley Cl. NG8: Bilb 2C **94**
Bingley Cres. NG17: Kirk A 1A **60**
Birch Av. DE7: Ilk 1A **92**
NG4: Carl 1G **97**
NG9: Bee 5C **106**
NG16: Nuth 1G **83**
NG21: Rain 2A **56**
NG22: Farns 4J **57**
Birch Cl. DN22: Ramp 6K **25**
DN22: Rans 2K **13**
NG15: Rave 3C **62**
NG16: Nuth 1G **83**
Birch Ct. NG21: Rain 2A **56**
NG22: Tuxf 7C **28**
Birch Cft. Dr. NG19: Mans W 7C **42**
Birchcroft Rd. DN22: Retf 2E **22**
Birchdale Av. NG15: Huck 1G **75**
Birchenall Ct. NG24: Farnd 7H **133**
Birches, The NG15: Rave 1C **62**
Birchfield Dr. S80: Work 3C **20**
Birchfield Rd. NG5: Arn 5J **77**
Birch Gro. NG18: Mans 6B **48**
Birchin Wlk. NG18: Mans 5K **47**
Birchlands, The
NG19: Mans W 1B **48**
Birch Lea LE12: East L 3K **121**
NG5: Redh 6F **77**
Birchover Rd. NG8: Bilb 3H **93**
Birch Pk. NG16: Gilt 7E **72**
Birch Pas. NG7: Radf 3A **6** (3H **95**)
Birch Ri. NG14: Woodbo 1G **79**
Birch Rd. NG22: New O 4C **38**
NG24: New B 4F **137**
Birch St. NG20: Chu W 2B **34**
Birch Tree Cl. NG19: Mans W 6F **43**
Birch Tree Cres. NG17: Kirk A 7K **51**
Birch Wlk. NG5: Sher 4A **86**
BIRCHWOOD 2D **147**
Birchwood Cl. NG15: Rave 3D **62**
NG17: Skeg 4J **45**
NG25: Sout 5G **131**
S81: Lango 1C **12**
Birchwood Dr. NG15: Rave 3C **62**
NG17: Skeg 4H **45**
Birchwood Pk. NG19: Mans W 6E **42**
Birchwood Pk. Homes NG21: Rain 1H **55**
Birchwood Rd. NG8: Woll 4H **93**
BIRCOTES 2F **9** (2B **144**)
Bircotes Leisure Cen. 1E **8**
Bird Cl. NG18: Mans 7J **47**
Birdcroft La. DN10: Walk 7J **11**
Birding St. NG19: Mans 1H **47**
Birdsall Av. NG8: Woll 4K **93**
Bird's La. NG17: Ann W 3J **59**
Birkdale S81: Work 6J **19**
Birkdale Av. NG22: New O 2D **38**
Birkdale Cl. NG12: Edwal 6D **108**
Birkdale Dr. NG17: Kirk A 5K **51**
Birkdale Gro. DN22: Ord 7D **22**
Birkdale Way NG5: Top V 6B **76**
Birkin Av. NG7: H Grn 1G **95**
NG9: Toton 7F **105**
NG11: Rudd 2K **115**
NG12: Rad T 4F **99**
Birkland Av. NG1: Nott 1E **6** (2K **95**)
NG3: Mapp 3D **86**
NG19: Mans W 6K **41**
NG20: Mkt W 3D **34**
Birkland Dr. NG21: Edwin 5E **36**
Birklands Av. NG22: New O 2C **38**
S80: Work 4J **21**
Birklands Cl. NG20: Mkt W 3D **34**
Birkland St. NG18: Mans 4K **47**
Birks Rd. NG19: Mans 3D **46**
Birley St. NG9: Stap 4C **104**

156 A-Z Nottinghamshire Atlas

Birling Cl. NG6: Bulw 7F 75
Birrell Rd. NG7: H Grn 7H 85
Bisham Dr. NG2: West Br 2E 108
Bishop Alexander Ct. NG24: New T 2B 136
Bishopdale S81: Work 5H 19
Bishopdale Dr. NG16: Want 7B 74
Bishopfield La. DN10: Scro 1G 13
　　DN22: Rans .1G 13
Bishops Cl. NG12: Key 6H 117
Bishop's Dr. NG25: Sout 6H 131
Bishops Hill NG21: Rain 2H 55
Bishops Rd. NG13: Bing 3E 100
Bishop St. NG16: Eastw 4D 72
　　NG17: Sut A 7K 45
　　NG18: Mans .5H 47
Bishop's Wlk. NG20: Chu W 2C 34
Bishops Way NG15: Huck 4H 67
Bispham Dr. NG9: Toton 6E 104
Blackacre NG14: Bur J 2D 88
Black Bank DN10: Eve 4E 10
Blackberry Way NG20: Mkt W 5C 34
　　NG24: Bald .7H 137
Blackbird Av. S81: Gate 5D 18
Blackbourn Cl. NG23: Coll 1J 129
Blackbrook Rd. NG24: New T 7G 135
Blackburn Vw. NG22: New O 1D 38
Blackburn Way NG5: Bestw 2H 85
Blackcliffe Farm M. NG11: Rudd 7B 116
Blackett's Wlk. NG11: Clif 2D 114
Blackfriars Cl. NG16: Nuth 5J 83
Blackhill Dr. NG4: Carl 7J 87
Black La. S81: Woods 1A 18
Blackmires Way NG17: Sut A 6B 46
Black Rock Way NG18: Mans 5K 47
Blackrod Cl. NG9: Toton 7F 105
Black Scotch Cl. NG18: Mans 6A 48
Black Scotch La. NG18: Mans 7A 48
　　　　　　　　　　　　　　　　　(not continuous)
Blackshale Rd. NG19: Mans W 7H 41
Blacksmith Ct. NG12: Cotg 5D 110
Blacksmith La. DN22: Torw 4J 13
　　NG23: Kel 1H 133
Blacksmiths Cl. NG15: Pap 2K 67
Blacksmiths M. DN10: Matt 2H 15
Blackstone Wlk. NG2: Nott 6K 95
Blackstope La. DN22: Retf 3G 23
　　　　　　　　　　　　　　　　　(not continuous)
Black Swan Cl. NG5: Sher 3A 86
Blackthorn Cl. NG4: Ged 5K 87
　　NG13: Bing .4H 101
Blackthorn Dr. NG14: Lowd 4D 80
　　NG16: Eastw 4C 72
　　NG18: Mans .5J 47
Blackthorne Cl. NG24: New B 4F 137
Blackthorne Dr. NG6: Cin 4C 84
Blackthorn Way NG17: Sut A 2G 51
BLACKWELL 3A 146
Blackwell Rd. NG17: Huth 1B 50
Bladon Cl. NG3: Mapp 5B 86
Bladon Rd. NG11: Rudd 3J 115
Blair Ct. NG2: Nott 7K 95
Blair Gro. NG10: Sand 5A 104
Blaise Cl. NG11: Clif 2F 115
Blake Cl. NG5: Arn 7J 77
Blake Cres. NG18: Mans 3K 47
Blakeley La. NG20: Mkt W 6F 35
Blakeney Ct. NG19: Mans W 5A 42
　　　　　　　　　　　　　　　　　(off Bow St.)
Blakeney Dr. NG18: Mans 6J 47
Blakeney Ho. NG7: H Grn 1G 95
　　　　　　　　　　　　　　　　(off St Paul's Av.)
Blakeney Rd. NG12: Rad T 5G 99
Blakeney Wlk. NG5: Arn 2C 86
Blake Rd. NG2: West Br 2C 108
　　NG9: Stap 3D 104
Blake St. NG19: Mans W 7H 41
Blanchbeck La. NG22: Farns 7J 57
Blandford Dr. DN22: Ord 6D 22
Blandford Rd. NG9: Chil 4H 105
Bland La. NG14: Epp 1A 80
Blanford Gdns. NG2: West Br 4K 107
Blankley's Yd. NG20: Chu W 2D 34
Blankney St. NG6: Basf 3F 85
Blants Cl. NG16: Kimb 1E 82
Blantyre Av. NG5: Top V 5A 76
Blatherwick Cl. NG15: Huck 5H 67
Blatherwick Rd. NG24: New T 1G 137
Blatherwick's Yd. NG5: Arn 6H 77
BLAXTON 1B 144
Bleaberry Cl. NG2: West Br 4F 109
Bleachers Yd. NG7: Basf 6F 85
BLEAK HILLS 6F 47
Bleak Hill Sidings NG18: Mans 5F 47
Bleak Hills La. NG18: Mans 7E 46
　　　　　　　　　　　　　　　　　(not continuous)
Bleak Hill Way NG18: Mans 6E 46
BLEASBY 2B 138 (1C 149)
Bleasby Cres. NG17: Sut A 2B 52
Bleasby Rd. NG14: Blea, Thur 6D 138
　　NG25: Fis 2E 138
Bleasby Station (Rail) 2A 138
Bleasby St. NG2: Nott 4C 96
Bleasdale Cl. NG4: Ged 5K 87
Blencathra Cl. NG2: West Br 4F 109
BLENHEIM 5F 75
Blenheim NG3: Nott 1K 95

Blenheim Av. NG3: Mapp 5F 87
　　NG14: Lowd .5E 80
Blenheim Cl. NG11: Rudd 3J 115
　　NG19: Mans W 1K 47
Blenheim Ct. NG6: Bulw 5E 74
Blenheim Dr. NG9: Chil 4H 105
Blenheim Gdns. NG13: East B 5E 90
Blenheim Ind. Est. NG6: Bulw 6F 75
Blenheim La. NG6: Bulw 4D 74
Blenheim Pk. Rd. NG6: Bulw 5E 74
Blenheim Pl. NG17: Huth 7C 44
Blenheim Ri. S81: Work 4F 19
Bley Av. LE12: East L 4K 121
BLIDWORTH 6J 55 (3A 146)
BLIDWORTH BOTTOMS 2J 63
Blidworth Cl. NG8: Stre 5K 83
Blidworth Community Leisure Cen. 6J 55
Blidworth Dale NG15: Rave 4E 62
Blidworth Ind. Pk. NG21: Blid 5J 55
Blidworth Rd. NG21: Blid 2J 63
　　NG21: Rain .1F 55
Blidworth Rd. NG17: Kirk A 7E 52
　　NG22: Farns 5J 57
Blidworth Waye NG15: Pap 1K 67
Blind La. NG12: Key 1H 119
　　NG25: Oxt 1G 71
Bloomer Wood Vw. NG17: Sut A 2G 51
Bloomsbury Ct. NG1: Nott 4G 7
　　　　　　　　　　　　　　　　　(off Beck St.)
Bloomsbury Dr. NG16: Nuth 4K 83
Bloomsbury M. NG12: Rad T 5K 99
Bloomsgrove Ind. Est. NG7: Radf 3G 95
Bloomsgrove St. NG7: Radf 3G 95
Blossom Ct. NG17: Kirk A 5C 52
Bluebell Bank NG13: Bing 5E 100
Blue Bell Cl. NG16: Unde 3D 64
Bluebell Cl. NG15: Huck 7C 66
　　NG17: Stant H 4F 45
Blue Bell Ct. DN22: Rans 2J 13
Bluebell Gro. NG17: Kirk A 4K 51
Blue Bell Hill Rd. NG3: Nott 1K 7 (2B 96)
Bluebell Pl. NG19: Mans W 5B 42
Bluebells, The NG17: Sut A 2B 52
Bluebell Wlk. NG24: New T 7G 135
　　　　　　　　　　　　　　　　　(not continuous)
Bluebell Wood La. NG21: C'tone 4H 43
Bluebell Wood Way NG17: Sut A 3G 51
Blue Bell Yd. NG22: Tuxf 6C 28
Blueberry Cft. NG17: Sut A 2G 51
Bluecoat Cl. NG1: Nott 2E 6 (2K 95)
Bluecoat Ho. NG1: Nott 2E 6 (2K 95)
Bluecoat St. NG1: Nott 2E 6 (2K 95)
Blundell Cl. NG2: Nott 7C 86
BLYBOROUGH 2D 145
BLYTH 6G 13 (3B 144)
Blyth Cl. NG19: Mans 1D 46
Blyth Ct. NG19: Mans 1D 46
Blyth Gdns. NG3: Mapp 5B 86
Blyth Gro. S81: Work 7H 19
Blyth Hall S81: Blyth 6G 13
Blyth Rd. DN10: Bawt, Serl 5F 9
　　DN11: Harwo .3C 8
　　DN11: Tick 1B 8
　　DN22: Rans .3F 13
　　NG22: Oll 4A 38
　　S81: Blyth 7J 13
　　S81: Oldc 6A 8
　　S81: Work 1G 21
Blyth St. NG3: Mapp 6B 86
BLYTON 2D 145
Blyton Wlk. NG5: Bestw 7D 76
Boarhill Gro. NG17: Sut A 2G 51
Boar La. NG24: New T 1C 136
Boat La. NG14: Blea 3D 138
　　NG14: Hove .4K 81
Boatswain Dr. NG15: Huck 5H 67
Bobbers Mill NG8: H Grn 1F 95
Bobbers Mill Bri. NG7: H Grn 1E 94
　　NG8: H Grn .1E 94
Bobbers Mill Rd. NG7: H Grn 1F 95
Boden Dr. NG16: Nuth 1H 83
Boden St. NG7: Radf 3A 6 (3G 95)
Bodill Gdns. NG15: Huck 7J 67
Bodmin Av. NG15: Huck 1C 74
Bodmin Ct. NG18: Mans 1C 54
Bodmin Dr. NG8: Aspl 5D 84
Body Rd. NG9: Chil 6G 105
BOGEND 4J 73
Bogg La. NG17: Huth 6G 27
Boggs Cotts. NG18: Mans 2C 54
Bohem Rd. NG10: Long E 6B 104
Bold Cl. NG6: Bulw 6H 75
BOLE 3C 145
Bolero Cl. NG8: Woll 3K 93
Bolero Sq. NG1: Nott 5H 7
BOLHAM 1F 23
Bolham La. DN22: Bol, Retf 1F 23
Bolham Rd. DN22: Bol 1F 23
Bolingey Way NG15: Huck 1C 74
Bollard's La. LE12: Sut B 5A 120
BOLSOVER 1A 146
Bolsover St. NG15: Huck 6H 67
　　NG18: Mans .4K 47
Bolton Av. NG9: Chil 5H 105
Bolton Cl. NG2: West Br 3D 108

Bolton Ter. NG12: Rad T 5E 98
BOLTON UPON DEARNE 1A 144
Bond Ho. NG5: Arn 6G 77
　　　　　　　　　　　　　　　　　(off Bond St.)
Bond St. NG2: Nott 5J 7 (4B 96)
　　NG5: Arn 6G 77
Bone Mill La. DN22: Welh 1J 23
　　S81: Work 7E 18
Bonetti Cl. NG5: Arn 2E 86
Boniface Gdns. NG5: Top V 5C 76
Bonington Cl. NG6: Bulw 1B 84
Bonington Dr. NG5: Arn 7H 77
Bonington Gallery, The 2D 6
Bonington Rd. NG3: Mapp 3C 86
　　NG19: Mans .4D 46
Bonington Theatre 6H 77
Bonner Hill NG14: Calv 7D 70
Bonner La. NG14: Calv 6E 70
Bonner's Rd. NG16: Aws 3B 82
Bonnington Cres. NG5: Sher 3K 85
Bonnymead NG12: Cotg 7D 110
Bonsal Ct. NG18: Mans 4D 48
Bonser Cl. NG4: Carl 1H 97
Bonser Cres. NG17: Huth 7C 44
Bonser Gdns. NG17: Sut A 1H 51
Booth Av. NG19: Plea 4A 40
Booth Cl. NG3: Nott 3G 7 (3A 96)
Booth Cres. NG19: Mans 7D 40
Booth St. NG19: Mans W 6H 41
Boots Yd. NG17: Huth 7D 44
Borders Av. NG17: Kirk A 3J 51
Borlace Cres. NG9: Stap 3D 104
Borman Cl. NG6: Bulw 2A 84
Borrow Bread La. NG14: Blea 3C 138
Borrowdale Cl. NG2: Gam 3G 109
　　NG18: Mans .7K 47
Borrowdale Ct. NG9: Chil 5G 105
Boscombe Rd. S81: Gate 4D 18
Bosden Cl. NG8: Bilb 2H 93
Bosley Sq. NG9: Lent A 1B 106
Bostocks La. NG10: Sand . . . . .6A 104 & 7A 104
Boston M. NG5: Sher 4G 85
Boston St. NG1: Nott 4H 7 (3A 96)
Boswell Cl. NG12: Kin 2C 142
　　NG18: Mans .7J 47
Boswell St. NG7: Radf 3F 95
Bosworth Cl. NG12: Shel 7H 89
Bosworth Dr. NG16: Newth 3F 73
Bosworth St. NG19: Mans 3D 46
Bosworth Wlk. NG2: Nott 7J 95
Botany Av. NG3: Nott 1C 96
　　NG18: Mans .4F 47
Botany Cl. NG2: West Br 6K 107
Botany Commercial Pk. NG18: Mans 4F 47
Botany Rd. NG18: Mans 1C 96
BOTHAMSALL 1B 144
BOTTESFORD
　　Nottingham .2D 149
　　Scunthorpe .1D 145
Bottesford La. NG13: Ors 2K 103
Bottle La. NG1: Nott 5F 7 (4K 95)
Bottom Grn. LE14: Upp B 3H 143
Bottom Row NG19: Plea 3E 40
　　NG22: Oll 6B 38
　　　　　　　　　　　　　　　　　(off Wellow Rd.)
　　NG24: New T .1E 136
Boudary Cl. NG13: What 4D 102
BOUGHTON 2F 39 (2B 146)
Boughton Cl. NG17: Skeg 5K 45
Boughton Ind. Est. (North) NG22: Bou 3G 39
Boughton Ind. Est. (South) NG22: Bou 4G 39
Boughton Pumping Station 1D 38
Boughton Rd. NG22: Wale 6G 27
　　S80: Rhod 7B 18
Boughton Way NG22: Bou 4G 39
Bould St. NG19: Mans 2F 47
Boulevard Ind. Pk. NG9: Bee 3C 106
BOULTHAM 2D 147
Boundary Cl. NG17: Kirk A 1A 60
Boundary Cl. NG21: Blid 5K 55
　　NG24: New T .2C 136
Boundary Cres. NG9: Bee 7A 94
　　NG21: Blid 6K 55
Boundary La. NG16: Lang M 3A 72
Boundary Rd. NG2: West Br 5B 108
　　NG9: Bee 7A 94
　　NG24: New T .2B 136
Boundary Row S80: Work 3G 21
Boundary Wlk. DN22: Retf 2B 22
　　NG20: Langw .6A 26
Bourne Av. NG16: Sels 5E 58
　　NG17: Kirk A .1B 60
Bourne Cl. NG9: Bram 7J 93
Bourne Dr. NG15: Rave 2C 62
Bourne M. NG4: Neth 2K 97
Bourne St. NG4: Neth 2K 97
Bournmoor Av. NG11: Clif 1F 115
Bovill St. NG7: Radf 2G 95
Bovington Ct. DN22: Retf 1E 22
Bowbridge La. NG24: New B, New T 5D 136
Bowbridge Rd. NG24: New T 2D 136
Bowden Av. NG5: Bestw V 2A 76
Bowden Cl. NG5: Sher 4K 85
Bowden Dr. NG9: Bee 3C 106
Bower Caravan Site
　　NG24: New T .7B 134

Bower Ct. NG24: New T 7D **134**
Bowers Av. NG3: Mapp P 1A **96**
Bowland Cl. NG3: Nott 1D **96**
Bowland Rd. NG13: Bing 4D **100**
Bowling St. NG18: Mans 4K **47**
Bowlwell Av. NG5: Top V 6B **76**
Bowman Pl. NG22: Well 7D **38**
Bowness Av. NG6: Basf 5D **84**
Bowness Cl. NG2: Gam 2F **109**
Bowne St. NG17: Sut A 7K **45**
Bowscale Cl.
NG2: West Br 4F **109**
Bow St. NG19: Mans W 5A **42**
Box Cres. NG17: Kirk A 5K **51**
Boxley Dr. NG2: West Br 5K **107**
Boxtree Av. NG15: Huck 7F **67**
Boyce Gdns. NG3: Mapp 6C **86**
Boycroft Av. NG3: Nott 7C **86**
Boyd Cl. NG5: Arn 5K **77**
Boy La. NG21: Edwin 7F **37**
Boynton Dr. NG3: Mapp 6C **86**
Bracadale Rd. NG5: Top V 5B **76**
BRACEBRIDGE 3H **21**
Bracebridge S80: Work 3H **21**
(not continuous)
Bracebridge Av. S80: Work 2J **21**
Bracebridge Ct. S80: Work 3H **21**
Bracebridge Dr. NG8: Bilb 2J **93**
Bracey Ri. NG2: West Br 6B **108**
Bracken Av. NG22: New O 2E **38**
Bracken Cl. NG4: Carl 5G **87**
NG8: Bilb 6A **84**
NG10: Long E 7A **104**
NG17: Kirk A 5K **51**
NG20: Mkt W 5E **34**
Bracken Ct. DN11: Harwo 2B **8**
NG22: Bils 6D **126**
Brackendale Av. NG5: Arn 6H **77**
Brackendale Dr. NG22: Wale 5G **27**
Brackenfield Av. NG19: Mans W 5A **42**
Brackenfield Dr. NG16: Gilt 6F **73**
Brackenfield Ri. NG15: Rave 1C **62**
Bracken Hill NG18: Mans 5C **48**
Brackenhill NG14: Cayt 6J **81**
Bracken Hill La. DN10: Miss 1B **10**
Bracken Ho. NG6: Bulw 7H **75**
Brackenhurst La. NG25: Sout 7G **131**
Bracken La. DN22: Retf 5G **23**
Bracken Rd. NG10: Long E 7A **104**
Bracken Way DN11: Harwo 2A **8**
Brackenwood Cl. NG19: Mans W 1C **48**
Brackmills Cl. NG19: Mans W 1A **48**
Bracknell Cres. NG8: Basf 6E **84**
BRACON 1C **145**
Bracton Dr. NG3: Nott 2C **96**
Bradbourne Av. NG11: Wilf 4H **107**
Bradbury Gdns. NG11: Rudd 3J **115**
Bradbury/Midway Ind. Est.
NG7: Lent 1F **107**
Bradbury St. NG2: Nott 4D **96**
Bradder Way NG18: Mans 5G **47**
Braddock Cl. NG7: Lent 4F **95**
Braddon Av. NG9: Stap 7D **92**
Bradfield Rd. NG8: Brox 6A **84**
Bradford Ct. NG6: Bulw 1B **84**
Bradford Way NG6: Bestw V 7D **68**
Bradforth Av. NG18: Mans 3C **48**
Bradgate Cl. NG10: Sand 5A **104**
Bradgate Rd. NG7: H Grn 7H **85**
Bradley Ct. NG9: Bee 3B **106**
Bradleys La. NG14: Hove 4J **81**
Bradley St. NG10: Sand 4B **104**
Bradleys Yd. NG12: Plum 3H **117**
NG20: Mkt W 4D **34**
Bradley Wlk. NG11: Clif 2G **115**
Bradman Gdns. NG5: Arn 1E **86**
BRADMORE 7C **116** (2A **148**)
Bradmore Av. NG11: Rudd 2K **115**
Bradmore Bus. Pk. NG11: Bunny 1B **118**
Bradmore Ct. NG18: Mans 7C **48**
Bradmore La. NG12: Plum 6F **117**
Bradmore Ri. NG5: Sher 3K **85**
Bradmore Rd. NG12: Wys 6E **118**
Bradshaw Cl. NG12: Kin 2C **142**
Bradstone Dr. NG3: Ged, Mapp 1G **87**
Bradwell Cl. NG16: Gilt 6G **73**
Bradwell Dr. NG5: Top V 6B **76**
Braefell Cl. NG2: West Br 4G **109**
Braemar Av. NG16: Eastw 6D **72**
Braemar Dr. NG4: Ged 6A **88**
Braemar Rd. NG6: Bulw 7J **75**
NG19: Mans W 6F **43**
Braemer Rd. NG23: Coll 2H **129**
Braidwood Ct. NG7: H Grn 1G **95**
Brail La. NG22: Eakr 4B **126**
Brailsford Ct. NG18: Mans 4D **48**
Brailsford Rd. NG7: Lent 7F **95**
Brailsford Way NG9: Chil 7H **105**
Brailwood Cl. NG22: Bils 5D **126**
Brailwood Rd. NG22: Bils 5D **126**
BRAITHWAITE 1B **144**
BRAITHWELL 2A **144**
Brake La. NG22: Wale 1D **38**
Brake Rd. NG22: Wale 6F **27**
Brake Vw. NG22: New O 2E **38**
Bramber Gro. NG11: Clif 3F **115**
Bramble Cl. DN22: Nth L 7C **24**
NG6: Basf 4E **84**
NG9: Atten 7J **105**
NG10: Long E 7A **104**
NG22: Bils 6D **126**
NG22: New O 2D **38**
Bramble Ct. NG4: Ged 6J **87**
NG10: Sand 4B **104**
Bramble Cft. NG17: Sut A 2G **51**
Bramble Dr. NG3: Nott 1D **96**
Bramble Gdns. NG8: Bilb 7B **84**
Bramble La. NG18: Mans 5C **48**
Bramble Rd. DN22: Retf 6H **23**
Brambles, The NG13: Barns 2G **141**
NG22: Wale 5G **27**
Bramble Way DN11: Harwo 2B **8**
NG12: Cotg 7F **111**
Brambling Cl. NG18: Mans 3A **48**
Bramblings, The S81: Gate 5D **18**
BRAMCOTE 1F **105** (2A **148**)
Bramcote Av. NG9: Chil 3H **105**
Bramcote Ct. NG18: Mans 7C **48**
Bramcote Crematorium
NG9: Bram 5F **93**
Bramcote Dr. DN22: Retf 5D **22**
NG8: Woll 5J **93**
NG9: Bee 2K **105**
Bramcote Dr. W. NG9: Bee 3J **105**
BRAMCOTE HILLS 7H **93**
Bramcote La. NG8: Woll 6J **93**
NG9: Chil 3H **105**
Bramcote Leisure Cen. 7G **93**
Bramcote Rd. NG9: Bee 2J **105**
Bramcote St. NG7: Radf 3F **95**
Bramcote Wlk. NG7: Radf 3F **95**
Bramerton Rd. NG8: Bilb 2H **93**
Bramhall Rd. NG8: Bilb 2H **93**
BRAMLEY 2A **144**
Bramley Cl. NG14: Gun 2B **90**
NG25: Sout 6J **131**
Bramley Ct. LE12: East L 3A **122**
NG16: Kimb 1E **82**
NG17: Sut A 7K **45**
Bramley Grn. NG8: Brox 6K **83**
Bramley Rd. NG8: Brox 6K **83**
BRAMLEY VALE 2A **146**
Bramley Wlk. NG19: Mans 3D **46**
Bramley Way DN10: Mist 4K **11**
BRAMPTON 1D **147**
Brampton Dr. NG9: Stap 4E **104**
BRAMPTON EN LE MORTHEN 3A **144**
Bramwell Dr. NG9: Bram 3H **105**
Brancaster Cl. NG6: Cin 3C **84**
Brancliffe La. S81: Shire 4A **18**
Brand Ct. NG17: Stant H 4G **45**
Brandish Cres. NG11: Clif 1E **114**
Brand La. NG17: Stant H 5G **45**
BRANDON 1D **149**
Brandon Cl. NG24: Bald 5H **137**
Brandon Wlk. NG17: Sut A 3H **51**
Brandreth Av. NG3: Nott 7C **86**
NG17: Sut A 6H **45**
Brandreth Dr. NG16: Gilt 6E **72**
Brand St. NG2: Nott 6C **96**
Brangwen Ho. *NG7: Lent* *4F* ***95***
(off Faraday Rd.)
Branklene Cl. NG16: Kimb 7J **73**
Branksome Wlk. NG2: Nott 6K **95**
BRANSBY 1D **147**
Bransdale S81: Work 4H **19**
Bransdale Av. NG19: Mans W 1A **48**
Bransdale Rd. NG11: Clif 1E **114**
BRANSTON 3D **149**
Branston Av. NG22: Farns 5K **57**
Branston Cl. NG24: Wint 2G **135**
Branston Gdns. NG2: West Br 5A **108**
Branston Wlk. NG5: Sher 3K **85**
BRANT BROUGHTON 3D **147**
Brantford Av. NG11: Clif 1G **115**
BRANTON 1B **144**
Brassington Cl. NG16: Gilt 7F **73**
Brassington Ct. NG19: Mans W 5A **42**
BRATTLEBY 3D **145**
Bratton Dr. NG5: Bestw 2H **85**
Braunton Cl. NG15: Huck 7D **66**
Braunton Cres. NG3: Mapp 1G **87**
Brayton Cres. NG6: Bulw 2E **84**
Breach Ho. *NG7: Lent* *4F* ***95***
(off Faraday Rd.)
Break La. NG15: Pap 7A **62**
BREASTON 2A **148**
Breaston Ct. *NG5: Top V* *6C* ***76***
(off Erewash Gdns.)
Brechin S81: Work 7J **19**
Brechin Cl. NG5: Arn 5K **77**
Brechin Ct. NG19: Mans W 3H **41**
Breck Bank NG22: New O 3C **38**
Breckbank NG19: Mans W 1A **48**
Breck Bank Cres. NG22: New O 3C **38**
Breckhill Rd. NG3: Mapp 2B **86**
NG5: Woodt 2B **86**
Breck La. DN10: Matt, Matt T 3F **15**
Brecks La. DN22: Tres 4K **25**
NG23: Elston 2E **140**
Brecks Rd. DN22: Ord 7D **22**
Breckswood Dr. NG11: Clif 3F **115**
Brecon Cl. NG8: Cin 4B **84**
NG21: Rain 2B **56**
Breconshire Gdns. NG6: Basf 3F **85**
Breedon St. NG10: Long E 6A **104**
Brendon Ct. NG9: Bram 1G **105**
Brendon Dr. NG8: Woll 3B **94**
NG16: Kimb 7K **73**
Brendon Gdns. NG8: Woll 3B **94**
Brendon Gro. NG13: Bing 3D **100**
Brendon Lawrence Sports Hall 7A **86**
Brendon Rd. NG8: Woll 3B **94**
Brendon Way NG10: Long E 7A **104**
Brentcliffe Av. NG3: Nott 1D **96**
BRENTINGBY 3C **149**
Brentnall Ct. NG9: Chil 6J **105**
Bressingham Dr. NG2: West Br 6K **107**
Bretby Ct. NG18: Mans 4D **48**
Brett Cl. NG15: Huck 1E **74**
Bretton Rd. NG15: Rave 1D **62**
Brettsil Dr. NG11: Rudd 3J **115**
Brewers Way NG18: Mans 5B **48**
Brewer's Wharf NG24: New T 7C **134**
Brewery La. DN10: Eve 6B **10**
DN22: Retf 4F **23**
Brewery St. NG16: Kimb 1E **82**
Brewhouse, The *NG24: New T* *1C* ***136***
(off Castle Brewery)
Brewhouse Yd. NG1: Nott 7D **6** (5J **95**)
Brewsters Cl. NG13: Bing 4F **101**
Brewsters Rd. NG3: Nott 7B **86**
Brewsters Way DN22: Retf 1C **22**
Brian Clough Way
NG7: Lent, Nott 5A **6** (6C **94**)
(not continuous)
NG9: Bram, Stap 4B **104**
(not continuous)
Briar Av. NG10: Sand 6A **104**
Briarbank Av. NG3: Nott 7D **86**
Briarbank Wlk.
NG3: Nott 1D **96**
Briar Cl. DN22: Elk 2G **27**
NG9: Bram 7K **93**
NG12: Key 6J **117**
NG15: Huck 1D **74**
NG17: Stant H 4G **45**
NG21: Rain 2K **55**
S80: Work 3D **20**
Briar Ct. DN11: Harwo 2B **8**
NG2: Nott 7J **95**
NG22: New O 3C **38**
Briar Gdns. NG14: Calv 5A **70**
Briar Ga. NG10: Long E 7A **104**
Briargate NG12: Cotg 7F **111**
Briar Gro. DN11: Harwo 2B **8**
Briar La. NG18: Mans 6C **48**
Briar Lea DN22: Ord 6D **22**
S80: Work 3D **20**
Briar Rd. NG16: Newth 6F **73**
NG22: New O 3C **38**
Briars, The DN10: Miss 2D **10**
Briarwood Av. NG3: Nott 1D **96**
Briarwood Cl. NG19: Mans W 1D **48**
Briarwood Ct. NG5: Sher 4B **86**
Briber Hill S81: Blyth 7G **13**
Briber Rd. S81: Blyth 7G **13**
Brickcliffe Rd. LE12: East L 2B **122**
Brickenell Rd. NG14: Calv 7D **70**
Brickenhole La. DN10: Walk 7H **11**
Brickings La. DN22: Sth L 2H **25**
Brickings Way DN22: Stu S 2C **24**
Brick Kiln La. NG18: Mans 3C **46**
NG19: Mans 3C **46**
Brickley Cres. LE12: East L 3B **122**
Brickyard NG15: Huck 7J **67**
Brickyard Cotts. NG16: Newth 5E **72**
Brickyard Dr. NG15: Huck 1J **75**
Brickyard La. DN10: Miss 1E **10**
LE12: West L 3F **121**
NG12: Rad T 5G **99**
NG13: East B 5E **90**
NG20: Cuck 2B **32**
NG22: Bou 3F **39**
NG22: Farns 5K **57**
Brickyard Plantation Nature Reserve 7D **82**
Brick Yard Rd. DN22: Gam 1G **27**
Bridegate La.
LE14: Hick, Hick P 7A **142**
Bridge Av. NG9: Chil 4K **105**
Bridge Ct. NG6: Bulw 5K **75**
NG9: Bee 2C **106**
NG15: Huck 7G **67**
NG24: Bald 5J **137**
Bridge End Av. NG16: Sels 4D **58**
Bridge Farm La. NG11: Clif 7F **107**
Bridgeford Ct. Caravan Pk.
NG13: East B 4C **90**
Bridgegate DN22: Retf 3E **22**
Bridgegate Cen. DN22: Retf 3E **22**
Bridge Grn. NG8: Brox 6K **83**
Bridge Grn. Wlk. NG8: Brox 6K **83**
Bridge Gro. NG2: West Br 1B **108**
Bridge Ho. Ct. S81: Carl L 7D **12**
Bridgend Cl. NG9: Stap 4C **104**
Bridge Pl. S80: Work 2G **21**
Bridge Rd. NG8: Woll 3J **93**
Bridge Row S81: Carl L 6D **12**

Bridge St. NG10: Long E 7C **104**
NG10: Sand 4B **104**
NG16: Lang M 3A **72**
NG18: Mans 3J **47**
NG24: New T .1C **136**
S80: Work 3F **21**
Bridgewater Ct. NG5: Woodt 2A **86**
Bridgeway Cen. NG2: Nott 6K **95**
Bridgeway Ct. NG2: Nott 6A **96**
Bridgford Rd. NG2: West Br 7B **96**
Bridgford St. NG13: East B 5D **90**
NG18: Mans 5B **48**
Bridgnorth Dr. NG11: Clif 7F **107**
Bridgnorth Way NG9: Toton 6D **104**
Bridle Cl. NG17: Stant H 4F **45**
Bridle Rd. NG9: Bram 7G **93**
NG14: Bur J 1C **88**
Bridlesmith Ga. NG1: Nott 5F **7** (4K **95**)
Bridlesmith Wlk. NG1: Nott 5F **7**
Bridleway, The NG19: Mans W 7B **42**
Bridle Ways NG13: East B 5E **90**
Bridlington St. NG7: H Grn 1F **95**
Bridport Av. NG8: Radf 3E **94**
Brielen Ct. NG12: Rad T 5F **99**
Brielen Rd. NG12: Rad T 5F **99**
Brierfield Av. NG11: Wilf 5J **107**
Brierley Bus. Pk. NG17: Stant H 5G **45**
Brierley Cotts. NG17: Sut A 7J **45**
Brierley Forest Golf Course 6D **44**
Brierley Forest Pk. Vis. Cen. 6E **44**
Brierley Grn. NG4: Neth 1K **97**
Brierley Pk. Cl. NG17: Stant H 5G **45**
Brierley Rd. NG17: Sut A 6H **45**
Brightmoor St. NG1: Nott 5G **7**
Brightmoor Pl. NG1: Nott 5G **7**
Brightmoor St. NG1: Nott 5G **7** (4A **96**)
Bright Sq. NG19: Mans 7D **40**
Bright St. NG7: Lent 3F **95**
NG16: Kimb 1D **82**
Brimblebeck La. NG23: Sut T 3A **128**
Brimington Ct. NG19: Mans W 5A **42**
(off Brackenfield Av.)
Brindley Cl. DN10: Gri H 3A **16**
Brindley Ct. NG5: Woodt 3A **86**
Brindley Rd. NG8: Bilb 3H **93**
Brinkhill Cres. NG11: Clif 6G **107**
BRINKLEY 3F **139**
BRINSLEY 7C **64** (1A **148**)
Brinsley Cl. NG8: Aspl 6B **84**
Brinsley Hill NG16: Brins 3A **64**
Brisbane Cl. NG19: Mans W 3J **41**
Brisbane Ct. NG24: Bald 5G **137**
Brisbane Dr. NG5: Top V 6A **76**
NG9: Stap 7E **92**
Bristol Cl. NG24: Codd 7H **135**
Bristol M. S81: Work 4F **19**
Britannia Av. NG6: Basf 2F **85**
Britannia Cl. NG4: Neth 7A **74**
Britannia Cl. NG4: Neth 2K **97**
Britannia Rd. NG10: Long E 7C **104**
British Coal Ent. Pk. DN11: Harwo 4B **8**
British Flds. NG22: Tuxf 7A **28**
British Geological Survey 6J **117**
Brittania Ct. NG24: New T 1B **136**
Britten Gdns. NG3: Nott 2C **96**
Brixham Rd. NG15: Huck 1D **74**
Brixton Rd. NG7: Radf 3F **95**
Brixworth Way DN22: Retf 2H **23**
B Road NG7: Nott 3E **106**
Broad Cl. NG14: Woodbo 2G **79**
Broad Dr. NG21: Edwin 4B **36**
Broad Eadow Rd. NG6: Bulw 7F **75**
Broadfields NG14: Calv 5D **70**
Broad Ga. NG22: East M 2E **28**
Broadgate NG9: Bee 2B **106**
Broadgate Av. NG9: Bee 2B **106**
Broadgate La. NG9: Bee 2B **106**
NG23: Kel 1G **133**
Broadgate Pk. NG9: Bee 1B **106**
Broad Gores DN22: Clar 7H **17**
(not continuous)
BROADHOLME .1D **147**
Broadholme St. NG7: Lent 5G **95**
Broadhurst Av. NG6: Basf 5E **84**
Broading La. DN22: Lane 1G **29**
NG22: Eakr 1D **126**
Broadlands NG10: Sand 6A **104**
Broadlands Cl. NG17: Sut A 6B **46**
Broad La. DN22: Cott, Sth L 1K **25**
NG16: Brins .4C **64**
S80: Work 7A **20**
Broadleigh Cl. NG2: West Br 6K **107**
Broadleigh Cl. DN22: Ord 6D **22**
Broad Marsh NG1: Nott 7F **7** (5K **95**)
Broad Marsh Shop. Cen. NG1: Nott . . .6F **7** (4K **95**)
Broadmead NG14: Bur J 2E **88**
Broadmeer NG12: Cotg 6D **110**
Broadmere Ct. NG5: Arn 5K **77**
Broad Oak Cl. NG3: Nott 1B **96**
Broad Oak Dr. NG9: Stap 3C **104**
NG16: Brins .4B **64**
Broadoak Pk. NG17: Nunc 3K **59**
Broadstairs Rd. NG9: Toton 7E **104**
Broadstone Cl. NG2: West Br 5J **107**
Broad St. NG1: Nott 4G **7** (3A **96**)
Broad Valley Dr. NG6: Bestw V 2A **76**

Broad Wlk. NG6: Basf 4D **84**
Broadway NG1: Nott 6G **7** (4A **96**)
Broadway, The NG18: Mans 4J **47**
Broadway Cinema
Nottingham .4G **7**
Broadway E. NG4: Carl 2G **97**
Broadwood Ct. NG9: Bee 1B **106**
Broadwood Rd. NG5: Bestw 6D **76**
Brockdale Gdns. NG12: Key 6H **117**
Brockenhurst Gdns. NG3: Nott 2C **96**
Brockenhurst Rd. NG19: Mans 4D **46**
Brockhole Cl. NG2: West Br 4G **109**
BROCKHOUSE .3A **144**
Brocklehurst Dr. NG21: Edwin 7H **37**
Brockley Rd. NG2: West Br 2E **108**
Brockton Av. NG24: Farnd 6J **133**
Brockwood Cres. NG12: Key 6H **117**
BRODSWORTH .1A **144**
Bromfield Cl. NG3: Nott 1F **97**
Bromley Av. NG24: New T 3D **136**
Bromley Cl. NG6: Bulw 1C **84**
Bromley Pl. NG1: Nott 5D **6** (4J **95**)
Bromley Rd. NG2: West Br 3B **108**
Brompton Cl. NG5: Arn 4C **76**
Brompton Way NG2: West Br 6K **109**
Bronte Ct. NG7: Radf 1B **6** (2H **95**)
Brook Av. NG5: Arn 6K **77**
Brook Chase Mdws. NG9: Chil 4H **105**
Brook Cl. NG6: Bulw 1C **84**
NG16: Newth 5F **73**
Brook Ct. NG7: Radf 2G **95**
NG16: Lang M 4A **72**
NG19: Mans .4D **46**
Brookdale Ct. NG5: Sher 2A **86**
Brookdale Rd. NG17: Sut A 7A **46**
Brook Dr. NG12: Kin 2B **142**
Brooke Cl. NG24: Bald 4G **137**
S81: Work 1K **21**
Brook End LE12: East L 2A **122**
Brooke St. DE7: Ilk 2A **92**
NG10: Sand .4A **104**
Brook Farm Ct. LE12: Will W 6F **143**
Brookfield Av. NG15: Huck 1G **75**
NG17: Sut A .6H **45**
Brookfield Cl. NG12: Rad T 5E **98**
Brookfield Ct. NG2: Nott 6K **95**
NG5: Arn 7J **77**
Brookfield Dr. NG14: Hove 3K **81**
Brookfield Gdns. NG5: Arn 7J **77**
Brookfield M. NG10: Sand 3B **104**
Brookfield Rd. NG5: Arn 7H **77**
Brookfields Way LE12: East L 2A **122**
Brookfield Way DE75: Hea 5A **72**
Brook Gdns. NG5: Arn 6J **77**
BROOK HILL 2H **115**
Brookhill Av. NG16: Pinx 7B **50**
Brookhill Ct. NG17: Sut A 1J **51**
(off Langton Rd.)
Brookhill Cres. NG8: Woll 5K **93**
Brookhill Dr. NG8: Woll 5K **93**
Brookhill Ind. Est. NG16: Pinx 2C **58**
Brookhill La. NG16: Pinx 7B **50**
Brookhill Leys Rd. NG16: Eastw 5C **72**
Brookhill Rd. NG16: Pinx 2B **58**
Brookhill St. NG9: Stap 4B **104**
Brookhouse Ct. NG20: Neth L 6B **26**
Brookland Av. NG18: Mans 3F **47**
Brookland Cl. NG14: Gun 2B **90**
Brookland Dr. NG9: Chil 4J **105**
Brooklands Cl. NG23: Coll 1H **129**
Brooklands Cres. NG4: Ged 6K **87**
Brooklands Dr. NG4: Ged 6K **87**
Brooklands Rd. NG3: Nott 1E **96**
Brooklyn Av. NG14: Bur J 2D **88**
Brooklyn Cl. NG6: Bulw 2E **84**
Brooklyn Rd. NG6: Bulw 1E **84**
Brook Rd. NG9: Bee 1A **106**
BROOKSBY 3B **143**
Brooksby La. NG11: Clif 5G **107**
Brooks Cl. NG13: East B 4E **90**
Brooks Cotts. NG4: Carl 1F **97**
Brookside LE12: East L 4A **122**
NG14: Lowd .5D **80**
NG15: Huck .1H **75**
NG16: Eastw .2D **72**
Brookside Av. LE12: East L 3K **121**
NG8: Woll 6J **93**
NG19: Mans W 4J **41**
Brookside Cotts. NG14: Bur J 2D **88**
Brookside Gdns. NG11: Rudd 2J **115**
Brookside Ind. Units NG9: Stap 1C **104**
Brookside Rd. NG11: Rudd 2J **115**
Brookside Wlk. DN11: Birc 2E **8**
Brookside Way NG17: Huth 2C **50**
Brook St. NG1: Nott 4G **7** (3A **96**)
NG15: Huck .5G **67**
NG17: Sut A .1J **51**
Brook Ter. S80: Work 3F **21**
Brookthorpe Way NG11: Wilf 5H **107**
Brookvale Cl. NG5: Arn 4C **48**
Brookvale Rd. NG16: Lang M 4A **72**
Brook Vw. Ct. NG12: Key 1H **119**
Brook Vw. Dr. NG12: Key 1H **119**
Brook Wlk. NG25: Sout 5G **131**
Brookwood Cres. NG4: Carl 1F **97**

Broom Cl. NG14: Calv 5D **70**
S81: Gate 3E **18**
Broome Acre DE55: Sth N 7A **50**
Broome Cl. NG24: New B 4E **136**
Broomfield Cl. NG10: Sand 4A **104**
Broomfield La. DN10: Matt T 1F **15**
NG22: Farns .5K **57**
BROOMHILL 1J **75**
Broomhill Av. S81: Work 4F **19**
Broomhill Cotts. NG15: Huck 1J **75**
Broomhill La. DN10: Eve 7A **10**
NG19: Mans .2F **47**
NG20: Mkt W 2F **35**
Broomhill Pk. Vw. NG15: Huck 1J **75**
Broomhill Rd. NG6: Bulw 1D **84**
NG15: Huck .1G **75**
NG16: Kimb .1F **83**
Broom Rd. NG14: Calv 6D **70**
Broom Wlk. NG3: Nott 7E **86**
Brora Rd. NG6: Bulw 7K **75**
Brotts La. NG23: Norm T 1K **125**
Brotts Rd. NG23: Norm T 1K **125**
BROUGH 3D **147**
Brougham Av. NG19: Mans 7D **40**
Brough La. DN22: Elk 3F **27**
Broughton Cl. NG21: C'tone 5H **43**
Broughton Dr. NG8: Woll 4D **94**
NG24: New T 4B **136**
Broughton Gdns. NG24: Bald 5H **137**
Broughton St. NG9: Bee 2A **106**
Brown Av. NG19: Mans W 5G **41**
Brown Cres. NG17: Sut A 4A **46**
Brownes Rd. NG13: Bing 3H **101**
Brownhill Cl. NG12: Crop Bi 5B **112**
Browning Cl. NG5: Arn 7F **77**
S81: Work 7J **19**
Browning Cl. NG5: Sher 4J **85**
Browning Rd. NG24: Bald 4H **137**
Browning St. NG18: Mans 3G **47**
Brown La. NG11: Bart F 7A **114**
Brownley Rd. NG21: C'tone 4H **43**
Brownlow Dr. NG5: Top V 5K **75**
Brownlow Rd. NG5: Sher 1F **47**
Brownlow's Hill NG24: Codd 7K **135**
Browns Cft. NG6: Basf 4E **84**
Brown's Flats NG16: Kimb 7K **73**
Brown's La. NG13: East B 4D **90**
(not continuous)
Brown St. NG7: H Grn 1G **95**
NG19: Mans .2F **47**
Brown Wood La. NG23: Thor 4J **31**
BROXHOLME 1D **147**
BROXTOWE 5B **84**
Broxtowe Av. NG8: Aspl 5D **84**
NG16: Kimb .1C **82**
Broxtowe Country Pk. 5K **83**
Broxtowe Dr. NG15: Huck 4G **67**
NG18: Mans .4J **47**
Broxtowe Hall Cl. NG8: Brox 5B **84**
Broxtowe La. NG8: Aspl, Brox 6A **84**
Broxtowe Pk. Bus. Cen. NG8: Stre 5J **83**
Broxtowe Ri. NG8: Cin 4C **84**
Broxtowe St. NG5: Sher 5K **85**
Bruce Cl. NG2: Nott 6A **96**
Bruce Dr. NG2: West Br 2A **108**
BRUMBY 1D **145**
Brunel Av. NG16: Newth 2F **73**
Brunel Bus. Pk. NG24: New T 7E **134**
Brunel Cl. DN11: Harwo 4C **8**
Brunel Ct. NG24: New T 6F **135**
Brunel Dr. NG24: New T 4F **135**
Brunel Dr. Workshops NG24: New T 4F **135**
Brunel Gate DN11: Harwo 4C **8**
Brunel Pk. Ind. Est. DN11: Harwo 4C **8**
Brunel Ter. NG7: Nott 4A **6** (3H **95**)
Brunswick Dr. NG9: Stap 4E **104**
Bruntings, The NG3: Mans 3B **48**
Bruntings Ct. NG18: Mans 4B **48**
Brunts Bus. Cen. NG18: Mans 2J **47**
(off Samuel Brunts Way)
Brunt's La. NG13: East B 6D **90**
Brunt St. NG18: Mans 4J **47**
Brushfield St. NG7: H Grn 1F **95**
Brusty Pl. NG14: Bur J 2D **88**
Bryan Ct. NG8: Aspl 7D **84**
Bryans Cl. DN11: Harwo 4D **8**
NG24: Codd .6H **135**
Bryans Cl. La. DN10: Miss 2A **10**
Bryans La. LE12: Will W 6H **143**
Brynsmoor Rd. NG16: Brins 6C **64**
Bryony Way NG19: Mans W 5B **42**
Buckfast Way NG2: West Br 2D **108**
Buckingham Av. NG15: Huck 5H **67**
Buckingham Cl. NG17: Kirk A 5K **51**
NG19: Mans W 4A **42**
Buckingham Ct. DN11: Harwo 1D **8**
NG10: Sand .6A **104**
Buckingham Dr. NG12: Rad T 6J **99**
Buckingham Ri. S81: Work 5E **18**
Buckingham Rd. NG5: Woodt 2B **86**
NG10: Sand .5A **104**
Buckingham Way NG16: Want 7B **74**
Buckland Cl. NG17: Sut A 2B **52**
Buckland Dr. NG14: Woodbo 2G **79**
Bucklee Dr. NG14: Calv 6C **70**
Bucklow Cl. NG8: Basf 6E **84**

BUCKMINSTER 3D 149
Buck's La. LE12: Sut B 5A 120
BUDBY 2B 146
Budby Av. NG18: Mans 4B 48
Budby Cres. NG20: Mede V 6G 33
Budby Dr. NG20: Mede V 4K 33
Budby Ri. NG15: Huck 6H 67
Budby Rd. NG20: Cuck 4D 32
BULCOTE 1G 89 (1B 148)
Bulcote Dr. NG14: Bur J 4C 88
Bulcote Ho. NG4: Carl 7H 87
                                      (off Garden City)
Bulcote Rd. NG11: Clif 6G 107
Bulham La. NG23: Sut T 2C 128
Bullace Ct. NG19: Mans W 1A 48
Bullace Rd. NG3: Nott 1K 7 (1C 96)
Bull Cl. Rd. NG7: Lent 1F 107
Bulldole La. DN22: Clay 7H 15
Buller Cl. NG23: Coll 1J 129
Buller St. DE7: Ilk 2A 92
Buller Ter. NG5: Sher 4A 86
BULL FARM 7E 40
Bullfinch Rd. NG6: Basf 3E 84
Bullins Cl. NG5: Arn 5E 76
Bullivant St. NG3: Nott 1G 7 (2A 96)
Bullock Cl. NG19: Mans W 4H 41
Bullpit Rd. NG24: Bald 5G 137
Bull Yd. NG25: Sout 5H 131
   S80: Work 3F 21
Bully La. NG19: Sook 5A 34
BULWELL 7J 75 (1A 148)
Bulwell Bus. Cen. NG6: Bulw 7G 75
BULWELL FOREST 6J 75
Bulwell Forest Golf Course 7A 76
Bulwell Forest Stop (NET) 6J 75
Bulwell Hall Pk. 4H 75
Bulwell High Rd. NG6: Bulw 1C 84
Bulwell La. NG6: Basf 3E 84
Bulwell Station (Rail) 1D 84
Bulwell Stop (NET) 1D 84
Bulwer Rd. NG7: Radf 3G 95
   NG17: Kirk A 6K 51
Bunbury St. NG2: Nott 7A 96
Bungalow La. NG22: Bils 6D 126
Bungalows, The DN11: Birc 2F 9
                                       (off White Ho. Rd.)
   NG22: Wale 5G 27
Bunnison La. NG12: Cols B 7H 141
BUNNY 3B 118 (3A 148)
Bunny Hall Pk. NG11: Bunny 4B 118
Bunny Hill LE12: Bunny, Costo 7A 118
   NG11: Bunny 7A 118
Bunny Hill Top LE12: Costo 6A 118
Bunny La. NG11: Bunny 1E 118
   NG12: Key 1E 118
Buntings La. NG4: Carl 1F 97
Bunting St. NG7: Lent 7F 95
Bunyan Grn. Rd. NG16: Sels 6B 58
Burbage Ct. NG18: Mans 4D 48
Burberry Av. NG15: Huck 2J 75
Burden Cres. DN22: Woodbe 7G 25
Burden La. NG12: Shel 6H 89
Burford Rd. NG7: H Grn 7G 85
Burford St. NG5: Arn 6G 77
Burgage NG25: Sout 5H 131
Burgage Cl. NG25: Sout 5H 131
Burgage La. NG25: Sout 5H 131
Burgass Rd. NG3: Nott 1D 96
Burge Cl. NG2: Nott 6K 95
Burgh Hall Cl. NG9: Chil 7H 105
BURGHWALLIS 1A 144
Burhill NG12: Cotg 7F 111
Burke St. NG7: Radf 3A 6 (3H 95)
Burleigh Cl. NG4: Carl 1J 97
Burleigh Ri. NG22: Tuxf 6C 28
Burleigh Rd. NG22: Tuxf 6C 28
Burleigh Rd. NG2: West Br 3C 108
Burleigh Sq. NG9: Chil 5H 105
Burley Cl. DN10: Walk 6G 11
Burlington Av. NG5: Sher 4J 85
Burlington Cl. NG5: Sher 4K 85
Burlington Dr. NG19: Mans 7E 40
Burlington Rd. NG4: Carl 7H 87
   NG5: Sher 4K 85
Burma Rd. NG21: Blid 5J 55
Burma Rd. Ind. Est. NG21: Blid 5K 55
Burnaby St. NG6: Basf 3E 84
Burnaston Cl. NG19: Mans W 5A 42
Burnaston Rd. NG18: Mans 4D 48
Burnbank Cl. NG2: West Br 4G 109
Burnbreck Gdns. NG8: Woll 4K 93
Burndale Wlk. NG5: Top V 6A 76
Burneham Cl. NG13: East B 5D 90
Burnell Cl NG23: Sibt 6E 140
Burnham Av. NG9: Chil 5A 106
Burnham Ct. NG18: Mans 6J 47
Burnham Lodge NG5: Top V 5A 76
Burnham St. NG5: Sher 5K 85
Burnham Way NG2: Nott 5K 95
Burnmoor La. NG22: Egma 2E 124
Burnor Pool NG14: Calv 6D 70
Burns, The NG20: Mkt W 3E 34
Burns Av. NG7: Radf 2B 6 (2H 95)
   NG19: Mans W .7J 41
Burns Ct. NG5: Sher 4J 85
Burnside Cl. NG17: Kirk A 4K 51

Burnside Dr. NG9: Bram 6H 93
   NG19: Mans 7E 40
Burnside Grn. NG8: Bilb 2J 93
Burnside Gro. NG12: Toll 1F 117
Burnside Rd. NG2: West Br 4B 108
   NG8: Bilb 2J 93
Burns La. NG20: Chu W, Mkt W 3D 34
Burns Rd. S81: Work 7J 19
Burns St. NG7: Radf 2A 6 (2H 95)
   NG18: Mans 3G 47
Burn St. NG17: Sut A 7A 46
Burnt Oak Cl. NG16: Nuth 4J 83
Burnt Oaks Cl. NG19: Mans W 6K 41
Burntstump Country Pk. 3F 69
Burntstump Hill NG5: Arn 3E 68
Burnwood Dr. NG8: Woll 3J 93
BURRINGHAM 1D 145
Burrows, The LE12: East L 2A 122
Burrows Av. NG9: Bee 7A 94
Burrows Ct. NG3: Nott 3C 96
Burrows Cres. NG9: Bee 7A 94
Burrow Wlk. NG17: Kirk A 7J 51
Bursar Way NG10: Long E 6B 104
Burtness Rd. NG11: Clif 1F 115
Burton Av. NG4: Carl 7E 86
Burton Cl. NG4: Carl 6K 87
   NG17: Sut A 7G 45
Burton Dr. NG22: Bils 5C 126
Burton Dr. NG9: Chil 5H 105
BURTON JOYCE 3E 88 (1B 148)
Burton Joyce Station (Rail) 4D 88
Burton La. DN22: Sth W 3K 17
   NG13: What 4E 102
BURTON LAZARS .3C 149
Burton Manderfield Ct.
   NG2: Nott 6K 95
BURTON ON THE WOLDS 3A 148
Burton Ri. NG17: Ann W 4A 60
   NG22: Wale 5G 27
Burton Rd. NG4: Carl, Ged 1H 97
   NG14: Bur J 5B 88
                                         (not continuous)
   NG17: Sut A 7G 45
Burton St. NG1: Nott 4E 6 (3K 95)
Burton Wlk. LE12: East L 3A 122
BURTON WOLDS .3B 148
Burwell Ct. NG19: Mans W 5A 42
Burwell St. NG7: H Grn 2G 95
Burwood Av. NG18: Mans 3C 48
Bush Cl. NG5: Top V 6B 76
Bushmead M. S80: Work 3G 21
                                         (off Pilgrim Way)
Bushstocks La. DN22: Tres 5G 25
Business Centre Beeston
   NG9: Bee 5B 106
Business Place, The NG19: Mans W 5H 41
Buskeyfield La. NG20: Cuck 3A 32
Bute Av. NG7: Lent 4G 95
Butler Av. NG12: Rad T 4F 99
Butler Cl. NG12: Crop Bu 3B 112
Butler Cres. NG19: Mans 7D 40
Butler Dr. NG21: Blid 7H 55
Butlers Cl. NG15: Huck 1J 75
Butlers Fld. NG13: Lang 7K 113
BUTLER'S HILL 7J 67
Butlerwood Cl. NG17: Ann W 3J 59
Butlers Hill Stop (NET) 1K 75
Buttercup Cl. NG24: New B 4F 137
Buttercup Mdw. NG21: C'tone 6J 43
Butterfield Ct. NG16: Want 7A 74
Buttergate, The NG24: New T 1C 136
                                         (off Market Pl.)
Buttermead Cl. NG9: Trow 6C 92
Buttermere Cl. NG2: Gam 2G 109
   NG10: Long E .7A 104
Buttermere Cl. NG5: Sher 5K 85
   NG19: Mans W .6K 41
Buttermere Dr. NG9: Bram 1J 105
Butterwick Cl. NG19: Mans W 1B 48
Buttery Gdns. NG11: Rudd 4K 115
Buttery La. NG17: Skeg, Teve 2G 45
Butt Houses NG7: Lent 4F 95
Butt La. LE12: Norm S 7G 121
   NG13: East B 5E 90
   NG19: Mans W .7J 41
Butt Rd. NG13: Bing 4H 101
Butt St. NG10: Sand 4A 104
Buxton Av. NG4: Carl 6G 87
Buxton Cl. NG5: Top V 6B 76
Buxton Rd. NG19: Mans 1D 46
Byard La. NG1: Nott 6F 7 (4K 95)
Bye Pass Rd. NG9: Chil 7J 105
Bye Path Rd. DN22: Retf 2F 23
Byfield Cl. NG7: Radf 2G 95
Byford Cl. NG3: Mapp 5B 86
Byley Rd. NG8: Bilb 3G 93
By-Pass Rd. NG14: Gun 2A 90
Byrne Ct. NG5: Arn 2E 86
Byron Av. NG10: Long E 6A 104
   NG17: Kirk A 4B 52
   NG17: Sut A 6B 46
   NG19: Mans W .7J 41
Byron Bingo
   Hucknall 6H 67
Byron Centre, The NG15: Huck 6G 67
Byron Cl. NG24: New T 3D 136

Byron Ct. NG2: Nott 5J 7 (4B 96)
   NG9: Stap 7D 92
   NG24: Bald 6H 137
Byron Cres. NG15: Rave 1A 62
   NG16: Aws 3B 82
Byron Flds. NG15: Ann 4C 60
Byron Gdns. NG25: Sout 5H 131
Byron Gro. NG5: Sher 4K 85
Byron Ind. Est. NG15: Ann 7J 77
Byron Pl. NG7: Lent 3F 95
                                         (off Wragby Rd.)
Byron Rd. NG2: West Br 2C 108
   NG15: Ann 4C 60
Byron Sq. NG15: Huck 6G 67
                                          (off Baker St.)
Byron St. NG5: Arn 7F 77
   NG15: Huck 7G 67
   NG15: News 6D 60
   NG18: Mans 3G 47
   NG21: Blid 6K 55
Byron Way S81: Work 1J 21
Bythorn Cl. NG17: Skeg 5B 46

C

Caddaw Av. NG15: Huck 7G 67
CADEBY 1A 144
Cadlan Cl. NG5: Bestw 7C 76
Cadlan Ct. NG5: Bestw 7C 76
Cad La. NG23: Norm T 1K 125
Caernarvon Pl. NG9: Chil 5G 105
Cafferata Way NG24: New T 7F 135
Caincross Rd. NG8: Bilb 1J 93
Cairngorm Dr. NG5: Arn 4D 76
   NG18: Mans 5K 47
Cairns Cl. NG5: Bestw 2H 85
Cairns St. NG1: Nott 3F 7 (3K 95)
Cairo St. NG7: Basf 6G 85
Caister Rd. NG11: Clif 2F 115
Caithness Ct. NG5: Sher 6J 85
Calcroft Cl. NG8: Aspl 5D 84
Caldbeck Cl. NG2: Gam 2F 109
Caldbeck Ct. NG9: Chil 5G 105
Caldbeck Wlk. NG5: Bestw 7D 76
Calderdale NG8: Woll 5G 93
Calder Gdns. NG13: Bing 5E 100
Calderhall Gdns. NG5: Bestw 6E 76
Calder Wlk. NG6: Bulw 4H 75
Caldon Grn. NG6: Bulw 4J 75
Caledonian Rd. DN22: Retf 5G 23
Caledon Rd. NG5: Sher 4J 85
California Rd. NG24: Farnd 7H 133
Calke Av. NG17: Huth 1C 50
Calladine Cl. NG17: Sut A 2H 51
Calladine Cl. NG6: Bulw 1B 84
Calladine Gro. NG17: Sut A 2H 51
Calladine La. NG17: Sut A 2H 51
Callaway Cl. NG8: Woll 3K 93
Calstock Rd. NG5: Woodt 2B 86
Calveley Rd. NG8: Bilb 7K 83
Calver Cl. NG8: Woll 4D 94
Calver St. NG19: Mans W 6A 42
Calvert Cl. NG9: Chil 5J 105
CALVERTON 6D 70 (1B 148)
Calverton Av. NG4: Carl 6E 86
Calverton Bus. Pk. NG14: Calv 4D 70
Calverton Cl. NG9: Toton 7F 105
Calverton Dr. NG8: Stre 5J 83
Calverton Leisure Cen. 5C 70
Calverton Rd. NG5: Arn 5H 77
   NG21: Blid 2J 63
Camberley Ct. NG6: Bulw 6G 75
Camberley Rd. NG6: Bulw 6G 75
Camborne Cl. DN22: Retf 2E 22
Camborne Cres. DN22: Retf 1E 22
Camborne Dr. NG8: Aspl 5D 84
Camborne M. DN22: Retf 1D 22
Cambourne Gdns. NG15: Rave 2B 62
Cambourne Pl. NG18: Mans 1D 54
Cambria M. NG3: Nott 1K 95
Cambria Rd. NG19: Plea 5C 40
Cambria Ter. S80: Work 1F 21
Cambridge Cl. NG21: Rain 3K 55
Cambridge Cl. NG2: West Br 1B 108
   NG7: Radf 2G 95
Cambridge Cres. NG9: Stap 6C 92
Cambridge Gdns. NG5: Woodt 2E 86
Cambridge Mdws. NG24: New T 1H 137
Cambridge Rd. DN11: Harwo 2C 8
   NG2: West Br 2D 108
   NG8: Woll 4B 94
   NG21: Rain 3J 55
Cambridge St. NG4: Carl 6H 87
   NG18: Mans 5G 47
Camb's La. DN22: Nth W 2J 17
Camdale Cl. NG9: Chil 3G 105
Camdale La. NG24: Bald 7J 137
Camden Cl. NG2: Nott 5K 7 (4B 96)
Camelia Av. NG11: Clif 1D 114
Camelot Av. NG5: Sher 5H 85
Camelot Cres. NG11: Rudd 2J 115
Camelot St. NG11: Rudd 2J 115
Cameo Cl. NG4: Colw 2J 97
Camer Ct. NG9: Bee 3B 106
                                       (off Waverley Av.)

Cameron La. NG24: Bald 7J **137**
Camerons, The NG19: Mans 5D **46**
Cameron St. NG5: Sher 5K **85**
Camish Ho. NG10: Sand 4A **104**
(off Bennett St.)
CAMMERINGHAM 3D **145**
Camomile Cl. NG5: Top V 7A **76**
Camomile Gdns. NG7: H Grn 1F **95**
Campbell Cl. NG8: Brox 6B **84**
    S81: Work 4G **19**
Campbell Dr. NG4: Carl 7F **87**
Campbell Gdns. NG5: Arn 5A **78**
Campbell Gro. NG3: Nott 3H 7 (3A **96**)
Campbell St. NG3: Nott 3J 7 (3B **96**)
    NG16: Lang M .2A **72**
Campden Grn. NG11: Clif 7F **107**
Campion Gdns. NG17: Kirk A 1A **60**
Campion St. NG5: Arn 6G **77**
Campion Way NG13: Bing 4E **100**
CAMPSALL 1A **144**
Camrose Cl. NG8: Bilb 7A **84**
Canal Rd. S80: Work 2G **21**
Canal Side NG9: Bee 6C **106**
Canalside NG1: Nott 7F 7 (5K **95**)
Canalside Ind. Pk. NG12: Crop Bi 7B **112**
Canalside M. S80: Work 2F **21**
Canalside Wlk. NG1: Nott 7C 6 (5K **95**)
Canalside Workshops DN22: Retf 3G **23**
Canal St. DN22: Retf 4F **23**
    NG1: Nott 7E 6 (5K **95**)
    NG10: Long E .7B **104**
    NG10: Sand 4A **104**
Canal Ter. S80: Work 2H **21**
Canberra Cl. NG9: Stap 7D **92**
Canberra Cres. NG2: West Br 5A **108**
Canberra Gdns. NG2: West Br 6A **108**
Candleby Cl. NG12: Cotg 6E **110**
Candleby Ct. NG12: Cotg 6E **110**
Candleby La. NG12: Cotg 6E **110**
Candlemass Ct. NG19: Mans W 7K **41**
Candle Mdw. NG2: Colw 4G **97**
Canning Cir. NG7: Nott 4B 6 (3H **95**)
Canning Ter. NG7: Nott 4B 6 (3H **95**)
Cannon Cl. NG24: New T 7H **135**
Cannon M. DN22: Retf 3F **23**
Cannon Sq. DN22: Retf 3F **23**
(off Churchgate)
Cannon St. NG5: Sher 4K **85**
    NG19: Mans 1F **47**
Canonbie Cl. NG5: Arn 5K **77**
Canon's Cl. NG25: Sout 5J **131**
Canon Stevens Cl. NG23: Coll 2H **129**
Cantabury Av. NG7: H Grn 7G **85**
Cantelupe Gdns. NG16: Gilt 6G **73**
Canterbury Cl. DN22: Ord 5E **22**
    NG16: Nuth 3J **83**
    NG19: Mans W 4J **41**
    S81: Work 5H **19**
Canterbury Ct. NG1: Nott 2D 6 (2J **95**)
Canterbury Rd. NG8: Radf 3E **94**
Canterbury Wlk. S81: Carl L 5B **12**
(off Beverley Wlk.)
CANTLEY 1B **144**
Cantley Av. NG4: Ged 5H **87**
Cantrell Rd. NG6: Bulw 1D **84**
Canver Cl. NG8: Bilb 2H **93**
Canwick Cl. NG8: Bilb 3H **93**
Capenwray Gdns. NG5: Bestw 6E **76**
Capes, The NG13: Aslo 4C **102**
Cape St. NG18: Mans 3F **47**
Capital FM Arena 5H 7 (4A **96**)
Capitol Cl. NG6: Woll 3B **94**
Caporn Cl. NG6: Bulw 2D **84**
Capps Pl. NG22: Tuxf 7D **28**
Captain Jacks Adventure 3E **22**
CARBURTON 1B **146**
Carburton Av. NG20: Mede V 7F **33**
Carburton La. NG20: Nort 3E **32**
Carburton Way NG17: Kirk A 5D **52**
CAR COLSTON 4K 91 (1C **149**)
CARCROFT 1A **144**
Cardale Rd. NG3: Nott 2D **96**
    NG19: Plea 5C **40**
Cardiff St. NG3: Nott 3K 7 (3C **96**)
Cardigan Cl. NG3: Nott 1F 7 (1K **95**)
Cardinal Cl. NG3: Nott 1K 7 (2B **96**)
Cardinal Ct. NG17: Sut A 2C **52**
Cardinal Hinsley Cl. NG24: New T 5A **136**
Cardinal Way NG21: C'tone 5J **43**
Carding Cl. NG22: Farns 6K **57**
Cardington Cl. NG5: Top V 5A **76**
Cardle Cl. NG19: Mans W 7C **42**
Cardwell St. NG7: H Grn 7G **85**
Carew Rd. NG11: Clif 7F **107**
Carey Rd. NG6: Bulw 6J **75**
Carisbrook Av. NG18: Mans 3C **48**
Carisbrooke Av. NG3: Mapp P 6K **85**
    NG4: Ged 6A **88**
    NG9: Bee 1B **106**
Carisbrooke Cl. NG17: Kirk A 7C **52**
Carisbrooke Dr. NG3: Mapp P 6K **85**
Carisbrook Rd. S81: Carl L 6B **12**
Car La. NG13: Car C 5K **91**
Carlight Gdns. Pk. Homes
    NG2: West Br 7E **96**
Carlile Rd. NG4: Carl 7H **87**

Carling Av. S80: Work 3E **20**
Carlingford Rd. NG15: Huck 5G **67**
Carlin St. NG6: Bulw 7H **75**
Carlisle Av. NG6: Bulw 7J **75**
Carlisle Av. NG18: Mans 5F **47**
Carlswark Gdns. NG5: Top V 5B **76**
CARLTON 1J 97 (1B **148**)
Carlton Av. S81: Work 6F **19**
Carlton Bus. Cen. NG4: Carl 1J **97**
Carlton Cl. NG19: Mans W 6F **43**
    NG24: New T .3D **136**
    S81: Work 5F **19**
Carlton Ct. S81: Work 5G **19**
Carlton Cres. LE12: East L 2B **122**
Carlton Ferry La. NG23: Coll 6E **128**
(Ferry La.)
    NG23: Coll 1F **129**
(Northcroft La.)
Carlton Fold NG1: Nott 5C **96**
Carlton Forum Leisure Cen. 6F **87**
Carlton Grange NG4: Carl 1F **97**
Carlton Hall La. S81: Carl L 7B **12**
Carlton Hgts. NG4: Carl 1F **97**
Carlton Hill NG4: Carl 1E **96**
CARLTON IN LINDRICK 7D 12 (3A **144**)
Carlton Lake Dr. NG23: Carl T 5D **128**
Carlton La. NG23: Carl T, Norw 7B **128**
    NG23: Carl T, Sut T 4E **128**
CARLTON-LE-MOORLAND 3D **147**
Carlton Mnr. Caravan Pk. NG23: Carl T . . .6C **128**
Carlton M. NG4: Carl 1F **97**
CARLTON-ON-TRENT 7D 128 (2D **147**)
Carlton Phoenix Ind. Est. S81: Work 1H **21**
Carlton Rd. NG3: Nott 5J 7 (4B **96**)
    NG24: New T .3C **136**
    S80: Work 2G **21**
    S81: Work 4G **19**
CARLTON SCROOP 1D **149**
Carlton Sq. NG4: Carl 1H **97**
Carlton Station (Rail) 1J **97**
Carlton St. NG1: Nott 5G 7 (4A **96**)
    NG18: Mans 1J **47**
Carlton Va. Cl. NG4: Carl 6G **87**
Carlyle Rd. NG2: West Br 2B **108**
Carman Cl. NG16: Want 6A **74**
Carmel Gdns. NG5: Arn 1C **86**
Carmelita Av. NG24: Bald 7J **137**
Carnaby Cl. NG12: Rad T 5K **99**
Carnarvon Cl. NG13: Bing 3F **101**
Carnarvon Dr. NG14: Bur J 2E **88**
Carnarvon Gro. NG4: Carl 7G **87**
    NG4: Ged 6J **87**
    NG17: Sut A 7F **45**
Carnarvon Pl. NG13: Bing 4E **100**
Carnarvon Rd. NG2: West Br 3C **108**
    NG17: Huth 1D **50**
Carnarvon St. NG4: Neth 2K **97**
    NG17: Teve 3F **45**
Carnell La. NG24: Bald 7J **137**
Carnforth Cl. NG9: Stap 4C **104**
Carnforth Ct. NG5: Bestw 6E **76**
Carnoustie S81: Work 7J **19**
Carnoustie Av. NG19: Mans 7D **40**
Carnoustie Cl. NG17: Kirk A 4J **51**
Carnwood Rd. NG5: Bestw 1H **85**
Carolgate DN22: Retf 3F **23**
Carolgate Ct. DN22: Retf 4F **23**
Caroline Cl. NG15: Rave 1D **62**
Caroline Ct. DE7: Ilk 2A **92**
Carpenter Av. NG19: Mans 7D **40**
Carpenters Cl. NG12: Crop Bu 3C **112**
(not continuous)
Carr, The DN22: Retf 4E **22**
Carradale Cl. NG5: Arn 6A **78**
Carr Farm Rd. NG17: Nunc 3K **59**
Carrfield Av. NG9: Toton 7E **104**
Carrfield Cl. NG17: Sut A 7H **45**
Carrgate La. NG23: Elston 1E **140**
Carr Gro. NG17: Kirk A 6J **51**
Carr Hill Way DN22: Retf 1F **23**
CARRHOUSE 1C **145**
CARRINGTON 5J **85**
Carrington Cl. NG5: Sher 6K **85**
Carrington La. NG14: Calv 4D **70**
Carrington St. NG1: Nott 7F 7 (5H **95**)
    NG2: Nott 7F 7 (5K **95**)
Carrion Vw. S81: Gate 6E **18**
Carr La. DN10: Mist 2G **11**
    NG20: Mkt W .4C **34**
    NG23: Upton 7C **132**
Carroll Gdns. NG2: Nott 7K **95**
Carr Rd. DN10: Gri H 1A **16**
    DN10: Matt 4J **15**
    DN22: Retf 4E **22**
    NG13: Bing 3J **101**
CARR VALE 2A **146**
Carr Vw. DN10: Eve 6B **10**
Carsic La. NG17: Sut A 7J **45**
Carsic Rd. NG17: Sut A 5H **45**
Carsington Ct. NG19: Mans W 6A **42**
Carswell Cl. NG24: New T 3C **136**
Cartbridge NG12: Cotg 7E **110**
Carter Av. NG11: Rudd 4K **115**
    NG12: Rad T 5G **99**
Carter Ga. NG1: Nott 6H 7 (4A **96**)
    NG24: New T .1C **136**

Carter La. NG18: Mans 4K **47**
    NG20: Chu W, Wars 4A **34**
Carter La. E. DE55: Sth N 5A **50**
Carter La. W. DE55: Sth N 6A **50**
Carter Rd. NG9: Chil 7F **105**
(not continuous)
Carterswood Dr. NG16: Nuth 4A **84**
Carters Yd. NG24: New T 1C **136**
(off Carter Ga.)
Cartledge Dr. NG3: Arn 1F **87**
Cartwright Cl. NG22: Dun T 5G **29**
Cartwright La. DE55: Sth N 4C **50**
Cartwright St. S81: Shire 5A **18**
Cartwright Way NG9: Bee 4A **106**
Carver Cl. NG21: Edwin 7F **37**
Carver St. NG7: H Grn 7G **85**
Carwood Rd. NG9: Bram 7J **93**
Casper Ct. NG5: Top V 6C **76**
(off Birkdale Way)
Castellan Ri. NG5: Bestw 6E **76**
Casterton Rd. NG5: Bestw 6D **76**
Castle Blvd. NG7: Lent, Nott 7A 6 (5G **95**)
Castle Brewery NG24: New T 1C **136**
Castle Brewery Ct. NG24: New T 1C **136**
Castlebridge Office Village NG7: Lent 6H **95**
Castle Bri. Rd. NG7: Lent 5H **95**
Castle Cl. NG14: Calv 6C **70**
Castle Cl. NG7: Nott 7D 6 (5J **95**)
CASTLE DONINGTON 3A **148**
Castle Exchange NG1: Nott 4G **7**
Castle Farm La. S80: Work 6D **20**
Castlefields NG2: Nott 6K **95**
Castle Gdns. NG7: Lent 5H **95**
Castle Gate NG1: Nott 6E 6 (4K **95**)
    NG24: New T .1C **136**
Castlegate Cen. 1C **136**
Castle Gro. NG7: Nott 6D 6 (4J **95**)
CASTLE HILL 7J **51**
Castle Hill LE12: East L 5B **122**
    NG23: Carl T .6B **128**
Castle Hill Cl. NG17: Kirk A 6J **51**
Castle Hill Sq. S80: Work 3F **21**
(off West St.)
Castle Ind. Pk. NG15: Huck 1F **75**
Castle Marina Pk. NG7: Lent 5H **95**
Castle Marina Rd. NG7: Lent 5H **95**
Castle Mdw. Retail Pk. NG7: Lent . . .7C 6 (5J **95**)
Castle Mdw. Rd. NG2: Nott 7E 6 (5J **95**)
Castle M. NG7: Nott 7A 6 (5H **95**)
    NG19: Mans W 6H **41**
Castle Museum & Art Gallery
    Nottingham 6D 6 (5J **95**)
Castle Pk. NG2: Nott 6J **95**
Castle Pk. Ind. Est. NG2: Nott 7J **95**
Castle Pl. NG1: Nott 6D 6 (4J **95**)
Castle Quay NG7: Nott 7C 6 (5J **95**)
Castle Quay Cl. NG7: Lent 5H **95**
Castle Retail Pk. NG7: Radf 2F **95**
Castlerigg Cl. NG2: West Br 4F **109**
Castle Rising NG24: New T 1C **136**
(off Lombard St.)
Castle Rd. NG1: Nott 6D 6 (4J **95**)
Castle Rock NG1: Nott 7D 6 (5J **95**)
Castle St. NG2: Nott 4C **96**
    NG16: Eastw .5E **72**
    NG18: Mans 3G **47**
    NG19: Mans W 6H **41**
    S80: Work 3F **21**
Castleton Av. NG4: Carl 6H **87**
    NG5: Arn 7H **77**
Castleton Cl. NG2: Nott 6J **95**
    NG15: Huck 7D **66**
    NG15: Rave 1C **62**
    NG16: Sels 5E **58**
    NG19: Mans W 5J **41**
Castle Vw. NG2: West Br 3A **108**
Castle Vw. Caravan Pk. NG24: New T 1A **136**
Castle Vw. Cotts. NG9: Bee 3D **106**
Castle Vw. Ct. NG24: New T 7C **134**
Castle Vs. NG2: Nott 6K **7**
Castle Wlk. NG7: H Grn 1G **95**
Castle Wharf NG1: Nott 7E 6 (5K **95**)
Castlewood Bus. Pk. NG17: Sut A 4D **50**
Castlewood Gro. NG17: Sut A 2H **51**
Caterham Cl. NG8: Bilb 1J **93**
Catfoot La. NG4: Lamb 6B **78**
Catherine Av. NG19: Mans W 6J **41**
Catherine Cl. NG6: Bulw 7G **75**
    NG17: Kirk A 4K **51**
Catherine St. NG6: Bulw 7G **75**
Catkin Dr. NG16: Gilt 6G **73**
Catkin Way NG24: New B 5E **136**
Catlow Wlk. NG5: Bestw 6E **76**
Caton Cl. NG17: Sut A 7H **45**
Cator Cl. NG4: Ged 4G **87**
Cator La. NG9: Chil 3J **105**
Cator La. Nth. NG9: Chil 3J **105**
Cator Rd. NG19: Plea 6C **40**
Catriona Cres. NG5: Arn 4J **77**
Catt Cl. NG9: Chil .7G **105**
Catterley Hill Rd. NG3: Nott 1D **96**
Cattle Mkt. Rd. NG2: Nott 6A **96**
Cattle Rd. DN10: Mist 2F **11**
Catton Rd. NG5: Arn 6J **77**
Caudale Ct. NG2: Gam 2F **109**

Caudwell Cl. NG25: Sout 4H **131**
Caudwell Dr. NG18: Mans 7H **47**
Cauldwell Rd. NG17: Sut A 1D **52**
   NG18: Mans 2H **53**
Caulton St. NG7: H Grn 2G **95**
      (not continuous)
CAUNTON 6J **127** (2C **147**)
Caunton Av. NG3: Nott 6B **86**
Caunton Cl. NG18: Mans 4F **47**
   NG20: Mede V 1F **35**
Caunton Rd. NG23: Norw 4G **127**
   NG25: Hock 1K **131**
Caunt's Cres. NG17: Sut A 7H **45**
Causeway La. NG25: Mort 5F **139**
Causeway M. NG2: Nott 6J **95**
Cavalier Building, The NG24: New T 6D **134**
      (off North Gate)
Cavan Ct. NG2: Nott 7K **95**
Cavell Cl. DN22: Woodbe 7G **25**
   NG11: Clif 7E **106**
Cavendish Av. NG4: Ged 5G **87**
   NG5: Sher 4A **86**
   NG17: Sut A 7J **45**
   NG21: Edwin 6D **36**
   NG24: New T 3D **136**
CAVENDISH BRIDGE 2A **148**
Cavendish Cl. NG15: Huck 7J **67**
Cavendish Ct. NG3: Mapp 4C **86**
   NG7: Nott 5B **6** (4H **95**)
Cavendish Cres. NG4: Carl 5F **87**
   NG9: Stap 6C **92**
   NG17: Ann W 3A **60**
Cavendish Cres. Nth. NG7: Nott 6A **6** (4H **95**)
Cavendish Cres. Sth. NG7: Nott 7A **6** (5H **95**)
Cavendish Dr. NG4: Carl 7H **87**
Cavendish Ho. NG4: Carl 7H **87**
      (off Garden City)
Cavendish M. NG7: Nott 5B **6** (4H **95**)
   NG12: Cotg 7E **110**
      (off Daleside)
Cavendish Pl. NG7: Nott 7A **6** (5H **95**)
   NG9: Bee 3A **106**
Cavendish Rd. DN22: Retf 6H **23**
   NG4: Carl 5F **87**
   NG10: Long E 7B **104**
   S80: Work 5H **21**
Cavendish Rd. E. NG7: Nott 5B **6** (4H **95**)
Cavendish Rd. W. NG7: Nott 6A **6** (4H **95**)
Cavendish St. NG5: Arn 6G **77**
   NG7: Lent 7F **95**
      (not continuous)
   NG17: Sut A 6A **46**
   NG18: Mans 5J **47**
   NG19: Mans W 6G **41**
   NG20: Langw 7A **26**
Cavendish Va. NG5: Sher 4A **86**
Cavendish Way NG21: C'tone 5H **43**
Cave's La. DN10: Walk 6F **11**
Cawdron Wlk. NG11: Clif 7F **107**
Cawston Gdns. NG6: Bulw 6H **75**
Cawthorne Cl. NG23: Coll 1J **129**
Cawthorne Way NG18: Mans 3B **48**
Caxmere Dr. NG8: Woll 3A **94**
Caxton Cl. NG4: Neth 1K **97**
Caxton Rd. NG5: Sher 6J **85**
CAYTHORPE
   Grantham 1D **149**
   Nottingham 6G **81** (1B **148**)
Caythorpe Ct. NG19: Mans W 6A **42**
      (off Chelmorton Cl.)
Caythorpe Cres. NG5: Sher 3K **85**
Caythorpe Ri. NG5: Sher 3K **85**
Caythorpe Rd. NG14: Cayt, Lowd . . .6E **80**
Cecil Cl. S80: Rhod 1B **20**
Cecil St. NG7: Lent 5G **95**
Cedar Av. LE12: East L 4K **121**
   NG9: Bee 2B **106**
   NG16: Nuth 3A **84**
   NG17: Kirk A 7K **51**
   NG19: Mans W 4H **41**
   NG24: New T 5E **134**
Cedar Cl. NG10: Sand 2A **104**
   NG13: Bing 4H **101**
   NG17: Skeg 3H **45**
   S81: Carl L 5B **12**
Cedar Ct. NG9: Bee 2B **106**
Cedar Dr. NG12: Key 1H **119**
   NG16: Sels 5D **58**
Cedar Grn. NG25: Sout 5G **131**
Cedar Gro. NG5: Arn 6K **77**
   NG8: Woll 4A **94**
   NG15: Huck 1H **75**
Cedarland Cres. NG16: Nuth 3A **84**
Cedar La. NG22: New O 2C **38**
Cedar Lodge NG7: Nott 5B **6** (4H **95**)
Cedar Lodge Caravan Pk. NG12: Hol P . .6B **98**
Cedar Rd. NG7: H Grn 7H **85**
   NG9: Chil 4K **105**
Cedars, The NG5: Sher 3A **86**
   NG23: Syer 3B **140**
Cedars St. NG18: Mans 5J **47**
Cedar Tree Rd. NG5: Arn 5D **76**
Cedar Tree Vw. DN22: Elk 3F **27**
Celandine Cl. NG5: Top V 7A **76**
Celandine Gdns. NG13: Bing 4D **100**

Celery Mdws. DN22: Clar 7H **17**
Celia Dr. NG4: Carl 1G **97**
Celtic Flds. S81: Work 5E **18**
Celtic Point S81: Work 5E **18**
Cemetery Rd. NG9: Stap 2D **104**
   S80: Work 3H **21**
Centenary Cl. NG24: New B 5F **137**
Central Av. NG2: West Br 1C **108**
   NG3: Mapp 3E **86**
   NG5: Arn 7H **77**
   NG7: Basf 6H **85**
   NG9: Bee 7K **93**
   NG9: Chil 3J **105**
   NG9: Stap 1D **104**
   NG10: Sand 3A **104**
   NG15: Huck 7G **67**
   NG17: Kirk A 1B **60**
   NG18: Mans 5J **47**
   NG21: Blid 6K **55**
   NG22: Wale 5G **27**
   S80: Work 3E **20**
Central Av. Sth. NG5: Arn 7H **77**
Central Ct. NG7: Lent 7G **95**
Central Dr. NG21: C'tone 7H **43**
   NG23: Elston 2E **140**
Central St. NG3: Nott 1K **7** (2B **96**)
Central Wlk. NG15: Huck 6G **67**
Centre Way NG12: Rad T 4D **98**
Centurion Bus. Pk. NG6: Bulw 5E **74**
Centurion Cl. NG15: Huck 5K **67**
Centurion Way NG2: Nott 1H **107**
Century Av. NG18: Mans 5F **47**
Century Ct. NG1: Nott 1D **6**
Century Rd. DN22: Ord 5E **22**
Century St. NG24: New T 1D **136**
Cernan Ct. NG6: Bulw 2A **84**
Cerne Cl. NG11: Clif 2G **115**
Chaceley Way NG11: Wilf 6H **107**
Chadborn Av. NG11: Goth 7G **115**
Chadburn Rd. NG18: Mans 2A **48**
Chaddesden, The NG3: Mapp P 1K **95**
Chad Gdns. NG5: Top V 4C **76**
CHADWELL 3C **149**
Chadwick Rd. NG7: H Grn 1F **95**
Chadwick Wlk. DN22: Woodbe 7G **25**
Chaffinch Cl. NG18: Mans 3B **48**
Chaffinch M. S81: Gate 5D **18**
Chainbridge La. DN22: Lound 4D **14**
Chainbridge Rd. DN22: Lound 4D **14**
Chain La. NG7: Lent 7F **95**
   NG24: New T 1C **136**
Chalet Caravan Site, The NG23: Bath . .6G **129**
Chalfield Cl. NG11: Clif 1E **114**
Chalfont Dr. NG8: Aspl 2D **94**
Challond Ct. NG5: Bestw 7E **76**
Chamberlain Cl. NG11: Clif 1D **114**
Chambers Av. DE7: Ilk 1A **92**
Chamber's Gdns. DN22: Clay 6H **15**
Champion Cres. NG19: Mans 2F **47**
Chancery, The NG9: Bram 2H **105**
Chancery Cl. NG17: Skeg 4A **46**
Chancery Ct. DN22: Retf 4E **22**
   NG11: Wilf 3H **107**
Chancery La. DN22: Retf 4E **22**
Chandos Av. NG4: Neth 7K **87**
Chandos St. NG3: Nott 1B **96**
   NG4: Neth 1K **97**
Chantrey Rd. NG2: West Br 2B **108**
Chantry, The NG18: Mans 5B **48**
Chantry Cl. NG9: Chil 5J **105**
   NG16: Kimb 2F **83**
   NG24: New T 4C **136**
Chantry Wlk. NG22: Tuxf 6C **28**
      (off Market Pl.)
Chapel Bar NG1: Nott 5D **6** (4J **95**)
Chapel Cl. DN10: Mist 2H **11**
   DN22: Clar 7J **17**
   NG11: Goth 7G **115**
   NG22: Wale 5G **27**
Chapel Ct. NG21: Edwin 7F **37**
   NG22: Edin 2A **130**
Chapelfield Gro. NG13: Bing 5F **101**
Chapel Flds. NG15: Rave 1D **62**
Chapel Gth. NG13: Ors 2J **103**
Chapel Ga. S81: Carl L 7D **12**
Chapelgate DN22: Retf 3F **23**
Chapelgate Ct. DN22: Retf 3F **23**
Chapel La. DN10: Eve 6B **10**
   DN10: Mist 2H **11**
   DN10: Scro 4K **9**
   LE12: Costo 3E **122**
   LE12: Will W 6G **143**
   LE14: Neth B 4K **143**
   LE14: Upp B 3H **143**
   NG4: Lamb 7F **79**
   NG5: Arn 6G **77**
   NG12: Cotg 6E **110**
   NG13: Aslo 3D **102**
   NG13: Bing 1E **100**
   NG13: Gran 1J **141**
   NG14: Epp 7K **71**
   NG15: Rave 4D **62**
   NG22: Farns 5K **57**
   NG22: Lax 6B **124**
   NG22: Wale 5G **27**
   NG23: Bath 5F **129**

Chapel La. NG23: Caun 6H **127**
   NG23: Nth M 5K **129**
   NG24: Codd 7K **135**
   NG24: Farnd 7G **133**
   NG24: Wint 2F **135**
   NG25: Oxt 1F **71**
Chapel Mews Ct.
   NG9: Bram 1G **105**
Chapel Pl. NG16: Kimb 1E **82**
Chapel Quarter NG1: Nott 5D **6** (4J **95**)
Chapel Rd. NG16: Sels 6C **58**
Chapel Side NG12: Wys 6K **123**
Chapel St. NG7: Radf 3A **6** (3H **95**)
   NG9: Bram 1G **105**
   NG11: Rudd 4K **115**
   NG13: Ors 2J **103**
   NG15: Huck 6G **67**
   NG16: Eastw 5D **72**
   NG16: Kimb 1E **82**
   NG16: Sels 5E **58**
   NG17: Kirk A 6J **51**
   NG17: Nunc 3A **60**
   NG19: New H 2A **40**
   NG20: Whal T 4B **26**
Chapel Ter. NG15: News 6D **60**
Chapel Wlk. NG13: What 4E **102**
   S80: Work 3F **21**
Chapel Yd. NG12: Norm W 3K **117**
Chapman Cl. NG8: Bilb 1C **94**
Chapmans Wlk. NG6: Bestw V 7D **68**
Chappel Gdns. NG22: Bils 7D **126**
Chapter Dr. NG16: Kimb 2F **83**
Chardlace Wlk. NG1: Nott 6H **7**
Chard St. NG7: Basf 5G **85**
Chard Ter. NG7: Basf 5G **85**
Charlbury Ct. NG9: Bram 4G **93**
Charlbury Rd. NG8: Woll 2B **94**
Charlecote Dr. NG8: Woll 5J **93**
Charlecote Pk. Dr.
   NG2: West Br 5K **107**
Charles Av. NG9: Chil 6H **105**
   NG9: Lent A 7B **94**
   NG9: Stap 1E **104**
   NG10: Sand 3A **104**
   NG16: Eastw 4F **73**
Charles Cl. DE7: Ilk 2A **92**
   NG4: Ged 5J **87**
Charles Ct. NG15: Huck 6G **67**
Charles Ho. NG1: Nott 6D **6**
Charles St. NG5: Arn 7G **77**
   NG11: Rudd 3K **115**
   NG15: Huck 6G **67**
   NG17: Sut A 7A **46**
   NG19: Mans 1G **47**
   NG19: Mans W 5J **41**
   NG24: New T 2E **136**
Charleston Ho. NG1: Nott 2D **6** (2J **95**)
Charles Way NG6: Bulw 2C **84**
Charles Way Bus. Pk.
   NG6: Bulw 2D **84**
Charlesworth Av. NG7: Basf 7F **85**
Charlesworth Ct. NG19: Mans W 6A **42**
      (off Calver St.)
Charlock Cl. NG5: Top V 7A **76**
Charlock Gdns. NG13: Bing 5E **100**
Charlotte Cl. NG5: Arn 4G **77**
   NG22: Kirt 2H **39**
   NG24: New T 1D **136**
Charlotte Ct. NG16: Eastw 3D **72**
Charlton Gro. NG9: Bee 5A **106**
Charnock Av. NG8: Woll 5E **94**
Charnos St. DE7: Ilk 4A **92**
Charnwood Av. LE12: Sut B 7C **120**
   NG9: Bee 3J **105**
   NG10: Sand 5A **104**
   NG12: Key 1H **119**
Charnwood Cl. NG15: Rave 4C **62**
Charnwood Flds. LE12: Sut B 7C **120**
Charnwood Gdns. NG5: Sher 6J **85**
Charnwood Gro. NG2: West Br 2B **108**
   NG13: Bing 4E **100**
   NG15: Huck 6G **66**
   NG18: Mans 3C **48**
   NG19: Mans W 4H **41**
Charnwood La. NG5: Arn 1D **86**
Charnwood St. NG17: Sut A 1F **51**
Charnwood Way NG14: Woodbo 2H **79**
Charta M. NG14: Lowd 5E **80**
Charter Ct. DN22: Retf 2E **22**
Charter Pl. NG22: Tuxf 6D **28**
Charters Cl. NG17: Kirk A 4K **51**
Chartwell Av. NG11: Rudd 3J **115**
Chartwell Gro. NG3: Mapp 2F **87**
Chartwell Rd. NG17: Kirk A 6C **52**
Chase Pk. NG2: Nott 5D **96**
Chatham Ct. NG6: Bulw 1D **84**
   NG24: New T 2C **136**
Chatham St. NG1: Nott 1E **6** (2K **95**)
   NG25: Sout 5J **131**
Chatsworth Av. NG4: Carl 7H **87**
   NG7: Basf 5G **85**
   NG9: Chil 7H **105**
   NG12: Rad T 4F **99**
   NG16: Sels 5E **58**
   NG25: Sout 6G **131**

Chatsworth Cl.—Church La.

Chatsworth Cl. NG10: Sand 5A **104**
NG15: Rave 1C **62**
NG17: Skeg 5K **45**
NG18: Mans 1A **54**
Chatsworth Ct. DN11: Birc 1E **8**
NG15: Huck 7G **67**
Chatsworth Dr. NG15: Huck 7G **67**
NG18: Mans 1K **53**
Chatsworth Rd. NG2: West Br 1E **108**
NG24: New T 4C **136**
S81: Work 5G **19**
Chatsworth St. NG17: Sut A 7K **45**
Chatsworth Ter. NG15: News 5D **60**
Chatterley Ct. *NG7: Lent* *3F* ***95***
(off Wragby Rd.)
Chatterley Parkway NG8: Stre 5H **83**
Chaucer Cres. NG17: Sut A 6B **46**
Chaucer Rd. NG24: Bald 5H **137**
Chaucer St. NG1: Nott 3D **6** (3J **95**)
NG18: Mans 3G **47**
Chaworth Av. NG16: Want 5K **73**
Chaworth Rd. NG2: West Br 3B **108**
NG4: Colw 2J **97**
NG13: Bing 4E **100**
Chaworth St. NG21: Blid 6K **55**
Cheadle Cl. NG3: Mapp 5E **86**
NG8: Bilb 7J **83**
Cheapside NG1: Nott 5F **7** (4K **95**)
S80: Work 3H **21**
Cheddar Cl. NG21: Rain 2A **56**
Cheddar Rd. NG11: Clif 2F **115**
Chedington Av. NG3: Mapp 1G **87**
Chediston Va. NG5: Bestw 6D **76**
Chedworth Cl. NG3: Nott 3C **96**
Chelmorton Cl. NG19: Mans W 6A **42**
Chelmsford M. DN22: Ord 6E **22**
Chelmsford Rd. NG7: Basf 5G **85**
Chelmsford Ter. *NG7: Basf* *5G* ***85***
(off Zulu Rd.)
Chelsbury Ct. NG5: Arn 7G **77**
Chelsea Cl. NG16: Nuth 4K **83**
Chelsea M. NG12: Rad T 5J **99**
Chelsea St. NG7: Basf 6G **85**
Cheltenham Cl. NG9: Toton 7E **104**
Cheltenham Ct. NG18: Mans 3B **48**
Cheltenham St. NG6: Basf 3F **85**
Chelwood Dr. NG3: Mapp 4F **87**
Chennel Nook NG12: Cotg 7F **111**
Chepstow Rd. NG11: Clif 2F **115**
Chepstow Wlk. NG18: Mans 3B **48**
Chequers La. NG22: Dun T 3H **29**
Cherhill Cl. NG11: Clif 3E **114**
Cheriton Cl. NG19: Mans 1E **46**
Cheriton Dr. NG15: Rave 2D **62**
Chermside Cl. NG15: Rave 3D **62**
Chernside NG15: Rave 1C **62**
Cherries, The NG11: Wilf 3J **107**
Cherry Av. NG15: Huck 1H **75**
NG17: Kirk A 4H **51**
Cherry Cl. NG2: West Br 7F **97**
NG5: Arn 6G **77**
NG5: Bestw 1J **85**
Cherry Gro. NG18: Mans 4E **46**
NG20: Mkt W 5E **34**
Cherry Hill NG12: Key 7J **117**
Cherry Holt DN22: Retf 2D **22**
NG24: New T 4C **136**
Cherryholt Cl. NG13: East B 3E **90**
Cherryholt La. NG13: East B 3E **90**
Cherry La. NG18: Mans 7H **47**
Cherry Orchard NG12: Cotg 6E **110**
Cherry Orchard Mt. NG5: Bestw 1J **85**
Cherry St. NG13: Bing 4G **101**
Cherry Tree Av. S81: Shire 5A **18**
Cherry Tree Cl. DN22: Rans 2J **13**
NG14: Calv 5C **70**
NG16: Brins 5C **64**
NG19: Mans W 5H **41**
NG22: Bou 3E **38**
Cherrytree Cl. NG12: Rad T 6E **98**
Cherry Tree La. NG12: Edwal 6E **108**
Cherry Tree Wlk. DN22: Rans 1K **13**
Cherry Tree Way NG16: Lang M 2A **72**
Cherry Wood Dr. NG8: Aspl 1C **94**
Cherrywood Gdns. NG3: Nott 7D **86**
Chertsey Cl. NG3: Nott 6C **86**
Cherwell Ct. NG6: Bulw 1A **84**
Cherwell Gdns. NG13: Bing 5D **100**
Chesham Dr. NG5: Sher 5J **85**
NG9: Bram 5G **93**
Cheshire Ct. NG2: West Br 4A **108**
Cheshire Way NG16: Westw 1A **64**
Chesil Av. NG8: Radf 3E **94**
Chesil Cotts. *NG8: Radf* *3E* ***94***
(off Chesil Av.)
Cheslyn Dr. NG8: Aspl 7D **84**
Chesnuts, The NG4: Ged 6A **88**
Chess Burrow NG19: Mans W 7K **41**
Chesterfield Av. NG4: Ged 4G **87**
NG13: Bing 4F **101**
Chesterfield Ct. NG4: Ged 4G **87**
Chesterfield Dr. DN22: Retf 3G **23**
NG14: Bur J 2F **89**
Chesterfield Rd. NG17: Huth, Teve 4B **44**
NG19: New H, Plea 3A **40**
S80: Darf 4A **20**
Chesterfield Rd. Nth. NG19: Plea 4B **40**
Chesterfield Rd. Sth. NG18: Mans 1F **47**
NG19: Mans 1F **47**
Chesterfield St. NG4: Carl 1G **97**
Chester Grn. NG9: Toton 7D **104**
Chester Ho. NG3: Mapp P 7K **85**
Chesterman Cl. NG16: Aws 3A **82**
Chester Pl. NG24: New T 2B **136**
Chester Rd. NG3: Nott 3F **97**
Chester St. NG19: Mans 1E **46**
Chesterton Dr. S81: Work 7J **19**
Chestnut Av. DN22: Ord 6D **22**
NG3: Mapp 5E **86**
NG9: Bee 3A **106**
NG13: Bing 4F **101**
NG15: Rave 3C **62**
NG17: Kirk A 7K **51**
NG22: Perl 1H **37**
NG24: New T 4E **134**
Chestnut Cl. DN10: Walk 7K **11**
NG12: Key 7H **117**
NG18: Mans 4A **54**
NG22: New O 2D **38**
NG23: Weston 2G **125**
S80: Work 4F **21**
Chestnut Copse NG24: New B 3E **136**
Chestnut Ct. NG16: Pinx 1C **58**
Chestnut Dr. NG16: Nuth 7B **74**
NG16: Sels 5D **58**
NG18: Mans 1A **54**
NG22: New O 2C **38**
Chestnut Gdns. NG17: Sut A 2H **51**
Chestnut Gro. NG2: West Br 2A **108**
NG3: Mapp P 1K **95**
NG4: Ged 6J **87**
NG5: Arn 5J **77**
NG10: Sand 2A **104**
NG12: Rad T 4E **98**
NG14: Bur J 3E **88**
NG15: Huck 2H **75**
NG17: Kirk A 6K **51**
NG19: Mans W 4H **41**
NG24: Farnd 7H **133**
Chestnut Hill NG18: Mans 1A **54**
Chestnut La. NG11: Bart F 7A **114**
Chestnut M. NG12: Toll 6J **109**
NG18: Mans 1A **54**
S81: Lango 1C **12**
Chestnut Rd. S81: Lango 1C **12**
Chestnuts, The NG3: Nott 6C **86**
NG12: Rad T 5D **98**
Chestnuts Cl. LE12: Sut B 2A **120**
Chestnut Wlk. NG5: Sher 4B **86**
Chestnut Way NG22: Tuxf 7D **28**
Chettles Ind. Est. NG7: Radf 3E **94**
Chettles Trade Pk. NG7: Radf 3E **94**
Chetwin Rd. NG8: Bilb 3J **93**
Chetwynd Bus. Pk. NG9: Chil 7G **105**
Chetwynd Rd. NG9: Chil 6F **105**
NG9: Toton 7F **105**
Chevin Gdns. NG5: Top V 5C **76**
Cheviot Cl. NG5: Arn 4D **76**
Cheviot Ct. NG9: Chil 6H **105**
S81: Carl L *5B* ***12***
(off Oak Tree Ri.)
Cheviot Dr. NG6: Bulw 6F **75**
Cheviot Rd. NG10: Long E 7A **104**
Chewton Av. NG16: Eastw 5E **72**
Chewton Cl. NG22: Bils 5B **126**
Chewton St. NG16: Eastw 5D **72**
Cheyne Dr. NG22: Bils 7D **126**
Cheyne Wlk. DN22: Ord 6D **22**
NG15: Huck 5H **67**
Cheyny Cl. NG2: Nott 7K **95**
Chichester Cl. DE7: Ilk 7A **82**
NG5: Top V 7A **76**
NG19: Mans 4C **46**
Chichester Dr. NG12: Cotg 5D **110**
Chichester Wlk. *S81: Carl L* *5B* ***12***
(off Lilac Tree Gro.)
Chidlow Rd. NG8: Bilb 1J **93**
Chidmere DN22: Ord 6D **22**
Chigwell Cl. NG16: Nuth 4K **83**
Chillon Way NG15: Huck 7D **66**
Chiltern Cl. NG5: Arn 4D **76**
Chiltern Way NG5: Bestw 1J **85**
S81: Carl L 5B **12**
Chilton Cres. NG19: Mans W 3J **41**
Chilton Dr. NG16: Want 7A **74**
Chilvers Cl. NG5: Bestw 7C **76**
CHILWELL 3H **105** (2A **148**)
Chilwell Ct. NG6: Bulw 7K **75**
Chilwell La. NG9: Bram 2G **105**
Chilwell Manor Golf Course 5K **105**
Chilwell Meadows Nature Reserve 5J **105**
Chilwell Olympia Leisure Cen. 6J **105**
Chilwell Retail Pk. NG9: Chil 7G **105**
Chilwell Rd. NG9: Bee 4K **105**
Chilwell St. NG7: Lent 5G **95**
Chimes Mdw. NG25: Sout 6J **131**
Chine, The DE55: Sth N 7A **50**
Chine Gdns. NG2: West Br 4K **107**
Chingford Rd. NG8: Bilb 7K **83**
Chipmunk Way NG13: Newton 1C **100**
Chippendale St. NG7: Lent 5G **95**
Chippenham Rd. NG5: Bestw 1J **85**
Chirnside NG19: Mans 5D **46**
Chisbury Grn. NG11: Clif 3E **114**
Chisholm Way NG5: Bestw 1H **85**
Chiswick Ct. NG5: Sher 4K **85**
Chisworth Ct. NG19: Mans W 6A **42**
Christchurch Rd. NG15: Huck 2D **74**
Christina Av. NG6: Cin 3D **84**
Christina Cres. NG6: Cin 3D **84**
Christine Cl. NG15: Huck 4J **67**
Christine Ct. NG3: Nott 1D **96**
Christopher Cl. NG8: Woll 2A **94**
Christopher Ct. NG15: Huck 2F **75**
Christopher Cres. NG24: New B 5F **137**
Chrysalis Way NG16: Eastw 3A **72**
Church Av. NG5: Arn 7G **77**
NG7: Lent 5G **95**
NG17: Sut A 1H **51**
Church Circ. NG22: New O 3C **38**
Church Cl. DN22: Nth W 2J **17**
LE12: East L 3A **122**
NG5: Arn 7G **77**
NG9: Trow 4B **92**
NG12: Rad T 5D **98**
NG13: Bing 3G **101**
NG20: Chu W 2D **34**
Church Ct. NG12: Cotg 6D **110**
NG23: Norw 2J **127**
Church Cres. NG5: Arn 7F **77**
NG9: Chil 5F **105**
Church Cft. NG2: West Br 1C **108**
Churchdale Av. NG9: Stap 7D **92**
Church Dr. DN10: Mist 2H **11**
NG2: West Br 2C **108**
NG5: Arn 7F **77**
NG5: Sher 6J **85**
NG10: Sand 2A **104**
NG12: Key 7H **117**
NG15: Huck 6G **67**
NG15: Rave 2B **62**
Church Dr. E. NG5: Arn 7G **77**
CHURCH END 7J **11**
Church End LE14: Neth B 3K **143**
Church Farm Gdns. NG22: Well 7E **38**
Church Fld. Cl. S81: Carl L 7D **12**
Churchfield Ct. NG5: Top V 5C **76**
Churchfield Dr. NG21: Rain 1H **55**
Churchfield La. NG7: Radf 1F **95**
Churchfield Ter. NG6: Basf 5F **85**
Churchfield Way NG5: Top V 5C **76**
Church Gdns. NG19: Mans W 6J **41**
Church Ga. NG12: Cols B 7H **141**
Churchgate DN22: Retf 3F **23**
Church Gro. NG7: Lent 5F **95**
Church Hill DN22: Nth W 2J **17**
NG12: Plum 4H **117**
NG16: Jack 7A **64**
NG16: Kimb 1E **82**
NG17: Kirk A 7H **51**
NG17: Sut A 1J **51**
NG19: Mans W 6J **41**
NG22: Bils 6D **126**
Church Hill Av. NG19: Mans W 6J **41**
Churchill Cl. NG5: Arn 1C **86**
Churchill Dr. NG9: Stap 1D **104**
NG11: Rudd 3J **115**
NG24: New T 4B **136**
Churchill Pk. NG4: Colw 3J **97**
Churchill Way S81: Gate 3E **18**
Church La. DN10: Mist 2G **11**
DN10: Scro 4K **9**
DN11: Harwo 2B **8**
DN22: Clar 7J **17**
DN22: Clay 6H **15**
DN22: Gam 2K **27**
DN22: Hay 6G **17**
DN22: Ord 6E **22**
LE12: Costo 3E **122**
LE12: Will W 6F **143**
LE14: Upp B 3H **143**
NG5: Arn 5H **77**
NG6: Bulw 7J **75**
NG9: Atten 7J **105**
NG9: Stap 2C **104**
NG11: Bart F 7A **114**
NG12: Cotg 6D **110**
NG12: Plum 3H **117**
NG12: Widm 6J **119**
NG13: Bing 4G **101**
NG13: Car C 4K **91**
NG13: Lang 7K **113**
NG14: Epp 7K **71**
NG14: Lowd 4C **80**
NG15: Lin 3G **67**
NG16: Brins 7C **64**
NG16: Coss 5B **82**
NG16: Sels 5B **58**
NG16: Unde 2E **64**
NG17: Sut A 1J **51**
NG18: Mans 4J **47**
NG19: Plea 4A **40**
(not continuous)
NG22: Bou 3F **39**
NG22: Eakr 2C **126**
NG22: Halam 5C **130**
NG22: Kirk 1C **132**
NG23: Aver 4F **133**

Church La. NG23: Best 7H 125
NG23: Carl T 7D 128
NG23: Coll 1H 129
NG23: Nth C, Sth C 5C 30
NG23: Nth M, Sth M 1B 134 & 7K 129
NG23: Sibt 6E 140
NG23: Sth C 7D 30
NG23: Upton 7C 132
NG24: Bald 6H 137
NG25: Mort 6G 139
S81: Carl L 7C 12 & 1G 19
CHURCH LANEHAM 1J 29 (1D 147)
Churchmead NG17: Huth 7D 44
Church Mdw. NG14: Calv 7D 70
Church Mdw. La. NG23: Upton 1H 139
Church M. NG2: Nott 7A 96
NG17: Kirk A 7J 51
NG17: Sut A 1J 51
S81: Lango 2C 12
Churchmoor Ct. NG5: Arn 5G 77
Churchmoor La. NG5: Arn 5G 77
Church Rd. DN11: Birc 2F 9
LN6: Swin 7K 31
NG3: Nott 1H 7 (1A 96)
NG6: Bestw V 2A 76
NG14: Bur J 3E 88
NG16: Grea, Want 3H 73
NG20: Chu W, Mkt W 2D 34
NG21: C'tone 6G 43
NG22: Bou 2F 39
NG23: Harby 7K 31
Church Row NG23: Nth M 6K 129
Church Side NG17: Huth 7D 44
NG18: Mans 3J 47
NG22: Farns 5K 57
Churchside Gdns. NG7: H Grn 7F 85
Church Sq. NG7: Lent 5G 95
Church St. DN10: Bawt 1K 9
DN10: Beck 6C 16
DN10: Eve 6B 10
DN10: Mist 2G 11
DN22: Nth W 2J 17
DN22: Sth L 1G 25
DN22: Stu S 3C 24
NG4: Carl 1H 97
NG4: Lamb 6G 79
NG5: Arn 6H 77
NG6: Basf 5F 85
NG7: Lent 5F 95
NG9: Bee 3A 106
NG9: Bram 1G 105
NG9: Stap 2C 104
NG10: Sand 2A 104
NG11: Bunny 3B 118
NG11: Goth 7G 115
NG11: Rudd 3K 115
NG12: Crop Bi 5B 112
NG12: Shel 6H 89
NG13: Bing 4G 101
NG13: Gran 1J 141
NG13: Ors 1J 103
NG13: What 5E 102
NG16: Eastw 4C 72
NG17: Kirk A 6H 51
NG17: Sut A 1H 51
NG18: Mans 3H 47
NG19: Mans W 6J 41
NG19: Plea 4B 40
NG20: Mkt W 4D 34
NG20: Whal T 5B 26
NG21: Edwin 5F 37
NG22: Bils 5C 126
NG22: East M 3D 28
NG22: Oll 5A 38
NG23: Coll 3G 129
NG23: Sut T 2E 128
NG24: Farnd 7G 133
NG24: New T 1C 136
NG25: Sout 6H 131
S81: Lango 2B 12
Church St. E. NG16: Pinx 1B 58
Church St. W. NG16: Pinx 1A 58
CHURCH TOWN 1C 145
Church Vw. DN10: Beck 6C 16
DN10: Scro 4K 9
NG4: Ged 6J 87
NG17: Stant H 4H 45
NG19: New H 2A 40
NG22: Egma 2E 124
NG22: Oll 5A 38
NG24: Bald 6G 137
NG25: Oxt 2F 71
Church Vw. Cl. NG5: Arn 5D 76
Church Vw. Gdns. NG17: Ann W 4J 59
Church Wlk. DN11: Harwo 2B 8
NG4: Carl 1H 97
NG9: Stap 2D 104
NG13: What 4D 102
NG14: Woodbo 2G 79
NG16: Brins 7C 64
NG16: Eastw 4D 72
NG22: Dun T 6J 29
NG23: Upton 7C 132
NG23: Weston 2F 125
NG24: New T 1C 136
S80: Work 2G 21
CHURCH WARSOP 1C 34 (2A 146)
Church Way DN22: Sut L 6B 14
CHURCH WILNE 2A 148
Churnet Cl. NG11: Clif 5F 107
Churston Ct. NG9: Bee 3B 106
Cider Orchard Pl. NG16: Kimb 1E 82
Cigar Factory, The *NG7: Nott 4B 6*
(off Derby Rd.)
CINDERHILL 3C 84
Cinderhill Footway NG6: Bulw 3E 84
Cinderhill Gro. NG4: Ged 5H 87
Cinderhill Gym 4C 84
Cinderhill Rd. NG6: Bulw, Cin 3C 84
Cinderhill Stop (NET) 3C 84
Cinderhill Wlk. NG6: Bulw 1C 84
Cinder La. NG22: Oll 6B 38
Cineworld Cinema
Nottingham 4E 6 (3K 95)
Circle, The NG19: Mans W 5H 41
NG21: C'tone 6J 43
Cirrus Dr. NG16: Want 7A 74
Citadel St. NG7: Radf 3F 95
City, The NG9: Bee 3B 106
(not continuous)
City Bus. Pk. NG4: Colw 2J 97
City Ground 7B 96
City Link NG2: Nott 7H 7 (5A 96)
City of Caves 6F 7
City Point NG1: Nott 6D 6 (4J 95)
City Rd. NG7: Nott 7E 94
NG9: Bee 2B 106
City Vw. NG3: Mapp 5C 86
Clandon Dr. NG5: Sher 5J 85
Clanfield Rd. NG8: Bilb 1K 93
Clapham St. NG7: Radf 3F 95
CLARBOROUGH 7J 17 (3C 145)
Clarborough Dr. NG5: Arn 1D 86
Clarborough Hill DN22: Clar 7J 17
Clare Cl. NG6: Basf 3F 85
Clarehaven NG9: Stap 4D 104
Clare Hill NG21: Blid 7J 55
Claremont Av. NG9: Bram 1H 105
NG15: Huck 1G 75
Claremont Cl. NG19: Mans W 5A 42
Claremont Dr. NG2: West Br 6K 107
Claremont Gdns. NG5: Sher 6J 85
Claremont Rd. NG5: Sher 6J 85
Clarence Ct. NG3: Nott 4K 7 (3B 96)
NG17: Sut A 7F 45
Clarence Rd. NG9: Chil 7J 105
S80: Work 1F 21
Clarence St. NG3: Nott 3K 7 (3B 96)
NG18: Mans 4G 47
NG19: Plea 6C 40
Clarendon Chambers NG1: Nott 3C 6 (3J 95)
Clarendon Ct. NG5: Sher 7J 85
Clarendon Dr. S81: Work 6E 18
Clarendon Ho. NG1: Nott 4C 6 (3J 95)
Clarendon Pk. NG5: Sher 7J 85
Clarendon Rd. NG19: Mans 2E 46
Clarendon St. NG1: Nott 3C 6 (3J 95)
Clare Rd. NG17: Sut A 3K 51
Clare St. NG1: Nott 4F 7 (3K 95)
Clare Valley NG7: Nott 6C 6 (4J 95)
Clarewood Gro. NG11: Clif 3F 115
Clarges St. NG6: Bulw 1D 84
Claricoates Dr. NG24: Codd 6H 135
Clarke Av. NG5: Arn 6H 77
NG24: New T 4B 136
Clarke Cl. NG12: Crop Bi 5B 112
Clarke Rd. NG2: Nott 6B 96
Clarke's La. NG9: Chil 5J 105
Clark La. NG22: Tuxf 7C 28
Clarks La. NG24: New T 6E 134
Clarkson Dr. NG9: Bee 3C 106
Clarkwoods Cl. NG22: Bou 4D 38
Clater's Cl. DN22: Retf 3G 23
Claude St. NG7: Lent 7F 95
CLAWSON HILL 3C 149
Clawson La. LE14: Hick 6E 142
LE14: Neth B 3K 143
Clay Av. NG3: Mapp 4D 86
Claybank Vs. NG21: Blid 7G 55
Clay Cross Dr. NG21: C'tone 6J 43
Clayfield Cl. NG6: Bulw 1B 84
Claygate NG3: Nott 1E 96
Clayhough La. DN22: Chu L 1J 29
Claylands Av. S81: Work 5C 18
Claylands Cl. S81: Work 6E 18
Claylands La. S81: Work 7E 18
Clay La. NG23: Harby 6K 31
NG24: New T 2E 136
Claymoor Cl. NG18: Mans 4F 47
Claypit La. NG25: Fis 5H 139
Claypit Wlk. NG11: Wilf 3H 107
CLAYPOLE 1D 149
Claypole Rd. NG7: H Grn 1G 95
CLAYTON 1A 144
Clayton Cl. NG24: New T 3D 136
Clayton Ct. NG7: Radf 3G 95
NG9: Bee 4B 106
Claytons Dr. NG7: Lent 6F 95
Claytons Wharf NG7: Lent 6F 95
CLAYWORTH 7J 15 (3C 145)
Clayworth Comn. DN22: Clay 7J 15
Clayworth Ct. NG18: Mans 7C 48
Clayworth Rd. DN10: Gri H 4B 16
Clegg Hill Dr. NG17: Huth 6C 44
Clement Av. NG24: Bald 6H 137
Clementine Dr. NG3: Mapp 2F 87
Clerkson's All. *NG18: Mans 3H 47*
(off Clumber St.)
Clerkson St. NG18: Mans 4H 47
Clether Rd. NG8: Bilb 2J 93
Cleve Av. NG9: Toton 6D 104
Clevedon Dr. NG5: Arn 5A 78
Cleveland Cl. NG7: Radf 3F 95
S81: Carl L 5B 12
Cleveland Hill NG22: West M 2A 28
Cleveland Sq. NG24: New T 3C 136
Cleveley's Rd. NG9: Toton 6D 104
Clevely Way NG11: Clif 6F 107
Cliff, The NG6: Bulw 3C 84
Cliff Blvd. NG16: Kimb 7K 73
Cliff Cres. NG12: Rad T 4E 98
Cliff Dr. NG12: Rad T 3F 99
Cliffe Hill Av. NG9: Stap 2C 104
Cliff Ga. DN22: Rock 1A 28
Cliffgrove Av. NG9: Chil 3J 105
Cliffhill La. NG13: Aslo 3D 102
Cliff La. NG16: Pinx 1D 58
Cliff La. Cotts. NG16: Pinx 7D 50
Cliffmere Wlk. NG11: Clif 1E 114
Cliff Nook DE55: Sth N 7A 50
Cliff Nook La. NG24: New T 7D 134
Clifford Av. NG9: Bee 1K 105
Clifford Cl. NG12: Key 6J 117
Clifford Ct. NG7: Radf 3A 6 (3G 95)
Clifford St. NG7: Radf 2A 6 (2G 95)
NG18: Mans 6H 47
Cliff Rd. NG1: Nott 6G 7 (4A 96)
NG4: Carl 2G 97
NG12: Rad T 4D 98
Cliffs, The NG12: Rad T 3F 99
Cliff St. NG18: Mans 3J 47
Cliff Way NG12: Rad T 4E 98
CLIFTON
Nottingham 1G 115 (2A 148)
Rotherham 2A 144
Clifton Av. NG11: Rudd 2K 115
Clifton Blvd. NG7: Lent, Nott 6E 94
NG11: Rudd, Wilf 4H 107
Clifton Cres. NG9: Atten 6K 105
NG24: New T 5F 135
Clifton Gdns. NG18: Mans 6B 48
Clifton Grn. NG11: Clif 7E 106
Clifton Gro. NG4: Ged 5H 87
NG18: Mans 6B 48
Clifton Hall Dr. NG11: Clif 7C 106
Clifton Ho. NG24: New T 5C 136
Clifton La. NG11: Clif, Wilf 2E 114
NG11: Rudd 2H 115
NG23: Thor 4F 31
Clifton Leisure Cen. 1G 115
Clifton M. NG7: Nott 5A 6 (4H 95)
Clifton Pastures NG11: Goth 3D 114
Clifton Pl. NG18: Mans 3H 47
Clifton Rd. NG11: Rudd 3J 115
Clifton St. NG9: Bee 3B 106
Clifton Ter. NG7: Nott 7B 6 (5H 95)
Clifton Way DN22: Retf 2C 22
Clinton Arms Ct. *NG24: New T 1C 136*
(off St Mark's Pl.)
Clinton Av. NG5: Sher 7J 85
NG16: Brins 7B 64
Clinton Ct. NG1: Nott 3E 6 (3K 95)
Clinton Ri. DN22: Gam 1K 27
Clinton St. NG5: Arn 7G 77
NG9: Bee 2K 105
NG24: New T 1C 136
S80: Work 4H 21
Clinton St. E. NG1: Nott 4F 7 (3K 95)
Clinton St. W. NG1: Nott 4F 7 (3K 95)
Clinton Ter. NG7: Nott 4A 6 (3H 95)
Clipsham Cl. NG24: Bald 4H 137
CLIPSTON 7C 110 (2B 148)
CLIPSTONE 7H 43 (2A 146)
Clipstone Av. NG1: Nott 1D 6 (2J 95)
NG3: Mapp 3D 86
NG17: Sut A 6A 46
NG18: Mans 2J 47
Clipstone Cl. NG8: Stre 5J 83
Clipstone Dr. NG19: Mans W 7E 42
NG21: Edwin 7H 35
Clipstone Rd. NG21: Edwin 7H 37
Clipstone Rd. E. NG19: Mans W 7E 42
Clipstone Rd. W. NG19: Mans W 2B 48
Clipstone Workshop Units NG21: C'tone 5K 43
Clipston La. NG12: Norm W 3J 117
Clive Cres. NG16: Kimb 2F 83
Cliveden Grn. NG11: Clif 1E 114
Cloister Ho. NG7: Lent 6F 95
Cloisters, The NG9: Bee 1B 106
Cloister St. NG7: Lent 6F 95
Close, The NG5: Sher 4K 85
NG9: Chil 5J 105
NG21: Rain 1G 55
NG23: Aver 3F 133
NG23: Upton 7C 132
NG24: New T 1D 136
Close Quarters NG9: Bram 1H 105
Closes Side La. NG13: East B 4E 90

Cloud Av. NG9: Stap 2E 104
Clouds Hill NG11: Clif 2F 115
Cloudside Ct. NG10: Sand 2A 104
Cloudside Rd. NG10: Sand 2A 104
Clough Ct. NG8: Bilb 1C 94
Clovelly Dr. NG3: Mapp 2F 87
Clover Cl. S81: Work 5J 19
Cloverdale NG12: Cotg 7F 111
Clover Flds. NG14: Calv 5E 70
Clover Gdns. NG24: New T 7G 135
Clover Grn. NG6: Basf 4E 84
Cloverlands NG2: West Br 6K 107
Cloverlands Ct. NG16: Want 7A 74
Cloverlands Dr. NG16: Want 7A 74
Clover Ri. NG16: Newth 5F 73
Clover St. NG17: Kirk A 5A 52
Clover Way NG19: Mans W 5B 42
CLOWNE 1A 146
Club Ct. NG24: Bald 5G 137
Cludd Av. NG24: New T 1H 137
Clumber Av. NG3: Mapp 3D 86
NG4: Neth 1K 97
NG5: Sher 7J 85
NG9: Chil 4J 105
NG16: Brins 4C 64
(not continuous)
NG21: Edwin 5D 36
NG21: Rain 2H 55
NG24: New T 3D 136
Clumber Ct. NG7: Nott 7A 6 (5H 95)
NG19: Mans 7E 40
NG20: Mkt W 4D 34
Clumber Cres. NG17: Stant H 4G 45
Clumber Cres. Nth. NG7: Nott 6A 6 (4H 95)
Clumber Cres. Sth. NG7: Nott 7A 6 (5H 95)
Clumber Dr. NG12: Rad T 3F 99
NG19: Mans 7E 40
Clumber Pk. 1B 146
Clumber Park Country Pk. 1B 146
Clumber Pl. S80: Work 2F 21
Clumber Rd. NG2: West Br 2C 108
Clumber Rd. E. NG7: Nott 6B 6 (4H 95)
Clumber Rd. W. NG7: Nott 6A 6 (4H 95)
Clumber St. DN22: Retf 4E 22
NG1: Nott 4F 7 (3K 95)
NG15: Huck 7J 67
NG17: Kirk A 6C 52
NG17: Sut A 1H 51
NG18: Mans 3H 47
NG20: Mkt W 4D 34
Clumber Way NG22: Bils 6D 126
Clun Ct. NG19: Mans W 7K 41
Clyro Pl. DN22: Sut L 6A 14
Coach Cl. S81: Shire 6B 18
Coach Cres. S81: Shire 5B 18
Coach Dr. NG16: Eastw 2D 72
Coach House, The NG18: Mans 6A 48
Coachmans Cft. NG8: Woll 3B 94
Coach Rd. NG20: Mkt W 6E 34
(not continuous)
S81: Shire 6A 18
Coalfield Cl. NG17: Sut A 2G 51
Coalpit La. DN22: Elk 2F 27
Coal Yd. La. NG23: Sth C 7C 30
COATES 3D 145
Coates Av. NG15: Huck 4F 67
Coatsby Rd. NG16: Kimb 7K 73
Cobblestone Dr. NG18: Mans 5K 47
Cobden Chambers NG1: Nott 5F 7
Cobden Pl. NG19: Mans 7E 40
Cobden St. NG7: Lent 3F 95
NG17: Kirk A 7A 52
Coburn St. NG17: Sut A 2K 51
Cobwell Rd. DN22: Retf 4E 22
Cochrane Ter. NG17: Stant H 4H 45
Cockayne Cl. NG10: Sand 6A 104
Cocker Beck NG4: Lamb 7G 79
Cockerhouse Rd. NG16: Eastw 2C 72
Cockett La. NG22: Farns 1H 57
Cockhill Cl. DN10: Bawt 1K 9
Cock Hill La. DN10: Bawt 1K 9
Cocking Hill NG22: Kirt 4H 39
Cocking La. DN22: Tres 5G 25
Cocking Moor La. NG22: Well 7F 39
Cockington Rd. NG8: Bilb 3H 93
Cockle Cl. NG18: Mans 5A 48
Cockshut La. NG20: Whal T 5B 26
CODDINGTON 6K 135 (3D 147)
Coddington Rd. NG24: Bald 5J 137
Codrington Gdns. NG5: Bestw 6E 76
Cogenhoe Wlk. NG5: Arn 4H 77
Coggins La. NG20: Chu W 2E 34
Coghill Ct. NG25: Sout 7G 131
Coging Cl. NG24: New B 6F 137
Cogley La. NG13: Bing 4H 101
NG23: Bath 5F 129
Cohen Cl. NG5: Arn 1E 86
NG9: Chil 7G 105
Cokefield Av. NG16: Nuth 4A 84
Cokefield Ter. DE55: Hilc 2A 50
Colbeck Ho. *S80: Work* 1F 21
(off Gateford Rd.)
Colbeck St. S80: Work 2F 21
Colborn St. NG3: Nott 1C 96
Colbrook Pl. NG4: Carl 1J 97
Colby Cl. NG19: Mans W 7D 42
Colchester Rd. NG8: Brox 6K 83
Coleby Av. NG7: Lent 6F 95
Coleby Rd. NG8: Brox 5A 84
Coledale NG2: West Br 3F 109
Coleman Av. NG24: New B 5E 136
Coleridge Cres. NG5: Arn 7F 77
Coleridge Rd. NG24: Bald 4H 137
S81: Work 7J 19
Coleridge St. NG7: Radf 2F 95
Colesbourne Rd. NG11: Clif 7G 107
Colin Broughton Ct. NG6: Bulw 7K 75
Colindale Gdns. NG16: Nuth 4K 83
Colinwood Av. NG5: Top V 5A 76
College Cl. NG24: New T 4A 136
College Ct. NG22: East M 2C 28
College Dr. NG11: Clif 7E 106
(not continuous)
College Ho. *NG18: Mans* 3G 47
(off The Connexion)
College La. NG22: East M 2D 28
S80: Work 4J 21
College Pines Golf Course 6H 21
College Rd. DN10: Walk 7G 11
LE12: Sut B 2A 120
NG3: Mapp 4F 87
NG9: Chil 4K 105
College Side NG18: Mans 1J 47
College St. NG1: Nott 4C 6 (3J 95)
NG10: Long E 6A 104
NG13: East B 4D 90
College Way NG8: Bilb 1H 93
Colley La. NG23: Weston 3G 125
Colleymoor Leys La. NG11: Clif 7G 107
Collier Av. NG19: Mans W 4H 41
Colliers Bus. Pk. NG12: Cotg 4F 111
Colliers Way NG8: Cin 3B 84
NG12: Cotg 4F 111
Colliery Cl. NG2: Nott 7J 95
Colliery Rd. DN11: Birc 3E 8
NG16: Pinx 2B 58
Colliery Vs. NG21: Edwin 6G 37
S81: Costh 3C 12
Collin Av. NG10: Sand 5A 104
COLLINGHAM 2G 129 (2D 147)
Collingham Rd. LN1: Newt T 2E 30
NG19: Mans 1D 46
NG23: Best 7H 125
Collingham Station (Rail) 2J 129
Collin Grn. NG5: Sher 3A 86
Collington St. NG9: Bee 3K 105
Collington Way NG2: West Br 4A 108
Collingwood Cl. NG11: Clif 5F 107
Collinridge Vw. NG22: Wale 5G 27
Collins Av. NG17: Sut A 2J 51
Collins Cl. NG6: Bulw 2A 84
Collins Homes NG9: Bee 7K 93
Collinson La. NG24: Bald 7H 137
Collin St. NG1: Nott 7F 7 (5K 95)
NG9: Bee 3A 106
Collins Wlk. *DN22: Retf* 3F 23
(off Wesley Rd.)
Collis Cl. NG24: New T 1G 137
Collison St. NG7: H Grn 2G 95
Collyer Rd. NG14: Calv 5A 70
Colly Ga. NG16: Kimb 2F 83
Collygate Rd. NG2: Nott 7A 96
Colmon Cl. NG5: Bestw 7C 76
Colmon Wlk. NG5: Bestw 7C 76
Colne Cl. NG19: Mans W 7K 41
Colonel's La. LE14: Upp B 3H 143
Colonsay Cl. NG9: Trow 5C 92
Colsterdale S81: Work 4J 19
COLSTERWORTH 3D 149
COLSTON BASSETT 7H 141 (2B 148)
Colston Ct. NG18: Mans 7C 48
Colston Cres. NG2: West Br 5A 108
Colston Ga. NG12: Cotg, Crop Bi 6E 110
Colston Rd. NG6: Bulw 6J 75
NG12: Crop Bi 6H 111
NG18: Mans 7C 48
Colton St. DN10: Mist 2G 11
Coltsfoot Cl. NG13: Bing 5D 100
Columbia Av. NG17: Sut A 1F 51
NG18: Mans 5B 48
Columbia Cl. NG16: Sels 5E 58
Columbia St. NG17: Huth 7D 44
Columbus Ct. S80: Work 3D 20
Colville Ct. NG1: Nott 1D 6 (1J 95)
Colville St. NG1: Nott 1D 6 (1J 95)
Colville Ter. NG1: Nott 1D 6 (2J 95)
Colville Vs. NG1: Nott 1D 6 (1J 95)
COLWICK 3H 97 (1B 148)
Colwick Bus. Pk. NG4: Colw 3J 97
Colwick Cl. NG19: Mans 1E 46
Colwick Country Pk. 5G 97
Colwick Crossing NG2: Nott 4D 96
Colwick Ind. Est. NG4: Colw 3J 97
(Private Rd. No. 2)
NG4: Colw 3A 98
(Private Rd. No. 5)
NG4: Colw 3H 97
(Private Rd. No. 8)
Colwick Lodge NG4: Carl 2J 97
Colwick Loop Rd.
NG4: Carl, Colw, Neth 7K 87
Colwick Mnr. Farm NG4: Colw 3H 97
Colwick Pk. Cl. NG4: Colw 3H 97
Colwick Quays Bus. Pk. NG4: Colw 3K 97
Colwick Rd. NG2: Nott 5C 96
NG2: West Br 7B 96
COLWICK VALE 2H 97
Colwick Woods Ct. NG2: Nott 4D 96
Combes, The NG25: Sout 4G 131
Combo Cft. NG21: Blid 6J 55
Combs La. NG22: Farns 7H 57
Comery Av. NG3: Nott 2D 96
Comet Dr. NG16: Eastw 4E 72
Comfrey Cl. NG5: Top V 7A 76
Comice Gdns. NG16: Brins 7B 64
Commerce Sq. NG1: Nott 6G 7 (4A 96)
Commercial Av. NG9: Bee 3A 106
Commercial Ga. NG18: Mans 4H 47
Commercial Rd. NG6: Bulw 7H 75
NG12: Key 1H 119
Commercial St. NG18: Mans 4H 47
Commodore Ct. NG8: Aspl 5D 84
Commodore Gdns. NG8: Aspl 5D 84
Common, The NG15: Huck 7C 66
Common La. DN11: Harwo 2A 8
DN22: Rans 2K 13
DN22: Stu S 1D 24
NG9: Bram 3F 105
NG15: Huck 7D 66
NG16: Want 7B 74
NG19: Plea 3A 40
(Chesterfield Rd.)
NG19: Plea 3F 41
(Meden La.)
S81: Blyth 5H 13
Common Rd. DN22: Retf 3F 23
NG17: Huth 7D 44
Commons Cl. NG16: Newth 6E 72
COMMONSIDE
Nottingham 4E 58
Sutton in Ashfield 1D 50
Commonside NG16: Sels 4C 58
Community Way S80: Work 4J 21
Compton Acres NG2: West Br 3J 107
Compton Acres Shop. Cen. NG2: West Br 4K 107
Compton Rd. NG5: Sher 4J 85
Compton St. NG20: Langw 7A 26
Comyn Gdns. NG3: Nott 2G 7 (2A 96)
Concorde Way NG19: Mans 6E 40
Conduit Cl. NG2: Nott 6K 95
Conery Gdns. NG13: What 5D 102
Conery La. NG13: What 7B 102
(not continuous)
Coney Wlk. NG5: Top V 6B 76
Conifer Cres. NG11: Clif 3F 115
Conifer Wlk. NG3: Nott 1D 96
Coningsby Av. S81: Gate 4D 18
Coningsby Gdns. E. NG5: Woodt 3C 86
Coningsby Rd. NG5: Woodt 2C 86
Coningswath Rd. NG4: Carl 5F 87
Conisborough Ter. NG2: Nott 7K 95
CONISBROUGH 2A 144
Conisbrough Av. NG4: Ged 6A 88
Coniston Av. NG6: Basf 5D 84
Coniston Cl. NG2: Gam 2F 109
NG19: Mans W 5A 42
Coniston Rd. NG9: Bram 7J 93
NG10: Long E 7A 104
NG15: Huck 5F 67
NG17: Kirk A 5C 52
S81: Work 4F 19
Connah La. NG22: Bou 7F 27
Connelly Cl. NG5: Arn 1F 87
Connelly Ct. NG6: Bulw 1D 84
Connery, The NG15: Huck 5H 67
Connery M. NG9: Toton 7G 105
Connexion, The NG18: Mans 3G 47
Conrad Cl. S80: Work 2J 21
Conrad Ct. NG6: Bulw 2A 84
Constance St. NG7: Basf 6H 85
Convent, The NG1: Nott 4C 6
Convent St. NG1: Nott 4G 7 (3A 96)
Conway Av. NG4: Carl 1K 97
Conway Cl. NG3: Nott 1F 7 (1K 95)
NG19: Mans 2D 46
Conway Cres. NG4: Carl 7K 87
Conway Dr. S81: Carl L 6C 12
Conway Gdns. DN22: Retf 2B 22
NG5: Arn 1B 86
Conway Rd. NG4: Carl 1J 97
NG15: Huck 3D 74
Conway Wlk. NG3: Nott 1F 7 (1K 95)
Cooks La. NG25: Fis 7G 139
NG25: Sout 6E 130
Cookson Av. NG4: Ged 5G 87
Cookson St. NG17: Kirk A 6J 51
Coombe Cl. NG8: Woll 5D 94
Coombe Rd. NG16: Newth 2F 73
Co-operative Av. NG15: Huck 5H 67
Co-operative St.
NG17: Stant H 4G 45
Cooper Cl. NG5: Arn 1F 87
NG6: Bulw 1A 84
NG12: Crop Bi 5B 112
Cooper Gdns. NG11: Rudd 3J 115
Coopers Grn. NG8: Woll 6K 93
Coopers Ri. NG21: Rain 2J 55
Cooper St. NG4: Neth 2K 97

Coopers Yd. NG20: Mkt W 4D **34**
NG24: New T 1B **136**
Copeland Av. NG9: Stap 1D **104**
NG17: Kirk A 5J **51**
Copeland Gro. NG13: Bing 3D **100**
Copeland Rd. NG15: Huck 5J **67**
NG17: Kirk A 5J **51**
Copenhagen Ct. NG3: Nott 6A **86**
Cope St. NG7: H Grn 2G **95**
Copper Hill NG23: Grass 3K **125**
Coppice Cl. NG15: Huck 1E **74**
Coppice Cft. NG17: Sut A 2G **51**
Coppice Dr. NG16: Eastw 3B **72**
Coppice Ga. NG5: Arn 6H **77**
Coppice Gro. NG3: Mapp 5C **86**
Coppice Lodge NG5: Arn 6J **77**
Coppice Rd. NG5: Arn 6H **77**
NG19: Mans W 6F **43**
S81: Work 5G **19**
Copplestone Dr. NG3: Mapp 1F **87**
Coppywood Cl. NG17: Teve 3F **45**
Copse, The NG9: Chil 3H **105**
NG15: Huck 7J **67**
NG17: Stant H 5G **45**
NG18: Mans 1J **53**
NG24: Farnd 7H **133**
Copse Cl. NG14: Bur J 2E **88**
NG15: Rave 1J **61**
Coral Cres. NG20: Mkt W 3C **34**
Corben Gdns. NG6: Bulw 7F **75**
Corbiere Av. NG16: Want 7A **74**
Corby Rd. NG3: Nott 6B **86**
Cordy La. NG16: Brins, Unde 6C **64**
Corene Av. NG17: Sut A 2J **51**
Coriander Dr. NG6: Basf 4E **84**
Corinthian Cl. NG15: Huck 4J **67**
Corinth Rd. NG11: Clif 7F **107**
Corke Ho. *NG7: Lent* *4F* ***95***
(off Faraday Rd.)
Corkhill La. NG22: Kirk 1D **132** & 1F **131**
NG25: Norm 1F **131**
Cormack La. NG24: Bald 7J **137**
Corn Cl. DE55: Sth N 5A **50**
NG12: Cotg 7D **110**
Corncrake Av. NG6: Basf 4E **84**
Corncrake Dr. NG5: Arn 7A **78**
Corncrake M. NG17: Kirk A 1A **60**
Corn Cft. NG11: Clif 1G **115**
Cornel Ct. NG19: Mans W 1A **48**
Cornelian Dr. NG17: Sut A 3H **51**
Cornell Dr. NG5: Arn 6K **77**
Corner, The NG14: Lowd 5D **80**
Corner Cft. NG17: Huth 7E **44**
Corner Farm Cl. DN22: Sut L 6B **14**
NG23: Roll 3K **139**
Cornerpin Dr. NG17: Kirk A 5B **52**
Cornfield Cl. S81: Carl L 5D **12**
Cornfield Rd. NG16: Kimb 7J **73**
Cornfields, The NG5: Bestw 6D **76**
Cornhill Rd. NG4: Carl 7E **86**
Cornley Rd. DN10: Mist 1F **11**
Cornmill Rd. NG17: Sut A 2B **52**
Cornwall Av. NG9: Bee 5D **106**
NG18: Mans 4B **48**
Cornwall Cl. NG16: Westw 1A **64**
Cornwall Dr. NG22: Oll 5B **38**
Cornwall Rd. DN22: Retf 1G **23**
NG5: Arn 7E **76**
S81: Shire 5A **18**
Cornwall's Hill NG4: Lamb 7H **79**
Coronation Av. DN10: Miss 2C **10**
NG10: Sand 2A **104**
NG11: Wilf 1J **107**
Coronation Dr. DE55: Sth N 5A **50**
NG19: Mans W 2B **48**
Coronation Pk. 4E **72**
Coronation Rd. DE7: Ilk 5A **82**
NG3: Mapp 4C **86**
NG6: Bestw V 1A **76**
NG15: Huck 5F **67**
NG16: Coss 5A **82**
NG16: Nuth 2G **83**
Coronation St. DN22: Retf 3E **22**
NG17: Sut A 2J **51**
NG18: Mans 4K **47**
NG24: New B 4F **137**
Coronation Ter. NG22: Dun T 5J **29**
Coronation Wlk. NG4: Ged 6K **87**
Corporation Cotts. NG14: Bulc 2G **89**
Corporation Oaks NG3: Nott 1K **95**
Corporation Rd. DE7: Ilk 3A **92**
Corporation St. NG18: Mans 3G **47**
CORRINGHAM 2D **145**
Corsham Gdns. NG3: Nott 1D **96**
Corve Dale Wlk. NG2: West Br 4C **108**
Cosby Dr. LE12: East L 1A **122**
Cosby Rd. NG2: Nott 5C **96**
Cosgrove Av. NG17: Skeg 5A **46**
COSSALL 6B **82** (1A **148**)
Cossall Ind. Est. DE7: Ilk 5A **82**
COSSALL MARSH 5B **82**
Cossall Rd. NG9: Trow 1B **92**
NG16: Coss 1B **92**
COSTHORPE 5C **12**
Costhorpe Ind. Est. S81: Costh 4B **12**
Costhorpe Vs. S81: Costh 3C **12**
COSTOCK 3E **122** (3A **148**)
Costock Av. NG5: Sher 3J **85**
Costock Rd. LE12: East L 3B **122**
NG12: Wys 2J **123**
COSTON 3D **149**
COTES 3A **148**
COTGRAVE 6E **110** (2B **148**)
Cotgrave Av. NG4: Ged 5J **87**
Cotgrave Cl. NG8: Stre 5K **83**
Cotgrave Country Pk. 3E **110**
Cotgrave La. NG12: Toll 6J **109**
Cotgrave Leisure Cen. 6F **111**
Cotgrave Rd. NG12: C'ton, Plum 3J **117**
NG19: Mans 7F **41**
Cotgrave Shop. Cen. NG12: Cotg 6E **110**
COTHAM 1C **149**
Cotham La. NG24: Haw 7A **136**
COTMANHAY 1A **148**
Coton Cl. NG11: Wilf 6H **107**
NG19: Mans W 5A **42**
Cotswold Ct. NG9: Bram 7J **93**
S81: Carl L 5B **12**
Cotswold Gro. NG18: Mans 4D **48**
Cotswold Rd. NG8: Stre 6K **83**
Cottage Av. NG13: What 4C **102**
Cottage Cl. LE12: East L 1A **122**
NG17: Stant H 4G **45**
NG21: Blid 7H **55**
NG24: Bald 7G **137**
Cottage Grn. NG2: West Br 7F **97**
Cottage La. NG20: Cuck 4D **32**
NG20: Mkt W 7D **34**
NG23: Coll 4G **129**
Cottage Mdw. NG4: Colw 4J **97**
Cottage Pasture La. NG14: Gun 7E **80**
Cottage Ter. NG1: Nott 4B **6** (3H **95**)
Cottage Wlk. NG8: Woll 3K **93**
COTTAM 1D **147**
Cottam Dr. NG5: Top V 6B **76**
Cottam Gdns. NG5: Top V 6C **76**
Cottam Gro. NG19: Mans 4D **46**
Cottam La. DN22: Tres 5H **25**
Cottam Rd. DN22: Sth L 1H **25**
DN22: Tres 4J **25**
Cottams Cl. NG25: Sout 6J **131**
Cotterdale Cl. NG19: Mans W 1A **48**
Cotterhill Cl. S81: Gate 3E **18**
Cottesmore Rd. NG7: Lent 4G **95**
Cotton Ho. *NG7: Radf* *2F* ***95***
(off Radford Blvd.)
Cotton Mill La. NG22: Farns 6K **57**
Coulton's Av. NG17: Sut A 7G **45**
Coulton's Cl. NG17: Sut A 7G **45**
County Archives 7E **6** (5K **95**)
County Bus. Pk. NG2: Nott 6B **96**
County Cl. NG9: Bee 4B **106**
County Court
Mansfield 2G **47**
Nottingham 7F **7** (5K **95**)
County Estate, The NG17: Huth 1C **50**
(not continuous)
County Rd. NG2: Nott 6B **96**
NG4: Ged 4F **87**
Coupe Gdns. NG15: Huck 7J **67**
Court, The NG9: Toton 7F **105**
Court Cres. NG8: Woll 4A **94**
Courtenay Gdns. NG3: Nott 1G **7** (1A **96**)
Courtfield Rd. NG17: Skeg 4A **46**
Court Gdns. NG2: West Br 5J **107**
Courtleet Way NG6: Bulw 2C **84**
Courtney Cl. NG8: Woll 3K **93**
Court St. NG7: H Grn 1G **95**
Court Vw. NG7: Nott 5B **6** (4H **95**)
Court Yd. NG9: Bram 1G **105**
Courtyard, The NG16: Kimb 6J **73**
NG18: Mans 6K **47**
NG24: Codd 6K **135**
NG24: New T *1C* ***136***
(off Castle Brewery)
Covedale Rd. NG5: Sher 2K **85**
Covent Gdns. NG12: Rad T 5K **99**
Coventry Ct. NG6: Bulw 2C **84**
Coventry Dr. S81: Work 6H **19**
Coventry La. NG9: Bram 7E **92**
Coventry Rd. NG6: Bulw 7H **75**
(Gilead St.)
NG6: Bulw 1C **84**
(Main St.)
NG9: Bee 2B **106**
Coverdale S81: Work 5J **19**
Covers, The NG2: West Br 7C **96**
Covert Cl. NG12: Key 6J **117**
NG14: Bur J 2D **88**
NG15: Huck 7J **67**
Covert Cres. NG12: Rad T 5G **99**
Covert Rd. NG2: West Br 3E **108**
Cowan St. NG1: Nott 4G **7** (3A **96**)
Cowdrey Gdns. NG5: Arn 1E **86**
Cowlairs NG5: Top V 7A **76**
Cow La. NG9: Bram 1G **105**
NG24: New T 7C **134**
Cowley St. NG6: Basf 4E **84**
Cow Pasture La. DN10: Miss 1E **10**
NG17: Kirk A 6H **51**
Cowpasture La. NG17: Sut A 2J **51**
Cowper Cl. S81: Work 7J **19**
Cowper Rd. NG5: Woodt 3B **86**
NG16: Newth 6E **72**
Cowpes Cl. NG17: Sut A 6H **45**
Cowslip Cl. NG13: Bing 4D **100**
COX MOOR 6C **52**
Coxmoor Cl. NG12: Edwal 5F **109**
Coxmoor Ct. NG5: Top V 5C **76**
Coxmoor Golf Course 4F **53**
Coxmoor Rd. NG17: Sut A, Kirk A 7B **46**
Cox's La. NG19: Mans W 4G **41**
Crabapple Dr. NG16: Lang M 2A **72**
Crab Apple Gro. NG15: Huck 2J **75**
Crab La. NG23: Nth M 7K **129**
Crabnook La. NG22: Farns 5K **57**
Crabtree Fld. NG2: Colw 4G **97**
Crabtree La. DN10: Beck 7A **16**
Crabtree Rd. NG6: Bulw 1B **84**
Crafts Way NG25: Sout 4H **131**
Cragdale Rd. NG5: Sher 2K **85**
Cragmoor Rd. NG14: Bur J 4D **88**
Craig Moray NG12: Rad T 4F **99**
Craigs Grn. NG19: Mans 5E **46**
Craigston Rd. S81: Carl L 6B **12**
Craithie Rd. S81: Carl L 6B **12**
Crammond Cl. NG2: Nott 6J **95**
Crampton Av. NG18: Mans 2A **48**
Crampton Cl. NG17: Sut A 7F **45**
Crampton Ct. NG5: Top V 6C **76**
Cramworth Gro. NG5: Sher 4A **86**
Cranberry Cl. NG2: West Br 3J **107**
Cranberry Pk. NG20: Mede V 7G **33**
Cranborne Cl. NG9: Trow 6C **92**
NG19: Mans 3D **46**
Cranbourne Gro. NG15: Huck 6E **66**
Cranbrook Ct. NG19: Mans W 3J **41**
Cranbrook Ho. NG1: Nott 5H **7**
Cranbrook St. NG1: Nott 4G **7** (3A **96**)
Cranfield Wlk. *NG11: Clif* *7G* ***107***
(off Southchurch Dr.)
Cranford Gdns. NG2: West Br 5K **107**
Crankley La. NG24: New T 4A **134**
Cranleigh Dr. NG14: Lowd 5D **80**
Cranmer Av. NG13: What 5B **102**
Cranmer Gro. NG3: Nott 1K **95**
NG19: Mans 6D **40**
Cranmer Rd. NG24: New T 4C **136**
Cranmer St. NG3: Nott 1K **95**
NG10: Long E 7C **104**
Cranmer Wlk. NG3: Nott 1F **7** (1K **95**)
Cranmore Cl. NG5: Arn 4J **77**
Cransley Av. NG8: Woll 6J **93**
Cranston Av. NG5: Arn 5H **77**
Cranston Rd. NG9: Bram 7H **93**
Cranswick Cl. NG19: Mans W 7C **42**
Cranthorne Dr. NG3: Nott 2F **97**
Crantock Gdns. NG12: Key 7J **117**
Cranwell Cl. NG24: New T 7G **135**
Cranwell Ct. NG6: Bulw 1A **84**
Cranwell Rd. NG8: Stre 6J **83**
Craster Dr. NG5: Arn 4J **77**
NG6: Bulw 6F **75**
Craster St. NG17: Sut A 2J **51**
Craven Rd. NG7: H Grn 1F **95**
Crawford Av. NG9: Stap 1C **104**
Crawford Cl. NG8: Woll 3K **93**
Crawford Ri. NG5: Arn 6A **78**
Crawfords Mdw. NG13: Aslo 3C **102**
Crawford Wlk. NG11: Clif 7G **107**
Creamery Cl. NG8: Bilb 1C **94**
Crees La. NG24: Farnd, New T 5J **133**
Crees Yd. NG17: Kirk A 6H **51**
Creeton Grn. NG11: Clif 2G **115**
Cremorne Dr. NG2: Nott 7J **95**
NG22: Bils 4B **126**
Crescent, The DN10: Beck 6D **16**
DN11: Birc 2F **9**
DN22: Retf 4D **22**
LE12: East L 2B **122**
NG3: Nott 7A **86**
NG5: Woodt 3B **86**
NG9: Chil 6H **105**
NG9: Stap 7D **92**
NG9: Toton 7F **105**
NG12: Rad T 5F **99**
NG16: Eastw 3E **72**
NG17: Skeg 3H **45**
NG18: Mans 7J **47**
NG21: Blid 6K **55**
NG22: Bils 5B **126**
NG24: New T 3D **136**
Crescent Av. NG4: Carl 6H **87**
Crescent Rd. NG16: Sels 6B **58**
Cresswell Rd. NG9: Chil 4G **105**
S80: Work 1F **21**
Cresswell St. S80: Work 2F **21**
Cressy Rd. NG11: Clif 7G **107**
Cresta Gdns. NG3: Mapp 5A **86**
Crest Vw. NG5: Sher 4J **85**
CRESWELL 1A **146**
Creswell Ct. NG19: Mans W 5A **42**
Creswell Crags Museum & Educational Cen. 1A **26**
Creswell Rd. NG20: Cuck 3A **32**
Crewe Cl. NG7: Radf 2G **95**
NG21: Blid 6J **55**
Crewe Rd. DN11: Birc 2E **8**
Crew La. NG25: Sout 6K **131** & 2F **139**

Crew La. Cl. NG25: Sout 6J **131**
Crew La. Ind. Est. NG25: Sout 6K **131**
Crew Rd. NG23: Coll 1J **129**
Cribb Cl. NG11: Wilf 2J **107**
Crich Vw. NG5: Sher 5K **85**
Cricket Cl. NG17: Nunc 3K **59**
Cricketers Ct. NG2: West Br 7C **96**
Cricket Fld. La. DN22: Retf 3E **22**
Criftin Ent. Cen. NG14: Epp 5H **71**
Criftin Rd. NG14: Bur J 3F **89**
Crink La. NG25: Sout 7H **131**
Cripps Hill NG7: Nott 6D **94**
Critch's Flats NG16: Kimb 1E **82**
Crocus Pl. NG2: Nott 5A **96**
Crocus St. NG2: Nott 6K **95**
   NG17: Kirk A .7B **52**
Croft, The DN10: Beck 7D **16**
   DN22: Retf 2F **23**
   NG17: Stant H 4G **45**
   NG17: Sut A 1K **51**
   NG24: New T .1D **136**
   S80: Work 3G **21**
Croft Av. NG15: Huck 1G **75**
   NG18: Mans 1K **53**
Croft Cl. NG16: Pinx 1A **58**
Croft Cres. NG16: Aws 2B **82**
Croft Farm Cl. DN10: Eve 6B **10**
   NG23: Roll 3K **139**
Crofton Cl. NG8: Bilb 2C **94**
   NG9: Chil 7J **105**
Crofton Rd. NG9: Chil 6J **105**
Croft Ri. NG13: East B 3D **90**
Croft Rd. NG5: Arn 6H **77**
   NG12: Edwal .5D **108**
   NG12: Key 7G **117**
Crofts, The NG13: Bing 4F **101**
Croft Way DN10: Eve 6B **10**
Cromarty Cl. NG19: Mans 5D **46**
Cromdale Cl. NG5: Arn 5A **78**
Cromer Cl. NG18: Mans 6J **47**
Cromer Rd. NG3: Nott 1B **96**
Cromford Av. NG4: Carl 7G **87**
   NG18: Mans 5G **47**
Cromford Cl. NG16: Lang M 2A **72**
Cromford Cl. NG15: Rave 1C **62**
Cromford Rd. NG2: West Br 3C **108**
   NG16: Lang M 2A **72**
   NG17: Nunc 3A **60**
Cromford Rd. Ind. Est. NG16: Lang M . . .2A **72**
Crompton Rd. DE7: Ilk, Stant D 6A **92**
   NG19: Plea 6D **40**
   NG22: Bils 5C **126**
Crompton Rd. Ind. Est. DE7: Ilk 5A **92**
Crompton St. NG17: Teve 3F **45**
   NG19: New H .2A **40**
CROMWELL 2C **147**
Cromwell Av. DE7: Ilk 3A **92**
Cromwell Cl. S81: Gate 4E **18**
Cromwell Cres. NG4: Lamb 7F **79**
Cromwell Dr. LE12: East L 3A **122**
Cromwell Rd. NG9: Bee 2K **105**
   NG13: What 5B **102**
   NG24: New T .2E **136**
Cromwell St. NG4: Carl 1H **97**
   NG7: Radf 3B **6** (3H **95**)
   NG16: Gilt 6F **73**
   NG18: Mans 5J **47**
Crook Dale Dr. NG21: Edwin 6A **36**
Crookdole La. NG14: Calv 6D **70**
Crookes Av. NG19: Mans W 6J **41**
   NG19: Plea 4A **40**
Crops, The NG22: Kirk 3C **132**
Cropston Cl. NG2: West Br 5B **108**
Cropton Cres. NG8: Bilb 2C **94**
Cropton Gro. NG13: Bing 4D **100**
CROPWELL BISHOP 5B **112** (2B **148**)
Cropwell Bishop Rd.
   NG12: Crop Bu 4C **112**
CROPWELL BUTLER 3C **112** (2B **148**)
Cropwell Butler Rd. NG12: Crop Bi 5C **112**
Cropwell Ct. NG18: Mans 3K **47**
Cropwell Gdns. NG12: Rad T 6F **99**
Cropwell Grn. NG3: Nott 2C **96**
Cropwell Mnr. Ct. NG12: Crop Bi 6C **112**
Cropwell Rd. NG12: Rad T 5E **98**
   NG13: Lang 7K **113**
CROSBY 1D **145**
Crosby Cl. NG19: Mans W 7C **42**
Crosby Rd. NG2: West Br 7C **96**
Cross, The NG12: Cotg 6D **110**
   S81: Carl L 6D **12**
Crossdale Dr. NG12: Key 6H **117**
Crossdale Wlk. NG5: Top V 6A **76**
Cross Dr. NG17: Kirk A 4B **52**
Crossfield Ct. NG5: Top V 6C **76**
Cross Fld. Dr. S81: Woods 1A **18**
Crossfield Dr. NG5: Top V 6C **76**
Crossgate Dr. NG2: Nott 1H **107**
Cross Hill DN10: Gri H 3A **16**
   LE12: Will W 6G **143**
   NG22: Lax 5B **124**
Crosshill NG12: Cotg 6F **111**
Crossings, The NG24: New T 1E **136**
Crossland Rd. NG5: Bestw 2H **85**
Crosslands Mdw. NG4: Colw 4J **97**

Cross La. NG13: East B 5E **90**
   NG17: Huth 1D **50**
   NG21: Blid 6E **54**
   NG23: Coll 1J **129**
   NG23: Harby 6K **31**
   NG24: Bald 7H **137**
   NG24: Barn W .7K **137**
   NG24: Farnd 7G **133**
   S81: Woods 1A **18**
Cross La. Cl. S81: Woods 1A **18**
Crossley Av. NG17: Huth 7E **44**
Crossley Hill La. S81: Work 1J **19**
Crossley St. NG5: Sher 5J **85**
Crossman St. NG5: Sher 5J **85**
Cross Rd. NG15: Ann 5C **60**
Cross Row NG17: Stant H 4G **45**
Cross St. DN22: Retf 4G **23**
   DN22: Stu S 2C **24**
   NG4: Carl 7G **87**
   NG4: Neth 1K **97**
   NG5: Arn 6F **77**
   NG9: Bee 2A **106**
   NG10: Sand 3B **104**
   NG16: Eastw 4E **72**
   NG19: Mans W 7H **41**
   NG22: Bils 5C **126**
   NG24: New T .1D **136**
   S81: Lango 2B **12**
Crossways DN22: Retf 2F **23**
   NG22: East M .2D **28**
Crossways Dr. NG13: East B 4E **90**
Crowborough Av. NG8: Woll 6K **93**
Crow Ct. NG13: Bing 4H **101**
Crowcroft Way NG10: Long E 7A **104**
Crow Hill NG19: Plea 4B **40**
Crow Hill Ct. NG19: Mans 2H **47**
Crow Hill Dr. NG19: Mans 2H **47**
Crow Hill La. NG19: Mans W 7H **41**
Crow Hill Ri. NG19: Mans 2H **47**
Crow Hill Rd. NG4: Carl 1J **97**
Crow La. NG23: Sth M 1A **134**
CROWLE 1C **145**
Crowley Cl. NG8: Bilb 2H **93**
Crown Av. NG19: Mans W 2C **48**
Crown Cl. NG21: Rain 3A **56**
   NG23: Coll 1H **129**
Crown Court
   Nottingham 7F **7** (5K **95**)
Crown Ct. DN22: Stu S 2C **24**
Crown Farm Ind. Pk. NG19: Mans W 2D **48**
Crown Farm La. NG18: Mans 3D **48**
Crown Farm Way NG19: Mans W 3C **48**
Crown Pl. S80: Work 1F **21**
Crown St. NG18: Mans 4B **48**
   NG24: New T .2C **136**
   S80: Work 1F **21**
Crown Wlk. NG18: Mans 3H **47**
Crown Way NG16: Lang M 2A **72**
Crow Pk. Av. NG23: Sut T 2C **128**
Crow Pk. Dr. NG14: Bur J 4D **88**
Crowthorne Cl. NG5: Top V 5A **76**
Crowthorne Gdns. NG5: Top V 5A **76**
Crowtrees Dr. NG17: Sut A 2G **51**
Croxall Cl. NG11: Clif 5F **107**
Croxley Gdns. NG16: Nuth 4J **83**
Croxton Ct. NG19: Mans W 6A **42**
CROXTON KERRIAL 3D **149**
Croydon Rd. NG7: Radf 3F **95**
Crummock Cl. NG9: Bram 1H **105**
Crusader Cl. NG11: Clif 1D **114**
Crusader Ho. NG1: Nott 4F **7** (4K **95**)
Cuckney Hill NG20: Chu W 7D **32**
Cuckney Rd. NG20: Neth L 6D **26**
Cuckoo Holt S81: Gate 5D **18**
Cuckstools, The NG23: Sut T 3D **128**
Cudworth Dr. NG3: Mapp 5C **86**
Cuillin Cl. NG5: Top V 4B **76**
Culbert Lodge NG7: Basf 6G **85**
Culbert Pl. NG7: Basf 6G **85**
Cul-de-Sac NG22: Bils 5C **126**
Cullen Cl. NG24: New T 7B **134**
Cullens Ct. NG5: Sher 5K **85**
Cumberland Av. NG9: Bee 3J **105**
   NG20: Mkt W .3B **34**
Cumberland Cl. DN11: Birc 2G **9**
   NG11: Rudd 3K **115**
   NG16: Westw .1A **64**
   S81: Costh 5C **12**
Cumberland Dr. NG19: Mans 3D **46**
Cumberland Ho. DN11: Birc 2G **9**
Cumberland Pl. NG1: Nott 5D **6** (4J **95**)
Cumbria Grange NG2: Gam 2F **109**
Cumbria Rd. S81: Work 6H **19**
Cundy Hill NG25: Sout 7E **130**
Cunningham Cl. DN10: Matt T 1F **15**
Cupar Cl. NG20: Chu W 2E **34**
Curbar Cl. NG18: Mans 5K **47**
Curie Ct. NG7: Nott 6F **95**
Curlew Cl. NG3: Nott 3F **97**
Curlew Wharf NG7: Lent 6H **95**
Currie Rd. NG24: New T 6D **134**
Cursham St. NG17: Sut A 1K **51**
Cursley Way NG9: Chil 7H **105**
Curtis Cl. NG23: Coll 1H **129**
Curtis St. NG15: Huck 7G **67**

Curzon Av. NG4: Carl 1E **96**
Curzon Cl. NG21: Rain 2J **55**
Curzon Ct. NG3: Nott 2H **7** (2A **96**)
Curzon Dr. S81: Work 6G **19**
Curzon Gdns. NG3: Nott 2H **7** (2A **96**)
Curzon Pl. NG3: Nott 3G **7** (3A **96**)
Curzon St. NG3: Nott 3G **7** (3A **96**)
   NG4: Neth 1K **97**
   NG10: Long E .7A **104**
   NG11: Goth 7G **115**
CUSWORTH 1A **144**
Cusworth Way S80: Work 2E **20**
Cuthrough La. NG7: Nott 1C **106**
Cutlers Ct. NG12: Rad T 5D **98**
Cutlersforth NG22: Halam 6A **130**
Cuttings Av. NG17: Sut A 3F **51**
Cuttle Hill Gdns. NG13: East B 4D **90**
Cutts Row NG17: Ann W 4K **59**
Cuxton Cl. NG8: Stre 6J **83**
Cycle Rd. NG7: Lent 4F **95**
Cygnet Fold NG19: Mans W 5J **41**
Cypress Ct. NG15: Huck 1C **74**
Cyprus Av. NG9: Bee 2A **106**
Cyprus Cl. NG3: Mapp P 7K **85**
Cyprus Dr. NG9: Bee 2A **106**
Cyprus Rd. NG3: Mapp P 7K **85**
Cyril Av. NG8: Aspl 7E **84**
   NG9: Bee 2K **105**
   NG9: Stap 2C **104**
Cyril Cotts. NG8: Aspl 7E **84**
Cyril Rd. NG2: West Br 1D **108**

D

Dabek Ri. NG17: Nunc 3A **60**
Dabell Av. NG6: Bulw 6E **74**
Dadley Rd. S81: Carl L 5C **12**
Dagmar Gro. NG3: Nott 6A **86**
   NG9: Bee 3B **106**
Dairy Cl. NG17: Sut A 7J **45**
Dairy Sq. NG8: Bilb 1C **94**
Daisy Cl. NG12: Cotg 7D **110**
Daisy Farm Rd. NG16: Newth 5F **73**
Daisy Rd. NG3: Nott 6D **86**
Dakeyne St. NG3: Nott 4J **7** (3B **96**)
Dakota Rd. NG13: Newton 1C **100**
Dalbeattie Cl. NG5: Arn 6K **77**
Dalby Sq. NG8: Woll 5D **94**
DALBY WOLDS .3B **148**
Dale Av. NG3: Mapp 5D **86**
   NG4: Carl 1F **97**
   NG10: Long E .7C **104**
Dalebrook Cres. NG15: Huck 7C **66**
Dale Cl. DN22: Ord 7E **22**
   NG2: West Br 2E **108**
   NG15: Huck 7C **66**
   NG17: Skeg 5A **46**
   NG19: Mans 2G **47**
   NG20: Langw .7A **26**
   NG21: Blid 6J **55**
Dale Cres. NG24: Bald 7H **137**
Dale Farm Av. NG3: Nott 3D **96**
Dale Gro. NG2: Nott 4C **96**
Dalehead Rd. NG11: Clif 7E **106**
Dale La. NG9: Chil 3K **105**
   NG21: Blid 6J **55**
Dalemoor Gdns. NG8: Bilb 7C **84**
Dale Rd. NG4: Carl 1F **97**
   NG12: Key 7H **117**
   NG16: Kimb 2E **82**
   NG20: Mkt W .3E **34**
Dales Av. NG17: Skeg 5K **45**
Dales Cl. LE12: Remp 7G **123**
Daleside NG12: Cotg 7D **110**
Daleside Rd. NG2: Nott 5C **96**
Daleside Rd. E. NG2: Nott 4E **96**
DALESTORTH 5B **46**
Dalestorth Av. NG19: Mans 1D **46**
Dalestorth Cl. NG17: Skeg 5A **46**
Dalestorth Gdns. NG17: Skeg 5A **46**
Dalestorth Rd. NG17: Skeg 5A **46**
Dalestorth St. NG17: Sut A 5A **46**
Dale St. NG2: Nott 6K **7** (4B **96**)
   NG19: Mans 1H **47**
Dale Ter. NG2: Nott 4C **96**
Dale Vw. Rd. NG3: Nott 1E **96**
Dale Way NG24: Bald 7J **137**
Dalkeith Ter. NG7: H Grn 1G **95**
Dallaglio M. NG9: Chil 7G **105**
Dallas St. NG18: Mans 4G **47**
Dallas York Rd. NG9: Bee 3C **106**
Dalley Cl. NG9: Stap 2D **104**
Dallman Cl. NG15: Huck 1G **75**
DALTON 2A **144**
Dalton Cl. NG9: Stap 4D **104**
DALTON MAGNA 2A **144**
Dame Flogan St. NG18: Mans 4H **47**
Dame La. DN10: Miss 3C **10**
Damson Wlk. NG3: Nott 7E **86**
Danbury Mt. NG5: Sher 5J **85**
Dane Cl. NG3: Nott 2G **7** (2A **96**)
Dane Ct. NG3: Nott 2G **7** (2A **96**)
Dane Gro. NG15: Ann 5D **60**
Danehurst Dr. NG4: Ged 6K **87**
Danes Cl. NG5: Arn 6F **77**

Danesfield Rd. S80: Work 4G **21**
Daneshill Gravel Pits (North) Nature Reserve 3B **144**
Daneshill Lakes (Nature Reserve) 3K **13**
Daneshill Rd. DN22: Lound 3A **14**
Danethorpe La. NG24: Dane 1K **135**
Danethorpe Va. NG5: Sher 3K **85**
Daniel Cres. NG18: Mans 3F **47**
Daniels Ct. NG16: Eastw 5D **72**
Daniels Way NG15: Huck 2E **74**
Dann Pl. NG11: Wilf 1J **107**
Danvers Dr. NG19: Mans 3E **46**
Darbyshire Cl. NG23: Harby 6K **31**
D'Arcy Ct. DN22: Retf 1D **22**
DARFOULDS 4A **20**
Darkey La. NG9: Stap 4D **104**
(not continuous)
Dark La. LE12: West L 2F **121**
NG13: Bing 4H **101**
NG13: What 4D **102**
NG14: Calv 7C **70**
NG24: Barn W 7K **137**
Darley Av. NG4: Carl 6H **87**
NG7: H Grn 1F **95**
NG9: Toton 6D **104**
NG17: Kirk A 5C **52**
Darleydale Cl. NG18: Mans 7J **47**
Darley Rd. NG7: H Grn 1F **95**
Darlison St. *NG15: Huck* *5G* ***67***
(off Ogle St.)
DARLTON 1C **147**
Darlton Dr. NG5: Arn 7J **77**
Darlton Rd. NG22: Darl, Dun T 6F **29**
NG22: Tuxf 6E **28**
Darlton St. NG19: Mans 4D **46**
Darnal Cl. NG5: Top V 7A **76**
Darnhall Cres. NG8: Bilb 1J **93**
Daron Gdns. NG5: Bestw 7C **76**
Darrel Rd. DN22: Retf 5E **22**
Darricott Cl. NG21: Rain 3K **55**
Dart Ct. NG13: Bing 5E **100**
Dartmeet Ct. NG7: Radf 1E **94**
Dartmoor Cl. NG11: Clif 2E **114**
Darvel Cl. NG8: Bilb 2C **94**
Darwin Cl. NG5: Top V 6A **76**
NG18: Mans 7J **47**
NG23: Elston 2E **140**
Darwin Dr. DN22: Woodbe 6G **25**
NG22: New O 5C **38**
Davey Cl. NG18: Mans 3G **47**
Davey Rd. NG18: Mans 3F **47**
David Gro. NG9: Bram 7J **93**
David La. NG6: Basf 4E **84**
David Lane Stop (NET) 4E **84**
David Lloyd Leisure
Nottingham 1E **94**
West Bridgford 3A **108**
Davids La. NG14: Gun 2B **90**
Davidson Cl. NG5: Arn 7A **78**
Davidson Gdns. NG11: Rudd 3H **115**
Davidson St. NG2: Nott 5C **96**
David St. NG17: Kirk A 4B **52**
Davies Av. NG17: Sut A 6J **45**
Davies Cl. NG17: Sut A 7J **45**
Davies Rd. NG2: West Br 2C **108**
Davies Way NG5: Bestw 2H **85**
Davis Cl. NG21: C'tone 5K **43**
Davis Rd. NG9: Chil 6G **105**
Davy Cl. NG15: Lin 3H **67**
Dawber St. S81: Work 5E **18**
Dawes Way NG7: Lent 3F **95**
Dawgates La. NG17: Skeg 1K **45**
NG19: Plea 7A **40** & 1K **45**
Dawlish Cl. NG3: Mapp 2F **87**
NG15: Huck 7D **66**
Dawlish Ct. NG3: Mapp 1G **87**
NG16: Eastw 3B **72**
Dawlish Dr. NG5: Bestw 2J **85**
Dawn Cl. NG15: Huck 4J **67**
Dawn's La. NG13: Aslo 3D **102**
Dawn Vw. NG9: Trow 6C **92**
Dawson Cl. NG16: Newth 5E **72**
Dawver Rd. NG16: Kimb 1E **82**
Daybill Cl. NG25: Mort 6G **139**
DAYBROOK 1B **86**
Daybrook Av. NG5: Sher 4K **85**
Daybrook Bus. Cen. NG5: Arn 1A **86**
DAYBROOK SQUARE 1B **86**
Daybrook St. NG5: Sher 4K **85**
D'Ayncourt Wlk. NG22: Farns 5K **57**
Day St. NG20: Mkt W 4D **34**
Deabill Ct. NG4: Neth 2K **97**
Deabill St. NG4: Neth 2K **97**
Dead La. NG16: Coss 6C **82**
Deadwong La. NG23: Sibt 6E **140**
Deakins Pl. NG7: Radf 3F **95**
Deal Gdns. NG6: Bulw 7F **75**
Dean Av. NG3: Mapp 4E **86**
Dean Cl. NG8: Woll 3J **93**
NG18: Mans 6J **47**
Deane Cl. NG23: Coll 1H **129**
Deane Ct. NG11: Wilf 3H **107**
Deane Rd. NG11: Wilf 3H **107**
Dean Rd. NG5: Woodt 2B **86**
Deans Cl. DN10: Mist 2G **11**
NG23: Caun 6J **127**
Deans Ct. NG12: Cotg 6F **111**
Deans Cft. NG9: Bram 7G **93**
Deansgate NG19: Plea 4A **40**
Dean St. NG1: Nott 6H **7** (4A **96**)
NG16: Lang M 3A **72**
DEARNE 1A **144**
Death La. DN22: Clay 4H **15**
Debdale Ga. NG19: Mans W 7G **41**
(not continuous)
Debdale La. NG12: Key 7G **117**
NG19: Mans, Mans W 7F **41**
Debdhill La. DN10: Mist 1F **11**
Debdhill Rd. DN10: Mist 2G **11**
Deben Down NG19: Mans W 6K **41**
De Buseli Cl. NG4: Ged 6K **87**
De Caldwell Dr. NG24: New T 3B **136**
Deddington La. NG9: Bram 6G **93**
Deeke Rd. NG24: Bald 7J **137**
Deeley Cl. NG16: Want 6A **74**
Deep Carrs La. S81: Work 3A **18**
Deepdale Av. NG9: Stap 3C **104**
Deepdale Cl. NG2: Gam 2F **109**
Deepdale Ct. *NG17: Sut A* *6K* ***45***
(off Slater St.)
Deepdale Gdns. NG17: Sut A 6K **45**
Deepdale Pk. NG17: Sut A 6K **45**
Deepdale Rd. NG8: Woll 4J **93**
NG19: Mans W 1K **47**
Deepdale St. NG17: Sut A 6K **45**
Deepdene Cl. NG8: Brox 5B **84**
Deepdene Way NG8: Brox, Cin 5B **84**
Deep Furrow Av. NG4: Carl 7G **87**
Deering Ct. NG2: Nott 6J **95**
Deerleap Dr. NG5: Arn 7E **76**
Deer Pk. NG8: Woll 4K **93**
Deer Pk. Dr. NG5: Arn 6D **76**
Deevon Farm Cl. NG24: New T 2A **136**
De Ferrers Cl. LE12: East L 3A **122**
De Havilland Way NG24: New T 5K **133**
De Lacy Ct. NG22: New O 4B **38**
Delamere Cl. NG18: Mans 6J **47**
Delamere Dr. NG18: Mans 5J **47**
Delia Av. NG15: Huck 4J **67**
Dell, The NG17: Ann W 4K **59**
Dell Lea NG18: Mans 7C **48**
Dell Way NG11: Clif 7G **107**
Dellwood Cl. NG4: Carl 5E **86**
Delta Ct. NG1: Nott 1D **6** (2K **95**)
Delta St. NG7: Basf 6G **85**
Deltic Cl. NG16: Want 7A **74**
Delville Av. NG12: Key 6H **117**
De Morgan Cl. NG16: Unde 3E **64**
DENABY MAIN 2A **144**
Denacre Av. NG10: Long E 7E **104**
Denbigh Av. S81: Work 5F **19**
Denbigh Cl. NG21: Rain 2A **56**
Denbigh Ct. NG23: Coll 1H **129**
Denbury Ct. NG3: Mapp 2G **87**
Denbury Rd. NG15: Rave 2C **62**
Denby Ct. NG4: Neth 1K **97**
Denby Dr. NG18: Mans 1K **53**
Dendy Dr. DN22: Woodbe 7G **25**
Dene, The S80: Work 3D **20**
Dene Cl. DN10: Matt 2H **15**
Denehurst Av. NG8: Aspl 6D **84**
Denewood Av. NG9: Bram 6H **93**
Denewood Cres. NG8: Bilb 7K **83**
Denholme Rd. NG8: Bilb 3J **93**
Denison Av. DN22: Retf 6G **23**
Denison Ct. NG7: Radf 2G **95**
Denison St. NG7: Radf 2G **95**
NG9: Bee 2K **105**
Denmam St. Central NG7: Radf 3F **95**
Denman Cl. DN22: Retf 2D **22**
Denman St. E. NG7: Radf 3A **6** (3G **95**)
Denman St. W. NG7: Radf 3F **95**
Denmark Gro. NG3: Nott 6A **86**
Dennett Cl. NG3: Nott 2J **7** (2B **96**)
Dennis Av. NG9: Bee 1K **105**
Dennis St. NG4: Neth 1K **97**
S80: Work 3G **21**
Dennor Dr. NG19: Mans W 4A **42**
Denstone Rd. NG3: Nott 4K **7** (3B **96**)
Dentdale Dr. NG8: Woll 4G **93**
DENTON 2D **149**
Denton Av. NG10: Sand 3A **104**
Denton Cl. NG19: Mans W 1A **48**
NG24: Bald 6F **137**
Denton Dr. NG2: West Br 5A **108**
Denton Grn. NG8: Brox 5A **84**
Denver Ct. NG9: Stap 7D **92**
Denz Childrens Play Cen. 3C **106**
Depot Yd. *NG24: New T* *7C* ***134***
(off Slaughter Ho. La.)
Deptford Cres. NG6: Bulw 1D **84**
Derby Gro. NG7: Lent, Radf 3G **95**
Derby Rd. NG1: Nott 4B **6** (3H **95**)
NG7: Lent, Nott 5A **6** (6E **94**)
NG9: Bee, Bram, Nott 1F **105**
NG9: Lent, Nott 7A **94**
NG9: Stap 4B **104**
NG10: Sand 4A **104**
NG15: Ann 5B **60**
NG16: Eastw 4B **72**
NG16: Lang M 3A **72**
NG17: Ann W, Kirk A 5B **60**
NG18: Mans 5B **60**
Derby Rd. Ind. Est. NG10: Sand 4A **104**
Derbyshire Av. NG9: Trow 4C **92**
Derbyshire Cres. NG8: Woll 3B **94**
Derbyshire Dr. NG16: Westw 1A **64**
Derbyshire La. NG15: Huck 6G **67**
Derby St. NG1: Nott 4C **6** (3J **95**)
NG5: Arn 7H **77**
NG9: Bee 2A **106**
NG18: Mans 4J **47**
Derby Ter. NG7: Nott 4A **6** (3H **95**)
Dereham Dr. NG5: Arn 1C **86**
Derry Dr. NG5: Arn 4H **77**
Derry Hill Rd. NG5: Arn 5G **77**
Derry La. NG13: Bing 5J **101**
DERRYTHORPE 1D **145**
Derwent Av. NG18: Mans 4C **48**
Derwent Cl. NG2: Gam 2F **109**
NG9: Atten 6K **105**
NG18: Mans 5C **48**
NG20: Mkt W 3E **34**
NG21: Rain 3K **55**
S81: Work 6G **19**
Derwent Ct. NG7: Radf 1B **6** (2H **95**)
NG24: Bald 6G **137**
Derwent Cres. NG5: Arn 1D **86**
Derwent Dr. NG15: Huck 2G **75**
NG16: Sels 5E **58**
NG17: Nunc 4A **60**
Derwent Ter. NG5: Sher 5K **85**
Derwent Way NG7: Lent 4E **94**
NG24: New T 6E **134**
Desborough Rd. NG16: Sels 5B **58**
Desford Cl. NG5: Sher 3H **85**
Desmond Ct. NG16: Unde 3E **64**
De Vere Gdns. NG5: Woodt 2C **86**
Devitt Dr. NG15: Huck 4J **67**
Devon Cir. NG5: Redh 5F **77**
Devon Cl. NG10: Sand 4A **104**
NG16: Newth 4F **73**
Devon Dr. NG5: Sher 5J **85**
NG11: Rudd 2A **116**
NG19: Mans 2F **47**
Devon Rd. NG24: New T 3B **136**
Devonshire Av. NG9: Bee 3A **106**
Devonshire Cl. NG17: Huth 1E **50**
Devonshire Cres. NG5: Sher 5J **85**
Devonshire Dr. NG9: Stap 6C **92**
NG16: Eastw 4D **72**
NG20: Langw 7A **26**
NG22: Oll 5A **38**
Devonshire Prom. NG7: Lent 5F **95**
Devonshire Rd. DN11: Harwo 2C **8**
DN22: Retf 4D **22**
NG2: West Br 3B **108**
NG5: Sher 5J **85**
Devonshire Sq. *NG17: Sut A* *1J* ***51***
(off Manor St.)
Devonshire St. NG19: New H 2A **40**
S80: Work 3E **20**
Devon St. DE7: Ilk 3A **92**
NG3: Nott 3C **96**
Dewberry Gdns. NG19: Mans W 7C **42**
Dewberry La. NG12: Rad T 6G **99**
Dexters Gro. NG15: Huck 6F **67**
DH Lawrence Birthplace Mus. 3D **72**
DH Lawrence Craft Cen. *3D* ***72***
(off Scargill Wlk.)
DH Lawrence Heritage Cen. 3C **72**
DH Lawrence 'Sons & Lovers' Cottage 3E **72**
Dial, The NG12: Cotg 7D **110**
Diamond Av. NG17: Kirk A 7B **52**
NG21: Rain 2A **56**
Diamond Ct. NG18: Mans 6K **47**
Dickens Ct. NG16: Newth 3F **73**
Dickens Rd. S81: Work 1J **21**
Dickinson St. NG3: Nott 1J **7** (2B **96**)
Dickinson Way NG23: Nth M 5K **129**
Dicks La. NG16: Newth 3G **73**
Dickson Dr. NG11: Rudd 4A **116**
Didcot Dr. NG8: Basf 6E **84**
Digby Av. NG3: Mapp 4E **86**
NG8: Woll 4B **94**
Digby Ct. NG7: Lent 5G **95**
NG19: Mans W 6J **41**
Digby Hall Dr. NG4: Ged 4F **87**
Digby Ind. Est. NG16: Kimb 7H **73**
Digby St. DE7: Ilk 6A **82**
NG16: Kimb 1C **82**
Dingle Ct. DN22: Rans 1J **13**
Dingley Cl. NG19: Mans W 4A **42**
DINNINGTON 3A **144**
Dirac Cl. NG11: Clif 2D **114**
DISEWORTH 3A **148**
Diseworth Gro. NG2: Nott 7A **96**
Distillery St. NG11: Rudd 4K **115**
Dixie St. NG16: Jack 6A **64**
Djanogly Community Leisure Cen. 1H **95**
Dobbin Cl. NG12: Crop Bi 5C **112**
Dobdykes La. DN22: Elk 4F **27**
DOBPARK 5F **67**
Dobsons M. NG17: Sut A 7B **46**
Dobsons Quay NG24: New T 7C **134**
Dockholm Rd. NG10: Long E 7B **104**
Dock Rd. S80: Work 2F **21**
DODDINGTON 2D **147**
Dodsley Way NG21: C'tone 5J **43**

DOE LEA 2A 146
Dog and Bear La. NG15: Ann 7A **60**
Doghill La. NG23: Syer 3B **140**
Dog Holes La. DN22: Stu S 4A **24**
Dog La. DN10: Scro 4K **9**
Dogwood Av. NG6: Bulw 7F **75**
Doles La. NG17: Kirk A 5F **51**
Dolphin Ct. NG5: Top V 6C **76**
Dominie Cross Rd. DN22: Retf 4F **23**
Donbas Cl. NG6: Bulw 3C **84**
DONCASTER 1A 144
Doncaster Av. NG10: Sand 3A **104**
Doncaster Gro. NG10: Long E 7E **104**
Doncaster Rd.
S81: Carl L, Costh, Lango, Oldc 6A **8** & 1C **12**
S81: Work 4G **19**
Doncaster Ter. NG2: Nott 7K **95**
Donington Rd. NG11: Clif 1F **115**
Donkey La. NG11: Rudd 7B **116**
Dooland Dr. NG3: Nott 6C **86**
Dorchester Cl. NG18: Mans 1K **53**
Dorchester Dr. NG18: Mans 1K **53**
Dorchester Gdns. NG2: West Br 6B **108**
Dorchester Rd. DN11: Birc 2E **8**
NG16: Kimb 7K **73**
NG17: Nunc 3B **60**
Doreen Dr. NG17: Sut A 1H **51**
Dorewood Ct. NG24: Bald 5H **137**
Doris Ct. NG9: Toton 7F **105**
Dorket Cl. NG5: Arn 5J **77**
Dorket Dr. NG8: Woll 5E **94**
DORKET HEAD 3J 77
Dorket Ho. *NG4: Carl 7H **87***
(off Garden City)
Dorking Rd. NG7: Radf 2F **95**
Dormy Cl. NG9: Bram 2H **105**
NG12: Rad T 5G **99**
NG19: Mans W 4A **42**
Dormy Ct. NG6: Bulw 7K **75**
Dorner Av. NG24: New T 2A **136**
Dornoch Av. NG5: Sher 5A **86**
NG25: Sout 5J **131**
Dorothy Av. NG10: Sand 4A **104**
NG15: Huck 4H **67**
NG16: Newth 3E **72**
NG19: Mans W 1J **47**
Dorothy Boot Homes, The NG11: Wilf 1J **107**
Dorothy Dr. NG19: Mans W 1B **48**
Dorothy Gro. NG8: Aspl 2D **94**
Dorset Dr. DN11: Harwo 2C **8**
Dorset Gdns. NG2: West Br 4K **107**
Dorset St. NG8: Radf 3E **94**
Dorset Way NG18: Mans 6C **48**
Dotterel Pl. NG20: Wars 3A **34**
Douglas Av. NG4: Carl 2G **97**
NG16: Aws 2B **82**
Douglas Cl. NG12: Rad T 6E **98**
Douglas Ct. NG9: Toton 7F **105**
Douglas Cres. NG4: Carl 2H **97**
Douglas Rd. NG7: Lent, Radf 4A **6** (3G **95**)
NG10: Long E 7A **104**
NG13: Bing 4J **101**
NG17: Sut A 1H **51**
NG19: Mans W 7D **42**
Douro Dr. NG5: Arn 5K **77**
Dove Cl. NG13: Bing 5G **101**
NG22: New O 4B **38**
S81: Work 5F **19**
Dovecote Cl. NG13: East B 4D **90**
Dovecote Dr. NG8: Woll 4K **93**
Dovecote La. NG9: Bee 3A **106**
NG13: Tith 3E **112**
Dovecote Rd. NG16: Eastw, Newth 4F **73**
Dovecotes, The NG9: Bee 4A **106**
Dove Cft. NG22: New O 4B **38**
Dovedale Av. NG17: Sut A 2H **51**
Dovedale Cl. NG18: Mans 7K **47**
NG21: Edwin 6D **36**
Dovedale Rd. NG2: West Br 4D **108**
NG3: Nott 2F **97**
Dovedale Ter. NG24: Bald 7H **137**
Dove Dr. NG16: Sels 5E **58**
DOVE GREEN 6C 58
Dovenby Rd. NG11: Clif 6G **107**
Dover Beck Cl. NG14: Calv 6E **70**
NG15: Rave 2B **62**
Doverbeck Dr. NG14: Woodbo 2G **79**
Dover Bottom DN22: Elk, West D 4J **27**
Doveridge Av. NG4: Carl 7K **87**
Doveridge Ct. NG15: Rave 1C **62**
Doveridge Rd. NG4: Carl 7J **87**
Dover St. NG25: Sout 5H **131**
Dove St. NG6: Bulw 7H **75**
Doveys Orchard NG14: Calv 6B **70**
Downes Cl. NG6: Bulw 7G **75**
Downham Cl. NG5: Arn 1D **86**
Downham Gdns. NG15: Rave 2D **62**
Downing Gdns. NG6: Bulw 6H **75**
Downing St. NG6: Bulw 6H **75**
NG17: Sut A 6K **45**
Downs, The NG11: Wilf 5H **107**
NG19: Mans W 1B **48**
Dowson Cl. NG12: Rad T 4G **99**
Dowson St. NG3: Nott 1K **7** (2C **96**)
Doyne Ct. NG2: Nott 7K **95**
Dragon St. NG13: Gran 1J **141**
DRAKEHOLES 7E 10
Drakemyre Cl. NG5: Arn 5K **77**
Drake Rd. NG4: Neth 2A **98**
Draymans Ct. NG7: Basf 6G **85**
Drayton Av. NG19: Mans 1D **46**
Drayton St. NG5: Sher 5K **85**
Drewry Island NG8: Brox 6A **84**
Drift, The NG11: Clif 6F **107**
NG15: Huck 4H **67**
DRINSEY NOOK 1K 31
Drinsey Nook La. NG23: Thor 2K **31**
Drive, The DN22: Retf 1G **23**
NG9: Atten 6K **105**
NG21: C'tone 6J **43**
NG24: Wint 2F **135**
Dronley Dr. NG20: Chu W 1E **34**
Drove La. NG24: Codd 2H **135**
(not continuous)
Droversdale Rd. DN11: Birc 2F **9**
Drummond Av. NG4: Neth 1A **98**
Drummond Dr. NG16: Nuth 3K **83**
Drummond Gro. NG23: Coll 2H **129**
Drury Cl. NG15: Huck 1D **74**
Drury Wlk. NG1: Nott 6F **7** (4K **95**)
Dryden Av. NG24: Bald 4H **137**
Dryden Ct. NG9: Stap 7D **92**
Dryden Dale S81: Work 1K **21**
Dryden St. NG1: Nott 2D **6** (2J **95**)
DRY DODDINGTON 1D 149
Drysdale Cl. NG6: Bulw 2C **84**
Duchess Gdns. NG6: Bulw 6H **75**
Duchess St. NG6: Bulw 6H **75**
Dudley Ct. NG9: Bram 1F **105**
Dudley Doy Rd. NG25: Sout 5F **131**
Duffield Ct. NG5: Top V 6B **76**
Duke Cl. NG6: Bulw 2A **84**
Duke Cres. NG16: Gilt 5G **73**
Duke Pl. S80: Work 2F **21**
Dukeries Cl. S81: Work 6D **18**
Dukeries Cres. NG21: Edwin 7F **37**
S80: Work 4K **21**
Dukeries Ind. Estate, The S81: Work 6C **18**
(not continuous)
Dukeries Leisure Cen. 3E 38
Dukeries Way S81: Work 6D **18**
Dukes Cl. NG17: Sut A 1C **52**
Dukes Ct. NG15: Huck 6H **67**
Dukes Pl. NG1: Nott 5H **7** (4A **96**)
Duke St. DN22: Retf 4E **22**
NG5: Arn 7F **77**
NG6: Bulw 7H **75**
NG7: Basf 7G **85**
NG15: Huck 6H **67**
NG17: Huth 7E **44**
*NG17: Sut A 1J **51***
(off King St.)
Duke St. E. NG15: Huck 6H **67**
Dukes Wharf NG7: Nott 7D **6** (5J **95**)
Duke William Mt. NG7: Nott 6A **6** (4H **95**)
Dulverton Va. NG8: Cin 4B **84**
Dulwich Rd. NG7: Radf 3F **95**
Dumbles, The NG4: Lamb 6F **79**
NG17: Sut A 2G **51**
Dunbar Dr. NG19: Mans 5D **46**
Dunblane Rd. NG11: Rudd 4K **115**
Duncan Av. NG15: Rave 3C **62**
Duncombe Cl. NG3: Nott 1J **7** (1B **96**)
Duncroft Av. NG4: Ged 6J **87**
Dundas Cl. NG1: Nott 2E **6** (2K **95**)
Dundee Dr. NG19: Mans W 3H **41**
Dunelm Cl. NG17: Sut A 7H **45**
Dunelm Dr. NG14: Calv 6E **70**
Dungannon Rd. NG11: Clif 2F **115**
Dunham Cl. NG25: Sout 6G **131**
DUNHAM-ON-TRENT 6J 29 (1D 147)
Dunham Rd. DN22: Lane 3G **29**
LN1: Newt T 5K **29**
NG22: Dun T 5K **29**
Dunholme Av. NG24: New T 2C **136**
Dunholme Cl. NG6: Bulw 6H **75**
Dunkery Rd. NG11: Clif 2G **115**
DUNKIRK 6F 95
Dunkirk Pl. NG7: Lent 7F **95**
Dunkirk Rd. NG7: Lent 7F **95**
(not continuous)
Dunlin Ct. S81: Gate 6D **18**
Dunlin Wharf NG7: Lent 6H **95**
Dunlop Av. NG7: Lent 4F **95**
Dunmore Dr. NG19: Mans 5D **46**
Dunn Brigg NG19: Mans W 7K **41**
Dunnett Rd. NG19: Mans 5E **46**
Dunnock Cl. NG15: Rave 4C **62**
Dunoon Cl. NG5: Top V 4A **76**
Dunoon Rd. NG19: Mans 5E **46**
Dunsby Cl. NG11: Clif 1F **115**
DUNSCROFT 1B 144
Dunsford Dr. NG3: Mapp 1G **87**
Dunsil Cl. NG19: Mans W 1H **47**
Dunsil Ct. NG19: Mans W 1H **47**
Dunsil Dr. NG2: Nott 1H **107**
Dunsil Rd. NG16: Newth 2F **73**
NG16: Pinx 2B **58**
NG19: Mans W 1H **47**
Dunsil Row NG21: C'tone 6J **43**
Dunsmore Cl. NG9: Bee 5C **106**
Dunstan Cres. S80: Work 4G **21**
Dunstan St. NG4: Neth 1K **97**
(not continuous)
Dunster Rd. NG2: West Br 3D **108**
NG16: Newth 4F **73**
DUNSVILLE 1B 144
Dunvegan Dr. NG5: Top V 4B **76**
Dunwoody Cl. NG18: Mans 3B **48**
Durham Av. NG2: Nott 4C **96**
Durham Chambers NG1: Nott 5F **7**
Durham Cl. NG2: Nott 4C **96**
NG19: Mans W 5K **41**
S81: Work 5H **19**
Durham Cres. NG6: Bulw 1D **84**
Durham Gro. DN22: Retf 1G **23**
Durham Ho. NG3: Mapp P 7K **85**
Durlston Cl. NG2: West Br 4J **107**
Durnford St. NG7: Basf 5G **85**
Dursley Cl. NG6: Bulw 2C **84**
DW Fitness
Nottingham 2A 98
Dyce Cl. NG6: Bulw 7F **75**
Dykes End NG23: Coll 3H **129**
Dylan M. NG8: Bilb 7K **83**
Dylan Thomas Rd. NG5: Bestw 6D **76**
Dyscarr Cl. S81: Lango 1C **12**
Dyscarr Wood (Nature Reserve) 1B 12

E

EAGLE 2D 147
EAGLE BARNSDALE 2D 147
Eagle Cl. NG5: Arn 7J **77**
NG9: Bee 1J **105**
Eagle Ct. NG6: Bulw 7K **75**
EAGLE MOOR 2D 147
Eagle Pl. DN22: Retf 3F **23**
Eagle Way NG19: Mans W 7B **42**
EAKRING 2C 126 (2B 146)
Eakring Cl. NG18: Mans 3B **48**
Eakring Ct. NG18: Mans 4A **48**
Eakring Rd. NG18: Mans 4A **48**
NG21: Rain 3E **48**
NG22: Bils 4C **126**
NG22: Kirk 1B **132**
NG22: Well 7D **38**
EALAND 1C 145
Ealing Av. NG6: Basf 3E **84**
Eardley Rd. NG5: Bestw 1F **85**
Earl Cres. NG4: Ged 4J **87**
Earl Dr. NG16: Gilt 5G **73**
Earles Ct. DN22: Retf 1C **22**
EARLESFIELD 2D 149
Earl Howe Cres. NG13: Lang 7K **113**
Earls Cl. NG8: Bilb 3H **93**
Earlsfield Dr. NG5: Top V 5K **75**
Earlswood Dr. NG12: Edwal 5E **108**
NG18: Mans 5B **48**
Earp Av. NG24: New T 2D **136**
Easedale Cl. NG2: Gam 2F **109**
Easegill Ct. *NG5: Top V 6B **76***
(off Aveline Cl.)
East Acres NG12: Cotg 6E **110**
E. Bridgeford Rd.
NG13: Newton 6C **90**
EAST BRIDGFORD 5D 90 (1B 148)
EAST BUTTERWICK 1D 145
E. Circus St. NG1: Nott 5D **6** (4J **95**)
Eastcliffe Av. NG4: Ged 4G **87**
East Cl. NG12: Key 1H **119**
Eastcote Av. NG9: Bram 6G **93**
East Cres. NG9: Bee 4C **106**
Eastdale Rd. NG3: Nott 2F **97**
EAST DRAYTON 1C 147
East Dr. NG7: Nott 7D **94**
Eastern Ct. NG24: New T 1D **136**
Eastern Ter. La. NG24: New T 1D **136**
Easter Pk. NG7: Lent 6G **95**
EAST FERRY 2D 145
Eastfield DN22: Nth W 2J **17**
NG23: Nth M 6K **129**
Eastfield Cl. NG21: C'tone 7H **43**
Eastfield Ct. NG25: Sout 6F **131**
Eastfield Pk. NG22: Tuxf 5E **28**
Eastfield Side NG17: Sut A 6A **46**
Eastgate NG23: Norm T 1K **125**
S80: Work 2G **21**
Eastglade Rd. NG5: Bestw 1G **85**
East Gro. NG7: Basf 7H **85**
NG13: Bing 4G **101**
Eastham Cl. NG3: Nott 2J **7** (2B **96**)
Eastham Rd. NG5: Arn 1E **86**
Eastholme Cft. NG2: Colw 3G **97**
EASTHORPE 2D 149
Easthorpe NG25: Sout 6J **131**
Easthorpe Cotts. NG11: Rudd 3A **116**
Easthorpe St. NG11: Rudd 3K **115**
Eastlands La. NG20: Chu W 2D **34**
Eastland Ter. NG20: Mede V 7G **33**
East La. NG21: Edwin 6F **37**
EAST LEAKE 3B 122 (3A 148)
East Leake Leisure Cen. 2B 122
E. Leake Rd. LE12: Stanf S 7A **122**
Eastleigh Dr. NG19: Mans W 3H **41**
EAST LOUND 2C 145
EAST MARKHAM 2D 28 (1C 147)

East Midlands Airport—Ely Cl.

EAST MIDLANDS AIRPORT .3A 148
East Midlands Conference Cen. .7C 94
E. Midlands Designer Outlet
DE55: Sth N .5C 50
East Moor NG12: Cotg .7F 111
Eastmoor Dr. NG4: Carl .7J 87
EASTON .3D 149
EAST RETFORD .3E 22
East Rd. NG7: Nott .6E 94
EAST STOCKWITH .2C 145
EAST STOKE .1C 149
East St. DN11: Harwo .1D 8
DN22: Retf .4F 23
NG1: Nott .4G 7 (3A 96)
NG11: Goth .7G 115
NG13: Bing .4G 101
NG17: Sut A .7A 46
NG20: Wars .3A 34
East Vw. NG2: West Br .3A 108
NG22: East M .3C 28
East Vw. Cl. NG17: Ann W .3C 60
Eastview Ter. NG16: Lang M .3A 72
East Wlk. DN22: Retf .2C 22
EASTWELL .3C 149
Eastwell Ct. *NG15: Huck* .*5G 67*
(off Annesley Rd.)
NG22: Bils .5B 126
Eastwell St. NG15: Huck .5G 67
Eastwold NG12: Cotg .7F 111
EASTWOOD .4D 72 (1A 148)
Eastwood Av. NG20: Mkt W .3D 34
Eastwood Cl. NG15: Huck .2E 74
Eastwood Community Sports Cen. .3C 72
Eastwood Ct. S81: Work .3G 19
Eastwood La. DN10: Miss .2E 10
Eastwood Rd. NG12: Rad T .5F 99
NG16: Kimb .7H 73
Eastwood St. NG6: Bulw .2D 84
Eastwood Town FC .4E 72
Eather Av. NG19: Mans W .5J 41
EATON
Grantham .3C 149
Retford .1C 147
Eaton Av. NG5: Arn .7J 77
Eaton Cl. NG9: Bee .3C 106
NG21: Rain .3J 55
NG22: Farns .5K 57
Eaton Ct. NG18: Mans .7C 48
Eaton Pl. NG13: Bing .4F 101
Eatons Rd. NG9: Stap .3C 104
Eaton St. NG3: Mapp .4C 86
Eaton Ter. NG3: Mapp .5C 86
Eaves La. NG23: Sut T .4C 128
Ebenezer St. NG16: Lang M .3A 72
Ebers Gro. NG3: Mapp P .7K 85
Ebers Rd. NG3: Mapp P .6K 85
Ebony Wlk. NG3: Nott .7E 86
Ebury Rd. NG5: Sher .6J 85
Eccleston's Yd. *NG24: New T* .*1C 136*
(off Market Pl.)
Eccles Way NG3: Nott .1C 96
Eckington Ter. NG2: Nott .7K 95
Eckington Wlk.
NG18: Mans .4D 48
Eclipse Yd. NG18: Mans .3H 47
Eco Ct. NG22: New O .4C 38
Ecton Cl. NG5: Top V .5B 76
Edale Cl. NG15: Huck .7C 66
NG18: Mans .7C 48
Edale Ct. NG17: Sut A .6J 45
Edale Ri. NG9: Toton .6D 104
Edale Rd. NG2: Nott .3D 96
NG18: Mans .4D 48
Eddery Vw. NG18: Mans .3B 48
Eddison Cl. S81: Work .5H 19
Eddison Pk. Av. S81: Work .3F 19
Eddlestone Dr. NG11: Clif .1G 115
Edenbridge Ct. NG8: Woll .6J 93
Eden Cl. NG5: Arn .1D 86
NG15: Huck .7C 66
Eden Ct. DN22: Ord .7E 22
Edenhall Gdns. NG11: Clif .7G 107
Eden Low NG19: Mans W .6K 41
EDENTHORPE .1B 144
Eden Wlk. NG13: Bing .5E 100
Edern Cl. NG5: Bestw .7C 76
Edern Gdns. NG5: Bestw .7C 76
Edgar Av. NG18: Mans .2J 47
Edgbaston Dr. DN22: Ord .6E 22
Edgbaston Gdns. NG8: Aspl .7E 84
Edge Cl. NG23: Nth M .4K 129
NG24: New T .2C 136
Edgecote Way NG5: Bestw .1H 85
Edgehill Dr. NG24: New T .1H 137
Edgehill Gro. NG19: Mans W .7J 41
Edgeway NG8: Stre .6J 83
Edgewood Dr. NG15: Huck .1D 74
Edgewood Leisure Cen. .2D 74
Edgington Cl. NG12: Cotg .7F 111
Edginton St. NG3: Nott .1C 96
Edginton Ter. NG3: Nott .1C 96
Edgware Rd. NG6: Bulw .7K 75
Edgwood Rd. NG16: Kimb .1E 82
Edinbane Cl. NG5: Top V .4B 76
Edinboro Row NG16: Kimb .7J 73
Edinburgh Dr. NG13: Bing .3E 100
Edinburgh Rd. S80: Work .5J 21
Edinburgh Wlk. S80: Work .5J 21
Edingale Ct. NG9: Bram .4G 93
EDINGLEY .2A 130 (3B 146)
Edingley Av. NG5: Sher .3K 85
NG19: Mans .3D 46
Edingley Hill NG22: Edin .2A 130
Edingley Sq. NG5: Sher .3J 85
Edison Ri. NG22: New O .4C 38
Edison St. NG17: Nunc .3K 59
Edison Village NG7: Nott .7F 95
Edison Way NG5: Arn .7A 78
Edith Ter. *NG7: Radf* .*2F 95*
(off Hartley Rd.)
Edlington Dr. NG8: Woll .5H 93
Edmond Gro. NG15: Huck .5J 67
Edmonds Cl. NG5: Arn .4C 76
EDMONDTHORPE .3D 149
Edmonstone Cres. NG5: Bestw .2G 85
Edmonton Ct. NG2: West Br .3A 108
Edmonton Rd. NG21: C'tone .7G 43
Ednaston Rd. NG7: Nott .7E 94
Edwald Rd. NG12: Edwal .6E 108
EDWALTON .6E 108 (2B 148)
Edwalton Av. NG2: West Br .2C 108
Edwalton Cl. NG12: Edwal .6E 108
Edwalton Ct. NG6: Bulw .1F 85
NG18: Mans .7C 48
Edwalton Golf Course .6F 109
Edwalton Hall NG12: Edwal .6D 108
Edwalton Lodge Cl. NG12: Edwal .6D 108
Edward Av. NG8: Aspl .7E 84
NG16: Jack .6A 64
NG17: Sut A .6K 45
NG24: New T .1B 136
Edward Cl. NG15: Huck .2D 74
Edward Ct. NG2: West Br .7C 96
Edward Jermyn Dr. NG24: New T .4E 134
Edward Rd. NG2: West Br .7C 96
NG16: Eastw .4E 72
NG16: Nuth .2H 83
Edwards Ct. NG5: Sher .2J 85
S80: Work .2E 20
Edwards La. NG5: Bestw, Sher .1J 85
Edward St. NG9: Stap .2C 104
NG16: Lang M .2A 72
NG17: Kirk A .5B 52
S80: Work .2G 21
EDWINSTOWE .6F 37 (2B 146)
Edwinstowe Av. NG2: West Br .2C 108
Edwinstowe Dr. NG5: Sher .3K 85
NG16: Sels .5F 59
Edwin St. NG5: Arn .1A 86
NG17: Sut A .7J 45
Eel Pool Rd. DN10: Drake, Eve .1J 15 & 7D 10
Eels La. NG22: Lax .6A 124
Eelwood Rd. NG15: Huck .2D 74
Egerton Cl. NG18: Mans .3C 48
Egerton Dr. NG9: Stap .6C 92
Egerton Rd. NG5: Woodt .3A 86
Egerton St. NG3: Nott .1E 6 (1K 95)
Egerton Wlk. NG3: Nott .1F 7 (1K 95)
Egham Cl. NG21: Rain .2A 56
Egling Cft. NG4: Colw .4J 97
EGMANTON .2D 124 (2C 147)
Egmanton Rd. NG18: Mans .7C 48
NG20: Mede V .7F 33
NG22: Tuxf .7B 28
Egmont Ct. NG2: Nott .6K 95
Egypt Rd. NG7: Basf .6G 85
(not continuous)
Eighth Av. NG7: Nott .4D 106
NG19: Mans W .2C 48
Eileen Rd. NG9: Bee .6B 106
Eisele Cl. NG6: Bulw .1A 84
Ekowe St. NG7: Basf .5G 85
Eland St. NG7: Basf .6G 85
Elder Cl. NG5: Arn .5J 77
Elder Ct. NG19: Mans W .1D 48
Elderfield Dr. NG17: Sut A .3K 51
Elder Gdns. NG5: Top V .6C 76
Elder Gro. NG15: Huck .2H 75
Elder St. NG17: Kirk A .5J 51
NG17: Skeg .3H 45
Eldon Chambers NG1: Nott .6E 6 (4K 95)
Eldon Grn. NG22: Tuxf .6C 28
Eldon Rd. NG9: Atten .7H 105
Eldon Rd. Ind. Est. NG9: Atten .7H 105
Eldon Rd. Trad. Est.
NG9: Chil .7H 105
Eldon St. NG22: Tuxf .6B 28
NG24: New T .2C 136
Eleanor Cres. NG9: Stap .2E 104
Electric Av. NG2: Nott .2H 107
Elford Ri. NG3: Nott .5K 7 (4C 96)
Elgar Gdns. NG3: Nott .2C 96
Eliot Wlk. NG11: Clif .2D 114
Elizabeth Cl. NG15: Huck .1E 74
Elizabeth Gro. NG4: Ged .5H 87
Elizabeth Ho. NG5: Woodt .2A 86
Elizabeth Rd. NG24: New T .4B 136
ELKESLEY .2G 27 (1B 146)
Elkesley Pk. DN22: Gam .2H 27
Elkesley Pl. NG20: Mede V .6G 33
Elkesley Rd. NG20: Mede V .6G 33
Elk Racing Outdoor Karting Circuit .1J 135
Ella Rd. NG2: West Br .7C 96
Ellastone Av. NG5: Bestw .6E 76
Ellerby Av. NG11: Clif .7F 107
Ellerslie Cl. NG24: New T .7D 134
Ellerslie Gro. NG10: Sand .4A 104
Ellesmere Bus. Pk. NG5: Sher .5J 85
Ellesmere Cl. NG5: Arn .7K 77
Ellesmere Cres. NG5: Sher .5J 85
Ellesmere Dr. NG9: Trow .3B 92
Ellesmere Rd. NG2: West Br .5C 108
NG19: Mans W .2B 48
Ellington Rd. NG5: Arn .4H 77
Elliot St. NG7: Nott .4B 6 (3H 95)
Ellis Av. NG15: Huck .7H 67
Ellis Ct. NG3: Nott .1G 7 (2A 96)
Ellis Gro. NG9: Bee .4A 106
Ellis St. NG17: Kirk A .6B 52
Ellsworth Ri. NG5: Bestw .1G 85
Ellwood Cres. NG8: Woll .3B 94
Elma La. NG20: Cuck .1A 32
S80: Holb W .4B 26
Elm Av. LE12: East L .1A 122
NG3: Nott .1E 6 (1K 95)
NG4: Carl .1J 97
NG9: Atten .7J 105
NG9: Bee .3K 105
NG10: Sand .2A 104
NG12: Key .1J 119
NG13: Bing .4H 101
NG15: Huck .1E 74
NG16: Nuth .1G 83
NG24: New T .3E 136
Elm Bank NG3: Mapp P .7K 85
Elm Bank Dr. NG3: Mapp P .7K 85
Elmbridge NG5: Bestw .7D 76
Elm Cl. NG3: Mapp P .1K 95
NG12: Key .1J 119
NG16: Pinx .1B 58
NG24: New T .3E 136
Elmcroft NG25: Oxt .2F 71
Elmdale Gdns. NG8: Bilb .7C 84
Elm Dr. NG4: Carl .1J 97
Elmfield NG20: Mkt W .5C 34
Elm Gro. NG5: Arn .5J 77
NG20: Chu W .2C 34
Elmhurst Av. NG3: Mapp .5F 87
Elmhurst Dr. NG17: Huth .7E 44
Elmhurst Rd. NG19: Mans W .1B 48
Elmore Ct. NG7: Radf .2A 6 (2H 95)
Elmore's Mdw. NG14: Blea .2B 138
Elms, The NG4: Colw .2J 97
NG16: Want .7K 73
Elms Cl. LE12: Remp .7F 123
NG11: Rudd .4A 116
Elmsdale Gdns. NG14: Bur J .3E 88
Elms Gdns. NG11: Rudd .4K 115
Elmsham Av. NG5: Top V .5A 76
Elmsmere Dr. S81: Oldc .6B 8
Elms Pk. NG11: Rudd .4A 116
Elms Rd. S80: Work .1F 21
Elmsthorpe Av. NG7: Lent .4F 95
Elmswood Gdns. NG5: Sher .4A 86
ELMTON .1A 146
Elm Tree Av. NG2: West Br .2A 108
NG19: Mans W .5G 41
Elmtree Av. NG16: Sels .5D 58
Elmtree Cl. S81: Shire .5A 18
Elm Tree Ct. S80: Work .3G 21
Elm Tree Pl. DN22: Elk .2G 27
Elm Tree Rd. NG17: Kirk A .5K 51
Elmtree Rd. NG14: Calv .6B 70
Elm Tree St. NG18: Mans .3J 47
Elm Vw. NG7: Radf .2G 95
Elm Wlk. DN22: Retf .5G 23
Elmwood Cl. DN22: Retf .2G 23
Elmwood Ct. S80: Work .3C 20
Elnor St. NG16: Lang M .4A 72
Elson St. NG7: Basf .7G 85
ELSTON .1D 140 (1C 149)
Elston Cl. NG19: Mans .1D 46
Elston Gdns. NG11: Clif .5F 107
Elston Hall NG23: Elston .2D 140
Elston La. NG23: East S, Elston .1D 140
Elston M. NG3: Nott .1E 96
Elstree Dr. NG8: Bilb .2B 94
Elswick Cl. NG5: Bestw .6D 76
Elswick Dr. NG9: Bee .5C 106
Elterwater Dr. NG2: Gam .2F 109
Eltham Cl. NG8: Cin .4A 84
Eltham Dr. NG8: Cin .4A 84
Eltham Rd. NG2: West Br .2C 108
ELTON .6J 103 (2C 149)
Elton and Orston Station (Rail) .3K 103
Elton Cl. NG9: Stap .1D 104
NG18: Mans .4D 48
NG24: Bald .6G 137
Elton M. NG5: Sher .6J 85
Elton Rd. NG18: Mans .4B 48
Elton Rd. Nth. NG5: Sher .6J 85
Elton Ter. NG7: H Grn .1G 95
Elvaston Ct. NG5: Bestw .2G 85
NG18: Mans .4D 48
Elvaston Rd. NG8: Woll .3B 94
Elwes Lodge NG4: Carl .2J 97
Elwin Dr. NG9: Bram .7H 93
Ely Cl. NG19: Mans W .5K 41
S80: Work .3H 21

Embley Rd. NG5: Sher 2H 85
Emerald Cl. NG17: Sut A 2C 52
   NG19: Mans 1F 47
Emerald Gro. NG17: Kirk A 7C 52
   NG21: Rain 2A 56
Emerys Rd. NG4: Ged, Neth 7A 88
Emma Bates Way NG21: Blid 5K 55
Emmanuel Av. NG3: Mapp 6D 86
   NG5: Arn 5C 76
Emmendingen Av. NG24: New T 5E 134
Emmerson Dr. NG21: C'tone 5J 43
Emneth Cl. NG3: Nott 7C 86
Emperor Cl. NG5: Sher 6J 85
Empingham Cl. NG9: Toton 7G 105
Empire St. NG18: Mans 4K 47
Emsworth Av. DN22: Retf 1E 22
Ena Av. NG2: Nott 3C 96
Enderby Cres. NG18: Mans 4B 48
Enderby Gdns. NG5: Redh 5G 77
Enderby Sq. NG9: Lent A 1A 106
Endsleigh Gdns. NG9: Bee 2A 106
   NG12: Edwal 5D 108
Enfield Chambers NG1: Nott 6F 7 (4K 95)
Enfield St. NG9: Bee 3K 105
Engine La. NG16: Newth 2F 73
Ennerdale Cl. NG2: Gam 2F 109
Ennerdale Ct. NG10: Long E 7A 104
Ennerdale Rd. NG5: Sher 2A 86
   NG10: Long E 7A 104
Ennismore Gdns. NG8: Aspl 2D 94
Ennismore M. NG2: West Br 6K 107
Enright Cl. NG24: New T 3C 136
Enterprise Cl. NG19: Mans 6E 40
   NG21: Blid 5J 55
Enterprise Pk. DN22: Retf 5F 23
   NG24: New T 5F 135
Enterprise Rd. NG19: Mans 7D 40
Enterprise Way DN22: Retf 5F 23
   NG2: Nott 6H 95
   NG16: Lang M 3A 72
Enthorpe St. NG8: Bilb 2C 94
EPPERSTONE 7K 71 (1B 148)
Epperstone By-Pass NG14: Woodbo 7J 71
Epperstone Ct. NG2: West Br 1B 108
   NG18: Mans 1C 54
Epperstone Rd. NG2: West Br 1B 108
   NG14: Lowd 3D 80
   NG25: Oxt 3F 71
Epping Way NG19: Mans W 2D 48
Epsom Rd. NG9: Toton 6D 104
Epsom St. NG18: Mans 4B 48
EPWORTH 1C 145
EPWORTH TURBARY 1C 145
Erdington Way NG9: Toton 6D 104
Erewash Ct. NG10: Long E 7C 104
Erewash Dr. DE7: Ilk 2A 92
Erewash Gdns. NG5: Top V 6C 76
Erewash Gro. NG9: Toton 7E 104
              (not continuous)
Erewash Rd. NG16: Pinx 2C 58
Erewash Sq. DE7: Ilk 2A 92
Erewash St. NG17: Kirk A 6A 52
Erewash Valley Golf Course 7A 92
Eric Av. NG15: Huck 4F 67
Erith Cl. NG8: Stre 6J 83
Ernehale Ct. NG5: Arn 6H 77
Ernest Rd. NG4: Carl 7E 86
Erskine Rd. NG5: Sher 6J 85
Escape Family Entertaiment Cen. 7G 73
Esher Gro. NG3: Mapp P 6K 85
Eskdale Cl. NG18: Mans 5B 48
Eskdale Ct. NG2: Gam 2F 109
Eskdale Dr. NG8: Aspl 7C 84
   NG9: Chil 4F 105
   S81: Work 4F 19
Esk Hause Cl. NG2: West Br 5F 109
Essex Dr. DN11: Birc 2G 9
Essex Rd. DN11: Birc 2F 9
Essex St. NG16: Eastw 4D 72
Estwic Av. NG16: Eastw 3D 72
Ethel Av. NG3: Mapp 6D 86
   NG15: Huck 4H 67
Ethelbert Av. NG17: Ann W 3C 60
Etheldene NG12: Crop Bi 5C 112
Ethel Rd. NG2: West Br 2C 108
Eton Av. NG24: New T 3B 136
Eton Cl. NG24: New T 3C 136
Eton Gro. NG8: Woll 4C 94
Eton Pl. NG2: West Br 4B 108
Eton Rd. NG2: West Br 3B 108
   NG5: Sher 6J 85
          (off Claremont Rd.)
Eucalyptus Av. NG11: Clif 1D 114
Eugene Gdns. NG2: Nott 6A 96
Eugene St. NG2: Nott 5A 96
Europa Way NG2: West Br 6K 107
Evans Av. NG17: Sut A 7G 45
Evans Rd. NG6: Basf 4E 84
Evedon Wlk. NG5: Top V 5D 76
Evelyn St. NG2: Nott 6J 7 (4B 96)
   NG9: Bee 2C 106
Everest Ct. NG24: Bald 5H 137
Eversley Wlk. NG5: Bestw 6D 76
EVERTON 6B 10 (2B 144)
Everton Rd. DN10: Matt 2H 15
Everton Sluice La. DN10: Eve 6B 10

Everton St. NG19: Mans 1E 46
Evesham Ct. NG9: Toton 7F 105
Evesham M. S80: Work 3G 21
Ewart Rd. NG7: H Grn 7G 85
Ewe Lamb Cl. NG9: Bram 7E 92
Ewe Lamb La. NG9: Bram 7E 92
Ewell Rd. NG8: Woll 3K 93
Exbourne Rd. NG8: Aspl 6A 84
Exbury Gdns. NG2: West Br 5J 107
Exchange Arc. NG1: Nott 5F 7
Exchange Rd. NG2: West Br 2C 108
Exchange Row NG18: Mans 3H 47
             (off Queen St.)
Exchange St. DN22: Retf 3E 22
Exchange Wlk. NG1: Nott 5F 7 (4K 95)
Excise Chambers NG1: Nott 5G 7
Exe Fold NG19: Mans W 7K 41
Exeter Cl. LE12: East L 3K 121
   NG4: Ged 5J 87
Exeter Rd. NG2: West Br 3C 108
   NG7: H Grn 7H 85
Exford Ct. NG19: Mans W 3J 41
Experian Way NG2: Nott 6H 95
Export Dr. NG17: Huth 3D 50
Exton Rd. NG5: Sher 4H 85
Eyam Cl. NG9: Bram 6H 93
   NG18: Mans 4D 48
Eyres Cl. NG17: Skeg 4K 45
Eyre St. NG2: Nott 5J 7 (4B 96)

F

Fabis Dr. NG11: Clif 5F 107
FACKLEY 3F 45
Fackley Rd. NG17: Stant H, Teve 3F 45
Fackley Way NG17: Stant H 4F 45
Factory La. NG9: Chil 4K 105
Factory Yd. NG17: Sut A 6A 46
Failsworth Cl. NG11: Clif 6F 107
Fairbank Cres. NG5: Sher 5A 86
Fairburn Cl. NG8: Woll 4H 93
Fairburn Way NG16: Want 7A 74
Faircroft Av. NG10: Sand 4A 104
Fairdale Dr. NG16: Newth 4F 73
Fairfax Av. NG24: New T 4B 136
   S81: Gate 4E 18
Fairfax Cl. NG5: Basf 5G 85
Fairfield Av. DE55: Hilc 2A 50
   NG24: Farnd 6H 133
   NG24: New B 4G 137
Fairfield Cl. NG11: Wilf 4J 107
   NG20: Neth L 5B 26
Fairfield Dr. NG18: Mans 3C 48
Fairfield Pk. NG22: Oll 5B 38
Fairfield Rd. NG17: Sut A 7B 46
Fairfields NG15: Rave 1J 61
Fairfield St. NG13: Bing 4F 101
Fairham Av. NG11: Goth 7G 115
Fairham Brook Nature Reserve 2G 115
Fairham Cl. NG11: Rudd 2J 115
Fairham Ct. NG11: Wilf 6H 107
Fairham Dr. NG8: Woll 4E 94
Fairham Rd. NG12: Key 7G 117
Fairhaven NG17: Kirk A 1B 60
Fairholm Ct. NG3: Nott 2K 7 (2B 96)
Fairholme Rd. NG21: C'tone 7H 43
Fairholme Dr. NG19: Mans 1E 46
Fairholme Pk. Homes NG22: Oll 5B 38
Fairisle Cl. NG11: Clif 1H 115
Fairland Cres. NG2: West Br 5A 108
Fairlawn Pl. NG5: Sher 5A 86
Fairlawns NG18: Mans 3D 48
Fairlie Av. NG19: Mans 5D 46
Fairlight Way NG5: Bestw 7D 76
Fairmaid Gro. NG11: Clif 7F 107
Fairmead Cl. NG3: Nott 7D 86
Fairnley Rd. NG8: Bilb 7J 83
Fair Va. NG23: Norw 2J 127
Fair Vw. NG19: Mans W 7C 42
Fairview Av. NG16: Unde 3D 64
Fairview Rd. NG2: West Br 7A 108
Fairview Rd. NG5: Woodt 3B 86
Fairway DN22: Ord 6D 22
   NG12: Key 7J 117
   NG24: New T 4A 136
Fairway, The NG4: Ged 4H 87
Fairway Cres. NG13: Newton 7C 90
Fairway Dr. NG4: Carl 7F 87
   NG6: Bulw 7K 75
   NG9: Chil 3J 105
Fairways, The NG19: Mans W 3K 41
Fairways Dr. NG17: Kirk A 4K 51
Fairweather Cl. NG22: Bou 2F 39
Falcon Cl. NG7: Lent 4F 95
Falcon Cl. NG17: Kirk A 5D 52
Falconers Wlk. NG5: Arn 6E 76
Falcon Gro. NG7: Basf 6H 85
Falcon St. NG7: Basf 6H 85
Falcon Way NG15: Huck 4K 67
Falconwood Gdns. NG11: Clif 1D 114
Fallow Cl. DN22: Retf 1E 22
Fallow Cl. NG11: Clif 7F 107
Fallow Ct. S81: Work 5J 19
Fal Paddock NG19: Mans W 7K 41
Falstaff M. NG7: Basf 6H 85

Falstone Av. NG24: New T 3E 136
Falston Rd. NG8: Bilb 2B 94
Faraday Av. NG22: Tuxf 6D 28
Faraday Bldg. NG7: Nott 7E 94
Faraday Cl. DN11: Harwo 3C 8
Faraday Ct. NG9: Stap 7D 92
Faraday Rd. NG7: Lent 3F 95
   NG18: Mans 5A 48
Far Back La. NG22: Farns 5K 57
Far Clay Gro. S81: Shire 5A 18
Farcroft Av. NG17: Sut A 7G 45
Farfield DN22: Ord 7E 22
Farfield Av. NG9: Bee 1K 105
Farfield Gro. NG9: Bee 1K 105
Farhill La. NG22: Ragn 7F 29
Far Holme La. NG23: Sut T 3E 128
Far La. LE12: Norm S 7G 121
FARLEYS 3H 75
Farleys Gro. NG15: Huck 1G 75
Farleys La. NG15: Huck 7G 67
           (not continuous)
Farley St. NG6: Bulw 7H 75
Farm Av. NG15: Huck 2D 74
Farm Cl. DN22: Nth L 6B 24
   NG11: Clif 7F 107
   NG13: East B 4E 90
   NG23: Bath 5F 129
Farm Ct. NG20: Neth L 6B 26
Farm Cft. Rd. NG19: Mans W 3J 41
Farmers Branch S81: Work 5H 19
Farmers Ct. NG17: Huth 2E 50
Farmer St. NG11: Rudd 7B 116
Farmers Wlk. NG24: New T 4F 135
Farm Gro. S81: Work 5J 19
Farmilo Cres. NG19: Mans 1E 46
Farm La. NG22: East M 2C 28
Farm Rd. NG5: Arn 7K 77
   NG9: Chil 4H 105
Farm Vw. DN22: Ord 7E 22
Farm Vw. Rd. NG17: Kirk A 6C 52
Farmway NG19: Mans W 7J 41
Farnborough Rd. NG11: Clif 5G 107
Farndale S81: Work 5J 19
Farndale Cl. NG17: Skeg 5K 45
Farndale Dr. NG8: Woll 4G 93
Farndale Rd. NG17: Skeg 5K 45
FARNDON 6G 133 (3C 147)
Farndon Dr. NG9: Toton 6E 104
Farndon Grn. NG8: Woll 4D 94
Farndon Gro. S81: Gate 5E 18
Farndon La. NG24: Haw 7A 136
Farndon M. NG3: Nott 7D 86
Farndon Rd. NG17: Sut A 2B 52
   NG24: New T 5K 133
Farndon Way NG19: Mans 3E 46
Farnes Ct. S81: Work 7J 19
Far New Cl. NG10: Sand 4A 104
FARNSFIELD 5K 57 (3B 146)
Farnsfield Av. NG14: Bur J 2F 89
Farnsfield Ct. NG18: Mans 1C 54
Farnsfield Rd. NG22: Bils . . . . .1J 57 & 7C 126
Farnsworth Av. NG21: Rain 1G 55
Farnsworth Cl. NG16: Want 5A 74
Farnsworth Gro. NG17: Huth 7D 44
Far Pastures Cl. NG12: Key 1H 119
Farrar Cl. NG24: New T 6F 135
Farrendale Cl. NG19: Mans W 1K 47
Farriers Grn. NG11: Clif 7D 106
Farringdon Cl. NG16: Nuth 4J 83
Farrington Way NG16: Eastw 4C 72
Farr Row NG5: Bestw 2H 85
Farr Way NG21: Blid 7J 55
Far Rye NG8: Woll 2A 94
Far St. NG11: Rudd 7B 116
Farthingate NG25: Sout 7H 131
Farthingate Cl. NG25: Sout 6J 131
Farthings, The NG7: Lent 4F 95
Farwells Cl. NG6: Basf 4D 84
Faulconbridge Cl. NG6: Bulw 1C 84
Faulks La. LE14: Hick 6E 142
Fearn Chase NG4: Carl 1H 97
Fearnleigh Dr. NG6: Basf 5E 84
Fearon Cl. NG14: Gun 2A 90
Featherbed La. S80: Darf 3A 20
Featherston Av. S80: Work 3J 21
Featherstone Cl. NG4: Ged 4G 87
   NG18: Mans 6D 46
Feignies Ct. NG12: Key 7H 117
Felen Cl. NG5: Bestw 7C 76
Fellbarrow Cl. NG2: West Br 4F 109
Fell Cft. NG24: Farnd 6G 133
Felley Av. NG17: Ann W 3J 59
Felley Cl. NG15: Huck 1E 74
Felley Mill La. (North) NG16: Unde 3F 65
Felley Mill La. (South) NG16: Unde 4E 64
Felley Priory Gdns. 2G 65
Fellows Rd. NG9: Bee 2K 105
Fellows Yd. NG12: Plum 3H 117
Fell Side NG5: Woodt 2D 86
Fellside Cl. NG2: Gam 3F 109
Fell Wilson Gro. NG20: Mkt W 4E 34
Fell Wilson St. NG20: Mkt W 4E 34
Felstead Ct. NG9: Bram 7H 93
Felstead Rd. NG8: Bilb 2B 94
Felton Av. NG19: Mans W 3J 41
Felton Cl. NG9: Chil 4G 105

Felton Rd. NG2: Nott 7A **96**
Fenchurch Cl. NG5: Arn 5C **76**
Fenimore Ct. NG12: Rad T 4G **99**
Fen La. NG24: Bald, Barn W 5J **137**
Fenroth Cl. NG6: Bulw 6F **75**
FENTON
Lincoln 1D **147**
Newark 3D **147**
Retford 4D **24** (3C **145**)
Fenton Cl. NG24: New T 6E **134**
Fenton Ct. NG5: Sher 3G **85**
Fenton Dr. NG6: Bulw 4J **75**
Fenton La. DN22: Fen 4D **24**
Fenton Rd. NG5: Sher 3G **85**
Fenwick Cl. NG8: Brox 5A **84**
Fenwick Ct. NG4: Neth 1K **97**
Fenwick Rd. NG8: Brox 5A **84**
Fenwick St. NG20: Mkt W 4D **34**
Fergus Cl. NG11: Clif 2G **115**
Ferguson Av. NG19: Mans W 5H **41**
Ferguson Cl. NG9: Chil 7H **105**
Fern Av. NG5: Sher 6J **85**
Fern Bank Av. NG22: Wale 6G **27**
Fern Cl. NG9: Bram 2G **105**
NG15: Rave 4D **62**
NG22: Bils 6D **126**
NG25: Sout 5G **131**
Fern Cres. NG16: Eastw 3C **72**
Ferndale NG18: Mans 5J **47**
Ferndale Cl. NG9: Atten 7J **105**
NG22: New O 2E **38**
Ferndale Gro. NG3: Nott 2E **96**
Ferndale Rd. NG3: Nott 2E **96**
Ferngill Cl. NG2: Nott 7J **95**
Fern Lea Av. NG12: Cotg 7D **110**
Fernleigh Av. NG3: Mapp 5E **86**
Fernleigh Ri. NG19: Mans W 7K **41**
Fern Rd. NG12: Cols B, Crop Bi 6C **112**
Ferns Mdw. DN22: Nth L 7B **24**
Fern St. NG17: Sut A 6J **45**
FERNWOOD 7H **137**
Fernwood Bus. Pk. NG24: Bald 7H **137**
Fernwood Cl. NG19: Mans W 1C **48**
Fernwood Commercial Workshops NG16: Want 6A **74**
Fernwood Cres. NG8: Woll 4H **93**
Fernwood Dr. NG12: Rad T 4E **98**
NG16: Want 6A **74**
Ferny Hollow Cl. NG5: Top V 6A **76**
Ferrers Wlk. NG3: Nott 3K **7** (3B **96**)
Ferriby Ter. NG2: Nott 7K **95**
Ferry Farm 5K **81**
Ferry La. DN10: Eve 6B **10**
NG23: Carl T 6D **128**
NG23: Nth M 6K **129**
Ferry Lodge NG4: Carl 2H **97**
Ferryman Rd. NG11: Wilf 3H **107**
Festival Av. DN11: Harwo 2D **8**
Festival Cres. NG9: Trow 4B **92**
Festival Hall Leisure Cen. 6A **52**
Festus Cl. NG3: Nott 1G **7** (2A **96**)
Festus St. NG4: Neth 1K **97**
NG17: Kirk A 7A **52**
Field, The DE75: Ship 7A **72**
Field Av. NG15: Huck 2D **74**
Field Cl. NG2: West Br 7F **97**
NG4: Ged 5J **87**
NG9: Chil 5F **105**
NG19: Mans W 4K **41**
S81: Work 5H **19**
Fielden Av. NG19: Mans 7D **40**
Field End Cl. LE12: East L 3J **121**
Fieldfare Cl. NG9: Bram 3H **105**
Fieldfare Dr. S81: Gate 5D **18**
Field Farm Cl. LE12: Will W 6G **143**
Field Ho. Cl. NG8: Woll 3J **93**
Field Ind. Est. NG17: Kirk A 5A **52**
Fieldings, The NG17: Huth 1F **51**
Field La. NG9: Chil 5F **105**
NG12: Crop Bi 5B **112**
NG12: Shel 7H **89**
NG12: Widm 7K **119**
NG14: Woodbo 2G **79**
NG21: Blid 7H **55**
Field Maple Dr. NG7: H Grn 7F **85**
Field Pl. NG17: Kirk A 3H **51**
Fields, The NG21: Rain 2A **56**
Fields Av. NG11: Rudd 5K **115**
Fields Dr. NG13: Aslo 3C **102**
Fields End DN10: Mist 3H **11**
Fields Vw. NG12: Cotg 5D **110**
Field Vw. NG12: Rad T 4H **99**
NG17: Sut A 2G **51**
Field Vw. Cl. NG16: Westw 1A **64**
Fieldway NG11: Wilf 5J **107**
Fiennes Cres. NG7: Nott 7A **6** (5H **95**)
Fifth Av. NG7: Nott 3D **106**
NG19: Mans W 2C **48**
NG21: C'tone 6H **43**
NG21: Edwin 6D **36**
Filey St. NG6: Bulw 6J **75**
FILLINGHAM 3D **145**
Finch Cl. NG7: Lent 1G **107**
Finchley Cl. NG11: Clif 1D **114**
Findern Ct. NG18: Mans 4D **48**
Findern Grn. NG3: Nott 2D **96**
Fingal Cl. NG11: Clif 1G **115**
Fingle St. DN22: Nth L 6C **24**
Fingleton S81: Work 7J **19**
Finkell St. DN10: Gri H 3B **16**
Finley Way DE55: Sth N 7A **50**
Finney La. NG22: East M 1C **28**
FINNINGLEY 2B **144**
Finningley Rd. NG18: Mans 1C **54**
Finsbury Av. NG2: Nott 4C **96**
Finsbury Pk. Cl. NG2: West Br 4K **107**
Finsbury Rd. NG5: Arn 4C **76**
NG9: Bram 5H **93**
Firbank Ct. NG9: Chil 4G **105**
FIRBECK 3A **144**
Firbeck Av. NG18: Mans 5B **48**
Firbeck Cres. S81: Lango 1B **12**
Firbeck Rd. NG5: Arn 6J **77**
NG8: Woll 4G **93**
Fir Cl. NG6: Bulw 7F **75**
NG15: Huck 2H **75**
Fircroft Av. NG8: Bilb 7K **83**
Fircroft Dr. NG15: Huck 1C **74**
Firdale NG12: Cotg 6F **111**
Firecrest Way NG6: Basf 3E **84**
Fire House, The NG5: Arn 1B **86**
Fireman's Row NG17: Sut A 1J **51**
Firs, The NG5: Sher 4A **86**
Firs Av. NG9: Bee 2A **106**
Firsby Rd. NG8: Brox 5A **84**
Firs Ho. NG5: Sher 4A **86**
Firs Rd. NG12: Edwal 4E **108**
First Av. NG4: Carl 1F **97**
NG4: Colw 3H **97**
NG4: Ged 6J **87**
NG6: Bulw 7H **75**
NG7: H Grn 7J **85**
NG7: Nott 3D **106**
NG19: Mans W 1C **48**
NG21: C'tone 6J **43**
NG21: Edwin 6E **36**
NG21: Rain 1H **55**
First Holme La. NG23: Sut T 3E **128**
First Oak Dr. NG21: C'tone 4H **43**
Firth Cl. NG5: Arn 5A **78**
Firth Dr. NG9: Chil 7H **105**
Firth Rd. DN22: Retf 2C **22**
Firth Way NG6: Bulw 6G **75**
Fir Tree Cl. NG19: Mans W 7F **43**
Fir Vw. NG22: New O 3D **38**
Fir Wlk. NG3: Nott 1E **96**
Fisher Av. NG5: Woodt 2C **86**
Fisher Cl. LE12: East L 2B **122**
NG17: Sut A 5H **45**
NG23: Coll 1J **129**
Fisher Ga. NG1: Nott 6H **7** (4A **96**)
Fisher La. NG13: Bing 4F **101**
NG18: Mans 5J **47**
Fishers St. NG17: Nunc 3A **60**
Fisher St. NG7: Basf 7G **85**
(not continuous)
FISHLAKE 1B **144**
Fishpond Dr. NG7: Nott 7B **6** (5H **95**)
FISHPOND HILL 3C **46**
Fishpool Rd. NG21: Blid 1F **63**
FISKERTON 6J **139** (3C **147**)
Fiskerton Ct. NG18: Mans 7C **48**
Fiskerton Rd. NG23: Roll . . . . . 3K **139** & 5K **139**
NG25: Brink, Sout . . . . . 7K **131** & 3F **139**
Fiskerton Station (Rail) 4H **139**
Fitzgerald Ct. NG15: Huck 7G **67**
Fitzherbert St. NG20: Mkt W 4E **34**
Fitzwilliam Dr. NG19: Mans W 7B **42**
Five Acres NG11: Wilf 5H **107**
Five Acres Pk. Home Est.
DN10: Bawt 2J **9**
Five Flds. Cl. DN22: Retf 6G **23**
Five Flds. La. DN22: Retf 6G **23**
Flagholme NG12: Cotg 7E **110**
Flamingo Ct. NG7: Lent 6H **95**
Flamstead Av. NG4: Lamb 7F **79**
Flamsteed Rd. NG8: Stre 6J **83**
Flatts, The NG9: Chil 4G **105**
Flatts La. NG14: Calv 3C **70**
NG16: Westw 2B **64**
FLAWBOROUGH 1C **149**
Flawborough Ri. NG2: West Br 6K **107**
Flawforth Av. NG11: Rudd 3A **116**
Flawforth La. NG11: Rudd 3A **116**
Flaxendale NG12: Cotg 7F **111**
Flaxton Way NG5: Top V 7B **76**
Fleam Rd. NG11: Clif 5F **107**
FLEDBOROUGH 3B **30** (1D **147**)
Fleeman Gro. NG2: West Br 7D **96**
Fleet Cl. NG7: Radf 2E **94**
Fleet La. NG23: Best 6H **125**
Fleetway S81: Work 5F **19**
Fleetway Cl. NG16: Newth 5F **73**
Fleetwith Cl. NG2: West Br 4F **109**
Fleming Av. NG22: Tuxf 6D **28**
Fleming Cl. NG16: Want 6A **74**
Fleming Dr. DN22: Woodbe 7G **25**
NG4: Carl 1F **97**
NG24: New T 4E **134**
Fleming Gdns. NG11: Clif 1D **114**
Fleming Ho. NG3: Mapp 5C **86**
Fletcher Ct. NG22: Farns 4J **57**
Fletcher Ga. NG1: Nott 5F **7** (4K **95**)
Fletcher Rd. NG9: Bee 2B **106**
Fletchers Way NG19: Mans W 2D **48**
Fletcher Ter. NG3: Mapp 5B **86**
Fletton Ct. NG3: Nott 1D **96**
Flewitt Gdns. NG3: Nott 2J **7** (2B **96**)
Flinders Orchard NG12: Key 1H **119**
Flint Av. NG19: Mans W 1B **48**
FLINTHAM 6A **140** (1C **149**)
Flintham Ct. NG18: Mans 7D **48**
Flintham Dr. NG5: Sher 3J **85**
Flintham Mus. 5A **140**
Flixton Rd. NG16: Kimb 7K **73**
Floral Vs. NG23: Sut T 4D **128**
Florence Av. NG10: Long E 7E **104**
Florence Boot Cl. NG7: Nott 1C **106**
Florence Cl. NG19: Plea 5A **40**
Florence Cres. NG4: Ged 7A **88**
Florence Gro. NG3: Nott 1D **96**
Florence Rd. NG2: West Br 1D **108**
NG3: Nott 6D **86**
NG4: Ged 6A **88**
Florence St. NG15: Huck 1G **75**
Florey Wlk. NG11: Clif 2D **114**
Florimel Ct. NG5: Arn 7E **76**
Flowers Cl. NG5: Arn 1E **86**
Flying Horse Wlk. NG1: Nott 5F **7** (4K **95**)
Foljambe Ter. NG3: Nott 3H **7** (3A **96**)
Folkton Gdns. NG3: Mapp 6C **86**
Folly La. LN6: Nth S 5K **125**
Folly Nook La. DN22: Rans 1J **13**
Fonton Hall Dr. NG17: Sut A 3F **51**
Footgap La. DN22: Stu S 1B **24**
Ford Cl. NG24: Bald 7J **137**
Fordham Grn. NG11: Clif 2F **115**
Ford La. NG23: Caun 6H **127**
Ford St. NG7: Basf 6H **85**
Ford St. Nth. NG7: Basf 6H **85**
Foredrift Cl. NG11: Goth 7F **115**
Forest Av. NG18: Mans 5J **47**
Forest Cl. NG12: Cotg 6D **110**
NG16: Sels 5F **59**
NG17: Ann W 4A **60**
NG21: Rain 2A **56**
Forest Cnr. NG21: Edwin 5E **36**
Forest Cotts. NG6: Bulw 5K **75**
Forest Ct. NG7: Radf 2A **6** (2H **95**)
NG18: Mans 3D **48**
Forester Cl. NG9: Chil 5H **105**
Forester Gro. NG4: Carl 1G **97**
Forester Rd. NG3: Nott 7D **86**
Foresters Ct. NG24: New T 1F **137**
Forester St. NG4: Neth 1K **97**
FOREST FIELDS 7H **85**
Forest Gdns. NG17: Ann W 4B **60**
Forest Gro. NG1: Nott 1J **95**
NG7: Radf 1A **6** (2H **95**)
Forest Hill NG18: Mans 1J **53**
S81: Work 5J **19**
Forest Hill Pk. S81: Work 5J **19**
Forest Hill Rd. S81: Work 5H **19**
Forest Ho. Pk. Homes NG22: Oll 5A **38**
Forest La. NG15: Pap 2K **67**
NG22: Wale 4F **27**
S80: Work 3K **21**
Forest Link NG22: Bils 6C **126**
Forest Pk. Mobile Homes
NG19: Mans W 7K **41**
Forest Ri S80: Work 3K **21**
Forest Ri. NG20: Mkt W 6E **34**
Forest Rd. NG13: Bing 4D **100**
NG14: Calv 5B **70**
NG17: Ann W 5K **59**
NG17: Skeg 4K **45**
NG18: Mans 6H **47**
NG20: Mkt W 6F **35**
NG21: Blid 6K **55**
NG21: C'tone 6G **43**
NG22: New O 4B **38**
NG25: Oxt 1F **71**
Forest Rd. E. NG1: Nott 1B **6** (2H **95**)
Forest Rd. W. NG7: Radf 2A **6** (2H **95**)
Forestry Houses NG22: Wale 5G **27**
Forest St. NG17: Ann W 4A **60**
NG17: Kirk A 7B **52**
NG17: Sut A 7J **45**
Forest, The (Park & Ride) (Nottingham) 1H **95**
Forest, The Stop (NET) 1H **95**
FOREST TOWN 1C **48** (2A **146**)
Forest Vw. DN22: Ord 7D **22**
NG21: Blid 7G **55**
NG22: New O 4B **38**
Forest Vw. Dr. NG15: Huck 6E **66**
Forest Wlk. S80: Work 4K **21**
Forewood La. DN22: Tres 5F **25**
Forge, The NG9: Trow 3A **92**
NG14: Lowd 4D **80**
Forge Av. NG14: Calv 5D **70**
Forge Cl. NG22: Kirk 1C **132**
NG23: Sth M 1A **134**
NG23: Sut T 3D **128**
Forge Cotts. NG23: Sth M 1B **134**
Forge Hill NG9: Chil 5J **105**
Forge La. NG19: Plea, Stony H 1B **40**
Forge Mill Gro. NG15: Huck 1K **75**
Forman Ho. NG5: Sher 6J **85**
Forman St. NG1: Nott 4E **6** (3K **95**)

Forrest's Yd. *S80: Work* .3F **21**
(*off Bridge St.*)
Forster Av. NG24: New T .5B **136**
Forster St. NG7: Radf .2F **95**
(not continuous)
NG17: Kirk A .6K **51**
Forsythia Gdns. NG7: Lent .6F **95**
Forum Rd. NG5: Bestw .1F **85**
Fosse, The NG12: Cotg, Crop Bi, Owt .7G **111**
Fosse Ct. NG24: Farnd .6J **133**
Fosse Rd. NG13: Bing, Newton, Saxon .4C **100**
NG13: Car C, East B, Knee, Scre .7F **91**
NG24: Farnd .7G **133**
Fossetts Av. NG16: Sels .5D **58**
Fosse Wlk. NG12: Cotg .7F **111**
Fosse Way NG12: Crop Bu .6B **100**
NG13: Bing .5C **100**
Foster Av. NG9: Bee .3A **106**
Foster Dr. NG5: Sher .3A **86**
Foster Rd. NG23: Coll .1H **129**
Fosters Cl. NG13: East B .4E **90**
Fosters La. NG13: Bing .4G **101**
Foster St. NG18: Mans .4J **47**
FOSTON .1D **149**
Foston Cl. NG18: Mans .4D **48**
Fothergill Ct. NG3: Mapp P .1K **95**
Foundry Cl. NG24: New T .6C **134**
Foundry Ter. NG15: News .5E **60**
Fountain Ct. NG19: Mans .6E **40**
NG22: New O .4C **38**
Fountain Dale Ct. NG3: Nott .1A **96**
Fountain Hill DN10: Walk .6F **11**
Fountain Hill Rd. DN10: Walk .5F **11**
Fountain Pk. NG22: New O .5C **38**
Fountains Cl. NG2: West Br .3E **108**
NG17: Kirk A .6C **52**
Fountains Ct. NG9: Bee .3B **106**
Four Seasons Shop. Cen.
NG18: Mans .3H **47**
Fourth Av. NG4: Carl .7E **86**
NG7: H Grn .7J **85**
NG7: Nott .3D **106**
NG19: Mans W .2C **48**
NG21: C'tone .6H **43**
NG21: Edwin .6D **36**
NG21: Rain .1H **55**
Fowler M. NG16: Want .7A **74**
Fowler St. NG3: Mapp P .7A **86**
Foxbridge Cl. NG17: Kirk A .7H **51**
Fox Covert NG4: Colw .4J **97**
Fox Covert Cl. NG17: Sut A .2G **51**
Fox Covert La. DN10: Mist .4J **11**
NG11: Clif .2C **114**
Fox Covert Way NG19: Mans W .3D **48**
Foxearth Av. NG11: Clif .7H **107**
Fox End NG5: Sher .5A **86**
Foxes Cl. NG7: Nott .7B **6**
Foxglove Cl. NG15: Huck .2J **75**
NG24: New B .5F **137**
S80: Work .3J **21**
Foxglove Gro. NG19: Mans W .5B **42**
Foxglove Rd. NG16: Newth .6F **73**
Foxgloves, The NG13: Bing .5E **100**
Fox Gro. NG5: Basf .4F **85**
Fox Gro. Ct. NG5: Basf .4F **85**
Foxhall Cl. NG23: Norw .2J **127**
Foxhall Rd. NG7: H Grn .7H **85**
Foxhill NG12: Cotg .7D **110**
Foxhill Cl. NG17: Sut A .7F **45**
Foxhill Ct. NG4: Carl .7H **87**
Foxhill Rd. NG4: Carl .7F **87**
NG14: Bur J .2D **88**
Foxhill Rd. Central NG4: Carl .7E **86**
Foxhill Rd. E. NG4: Carl .7G **87**
Foxhill Rd. W. NG4: Carl .7D **86**
Foxhollies Gro. NG5: Sher .4J **85**
Fox Hollow NG15: Rave .4C **62**
Fox Mdw. NG15: Huck .7F **67**
Fox Rd. NG2: West Br .7C **96**
Fox St. NG17: Ann W .4A **60**
NG17: Sut A .7K **45**
Foxton Cl. NG6: Bulw .6F **75**
Foxton Gdns. NG8: Bilb .1B **94**
Foxwood Cl. S81: Gate .3E **18**
Foxwood Gro. NG14: Calv .6D **70**
Foxwood La. NG14: Woodbo .7D **70**
Fradley Cl. NG6: Bulw .4J **75**
Frampton Rd. NG8: Bilb .1B **94**
Frances Gro. NG15: Huck .4H **67**
Frances St. NG16: Brins .4B **64**
Francis Ct. NG16: Jack .6A **64**
Francis Gro. NG6: Basf .4F **85**
Francis Mill NG9: Bee .2A **106**
Francis Rd. NG4: Carl .7J **87**
Francis St. NG7: Radf .2B **6** (2H **95**)
(not continuous)
NG18: Mans .3A **48**
Francis Way NG18: Mans .6E **46**
Francklin Rd. NG14: Lowd .4D **80**
Franderground Dr. NG17: Kirk A .6J **51**
Frank Av. NG18: Mans .5F **47**
Franklin Cl. NG5: Arn .6E **76**
Franklin Dr. NG12: Toll .1G **117**
Franklin Ho. *NG3: Mapp* .5C **86**
(*off Ockbrook Dr.*)
Franklin Rd. NG16: Jack .6A **64**
Franklyn Gdns. NG8: Aspl .2D **94**
NG12: Key .6H **117**
Fraser Cres. NG4: Carl .6E **86**
Fraser Rd. NG2: Nott .1A **108**
NG4: Carl .5E **86**
Fraser Sq. NG4: Carl .6E **86**
Fraser St. NG15: News .6D **60**
Frearson Farm Ct.
NG16: Eastw .5D **72**
Freckingham St. NG1: Nott .4J **7** (3A **96**)
Freda Av. NG4: Ged .5G **87**
Freda Cl. NG4: Ged .4G **87**
Frederick Av. NG4: Carl .1E **96**
NG17: Kirk A .5H **51**
Frederick Gro. NG7: Lent .5G **95**
Frederick Rd. NG9: Stap .2C **104**
Frederick St. DN22: Retf .5E **22**
NG17: Sut A .2F **51**
NG18: Mans .4J **47**
S80: Work .2F **21**
FREEBY .3D **149**
Freeby Av. NG19: Mans W .4K **41**
Freeland Cl. NG9: Toton .6E **104**
Freemans La. DN22: Stu S .3A **24**
Freemans Rd. NG4: Carl .7K **87**
Freemans Ter. NG4: Carl .7J **87**
Freemantle Wlk. NG5: Top V .6A **76**
Freeston Dr. NG6: Bulw .6F **75**
Freeth Ct. NG2: Nott .6C **96**
Freeth St. NG2: Nott .6B **96**
Freeth Ter. NG23: Nth C .3D **30**
Freiston St. NG7: H Grn .1F **95**
Fremount Dr. NG8: Bilb .2A **94**
French St. DE7: Ilk .2A **92**
French Ter. NG20: Whal T .5B **26**
Fretwell St. NG7: H Grn .1F **95**
Freya Rd. NG22: New O .5C **38**
Friar La. NG1: Nott .6D **6** (4J **95**)
NG20: Mkt W .6E **34**
Friars Cl. NG16: Sels .5F **59**
Friars Ct. NG7: Nott .7B **6** (5H **95**)
Friars Cres. NG24: New T .4C **136**
Friar St. NG7: Lent .6F **95**
Friar Wlk. NG13: Newton .7D **90**
Friary, The NG7: Lent .6F **95**
Friary Cl. NG7: Lent .6F **95**
Friary Gdns. NG24: New T .7D **134**
Friary M. NG24: New T .7D **134**
Friary Rd. NG24: New T .1D **136**
Friary Vs. NG24: New T .7D **134**
Friday La. NG4: Ged .5J **87**
Friend La. NG21: Edwin .7F **37**
FRIESTON .1D **149**
FRIEZELAND .3F **65** (3A **146**)
Frinton Rd. NG8: Brox .6K **83**
FRISBY ON THE WREAKE .3B **148**
Fritchley Ct. NG18: Mans .4D **48**
Frith Cl. LE12: East L .1A **122**
Frith Gro. NG19: Mans .3E **46**
Frobisher Gdns. NG5: Arn .1A **86**
FRODINGHAM .1D **145**
Frogmore St. NG1: Nott .1E **6** (2K **95**)
Frome Gdns. NG13: Bing .5E **100**
Front St. NG5: Arn .7H **77**
NG23: Sth C .7D **30**
NG24: Barn W .7K **137**
Fryar Rd. NG16: Eastw .2D **72**
Fuchsia Way NG19: Mans W .1C **48**
FULBECK .3D **147**
Fulford Av. DN22: Retf .2C **22**
Fulforth St. NG1: Nott .2E **6** (2K **95**)
Fuller Cl. NG18: Mans .6H **47**
Fuller St. NG11: Rudd .4K **115**
Fulmar Cl. NG19: Mans W .1A **48**
Fulmar Way S81: Gate .5D **18**
FULWOOD .3F **51** (3A **146**)
Fulwood Cl. NG9: Chil .5H **105**
NG17: Huth .3E **50**
Fulwood Cres. NG8: Aspl .6B **84**
Fulwood Ind. Est. NG17: Huth .3D **50**
Fulwood Ri. NG17: Huth .3E **50**
Fulwood Rd. Nth. NG17: Huth .3D **50**
Fulwood Rd. Sth. NG17: Huth .3D **50**
Funky Pots
West Bridgeford .3B **108**
Furleys Cotts. NG14: Lowd .3B **80**
Furlong Av. NG5: Arn .6G **77**
Furlong Cl. NG9: Stap .1C **104**
Furlong Ct. NG5: Arn .6G **77**
Furlong St. NG5: Arn .7G **77**
Furnace Rd. DE7: Ilk .1A **92**
Furness Cl. NG2: West Br .2E **108**
Furness Rd. NG6: Basf .4D **84**
Furnival St. S80: Work .4H **21**
Furrows, The NG21: Rain .2A **56**
Furze, The NG22: Kirt .2J **39**
Furzebrook Rd. NG4: Colw .3H **97**
Furze Gdns. NG3: Nott .1G **7** (1A **96**)
Fylde Cl. NG9: Toton .7D **104**
Fylingdale Way NG8: Woll .5G **93**

G

Gables, The NG3: Mapp .3D **86**
NG7: Basf .6H **85**
Gables, The NG19: Mans W .1B **48**
NG22: Bils .6D **126**
Gables Dr. NG25: Hock .1K **131**
Gables Farm Dr. LE12: Costo .3E **122**
Gable's Lea LE12: Sut B .6B **120**
Gabor Cl. NG11: Clif .2D **114**
Gabor Ct. NG11: Clif .1D **114**
Gabrielle Cl. NG6: Bulw .3E **84**
Gaddick Vw. NG22: Egma .2E **124**
Gadd St. NG7: Radf .1A **6** (2G **95**)
Gadwall Cres. NG7: Lent .6H **95**
Gainborough Rd. DN22: Nth W .2G **17**
GAINSBOROUGH .2D **145**
Gainsborough Cl. NG9: Stap .3D **104**
NG12: Kin .2B **142**
Gainsborough Ct. NG9: Bee .2B **106**
Gainsborough Dr. NG24: New T .5E **134**
Gainsborough Rd. DN10: Bawt .1K **9**
DN10: Drake, Eve .7B **10**
DN10: Gri H .3A **16**
DN22: Stu S .1B **24**
LN1: Dri N, Sax .1K **31**
NG23: Girt .5H **125**
NG24: Wint .3F **135**
Gainsford Cl. NG5: Bestw .2G **85**
Gainsford Cres. NG5: Bestw .2G **85**
Gaitskell Cres. NG21: Edwin .7G **37**
Gaitskell Way NG24: Bald .5H **137**
Gala Bingo
Mansfield .4H **47**
Nottingham Castle .2F **95**
Nottingham St Anns .3G **7** (3A **96**)
Nottingham Top Valley .1F **85**
Gala Way DN22: Retf .5F **23**
NG5: Bestw .1F **85**
Galeb, The *NG7: Lent* .6F **95**
(*off Leen Ct.*)
Gale Cl. NG9: Bee .3C **106**
Galena Dr. NG3: Nott .1D **96**
Galen Av. DN22: Woodbe .6F **25**
Gallery, The NG7: Nott .7D **6** (5J **95**)
Galley Hill Rd. NG25: Sout .5K **131**
GALLOWS INN .2A **92**
Gallows Inn Cl. DE7: Ilk .2A **92**
Gallows Inn Ind. Est. DE7: Ilk .2A **92**
Galway Av. DN11: Birc .1G **9**
Galway Cres. DN22: Retf .2C **22**
Galway Dr. DN11: Birc .1G **9**
Galway M. DN11: Harwo .3D **8**
Galway Rd. DN11: Birc .1G **9**
NG5: Arn .6F **77**
NG7: Lent .7A **6** (5G **95**)
Gamage Cl. NG24: Bald .6H **137**
Gamble St. NG7: Radf .2A **6** (2H **95**)
GAMSTON
Nottingham .2F **109** (2B **148**)
Retford .1K **27** (1C **147**)
Gamston Cres. NG5: Sher .4K **85**
Gamston District Cen. NG2: West Br .3F **109**
Gamston Lings Bar Rd. NG2: Gam .2G **109**
NG12: Toll, Edwal .1D **116**
Gamston Lodge NG4: Carl .2H **97**
Gamston Rd. NG18: Mans .7D **48**
Ganton Cl. NG3: Mapp .6C **86**
Garbsen Ct. S80: Work .4F **21**
Garden Av. NG4: Carl .1G **97**
NG21: Rain .2J **55**
Garden, The (Caravan Pk.) DN22: Welh .2K **23**
Garden City NG4: Carl .7H **87**
Gardendale Av. NG11: Clif .1E **114**
Gardeners Cl. NG4: Carl .6G **87**
NG13: Bing .3E **100**
NG15: Huck .6F **67**
Gardeners Wlk. NG5: Sher .3G **85**
Gardenia Cl. NG9: Toton .7F **105**
Gardenia Cres. NG3: Mapp .5E **86**
Gardenia Gro. NG3: Mapp .5E **86**
Garden La. NG17: Sut A .7A **46**
Garden Rd. NG13: Bing .4E **100**
NG15: Huck .6F **67**
NG16: Eastw .3D **72**
NG18: Mans .4H **47**
Gardens Ct. NG2: West Br .2D **108**
Garden St. NG7: Radf .3G **95**
Garden Ter. NG15: News .5D **60**
Gardiner Av. NG24: Bald .7J **137**
Gardiners Ct. NG19: Mans W .6J **41**
Gardiner Ter. NG17: Stant H .4H **45**
Gardner Dr. NG12: Kin .1B **142**
Garfield Cl. NG9: Stap .7D **92**
Garfield Ct. NG7: Radf .3G **95**
Garfield Rd. NG7: Radf .2F **95**
(not continuous)
Garforth Cl. NG8: Basf .7F **85**
Garibaldi Rd. NG19: Mans W .7F **43**
Garland, The *NG7: Lent* .6F **95**
(*off Leen Ct.*)
Garners Hill NG1: Nott .6F **7** (4A **96**)
Garnet Cl. NG18: Mans .6K **47**
Garnet Ct. NG3: Nott .3K **7** (3B **96**)
Garnet St. NG4: Neth .1J **97**
Garnon St. NG18: Mans .5E **46**
Garood Cl. NG24: New T .5K **133**
Garratt Av. NG18: Mans .3J **47**
Garrett Gro. NG11: Clif .7D **106**
Garsdale Cl. NG2: Gam .3F **109**

Garsdale Dr.—Goodwin St.

Garsdale Dr. NG11: Wilf .6H 107
Garside Av. NG17: Sut A .1H 51
Garside St. S80: Work .2H 21
Garth Av. NG17: Kirk A .3J 51
GARTHORPE .3D 149
Garth Rd. NG18: Mans .6G 47
Garton Cl. NG6: Bulw .2C 84
NG9: Chil .4G 105
Garwick Cl. NG19: Mans W .7D 42
Gas St. NG10: Sand .3B 104
Gatcombe Cl. NG12: Rad T .5F 99
Gatcombe Gro. NG10: Sand .6A 104
GATE BURTON .3D 145
GATEFORD .5D 18
Gateford Av. S81: Work .6E 18
Gateford Chambers S80: Work .2G 21
(off Gateford Rd.)
Gateford Cl. NG9: Bram .6H 93
S81: Work .5E 18
GATEFORD COMMON .5B 18
Gateford Dr. S81: Work .6E 18
Gateford Gdns. S81: Work .6E 18
Gateford Glade S81: Work .6F 19
Gateford Ri. S81: Work .5E 18
Gateford Rd. S80: Work .1F 21
S81: Gate, Work .4B 18
Gateford Toll Bar S81: Gate .5B 18
Gatehouse Ct. NG9: Chil .4J 105
Gateside Rd. NG2: Nott .7H 95
Gateway, The NG24: New T .1E 136
Gatling St. NG7: Radf .3F 95
Gattlys La. NG22: New O .3B 38
Gaul St. NG6: Bulw .7H 75
Gauntley Ct. NG7: Basf .7G 85
Gauntley St. NG7: Basf .7F 85
Gautries Cl. NG5: Top V .6C 76
Gavin M. NG7: H Grn .7G 85
Gawthorne St. NG7: Basf .6G 85
Gayhurst Grn. NG6: Bulw .2F 85
Gayhurst Rd. NG6: Bulw .2F 85
Gaynor Ct. NG8: Bilb .2C 94
Gayrigg Ct. NG9: Chil .4G 105
Gayton Cl. NG8: Bilb .7J 83
Gaywood Cl. NG11: Clif .2G 115
GEDLING .5J 87 (1B 148)
Gedling Gro. NG5: Arn .7H 77
NG7: Radf .1B 6 (2H 95)
Gedling Rd. NG4: Carl .7J 87
NG5: Arn .7H 77
Gedling St. NG1: Nott .5H 7 (4A 96)
NG18: Mans .5H 47
Gedney Av. NG3: Nott .7C 86
Gell Rd. NG9: Chil .5F 105
GELSTON .1D 149
Genesis Pk. NG7: Radf .3E 94
George Av. NG9: Bee .4A 106
George Dere Cl. NG22: New O .2D 38
George Grn. Ct. NG2: Nott .4C 96
(off Sneinton Blvd.)
George Grn. Way NG7: Nott .1E 106
George Rd. NG2: West Br .2B 108
NG4: Carl .1H 97
George Shooter Ct. NG20: Mkt W .3E 34
George's La. NG5: Calv, Woodbo .1K 77
NG14: Calv .1K 77
George St. DN22: Retf .5F 23
NG1: Nott .4G 7 (3A 96)
NG5: Arn .1B 86
NG15: Huck .5G 67
NG16: Pinx .7A 50
NG17: Kirk A .6H 51
NG17: Sut A .7F 45
NG19: Mans .2F 47
NG19: Mans W .1C 48
(Attlee Av.)
NG19: Mans W .6K 41
(Warsop Rd.)
NG20: Mkt W .4D 34
NG20: Whal T .5B 26
NG24: New T .7D 134
S80: Work .2G 21
George St. Trad. Ho. NG1: Nott .5G 7
Georgia Dr. NG5: Arn .4G 77
Georgina Rd. NG9: Bee .4A 106
Gerbera Dr. NG24: New T .7G 135
Gerrard Cl. NG5: Arn .4C 76
Gertrude Rd. NG2: West Br .1D 108
Gervase Gdns. NG11: Clif .7D 106
Ghest Vs. S81: Costh .3C 12
Ghost Ho. La. NG9: Chil .4G 105
(not continuous)
Gibbet Hill La. DN10: Bawt .2J 9
Gibbons Av. NG9: Stap .2C 104
Gibbons Ct. DN22: Nth W .2J 17
Gibbons Rd. NG18: Mans .5F 47
Gibbons St. NG7: Lent .1F 107
Gibdyke DN10: Miss .3D 10
GIBSMERE .4D 138 (1C 149)
Gibson Ct. NG22: Bou .3E 38
S81: Work .3F 19
Gibson Cres. NG24: New B .6F 137
Gibson Rd. NG7: H Grn .7H 85
Gifford Gdns. NG2: Nott .6K 95
Gilbert Av. NG11: Goth .7G 115
NG22: Tuxf .6D 28
Gilbert Blvd. NG5: Arn .7A 78
Gilbert Cl. NG5: Bestw .2H 85
Gilbert Gdns. NG3: Nott .2D 96
Gilbert Rd. DN11: Birc .2E 8
Gilbert St. NG15: Huck .6G 67
(not continuous)
Gilbert Way NG21: Blid .5K 55
NG24: Bald .7J 137
Gilcroft St. NG17: Skeg .4J 45
NG18: Mans .4H 47
GILDINGWELLS .3A 144
Gilead St. NG6: Bulw .7H 75
Giles Av. NG2: West Br .3A 108
Giles Ct. NG2: West Br .2B 108
Gillercomb Cl. NG2: West Br .4G 109
Gill Grn. Wlk. DN22: Clar .7H 17
Gill Ho. NG24: New T .5D 136
Gillies, The NG19: Mans .5E 46
Gilliver La. NG12: C'ton .7B 110
Gill La. DN10: Beck .6C 16
Gillotts Cl. NG13: Bing .3F 101
Gill St. NG1: Nott .2D 6 (2J 95)
NG16: Sels .6E 58
NG17: Sut A .1G 51
Gilmores La. NG24: Bald .7J 137
Gilpet Av. NG3: Nott .7C 86
Gilstrap Cl. NG24: New T .1G 137
GILTBROOK .6G 73 (1A 148)
Giltbrook Cres. NG16: Gilt .6G 73
Giltbrook Ind. Est. NG16: Gilt .7G 73
Giltbrook Retail Pk. NG16: Gilt .7G 73
Gilt Hill NG16: Kimb .7H 73
Giltway NG16: Gilt .7G 73
Gin Cl. Way NG16: Aws, Gilt .1B 82
Gipsy La. NG11: Clif .7D 106
NG15: Huck .3D 66
NG20: Chu W .2B 34
GIRTON .4H 125 (2D 147)
Girton Ct. NG18: Mans .1D 54
Girton Rd. NG5: Sher .4H 85
Gisburn Cl. NG11: Wilf .5H 107
Gisburn Gro. NG19: Mans W .2D 48
Glade, The NG11: Clif .3F 115
Glade Av. NG8: Woll .3D 94
Glade Bus. Centre, The NG5: Bestw .1F 85
Gladehill Rd. NG5: Arn, Bestw .7E 76
Glades, The NG5: Top V .6B 76
Gladstone Av. NG11: Goth .7G 115
Gladstone Dr. NG16: Brins .6C 64
Gladstone Pl. S80: Work .2G 21
Gladstone Rd. NG24: New T .3C 136
Gladstone St. NG4: Carl .1G 97
NG7: Basf, H Grn .7G 85
(not continuous)
NG9: Bee .4K 105
NG16: Lang M .3A 72
NG17: Kirk A .6B 52
NG18: Mans .3K 47
(not continuous)
NG19: Mans W .7J 41
S80: Work .2F 21
Gladstone Ter. NG17: Kirk A .6K 51
NG19: Mans W .7J 41
Gladys St. NG7: Basf .6H 85
Glaisdale S81: Work .5J 19
Glaisdale Dr. E. NG8: Bilb .2J 93
Glaisdale Dr. W. NG8: Bilb .3J 93
Glaisdale Pk. Ind. Est. NG8: Bilb .2J 93
Glaisdale Parkway NG8: Bilb .3J 93
Glamis Cl. NG17: Sut A .2B 52
Glamis Rd. NG5: Sher .5H 85
S81: Carl L .6B 12
Glannis Sq. NG20: Chu W .2E 34
Glanton Way NG5: Arn .4J 77
Glapton La. NG11: Clif .7E 106
Glapton Rd. NG2: Nott .7K 95
GLAPWELL .2A 146
Glaramara Cl. NG2: Nott .7J 95
Glasby Cl. NG22: New O .4B 38
Glasby Ct. NG22: New O .4B 38
(off Glasby Cl.)
Glasshouse, The NG3: Nott .3G 7 (3K 95)
Glasshouse St. NG1: Nott .3F 7 (3K 95)
Glastonbury Cl. NG19: Mans W .5K 41
Glaven Cl. NG19: Mans W .7K 41
Glebe, The DN22: Retf .2D 22
NG16: Coss .3A 82
Glebe Av. NG16: Pinx .1B 58
NG20: Mkt W .4E 34
Glebe Cl. DN22: Nth W .2J 17
S80: Work .2D 20
Glebe Cotts. NG11: Wilf .1J 107
Glebe Cres. DE7: Ilk .1A 92
Glebe Dr. NG14: Bur J .4C 88
Glebe Farm Cl. NG2: West Br .5K 107
Glebe Farm Vw. NG4: Ged .4J 87
Glebelands NG23: Nth M .7K 129
Glebe La. NG12: Rad T .5E 98
Glebe Pk. NG24: New B .3F 137
Glebe Rd. NG2: West Br .2C 108
NG4: Carl .5F 87
NG16: Nuth .1H 83
Glebe St. NG9: Bee .3K 105
NG15: Huck .5G 67
NG17: Ann W .4K 59
Glebe Vw. NG19: Mans W .2K 47
Gledhill Dr. S81: Gate .5C 18
Glen, The NG11: Clif .1F 115
Glen Av. NG16: Eastw .5F 73
Glenbrook NG12: Cotg .6F 111
Glenbrook Cres. NG8: Bilb .1B 94
Glencairn Dr. NG8: Bilb .7B 84
Glencairn M. NG8: Bilb .7B 84
Glencoe Rd. NG11: Clif .1H 115
Glencoyne Rd. NG11: Clif .2F 115
Glencross Cl. NG2: West Br .7F 97
Glendale Cl. NG4: Carl .5G 87
Glendale Ct. NG9: Chil .6K 105
Glendale Gdns. NG5: Arn .7H 77
Glendoe Gro. NG13: Bing .4D 100
Glendon Dr. NG5: Sher .4H 85
NG15: Huck .1G 75
Gleneagles Ct. NG12: Edwal .6E 108
Gleneagles Dr. NG5: Arn .5K 77
NG17: Kirk A .4J 51
Glen Eagles Way DN22: Ord .7D 22
Glenfield Av. NG16: Kimb .7H 73
Glenfields NG25: Sout .5G 131
Glen Helen NG4: Colw .2J 97
Glenlivet Gdns. NG11: Clif .1G 115
Glenloch Dr. NG11: Clif .2G 115
Glen Mooar Cl. NG19: Mans W .7C 42
Glenmore Rd. NG2: West Br .3E 108
Glenorchy Cres. NG5: Top V .6A 76
Glen Parva Av. NG5: Redh .5G 77
Glenridding Cl. NG2: West Br .4G 109
Glen Rd. NG14: Bur J .2D 88
Glensford Gdns. NG5: Top V .4A 76
Glenside NG5: Woodt .2E 86
NG17: Kirk A .6C 52
Glenside Rd. NG9: Bram .7H 93
Glenstone Ct. NG7: H Grn .7G 85
Glen St. NG17: Sut A .6J 45
Glenthorn Cl. S81: Shire .5A 18
GLENTWORTH .3D 145
Glentworth Rd. NG7: Radf .2F 95
Glenwood Av. NG8: Woll .4J 93
Glins Rd. NG5: Top V .6B 76
Glossop Av. NG18: Mans .4D 48
Gloucester Av. NG7: Lent .4F 95
NG9: Bee .4A 106
NG16: Nuth .4A 84
Gloucester Rd. S81: Work .5H 19
Glover Av. NG8: Woll .4J 93
Glover Cl. DN22: Sth L .2G 25
Glover Ho. NG5: Arn .1D 86
(off Derwent Cres.)
Glovers Cl. NG20: Cuck .4C 32
Glovers La. NG24: Bald .5G 137
Goacher's La. DN22: Nth W .2H 17
GOADBY MARWOOD .3C 149
Goatchurch Ct. NG5: Top V .6C 76
Goathland Cl. NG5: Bestw .6D 76
Godber Cl. NG16: Gilt .6E 72
Godber Rd. NG15: Huck .1E 74
Goddard Ct. NG3: Arn .1F 87
Godfrey's Ct. S80: Work .2F 21
Godfrey St. NG4: Neth .2K 97
Godley Vs. S80: Work .2G 21
Goit La. DN22: Hay .5K 17
Goldcrest Ct. NG13: Bing .5H 101
Goldcrest Ri. S81: Gate .5D 18
Goldcrest Rd. NG6: Cin .4C 84
NG19: Mans W .7B 42
Golden Hill La. NG22: Kirt .2K 39
Goldenholme La. DN22: Ramp .7K 25
Goldfinch Cl. NG18: Mans .3A 48
Goldham Rd. NG8: Stre .7J 83
Goldies Dr. NG18: Mans .2K 47
Goldrill Cl. NG2: Gam .2E 108
Goldsmith Ct. NG1: Nott .3D 6
Goldsmith Ho. NG18: Mans .3G 47
(off The Connexion)
Goldsmith Rd. NG24: Bald .4G 137
S81: Work .7J 19
Goldsmith St. NG1: Nott .3D 6 (3J 95)
NG18: Mans .3G 47
Goldson Way NG23: Nth M .7K 129
Goldstraw La. NG24: Bald .7H 137
Goldswong Ter. NG3: Nott .1K 95
GOLDTHORPE .1A 144
Goldthorpe Av. S81: Lango .1C 12
Goldthorpe Cl. S81: Lango .1C 12
Golf Cl. NG6: Bulw .4J 75
Golf Club Rd. DE7: Stant D .7A 92
Golf Rd. NG12: Rad T .5F 99
Gomersall Cl. DN22: Retf .4G 23
GONALSTON .3F 81 (1B 148)
Gonalston La. NG14: Epp, Gon, Hove .1B 80
GONERBY HILL FOOT .2D 149
Goodacre St. NG18: Mans .3J 47
Goodall Cres. NG15: Huck .7J 67
Goodall St. NG7: H Grn .1G 95
Goodhand Cres. NG18: Mans .4E 46
Goodliffe St. NG7: H Grn .7G 85
Goodman Cl. NG16: Gilt .6G 73
Goodwill Rd. NG22: New O .5D 38
Goodwin Cl. NG24: New T .1G 137
Goodwin Ct. NG22: Farns .4K 57
Goodwin Dr. NG16: Kimb .1D 82
Goodwin La. NG24: Bald .7J 137
Goodwins Ct. NG23: Roll .3K 139
Goodwin St. NG7: Radf .2B 6 (2H 95)

Goodwood Av. NG5: Arn 6G **77**
Goodwood Dr. NG9: Toton 7E **104**
Goodwood Rd. NG8: Woll 4J **93**
Goodwood Way NG18: Mans 3B **48**
Goosedale La. NG6: Bestw V 6A **68**
Goose Ga. NG1: Nott 5G **7** (4A **96**)
NG12: Cotg 6D **110**
Goosemoor La. DN22: Retf 6F **23**
Gopher Rd. NG24: New T 4C **136**
Gordon Av. NG18: Mans 4A **48**
Gordon Brae NG18: Mans 7J **47**
Gordon Cl. NG9: Atten 7J **105**
NG22: Farns 6K **57**
S80: Work 2J **21**
Gordondale Rd. NG19: Mans 1H **47**
Gordon Gro. NG7: Basf 6G **85**
Gordon Ri. NG3: Mapp 5B **86**
Gordon Rd. NG2: West Br 2C **108**
NG3: Nott 2K **7** (2B **96**)
NG14: Bur J 2F **89**
Gordon Sq. NG2: West Br 2C **108**
Gordon St. NG6: Basf 3E **84**
Gorman Ct. NG5: Arn 7K **77**
Gorse Av. NG18: Mans 5C **48**
Gorse Cl. NG10: Long E 7A **104**
NG14: Calv 6B **70**
NG16: Newth 5F **73**
Gorse Ct. NG6: Bulw 2F **85**
Gorse Hill NG15: Rave 3C **62**
Gorselands Av. S80: Work 4K **21**
Gorse Rd. NG12: Key 7G **117**
NG24: New T 4C **136**
Gorsethorpe Cotts. NG21: Edwin 1J **43**
Gorsethorpe La. NG21: Edwin, K Cli 7H **35**
Gorse Vw. NG23: Roll 3K **139**
Gorse Wlk. NG3: Nott 1E **96**
Gorseway NG21: C'tone 6J **43**
Gorsey Rd. NG3: Mapp P 1A **96**
Gorsy La. NG25: Fis 7F **139**
Gosforth Ct. NG2: Nott 7A **96**
GOTHAM 7G **115** (2A **148**)
Gotham La. NG11: Bunny 4A **118**
Gotham Rd. LE12: East L 1A **122**
NG11: King 1A **120**
Gothic Cl. NG6: Basf 3F **85**
GOVERTON 5E **138** (1C **149**)
Goverton Hill NG14: Blea 1A **138**
Goverton Sq. NG6: Bulw 2E **84**
Gowan Cl. NG9: Chil 7H **105**
Goyden Cl. NG5: Top V 6C **76**
Grace Av. NG9: Bee 3C **106**
Grace Dr. NG8: Aspl 7E **84**
Gracefield La. NG23: Norm T 1K **125**
Grace Rd. DN22: Ord 6E **22**
Grafton Av. NG5: Woodt 2B **86**
Grafton Cl. NG17: Skeg 5B **46**
Grafton Ct. NG7: Radf 4A **6** (3H **95**)
Grafton St. S80: Work 1F **21**
Graham Cl. NG24: New B 5E **136**
Graham St. NG7: Radf 3G **95**
Grainger Av. NG2: West Br 6B **108**
NG17: Nunc 3B **60**
Graingers Ter. NG15: Huck 7H **67**
Grainger St. NG2: Nott 6B **96**
GRAISELOUND 2C **145**
Grampian Dr. NG5: Arn 4D **76**
Granary, The NG18: Mans 3K **47**
Granary Ct. S81: Carl L 6D **12**
GRANBY 1J **141** (2C **149**)
Granby Av. NG19: Mans 2H **47**
NG24: New T 3D **136**
Granby Ct. NG13: Bing 4E **100**
Granby Dr. NG24: Bald 6G **137**
Granby Hill NG13: Gran 1J **141**
Granby La. NG13: Bing, What 5A **102**
Granby Vs. NG2: Nott 4C **96**
Grandfield Av. NG12: Rad T 4E **98**
Grandfield Cres. NG12: Rad T 4E **98**
Grange, The DN22: Ord 7E **22**
NG23: Nth M 5K **129**
Grange Av. DN10: Mist 4J **11**
NG9: Bee 3A **106**
NG11: Rudd 2J **115**
NG18: Mans 5F **47**
NG22: Oll 5B **38**
S81: Woods 1A **18**
Grange Cl. DN10: Mist 3J **11**
NG4: Lamb 7G **79**
NG11: Wilf 1J **107**
NG17: Teve 2G **45**
S81: Carl L 6D **12**
Grange Ct. NG11: Rudd 7K **107**
NG17: Kirk A 6D **52**
Grange Cres. NG4: Ged 4J **87**
Grange Dr. DN10: Mist 4J **11**
DN11: Harwo 1D **8**
Grange Est. NG16: Coss 6C **82**
Grange Farm NG2: Gam 2F **109**
Grange Farm Cl. NG9: Toton 7F **105**
NG17: Sut A 3G **51**
Grange Farm Cotts. NG14: Lowd 3K **79**
Grangelea Gdns. NG9: Bram 1G **105**
Grange M. NG11: Rudd 7K **107**
Grangemoor NG15: Pap 4K **67**
Grange Pk. NG2: West Br 4E **108**
NG12: Crop Bu 2B **112**
Grange Rd. DN22: Ord 7E **22**
NG5: Woodt 3B **86**
NG6: Basf 4E **84**
NG12: Edwal 5D **108**
NG21: Blid 6K **55**
NG24: New T 4A **136**
Grange Vw. DN11: Harwo 1D **8**
NG16: Eastw 3D **72**
Grange Vw. Rd. NG4: Ged 5J **87**
Grange Wlk. DN10: Mist 3J **11**
Grangewood Ct. NG8: Woll 5H **93**
Grangewood Rd. NG8: Woll 5H **93**
NG17: Kirk A 4K **51**
Grannis Dr. NG8: Bilb 7B **84**
GRANTHAM 2D **149**
Grantham Cl. NG16: Gilt 7G **73**
Grantham Rd. NG12: Rad T 6C **98**
NG13: Bing, Aslo, What 4G **101**
Grantleigh Cl. NG8: Woll 3A **94**
Granton Av. NG11: Clif 2G **115**
Granton Ri. NG19: Mans 5D **46**
Grant St. NG7: Radf 3A **6** (3G **95**)
Granville Av. NG10: Long E 7C **104**
Granville Ct. NG3: Nott 3C **96**
Granville Cres. NG12: Rad T 6D **98**
Granville Gro. NG3: Nott 3C **96**
Grasby Wlk. NG11: Clif 7E **106**
Grasmere Av. NG8: Aspl 5D **84**
Grasmere Cl. NG15: Huck 5F **67**
Grasmere Ct. NG10: Long E 7A **104**
NG18: Mans *3G* ***47***
(off Layton Av.)
Grasmere Gdns. NG11: Goth 6G **115**
Grasmere Rd. NG9: Bram 1J **105**
NG10: Long E 7A **104**
S81: Work 5G **19**
Grasmere St. NG10: Sand 4A **104**
Grasmoor Cl. NG3: Nott 7C **86**
Grassingdale Cl. NG4: Carl 5G **87**
Grassington Rd. NG8: Aspl 2E **94**
Grasslands, The NG21: Rain 2A **56**
Grassmere NG12: Cotg 6F **111**
GRASSTHORPE 3K **125** (2C **147**)
Grassthorpe La. NG23: Grass, Weston 4H **125**
Grassthorpe Rd.
NG23: Grass, Norm T 3K **125**
NG23: Sut T 4K **125** & 1C **128**
Grassy La. NG9: Bee 4B **106**
Gratton Ct. NG17: Kirk A 4J **51**
Gravelholes La. DN10: Mist 3G **11**
Gravel La. NG22: Egma 1C **124**
Gravelly Hollow NG14: Calv 3H **69**
Gravelly La. NG25: Fis 6G **139**
Graveney Gdns. NG5: Arn 1E **86**
Graves Moor La. S81: Blyth 7K **13**
Gray Fallow DE55: Sth N 7A **50**
GRAYINGHAM 2D **145**
Graylands Rd. NG8: Bilb 1J **93**
Gray La. NG22: Edin, Halam 4A **130**
Grays Ct. NG24: Farnd 7H **133**
Grays Dr. NG15: Rave 6D **62**
Grayson M. NG9: Chil 7G **105**
Graystones Cl. NG2: West Br 4F **109**
Grazingfield NG11: Wilf 5H **107**
GREASLEY 3J **73**
Greasley Av. NG16: Newth 4G **73**
Greasley Ct. NG18: Mans 7D **48**
Greasley Sports & Community Cen. 4F **73**
Greasley St. NG6: Bulw 7H **75**
Gt. Black La. DN11: Tick 1A **8**
Great Central Railway
Ruddington Station 5K **115**
Rushcliffe Halt Station 1A **122**
Gt. Central Rd. NG18: Mans 4J **47**
Gt. Freeman St. NG3: Nott 2F **7** (2K **95**)
GREAT GONERBY 2D **149**
Gt. Hoggett Dr. NG9: Chil 3F **105**
Great La. NG22: East M 2B **28**
Gt. Northern Close, The NG2: Nott 7H **7** (5A **96**)
Gt. Northern Cotts. NG15: Huck 4H **67**
NG19: Plea *4A* ***40***
(off Chesterfield Rd.)
Gt. Northern Rd. NG16: Eastw 4B **72**
Gt. Northern Way NG4: Neth 2A **98**
Great Nth. Rd. DN10: Bawt, Scro 1J **9**
DN22: Rans, Torw 1H **13**
NG22: Tuxf 7D **28**
NG22: West M 3A **28**
NG23: Carl T, Sut T, Weston 3F **125** & 1A **128**
(not continuous)
NG23: Nth M, Sth M 1A **134** & 7J **129**
(not continuous)
NG24: New T 6B **134**
GREAT PONTON 2D **149**
GREAT WILNE 2A **148**
Greaves Cl. NG5: Arn 2E **86**
NG8: Stre 6J **83**
NG24: New T 1G **137**
Greaves La. NG22: Edin 3A **130**
Grebe Cl. NG24: New B 4F **137**
Greek St. NG7: Radf 4A **6** (3H **95**)
Green, The DN10: Beck 7D **16**
DN11: Harwo 3B **8**
LE12: East L 3A **122**
LE14: Hick 6E **142**
NG4: Carl 7F **87**
Green, The NG9: Chil 5K **105**
NG11: King 1A **120**
NG11: Rudd 4K **115**
NG12: Rad T 5D **98**
NG13: Ors 1J **103**
NG14: Lowd 4K **79**
NG17: Huth 1E **50**
NG19: Mans W 4G **41**
NG22: Bils 4C **126**
NG22: Dun T 6J **29**
NG22: Kirk 1C **132**
NG23: Coll 3G **129**
NG23: Elston 2D **140**
NG24: Codd 6K **135**
S81: Carl L 6D **12**
Green Acre NG8: Woll 3G **93**
Greenacre NG12: Edwal 5E **108**
NG14: Bur J 2D **88**
NG17: Stant H 5G **45**
NG18: Mans 5B **48**
Greenacre Rd. S81: Work 6H **19**
Greenacres NG17: Kirk A 2B **60**
Greenacres Caravan Pk.
NG22: Tuxf 5E **28**
Greenacres Cl. NG16: Newth 4G **73**
Greenacres Pk. NG2: West Br 7G **97**
Green App. NG4: Carl 7F **87**
Green Av. NG4: Neth 1K **97**
Greenaway NG23: Roll 3K **139**
Green Bank NG21: Rain 3A **56**
Greenbank NG4: Carl 2G **97**
Greenbank Ct. NG5: Sher 5K **85**
Greenbank Dr. NG17: Sut A 6J **45**
Greenbanks NG5: Woodt 3B **86**
Greenburn Cl. NG2: Gam 3G **109**
Green Cl. NG7: Nott 6D **94**
NG12: Key 6J **117**
NG15: Huck 1J **75**
NG21: Blid 7J **55**
Green Ct. NG13: Bing 3F **101**
Green Cres. NG16: Sels 6C **58**
Greencroft NG11: Clif 6G **107**
Greendale Av. NG21: Edwin 5D **36**
Greendale Cl. NG17: Stant H 4G **45**
NG20: Mkt W 4C **34**
Greendale Cres. NG21: C'tone 5K **43**
Greendale Gdns. NG8: Bilb 7C **84**
Greendale Rd. NG3: Nott 2F **97**
NG5: Arn 1C **86**
Green Dr. NG21: Edwin 5K **35**
NG25: Fis 6J **139**
Green Farm Ct. S81: Carl L 6D **12**
Green Farm Rd. NG16: Sels 6B **58**
Greenfield Cl. NG19: Mans W 1D **48**
NG21: Edwin 7H **37**
NG24: Codd 7H **135**
Greenfield Gro. NG4: Carl 7E **86**
Greenfields Cres. NG22: New O 4C **38**
Greenfields Dr. NG12: Cotg 7E **110**
Greenfield St. NG7: Nott 7E **94**
Greenfields Way S81: Carl L 5C **12**
Greenfinch Dale S81: Gate 5D **18**
Greenford Cl. NG16: Nuth 4K **83**
Greengate NG23: Syer 2A **140**
Greengates Av. NG3: Mapp 4C **86**
Greenhill Cres. NG4: Carl 2H **97**
Greenhill La. NG17: Nunc 4K **59**
Greenhill Ri. NG4: Carl 1H **97**
Greenhill Rd. NG4: Carl 2H **97**
Greenhills Av. NG16: Eastw 3E **72**
Greenhills Rd. NG16: Eastw 3D **72**
Greenholme Cl. NG17: Kirk A 7A **52**
Greenholme Pk. NG19: Mans W 3A **42**
Greenland Cres. NG9: Chil 5H **105**
Greenland Rd. NG17: Skeg 3J **45**
Green La. DE7: Ilk 1A **92**
DN10: Scro 7H **9**
DN22: Sth L 2H **25**
DN22: Tres 5H **25**
LE12: Will W 6F **143**
LE14: Hick, Hick P 1F **143** & 7D **142**
NG4: Lamb 5F **79**
NG11: Clif 7E **106**
NG13: Gran 1K **141**
NG18: Mans 7J **47**
NG19: Mans W 4B **42**
NG19: Plea 1K **45**
NG22: Dun T 6K **29**
NG22: Lax, Moor 7C **124**
NG22: Wale 4G **27**
NG23: Bath 6F **129**
NG23: Coll 4J **129**
NG23: Girt 4G **125**
S81: Carl L 6A **12**
Green Leys NG2: West Br 5K **107**
Green Mews, The NG5: Bestw 2H **85**
Green Mile La. DN22: Babw 4A **22**
Green Platt NG12: Cotg 6D **110**
Green Rd. DN10: Gri H 3C **16**
Greens Farm La. NG4: Ged 5K **87**
Greensfields NG17: Skeg 5A **46**
Green Side NG16: Sels 6B **58**
Greenside DN22: Ramp 6K **25**
Greenside Av. DN22: Ramp 6K **25**
Greenside Wlk. NG3: Nott 2F **97**
Greens La. NG16: Kimb 1E **82**

Green Sq. Rd.—Hambling Cl.

Green Sq. Rd. NG16: Pinx 2C 58
Green St. NG2: Nott 7A 96
NG11: Bart F, Thru 5A 114
Green's Windmill & Science Cen. 5K 7 (4C 96)
Greentrees Ct. NG17: Sut A 2H 51
Greenvale NG22: Farns 5K 57
Green Vw. Bungs. S81: Blyth 7G 13
Greenview Cl. NG19: Mans W 1D 48
Green Wlk. NG13: What 4D 102
Greenway DN22: Ord 7D 22
NG19: Mans W 6F 43
NG24: New T 4B 136
S81: Carl L 6D 12
Greenway, The NG10: Sand 3A 104
Greenway Cl. NG12: Rad T 5D 98
Greenwich Av. NG6: Basf 3D 84
Greenwich Pk. Cl. NG2: West Br 4K 107
Greenwood NG22: Bils 5C 126
Greenwood Av. DE7: Ilk 1A 92
DN11: Harwo 1C 8
NG3: Nott 3G 97
NG15: Huck 5F 67
NG17: Huth 1D 50
NG19: Mans W 5H 41
NG21: Edwin 6F 37
Greenwood Bonsai Studio 6G 69
Greenwood Cl. NG22: Farns 5K 57
S81: Gate 3E 18
Greenwood Cotts. NG18: Mans 2B 48
Greenwood Ct. NG9: Chil 4J 105
Greenwood Cres. NG4: Carl 2H 97
NG22: Bou 3E 38
Greenwood Dr. NG17: Kirk A 6J 51
Greenwood Gdns. NG8: Bilb 1H 93
NG11: Rudd 4A 116
Greenwood Rd. NG3: Nott 3D 96
NG4: Carl 3F 97
Greenwood Va. NG15: Huck 5E 66
Greet Ct. NG7: Radf 1E 94
Greet Lily Mill *NG25: Sout* *5J 131*
(off Mill Pk.)
Greet Pk. Cl. NG25: Sout 5J 131
Greetwell Cl. NG8: Bilb 2B 94
Gregory, The *NG7: Lent* *6F 95*
(off Leen Ct.)
Gregory Av. NG3: Mapp 5D 86
NG7: Lent 5G 95
Gregory Blvd. NG7: H Grn 1F 95
Gregory Cl. NG9: Stap 1E 104
Gregory Ct. NG7: H Grn 7G 85
NG7: Lent 5F 95
NG9: Chil 5G 105
Gregory Cres. DN11: Harwo 2B 8
Gregory Gdns. NG22: Farns 6K 57
Gregory St. NG7: Lent 5F 95
Gregson Gdns. NG9: Toton 7G 105
Gregson Rd. NG9: Chil 6F 105
Grenay Ct. NG11: Rudd 2J 115
Grendon Way NG17: Skeg 5B 46
Grenfell Ter. NG6: Basf 3F 85
Grenville Dr. NG9: Stap 1D 104
Grenville Ri. NG5: Arn 5H 77
Grenville Rd. NG9: Bee 5C 106
Gresham Cl. NG2: West Br 2K 107
NG17: Sut A 7K 45
NG24: New T 1H 137
Gresham Gdns. NG2: West Br 2A 108
NG5: Woodt 2D 86
Gresham Pk. Rd. NG2: West Br 2K 107
Gresley Dr. NG2: Nott 7K 7 (5C 96)
Gresley Rd. DN22: Retf 5D 22
Gretton Rd. NG3: Mapp 3D 86
Greyfriar Ga. NG1: Nott 7E 6 (5K 95)
GREY GREEN 1C 145
Greyhound St.
NG1: Nott 5F 7 (4K 95)
Greys Rd. NG5: Woodt 3C 86
Greystoke Dr. NG8: Bilb 1H 93
Grey St. NG16: Newth 5E 72
NG17: Kirk A 6H 51
Greythorn Dr. NG2: West Br 5A 108
Griceson Cl. NG22: Oll 6B 38
Grierson Av. NG5: Bestw 6D 76
Grieves Cl. DN22: Retf 5F 23
Griffins End NG13: What 5E 102
Griffiths Way NG15: Huck 7H 67
Griffs Hollow NG4: Carl 1H 97
Grimesmoor Rd. NG14: Calv 5E 70
Grimsby Ter. NG3: Nott 2F 7 (2K 95)
GRIMSTON 3B 148
Grimston Rd. NG7: Radf 2F 95
Grindle Ford Grange
NG18: Mans 5D 48
Grindon Cres. NG6: Bulw 4J 75
Gringley Ct. DN10: Gri H 3A 16
GRINGLEY ON THE HILL 3B 16 (2C 145)
Gringley Rd. DN10: Beck 6A 16
DN10: Gri H 6J 15
DN10: Mist 4F 11
DN10: Walk 7F 11
DN22: Clay, Gri H 6J 15
Gringley Vw. DN10: Harwe 5A 10
Grinsbrook NG7: Lent 4F 95
Gripps, The *NG12: Cotg* *7E 110*
(off Owthorpe Rd.)
Gripps Comn. NG12: Cotg 7E 110
Grisedale Ct. NG9: Chil 5F 105
Gritley M. NG2: Nott 6J 95
Grives La. NG17: Kirk A 2B 60
Grizedale Cl. NG19: Mans W 2D 48
Grizedale Gro. NG13: Bing 4C 100
Grizedale Ri. NG19: Mans W 2C 48
Grosvenor Av. NG3: Mapp P 6K 85
NG17: Sut A 1H 51
Grosvenor Cl. DN22: Retf 6G 23
NG12: Rad T 5J 99
Grosvenor Ct. NG3: Mapp P 7K 85
Grosvenor Pl. *NG17: Sut A* *1H 51*
(off Grosvenor Av.)
Grosvenor Rd. DN11: Birc 2E 8
NG16: Eastw 3D 72
NG24: New B 5E 136
S81: Lango 1C 12
Grouville Dr. NG5: Woodt 2D 86
GROVE 1C 147
Grove, The DN10: Beck 6C 16
NG5: Sher 5J 85
NG7: Radf 1A 6 (2G 95)
NG14: Calv 6E 70
NG15: Ann 4B 60
S81: Work 5G 19
Grove Av. NG7: Radf 1A 6 (2H 95)
NG9: Chil 3K 105
Grove Cl. NG14: Bur J 2E 88
Grove Coach Rd. DN22: Retf 6G 23
(not continuous)
Grove Cotts. NG19: Plea 4B 40
NG24: New T 2F 137
Grove Ct. NG9: Chil 3J 105
S80: Work 3F 21
Grove Dr. DN22: Grove 6K 23
Grove La. DN22: Lit G, Retf 3G 23
Grove Leisure Cen. 3F 137
Grove M. NG16: Eastw 5C 72
Grove Pk. DN10: Mist 3H 11
Grover Av. NG3: Mapp 4D 86
Grove Rd. DN22: Grove, Retf 7G 23
NG7: Lent 5G 95
NG13: Bing 3G 101
NG17: Sut A 7B 46
NG20: Chu W 2C 34
Groveside Cres. NG11: Clif 6D 106
Grove St. DN22: Retf 3F 23
NG9: Bee 4B 106
NG18: Mans 4H 47
NG19: Mans W 6H 41
NG24: New B 4E 136
Groveview Rd. NG24: New B 4F 137
Grove Way NG19: Mans W 6H 41
Grovewood Cl. DN10: Mist 4H 11
Grovewood Rd. DN10: Mist 3H 11
Grovewood Ter. DN10: Mist 3H 11
Grundy Av. NG16: Sels 5B 58
Grundy St. NG7: H Grn 1F 95
Guardian Ct. NG8: Aspl 7D 84
Guildford Av. NG19: Mans W 3J 41
Guildhall Dr. NG16: Sels 2C 58
Guildhall St. NG24: New T 1D 136
GUNBY 3D 149
Gunn Cl. NG6: Bulw 7G 75
Gunnersbury Way
NG16: Nuth 4J 83
GUNNESS 1D 145
GUNTHORPE
Gainsborough 2D 145
Nottingham 2B 90 (1B 148)
Gunthorpe Cl. NG5: Sher 4J 85
Gunthorpe Ct. NG18: Mans 7D 48
Gunthorpe Dr. NG5: Sher 4J 85
Gunthorpe Rd. NG4: Ged 4F 87
NG14: Lowd 6E 80
Gutersloh Ct. NG9: Stap 1E 104
Guy Cl. NG9: Stap 3D 104
Guylers Hill Dr. NG21: C'tone 7H 43
Gwenbrook Av. NG9: Chil 4K 105
Gwenbrook Rd. NG9: Chil 4K 105
Gwndy Gdns. NG5: Bestw 7C 76
Gypsum Way NG11: Goth 7F 115
Gypsy La. NG14: Blea 2C 138
NG25: Fis 2C 138

H

H2 Fitness
Nottingham 3F 7 (3K 95)
HABBLESTHORPE 6D 24 (3C 145)
Habblesthorpe Cl. DN22: Habb 6D 24
Habblesthorpe Rd. DN22: Habb 6D 24
Habitat, The NG1: Nott 5G 7
Hackers Cl. NG13: East B 4D 90
Hack La. NG17: Sut A 1J 51
Hackworth Cl. NG16: Newth 3F 73
Hadbury Rd. NG5: Sher 4G 85
Hadden Ct. NG8: Bilb 3J 93
HADDINGTON 2D 147
Haddon Cl. NG4: Carl 5G 87
NG15: Huck 7G 67
NG16: Sels 5E 58
Haddon Ct. NG4: Ged 6A 88
Haddon Cres. NG9: Chil 6H 105
Haddon Dr. NG24: Bald 6G 137
Haddon Rd. DN22: Retf 6H 23
NG2: West Br 3C 108
NG15: Rave 1C 62
NG19: Mans 2H 47
Haddon St. NG5: Sher 5J 85
NG17: Sut A 6J 45
Haddon Way NG12: Rad T 4F 99
Hades La. LE12: Will W, Wym 7F 143
Hadfield Wlk. *NG18: Mans* *4D 48*
(off Edale Rd.)
Hadleigh Cl. NG9: Toton 7D 104
Hadley St. DE7: Ilk 3A 92
Hadrian Gdns. NG5: Top V 4C 76
Hadstock Cl. NG10: Sand 5A 104
Hagg La. NG14: Epp 1B 80
Haggnook Wood NG15: Rave 1K 61
Haggonfields S80: Rhod 1B 20
Hagley Cl. NG3: Nott 2D 96
Haileybury Cres. NG2: West Br 4C 108
Haileybury Rd. NG2: West Br 4C 108
Haise Ct. NG6: Bulw 2A 84
HALAM 4C 130 (3B 146)
Halam Cl. NG19: Mans 3D 46
Halam Hill NG22: Halam 5C 130
NG25: Sout 5C 130
Halam Rd. NG25: Sout 5D 130
Halberton Dr. NG2: West Br 5A 108
Haldon Way S81: Gate 4D 18
Hales Cl. NG12: Cotg 6D 110
Halfmoon Dr. NG17: Kirk A 1A 60
Halfpenny Wlk. NG11: Wilf 3H 107
Halifax Av. NG20: Chu W 1D 34
Halifax Ct. NG8: Stre 5J 83
NG24: Bald 7H 137
Halifax Dr. S81: Work 4F 19
Halifax Pl. NG1: Nott 6G 7 (4A 96)
Halina Ct. NG9: Bee 2A 106
HALLAM FIELDS 1A 148
Hallam Flds. Rd. DE7: Ilk 4A 92
Hallam Rd. NG3: Mapp 5D 86
NG9: Bee 3A 106
NG22: New O 2D 38
Hallams La. NG5: Arn 7H 77
NG9: Chil 5H 105
Hallam Way NG16: Lang M 3A 72
Hallamway NG19: Mans W 1J 47
Hall Barn La. NG19: Mans 2D 46
Hall Cl. NG12: Rad T 5D 98
NG21: Rain 3K 55
NG22: Farns 6J 57
Hall Close, The NG22: East M 2D 28
Hall Cft. NG9: Bee 4A 106
Hallcroft Av. DN22: Retf 2E 22
Hallcroft Ind. Est. DN22: Retf 1D 22
Hallcroft Rd. DN22: Retf 1C 22
Hall Dr. DN22: Clay 6H 15
NG5: Arn 6J 77
NG8: Woll 5K 93
NG9: Chil 4H 105
NG10: Sand 3A 104
NG11: Goth 7F 115
NG12: Crop Bi 5B 112
S80: Work 3E 20
Hall Farm NG24: Codd 6K 135
Hall Farm Cl. NG12: Toll 1G 117
Hall Farm Ct. NG2: Gam 2F 109
Hallfields NG12: Edwal 6E 108
Hall Gdns. LE12: East L 4B 122
NG9: Bram 2G 105
HALL GREEN 4C 58
Hall Grounds NG12: Cols B 6G 141
Hall Grounds Dr.
NG12: Cols B 6G 141
Halliday Cl. S80: Work 2E 20
Halliwell Cl. NG24: New T 4E 134
Hall La. NG12: Cols B 7G 141
NG12: Kin 1C 142
NG15: Pap 7K 61
NG16: Brins 6B 64
NG22: East M 3D 28
NG22: Lax 5A 124
Hall Mews NG15: Pap 1K 67
HALLOUGHTON 3B 146
Halloughton Rd. NG25: Sout 6G 131
Hallowell Dr. NG8: Woll 2A 94
Hall Pk. Dr. NG16: Eastw 3C 72
Hall Rd. NG16: Lang M 2A 72
Halls Brook LE12: East L 2A 122
Halls La. NG16: Newth 6E 72
Halls Rd. DN10: Gri H 2C 16
NG9: Stap 3C 104
Hall St. NG5: Sher 4A 86
NG17: Skeg 4J 45
NG18: Mans 4A 48
Hall Vw. DN10: Matt 2H 15
S80: Work 3E 20
Hall Vw. Dr. NG8: Bilb 2J 93
Halstead Cl. NG8: Cin 4C 84
NG9: Chil 5H 105
NG19: Mans W 7B 42
Haltham Wlk. NG11: Clif 2E 114
Hamble Cl. NG19: Mans W 6K 41
Hambledon Dr. NG8: Woll 3C 94
Hambleton Ct. S81: Carl L 5B 12
Hambleton Ri. NG19: Mans W 1B 48
Hambling Cl. NG6: Bulw 7G 75

Hamilton, The—Hawkins Cl.

Hamilton, The *NG7: Lent 6F 95*
(off Leen Ct.)
Hamilton Cl. NG5: Arn 5A 78
NG9: Toton 7E 104
Hamilton Ct. NG7: Nott 7C 6 (5J 95)
NG11: Clif 6G 107
NG18: Mans 6F 47
Hamilton Dr. NG7: Nott 7C 6 (5J 95)
NG12: Rad T 4E 98
NG20: Mkt W 4C 34
Hamilton Gdns. *NG5: Sher 6J 85*
(off Alexandra St.)
Hamilton Pl. NG2: Nott 4C 96
NG18: Mans 6F 47
Hamilton Rd. NG5: Sher 7J 85
NG17: Sut A 1C 52
Hamilton St. NG18: Mans 4A 48
S81: Work 6E 18
Hamilton Way NG18: Mans 7E 46
Hammer Leys DE55: Sth N 7A 50
Hammersmith Cl.
NG12: Rad T 6J 99
NG16: Nuth 3K 83
Hammerwater Dr. NG20: Mkt W 5C 34
Hammond Gro. NG17: Kirk A 2B 60
Hampden NG1: Nott 2D 6 (2J 95)
Hampden Gro. NG9: Bee 3K 105
Hampden Rd. NG13: Newton 1C 100
Hampdens Cl. NG24: Codd 6H 135
Hampden St. NG1: Nott 2D 6 (2J 95)
NG16: Gilt 6F 73
NG17: Kirk A 6K 51
HAMPOLE 1A 144
Hampshire Ct. NG16: Jack 6A 64
Hampshire Dr. NG10: Sand 4A 104
Hampstead Ct. *NG5: Sher 4K 85*
(off St Albans St.)
Hampstead Rd. NG3: Nott 6B 86
Hampton Cl. NG9: Toton 6D 104
Hampton Rd. NG2: West Br 3B 108
Hanbury Ct. NG18: Mans 4D 48
Handel St. NG3: Nott 4J 7 (3B 96)
Handford Ct. NG25: Sout 6F 131
Handley Arc. NG18: Mans 3H 47
Handley Ct. NG24: New T 7C 134
HANDSTUBBIN 6D 58
Hanger Hill Dr. NG20: Mkt W 6K 33
Hangingside La. DN22: Hay 5J 17
Hankin Av. NG16: Unde 3E 64
Hankin St. NG15: Huck 7J 67
Hanley Av. NG9: Bram 1G 105
Hanley St. NG1: Nott 4D 6 (3J 95)
Hannah Cres. NG11: Wilf 2J 107
Hannah Pk. Vw. S80: Work 5H 21
Hanover Cl. NG19: Mans W 2B 48
Hanover Ct. NG8: Bilb 2J 93
Hanselin Ct. NG4: Ged 6K 87
Hanslope Cres. NG8: Bilb 2J 93
Hanson Cres. NG15: Huck 6G 67
Hanstubbin Rd. NG16: Sels 6D 58
Hanworth Gdns. NG5: Arn 6F 77
Happy Days Play Den
Kirkby-in-Ashfield *6B 52*
(off Station St.)
Harberton Cl. NG5: Redh 5G 77
HARBY
Melton Mowbray 2C 149
Newark 6K 31 (1D 147)
Harby Av. NG17: Sut A 2C 52
NG19: Mans W 4K 41
Harby Cl. NG24: Bald 6G 137
Harby Dr. NG8: Woll 4D 94
Harby La. NG12: Cols B 7J 141
Harby Rd. NG13: Lang 7K 113
NG23: Harby, Wigs 7G 31
Harcourt Cres. NG16: Nuth 4A 84
Harcourt Pl. DN22: Retf 6G 23
Harcourt Rd. NG7: H Grn 7H 85
Harcourt St. NG9: Bee 3K 105
NG17: Kirk A 6A 52
NG18: Mans 4K 47
NG24: New T 2E 136
Harcourt Ter. NG3: Nott 3H 7 (3A 96)
Harden Ct. NG11: Clif 2D 114
Hardigate Rd. NG12: Crop Bu 1A 112
Hardstaff Almshouses NG4: Ged 5H 87
Hardstaff Cl. DN22: Retf 1C 22
NG17: Ann W 3J 59
Hardstaff Homes, The NG16: Gilt 6G 73
NG19: Mans W 6H 41
Hardstaff Rd. NG2: Nott 3D 96
HARDWICK 3A 144
Hardwick Av. NG17: Skeg 4A 46
NG21: Rain 2H 55
NG24: New T 2C 136
Hardwick Cl. NG17: Skeg 4A 46
Hardwick Ct. DE55: Sth N 5A 50
DN11: Birc 1E 8
Hardwick Cres. S80: Work 3J 21
Hardwick Dr. NG16: Sels 5F 59
NG22: Oll 5A 38
Hardwicke Rd. NG9: Chil 6H 105
Hardwick Gro. NG2: West Br 7C 96
NG7: Nott 6A 6 (4H 95)
NG13: Bing 4E 100
Hardwick La. NG17: Sut A 1K 51
Hardwick Rd. NG5: Sher 4K 85
NG7: Nott 7A 6 (5H 95)
Hardwick Rd. E. S80: Work 3J 21
Hardwick Rd. W. S80: Work 3J 21
Hardwick St. NG17: Sut A 1K 51
NG18: Mans 3K 47
NG20: Langw 7A 26
Hardwick Vw. NG17: Skeg 4A 46
HARDWICK VILLAGE 1B 146
Hardwood Cl. NG6: Bulw 7G 75
Hardy Cl. NG16: Kimb 7K 73
Hardy Pl. NG18: Mans 4F 47
Hardys Cl. NG12: Crop Bi 5C 112
Hardy's Dr. NG4: Ged 6J 87
Hardy St. NG7: Radf 1A 6 (2H 95)
NG16: Kimb 7K 73
S80: Work 3F 21
Hardy Way LE12: East L 1A 122
Harebell Cl. NG17: Kirk A 1A 60
Harebell Gdns. NG13: Bing 4D 100
Harefield LE12: East L 1A 122
Hareholme St. NG19: Mans 2G 47
Harewood Av. DN22: Retf 5C 22
NG6: Bulw 2E 84
NG24: New T 2C 136
Harewood Cl. NG10: Sand 5A 104
NG12: Rad T 5F 99
Harewood Ct. DN11: Birc 1E 8
Harewood Rd. S81: Work 5G 19
Hargon La. NG24: Wint 2G 135
Harkstead Rd. NG5: Top V 5D 76
HARLAXTON 2D 149
Harlaxton Dr. NG7: Lent 5A 6 (4G 95)
(not continuous)
Harlaxton Wlk. NG3: Nott 1F 7 (2K 95)
Harlech Ri. NG9: Chil 5G 105
HARLEQUIN 5G 99 (2B 148)
Harlequin Cl. NG12: Rad T 5G 99
Harlequin Ct. NG16: Eastw 3B 72
Harlequin M. NG12: Rad T 4G 99
Harles Acres LE14: Hick 6E 142
Harley Cl. S80: Work 5F 21
Harley Gallery, The 1B 26
Harley St. NG7: Lent 5G 95
HARLINGTON 1A 144
Harlow Av. NG18: Mans 7J 47
Harlow Cl. NG17: Skeg 4K 45
NG19: Mans W 3J 41
Harlow Gro. NG4: Ged 5H 87
Harlow St. NG21: Blid 6K 55
Harlow Ter. DN22: Ord 5E 22
Harmans Wlk. *NG25: Sout 6H 131*
(off Queen St.)
Harmston Ri. NG5: Sher 3G 85
(not continuous)
Harnett Cl. NG1: Nott 6G 7 (4A 96)
Harold Ct. NG2: Nott 5K 7 (4B 96)
Harold La. NG22: East M 2B 28
Harold St. NG2: Nott 5K 7 (4B 96)
Harpenden Sq. NG8: Cin 4B 84
Harpole Wlk. NG5: Arn 4H 77
HARPSWELL 3D 145
Harrier Gro. NG15: Huck 2E 74
Harriers Gro. NG17: Sut A 6B 46
Harriett St. NG9: Stap 2C 104
Harrimans Ct. NG7: Lent 1F 107
Harrimans La. NG7: Lent 1E 106
Harrington Cl. NG4: Ged 6A 88
Harrington Dr. NG7: Lent 6A 6 (4G 95)
(not continuous)
Harrington St. NG18: Mans 4F 47
S80: Work 3E 20
Harris Cl. NG8: Woll 3A 94
Harrison Ct. NG13: Bing 4D 100
Harrison Dr. S81: Lango 1B 12
Harrison Dr. Bus. Cen. S81: Lango 1C 12
Harrison Rd. NG9: Stap 1C 104
NG18: Mans 4E 46
Harrison's Plantation Nature Reserve 3B 94
Harrisons Way NG24: New T 7E 134
Harris Rd. NG9: Chil 3J 105
NG17: Kirk A 6D 52
Harrogate Rd. NG3: Nott 3F 97
Harrogate St. NG4: Neth 1J 97
Harrop White Rd. NG19: Mans 2F 47
Harrowby M. NG7: Lent 4G 95
Harrowby Rd. NG7: Lent 6A 6 (4G 95)
Harrow Cl. NG21: Rain 3J 55
Harrow Gdns. NG8: Woll 4D 94
Harrow La. NG22: Bou 3F 39
Harrow La. Caravan Site NG22: Bou 3F 39
Harrow Rd. NG2: West Br 4B 108
NG8: Woll 4B 94
NG15: Huck 1D 74
Harry Peel Ct. NG9: Bee 3B 106
Harstoft Av. S81: Work 7G 19
HARSTON 2D 149
Harston Gdns. NG2: West Br 6J 107
Hart Av. NG10: Sand 3A 104
Hartcroft Rd. NG5: Bestw 1H 85
Hartford Cl. NG2: Nott 6A 96
HARTHILL 3A 144
Harthill Dr. NG19: Mans 5D 46
Hartill Cl. NG9: Chil 7H 105
Hartington Av. NG4: Carl 6G 87
NG15: Huck 7C 66
Hartington Ct. NG18: Mans 4D 48
Hartington Dr. NG16: Sels 5E 58
NG17: Sut A 6B 46
Hartington Rd. NG5: Sher 4K 85
Hartington St. NG20: Langw 7A 26
Hartland Rd. S80: Work 3F 21
Hart Lea NG10: Sand 3A 104
(Charles Av.)
NG10: Sand 3A 104
(Hall Dr.)
Hartley Ct. NG7: Radf 2G 95
Hartley Dr. NG9: Bee 3C 106
Hartley Rd. NG7: Radf 2F 95
NG17: Kirk A 5K 51
Hartness Rd. NG11: Clif 1D 114
Harton Cl. NG17: Skeg 4H 45
Hartside Cl. NG2: Gam 2F 109
Hartside Way DE75: Hea 5A 72
Hart St. NG7: Lent 5G 95
Hartwell St. NG3: Nott 1G 7 (2A 96)
Hartwood Dr. NG9: Stap 7C 92
Harvard Ct. NG22: New O 5D 38
Harvest Cl. NG5: Top V 6B 76
NG13: Bing 4E 100
S81: Carl L 5C 12
S81: Work 5J 19
Harvest Dr. NG24: New T 4F 135
Harvest La. NG17: Huth 2E 50
Harvey Cl. NG11: Rudd 5A 116
Harvey Ct. NG7: Nott 6F 95
Harvey Cft. NG9: Trow 4B 92
Harvey Hadden Sports Complex 1A 94
Harvey Hadden Stadium 1A 94
Harvey Rd. NG7: Nott 6E 94
NG8: Bilb 1A 94
NG18: Mans 5A 48
Harvey's Fld. NG25: Sout 6H 131
HARWELL 5A 10
Harwell La. DN10: Harwe 5A 10
Harwell Sluice La. DN10: Harwe 4A 10
Harwich Cl. NG6: Bulw 6G 75
Harwill Cres. NG8: Aspl 5C 84
Harwood Cl. NG5: Arn 6K 77
NG17: Sut A 6A 46
Harwood Pl. NG17: Sut A 6A 46
HARWORTH 2C 8 (2B 144)
Harworth Av. S81: Blyth 7D 8
Harworth Cl. NG19: Mans 4D 46
Harworth Pk. Ind. Est. DN11: Harwo 5D 8
Harworth Rd. S81: Blyth 7D 8
Haslam Ho. NG24: New T 5C 136
Haslam St. NG7: Nott 7D 6 (5J 95)
Haslehurst Gdns. S80: Work 3F 21
Haslemere Gdns. NG15: Rave 2B 62
Haslemere Rd. NG8: Aspl 7E 84
Hassall Ct. NG13: Bing 4G 101
Hassock La. Nth. DE75: Ship 7A 72
Hassocks Cl. NG9: Bee 2C 106
Hassocks La. NG9: Bee 2C 106
Hassop Wlk. *NG18: Mans 4D 48*
(off Edale Rd.)
Hastings St. NG4: Carl 1F 97
Haswell Rd. NG6: Bulw 2C 84
Hatchet's La. NG24: New T 5D 134
HATFIELD 1B 144
Hatfield Av. NG10: Sand 5A 104
NG20: Mede V 7H 33
Hatfield Cl. NG21: Rain 2K 55
Hatfield Dr. NG2: West Br 5K 107
Hatfield La. NG25: Oxt 1E 70
Hatfield Rd. NG3: Mapp P 6K 85
Hatfield St. DN22: Retf 4G 23
HATFIELD WOODHOUSE 1B 144
Hatherleigh Cl. NG3: Mapp 1F 87
HATHERN 3A 148
Hathern Grn. NG9: Lent A 1B 106
Hathernware Ind. Est. LE12: Norm S 7C 120
Hathersage Cl. NG5: Top V 6B 76
Hathersage Ri. NG15: Rave 1C 62
Hathersage Wlk. *NG18: Mans 4D 48*
(off Hindlow Ct.)
Hathersage Way NG17: Sut A 6J 45
Hatley Cl. NG2: Nott 7J 95
Hatton Cl. NG5: Arn 4C 76
NG23: Nth M 6K 129
Hatton Ct. NG18: Mans 4D 48
Hatton Gdns. NG16: Nuth 4K 83
NG24: New T 2D 136
Haughgate Hill DN22: Nth W 1F 17
HAUGHTON 1B 146
Havelock Gdns.
NG3: Nott 2H 7 (2A 96)
Haven, The NG22: Kirt 7J 27
S81: Carl L 6D 12
Haven Cl. NG2: West Br 4A 108
NG17: Sut A 7H 45
NG21: C'tone 6H 43
Havenwood Ri. NG11: Clif 2E 114
Haverhill Cres. NG5: Top V 4K 75
Haversham Cl. NG6: Basf 5E 84
Hawarden Ter. NG7: H Grn 1G 95
Hawbush Rd. NG23: Weston 1F 125
Hawker Cl. NG9: Chil 4G 105
Hawkhill Cl. NG22: Oll 6A 38
Hawkhurst Dr. NG8: Woll 6J 93
Hawkins Cl. DN11: Harwo 1D 8

Hawkridge Gdns. NG3: Nott . . . 3H 7 (3B 96)
(not continuous)
Hawkshead Cl. NG2: West Br . . . 4G 109
Hawksley Gdns. NG11: Clif . . . 7D 106
Hawksley Rd. NG7: H Grn . . . 1G 95
Hawkswood Cl. NG9: Chil . . . 5G 105
HAWKSWORTH . . . 1C 149
Hawksworth Av. NG5: Sher . . . 3A 86
NG19: Mans W . . . 1D 48
Hawksworth Rd. NG2: West Br . . . 7C 96
NG13: Scar . . . 1C 102
NG23: Syer . . . 4B 140
Hawksworth St. NG3: Nott . . . 4K 7 (3B 96)
Hawley Cl. LE12: East L . . . 3B 122
Hawley Mt. NG5: Sher . . . 4C 86
Haworth Ct. NG11: Clif . . . 1D 114
Haworth Ind. Est. DN11: Harwo . . . 4D 8
Hawson Way S81: Gate . . . 5D 18
Hawthorn Cl. DN10: Beck . . . 7C 16
NG2: Nott . . . 7J 95
NG12: Edwal . . . 5E 108
NG12: Key . . . 1H 119
NG12: Shel . . . 6H 89
NG14: Blea . . . 2C 138
NG14: Woodbo . . . 2G 79
NG19: Mans W . . . 4A 42
NG22: New O . . . 3D 38
Hawthorn Cres. NG5: Arn . . . 5J 77
NG17: Kirk A . . . 5A 52
Hawthorn Cft. DN10: Mist . . . 2J 11
Hawthorn Dr. NG22: New O . . . 3D 38
Hawthorne Av. NG9: Stap . . . 3C 104
NG12: Cotg . . . 7E 110
NG15: Huck . . . 6F 67
Hawthorne Cl. DN22: Nth L . . . 7C 24
NG17: Stant H . . . 4G 45
Hawthorne Ct. DN22: Ord . . . 6E 22
Hawthorne Cres. NG24: Farnd . . . 7H 133
Hawthorne Gro. NG9: Bee . . . 3C 106
Hawthorne Leys NG23: Norm T . . . 1K 125
Hawthorne Lodge NG2: West Br . . . 7E 96
Hawthorne Ri. NG16: Aws . . . 3A 82
Hawthorne Rd. NG16: Pinx . . . 1B 58
Hawthorne Way NG21: Edwin . . . 7H 37
Hawthorns, The NG17: Kirk A . . . 5K 51
NG20: Mkt W . . . 4C 34
NG22: Dun T . . . 6J 29
NG22: Wale . . . 5G 27
Hawthorn Vw. NG2: Nott . . . 6J 95
Hawthorn Wlk. NG3: Nott . . . 1E 96
Hawthorn Way S81: Carl L . . . 5B 12
HAWTON . . . 6A 136 (3C 147)
Hawton Cl. NG19: Mans . . . 1F 47
Hawton Cres. NG8: Woll . . . 4D 94
Hawton La. NG24: Farnd . . . 7H 133
NG24: New B . . . 5D 136
Hawton Rd. NG24: New T . . . 5A 136
Hawton Spinney NG8: Woll . . . 4D 94
HAXEY . . . 2C 145
Haxey Rd. DN10: Mist . . . 2H 11
Haycroft Cl. NG19: Mans W . . . 4K 41
Haycroft Way NG13: East B . . . 4D 90
Hayden La. NG15: Lin . . . 3H 67
Haydn Av. NG5: Sher . . . 5J 85
Haydn Rd. NG5: Sher . . . 5H 85
Haydock Cl. NG16: Kimb . . . 7J 73
Hayes Cl. NG16: Pinx . . . 1A 58
Hayes Ct. DN22: Rans . . . 2J 13
Hayes Rd. NG12: Key . . . 7G 117
Hayfield Gro. NG23: Weston . . . 3F 125
Hay Fields, The NG21: Rain . . . 2K 55
Hayles Cl. NG5: Bestw . . . 1J 85
Hayley Cl. NG16: Kimb . . . 1C 82
Hayling Dr. NG8: Basf . . . 6E 84
Hayloft, The NG18: Mans . . . 6K 47
Hayman Cl. NG19: Mans W . . . 6J 41
Haynes Av. NG9: Trow . . . 3B 92
Haynes Cl. NG11: Clif . . . 6G 107
NG22: Tuxf . . . 6D 28
Hayside Av. NG24: Bald . . . 6E 136
HAYTON . . . 6H 17 (3C 145)
Haywood Av. NG21: Blid . . . 6J 55
Haywood Ct. NG2: Nott . . . 5J 7 (4B 96)
NG21: Rain . . . 1G 55
Haywood Oaks La. NG21: Blid . . . 7J 55
Haywood Rd. NG3: Mapp . . . 5C 86
Haywoods, The NG20: Chu W . . . 2D 34
Haywood St. NG2: Nott . . . 5J 7 (4B 96)
Hayworth Rd. NG10: Sand . . . 4A 104
Hazelas Dr. NG14: Gun . . . 2B 90
Hazel Bank NG19: Mans W . . . 2A 48
Hazelbank Av. NG3: Nott . . . 6C 86
Hazel Cl. NG2: West Br . . . 7F 97
NG13: Bing . . . 4H 101
Hazel Ct. NG21: Blid . . . 5K 55
Hazel Dr. NG16: Nuth . . . 1G 83
Hazelford Way NG15: News . . . 5D 60
HAZELGROVE . . . 2H 75
Hazel Gro. DE55: Sth N . . . 6A 50
NG3: Mapp . . . 3D 86
NG15: Huck . . . 1G 75
NG17: Kirk A . . . 6C 52
NG19: Mans W . . . 4H 41
NG21: Edwin . . . 7F 37
NG24: New B . . . 4F 137
Hazel Hill Cres. NG5: Bestw . . . 6D 76
Hazelhurst Gdns. NG6: Bulw . . . 7H 75
Hazel Mdws. NG15: Huck . . . 1G 75
Hazelmere Gro. NG7: Lent . . . 4F 95
Hazel Rd. NG22: New O . . . 3D 38
Hazel St. NG6: Bulw . . . 6H 75
(not continuous)
NG17: Skeg . . . 3H 45
Hazel Way NG15: Lin . . . 3H 67
Hazelwood NG12: Cotg . . . 6F 111
Hazelwood Cl. NG16: Newth . . . 4F 73
NG19: Mans W . . . 7D 42
Hazelwood Dr. NG15: Huck . . . 7C 66
Hazelwood Gro. S80: Work . . . 3C 20
Hazelwood Rd. NG7: H Grn . . . 1F 95
Headingley Gdns. NG8: Aspl . . . 7E 84
Headingley Rd. DN22: Ord . . . 6E 22
Headland Av. DN22: Elk . . . 2F 27
Headland La. DN22: Rans . . . 2K 13
Headlands La. DN22: Rans . . . 3J 13
HEADON . . . 1C 147
Headstocks, The NG17: Huth . . . 1E 50
Healdswood St. NG17: Skeg . . . 3H 45
Healey Cl. NG2: Nott . . . 6K 95
NG23: Coll . . . 2H 129
Heanor Wlk. *NG18: Mans . . . 4D 48*
(off Hanbury Ct.)
HEAPHAM . . . 3D 145
Heard Cres. NG9: Bee . . . 1A 106
HEATH . . . 2A 146
Heath, The NG16: Gilt . . . 6E 72
Heath Av. NG18: Mans . . . 3D 48
Heathcoat Bldg. NG7: Nott . . . 7E 94
Heathcoat Ho. NG1: Nott . . . 6G 7 (4A 96)
Heathcoat St. NG1: Nott . . . 5G 7 (4A 96)
Heathcote Ct. NG17: Sut A . . . 2J 51
Heathcote Pl. NG17: Sut A . . . 2A 52
Heather Cl. NG3: Nott . . . 1A 96
NG16: Newth . . . 5F 73
NG17: Kirk A . . . 4K 51
NG18: Mans . . . 4G 47
Heather Ct. DE75: Hea . . . 5A 72
Heather Cft. NG2: West Br . . . 5K 107
Heatherington Gdns. NG5: Top V . . . 5C 76
Heather La. NG15: Rave . . . 4D 62
Heatherley Dr. NG6: Basf . . . 3G 85
NG19: Mans W . . . 1A 48
Heather Ri. NG9: Bram . . . 7K 93
Heather Rd. NG4: Carl . . . 6G 87
Heathers, The NG22: Bou . . . 3E 38
Heathervale NG2: West Br . . . 3J 107
Heather Way NG18: Mans . . . 4C 48
Heathfield Av. DE7: Ilk . . . 7A 82
Heathfield Ct. NG17: Kirk A . . . 4J 51
Heathfield Gdns. DN22: Retf . . . 2E 22
Heathfield Gro. NG9: Chil . . . 6H 105
Heathfield Rd. NG5: Sher . . . 3G 85
Heathfield Way NG18: Mans . . . 5K 47
Heathland Cl. NG18: Mans . . . 4C 48
Heaton Cl. NG3: Nott . . . 6C 86
NG24: New T . . . 1G 137
Heavenside LE12: East L . . . 1A 122
Heavytrees Av. NG15: Rave . . . 3C 62
Hecadeck La. LE14: Neth B . . . 4K 143
HECKDYKE . . . 2C 145
Heckington Dr. NG8: Woll . . . 3C 94
Hedderley Wlk. NG3: Nott . . . 2G 7 (2A 96)
Heddington Gdns. NG5: Arn . . . 6F 77
Heddon Bar NG19: Mans W . . . 6A 42
Hedgerow Cl. NG17: Sut A . . . 2G 51
Hedgerows, The NG21: Rain . . . 2K 55
Hedley St. NG7: Basf . . . 7H 85
Hedley Vs. NG7: Basf . . . 6H 85
Helen Cl. NG9: Chil . . . 3J 105
Hellebore Cl. NG5: Top V . . . 7A 76
Helm Cl. NG6: Bulw . . . 7F 75
Helmsdale Cl. NG5: Arn . . . 5K 77
NG19: Mans . . . 5E 46
Helmsdale Gdns. NG5: Top V . . . 5B 76
Helmsley Dr. NG16: Eastw . . . 3B 72
Helmsley Rd. NG21: Rain . . . 1G 55
Helston Dr. NG8: Stre . . . 5J 83
Helvellyn Cl. NG2: West Br . . . 6K 95
Helvellyn Way NG10: Long E . . . 7A 104
HEMINGTON . . . 3A 148
Hemingway Cl. NG4: Carl . . . 1F 97
NG16: Newth . . . 5G 73
Hemlock Av. NG9: Stap . . . 1D 104
NG10: Long E . . . 7C 104
Hemlock Gdns. NG6: Bulw . . . 1A 84
Hemmingfield Cl. S81: Work . . . 4G 19
Hemmingfield Cres. S81: Work . . . 4G 19
Hemmingfield Ri. S81: Work . . . 4G 19
Hemmingfield Rd. S81: Work . . . 5G 19
Hemmingfield Way S81: Work . . . 4H 19
Hemplands, The NG23: Coll . . . 1H 129
Hemplands La. NG23: Sut T . . . 3C 128
Hempshill Barns NG6: Bulw . . . 2K 83
Hempshill La. NG6: Bulw . . . 1C 84
(Lillington Rd.)
NG6: Bulw . . . 1A 84
(Rochester Ct.)
HEMPSHILL VALE . . . 2A 84
Hemsby Ct. NG5: Arn . . . 1C 86
Hemsby Gdns. NG6: Bulw . . . 6H 75
(not continuous)
Hemscott Cl. NG6: Bulw . . . 6F 75
HEMSWELL . . . 2D 145
HEMSWELL CLIFF . . . 3D 145
Hemswell Cl. NG3: Nott . . . 3D 96
Hen & Chicken Yd. NG24: Barn W . . . 7K 137
Hendon Ct. NG3: Nott . . . 7C 86
Hendon Ri. NG3: Nott . . . 7C 86
Hendre Gdns. NG5: Top V . . . 7C 76
Henfrey Dr. NG15: Ann . . . 5D 60
Henley Cl. NG4: Neth . . . 2K 97
Henley Gdns. NG9: Stap . . . 7D 92
Henley Ri. NG5: Sher . . . 4H 85
Hennessey Cl. NG9: Chil . . . 7H 105
Henning Gdns. NG5: Top V . . . 6C 76
Henning La. NG17: Sut A . . . 2F 51
Henrietta St. NG6: Bulw . . . 1D 84
Henry Av. NG19: Mans W . . . 4H 41
Henry Ct. NG2: Nott . . . 6K 95
Henry Rd. NG2: West Br . . . 1B 108
NG7: Lent . . . 5G 95
NG9: Bee . . . 3B 106
Henry St. NG2: Nott . . . 5K 7 (4B 96)
NG5: Redh . . . 4G 77
NG15: Huck . . . 7H 67
NG17: Sut A . . . 2K 51
Henson Cl. NG12: Rad T . . . 5K 99
Henson La. NG12: Crop Bu, Rad T . . . 4K 99
Hensons Row NG6: Basf . . . 5E 84
Hensons Sq. NG9: Bram . . . 1G 105
(not continuous)
Henton Cl. NG24: Codd . . . 6H 135
Henton Rd. NG21: Edwin . . . 7F 37
Hepple Dr. NG6: Bulw . . . 7F 75
Herald Cl. NG9: Bee . . . 2C 106
Herbert Buzzard Ct. *NG15: Huck . . . 7J 67*
(off Hankin St.)
Herbert Rd. NG5: Sher . . . 6H 85
NG17: Nunc . . . 3B 60
Herbert St. NG18: Mans . . . 4G 47
Hercules Dr. NG24: New T . . . 2E 136
Hereford Av. NG19: Mans W . . . 4J 41
NG22: Oll . . . 4B 38
Hereford Cl. S81: Work . . . 6H 19
Hereford Rd. NG3: Nott . . . 3E 96
NG4: Ged . . . 4J 87
NG5: Woodt . . . 2B 86
NG15: Rave . . . 1C 62
Hermitage, The NG18: Mans . . . 6E 46
Hermitage Av. NG18: Mans . . . 5F 47
Hermitage La. NG18: Mans . . . 6E 46
Hermitage Sq. NG2: Nott . . . 4C 96
Hermitage Wlk. NG7: Nott . . . 7B 6 (5H 95)
Hermitage Way NG18: Mans . . . 6E 46
Hermon St. NG7: Nott . . . 4A 6 (3H 95)
Herne St. NG17: Sut A . . . 6A 46
Heron Dr. NG7: Lent . . . 4F 95
Heron Glade S81: Gate . . . 5D 18
Herons Ct. NG2: West Br . . . 5F 109
Heron Way NG19: Mans . . . 1C 46
NG24: New B . . . 4F 137
Heron Wharf NG7: Lent . . . 6G 95
Herrick Dr. S81: Work . . . 1K 21
Herriot Gro. DN11: Birc . . . 2D 8
Herrod Cl. NG23: Sut T . . . 3E 128
Herrods Vw. NG17: Stant H . . . 4G 45
Hertford M. NG4: Carl . . . 7F 87
Hervey Grn. NG11: Clif . . . 7F 107
Heskey Cl. NG3: Nott . . . 1F 7 (2K 95)
Heskey Wlk. NG3: Nott . . . 1F 7 (2K 95)
Heslington Av. NG8: Basf . . . 7F 85
Heslop Ct. S80: Work . . . 2E 20
Hethbeth Ct. NG2: Nott . . . 6K 95
Hethersett Gdns. NG6: Bulw . . . 6H 75
Hetley Rd. NG9: Bee . . . 1A 106
Hett's La. NG20: Mkt W . . . 3D 34
Hewett St. NG20: Wars . . . 3A 34
Hexham Cl. NG2: West Br . . . 3D 108
NG18: Mans . . . 5B 48
Hexham Gdns. NG5: Top V . . . 4C 76
Heyes, The NG15: Rave . . . 3B 62
Heywood Cl. NG25: Sout . . . 5J 131
Heywood St. NG18: Mans . . . 3K 47
Hibbert Cres. NG17: Sut A . . . 7A 46
Hibbert Rd. NG18: Mans . . . 3K 47
Hicking Building, The NG2: Nott . . . 5A 96
Hickings La. NG9: Stap . . . 1D 104
HICKLETON . . . 1A 144
HICKLING . . . 6E 142 (3B 148)
Hickling Ct. NG18: Mans . . . 3K 47
Hickling La. LE14: Upp B . . . 3H 143
NG12: Kin . . . 2C 142
Hickling Rd. LE14: Hick . . . 3D 142
NG3: Mapp . . . 5D 86
Hickory Cl. NG17: Kirk A . . . 4K 51
Hickton Dr. NG9: Chil . . . 7G 105
Higgins Cl. NG24: New T . . . 6D 134
Highbank Dr. NG11: Clif . . . 2F 115
Highbury Av. NG6: Bulw . . . 2D 84
Highbury Cl. NG16: Nuth . . . 4J 83
Highbury Rd. NG6: Bulw . . . 7J 75
NG12: Key . . . 6H 117
HIGHBURY VALE . . . 2E 84
Highbury Vale Stop (NET) . . . 3E 84
Highbury Wlk. NG6: Bulw . . . 1D 84
High Chu. St. NG7: Basf . . . 6G 85
(not continuous)
Highclere Dr. NG4: Carl . . . 7J 87

Highcliffe Rd. NG3: Nott 3D 96
High Cl. NG17: Ann W 3B 60
High Cres. NG17: Ann W 3B 60
Highcroft NG3: Mapp 3C 86
Highcroft Dr. NG8: Woll 3G 93
High Cross NG14: Blea 1A 138
Highcross Ct. NG7: Radf 2A 6 (2G 95)
High Cross Leys NG3: Nott 2F 7 (2K 95)
High Cross St. NG1: Nott 4G 7 (3A 96)
Highfield DN22: Retf 1C 22
Highfield Av. NG17: Kirk A 5J 51
NG19: Mans 1H 47
Highfield Cl. NG15: Rave 2C 62
NG19: Mans 1H 47
NG21: C'tone 5J 43
Highfield Ct. NG9: Bee 3A 106
Highfield Dr. DE55: Sth N 6A 50
NG4: Carl 1E 96
NG16: Nuth 3A 84
Highfield Farm Courtyard DN22: Lound 3C 14
Highfield Gro. NG2: West Br 2C 108
S81: Carl L 7E 12
Highfield La. S80: Work 4K 21
Highfield Rd. NG2: West Br 2C 108
NG7: Nott 7E 94
NG9: Chil 5F 105
NG12: Key 6H 117
NG16: Nuth 3K 83
NG17: Sut A 7G 45
NG21: C'tone 5J 43
Highfields Ct. NG15: Huck 7G 67
Highfields Dr. NG22: Bils 7C 126
Highfield St. NG10: Long E 7B 104
Highfield Vs. S81: Costh 4C 12
Highfield Way NG18: Mans 5G 47
Highgate Cl. NG4: Carl 5F 87
High Grounds Rd. S80: Rhod 1D 20
High Grounds Way S80: Rhod 1C 20
High Gro. NG19: Mans W 1A 48
Highgrove Av. NG9: Chil 3J 105
Highgrove Gdns. NG12: Edwal 5D 108
High Hazel Dr. NG19: Mans W 1H 47
High Hazels Ct. NG16: Newth 2F 73
High Hazles Cl. NG4: Ged 4H 87
High Hazles Dr. NG17: Huth 1E 50
High Hazles Rd. NG12: Cotg 5F 111
High Hoe Ct. S80: Work 2H 21
High Hoe Dr. S80: Work 2H 21
High Hoe Rd. S80: Work 2H 21
High Ho. Rd. DN22: Stu S 3A 24
High Hurst NG14: Calv 6C 70
Highland Cl. NG19: Mans W 6K 41
Highland Ct. NG5: Basf 5G 85
Highland Dr. NG17: Sut A 2H 51
Highland Gro. S81: Work 7H 19
Highland Rd. NG18: Mans 1A 54
High Leys Dr. NG15: Rave 1J 61
High Leys Rd. NG15: Huck 7F 67
High Main Dr. NG6: Bestw V 2A 76
HIGH MARNHAM 7A 30 (1D 147)
High Mdw. NG12: Toll 1G 117
HIGH MELTON 1A 144
High Oakham Cl. NG17: Sut A 6B 46
High Oakham Dr. NG18: Mans 7H 47
High Oakham Grange NG18: Mans 7G 47
High Oakham Hill NG18: Mans 6G 47
High Oakham Rd. NG18: Mans 7H 47
High Pk. S80: Darf 4A 20
High Pk. Cotts. NG16: Newth 7H 65
High Pavement NG1: Nott 6G 7 (4A 96)
NG17: Sut A 1J 51
High Ridge NG19: Mans W 7B 42
High Rd. NG9: Bee 3A 106
NG9: Chil 6H 105
NG9: Toton 7F 105
S81: Carl L 7D 12
High School Stop (NET) 1B 6 (2H 95)
High Spannia NG16: Kimb 7K 73
High St. DN10: Beck 6C 16
DN10: Eve 6B 10
DN10: Gri H 3B 16
DN10: Miss 3C 10
DN10: Mist 2H 11
DN10: Walk 6H 11
DN22: Elk 2G 27
DN22: Ord 7E 22
DN22: Sth L 2G 25
NG1: Nott 5F 7 (4K 95)
NG5: Arn 7G 77
NG9: Stap 2D 104
NG11: Rudd 3K 115
NG13: Ors 1J 103
NG15: Huck 6G 67
NG16: Brins 4B 64
NG16: Kimb 1E 82
NG17: Huth 7E 44
NG17: Stant H 4G 45
NG17: Sut A 1J 51
NG19: Mans W 6J 41
NG19: Plea 4B 40
NG20: Mkt W 4C 34
NG21: Edwin 6F 37
NG22: East M 2B 28
NG22: Lax 5A 124
NG23: Coll 3G 129
NG23: Girt 4G 125
High St. NG23: Harby 6K 31
NG23: Hol 6K 129
NG23: Nth C 3D 30
NG23: Sth C 7D 30
NG23: Sut T 3D 128
S81: Blyth 6H 13
High St. Av. NG5: Arn 7G 77
High St. Pl. NG1: Nott 5F 7 (4K 95)
High Tor NG17: Skeg 3J 45
NG18: Mans 1J 53
Highurst Ct. NG7: Radf 3A 6 (3H 95)
Highurst St. NG7: Radf 4A 6 (3H 95)
High Vw. Av. NG12: Key 7J 117
High Vw. Ct. NG3: Mapp P 7A 86
High Vw. Gdns. NG17: Ann W 3B 60
High Vw. Rd. DE55: Sth N 4A 50
Highwood Av. NG8: Bilb 7A 84
Highwray Gro. NG11: Clif 1E 114
Hilary Cl. NG8: Woll 5J 93
Hilcot Dr. NG8: Aspl 6C 84
HILCOTE 2A 50
Hilcote Dr. NG21: C'tone 5H 43
Hilcote La. DE55: Blac, Hilc 2A 50
Hill, The NG17: Kirk A 6J 51
Hillary Way NG24: Bald 5H 137
Hill Bank Cotts. NG16: Sels 3C 58
Hillbeck Cres. NG8: Woll 4H 93
Hill Cl. NG2: West Br 3E 108
NG16: Newth 5G 73
Hill Cres. NG17: Sut A 6A 46
Hill Crest NG22: Bou 3E 38
Hillcrest NG25: Sout 6G 131
Hillcrest Cl. NG16: Want 7A 74
Hillcrest Dr. NG15: Huck 7D 66
Hillcrest Gdns. NG14: Bur J 2D 88
Hillcrest Gro. NG5: Sher 4J 85
Hillcrest M. DN22: Retf 3G 23
Hill Crest Pk. NG14: Calv 4D 70
Hillcrest Rd. NG12: Key 6H 117
Hillcrest Vw. NG4: Carl 6E 86
Hill Dr. NG13: Bing 3E 100
Hill Farm Ct. NG12: Edwal 7D 108
Hillfield Gdns. NG5: Top V 4A 76
Hillfield Rd. NG9: Stap 1E 104
Hill Gdns. DN11: Harwo 2D 8
Hillgrove Gdns. *NG5: Top V* 6C 76
(off Whitchurch Cl.)
Hilliers Ct. NG5: Top V 6B 76
Hillingdon Av. NG16: Nuth 4J 83
Hillington Ri. NG5: Bestw 7E 76
Hillmoor St. NG19: Plea 5B 40
Hillocks, The NG17: Sut A 7B 46
Hill Ri. NG9: Trow 4B 92
Hill Rd. DN11: Harwo 2C 8
NG6: Bestw V 2A 76
NG9: Chil 6G 105
NG13: Ors 2K 103
Hillsborough Av. NG17: Sut A 3H 51
Hillsborough Way NG17: Sut A 3H 51
Hillsford Cl. NG8: Woll 3B 94
Hillside NG7: Nott 5E 94
NG22: Tuxf 6E 28
Hillside Av. NG3: Mapp 3D 86
Hillside Ct. NG22: New O 5C 38
Hillside Cres. NG9: Bram 1K 105
S81: Work 7G 19
Hillside Dr. NG14: Bur J 2E 88
NG25: Sout 6G 131
Hillside Gro. NG10: Sand 3A 104
Hillside Rd. NG9: Bram 7H 93
NG9: Chil 6F 105
NG12: Rad T 5F 99
NG21: Blid 7J 55
Hillside Wlk. NG21: Blid 7J 55
Hills Rd. NG5: Woodt 3B 86
HILLSTOWN 2A 146
Hill St. DN22: Ord 6E 22
S80: Work 3F 21
Hillsview Ct. NG19: Plea 4A 40
Hillsway Cres. NG18: Mans 6G 47
Hillsyde Av. DN10: Mist 2H 11
Hill Syke NG14: Lowd 4A 80
HILL TOP 4F 73
Hill Top NG13: Ors 2K 103
Hill Top Cotts. NG21: K Cli 3K 43
Hill Top Ct. DN11: Harwo 2D 8
Hilltop Ri. NG16: Eastw 4F 73
Hilltop Rd. NG16: Pinx 7A 50
Hill Top Vw. NG17: Sut A 2G 51
Hillview DN22: Ord 7E 22
Hillview Av. NG3: Mapp 5A 86
Hillview Ct. NG19: Mans W 5K 41
Hill Vw. Cres. DN22: Clar 7J 17
Hillview Rd. NG4: Carl 6D 86
NG9: Toton 7F 105
NG17: Kirk A 6C 52
Hill Vue Av. NG24: New T 1E 136
Hill Vue Gdns. NG24: New T 1E 136
Hillwood Cl. S80: Work 3C 20
Hilton Ct. NG2: West Br 4E 108
Hilton Cres. NG2: West Br 4E 108
Hilton Pk. NG21: Blid 6H 55
Hilton Rd. NG3: Mapp 5C 86
Hinchin Brook NG7: Lent 4F 95
Hindlow Ct. NG18: Mans 4D 48
Hind St. DN22: Retf 5G 23
Hine Av. NG24: New T 1G 137
Hine Hall NG3: Nott 6C 86
Hinshelwood Ct. NG11: Clif 1D 114
Hinsley Cl. NG5: Arn 6K 77
Hinsley Ct. NG8: Bilb 3H 93
Hirst Cl. NG5: Arn 4H 77
Hirst Ct. NG7: Radf 3A 6 (3H 95)
Hirst Cres. NG8: Woll 4A 94
Hirst Rd. DN22: Retf 2G 23
HMP Lowdham Grange NG14: Lowd 4J 79
HMP Nottingham NG5: Sher 4J 85
HMP Whatton NG13: What 5B 102
Hobart Cl. NG2: Nott 7K 95
Hobart Dr. NG9: Stap 7E 92
Hobben Cres. NG15: Huck 4K 67
Hobhouse Rd. NG19: Mans 7D 40
HOBSIC 5B 64
Hobsic Cl. NG16: Brins 5B 64
Hobsic La. NG16: Sels 4B 58
Hobson's Acre NG14: Gun 2A 90
HOBY 3B 148
HOCKERTON 1K 131 (3C 147)
Hockerton Rd. NG22: Kirk 1D 132
NG23: Upton 6C 132
NG25: Hock, Norm 4K 131
Hockerwood NG11: Clif 5F 107
Hockley NG1: Nott 5H 7 (4A 96)
Hockley Ho. NG1: Nott 5H 7
Hockley Pl. NG17: Kirk A 7J 51
Hockley Valley NG17: Kirk A 7J 51
Hodgkin Cl. NG11: Clif 1D 114
Hodgkinson Rd. NG17: Kirk A 7B 52
Hodgkinson St. NG4: Neth 2K 97
Hodsock La. S81: Carl L, Hods 6E 12
Hodsock Priory Gdns. 3B 144
Hodson Ho. NG5: Sher 5K 85
HODTHORPE 1A 146
Hoefield Cres. NG6: Bulw 1B 84
Hoe Hill Vw. NG12: Toll 1G 117
Hoe La. NG12: Crop Bu 4B 112
Hoe Nook NG12: Crop Bi 5B 112
Hoe Vw. Rd. NG12: Crop Bi 5B 112
Hoewood Rd. NG6: Bulw 7G 75
Hogan Gdns. NG5: Top V 5C 76
Hogarth Cl. NG9: Stap 3D 104
Hogarth St. NG3: Nott 2C 96
Hoggetts Cl. NG9: Chil 3G 105
Hogg La. NG12: Rad T 5D 98
nuous)
Hoggs Fld. NG16: Eastw 4D 72
HOLBECK 3A 26 (1A 146)
Holbeck La. S80: Holb 3B 26
Holbeck Rd. NG8: Aspl 2D 94
NG15: Huck 4H 67
Holbeck Way NG21: Rain 2K 55
HOLBECK WOODHOUSE 3B 26 (1A 146)
Holborn Av. NG2: Nott 3C 96
Holborn Cl. NG16: Nuth 4J 83
Holborn Pl. NG6: Bulw 7J 75
HOLBROOK 3A 144
Holbrook Cl. NG19: Plea 4A 40
Holbrook Ct. NG11: Clif 2F 115
NG18: Mans 4D 48
Holbrook Cres. NG21: K Cli 3K 43
Holby Cl. NG5: Top V 6B 76
Holcombe Cl. NG8: Aspl 5C 84
Holdale Rd. NG3: Nott 2E 96
Holdenby Cl. DN22: Retf 2G 23
Holden Ct. NG7: Radf 3A 6 (3H 95)
Holden Cres. NG16: Nuth 1H 83
NG24: New T 3C 136
Holden Gdns. NG9: Stap 3D 104
Holden Rd. NG9: Bee 2K 105
Holden St. NG7: Radf 3A 6 (3H 95)
NG18: Mans 4G 47
Holderness Cl. DN11: Harwo 2D 8
Holdin C'way. DN10: Miss 2A 10
Holding S81: Work 7J 19
Holds La. DN22: Torw 4J 13
Holgate NG11: Clif 7D 106
Holgate Rd. NG2: Nott 7K 95
Holgate Wlk. NG15: Huck 7E 66
Holkham Av. NG9: Chil 4H 105
Holkham Cl. NG5: Arn 1D 86
Holland Cl. NG11: Goth 7G 115
Holland Cres. NG16: Sels 5F 59
Holland St. NG7: H Grn 1G 95
Holles Cl. NG22: Bou 3E 38
Holles Ct. S80: Work 4G 21
Holles Cres. NG7: Nott 7B 6 (5H 95)
Holles St. S80: Work 4G 21
Hollies, The NG15: Rave 3B 62
NG16: Eastw 4D 72
NG21: Rain 2K 55
S81: Blyth 7H 13
Hollies Av. NG24: New T 4E 134
Hollies Dr. NG12: Edwal 5D 108
Hollington Rd. NG8: Bilb 2B 94
Hollington Way NG18: Mans 4D 48
Hollingwell Dr. NG18: Mans 3D 48
Hollingworth Av. NG10: Sand 6A 104
Hollins, The NG14: Calv 5E 70
Hollinwell Av. NG8: Woll 3C 94
Hollinwell Cl. NG17: Kirk A 4J 51
Hollinwell Ct. NG12: Edwal 6E 108
Hollinwood La. NG14: Calv 6K 69

Hollis Mdw. LE12: East L . . . 1A 122
Hollis St. NG7: Basf . . . 6H 85
Holloway Cl. NG13: East B . . . 4E 90
Hollowdyke La. NG24: Bald . . . 6J 137
Hollowgate La. NG23: High M . . . 7A 30
Hollows, The NG11: Wilf . . . 5H 107
NG14: Thur . . . 6C 138
Hollowstone NG1: Nott . . . 6H 7 (4A 96)
Holly Av. NG3: Nott . . . 1D 96
NG4: Carl . . . 1G 97
NG11: Wilf . . . 1J 107
Holly Bank Cl. NG19: New H . . . 3A 40
Hollyberry Cft. NG17: Sut A . . . 2H 51
Hollybrook Gro. NG16: Want . . . 7B 74
Holly Bush Cl. DN22: Elk . . . 2G 27
Holly Cl. NG13: Bing . . . 4H 101
NG15: Huck . . . 1H 75
Holly Copse Nature Reserve . . . 5E 82
Holly Ct. DN11: Harwo . . . 2B 8
DN22: Retf . . . 4F 23
NG3: Nott . . . 1C 96
NG9: Bram . . . 1H 105
NG19: Mans W . . . 1A 48
NG23: Roll . . . 4K 139
NG24: New T . . . 7G 135
Hollycroft NG2: West Br . . . 5D 108
Hollydale Rd. NG3: Nott . . . 2E 96
Hollydene Cl. NG15: Huck . . . 1C 74
Hollydene Cres. NG6: Cin . . . 3C 84
Holly Dr. NG19: Mans W . . . 1C 48
Holly Farm Cotts. NG12: Key . . . 2H 119
Holly Farm Ct. NG16: Newth . . . 5G 73
Holly Gdns. NG3: Nott . . . 1C 96
Hollygate Ind. Pk. NG12: Cotg . . . 5F 111
Hollygate La. NG12: Cotg . . . 6E 110
Holly Gro. NG17: Kirk A . . . 5K 51
Holly Hill Rd. NG16: Sels . . . 6D 58
Hollyhock Dr. NG19: Mans . . . 1F 47
Holly La. NG9: Chil . . . 4K 105
Holly Leaf Rd. NG15: Huck . . . 2J 75
Holly Lodge NG2: West Br . . . 7E 96
Holly M. NG24: New B . . . 4F 137
Hollymount DN22: Retf . . . 4F 23
Holly Ri. NG22: New O . . . 3D 38
Holly Rd. DN22: Retf . . . 4F 23
NG16: Want . . . 7K 73
NG19: Mans W . . . 7B 42
Hollythorpe Pl. NG15: Huck . . . 1C 74
HOLME
Newark . . . 5K 129 (3D 147)
Scunthorpe . . . 1D 145
Holme, The NG25: Sout . . . 6E 130
Holme Av. LE12: East L . . . 1A 122
Holme Bus. Pk. S81: Work . . . 1E 18
Holme Cl. NG14: Woodbo . . . 2H 79
Holme Farm Cl. LE12: Will W . . . 6H 143
Holmefield NG24: Farnd . . . 7H 133
Holmefield Cl. S81: Work . . . 7H 19
Holmefield Cres. DE7: Ilk . . . 7A 82
Holmefield Cft. DN10: Scro . . . 4K 9
Holme Gro. NG2: West Br . . . 6E 96
Holme La. NG12: Hol P, Rad T . . . 5A 98
NG12: Rad T . . . 1J 109
NG22: Edin, Halam . . . 1C 130
NG22: Egma . . . 3A 124
NG24: Wint . . . 1F 135
Holme Lea NG10: Sand . . . 3A 104
Holme Lodge NG4: Carl . . . 2H 97
HOLME PIERREPONT . . . 5K 97 (2B 148)
Holme Pierrepont Country Pk. . . . 5K 97
Holme Pierrepont Hall . . . 5A 98
Holme Rd. NG2: West Br . . . 7C 96
NG13: Bing . . . 4G 101
Holmesfield Wlk. NG18: Mans . . . 4D 48
Holmes Rd. DN10: Walk . . . 7K 11
DN22: Retf . . . 3F 23
Holmestead Cl. LE12: Costo . . . 3E 122
Holme St. NG2: Nott . . . 6B 96
Holme Way S81: Gate . . . 3E 18
Holmewood Cres. NG5: Bestw . . . 1H 85
Holmewood Dr. NG16: Gilt . . . 6F 73
Holmfield Rd. NG9: Chil . . . 6H 105
Holmhurst Cl. S81: Work . . . 7E 18
Holmsfield NG12: Key . . . 1H 119
Holmwood Rd. NG21: Rain . . . 2A 56
Holroyd Av. NG2: Nott . . . 4C 96
Holt, The NG24: New T . . . 5K 133
Holt Gro. NG14: Calv . . . 5D 70
HOLWELL . . . 3C 149
Holwood Ct. NG6: Bulw . . . 1B 84
Holyoake Rd. NG3: Mapp . . . 4F 87
Holyoake Vs. NG4: Colw . . . 2J 97
Holyrood Ct. NG9: Bram . . . 7H 93
Home Cl. NG5: Arn . . . 6F 77
Home Croft, The NG9: Bram . . . 2G 105
Homecroft Av. NG17: Skeg . . . 4K 45
Homecroft Dr. NG16: Sels . . . 4C 58
Home Farm Cl. NG11: Goth . . . 7F 115
NG23: Kel . . . 1H 133
Home Farm Ct. NG16: Sels . . . 6A 58
Home Farm La. NG12: Rad T . . . 5K 99
NG22: Kirk . . . 1C 132
Homefarm La. NG23: Thor . . . 3H 31
Homefield Av. NG5: Arn . . . 4J 77
Homefield Rd. NG8: Aspl . . . 1E 94
Homelands, The NG17: Sut A . . . 1K 51
Homeleigh La. NG14: Hove . . . 4K 81
Homesteads, The NG17: Kirk A . . . 5K 51
NG20: Mkt W . . . 4D 34
Homewell Wlk. NG11: Clif . . . 6G 107
Homewood Dr. NG17: Kirk A . . . 4J 51
Honey Cft. Ct. DE55: Sth N . . . 7A 50
Honeyknab La. NG25: Oxt . . . 1G 71
Honeysuckle Cl. NG8: Brox . . . 6K 83
NG24: New B . . . 4F 137
Honeysuckle Gro. NG6: Cin . . . 3C 84
NG13: Bing . . . 5E 100
Honeywood Ct. NG3: Nott . . . 1D 96
Honeywood Dr. NG3: Nott . . . 1D 96
Honing Dr. NG25: Sout . . . 6G 131
Honingham Cl. NG5: Arn . . . 2C 86
HONINGTON . . . 1D 149
Honister Cl. NG2: Gam . . . 2F 109
NG11: Clif . . . 3E 114
NG18: Mans . . . 6J 47
Honister Ct. NG18: Mans . . . 6J 47
Honiton Cl. NG9: Toton . . . 7F 105
Honiton Rd. NG8: Brox . . . 6K 83
Hood Cotts. NG5: Sher . . . 5A 86
Hood St. NG5: Sher . . . 5A 86
Hook Cl. NG9: Chil . . . 7H 105
Hoo La. DN22: Lane . . . 4F 29
Hooley Pl. NG5: Sher . . . 4A 86
Hooley St. NG16: Sels . . . 6D 58
Hoopers Wlk. NG2: Nott . . . 6K 95
HOOTON LEVITT . . . 2A 144
HOOTON PAGNELL . . . 1A 144
Hooton Rd. NG4: Carl . . . 1F 97
HOOTON ROBERTS . . . 2A 144
Hooton St. NG3: Nott . . . 3C 96
Hope Cl. NG2: Nott . . . 6J 95
Hopedale Cl. NG7: Radf . . . 3F 95
Hope Dr. NG7: Nott . . . 7C 6 (5J 95)
Hope St. NG9: Bee . . . 2K 105
NG18: Mans . . . 4K 47
Hopewell Cl. NG12: Rad T . . . 3F 99
Hopkiln La. NG25: Sout . . . 5F 131
Hopkin Ct. NG3: Mapp . . . 1F 87
Hopkins Ct. NG16: Eastw . . . 3D 72
Hopkinson Ct. NG6: Bestw V . . . 3A 76
Hop Yd. NG25: Sout . . . 3G 131
Hopyard La. NG22: Tuxf . . . 1B 124
NG23: Bath . . . 6F 129
Horace Av. NG9: Stap . . . 2B 104
Horizon Pl. NG8: Stre . . . 5H 83
Hornbeam Cl. DE7: Ilk . . . 1A 92
Hornbeam Gdns. NG6: Bulw . . . 7F 75
Hornbeam Way NG17: Kirk A . . . 1A 60
Hornbuckle Ct. NG7: Radf . . . 3G 95
Hornchurch Rd. NG8: Bilb . . . 7J 83
Horne La. NG22: Dun T . . . 6J 29
Hornsby Wlk. NG5: Top V . . . 6A 76
Horsendale Av. NG16: Nuth . . . 3K 83
Horseshoe Cl. LE12: Will W . . . 6G 143
Horseshoe Cotts. NG23: Coll . . . 2J 129
Horseshoe Ri. DN10: Walk . . . 7J 11
Horsewells St. DN10: Gri H . . . 3B 16
Horsham Dr. NG5: Top V . . . 6B 76
HOSE . . . 3C 149
Hosiery St. NG17: Kirk A . . . 6A 52
Hospital Rd. DN22: Retf . . . 3E 22
Hoten Rd. NG2: Nott . . . 5C 96
HOTON . . . 3A 148
Hotspur Cl. NG6: Basf . . . 2F 85
Hotspur Dr. NG4: Colw . . . 2H 97
Houfton Rd. NG18: Mans . . . 2A 48
HOUGHAM . . . 1D 149
HOUGH-ON-THE-HILL . . . 1D 149
Houghton Cl. NG16: Nuth . . . 3K 83
Houldsworth Ri. NG5: Arn . . . 4G 77
Hound Rd. NG2: West Br . . . 1B 108
Hounds Gate NG1: Nott . . . 6D 6 (4K 95)
(not continuous)
Hounsfield Cl. NG24: New T . . . 1H 137
Hounsfield Way NG23: Sut T . . . 3D 128
Houseman Gdns. NG2: Nott . . . 6K 95
Houston Cl. NG5: Top V . . . 5A 76
Hove Chase DN22: Ord . . . 6E 22
Hovenden Gdns. NG7: H Grn . . . 1F 95
HOVERINGHAM . . . 4K 81 (1C 149)
Hoveringham La. NG14: Hove . . . 1K 81
Hoveringham Rd. NG14: Cayt, Hove . . . 6J 81
Hove Rd. NG5: Bestw . . . 2F 85
Howard Rd. DN11: Birc . . . 2F 9
NG19: Mans . . . 2F 47
Howard's NG25: Sout . . . 6G 131
Howard's Gdns. NG24: New B . . . 5F 137
Howard St. NG1: Nott . . . 3G 7 (3K 95)
NG17: Sut A . . . 6K 45
S80: Work . . . 3H 21
Howbeck La. DN22: Clar . . . 7J 17
Howbeck Rd. NG5: Arn . . . 5K 77
Howden Rd. NG6: Bulw . . . 4J 75
Howell Jones Rd. NG9: Chil . . . 6G 105
Howells Cl. NG5: Arn . . . 6E 76
Howes Ct. NG24: New T . . . 1D 136
Howick Dr. NG6: Bulw . . . 7F 75
Howieson Ct. NG3: Mapp . . . 2E 86
Howitts Fld. NG24: Farnd . . . 7G 133
Hoylake Cl. NG19: Mans W . . . 3A 42
Hoylake Cres. NG8: Bilb . . . 1J 93
Hoyland Av. NG7: Lent . . . 6F 95
Hoyle Rd. NG14: Calv . . . 4D 70
Hubert Ct. NG7: H Grn . . . 2G 95
Hubert St. NG7: H Grn . . . 2G 95
Huckerbys Fld. NG4: Carl . . . 6F 87
Hucklow Ct. NG18: Mans . . . 4D 48
HUCKNALL . . . 6G 67 (1A 148)
Hucknall (Park & Ride) . . . 6J 67
Hucknall By-Pass NG15: Huck . . . 6E 66
Hucknall Cl. NG8: Stre . . . 5J 83
Hucknall Cres. NG4: Ged . . . 5H 87
Hucknall Golf Course . . . 6J 67
Hucknall Ind. Pk. NG15: Huck . . . 2F 75
Hucknall La. NG6: Bulw . . . 6J 75
Hucknall Leisure Cen. . . . 5H 67
Hucknall Rd.
NG5: Bestw, Sher, Top V . . . 5K 75
NG6: Bulw . . . 5K 75
NG15: Ann, News . . . 5D 60
Hucknall Station (Rail & NET) . . . 6J 67
Huddlestones Wharf NG24: New T . . . 1B 136
Hudson St. NG3: Nott . . . 1K 7 (2C 96)
Hudson Way NG12: Rad T . . . 4G 99
Hugessen Av. NG15: Huck . . . 5J 67
Huggett Gdns. NG5: Top V . . . 6C 76
Humber Cl. NG2: Nott . . . 6K 95
Humber Lodge NG9: Bee . . . 2B 106
Humber Mdw. La. DN22: Sth L . . . 3K 25
Humber Rd. NG9: Bee . . . 2B 106
(not continuous)
NG10: Long E . . . 7B 104
Humber Rd. Sth. NG9: Bee . . . 3C 106
Humberstone Rd. NG25: Sout . . . 5G 131
Humberston Rd. NG8: Woll . . . 5H 93
Humber St. DN22: Retf . . . 4G 23
S80: Work . . . 1F 21
Humphries Gdns. S80: Work . . . 4F 21
Hundred Acre La. S81: Work . . . 1J 19
Hundred Acres La. NG24: Bald . . . 7F 137
Hungary La. LE12: Sut B . . . 6B 120
HUNGERHILL GARDENS . . . 1A 96
Hungerhill La. NG14: Woodbo . . . 4D 78
Hungerhill Rd. NG3: Nott . . . 1A 96
HUNGERTON . . . 2D 149
Hungerton St. NG7: Lent . . . 5G 95
Hunston Cl. NG8: Bilb . . . 1B 94
Hunt Cl. NG12: Rad T . . . 5E 98
NG17: Kirk A . . . 4C 52
Hunter Rd. NG5: Arn . . . 1F 87
Hunters Chase NG19: Mans W . . . 7H 41
Hunters Cl. NG11: Wilf . . . 3H 107
Hunters Ct. NG17: Kirk A . . . 6J 51
Hunter's Dr. DN10: Gri H . . . 3A 16
Hunters Rd. NG24: Bald . . . 6J 137
Hunter St. NG2: Nott . . . 1A 108
Huntingdon Dr. NG7: Nott . . . 6C 6 (4J 95)
Huntingdon St. NG1: Nott . . . 1E 6 (2K 95)
Huntingdon Wlk. NG10: Sand . . . 4A 104
Huntingdon Way NG9: Toton . . . 7E 104
Huntly Cl. NG11: Clif . . . 1H 115
NG18: Mans . . . 5D 46
Huntsman Pl. DN22: Torw . . . 3J 13
Hurcomb St. NG3: Nott . . . 1C 96
Hurst Cl. NG21: Rain . . . 2H 55
Hurts Cft. NG9: Chil . . . 5J 105
Hurt's Yd. NG1: Nott . . . 4E 6 (3K 95)
Hutchinson Grn.
NG3: Nott . . . 2G 7 (2A 96)
Hutchinson Rd. NG24: New T . . . 1H 137
HUTHWAITE . . . 7D 44 (3A 146)
Huthwaite La. DE55: Blac . . . 1A 50
Huthwaite Leisure Cen. . . . 7D 44
Huthwaite Rd. NG17: Sut A . . . 7F 45
Hutt Farm Ct. NG15: Rave . . . 3B 62
Hutton Cl. NG9: Bram . . . 7J 93
Hutton St. NG2: Nott . . . 5C 96
Huxley Cl. NG8: Bilb . . . 1J 93
Hyde Cl. NG11: Clif . . . 5G 107
HYDE PARK . . . 1A 144
Hyde Pk. Cl. NG2: West Br . . . 4K 107
Hyson Cl. NG7: H Grn . . . 7G 85
HYSON GREEN . . . 1G 95
Hyson Green Market Stop (NET) . . . 1G 95
Hyson St. NG7: H Grn . . . 1G 95

I

Ian Gro. NG4: Carl . . . 7J 87
Ice House, The NG1: Nott . . . 5H 7
Idle Valley Rd. DN22: Retf . . . 3E 22
Idle Vw. DN22: Retf . . . 1F 23
Idlewells Shop. Cen. NG17: Sut A . . . 1J 51
Ikea Way NG16: Gilt . . . 7G 73
Ilion St. NG19: Mans . . . 7F 41
ILKESTON . . . 1A 92 (1A 148)
ILKESTON JUNCTION . . . 6A 82
Ilkeston Rd. DE7: Stant D . . . 7B 92
NG7: Lent, Nott, Radf . . . 4A 6 (3E 94)
NG9: Stap, Bram . . . 6D 92
NG9: Trow . . . 3A 92
NG10: Sand . . . 7B 92
Imex Ent. Pk. NG15: Huck . . . 7K 67
Imperial Av. NG4: Ged . . . 6H 87
NG9: Bee . . . 3K 105
Imperial Rd. NG6: Bulw . . . 1E 84
NG9: Bee . . . 3K 105

Incher M. NG4: Carl 6F 87
Inchwood Cl. NG9: Toton 7E 104
Incinerator Rd. NG2: Nott 6B 96
Independent St.
NG7: Radf 2A 6 (2G 95)
Indigo Ct. NG18: Mans 3J 47
Infield La. DN22: Habb 6D 24
NG20: Nort 2C 32
NG23: Weston 4G 125
INGHAM 3D 145
Ingham Bungs. S81: Costh 4C 12
Ingham Gro. NG7: Lent 5F 95
Ingham Rd. NG10: Long E 7B 104
Ingleby Cl. NG8: Woll 4G 93
NG12: Cotg 7D 110
Inglemere Cl. S81: Work 7H 19
Inglewood Cl. NG24: Bald 7G 137
Inglewood Rd. NG11: Clif 1F 115
Ingram La. NG23: Grass 3K 125
NG23: Sut T 2E 128
Ingram Rd. NG6: Bulw 1D 84
Ingram Ter. NG6: Bulw 1E 84
Ings Rd. DN10: Gri H 1B 16
Inham Cir. NG9: Chil 3H 105
Inham Cl. NG9: Chil 4F 105
Inham Flds. Cl. NG14: Gun 2B 90
Inham Rd. NG9: Chil 4F 105
Inholms Gdns. NG23: Flin 4A 140
Inholms Rd. NG23: Flin 4A 140
Inkerman Rd. NG16: Sels 7D 58
Inkerman St. NG16: Sels 7D 58
Inkersall La. NG22: Bils 5A 126
Innes Cl. NG4: Carl 1F 97
Innovation Pk. NG7: Lent 4E 94
Institute St. NG17: Stant H 4G 45
Instow Ri.
NG3: Nott 2H 7 (2A 96)
Intake Av. NG18: Mans 5F 47
Intake Rd. NG12: Key 7G 117
NG21: C'tone 5J 43
Iona Dr. NG9: Trow 5C 92
Iona Gdns. NG5: Top V 5C 76
Ipswich Cir. NG3: Nott 3D 96
Ireland Av. NG9: Bee 4B 106
Ireland Cl. NG9: Bee 4B 106
Iremonger Rd. NG2: Nott 6A 96
Irene Ter. NG7: Basf 5G 85
Ireton Av. NG24: New T 1H 137
Ireton Gro. NG9: Atten 7J 105
Ireton St. NG7: Radf 3B 6 (3H 95)
NG9: Bee 3K 105
Irving Cl. NG22: Farns 6K 57
Irwin Dr. NG6: Bulw 2A 84
Isaac Newton Cen. NG7: Nott 7E 94
Isaacs La. NG9: Stap 2C 104
Isabella St. NG1: Nott 7E 6 (5K 95)
Isandula Rd. NG7: Basf 5G 85
Island, The NG16: Eastw 5D 72
Island La. NG12: Rad T 4C 98
Islay Cl. NG5: Arn 5H 77
NG9: Trow 5C 92
Ivatt Dr. NG2: Nott 5C 96
Iveagh Cl. NG20: Mkt W 3E 34
Ives Cl. NG2: West Br 5K 107
Ivies, The NG24: New T 5K 133
Ivy Cl. NG16: Want 5K 73
Ivy Gro. NG4: Carl 1G 97
NG7: Basf 7H 85
NG17: Kirk A 5K 51
Ivy La. NG16: Eastw 4C 72
Ivy Row NG13: What 5E 102

J

Jacklin Ct. NG17: Kirk A 5K 51
Jacklin Gdns. NG5: Top V 5C 76
JACKSDALE 7A 64 (3A 146)
Jacksdale Nature Reserve 7A 64
Jackson Av. NG10: Sand 3A 104
Jackson Ct. NG24: Farnd 7H 133
Jackson Cres. LE12: East L 1A 122
Jackson Dr. NG5: Bestw 2H 85
Jackson Ter. NG20: Mede V 7G 33
Jade Ct. NG18: Mans 6K 47
Jadella Cl. NG18: Mans 5F 47
Jake Rd. NG9: Bee 6B 106
Jalland's Row NG24: New T 7D 134
James Cl. NG22: New O 3C 38
James Dr. NG14: Calv 4C 70
James Hince Ct. S81: Carl L 6B 12
James Murray M. *NG18: Mans 3J 47*
(off Rock Valley)
James St. NG5: Arn 6G 77
NG16: Kimb 1E 82
NG17: Nunc 3A 60
S81: Work 7F 19
James Watt Rd. NG24: New T 5F 135
James William Turner Av.
NG17: Sut A 2J 51
James' Yd. *NG18: Mans 3J 47*
(off Rock Ct.)
Japonica Dr. NG6: Cin 3C 84
Jardine S81: Work 6J 19
Jardines, The NG9: Bram 7H 93
Jarrow Gdns. NG5: Top V 4B 76
Jarvis Av. NG3: Nott 2E 96
Jasmine Cl. NG8: Brox 6K 83
NG9: Bram 7J 93
NG11: Clif 1D 114
Jasmine Ct. DE75: Hea 5A 72
NG24: Bald 4H 137
Jasmine Rd. NG5: Basf 4F 85
Jasper Cl. NG12: Rad T 6D 98
Jayne Cl. NG4: Ged 5K 87
NG8: Woll 2K 93
Jeacock Dr. NG21: Rain 3A 56
Jebb's La. NG13: Bing 4G 101
Jedburgh Cl. NG3: Nott 2H 7 (2A 96)
NG16: Kimb 7J 73
Jedburgh Wlk. NG3: Nott 2H 7 (2A 96)
Jellicoe St. NG20: Whal T 5B 26
Jenford St. NG18: Mans 4E 46
Jenison Ho. NG24: New T 5C 136
Jenkins Av. NG19: Mans 3D 46
Jenned Rd. NG5: Arn 4J 77
Jenner Ho. NG3: Mapp 5C 86
Jenner St. NG5: Sher 6J 85
Jenness Av. NG5: Top V 5A 76
Jennison St. NG6: Bulw 7J 75
NG19: Mans 1G 47
Jenny Becketts La. NG18: Mans 5A 48
Jenny Burton Way NG15: Huck 1J 75
Jensen Way NG5: Sher 6J 85
Jephson Bldgs. NG17: Sut A 3K 51
Jephson Rd. NG17: Sut A 3K 51
Jericho Rd. NG24: Bald 7G 137
Jermyn Dr. NG5: Arn 5C 76
Jersey Gdns. NG3: Nott 2K 7 (2B 96)
NG18: Mans 5B 48
Jersey St. NG24: New T 4B 136
Jesmond Rd. NG6: Bulw 1E 84
Jessamine Ct. NG9: Bee 3B 106
Jesse Boot Av. NG7: Nott 7E 94
Jessop Cl. NG24: New T 7F 135
Jessops La. NG4: Ged 4J 87
Jessop Way NG24: New T 7F 135
Jewitt Way NG11: Rudd 3J 115
Jill-lain Ct. NG9: Stap 3D 104
Job La. DN10: Matt 2H 15
Jockey La. DN22: Elk 1F 27
John & Eliza Jelley Homes
NG7: Nott 5E 94
John Barrow Cl. NG21: Rain 3A 56
John Carroll Ct. NG3: Nott 2C 96
John Carroll Leisure Cen. 3G 95
John Davies Workshop
NG17: Huth 6D 44
John Gold Av. NG24: New T 2E 136
John Pope Way NG24: New T 4E 134
John Quinn Ct. NG7: Basf 6G 85
Johnson Av. NG15: Huck 1H 75
Johnson Cl. NG16: Want 7A 74
Johnson Ct. *S80: Work 2F 21*
(off Sandhill St.)
Johnson Dr. NG18: Mans 7J 47
Johnson Rd. NG7: Lent 4F 95
Johnsons Rd. NG24: Bald 7J 137
Johnson Way NG9: Chil 7G 105
Johns Rd. NG9: Bee 6B 106
NG12: Rad T 5F 99
Johnstone Way NG6: Bestw V 7D 68
John St. NG7: Basf 6G 85
NG17: Sut A 6K 45
S80: Work 1F 21
John Woodhead Ct. NG19: Mans 2F 47
John Wright Cl. NG6: Bulw 5K 75
Jolly Jungle Playland 6D 134
Joshua Bus. Pk. NG16: Lang M 3A 72
Joyce Av. NG5: Sher 3A 86
NG9: Toton 6E 104
Joyce Cl. NG5: Sher 3A 86
Jubilee, The NG25: Sout 5F 131
Jubilee Bldgs. *NG17: Sut A 1K 51*
(off Outram St.)
Jubilee Cl. DN10: Miss 2C 10
Jubilee Ct. NG8: Stre 6J 83
NG15: Huck 1E 74
NG16: Pinx 1B 58
Jubilee Rd. DN22: Retf 5D 22
NG5: Arn 1B 86
NG17: Sut A 7H 45
Jubilee St. NG2: Nott 4C 96
NG16: Kimb 7J 73
NG24: New T 2D 136
Jubilee Way Nth. NG18: Mans 3D 48
Jubilee Way Sth.
NG18: Mans 5D 48
Judes Ct. NG3: Mapp 5B 86
Judson Av. NG9: Stap 3E 104
Julian Cl. DE7: Ilk 2A 92
Julian La. NG12: Shel 6H 89
Julian Rd. NG2: West Br 1E 108
Julias Way NG17: Kirk A 3B 52
Jumelles Dr. NG14: Calv 6B 70
Junction, The NG15: Huck 6H 67
Junction Rd. NG17: Sut A 1B 52
Jungletastic Play Cen. 3A 84
Juniper Cl. NG11: Clif 1D 114
NG22: Bils 6D 126
Juniper Ct. NG7: Radf 2A 6
NG16: Gilt 6G 73
Juniper Gdns. NG13: Bing 4H 101
Justnian Cl. NG15: Huck 5J 67

K

Kappler Cl. NG4: Neth 1K 97
Karen Gdns. NG9: Chil 5J 105
Karen Ri. NG5: Arn 5J 77
Katherine Dr. NG9: Toton 5E 104
Kaye Rd. NG19: Mans 3D 46
Kayes Ct. NG9: Stap 2C 104
Kayes Wlk. NG1: Nott 6G 7 (4A 96)
Kay's Mdw. NG9: Bee 2B 106
KEADBY 1D 145
Keane Cl. NG21: Blid 6H 55
Keats Av. NG17: Sut A 7F 45
Keats Cl. NG5: Arn 7F 77
NG16: Nuth 1G 83
NG18: Mans 3G 47
Keats Cres. S81: Work 7J 19
Keats Dr. NG15: Huck 7D 66
Keats Rd. NG24: Bald 4G 137
Kedleston Cl. NG9: Chil 4H 105
NG17: Huth 1D 50
Kedleston Rd. S81: Work 6G 19
Kedleston Wlk. *NG18: Mans 4D 48*
(off Kelstedge Dr.)
Keeling Cl. NG16: Newth 5F 73
Keep, The LE12: East L 3B 122
Keepers Av. NG17: Kirk A 1A 60
Keepers Cl. NG6: Bestw V 2A 76
Keeton Way DN22: Nth L 6C 24
KEGWORTH 3A 148
Kegworth Rd. NG11: Goth 7F 115
NG11: King 1A 120
Keighton Dr. NG7: Nott 7D 94
KELFIELD 1D 145
Kelfield Cl. NG6: Bulw 2F 85
KELHAM 1H 133 (3C 147)
Kelham Cotts. NG17: Skeg 4A 46
Kelham Dr. NG5: Sher 5H 85
Kelham Grn. NG3: Nott 2C 96
Kelham La. NG23: Sth M 2A 134
NG24: New T 5A 134
Kelham M. NG3: Nott 7E 86
Kelham Rd. NG18: Mans 3E 46
NG24: New T 2J 133
(not continuous)
Kelham Way NG16: Eastw 3C 72
Keller Ct. DN22: Woodbe 7G 25
Kelling Cl. NG5: Bestw 1H 85
Kelly Wlk. NG11: Wilf 2J 107
Kelsey Av. NG22: New O 5D 38
Kelsey Cl. NG9: Atten 6K 105
Kelso Gdns. NG2: Nott 6J 95
Kelstedge Dr. NG18: Mans 4D 48
Kelstern Cl. NG8: Cin 4C 84
NG18: Mans 3C 48
Kelvedon Gdns. NG3: Nott 2J 7 (2B 96)
Kelvin Cl. NG9: Stap 4B 104
NG19: Mans W 6F 43
Kelvin Rd. NG3: Nott 1D 96
Kemmel Rd. NG6: Bulw 2E 84
Kempsey Cl. NG5: Top V 6A 76
Kempson St. NG11: Rudd 3K 115
Kempton Cl. NG16: Kimb 7J 73
Kempton Dr. NG5: Arn 5J 77
Kempton Rd. NG18: Mans 3B 48
Kenbrook Rd. NG15: Huck, Pap 4J 67
Kendal Cl. NG15: Huck 5F 67
NG17: Nunc 4K 59
S81: Work 4F 19
Kendal Ct. NG2: West Br 1E 108
Kendal Dr. NG9: Bram 1J 105
Kendale Ct. NG3: Nott 6C 86
Kendal Rd. NG12: Crop Bi 5B 112
Kendrew Ct. NG11: Clif 1D 114
Kenia Cl. NG4: Carl 7G 87
Kenilworth Av. NG17: Sut A 6B 46
Kenilworth Cl. S80: Work 4H 21
Kenilworth Ct. NG7: Nott 7C 6 (5J 95)
NG9: Bee 1B 106
Kenilworth Dr. S81: Carl L 6C 12
Kenilworth Rd. NG7: Nott 7C 6 (5J 95)
NG9: Bee 2B 106
Kenley Cl. S81: Gate 4E 18
Ken Martin Leisure Cen. 5J 75
Kenmore Cl. NG19: Mans 5E 46
Kenmore Gdns. NG3: Nott 2H 7 (2A 96)
Kennack Cl. DE55: Sth N 5A 50
Kennedy Av. NG19: Mans W 5K 41
Kennedy Cl. NG5: Arn 7F 77
Kennedy Ct. NG22: Wale 5G 27
Kennedy Dr. NG9: Stap 7D 92
Kennedy Ri. NG22: Wale 5G 27
Kennedy Wlk. NG24: Bald 5H 137
Kennel La. NG15: Ann 1K 65
Kenneth Rd. NG5: Arn 4H 77
Kennet Paddock NG19: Mans W 6K 41
Kennington Rd. NG8: Radf 3E 94
Ken Reid Gdns. *NG6: Bulw 6J 75*
(off Ragdale Rd.)
Kenrick Rd. NG3: Mapp 6D 86
Kenrick St. NG4: Neth 1K 97
Kensal Ct. NG2: West Br 1B 108

Kensington Cl. NG9: Toton 7F 105
  NG17: Sut A 1J 51
  NG19: Mans W .4A 42
Kensington Ct. NG5: Sher 4K 85
  (off St Albans St.)
Kensington Gdns. NG4: Carl 1H 97
Kensington Pk. Cl. NG2: West Br 4K 107
Kensington Rd. NG10: Sand 5A 104
Kensington Way S81: Work 5G 19
Kenslow Av. NG7: H Grn 1F 95
Kent Av. NG9: Bee 5A 106
  NG16: Jack 6A 64
Kent Cl. S81: Work 6H 19
Kentmere Cl. NG2: Gam 2F 109
Kenton Av. NG16: Nuth 4J 83
Kenton Ct. NG2: Nott 7A 96
Kent Rd. NG3: Mapp 5C 86
  NG16: Gilt 5G 73
Kent St. NG1: Nott 4G 7 (3A 96)
Kentwood Rd. NG2: Nott 4C 96
Kenyon Rd. NG7: Lent 5E 94
Kerrs Wlk. NG12: Crop Bi 5C 112
Kerry Cl. NG21: C'tone 4H 43
KERSALL 2C 147
Kersall Ct. NG6: Bulw 2E 84
Kersall Dr. NG6: Bulw 2E 84
Kersall Gdns. NG15: Huck 6H 67
Kestral Rd. NG18: Mans 6E 46
Kestrel Cl. NG4: Carl 6E 86
Kestrel Dr. NG13: Bing 5G 101
Kestrel Gro. NG15: Huck 7F 67
Kestrel M. S81: Gate 5E 18
Kestrel Ri. NG21: Rain 3K 55
Keswick Cl. NG2: Gam 2F 109
  NG9: Bram .1J 105
Keswick Ct. NG2: Nott 5J 7 (4B 96)
  NG10: Long E 7A 104
Keswick Rd. S81: Work 4F 19
Keswick St. NG2: Nott 5J 7 (4B 96)
Ketlock Hill La. DN22: Nth L 6B 24
KETTLETHORPE 1D 147
Kett St. NG6: Bulw 7H 75
Keverne Cl. NG8: Aspl 5D 84
  (not continuous)
Kevin Rd. NG8: Woll 6J 93
Kew Cl. NG2: West Br 6K 107
Kew Cres. DE75: Hea 5A 72
Kew Gdns. NG16: Nuth 4K 83
  NG24: New B 5E 136
KEXBY 3D 145
Key VI Fitness 1H 119
Keyes Cl. DN10: Matt T 1F 15
Keyes Ct. DN10: Matt T 1G 15
  (off Keyes Ri.)
Keyes Ri. DN10: Matt T 1F 15
Keys Cl. NG6: Bulw 7G 75
Key St. NG3: Nott 3C 96
KEYWORTH 1H 119 (2B 148)
Keyworth Cl. NG19: Mans 3E 46
Keyworth Dr. NG19: Mans W 1D 48
Keyworth La. NG11: Bunny 2C 118
Keyworth Leisure Cen. 7J 117
Keyworth Rd. NG4: Ged 4G 87
  NG12: Widm 6K 119
  NG12: Wys .6J 123
Kibworth Cl. NG5: Sher 3G 85
Kiddier Av. NG5: Arn 7K 77
Kielder Dr. NG13: Bing 4D 100
Kighill La. NG15: Rave 5C 62
Kilbourne Rd. NG5: Arn 5K 77
Kilbourn St. NG3: Nott 1E 6 (2K 95)
Kilburn Cl. NG9: Bram 6G 93
Kilby Av. NG3: Nott 2D 96
Kildare Rd. NG3: Nott 7C 86
Kildonan Cl. NG8: Stre 5J 83
KILLAMARSH 3A 144
Killarney Pk. NG6: Bestw V 7D 68
Killerton Grn. NG11: Clif 3G 115
Killerton Pk. Dr. NG2: West Br 5J 107
Killisick La. NG5: Arn 4K 77
Killisick Rd. NG5: Arn 6K 77
Kilnbrook Av. NG5: Arn 5K 77
KILNHURST 2A 144
Kilnwood Cl. NG3: Nott 1D 96
Kilsby Rd. NG11: Clif 7G 107
KILTON 1J 21
Kilton Av. NG18: Mans 3D 48
Kilton Cl. S81: Work 1H 21
Kilton Cres. S81: Work 1H 21
Kilton Forest Golf Course 6J 19
Kilton Glade S81: Work 1J 21
Kilton Hill S81: Work 1H 21
Kilton Rd. S80: Work 2H 21
Kilton Ter. S80: Work 2H 21
Kilton Ter. Ind. Est. S80: Work 2H 21
Kilverston Rd. NG10: Sand 3A 104
Kilverton Cl. NG8: Woll 4D 94
KILVINGTON 1D 149
Kilvington Rd. NG5: Arn 7K 77
Kimber Cl. NG8: Bilb 2J 93
KIMBERLEY 1E 82 (1A 148)
Kimberley Cl. NG16: Kimb 2E 82
Kimberley Eastwood By-Pass NG8: Cin 2F 83
  NG16: Eastw, Gilt, Kimb, Newth, Nuth 4B 72
Kimberley Leisure Cen. 1F 83
Kimberley Rd. NG16: Nuth 2G 83

Kimberley St. NG2: Nott 4D 96
Kimbolton Av. NG7: Lent, Radf 3G 95
Kindlewood Dr. NG9: Toton 7G 105
King Charles St. NG1: Nott 6D 6 (4J 95)
King Edward Av. NG18: Mans 6G 47
King Edward Cl. NG16: Jack 4G 7 (3A 96)
King Edward Gdns. NG10: Sand 3A 104
King Edward St. NG1: Nott 4G 7 (3A 96)
  NG10: Sand .3A 104
  NG15: Huck 7G 67
King Edward Ter. DN22: Retf 4F 23
King Edwins Cl. NG21: Edwin 7E 36
Kingfield Cl. NG21: Rain 3K 55
Kingfisher Cl. NG6: Basf 3E 84
  NG9: Bee 4C 106
  NG24: New B 5F 137
Kingfisher Ct. NG14: Lowd 3D 80
Kingfisher Rd. NG19: Mans 1C 46
Kingfishers Ct. NG2: West Br 5F 109
Kingfisher Wlk. S81: Gate 6D 18
Kingfisher Way NG17: Sut A 7B 46
Kingfisher Wharf NG7: Lent 6H 95
King George IV M. NG19: Mans 7E 40
King George V Av. NG18: Mans 5K 47
King John's Arc. NG1: Nott 5F 7
King John's Chambers NG1: Nott 5F 7
King John's Rd. NG21: C'tone 5J 43
King John Workshop Museum, The 1B 58
Kinglake Pl. NG2: Nott 6K 95
King Rd. NG20: Mkt W 4C 34
Kingrove Av. NG9: Chil 3J 105
Kings Av. NG4: Ged 5H 87
Kingsbridge Av. NG3: Mapp 1F 87
Kingsbridge Way NG9: Bram 3H 105
Kings Brook Cl. LE12: Remp 6F 123
Kingsbrook Ct. LE12: Stanf S 7A 122
Kingsbury Dr. NG8: Bilb 7B 84
KINGS CLIPSTONE 3K 43 (2B 146)
Kings Ct. NG17: Nunc 4B 60
  NG25: Sout .5H 131
Kingsdale S81: Work 4J 19
Kingsdown Mt. NG8: Woll 6K 93
Kings Dr. NG16: Brins 6C 64
Kingsford Av. NG7: Radf 2F 95
Kingsley Av. NG19: Mans W 4K 41
Kingsley Cl. NG19: Mans W 5K 41
Kingsley Ct. NG19: Mans W 4K 41
  S81: Work 1H 21
Kingsley Dr. NG4: Neth 2K 97
Kingsley Rd. NG2: Nott 4D 96
Kingsley St. NG17: Kirk A 7B 52
Kings Lodge Dr. NG18: Mans 6E 46
Kingsmead NG22: Ord 7D 22
Kingsmead Av. NG9: Trow 6C 92
Kings Mdw. NG21: Rain 3A 56
Kings Mill Rd. E. NG17: Sut A 5B 46
Kings Mill Rd. W. NG17: Sut A 4F 51
Kings Mill Way NG18: Mans 6E 46
Kingsmoor Cl. NG5: Top V 7A 76
Kingsnorth Cl. NG24: New T 1D 136
King's Pl. NG1: Nott 5G 7 (4A 96)
Kings Rd. NG10: Sand 3A 104
  NG24: New T 7C 134
Kings Sconce Av. NG24: New T 5D 134
Kings Stand NG18: Mans 6A 48
Kingsthorpe Cl. NG3: Nott 6C 86
  NG19: Mans W 1A 48
Kingston Av. DE7: Ilk 4A 92
Kingston Cl. S80: Work 5K 21
Kingston Ct. NG2: Nott 5K 7 (4B 96)
  NG12: Rad T .5E 98
  (off Bingham Rd.)
Kingston Dr. NG12: Cotg 7E 110
  NG22: Oll 3A 38
KINGSTON ON SOAR 1A 120 (3A 148)
Kingston Rd. NG2: West Br 3B 108
  NG18: Mans .3K 47
  S80: Work 4J 21
  S81: Carl L 6B 12
King St. NG1: Nott 4E 6 (4K 95)
  NG9: Bee 3B 106
  NG16: Eastw .4D 72
  NG16: Pinx 7B 50
  NG17: Huth 7F 45
  NG17: Kirk A .7A 52
  NG17: Sut A .1J 51
  NG18: Mans .3K 47
  NG19: Mans W 7J 41
  NG20: Wars 3A 34
  NG24: New T 2B 136
  NG25: Sout .6H 131
  S80: Work 2F 21
Kings Wlk. NG1: Nott 4E 6 (3K 95)
  NG18: Mans .6K 47
Kingsway NG12: Rad T 6D 98
  NG17: Kirk A .7B 52
  NG19: Mans W 1C 48
  NG24: New B 5F 137
  S81: Work 1H 21
Kingsway Av. NG22: New O 2D 38
Kingsway Gdns. NG15: Huck 2E 74
Kingsway Rd. NG15: Huck 2E 74
Kingswell Av. NG5: Arn 7H 77
Kingswell Rd. NG5: Arn 7H 77
Kingswood Cl. NG2: West Br 4A 108

Kingswood Dr. NG17: Kirk A 4K 51
Kingswood Rd. NG2: West Br 4A 108
  NG8: Woll 3C 94
Kinlet Rd. NG5: Bestw 1H 85
KINOULTON 2B 142 (2B 148)
Kinoulton La. NG12: Kin 1B 142
Kinoulton Rd. NG12: Crop Bi 7A 112
Kinross Cres. NG8: Bilb 2B 94
Kinsale Wlk. NG11: Clif 7F 107
Kipling Cl. NG11: Clif 2D 114
  S81: Work 7J 19
Kipling St. NG18: Mans 3G 47
Kipps St. NG1: Nott 4G 7 (3A 96)
KIRBY BELLARS .3C 149
Kirby Cl. NG16: Newth 3E 72
  NG21: Blid 7J 55
Kirby Rd. NG16: Newth 3E 72
KIRK BRAMWITH 1B 144
Kirkbride Ct. NG9: Chil 5G 105
Kirkby Cl. NG25: Sout 4H 131
Kirkby Folly Rd. NG17: Sut A 2B 52
Kirkby Gdns. NG2: Nott 6A 96
KIRKBY HARDWICK 3B 52
Kirkby Hardwick NG17: Sut A 3A 52
Kirkby Ho. Dr. NG17: Kirk A 6J 51
KIRKBY-IN-ASHFIELD 6B 52 (3A 146)
Kirkby-in-Ashfield Station (Rail) 6A 52
Kirkby La. NG16: Pinx 1D 58
Kirkby Mill Vw. NG17: Kirk A 7J 51
Kirkby Rd. NG15: Rave 7J 53
  NG17: Sut A .3J 51
KIRKBY WOODHOUSE 3J 59
Kirk Cl. NG9: Chil .5J 105
Kirkdale Cl. NG8: Woll 4G 93
Kirkdale Rd. NG3: Nott 2E 96
Kirk Dr. NG22: Bou .2E 28
Kirke Cl. NG22: East M 2E 28
Kirke St. DN22: Retf 3F 23
Kirkewhite Ct. NG2: Nott 6A 96
Kirkewhite St. W. NG2: Nott 6K 95
Kirkewhite Wlk. NG2: Nott 6K 95
Kirkfell Cl. NG2: West Br 4F 109
Kirk Ga. NG24: New T 7C 134
KIRK HALLAM 1A 148
Kirkham Dr. NG9: Toton 7E 104
Kirk Hill NG13: East B 5D 90
Kirkhill NG13: Bing .3F 101
Kirkland Av. NG18: Mans 4F 47
Kirkland Cl. NG17: Sut A 2B 52
Kirkland Dr. NG9: Chil 7H 105
Kirk La. NG11: Rudd 3K 115
Kirkley Gdns. NG5: Arn 6J 77
Kirk Ley Rd. LE12: East L 5K 121
KIRKLINGTON 1C 132 (3B 146)
Kirklington Cl. NG25: Sout 5G 131
Kirklington Rd.
  NG21: Rain 2J 55
  NG22: Bils 7D 126
  NG22: Eakr 4C 126
  NG22: Farns .1G 57
  NG22: Kirk 1B 132
  NG25: Hock .1K 131
  NG25: Sout .4G 131
Kirkpatrick Dr. S81: Gate 1C 18
Kirk Pl. NG16: Pinx .1C 58
Kirk Rd. NG3: Mapp 5D 86
KIRK SANDALL 1B 144
Kirk's Bldgs. NG4: Carl 1G 97
Kirks Cft. NG21: Blid 7H 55
KIRKSTEAD 1A 58
Kirkstead Cl. NG16: Pinx 1B 58
Kirkstead Gdns. NG7: H Grn 1G 95
Kirkstead Rd. NG16: Pinx 1B 58
Kirkstead St. NG7: H Grn 1G 95
Kirkstone Av. DE75: Hea 5A 72
Kirkstone Ct. NG10: Long E 7A 104
Kirkstone Dr. NG2: Gam 2F 109
Kirtle Cl. NG8: Aspl .7C 84
Kirtley Cl. NG16: Want 6A 74
Kirtley Dr. NG7: Lent 6H 95
Kirtling Cl. NG5: Bestw 6E 76
KIRTON .7J 27 (2B 146)
Kirton Cl. NG19: Mans 3D 46
  NG20: Mede V 7G 33
  NG24: Bald 7G 137
Kirton Ct. NG22: Kirt 2H 39
KIRTON IN LINDSEY 2D 145
Kirton Pk. NG22: Kirt 2J 39
Kirton Rd. NG22: Egma 2A 124
Kitchener Dr. NG18: Mans 4J 47
Kitchener Gdns. S81: Gate 4F 19
Kitchener Ter. NG20: Whal T 5B 26
Kitson Av. NG16: Jack 1A 64
Kittiwake M. NG7: Lent 4F 95
KIVETON PARK 3A 144
Kiwi Cl. NG15: Huck 1D 74
KK Sports & Leisure Cen. 2D 96
KNAITH 3D 145
KNAITH PARK 3D 145
Knapp Av. NG16: Eastw 5D 72
Knaton Rd. S81: Carl L 6B 12
Kneesal Cl. NG20: Mede V 1F 35
KNEESALL 2C 147
Kneesall Gro. NG15: Huck 6H 67
Kneesall Rd. NG22: Lax 7A 124
KNEETON 1C 149

Kneeton Cl. NG4: Ged 3G 87
NG5: Sher 3K 85
Kneeton Rd. NG13: East B 4D 90
Kneeton Va. NG5: Sher 3K 85
Kneeton Vw. NG14: Hove 4K 81
Knighton Av. NG7: Radf 2F 95
Knighton Rd. NG5: Woodt 2A 86
Knightsbridge Ct. *NG5: Sher 4K 85*
(off St Albans St.)
Knightsbridge Dr. NG2: West Br 5K 107
NG16: Nuth 4K 83
Knightsbridge Gdns. NG15: Huck 3F 67
Knightsbridge Way NG15: Huck 4F 67
Knights Cl. NG2: West Br 6K 107
NG5: Top V 6B 76
NG9: Toton 7E 104
Knight's Ct. NG24: New T 1D 136
Knight St. NG4: Neth 2J 97
Knightwood Dr. NG6: Bestw V 1D 76
KNIPTON 2D 149
Knipton Cl. NG24: Bald 6G 137
Knole Rd. NG8: Woll 3K 93
Knoll, The NG18: Mans 4E 46
Knoll Av. NG15: Huck 1D 74
Knott End S81: Lango 1B 12
Knott's Ct. NG24: Bald 5G 137
Knowle Hill NG16: Kimb 2F 83
Knowle La. NG16: Kimb 3F 83
Knowle Pk. NG16: Kimb 2F 83
Knowles Wlk. NG5: Arn 6F 77
Kozi Kots NG4: Neth 1J 97
Krebs Cl. NG11: Clif 1D 114
Kurburgring, The (Karting) 2D 50
Kyle Vw. NG5: Top V 5C 76
Kyme St. NG7: Radf 3A 6 (3G 95)
Kynance Cl. DE55: Sth N 5A 50
Kynance Gdns. NG11: Wilf 4J 107

L

Labray Rd. NG14: Calv 5C 70
Laburnum Av. NG12: Key 1K 119
NG17: Kirk A 1H 59
Laburnum Cl. NG10: Sand 2A 104
NG24: New B 4F 137
S80: Work 4E 20
Laburnum Gdns. NG6: Bulw 2F 85
Laburnum Gro. NG9: Bee 4C 106
NG15: Huck 1H 75
NG19: Mans W 5G 41
Laburnum Rd. S81: Lango 1C 12
Laburnum St. NG3: Nott 1A 96
Laceby Ct. NG19: Mans W 5A 42
Lace Ct. NG10: Long E 7B 104
LACE MARKET 6G 7 (4A 96)
Lace Mkt. Sq. NG1: Nott 5G 7
Lace Market Stop (NET) 5F 7 (4K 95)
Lace Market Theatre 6G 7 (4A 96)
Lace Mill Ct. NG6: Basf 4E 84
Lace Rd. NG9: Bee 2A 106
Lace St. NG7: Nott, Lent 7E 94
Lace Way NG1: Nott 6J 7 (4B 96)
Lacey Av. NG15: Huck 1G 75
Laceyfields Rd. DE75: Hea 5A 72
Lacey Grn. NG24: Bald 6H 137
Lacey Gro. NG15: Ann 5D 60
Ladbrooke Cres. NG6: Basf 4D 84
Ladybank Ri. NG5: Arn 6A 78
Lady Bay Av. NG2: West Br 7C 96
Lady Bay Bri. NG2: Nott, West Br 6B 96
Lady Bay Ct. NG2: West Br 7D 96
Lady Bay Rd. NG2: West Br 7D 96
Ladybay Workshops *NG2: West Br 7C 96*
(off Lady Bay Av.)
Ladybridge Cl. NG9: Atten 6K 105
LADYBROOK 3E 46
Ladybrook La. NG18: Mans 4E 46
NG19: Mans 4D 46
Ladybrook Pl. NG18: Mans 3E 46
Ladycroft Av. NG15: Huck 6G 67
Lady Lea Cl. S80: Work 3C 20
Lady Lee Quarry Nature Reserve 1C 20
Lady Margarets Cres. NG20: Nort 2E 32
Lady's Holt La. DN10: Bawt 1H 9
Ladysmith St. NG2: Nott 4D 96
Ladysmock Gdns. NG2: Nott 6A 96
Lady Wlk. S81: Gate 5D 18
LA Fitness
Newark-on-Trent 6E 134
Lake Av. NG19: Mans 3D 46
Lake Farm Rd. NG21: Rain 2H 55
Lakehead Ho. NG11: Clif 1F 115
Lakeland Av. NG15: Huck 1J 75
Lakeland Rd. NG14: Calv 7G 71
Lakeside Arts Cen. 7D 94
Lakeside Cen. NG24: New B 4F 137
Lakeside Ct. NG15: Ann 6A 60
NG22: Bils 5D 126
Lakeside Point NG17: Sut A 6B 46
Lakeside Vw. NG17: Sut A 6B 46
Lake St. NG7: Radf 1A 6 (2G 95)
Lake Vw. Dr. NG15: Ann 6K 59
Lamartine St. NG3: Nott 3H 7 (3A 96)
Lamb Cl. NG16: Eastw 7F 65
NG24: New T 3A 136
Lamb Cl. Dr. NG16: Eastw, Newth 2E 72
Lambcroft Rd. NG16: Pinx 7B 50
Lambert Gdns. NG8: Aspl 7D 84
Lambert Hill NG15: Huck 6F 67
Lambert St. NG7: H Grn 1F 95
Lambeth Ct. NG9: Bee 2C 106
Lambeth Rd. NG5: Arn 4C 76
Lambie Cl. NG8: Woll 3D 94
Lamb La. S81: Fir 7A 8
LAMBLEY 7G 79 (1B 148)
Lambley Almshouses NG3: Nott 7A 86
Lambley Av. NG3: Mapp 4E 86
NG18: Mans 5B 48
Lambley Bridle Rd. NG14: Bur J 1C 88
Lambley Ct. NG3: Mapp 4C 86
Lambley La. NG4: Ged 4H 87
NG14: Bur J 2C 88
Lambley Rd. NG14: Lowd 6K 79
Lambourne Cl. NG9: Bram 1H 105
Lambourne Cres. NG14: Lowd 5E 80
Lambourne Dr. NG8: Woll 3A 94
Lambourne Gdns. NG5: Woodt 2D 86
Lamcote Gdns. NG12: Rad T 5D 98
Lamcote Gro. NG2: Nott 7A 96
Lamcote M. NG12: Rad T 5D 98
Lamcote St. NG2: Nott 7A 96
Lamins La. NG6: Bestw V 1D 76
Lammas Cl. NG17: Sut A 1J 51
Lammas Gdns. NG2: Nott 6A 96
NG13: East B 3E 90
Lammas La. NG13: East B 3E 90
Lammas Leisure Cen. 7J 45
Lammas Rd. NG17: Sut A 1H 51
Lamond Cl. NG19: Mans 5E 46
Lamorna Gro. NG11: Wilf 3J 107
Lamplands NG12: Cotg 6D 110
Lamp Wood Cl. NG14: Calv 6C 70
Lanark Cl. NG8: Woll 5D 94
Lancaster Av. NG9: Stap 3D 104
NG10: Sand 5A 104
Lancaster Ct. NG3: Nott 1E 96
Lancaster Rd. DN10: Gri H 3C 16
NG3: Nott 1E 96
NG6: Bestw V 2A 76
NG15: Huck 2D 74
NG24: Codd 6H 135
Lancaster Wlk. S81: Work 4F 19
Lancaster Way NG8: Stre 5J 83
Lancastrian Way S81: Work 6H 19
Lancelot Dr. NG16: Want 5K 73
Lancelyn Gdns. NG2: West Br 5B 108
Lanchester Gdns. S80: Work 3H 21
Landa Gro. NG22: Tuxf 6D 28
Landcroft Cres. NG5: Bestw 1H 85
Landcroft La. LE12: Sut B 4B 120
Landmere Gdns. NG3: Nott 6C 86
Landmere La. NG2: West Br 6J 107
NG11: Rudd 7A 108
NG12: Edwal 1C 116
Landseer Cl. NG7: Radf 2F 95
NG25: Sout 6F 131
Landseer Rd. NG25: Sout 6F 131
Lane, The NG16: Aws 3B 82
Lane End NG17: Kirk A 4A 52
LANEHAM 2G 29 (1D 147)
Laneham Av. NG5: Arn 7J 77
Laneham Rd. DN22: Lane 2F 29
NG22: Dun T 2F 29
Laneham St. DN22: Ramp 7K 25
Lanercost M. *S80: Work 3G 21*
(off Pilgrim Way)
Laneside Av. NG9: Toton 7D 104
LANGAR 7K 113 (2C 149)
Langar Cl. NG5: Sher 3K 85
Langar La. NG12: Cols B 7J 141
NG13: Lang 7J 113 & 7J 141
Langar Pl. NG19: Mans W 2D 48
Langar Rd. NG12: Cols B 6F 113
NG13: Bing 5F 101
NG13: Cols B, Lang 6F 113 & 4K 141
Langbank Av. NG5: Top V 5A 76
Langdale Cl. NG24: New T 5B 136
Langdale Gro. NG13: Bing 4C 100
Langdale Rd. NG3: Nott 3E 96
S81: Work 5G 19
Langdon Cl. NG5: Sher 5H 85
Langdown Cl. NG6: Bulw 6G 75
LANGFORD 3D 147
Langford La. NG23: Hol 5K 129
Langford Rd. NG5: Arn 7K 77
NG19: Mans 4D 46
Langford St. NG17: Sut A 7J 45
Langham Av. NG3: Nott 2D 96
Langham Dr. NG14: Bur J 2E 88
Langham Pk. DE7: Stant D 7A 92
DE55: Sth N 4B 50
Langham Pl. NG18: Mans 3F 47
LANGLEY 5A 72 (1A 148)
Langley Av. NG5: Arn 1C 86
Langley Bus. Pk. NG16: Lang M 4A 72
Langley Cl. NG6: Bestw V 2A 76
NG19: Mans 1E 46
LANGLEY MILL 3A 72
Langley Mill By-Pass NG16: Lang M 1A 72
Langley Mill Station (Rail) 3A 72
Langley Pk. NG16: Lang M 3A 72
Langley St. S80: Work 3G 21
LANGOLD 1C 12 (3A 144)
Langold Country Pk. 2B 12
Langstrath Dr. NG2: West Br 5F 109
Langstrath Rd. NG11: Clif 1F 115
Langton Av. NG17: Kirk A 5H 51
Langton Cl. NG4: Colw 2H 97
Langton Ct. NG17: Sut A 1J 51
Langton Hollow NG16: Sels 6B 58
Langton Rd. NG17: Sut A 1J 51
Langtry Gdns. NG13: Bing 3G 101
Langtry Gro. NG7: Basf 6H 85
Langwell Dr. NG19: Mans W 7E 42
LANGWITH 6A 26 (2A 146)
Langwith Dr. NG20: Langw 6A 26
Langwith Lodge Dr. NG20: Neth L 5C 26
Langwith Maltings NG20: Langw 7A 26
Langwith Rd. NG20: Cuck 5B 32
Langwith-Whaley Thorns Station (Rail) 5A 26
Lanky Bills Fun Shack 2A 72
Lansbury Av. NG22: New O 2C 38
Lansbury Dr. NG22: Bils 4C 126
Lansbury Gdns. NG18: Mans 2A 48
Lansbury Rd. NG17: Sut A 2K 51
NG21: Edwin 6F 37
NG22: Bils 4B 126
NG24: New B 5F 137
Lansdown Cl. NG9: Chil 5G 105
Lansdown Dr. DN22: Ord 7E 22
Lansdowne Av. NG18: Mans 1K 53
Lansdowne Ct. DN22: Ord 6D 22
Lansdowne Dr. NG2: West Br 5A 108
Lansdowne Rd. NG6: Basf 3F 85
Lansic La. NG14: Hove 5J 81
Lansing Cl. NG11: Clif 2G 115
Lantern La. LE12: East L 2B 122
Lanthwaite Cl. NG11: Clif 1F 115
Lanthwaite Rd. NG11: Clif 1G 115
Lapford Cl. NG3: Mapp 1G 87
Larch Av. NG19: Mans W 4H 41
Larch Cl. NG2: West Br 7F 97
NG5: Arn 6E 76
NG13: Bing 4H 101
NG15: Huck 1H 75
NG16: Unde 2F 65
Larch Cres. NG9: Bee 2K 105
NG16: Eastw 4C 72
Larchdene Av. NG8: Woll 5J 93
Larch Dr. NG10: Sand 2A 104
Larch Gdns. NG6: Bulw 7G 75
Larch Ho. NG5: Sher 4A 86
NG17: Sut A 5D 46
Larch Rd. NG22: New O 3D 38
Larch Way NG12: Key 1K 119
Largs Cl. NG5: Top V 4A 76
Lark Cl. NG9: Chil 4F 105
Larkdale St. NG7: Radf 2A 6 (2H 95)
Larkfield Av. NG17: Ann W 3J 59
Larkfield Rd. NG16: Nuth 2G 83
LARKFIELDS 2G 83
Larkfields NG24: New T 4A 136
Larkhall Pl. NG19: Mans 5E 46
Lark Hill Village NG11: Clif 2D 114
Larkland's Av. DE7: Ilk 1A 92
Lark Spinney S81: Gate 6D 18
Larkspur Av. NG5: Redh 4G 77
Larkspur Cl. NG19: Mans W 7K 41
Larkwood Cl. NG8: Bilb 7B 84
Larwood Av. S81: Work 6J 19
Larwood Cres. NG17: Nunc 3K 59
Larwood Gro. NG5: Sher 3K 85
Larwood Ho. S81: Work 6J 19
Lascelles Av. NG4: Ged 5G 87
Latham St. NG6: Bulw 7H 75
Lathkill Cl. NG6: Bulw 7H 75
Lathkill Dr. NG16: Sels 5D 58
Latimer Cl. NG6: Bulw 1D 84
Latimer Dr. NG9: Bram 5G 93
Latimer Way NG22: New O 5C 38
Latin Gro. NG15: Huck 5J 67
LAUGHTERTON 1D 147
LAUGHTON 2D 145
Laughton Av. NG2: West Br 5K 107
LAUGHTON COMMON 3A 144
Laughton Cres. NG15: Huck 2E 74
LAUGHTON EN LE MORTHEN 3A 144
Launceston Cres. NG11: Wilf 5H 107
Launder St. NG2: Nott 6K 95
NG13: Ors 1J 103
Launds Av. NG16: Sels 5B 58
Laurel Av. NG12: Key 1J 119
NG18: Mans 5J 47
NG19: Mans W 1B 48
NG20: Chu W 1C 34
Laurel Cl. NG12: Wys 6J 123
Laurel Cres. NG16: Nuth 7B 74
Laurel Gro. DN22: Retf 5F 23
NG17: Kirk A 6C 52
Laurel Rd. NG4: Carl 7G 87
Lauren Gro. NG9: Toton 7E 104
Laurie Av. NG7: H Grn 7H 85
Laurie Cl. NG7: H Grn 7H 85
Lauriston Dr. NG6: Bulw 3E 84
Lavelle Ct. NG9: Chil 7H 105
Lavender Cl. NG8: Brox 6K 83
Lavender Cres. NG4: Carl 6G 87

Lavender Gdns. DE75: Hea 5A 72
Lavender Gro. NG9: Bee 4C 106
Lavender Wlk. NG3: Nott 1A 96
Lavender Way NG24: New T 7H 135
Lavenham M. S80: Work 3G 21
(off Abbey St.)
Laver Cl. NG5: Arn 7K 77
Laverick Rd. NG16: Jack 6A 64
Laverock Cl. NG16: Kimb 1E 82
Lawdon Rd. NG5: Arn .5J 77
Lawley Av. NG9: Lent A 7B 94
Lawn Av. NG17: Sut A .1K 51
Lawn Ct. S81: Costh 4B 12
Lawn Gro. NG4: Carl, Ged 6K 87
Lawn La. NG17: Sut A .1K 51
Lawn Mill Rd. NG16: Kimb 7J 73
Lawn Mills NG16: Kimb 7H 73
Lawn Pleasure Grounds, The 1K 51
Lawn Rd. NG17: Sut A .7B 46
S81: Costh 4B 12
Lawns, The NG13: What 5D 102
NG23: Coll 1J 129
Lawns Rd. NG17: Ann W 4K 59
Lawnwood Av. DN22: Elk 3F 27
Lawnwood La. DN22: Elk 3F 27
Lawrence Av. NG4: Colw 3H 97
NG16: Aws 3B 82
NG16: Eastw 4D 72
NG17: Kirk A 6J 51
NG19: Mans W 5G 41
Lawrence Cl. NG12: Cotg 6E 110
Lawrence Cres. NG17: Sut A 6B 46
Lawrence Dr. NG8: Stre 5H 83
NG16: Brins 5B 64
Lawrence M. NG12: Cotg 6E 110
Lawrence Pk. NG16: Unde 2F 65
Lawrence Pl. NG24: New T 7D 134
Lawrence St. NG9: Stap 3C 104
NG10: Sand 2A 104
NG24: New T 7D 134
Lawrence Way NG7: Lent 6H 95
Lawson Sq. S81: Blyth 7H 13
Lawson St. NG7: Radf 1A 6 (2H 95)
Lawton Dr. NG6: Bulw 5J 75
LAXTON 5B 124 (2C 147)
Laxton Av. NG6: Bulw .2E 84
NG17: Sut A 2C 52
Laxton Dr. NG15: Huck 7E 66
NG20: Mede V 7F 33
Laxton Rd. NG22: Egma, Lax 5C 124
Laxton Vis. Cen. 5B 124
Laycock Av. DN10: Gri H 3A 16
Layton Av. NG18: Mans 3G 47
Layton Burroughs NG18: Mans 3G 47
LEA 3D 145
Leabrook Cl. NG11: Clif 6D 106
Leabrook Gdns. NG15: Huck 5J 67
Leabrooks Av. NG17: Sut A 3C 52
NG19: Mans W 4K 41
Leach Cl. NG22: Dun T 6J 29
Leachcroft Hill NG25: Sout 6E 130
Leach's Bldgs. NG24: New T 2B 136
Leach Way NG21: Blid .5K 55
Lea Cl. NG15: Rave 2C 62
Lea Ct. S80: Work 3D 20
Leacroft Rd. NG8: Aspl 1E 94
Leadale Av. NG15: Huck 5J 67
Leadale Cres. NG19: Mans W 4A 42
LEADENHAM 3D 147
Lead Hill S80: Work 3F 21
Leaf Cl. NG15: Huck 4H 67
Leafe Cl. NG9: Chil 7H 105
Leafield DN22: Retf 2D 22
Leafield Grn. NG11: Clif 7F 107
Leahurst Gdns. NG2: West Br 4E 108
Leahurst Rd. NG2: West Br 4D 108
Leahy Gdns. NG5: Bestw 1G 85
Leake La. LE12: Stanf S 7K 121
Leake Rd. LE12: Costo 3C 122
NG11: Goth 7G 115
Lea La. NG16: Sels 6D 58
Leam Glen NG19: Mans W 7K 41
Leamington Bldgs. NG17: Sut A 2K 51
(off Leamington Dr.)
Leamington Dr. DE55: Sth N 6A 50
NG9: Chil 5H 105
NG17: Sut A 3J 51
Leamington Hall Bungs. NG17: Sut A 2J 51
Leamington Hall Flats NG17: Sut A 2J 51
(off Stuart St.)
Leander Cl. NG11: Wilf 3J 107
NG17: Sut A 1B 52
Lea Rd. NG15: Rave 3D 62
NG20: Mkt W 5E 34
Leas, The NG14: Bulc 2G 89
Leas Av. NG19: Plea 4A 40
Leas Rd. NG19: Mans W 5K 41
Lea Vw. NG21: Rain 2K 55
Le Brun Sq. S81: Carl L 5B 12
Lechlade Rd. NG5: Bestw 1H 85
Ledbury Va. NG8: Aspl 7C 84
Ledger Wlk. NG5: Sher 6J 85
(off Jensen Way)
Leech Ct. NG16: Gilt 7F 73
Lee Cres. DE7: Ilk 7A 82
Leeds Rd. S81: Shire 5A 18

Leeks Cl. NG25: Sout .5H 131
Lee La. DE75: Hea 5A 72
Leeming Cl. NG20: Mkt W 3E 34
Leeming Ct. DN10: Bawt 1J 9
Leeming La. NG19: Mans W 3A 42
Leeming La. Nth. NG19: Mans W 6K 41
Leeming La. Sth. NG19: Mans W 1J 47
Leeming Pk. NG19: Mans W 6J 41
Leeming St. NG18: Mans 3H 47
Leen Cl. NG5: Bestw V 2B 76
NG15: Huck 5J 67
Leen Ct. NG7: Lent 6F 95
NG22: Bou 4G 39
Leen Dr. NG6: Bulw 5J 75
NG15: Huck 4H 67
Leen Ga. NG7: Lent, Nott 6E 94
Leen Mills NG15: Huck 4H 67
Leen Pl. NG7: Radf 3F 95
Leen Valley Country Pk. 1K 75
Leen Valley Way NG15: Huck 1J 75
Lee Rd. NG7: Bur J 2F 89
NG14: Calv 5B 70
Lees Av. NG19: Mans .3D 46
Lees Barn Rd. NG12: Rad T 6C 98
Lees Fld. NG25: Sout .7G 131
Lees Hill Footpath NG2: Nott 7K 7 (5B 96)
Lees Hill St. NG2: Nott 6K 7 (4B 96)
Lees Rd. NG3: Mapp 6D 86
Leeway Cl. NG21: Rain 1G 55
Leeway Rd. NG21: Rain 1G 55
NG25: Sout 5G 131
Lee Westwood Sports Cen. 6E 106
Legion Dr. NG17: Skeg 4H 45
Leicester Cres. S81: Work 5F 19
Leicester Ho. NG9: Bram 1E 104
Leigh Cl. NG2: West Br 3K 107
Leigh Rd. NG9: Toton 6E 104
Leighton Pk. NG22: Bils 4B 126
Leighton St. NG3: Nott 2C 96
Leiston Gdns. NG5: Top V 6C 76
Leivers Av. NG5: Arn 6H 77
Leivers Cl. LE12: East L 3K 121
Leivers Ho. NG5: Arn .1D 86
(off Derwent Cres.)
Lema Cl. NG6: Bulw 6K 75
Lemont Rd. NG19: Mans W 7C 42
Lendal Ct. NG7: Radf 3A 6 (3H 95)
Lendrum Ct. NG14: Bur J 3E 88
Len Maynard Ct. NG3: Nott 2D 96
Lennox St. NG1: Nott 4H 7 (3A 96)
LENTON ABBEY 7B 94
Lenton Av. NG7: Nott 6A 6 (4H 95)
NG12: Toll 1F 117
Lenton Blvd. NG7: Lent 3G 95
Lenton Bus. Pk. NG7: Lent 4F 95
Lenton Cir. NG12: Toll 1F 117
Lenton Ct. NG7: Lent .4G 95
NG7: Nott .7A 6 (5H 95)
Lenton Hall Dr. NG7: Nott 6D 94
Lenton Ind. Est. E. NG7: Lent 2G 107
Lenton Ind. Est. W. NG7: Lent 1G 107
Lenton La. NG7: Lent .6G 95
Lenton Mnr. NG7: Lent 5F 95
Lenton Rd. NG7: Nott 7A 6 (5H 95)
Lenton St. NG10: Sand 3B 104
Lenton Ter. NG24: New T 1B 136
Leonard Av. NG5: Sher 5J 85
Leonard M. NG9: Chil 7G 105
Leonard St. NG6: Bulw 2C 84
Leopold St. NG17: Sut A 2J 51
Le Page Ct. NG8: Bilb .7B 84
Leroy Wallace Av. NG7: Radf 2G 95
Lerwick Cl. NG11: Clif 1H 115
S81: Work 3F 19
Leslie Av. NG7: H Grn .7H 85
NG9: Bee 4A 106
NG16: Kimb 2E 82
Leslie Gro. NG14: Calv 6D 70
Leslie Rd. NG7: H Grn 7H 85
(not continuous)
Letchworth Cres. NG9: Chil 5H 105
Letcombe Rd. NG11: Clif 6F 107
LETWELL 3A 144
Levellers Way NG24: New T 1H 137
Levens Cl. NG2: West Br 4F 109
Leverton Cl. NG2: West Br 4C 108
Leverton Grn. NG11: Clif 7F 107
Leverton Rd. DN22: Retf 3G 23
DN22: Stu S 5C 24
NG18: Mans 3E 46
Levertons Pl. NG15: Huck 2H 75
Leverton Wlk. NG5: Arn 6J 77
Levick Ct. NG2: Nott 6K 95
Lewindon Ct. NG5: Woodt 3B 86
Lewis Cl. NG3: Nott 1G 7 (2A 96)
Lewis Way NG6: Bestw V 1D 76
Lewsey Cl. NG9: Chil .7G 105
Lexington Ct. NG22: Tuxf 7C 28
Lexington Gdns. NG5: Sher 3A 86
NG22: Tuxf 7C 28
Lexington Pl. NG1: Nott 5H 7
Leybourne Dr. NG5: Bestw 1F 85
Ley Cft. NG19: Mans W 4K 41
Leyland Cl. NG9: Toton 7E 104
Ley La. NG19: Mans W 5J 41

Leys, The NG11: Clif 7D 106
NG12: Norm W 3J 117
NG14: Lowd 4D 80
Leys Ct. NG11: Rudd .4K 115
Leys La. DN10: Gri H 3A 16
Leys Rd. NG11: Rudd .4K 115
Leyton Av. NG17: Skeg 5K 45
Leyton Cres. NG9: Bee 4C 106
Liber Cl. NG19: Mans W 2C 48
Library Rd. NG7: Nott .7D 94
Lichfield Av. NG18: Mans 1J 53
Lichfield Cl. NG9: Toton 6D 104
NG18: Mans 1J 53
S81: Work 5H 19
Lichfield La. NG18: Mans 7K 47
Lichfield Rd. NG2: Nott 4D 96
Lichfield Wlk. S81: Carl L 5B 12
Liddell Gro. NG8: Woll .3A 94
Liddington St. NG7: Basf 6G 85
Lidget La. DN22: Retf .3G 23
LIDGETT 7J 37 (2B 146)
Lido Cl. NG6: Bulw 5J 75
Lifton Av. DN22: Retf 1E 22
Lightfoot Cl. NG24: New T 1H 137
Lilac Av. NG4: Carl 7F 87
Lilac Cl. NG8: Brox 6K 83
NG12: Key 1K 119
NG24: New T 5C 136
Lilac Ct. NG11: Clif 1D 114
Lilac Cres. NG9: Bee .4C 106
Lilac Gro. NG9: Bee 4C 106
NG17: Kirk A 7H 51
NG19: Mans W 7F 43
NG20: Chu W 1B 34
Lilac Rd. NG15: Huck .1H 75
Lilacs, The NG9: Bee .3A 106
Lilac Tree Gro. S81: Carl L 5B 12
Lilburne Cl. NG24: New T 1H 137
Lilian Hind Ct. NG6: Bulw 6F 75
Lillee Ct. S81: Work 7J 19
Lilleker Ri. NG5: Arn 5G 77
Lilley Cl. NG16: Sels 6C 58
Lillie Ter. NG2: Nott 4C 96
Lillington Rd. NG6: Bulw 7H 75
Lily Av. NG4: Neth 1K 97
Lily Cl. NG24: New T .7G 135
Lily Gro. NG9: Bee 4C 106
Limb Cres. NG17: Sut A 2K 51
Lime Acres NG20: Neth L 5B 26
Lime Av. NG16: Lang M 4A 72
NG17: Huth 7E 44
NG17: Sut A 6K 45
Lime Cl. NG12: Rad T .5E 98
NG16: Nuth 1F 83
NG16: Pinx 1B 58
Lime Cres. NG20: Chu W 2B 34
Limefield Ct. NG2: West Br 7D 96
Lime Gro. DN22: Retf .3D 22
NG9: Stap 4C 104
NG10: Sand 3A 104
NG19: Mans W 7E 42
NG24: New T 2C 136
Lime Gro. Av. NG9: Chil 4K 105
Limekiln Ct. NG6: Bulw 6G 75
Lime Kiln Pl. NG18: Mans 4G 47
Limekiln Way S81: Shire 5A 18
Lime La. NG5: Arn 1G 77
Limes, The DN10: Beck 6C 16
NG11: Bart F 7A 114
Limes Av. NG20: Neth L 5B 26
Limes Cl. NG16: Lang M 2A 72
Limes Cres. NG17: Sut A 1C 52
Limestone Cl. S81: Woods 1A 18
Limestone Ri. NG19: Mans 2G 47
Limestone Ter. NG19: Mans W 5H 41
Lime St. NG6: Bulw 7H 75
NG17: Kirk A 7A 52
NG17: Sut A 6A 46
Lime Tree Av. DN22: Retf 3D 22
NG8: Cin 4C 84
NG8: Woll 5C 94
NG17: Kirk A 6K 51
NG17: Skeg 4H 45
NG19: Mans W 5G 41
S81: Carl L 5B 12
Limetree Av. S80: Carb, Nort 2J 33
NG23: Coll 2H 129
Limetree Cl. NG12: Key 1J 119
Lime Tree Cl. NG18: Mans 7B 94
Lime Tree Dr. NG18: Mans 4A 94
Lime Tree Gdns. NG14: Lowd 5E 80
Lime Tree Pl. NG18: Mans 4J 47
NG21: Rain 2A 56
Lime Tree Rd. DN22: Elk 3G 27
NG15: Huck 2H 75
NG22: New O 3C 38
Limmen Gdns. NG3: Nott 2J 7 (2B 96)
Limpenny St. NG7: Radf 2A 6 (2G 95)
LINBY .2H 67 (3A 146)
Linby Av. NG15: Huck .6H 67
NG19: Mans 4D 46
Linby Cl. NG4: Ged 5H 87
NG5: Sher 2A 86
Linby Dr. NG8: Stre 5J 83

Linby Gro. NG15: Huck 5H **67**
Linby Ho. NG15: Lin 2H **67**
Linby La. NG15: Lin, Pap 2H **67**
Linby Rd. NG15: Huck 5H **67**
Linby St. NG6: Bulw 6J **75**
Linby Wlk. NG15: Huck 5G **67**
Lincoln Av. NG10: Sand 5A **104**
Lincoln Cir. NG7: Nott 6A **6** (4H **95**)
Lincoln Cl. NG9: Stap 7D **92**
Lincoln Ct. NG8: Bilb 1J **93**
NG24: New T 5E **134**
Lincoln Dr. NG19: Mans W 5K **41**
Lincoln Gro. NG12: Rad T 5E **98**
Lincoln Ho. NG3: Mapp P 7A **86**
Lincoln Rd. NG22: East M 2D **28**
NG22: Tuxf 6C **28**
NG24: New T 5E **134**
Lincoln Rd. Bri. NG24: New T 6D **134**
Lincoln St. NG1: Nott 4F **7** (3K **95**)
NG6: Basf 4F **85**
NG24: New T 6D **134**
S80: Work 4H **21**
Lincoln Vw. S80: Work 3H **21**
Lindale Cl. NG2: Gam 3F **109**
Lindbergh Cl. S80: Work 3D **20**
Lindbridge Rd. NG8: Brox 5A **84**
Lind Cl. NG21: Rain 2H **55**
Linden Av. NG11: Clif 1D **114**
NG22: Tuxf 6D **28**
NG24: New B 3E **136**
Linden Ct. NG9: Bee 4B **106**
NG21: Edwin 6F **37**
Linden Gro. NG4: Ged 6A **88**
NG9: Bee 4B **106**
NG9: Stap 3D **104**
NG10: Sand 2A **104**
NG17: Kirk A 5H **51**
Linden Pl. NG3: Mapp 1F **87**
Linden Rd. NG19: Mans W 2B **48**
Linden St. NG3: Nott 1A **96**
NG19: Mans 1G **47**
Lindfield Cl. NG8: Brox 5B **84**
Lindfield Rd. NG8: Brox 5A **84**
Lindholme Way NG17: Skeg 5K **45**
Lindhurst La. NG18: Mans 1C **54**
(Syerston Rd.)
NG18: Mans 6B **48**
(Woodland Dr.)
Lindisfarne Gdns. NG5: Top V 5C **76**
Lindley Av. NG17: Sut A 1H **51**
Lindleys Ct. NG17: Kirk A 7A **52**
Lindley's La. NG17: Kirk A 1A **60**
Lindley St. NG16: Newth 2F **73**
NG16: Sels 6B **58**
NG18: Mans 3G **47**
Lindley Ter. NG7: H Grn 1F **95**
Lindrick Cl. NG12: Edwal 5F **109**
NG19: Mans W 3K **41**
S81: Carl L 6C **12**
S81: Work 7G **19**
Lindrick Ct. DN22: Ord 7D **22**
S81: Woods 1A **18**
Lindrick Rd. NG17: Kirk A 4K **51**
Lindsay Av. NG17: Nunc 3B **60**
NG24: New T 5C **136**
Lindsay Cl. NG18: Mans 4G **47**
Lindsay St. NG7: H Grn 1G **95**
Lindsey Dr. NG18: Mans 7C **48**
Lindsey Rd. DN11: Harwo 1D **8**
Lindum Cotts. NG14: Hove 4K **81**
Lindum Gro. NG2: Nott 5C **96**
Lindum M. NG24: New T 1D **136**
Lindum Rd. NG6: Basf 4E **84**
Lindum St. NG24: New T 1D **136**
Lindwall Ct. S81: Work 7J **19**
Lindy Cl. NG12: Kin 2B **142**
Linecroft La. DN10: Walk 5K **11**
Lineham La. NG23: Elston 4E **140**
Linen Ho. *NG7: Radf 2F **95***
(off Hartley Rd.)
Linette Cl. NG5: Sher 5H **85**
Linford Ct. NG9: Bram 4G **93**
Ling Beeches DN22: Ord 6D **22**
Ling Cres. NG11: Rudd 2K **115**
Lingfield Cl. NG18: Mans 5B **48**
Lingfield Ct. NG8: Woll 5J **93**
Lingford NG12: Cotg 6F **111**
Lingford St. NG15: Huck 7H **67**
Ling Forest Cl. NG18: Mans 5C **48**
Lingforest Ct. NG18: Mans 5C **48**
Lingforest Rd. NG18: Mans 4C **48**
Ling La. NG20: Mkt W 5G **35**
Lingmell Cl. NG2: West Br 3F **109**
Lings Bar Rd. *NG2: Gam 3G **109***
(off Ambleside)
Lings La. NG12: Key 2H **119**
Lings Vw. NG20: Mkt W 5E **34**
Lingwood Gro. NG18: Mans 3B **48**
Lingwood La. NG14: Woodbo 4F **79**
Linkin Rd. NG9: Chil 3H **105**
Linkmel Cl. NG2: Nott 7H **95**
Linkmel Rd. NG16: Eastw 3A **72**
Links, The NG16: Sels 6B **58**
NG18: Mans 4C **48**
Linksfield Ct. NG2: West Br 7K **107**
Linley Cl. NG23: Coll 2H **129**
Linley Ct. *NG13: Bing 4F **101***
(off Long Acre)
Linnell St. NG3: Nott 2C **96**
Linnet Cl. NG17: Kirk A 1A **60**
Linnet Dr. NG18: Mans 3A **48**
Linnets, The S81: Gate 5E **18**
Linnet Way NG15: Huck 6F **67**
Linsdale Cl. NG8: Bilb 3G **93**
Linsdale Gdns. NG4: Ged 3G **87**
Linseed Av. NG24: New T 4E **134**
Lintin Av. NG21: Edwin 6D **36**
Linton Cl. NG18: Mans 4D **48**
NG24: Farnd 6J **133**
Linton Dr. NG22: Bou 3E **38**
Linton Ri. NG3: Nott 2D **96**
Linwood Ct. NG19: Mans W 5A **42**
Linwood Cres. NG15: Rave 1B **62**
NG16: Eastw 5D **72**
Lion Cl. NG8: Aspl 5D **84**
Liquorice La. S81: Wigt 1H **19**
Lismore Cl. NG7: Radf 3F **95**
Lismore Ct. NG19: Mans 5D **46**
Lister Ga. NG1: Nott 6F **7** (4K **95**)
Listergate Sq. NG1: Nott 6F **7** (4K **95**)
Lister Ho. NG3: Mapp 5C **86**
Lister Rd. NG7: Nott 6F **95**
Listowel Cres. NG11: Clif 2F **115**
Litchfield Ri. NG5: Arn 4G **77**
Litmus Building, The NG1: Nott 3G **7**
Little Acre NG19: Mans W 4A **42**
Lit. Barn Ct. NG18: Mans 4B **48**
Lit. Barn Gdns. NG18: Mans 5B **48**
Lit. Barn La. NG18: Mans 5B **48**
LITTLEBOROUGH 3D **145**
Littleborough Rd. DN22: Stu S 3E **24**
Little Bounds NG2: West Br 2A **108**
LITTLE CARLTON 1A **134** (3C **147**)
Lit. Carter La. NG18: Mans 3A **48**
Lit. Debdale La. NG19: Mans 7F **41**
Little Drivers Soft Play Cen. 3C **104**
LITTLE GREEN 4K **91**
Littlegreen Rd. NG5: Woodt 3B **86**
Lit. Gringley La. DN22: Welh 2K **23**
Lit. Hallam La. DE7: Ilk 2A **92**
Little Hayes NG2: West Br 5K **107**
Lit. Holland Gdns. NG16: Nuth 1G **83**
Little Hollies NG19: Mans W 7C **42**
Lit. John Av. NG20: Mkt W 6D **34**
Lit. John Cl. NG22: New O 2D **38**
Lit. John Dr. NG21: Rain 2J **55**
Lit. John Wlk. NG3: Nott 1G **7** (1A **96**)
Little La. DN10: Gri H 3B **16**
DN22: Clar 7H **17**
NG12: Toll 6H **109**
NG14: Calv 6B **70**
NG16: Kimb 2E **82**
NG17: Huth 1C **50**
NG19: Plea 4B **40**
NG22: Edin 3A **130**
NG23: Coll 3G **129**
S81: Blyth 6H **13**
Lit. Lime La. NG5: Arn 1G **77**
Little Lincoln NG12: Wys 6J **123**
Lit. London La. NG12: Wys 6J **123**
Little Lunnon NG11: Bart F 7A **114**
Little Meadow NG12: Cotg 7F **111**
Littlemoor La. NG11: Rudd 7B **116**
Lit. Oak Av. NG17: Ann W 4B **60**
Lit. Oak Dr. NG15: Ann 5K **59**
Lit. Oakwood Dr. NG5: Top V 4K **75**
Littleover Av. NG18: Mans 4D **48**
Little Ox NG4: Colw 4J **97**
LITTLE PONTON 2D **149**
Lit. Ricket La. NG15: Rave 1K **61**
Lit. Robins Ct. NG19: Mans 5E **46**
Lit. Tennis St. NG2: Nott 5D **96**
Lit. Tennis St. Sth. NG2: Nott 6D **96**
Little Top La. DN22: Lound 3D **14**
Lit. Wood Ct. NG15: Huck 1E **74**
Littlewood Gdns. NG8: Bilb 3H **93**
Littlewood La. NG19: Mans W 2A **42**
(Leeming La.)
NG19: Mans W 2G **41**
(Scotswood Rd.)
Littleworth NG18: Mans 4J **47**
Litton Av. NG17: Skeg 5A **46**
Litton Cl. NG5: Woodt 3B **86**
NG15: Rave 1C **62**
Littondale S81: Work 5H **19**
Litton Rd. NG19: Mans W 5A **42**
Liverpool St. NG3: Nott 4J **7** (3B **96**)
Livingstone Rd. NG3: Nott 1J **7** (2B **96**)
Livingstone St. NG15: News 6E **60**
LivingWell Health Club
Nottingham 4F **7** (3K **95**)
Llanberis Gro. NG8: Aspl 5D **84**
Lloyd St. NG5: Sher 5K **85**
Loach Ct. NG8: Woll 3D **94**
Lobelia Cl. NG3: Nott 1A **96**
Lochbuie Ct. NG18: Mans 1J **47**
Lock Cl. NG9: Bee 6B **106**
Lockerbie St. NG4: Colw 2J **97**
LOCKINGTON 3A **148**
Lock La. NG10: Sand 4A **104**
Locksley Ho. NG3: Nott 1H **7** (2A **96**)
Locksley La. NG11: Clif 5F **107**
Lockwood Cl. NG5: Top V 5C **76**
NG9: Bee 5C **106**
Lockwood Dr. DN22: Ord 7D **22**
Lodge Cl. NG5: Redh 4G **77**
NG8: Aspl 7E **84**
Lodge Farm La. NG5: Arn 5G **77**
Lodge La. NG13: Scre 1K **91**
NG17: Kirk A 7D **52**
NG22: Tuxf 7D **28**
NG23: Elston 1B **140**
Lodge La. Ind. Est. NG22: Tuxf 7E **28**
Lodge Rd. NG16: Newth 6E **72**
Lodgewood Cl. NG6: Bulw 1B **84**
Lodore Cl. NG2: West Br 3F **109**
Lodore Rd. S81: Work 5G **19**
Logan Sq. NG6: Basf 2F **85**
Logan St. NG6: Bulw 1D **84**
Lois Av. NG7: Lent 5G **95**
Lombard Cl. NG7: Lent 4G **95**
Lombard St. NG13: Ors 2J **103**
NG24: New T 1C **136**
Lombardy Lodge NG9: Toton 7F **105**
Lonan Cl. NG19: Mans W 7C **42**
London La. LE12: Will W 6G **143**
London Rd. DN22: Eaton, Retf 4F **23**
NG2: Nott 6H **7** (4A **96**)
NG24: Bald, New B, New T 1C **136**
London Rd. Bus. Pk.
DN22: Retf 5F **23**
London Row NG23: Sth C 7D **30**
LONDONTHORPE 2D **149**
Long Acre NG13: Bing 4F **101**
NG15: Huck 6D **66**
Longacre NG5: Woodt 3C **86**
Long Acre E. NG13: Bing 4G **101**
Longbeck Av. NG3: Nott 6D **86**
LONG BENNINGTON 1D **149**
Longbourne Ct. NG19: Mans W 7B **42**
Long Brecks La. S81: Blyth 7K **13**
LONG CLAWSON 3C **149**
Longclose Ct. NG6: Bulw 1B **84**
LONG DALE 6F **63**
Longdale NG19: Mans W 1A **48**
Longdale Av. NG15: Rave 3C **62**
Longdale Craft Cen. 6F **63**
Longdale La. NG14: Calv 7G **63**
NG15: Rave 3B **62**
Longdale Rd. NG5: Arn 1A **86**
Longden Cl. NG9: Bram 6E **92**
Longden Mill NG3: Nott 4J **7**
Longden St. NG3: Nott 4J **7** (3B **96**)
Longden Ter. NG17: Stant H 4H **45**
NG20: Mkt W 4D **34**
LONG EATON 7A **104** (2A **148**)
Longfellow Dr. NG24: Bald 4G **137**
S81: Work 1J **21**
Longfellows Cl. NG5: Bestw 6D **76**
Longfield Av. NG8: Bilb 1H **93**
Longford Cres. NG6: Bulw 4J **75**
Longford Wlk. NG18: Mans 4D **48**
Longhedge La. NG19: Plea 5A **40**
NG23: Syer 2A **140**
Long Hill Ri. NG15: Huck 7F **67**
NG17: Nunc 3K **59**
Long Hollow Way NG24: Wint 4G **135**
Longholme Rd. DN22: Retf 2H **23**
Longhurst S81: Work 7J **19**
Longhurst Dr. NG5: Arn 4H **77**
Longland La. NG22: Farns 7F **57**
Longlands Cl. NG9: Bee 5C **106**
Longlands Dr. NG2: West Br 4G **109**
Longlands Rd. NG9: Bee 5C **106**
Long La. DE75: Ship 7B **72**
LE14: Hick 6E **142**
NG9: Atten 7J **105**
NG16: Want 5A **74**
NG22: Tuxf 7A **28**
NG24: Barn W 6K **137**
NG24: Farnd 4H **133**
S81: Carl L 6B **12**
Longleat Cres. NG9: Chil 4H **105**
Longmead Cl. NG5: Bestw 1K **85**
Longmead Dr. NG5: Bestw 1K **85**
NG25: Fis 6H **139**
Long Meadow NG19: Mans W 4K **41**
NG22: Farns 5K **57**
Long Meadow Hill NG14: Lowd 4K **79**
Long Meadows DN10: Eve 6A **10**
Longmoor Av. NG14: Lowd 6E **80**
Longmoor Gdns. NG10: Long E 7A **104**
Longmoor La. NG10: Sand 6A **104**
NG13: Aslo 1E **102**
Longmoor Rd.
NG10: Long E, Sand 7A **104**
Longnor Wlk. NG18: Mans 4D **48**
Longore Sq. NG8: Woll 4E **94**
Longridge Rd. NG5: Woodt 3C **86**
Long Row NG1: Nott 5E **6** (4K **95**)
(not continuous)
NG11: King 1A **120**
NG24: New T 1E **136**
Long Row W. NG1: Nott 5E **6** (4K **95**)
Longshaw Rd. NG18: Mans 4D **48**
Long Sleets DE55: Sth N 7A **50**
Long Stairs NG1: Nott 6H **7**
Longstone Way NG19: Mans 4D **46**

Long Stoop Way NG19: Mans W .3C **48**
Longthorpe Ct. NG5: Arn .7H **77**
Longue Dr. NG14: Calv .6B **70**
Long Wlk. DN22: Retf .2C **22**
Longwall Av. NG2: Nott .7H **95**
Long West Cft. NG14: Calv .6A **70**
LONG WHATTON .3A **148**
Longwood Ct. NG5: Top V .6B **76**
Longwood Dr. NG17: Sut A .3H **51**
Longwood Rd. NG16: Pinx .2C **58**
Lonscale Cl. NG2: West Br .4F **109**
Lonsdale Dr. NG9: Toton .7D **104**
Lonsdale Rd. NG7: Radf .2F **95**
Lord Nelson St. NG2: Nott .4C **96**
Lordship La. NG13: Ors .2K **103**
Lord St. NG2: Nott .5K **7** (4C **96**)
NG18: Mans .5H **47**
Lorimer Av. NG4: Ged .4J **87**
Lorna Ct. NG3: Nott .6A **86**
Lorne Gro. NG12: Rad T .5E **98**
Lorne Wlk. NG3: Nott .1F **7** (1K **95**)
Lortas Rd. NG5: Sher .5G **85**
Loscoe Gdns. NG5: Sher .6J **85**
Loscoe Mt. Rd. NG5: Sher .5K **85**
Loscoe Rd. NG5: Sher .6K **85**
Lothian Rd. NG12: Toll .1F **117**
Lothmore Ct. NG2: Nott .6J **95**
Lotus Cl. NG3: Nott .1B **96**
Loughbon NG13: Ors .1K **103**
LOUGHBOROUGH .3A **148**
Loughborough Av. NG2: Nott .4C **96**
Loughborough Rd. LE12: Costo, Remp .7E **122**
LE12: Stanf S .6A **122**
NG2: West Br .3B **108**
NG11: Bunny, Rudd .7A **108**
Loughrigg Cl. NG2: Nott .7J **95**
Louis Av. NG9: Bee .2K **105**
Louise Av. NG4: Neth .7K **87**
LOUND .3D **14** (3B **144**)
Lound Ho. Cl. NG17: Skeg .5K **45**
Lound Ho. Rd. NG17: Skeg .5K **45**
Lound Low Rd. DN22: Sut L .6B **14**
Louwil Av. NG19: Mans W .4A **42**
Loveden Cl. NG24: Bald .6G **137**
Lovelace Wlk. NG15: Huck .5H **67**
Lovell Cl. NG6: Bulw .2A **84**
Loveridge M. NG24: New T .1C **136**
LOVERSALL .2A **144**
Lover's La. NG24: New T .7D **134**
Lovers' Wlk. DN22: Hay .4J **17**
Lowater Pl. NG4: Carl .1E **96**
Lowater St. NG4: Carl .1E **96**
LOW BURNHAM .1C **145**
Low Common DN11: Harwo .2A **8**
Lowcroft NG5: Woodt .3C **86**
LOWDHAM .4D **80** (1B **148**)
Lowdham La. NG14: Woodbo .2H **79**
Lowdham Rd. NG4: Ged .4F **87**
NG14: Epp .2A **80**
NG14: Gun .6E **80**
Lowdham Station (Rail) .6E **80**
Lowdham St. NG3: Nott .4J **7** (3B **96**)
Lower Bagthorpe NG16: Bagt .1D **64**
LOWER BEAUVALE .3E **72**
Lower Beauvale NG16: Newth .3E **72**
Lower Canaan NG11: Rudd .2A **116**
Lower Ct. NG9: Bee .2B **106**
Lwr. Eldon St. NG2: Nott .6K **7** (4B **96**)
Lwr. Kirklington Rd. NG25: Sout .3E **130**
Lwr. Meadow La. NG17: Huth .1E **50**
Lwr. Middleton St. DE7: Ilk .6A **82**
Lwr. Oakham Way NG18: Mans .7F **47**
Lwr. Orchard St. NG9: Stap .2D **104**
Lwr. Park St. NG9: Stap .3B **104**
Lwr. Parliament St. NG1: Nott .4F **7** (3K **95**)
Lwr. Regent St. NG9: Bee .3B **106**
Lower Rd. NG9: Bee .2C **106**
Loweswater Ct. NG2: Gam .2F **109**
Lowes Wong NG25: Sout .6G **131**
Lowfield DN22: Retf .1D **22**
Lowfield Cl. DN22: Rans .2K **13**
Lowfield Cotts. NG24: New B .6D **136**
Lowfield La.
NG24: Bald, New B .6E **136**
Low Holland La. DN22: Stu S .3D **24**
Lowlands Dr. NG12: Key .6J **117**
LOW MARNHAM .2D **147**
Low Mdw. Row S81: Shire .5A **18**
Lowmoor Bus. Pk. NG17: Kirk A .4C **52**
Lowmoor Ct. NG17: Kirk A .5C **52**
Lowmoor Rd. NG17: Kirk A .5B **52**
Lowmoor Rd. Ind. Est.
NG17: Kirk A .4B **52**
Low Pasture La. DN22: Nth W .2J **17**
Low Pavement NG1: Nott .6F **7** (4K **95**)
Low Rd. DN10: Scro .4K **9**
NG17: Skeg .3K **45**
NG23: Best .7H **125**
Lows La. DE7: Stant D .6A **92**
Low St. DN10: Beck .5C **16**
DN10: Gri H .3A **16**
DN22: Nth W .2H **17**
DN22: Torw .4J **13**
NG17: Sut A .1K **51**
NG22: Dun T .5H **29**
NG22: East M .2C **28**
Low St. NG23: Coll .3G **129**
NG23: Elston .1D **140**
NG23: Harby .6K **31**
S81: Carl L .7D **12**
Lowther Sq. S81: Carl L .5B **12**
Lowtown Cl. S80: Work .3H **21**
Lowtown St. S80: Work .3H **21**
Lowtown Vw. S80: Work .3H **21**
Low Wood Rd. NG6: Bulw .2K **83**
Loxley Cl. NG15: Huck .1E **74**
Loxley Dr. NG18: Mans .7C **48**
Loxley Mdw. NG14: Bur J .3D **88**
Lucerne Cl. NG11: Wilf .3J **107**
Lucknow Av. NG3: Mapp P .7A **86**
Lucknow Ct. NG3: Mapp P .6A **86**
Lucknow Dr. NG3: Mapp P .7A **86**
NG17: Sut A .7B **46**
NG18: Mans .5E **46**
Lucknow Rd. NG3: Mapp P .7A **86**
Ludborough Wlk. NG19: Mans W .5A **42**
Ludford Rd. NG6: Bulw .6J **75**
Ludgate Cl. NG5: Arn .4C **76**
Ludgate Dr. NG13: East B .5E **90**
Ludham Av. NG6: Bulw .6H **75**
Ludlam Av. NG16: Gilt .7E **72**
Ludlow Av. NG2: West Br .2C **108**
Ludlow Cl. NG9: Bram .7J **93**
Ludlow Hill Rd. NG2: West Br .4C **108**
Lulworth Cl. NG2: West Br .4K **107**
Lulworth Ct. NG16: Kimb .7K **73**
Lumley Cl. NG22: Bils .4B **126**
Lune Cl. NG9: Atten .6K **105**
Lune Mdw. NG19: Mans W .6K **41**
Lune Way NG13: Bing .5E **100**
Lunness Ct. NG18: Mans .4K **47**
Lunn La. NG23: Coll .3G **129**
Lupin Cl. NG3: Nott .1A **96**
Luther Av. NG17: Sut A .1J **51**
Luther Cl. NG3: Nott .1B **96**
Luton Cl. NG8: Aspl .6E **84**
Lutterell Ct. NG2: West Br .4A **108**
Lutterell Way NG2: West Br .4E **108**
Lybster M. NG2: Nott .6J **95**
Lychgate Ct. NG16: Want .6K **73**
Lydia Gdns. NG16: Eastw .5C **72**
Lydney Pk. NG2: West Br .3J **107**
Lyle Cl. NG16: Kimb .7J **73**
Lyme Pk. NG2: West Br .4J **107**
Lymington Gdns. NG3: Nott .2D **96**
Lymington Rd. NG19: Mans .4D **46**
Lymn Av. NG4: Ged .5J **87**
Lynam Ct. NG6: Bulw .7H **75**
Lynchet La. S81: Work .5E **18**
Lyncombe Ct. DN22: Ord .6D **22**
Lyncombe Gdns. NG12: Key .6J **117**
Lyndale Rd. NG9: Bram .1F **105**
Lynd Cl. NG16: Sels .5F **59**
Lyndhurst Av. NG21: Blid .6K **55**
Lyndhurst Gdns. NG2: West Br .5A **108**
Lyndhurst Rd. NG2: Nott .4C **96**
Lynds Cl. NG21: Edwin .6F **37**
Lynemouth Ct. NG5: Arn .4J **77**
Lyn Gilzean Ct. NG3: Nott .2H **7** (2A **96**)
Lyngs, The NG13: East B .5D **90**
Lynmoor Ct. NG15: Huck .4J **67**
Lynmouth Cres. NG7: Radf .1F **95**
Lynncroft NG16: Eastw .3E **72**
Lynnes Cl. NG21: Blid .7J **55**
Lynstead Dr. NG15: Huck .1C **74**
Lynton Ct. NG3: Nott .1C **96**
Lynton Dr. NG17: Sut A .3H **51**
Lynton Gdns. NG5: Arn .6J **77**
Lynton Rd. NG9: Chil .3H **105**
Lyons Cl. NG11: Rudd .2J **115**
Lysander Way S81: Work .4F **19**
Lytham Dr. NG12: Edwal .6F **109**
Lytham Gdns. NG5: Top V .5C **76**
Lytham Rd. NG17: Kirk A .4J **51**
Lythe Cl. NG11: Wilf .4H **107**
Lytton Cl. NG3: Nott .3J **7** (3B **96**)

M

Mabel Av. NG17: Sut A .2A **52**
Mabel Gro. NG2: West Br .1D **108**
Mabel St. NG2: Nott .6A **96**
Mable St. S80: Rhod .1B **20**
Macaulay Cl. NG24: Bald .4G **137**
S81: Work .1K **21**
Macaulay Dr. NG24: Bald .4G **137**
Macaulay Gro. NG16: Nuth .1G **83**
McClelland Av. NG6: Bestw V .1D **76**
Machin Cl. NG22: Tuxf .6D **28**
Machin Gro. S81: Gate .5D **18**
Machins La. NG12: Edwal .6D **108**
McIntosh Rd. NG4: Ged .4G **87**
Mackinley Av. NG9: Stap .7D **92**
Mackleys La. NG23: Nth M .6K **129**
Mackworth Ct. NG18: Mans .5D **48**
Maclaren Gdns. NG11: Rudd .4A **116**
Maclean Rd. NG4: Carl .1F **97**
Macmillan Cl. NG3: Mapp .5C **86**
Madden Cl. NG5: Bestw .2G **85**
Madeline Ct. NG18: Mans .6K **47**
Madford Bus. Pk. NG5: Arn .1A **86**
Madison Ct. NG7: Lent .4E **94**
Madryn Wlk. NG5: Bestw .7C **76**
Mafeking St. NG2: Nott .4D **96**
Magadales Dr. NG14: Thur .5B **138**
Magdala Rd. NG3: Mapp P .7K **85**
Magdalen Dr. NG13: East B .4E **90**
Magdalene Vw. NG24: New T .1E **136**
Magdalene Way NG15: Huck .5G **67**
Magellan Dr. S80: Work .3D **20**
Magistrates' Court
Mansfield .2G **47**
Nottingham .7F **7** (5K **95**)
Worksop & Retford .3G **21**
Magna Cl. NG14: Lowd .5E **80**
Magnolia Cl. NG8: Brox .6K **83**
Magnolia Ct. NG9: Bram .7J **93**
Magnolia Gro. NG15: Huck .2H **75**
Magnus Ct. NG9: Bee .3B **106**
Magnus Rd. NG5: Sher .4K **85**
Magnus St. NG24: New T .7D **134**
Magpie Cl. S81: Gate .5D **18**
Magpie La. DN22: Habb .6D **24**
Magson Cl. NG3: Nott .3K **7** (3B **96**)
Maida La. NG22: New O .4B **38**
(not continuous)
Maiden La. NG1: Nott .5H **7** (4A **96**)
Maidens Dale NG5: Arn .6F **77**
Maid Marian Av. NG22: Bils .7D **126**
Maid Marian Way NG1: Nott .5D **6** (4J **95**)
Maid Marion Av. NG16: Sels .5F **59**
Maid Marion Dr. NG21: Edwin .6G **37**
Maid Marion Ri. NG20: Mkt W .4D **34**
Maid Marion Way NG22: New O .2D **38**
Maidstone Dr. NG8: Woll .6J **93**
Main Av. NG19: Mans W .1C **48**
Main Bright Rd. NG19: Mans W .1H **47**
Main Bright Wlk. NG19: Mans W .1H **47**
Main Rd. LE14: Neth B, Upp B .3G **143**
NG4: Ged .6J **87**
NG7: Nott .3D **106**
NG11: Wilf .3J **107**
NG12: Cotg, Rad T .2C **110**
NG12: Plum .2H **117**
NG12: Rad T .5D **98**
NG12: Shel .7H **89**
NG13: Barns .3F **141**
NG13: Elton .6G **103**
NG14: Bulc, Lowd .2F **89**
NG15: Rave .1A **62**
NG16: Jack, Westw .7A **64**
NG16: Unde .2C **64**
NG16: Want .5K **73**
NG17: Ann W, Nunc .3J **59**
NG20: Langw, Neth L .6A **26**
NG22: Bou .3E **38**
NG23: Aver, Upton .7C **132**
NG23: Best .7H **125**
NG23: Kel .2G **133**
NG23: Nth C, Sth C .2E **30**
Mainside Cres. NG16: Unde .4E **64**
Main St. DN10: Matt .2H **15**
DN11: Harwo .2B **8**
DN11: Sty .5A **8**
DN22: Clar, Hay .4H **17**
DN22: Lane .2G **29**
DN22: Nth L .7A **24**
DN22: Ramp .7K **25**
LE12: Costo .3E **122**
LE12: East L .3A **122**
LE12: Norm S .7G **121**
LE12: Remp .7F **123**
LE12: Sut B .4A **120**
LE12: West L .3F **121**
LE12: Will W .6F **143**
LE14: Hick .5E **142**
NG2: Gam .2F **109**
NG4: Lamb .7F **79**
NG6: Bulw .1C **84**
(not continuous)
NG8: Stre .6G **83**
NG11: Bunny .3B **118**
NG11: Rudd .7B **116**
NG12: Crop Bu .2B **112**
NG12: Key .2H **119**
NG12: Kin .3A **142**
NG12: Shel .6H **89**
NG12: Widm .6K **119**
NG12: Wys .6J **123**
NG13: Aslo .4D **102**
NG13: East B .4D **90**
NG13: Gran .1J **141**
NG13: Lang .7K **113**
NG13: Newton .7C **90**
NG13: Scar .1B **102**
NG13: What .5E **102**
NG14: Blea .2B **138**
NG14: Bur J .3E **88**
NG14: Calv .5K **69**
NG14: Cayt .6H **81**
NG14: Epp .7J **71**
NG14: Gun .2A **90**
NG14: Hove .4K **81**
NG14: Lowd .4D **80**
NG14: Thur .6C **138**
NG14: Woodbo .2F **79**
NG15: Lin .2G **67**

Main St. NG15: Pap	.2K **67**	**Manly Cl.** NG5: Top V
NG16: Aws	.2B **82**	**Manners Rd.** NG24: Bald
NG16: Brins	.4B **64**	NG24: New T
NG16: Eastw	.5D **72**	**Manning St.** NG3: Nott
NG16: Kimb	.1E **82**	**Manns Leys** NG12: Cotg
NG16: Newth	.4G **73**	**Mann St.** NG7: Basf
NG17: Ann W	.4K **59**	**Manor Av.** NG2: Nott
NG17: Huth	.7D **44**	NG9: Atten
NG20: Nort	.3E **32**	NG9: Bee
NG20: Whal T	.5B **26**	NG9: Stap
NG21: Blid	.7H **55**	**Manor Cl.** DN10: Miss
NG22: Dun T	.5J **29**	LE12: Costo
NG22: Eakr	.2C **126**	NG12: Edwal
NG22: Edin	.2A **130**	NG14: Blea
NG22: Egma	.2E **124**	NG17: Teve
NG22: Farns	.5K **57**	NG22: Bou
NG22: Kirk	.1D **132**	NG22: Wale
NG22: Kirt	.3H **39**	NG25: Oxt
NG22: Lax	.5B **124**	NG25: Sout
NG22: Oll	.5A **38**	S80: Work
NG22: Wale	.5G **27**	**Manor Ct.** LE12: Will W
NG22: West M	.4A **28**	NG4: Carl
NG23: Aver, Upton	.7B **132**	NG9: Bram
NG23: Bath	.5F **129**	NG20: Chu W
NG23: Carl T	.7D **128**	**Manor Cres.** NG4: Carl
NG23: Caun	.6J **127**	NG17: Kirk A
NG23: Flin	.5A **140**	**Manor Dr.** NG25: Mort
NG23: Norw	.2J **127**	**Manor Farm & Woodland**
NG23: Nth M	.5K **129**	**Mnr. Farm Cl.** NG11: Rudd
NG23: Sibt	.6E **140**	NG23: Roll
NG23: Sth M	.2A **134**	**Mnr. Farm Ct.** NG11: King
NG23: Sut T	.4D **128**	**Mnr. Farm La.** NG11: Clif
NG23: Syer	.2B **140**	**Mnr. Farm Mdw.** LE12: East L
NG23: Thor	.2G **31**	**Mnr. Farm Ri.** DN22: Nth L
NG23: Weston	.3F **125**	NG22: Well
NG24: Bald	.5G **137**	
NG24: Codd	.7K **135**	**Manor Flds.** NG22: Halam
NG24: Farnd	.7G **133**	**Manor Gdns.** NG13: Barns
NG25: Fis	.7H **139**	**Manor Grn.** NG4: Carl
NG25: Mort	.7G **139**	**Manor Grn. Wlk.** NG4: Carl
NG25: Oxt	.2F **71**	**Manor Gro.** DN22: Nth L
S81: Oldc	.6A **8**	**Manor Ho.** NG19: Mans W
Maisies Way DE55: Sth N	.5B **50**	**Manor Ho. Cl.** NG11: Wilf
Maitland Av. NG5: Woodt	.3C **86**	NG14: Lowd
Maitland Rd. NG5: Woodt	.3C **86**	**Manor Ho. Ct.** NG17: Kirk A
Majestic Theatre	.3E **22**	**Manor Ho. Dr.** NG12: Wys
Major Oak, The		NG23: Nth M
Sherwood Forest Country Pk.	.4E **36**	**Manor Ho. Pk.** DN22: Chu L
Major St. NG1: Nott	.3E **6** (3K **95**)	**Manor La.** NG12: Shel
Making It! Discovery Cen.	.4J **47**	NG13: What
Malbon Cl. NG3: Nott	.7C **86**	**Manor Pk.** NG11: Rudd
Malcolm Cl. NG3: Mapp P	.1K **95**	**Manor Pk. La.** NG14: Epp
Maldon Cl. NG9: Chil	.5H **105**	**Manor Ri.** NG13: East B
Malin Cl. NG5: Arn	.6K **77**	**Manor Rd.** DN10: Scro
Malin Hill NG1: Nott	.6G **7**	LE12: East L
Malkin Av. NG12: Rad T	.4F **99**	NG4: Carl
Mallard Cl. NG6: Basf	.3G **85**	NG11: Bart F
NG13: Bing	.5H **101**	NG12: Key
NG22: Bils	.6C **126**	NG13: Bing
Mallard Ct. NG9: Bee	.4B **106**	NG14: Calv
NG19: Mans W	.7G **41**	NG16: Eastw
Mallard Grn. NG24: New B	.4F **137**	NG17: Skeg
Mallard Rd. NG4: Neth	.2A **98**	NG19: Mans W
Mallards, The S81: Gate	.5D **18**	NG20: Chu W
Mallatratt Pl. NG19: Mans W	.5H **41**	NG23: Caun
Mallory Dr. S80: Work	.3D **20**	NG23: Coll
Mallow Way NG13: Bing	.4D **100**	**Manor St.** NG2: Nott
Malmesbury Rd. NG3: Mapp	.3D **86**	NG17: Sut A
MALTBY	.2A **144**	**Manor Vw.** NG23: Caun
Maltby Cl. NG8: Aspl	.5C **84**	**Manor Wlk.** NG4: Carl
Maltby Rd. NG3: Mapp	.3D **86**	**Manorwood Rd.** NG12: Cotg
NG18: Mans	.5A **48**	**Mansell Cl.** NG16: Eastw
S81: Oldc	.6A **8**	**MANSFIELD**
Malt Cotts. NG7: Basf	.6G **85**	**Mansfield & District Crematorium** NG18: Mans
Malt Cross Gallery, The	.5E **6**	**Mansfield Bus. Cen.** NG19: Mans
Malthouse Cl. NG16: Eastw	.5D **72**	**Mansfield Ct.** NG5: Sher
Malthouse Ct. NG13: East B	.4D **90**	**Mansfield Golf Course**
Malting Cl. NG11: Rudd	.4K **115**	**Mansfield Gro.** NG1: Nott
Maltings, The NG3: Nott	.1C **96**	**Mansfield La.** NG14: Calv
NG6: Basf	.5F **85**	NG17: Skeg
NG12: Crop Bi	.5B **112**	**Mansfield Leisure Pk.** NG18: Mans
S81: Blyth	.6H **13**	**Mansfield Mus.**
Maltings Cl. NG17: Skeg	.4A **46**	**Mansfield Rd.**
Malt Kiln Cl. NG22: Oll	.6B **38**	DE55: Sth N
Maltkiln La. NG24: New T	.6D **134**	
Maltkiln Row NG20: Cuck	.4C **32**	DE55: Tibs
Maltkins, The DN22: Nth L	.7B **24**	DN22: Babw, Retf
Maltmill La. NG1: Nott	.6G **7** (4A **96**)	NG1: Nott
Malton Rd. NG5: Sher	.5G **85**	NG5: Arn, Redh, Sher
Maltsters, The NG24: New T	.5K **133**	NG15: Ann
Malt St. NG11: Goth	.7G **115**	NG15: Pap, Rave
Malvern Cl. NG3: Nott	.6B **86**	NG15: Rave
Malvern Ct. NG3: Mapp P	.1K **95**	NG16: Brins, Eastw
NG9: Bee	.3C **106**	NG16: Sels
Malvern Cres. NG2: West Br	.4C **108**	NG16: Unde
Malvern Rd. NG2: West Br	.4B **108**	NG17: Skeg
NG3: Nott	.6B **86**	NG17: Sut A
Manby Ct. NG20: Mede V	.7F **33**	NG19: Mans W
Mandalay St. NG6: Basf	.3E **84**	NG20: Cuck
Mandarin Cl. NG19: Mans W	.7A **42**	NG20: Mkt W
Mandeen Gro. NG18: Mans	.6C **48**	NG21: Blid
Mandeville Cl. NG15: Huck	.6J **67**	NG21: C'tone, K Cli
Manesty Cres. NG11: Clif	.3F **115**	
Manifold Dr. NG16: Sels	.5E **58**	
Manifold Gdns. NG2: Nott	.6K **95**	
Manitoba Way NG16: Sels	.5D **58**	

Manly Cl. NG5: Top V	.6A **76**
Manners Rd. NG24: Bald	.6F **137**
NG24: New T	.7B **134**
Manning St. NG3: Nott	.1A **96**
Manns Leys NG12: Cotg	.7D **110**
Mann St. NG7: Basf	.7G **85**
Manor Av. NG2: Nott	.6K **7** (4B **96**)
NG9: Atten	.6K **105**
NG9: Bee	.3A **106**
NG9: Stap	.1C **104**
Manor Cl. DN10: Miss	.2D **10**
LE12: Costo	.3E **122**
NG12: Edwal	.6E **108**
NG14: Blea	.2B **138**
NG17: Teve	.2G **45**
NG22: Bou	.2F **39**
NG22: Wale	.5G **27**
NG25: Oxt	.2F **71**
NG25: Sout	.5H **131**
S80: Work	.3D **20**
Manor Ct. LE12: Will W	.6F **143**
NG4: Carl	.1J **97**
NG9: Bram	.2H **105**
NG20: Chu W	.2E **34**
Manor Cres. NG4: Carl	.7J **87**
NG17: Kirk A	.1B **60**
Manor Dr. NG25: Mort	.6G **139**
Manor Farm & Woodland	.4B **122**
Mnr. Farm Cl. NG11: Rudd	.7B **116**
NG23: Roll	.3K **139**
Mnr. Farm Ct. NG11: King	.1A **120**
Mnr. Farm La. NG11: Clif	.7F **107**
Mnr. Farm Mdw. LE12: East L	.3A **122**
Mnr. Farm Ri. DN22: Nth L	.6B **24**
NG22: Well	.7E **38**
	(off Eakring Rd.)
Manor Flds. NG22: Halam	.5B **130**
Manor Gdns. NG13: Barns	.3F **141**
Manor Grn. NG4: Carl	.7J **87**
Manor Grn. Wlk. NG4: Carl	.7J **87**
Manor Gro. DN22: Nth L	.6B **24**
Manor Ho. NG19: Mans W	.6H **41**
Manor Ho. Cl. NG11: Wilf	.1J **107**
NG14: Lowd	.4D **80**
Manor Ho. Ct. NG17: Kirk A	.7H **51**
Manor Ho. Dr. NG12: Wys	.6K **123**
NG23: Nth M	.5K **129**
Manor Ho. Pk. DN22: Chu L	.1J **29**
Manor La. NG12: Shel	.6H **89**
NG13: What	.7C **102**
Manor Pk. NG11: Rudd	.3J **115**
Manor Pk. La. NG14: Epp	.1A **80**
Manor Pk. Sports Complex	.4K **41**
Manor Ri. NG13: East B	.3D **90**
Manor Rd. DN10: Scro	.4K **9**
LE12: East L	.1B **122**
NG4: Carl	.7J **87**
NG11: Bart F	.7A **114**
NG12: Key	.7H **117**
NG13: Bing	.4G **101**
NG14: Calv	.6C **70**
NG16: Eastw	.5D **72**
NG17: Skeg	.3J **45**
NG19: Mans W	.5G **41**
NG20: Chu W	.2E **34**
NG23: Caun	.7H **127**
NG23: Coll	.1H **129**
Manor St. NG2: Nott	.7K **7** (4B **96**)
NG17: Sut A	.1J **51**
Manor Vw. NG23: Caun	.7H **127**
Manor Wlk. NG4: Carl	.1A **80**
Manorwood Rd. NG12: Cotg	.7E **110**
Mansell Cl. NG16: Eastw	.5F **73**
MANSFIELD	.3H **47** (2A **146**)
Mansfield & District Crematorium NG18: Mans	.1H **53**
Mansfield Bus. Cen. NG19: Mans	.2H **47**
Mansfield Ct. NG5: Sher	.7J **85**
Mansfield Golf Course	.5E **48**
Mansfield Gro. NG1: Nott	.2D **6** (2J **95**)
Mansfield La. NG14: Calv	.4D **70**
NG17: Skeg	.4A **46**
Mansfield Leisure Pk. NG18: Mans	.5G **47**
Mansfield Mus.	.3J **47**
Mansfield Rd.	
DE55: Sth N	.6A **50**
	(not continuous)
DE55: Tibs	.3A **44**
DN22: Babw, Retf	.5A **22**
NG1: Nott	.1E **6** (1J **95**)
NG5: Arn, Redh, Sher	.4E **68**
NG15: Ann	.3F **65**
NG15: Pap, Rave	.4B **62**
NG15: Rave	.1A **62**
NG16: Brins, Eastw	.7C **64**
NG16: Sels	.6D **58**
NG16: Unde	.3F **65**
NG17: Skeg	.4H **45**
NG17: Sut A	.6A **46**
NG19: Mans W	.7J **41**
NG20: Cuck	.4D **32**
NG20: Mkt W	.7B **34**
NG21: Blid	.4H **55**
NG21: C'tone, K Cli	.7H **43**

Mansfield Rd. NG21: Edwin	.7B **36**
NG21: Rain	.3A **56**
NG22: Edin, Halam	.2A **130**
NG22: Farns	.4F **57**
NG22: Oll	.5K **37**
S80: Work	.7A **20**
Mansfield Station (Rail)	.4H **47**
Mansfield St. NG5: Sher	.5K **85**
Mansfield Town FC	.5G **47**
MANSFIELD WOODHOUSE	.6J **41** (2A **146**)
Mansfield Woodhouse Golf Course	.3A **42**
Mansfield Woodhouse Station (Rail)	.6G **41**
MANTHORPE	.2D **149**
Manthorpe Cres. NG5: Sher	.4C **86**
Manthorpe Ho. NG24: Bald	.5H **137**
Manthorpe Way NG24: Bald	.5H **137**
MANTON	
Scunthorpe	.1D **145**
Worksop	.4J **21** (1A **146**)
Manton Cl. NG21: Rain	.3K **55**
Manton Cres. NG9: Lent A	.1A **106**
S80: Work	.4J **21**
Manton Dale S80: Work	.4J **21**
Manton Vs. S80: Work	.3K **21**
Manvers Bus. Pk. NG12: Cotg	.5F **111**
Manvers Ct. NG2: Nott	.5J **7** (4B **96**)
Manvers Cres. NG21: Edwin	.6D **36**
Manvers Gro. NG12: Rad T	.5E **98**
Manvers Rd. DN22: Retf	.5D **22**
NG2: West Br	.3C **108**
Manvers St. NG2: Nott	.5J **7** (4B **96**)
NG4: Neth	.2K **97**
NG18: Mans	.3G **47**
NG20: Mkt W	.5D **34**
S80: Work	.2F **21**
	(off Portland St.)
Manvers Vw. NG22: Bou	.2E **38**
Manville Cl. NG8: Aspl	.2D **94**
NG9: Bram	.5G **93**
Maori Av. NG15: Huck	.1D **74**
Maple Av. NG9: Bee	.4C **106**
NG10: Sand	.2A **104**
MAPLEBECK	.2C **147**
Maplebeck Av. NG20: Mede V	.7F **33**
Maplebeck Rd. NG5: Arn	.7J **77**
NG23: Caun	.6F **127**
Maple Cl. LE12: East L	.4K **121**
NG12: Key	.1K **119**
NG12: Rad T	.6E **98**
NG13: Bing	.4H **101**
NG14: Calv	.6B **70**
NG19: Mans W	.1A **48**
NG22: Tuxf	.7D **28**
Maple Ct. NG7: Lent	.7A **6** (5G **95**)
NG16: Kimb	.1E **82**
Maple Cres. NG17: Kirk A	.5K **51**
Maple Cft. NG18: Mans	.5B **48**
Mapledene Cres. NG8: Woll	.5H **93**
Maple Dr. DN22: Elk	.3G **27**
NG4: Ged	.5A **88**
NG15: Huck	.1E **74**
NG16: Nuth	.1G **83**
NG18: Mans	.4K **53**
S81: Work	.5G **19**
Maple Gdns. NG16: Lang M	.3A **72**
Maple Gro. NG24: New T	.5C **136**
Maple Leaf Ct. NG24: New T	.5E **134**
Maple Leaf Gdns. S80: Work	.3H **21**
Maple Leaf Way NG15: Huck	.2J **75**
Maples St.	
NG7: H Grn	.1A **6** (1G **95**)
Maplestead Av. NG11: Wilf	.3J **107**
Mapletoft Av. NG19: Mans W	.4G **41**
Mapleton Way NG17: Sut A	.6A **46**
Mapletree Cl. NG5: Bestw	.7D **76**
Maple Vw. NG11: Wilf	.5J **107**
Maple Way NG2: West Br	.5A **108**
NG16: Sels	.5D **58**
MAPPERLEY	.4C **86** (1A **148**)
Mapperley Cres. NG3: Mapp	.5B **86**
Mapperley Golf Course	.3E **86**
Mapperley Hall Dr. NG3: Mapp P	.6K **85**
Mapperley Hall Gdns.	
NG3: Mapp P	.6A **86**
Mapperley Hgts. NG5: Woodt	.2E **86**
Mapperley Orchard NG5: Arn	.7K **77**
MAPPERLEY PARK	.6K **85** (1A **148**)
Mapperley Pk. Dr.	
NG3: Mapp P	.7K **85**
Mapperley Plains NG3: Mapp	.2E **86**
Mapperley Ri. NG3: Mapp	.5B **86**
Mapperley Rd. NG3: Mapp P	.1K **95**
Mapperley Sports Village	.6B **86**
Mapperley St. NG5: Sher	.5K **85**
Mappleton Dr. NG18: Mans	.5D **48**
Mapplewells NG17: Ann W	.3K **59**
Mapplewells Cres. NG17: Sut A	.2F **51**
Mapplewells Rd. NG17: Sut A	.2F **51**
March Cl. NG5: Top V	.7A **76**
Marchesi Cl. NG15: Huck	.2E **74**
Marchwood Cl. NG8: Radf	.3E **94**
Marco Island NG1: Nott	.4H **7**
Mardale Cl. NG2: West Br	.4F **109**
Mardling Av. NG5: Bestw	.2H **85**

Margaret Av.—Meden Bank

Margaret Av. NG10: Long E 7E 104
NG10: Sand 5A 104
Margaret Cres. NG4: Ged 5H 87
Margaret Pl. NG13: Bing 3E 100
Margarets Ct. NG9: Bram 1F 105
Marham Cl. NG2: Nott 7K 7 (5B 96)
Marhill Rd. NG4: Carl 1J 97
Maria Ct. NG7: Nott 7B 6 (5H 95)
Marie Gdns. NG15: Huck 1G 75
Marina Av. NG9: Bee 4A 106
Mariner Ct. NG6: Bulw 1B 84
Marion Av. NG15: Huck 4J 67
NG17: Kirk A 2B 60
Maris Cl. NG11: Clif 7D 106
Maris Dr. NG14: Bur J 3D 88
Marjorie St. S80: Rhod 1B 20
Markeden Ct. NG22: New O 4C 38
Market Ho. Pl. *NG18: Mans* *3H 47*
(off Queen St.)
MARKET OVERTON 3D 149
Market Pl. DN22: Retf 3F 23
NG5: Arn 7H 77
NG6: Bulw 7H 75
NG13: Bing 4F 101
NG15: Huck 6G 67
NG17: Huth 7D 44
NG17: Sut A 1J 51
NG18: Mans 3H 47
NG19: Mans W 6J 41
NG22: Oll 5A 38
NG22: Tuxf 6C 28
NG24: New T 1C 136
NG25: Sout 6H 131
Market Side *NG6: Bulw* *7H 75*
(off Duke St.)
Market Sq. NG25: Sout 5H 131
Market St. NG1: Nott 4E 6 (3K 95)
NG13: Bing 4F 101
NG17: Huth 7D 44
NG17: Sut A 1J 51
NG18: Mans 4H 47
S80: Work 2G 21
Markham Av. NG24: New T 5E 134
Markham Cl. NG22: New O 4B 38
Markham Cres. NG5: Sher 3K 85
Markham Pl. NG19: Mans 3D 46
Markham Rd. NG9: Bram 7J 93
NG22: Tuxf 5C 28
S81: Lango 1B 12
Markhams, The NG22: New O 4B 38
Markham St. NG15: News 6D 60
Mark La. NG22: East M 3C 28
Marklew Cl. NG21: Blid 6J 55
Mark St. NG10: Sand 4B 104
Markwick Cl. NG24: New T 1G 137
Marlborough, The NG3: Nott 1K 95
Marlborough Cl. NG24: New T 4A 136
S81: Gate 4E 18
Marlborough Ct. NG2: West Br 2C 108
NG9: Bee 1A 106
NG24: New T 4A 136
Marlborough Rd. NG5: Woodt 2A 86
NG9: Bee 1A 106
NG17: Kirk A 6B 52
NG19: Mans 1F 47
Marlborough St. NG7: Lent 7F 95
Marldon Cl. NG8: Bilb 3G 93
Marle Pit Hill LE12: Sut B 4A 120
Marles Cl. NG24: New T 6F 135
Marlock Cl. NG25: Fis 6H 139
Marlow Av. NG6: Basf 5F 85
Marlowe Dr. NG24: Bald 5H 137
Marlowe Gdns. S81: Work 1J 21
Marl Rd. NG12: Rad T 5G 99
Marlwood NG12: Cotg 7F 111
Marly Bank NG18: Mans 5A 48
Marmion Ct. NG3: Nott 2C 96
Marmion Rd. NG3: Nott 1D 96
Marnham Dr. NG3: Nott 6B 86
Marnham Mdw. Holiday Pk.
NG23: High M 7A 30
Marnham Rd. NG22: Tuxf 6E 28
Marples Av. NG19: Mans W 4A 42
Marquis Av. NG24: Bald 6G 137
Marquis Gdns. DN22: Retf 6G 23
MARR 1A 144
Marriott Av. NG9: Chil 4F 105
NG18: Mans 4F 47
Marriott Cl. NG9: Chil 4F 105
Marriott La. NG21: Blid 7H 55
Marrison Ct. NG24: Farnd 7G 133
Marrison Way NG25: Sout 5J 131
Marron Cl. NG24: Bald 7J 137
Marron Ct. NG24: Bald 7J 137
Marsant Cl. NG8: Woll 3D 94
Marsden Cl. NG6: Bulw 2F 85
Marshall Av. NG17: Kirk A 7C 52
Marshall Cl. NG14: Calv 5B 70
Marshall Ct. NG24: Bald 5H 137
Marshall Dr. NG9: Bram 1E 104
Marshall Hill Dr. NG3: Mapp 6D 86
Marshall Rd. NG3: Mapp 6D 86
NG12: Crop Bi 5B 112
Marshall St. NG5: Sher 5K 85
Marshall Ter. NG17: Stant H 4H 45
Marsham Dr. NG5: Arn 1C 86
Marsh La. DN10: Mist 3K 11
NG22: Dun T 5K 29
NG23: Nth M 6K 129
NG24: Farnd 7G 133
Marsh Rd. DN10: Walk 7K 11
Marsh's Paddock LE14: Hick 6E 142
MARSTON 1D 149
Marston Av. NG20: Mede V 7F 33
Marston Cl. NG24: Bald 6F 137
Marston Moor Rd. NG24: New T 1H 137
Marston Rd. NG3: Nott 1E 96
Martell Ct. NG9: Chil 6H 105
Martin Cl. NG6: Bulw 6F 75
Martin Ct. NG6: Bulw 6G 75
Martin Cres. NG11: Rudd 3J 115
Martindale Cl. NG2: Gam 2F 109
Martindale La. NG24: New T 1C 136
Martinmass Cl. NG7: Lent 5F 95
Martin's Hill NG4: Carl 1H 97
Martin's Pond Nature Reserve 3K 93
Martlet Way S80: Work 5H 21
MARTON 3D 145
Marton Rd. NG6: Bulw 5J 75
NG9: Chil 6H 105
NG24: New T 3E 136
Martyn Av. NG17: Sut A 2K 51
Marvyn Cl. NG6: Bulw 1F 85
Marwood Cres. NG4: Carl 5F 87
Marwood Rd. NG4: Carl 6F 87
Mary Ct. NG3: Nott 6B 86
Maryfield Cl. DN22: Retf 1E 22
Maryland Ct. NG9: Stap 7D 92
Mary Rd. NG16: Eastw 5F 73
Mary St. NG17: Kirk A 4B 52
NG20: Whal T 5B 26
S80: Rhod 7B 18
Masefield Cres. NG24: Bald 5G 137
Masefield Pl. S81: Work 1J 21
Masonic Pl. NG1: Nott 4D 6 (3J 95)
Mason St. NG17: Sut A 6B 46
Massey Cl. NG14: Bur J 4D 88
Massey Ct. NG24: New T 1E 136
Massey Gdns. NG3: Nott 1K 7 (2B 96)
Massey St. NG24: New T 1E 136
Masson Ct. NG5: Top V 5C 76
MASTIN MOOR 1A 146
Mather Rd. NG24: New T 7C 134
Matlock Av. NG18: Mans 6G 47
Matlock Cl. NG17: Nunc 3A 60
Matlock Ct. NG1: Nott 3E 6 (3K 95)
Matlock St. NG4: Neth 1J 97
MATTERSEY 2J 15 (3B 144)
Mattersey Ct. *NG19: Mans* *1H 47*
(off W. Bank Av.)
Mattersey Hall 2J 15
Mattersey Priory (remains of) 3C 145
Mattersey Rd. DN10: Eve, Matt 1H 15 & 7B 10
DN22: Lound, Sut L 6B 14
DN22: Rans 2J 13
MATTERSEY THORPE 1G 15 (3B 144)
Matthews Ct. NG9: Stap 6E 92
Matthew Thomas Ct. NG9: Bee 3B 106
Mattingly Rd. NG6: Bulw 1B 84
Mattley Av. NG17: Nunc 3A 60
Maud St. NG7: Basf 6H 85
Maun Av. NG7: Radf 2E 94
NG17: Kirk A 4B 52
Maun Cl. DN22: Retf 5F 23
NG17: Sut A 1B 52
NG18: Mans 6F 47
Maun Cres. NG22: New O 3C 38
Maundale Av. NG17: Sut A 6B 46
Maun Gdns. NG7: Radf 2E 94
Maun Grn. NG24: New T 6E 134
Maunleigh NG19: Mans W 1A 48
Maunside NG18: Mans 6F 47
Maunside Av. NG17: Sut A 2B 52
Maun Valley Ind. Pk. NG17: Sut A 1B 52
Maun Vw. NG18: Mans 3J 47
Maun Vw. Gdns. NG17: Sut A 2B 52
Maun Way NG18: Mans 6F 47
NG22: Bou 4G 39
Maurice Dr. NG3: Mapp 5B 86
Mavis Av. NG15: Rave 3C 62
Mavis Wood M. NG21: Blid 6K 55
Mawkin La. NG16: Pinx 6D 50
Maws La. NG16: Kimb 7J 73
Maxtoke Rd. NG7: Nott 7A 6 (5H 95)
Maxwell Cl. NG7: Lent 5G 95
May Av. NG8: Woll 4K 93
May Ct. NG5: Sher 6J 85
Maycroft Gdns. NG3: Nott 1D 96
NG17: Huth 7F 45
Maydene Cl. NG11: Clif 1E 114
Mayes Ri. NG6: Bestw V 2A 76
Mayfair NG12: Rad T 5J 99
Mayfair Av. NG18: Mans 4K 47
Mayfair Cl. DN11: Harwo 2C 8
Mayfair Gdns. NG5: Sher 2G 85
Mayfair Pl. NG22: Tuxf 7D 28
Mayfield Av. NG14: Bur J 2E 88
Mayfield Cl. NG18: Mans 5D 48
Mayfield Ct. NG2: Nott 6K 95
Mayfield Dr. NG9: Stap 6E 92
Mayfield Pl. NG17: Sut A 1H 51
Mayfield Rd. NG4: Carl 1E 96
Mayfield St. NG17: Kirk A 1H 59
Mayfield Ter. NG20: Mkt W 5D 34
Mayflower Av. DN10: Scro 4K 9
Mayflower Cl. NG2: West Br 2D 108
Mayflower Ct. NG18: Mans 7H 47
Mayflower Rd. NG16: Newth 6F 73
Mayhall Av. NG19: Mans W 5G 41
May Hill NG25: Sout 6F 131
Mayland Cl. NG8: Bilb 2H 93
Mayo Rd. NG5: Sher 6J 85
Maypole NG11: Clif 6F 107
Maypole Grn. NG22: Well 7D 38
Maypole Rd. NG22: Well 7E 38
Maypole Yd. NG1: Nott 4F 7 (3K 95)
May's Av. NG4: Carl 2F 97
Mays Cl. NG4: Carl 2F 97
Maythorn Cl. NG2: West Br 6K 107
Maythorne Cl. NG5: Arn 7K 77
NG24: New B 4F 137
Maythorne Ind. Est.
NG25: Mayt 2F 131
Maythorne La. NG25: Mayt 3F 131
Maythorne Wlk. NG5: Bestw 6E 76
Maythorn Gro. NG21: Edwin 5F 37
Meade Dr. S81: Work 5H 19
Meadow, The DN22: Retf 2F 23
Meadow Av. NG18: Mans 5J 47
Meadow Bank NG19: Mans W 3A 42
Meadowbank Ct. NG16: Eastw 3B 72
Meadowbank Way NG16: Eastw 3B 72
Meadow Brown Rd. NG7: H Grn 7F 85
Meadow Cl. DN22: Retf 1E 22
NG2: Nott 6B 96
NG13: Aslo 3D 102
NG15: Huck 1D 74
NG16: Eastw 2D 72
NG17: Kirk A 5J 51
NG21: Edwin 6E 36
NG22: Farns 5K 57
NG23: Nth M 7K 129
Meadow Cotts. NG4: Neth 1J 97
NG19: Mans W 6J 41
Meadow Ct. NG2: Nott 6C 96
Meadow Cft. Gdns. NG15: Huck 1F 75
Meadow Dike La. DN22: Sth L 2H 25
Meadow Dr. DN10: Mist 2H 11
NG12: Key 7K 117
NG17: Sut A 7G 45
S80: Work 3D 20
Meadow End NG11: Goth 7G 115
NG12: Rad T 5H 99
Meadow Farm Vw. NG17: Kirk A 6J 51
Meadow Gdns. DE75: Hea 5A 72
NG9: Chil 5K 105
Meadow Gro. NG2: Nott 6B 96
NG22: Bils 7D 126
Meadow Lane 6B 96
Meadow La. DN22: Clay 6F 15
DN22: Hay 5G 17
NG2: Nott 7K 7 (6B 96)
(not continuous)
NG9: Chil 4K 105
NG13: Tith 3D 112
NG14: Bur J 3E 88
NG21: Blid 7H 55
NG23: Weston 3G 125
Meadow Lark Cl. NG17: Sut A 2H 51
Meadow Lea S80: Work 3D 20
Meadow Pl. NG20: Mkt W 4C 34
Meadow Rise NG6: Bulw 1A 84
Meadow Rd. DN22: Retf 2G 23
NG4: Neth 2J 97
NG9: Bee 4B 106
NG16: Aws 2B 82
NG21: Blid 6J 55
NG24: New B 5F 137
S80: Work 3D 20
MEADOWS 6K 95 (2A 148)
Meadows, The DN10: Beck 7C 16
DN22: Sth W 2K 17
NG14: Woodbo 2F 79
NG16: Aws 2B 82
NG21: Blid 7H 55
NG24: Farnd 6H 133
Meadows Way NG2: Nott 7J 95
Meadowsweet Hill NG13: Bing 4D 100
Meadow Trad. Est. NG2: Nott 7K 7 (5B 96)
Meadowvale Cres. NG11: Clif 1F 115
Meadow Vw. NG9: Stap 1C 104
NG16: Sels 6C 58
NG25: Sout 5J 131
S80: Work 3H 21
Meadow Way DN11: Harwo 1C 8
NG12: Kin 2B 142
NG19: New H 2A 40
NG21: C'tone 4H 43
Mead Way NG24: Bald 6E 136
Mecca Bingo
Beeston 3C 106
Medawar Cl. NG11: Clif 1D 114
Medbank Ct. NG11: Wilf 4H 107
Meden Av. NG19: New H 2A 40
NG20: Mkt W 4E 34
MEDEN BANK 4F 45
Meden Bank NG17: Stant H 4G 45
NG19: Plea 4B 40

Meden Cl. NG11: Clif 6F **107**
  NG19: Plea .4B **40**
Meden Ct. NG22: Bou 4H **39**
Meden Cres. NG17: Sut A 6G **45**
Meden Gdns. NG7: H Grn 1E **94**
Meden Glen NG20: Chu W 1E **34**
Meden La. NG19: Plea 3F **41**
Meden Pl. NG20: Mkt W 3D **34**
Meden Rd. NG19: Mans W 5K **41**
  NG22: Bou .4H **39**
Meden Side NG20: Mede V 1F **35**
Meden Sports Cen. 3D **34**
Meden Sq. NG19: Plea 4B **40**
MEDEN VALE 7G **33** (2A **146**)
Meden Way DN22: Retf 5F **23**
Medina Dr. NG12: Toll 1G **117**
Medway DN22: Retf 1D **22**
Medway Cl. NG9: Chil 4H **105**
Medway Dr. NG13: Bing 5D **100**
Medway St. NG8: Radf 3E **94**
Meeks Rd. NG5: Arn 6K **77**
Meering Av. NG24: New T 4E **134**
Meering Cl. NG23: Coll 1H **129**
Meering La. NG23: Best 7G **125**
Meerings, The NG23: Sut T 2C **128**
Meer Rd. NG9: Chil 4F **105**
Meeting Ho. Cl. LE12: East L 3B **122**
Meeting Ho. La. DN22: Sth L . . . . .1F **25** & 2F **25**
Melbourne Ct. NG8: Aspl 6D **84**
  NG18: Mans 4D **48**
Melbourne Gro. DN11: Harwo 2C **8**
Melbourne Rd. NG2: West Br 7C **96**
  NG8: Aspl 7C **84**
  NG9: Stap 6D **92**
Melbourne St. NG16: Sels 6F **59**
  NG19: Mans W 4J **41**
Melbury Rd. NG5: Woodt 3C **86**
  NG8: Bilb 7J **83**
Meldreth Rd. NG8: Bilb 2K **93**
Meldrum Cres. NG24: New T 4B **136**
Melford Hall Dr. NG2: West Br 5K **107**
Melford Rd. NG8: Bilb 7J **83**
Melksham Rd. NG5: Bestw 6E **76**
Mellbreak Cl. NG2: West Br 3F **109**
Mellers Ct. NG3: Nott 1D **96**
Mellish Rd. S81: Lango 2B **12**
Mellish Sports Cen. 2E **84**
Mellors Rd. NG2: West Br 4C **108**
  NG5: Arn 5H **77**
  NG19: Mans 2D **46**
  NG21: Edwin 7D **36**
Mellors Way NG8: Stre 5H **83**
Melrose Av. NG5: Sher 4K **85**
  NG9: Bee 4B **106**
  NG18: Mans 5K **47**
Melrose Gdns. NG2: West Br 5A **108**
Melrose St. NG5: Sher 4K **85**
Melrose Wlk. S80: Work 3G **21**
                  (off Pilgrim Way)
Melton Ct. NG10: Sand 4A **104**
Melton Gdns. NG12: Edwal 5D **108**
Melton Gro. NG2: West Br 2B **108**
Melton Hall NG8: Woll 4D **94**
Melton La. LE12: Sut B 2A **120**
MELTON MOWBRAY 3C **149**
Melton Rd. LE12: Norm S, Stanf S 6J **121**
  LE14: Hick P, Upp B 1F **143**
  NG2: West Br 2B **108**
  NG12: Edwal, Key, Plum, Stant W . . .1D **116**
Melton Way NG18: Mans 7E **46**
Melville Ct. NG3: Mapp P 7K **85**
  NG20: Mede V 7F **33**
Melville Gdns. NG3: Nott 2K **7** (2B **96**)
Melville St. NG1: Nott 7F **7** (5K **95**)
Melvyn Dr. NG13: Bing 4F **101**
Memorial Av. S80: Work 3G **21**
Memorial Dr. NG25: Sout 6H **131**
Mendip Cl. NG18: Mans 6A **48**
Mendip Ct. NG5: Top V 6B **76**
  S81: Carl L .5B **12**
            (off Salisbury Wlk.)
Mensing Av. NG12: Cotg 6D **110**
Merchant St. NG6: Bulw 6H **75**
               (not continuous)
Mercia Av. NG12: Crop Bi 5B **112**
Mercia Cl. NG16: Gilt 6E **72**
  S81: Work 5H **19**
Mercia Ct. NG17: Huth 1E **50**
Mercia Rd. NG24: New T 4C **136**
Mercury Cl. NG6: Basf 2F **85**
Mere Av. NG14: Calv 6D **70**
Mere Cl. NG14: Calv 6D **70**
Meredith Cl. NG2: Nott 7J **95**
Meredith Cl. NG9: Stap 6D **92**
Meregill Cl. NG5: Top V 5B **76**
Merevale Av. NG11: Clif 5G **107**
Merevale Cl. NG14: Lowd 5E **80**
Mere Way NG11: Rudd 6A **116**
Meriac Cl. NG5: Top V 6B **76**
Meriden Av. NG9: Lent A 1B **106**
Meridian Cl. NG5: Sher 5H **85**
Merlin Cl. NG11: Clif 7F **107**
Merlin Dr. NG15: Huck 2E **74**
Merlin Rd. NG19: Mans W 7H **41**
Merlin Way DE7: Ilk 5A **92**
Merrivale Ct. NG3: Mapp P 7K **85**

Merry Rd. NG22: New O 5D **38**
Merryvale Dr. NG19: Mans 4D **46**
Merryweather Cl. NG21: Edwin 7J **37**
  NG25: Sout 4H **131**
Mersey St. NG6: Bulw 7H **75**
Merton Av. DN22: Retf 1E **22**
Merton Cl. NG5: Arn 5K **77**
Merton Ct. NG9: Stap 7D **92**
Meryton Gro. NG17: Kirk A 1A **60**
MESSINGHAM 1D **145**
Metcalfe Cl. NG22: Bils 4C **126**
  NG25: Sout 6J **131**
Metcalf Rd. NG16: Newth 3F **73**
Meteor Cl. NG13: Newton 1C **100**
Methuen Av. NG18: Mans 4A **48**
Mettham St. NG7: Lent 5G **95**
Mevell Ct. NG7: Nott 6B **6** (4H **95**)
Mews, The NG7: Basf 7H **85**
  NG12: Cols B 6G **141**
  S81: Blyth 6G **13**
Mews La. NG14: Calv 6C **70**
MEXBOROUGH 1A **144**
Meynell Gro. NG7: Basf 6H **85**
Meyrick Rd. NG24: New T 7D **134**
Miall Ct. NG7: Lent 3F **95**
Miall St. NG7: Lent 3F **95**
Michael Gdns. NG5: Sher 6J **85**
Michael Rayner Ct. NG6: Basf 4E **84**
Micklebarrow Cl. NG25: Sout 6F **131**
MICKLEBARROW HILL 4E **132**
Mickleborough Av. NG3: Nott 7C **86**
Mickleborough Way NG2: West Br 6K **107**
MICKLEBRING 2A **144**
Mickledale Cl. NG22: Bils 4B **126**
Mickledale La. NG22: Bils 3A **126**
Mickledon Cl. NG2: Nott 6K **95**
Micklemoor La. NG13: Car C 7J **91**
Middle Av. NG4: Carl 7F **87**
Middlebeck Av. NG5: Arn 6A **78**
Middlebeck Dr. NG5: Arn 6K **77**
Middlebridge Rd. DN10: Gri H 1A **16**
Middlebrook Rd. NG16: Unde 1E **64**
Middle Cross La. DN10: Eve, Harwe 5A **10**
Middledale Rd. NG4: Carl 2F **97**
Middlefell Way NG11: Clif 1E **114**
Middlefield La. NG22: Oll 5B **38**
Middlefield Rd. DN22: Nth W 2J **17**
  NG25: Mort .5F **139**
Middle Furlong Gdns. NG2: Nott 6J **95**
Middle Furlong M. NG2: Nott 6J **95**
Middle Ga. NG24: New T 1C **136**
Middle Hill NG1: Nott 6F **7** (4K **95**)
Middle Hill Rd. DN22: Nth W 2F **17**
Middle Holme La. NG23: Sut T 3E **128**
Middle La. LE14: Neth B 4K **143**
  NG9: Chil 4K **105**
  NG25: Mort .6F **139**
Middle Mdw. S81: Shire 5A **18**
Middle Nook NG8: Woll 3K **93**
             (off Cottage Wlk.)
Middle Orchard St. NG9: Stap 2C **104**
Middle Pavement NG1: Nott 6F **7** (4K **95**)
Middle St. DN10: Miss 2D **10**
  NG9: Bee 3A **106**
Middleton Blvd. NG8: Woll 4D **94**
Middleton Cl. NG16: Nuth 1H **83**
  NG16: Sels .5F **59**
Middleton Ct. NG8: Bilb 3J **93**
  NG18: Mans 4D **48**
  NG22: New O 3C **38**
Middleton Cres. NG9: Bee 7K **93**
Middleton Dr. DE7: Ilk 3A **92**
  NG19: Mans W 4J **41**
  NG21: C'tone 5H **43**
  NG24: New T 5E **134**
Middleton St. DE7: Ilk 6A **82**
  NG7: Lent 3F **95**
  NG9: Bee 2K **105**
  NG16: Aws .3B **82**
Middlewood Cl. NG17: Sut A 6H **45**
Midfield Rd. NG17: Nunc 3B **60**
Midhurst Cl. NG9: Chil 5H **105**
Midhurst Way NG11: Clif 7F **107**
Midlame Gdns. NG6: Bulw 7F **75**
Midland Av. NG4: Neth 1K **97**
  NG7: Lent 5F **95**
  NG9: Stap 4B **104**
Midland Bank Chambers
  NG18: Mans 3H **47**
             (off Leeming St.)
Midland Cotts. NG2: West Br 2C **108**
  NG19: Plea .3A **40**
Midland Ct. NG7: Radf 2E **94**
Midland Cres. NG4: Carl 1J **97**
Midland Gro. NG4: Neth 7K **87**
Midland Rd. NG4: Carl 1J **97**
  NG16: Eastw 4D **72**
  NG17: Sut A 1B **52**
Midland Ter. NG24: New T 7B **134**
Midland Way NG7: Radf 2E **94**
  NG18: Mans 5G **47**
Midway, The NG7: Lent 1F **107**
Midworth St. NG18: Mans 4H **47**
Milburn Gro. NG13: Bing 4D **100**
Mildenhall Cres. NG5: Bestw 6E **76**
Mile End Rd. NG4: Colw 3H **97**

Milford Av. NG10: Long E 6A **104**
Milford Cl. NG6: Bulw 6G **75**
Milford Ct. NG5: Arn 1A **86**
Milford Cres. NG19: Mans 3D **46**
Milford Dr. NG3: Nott 1F **97**
Mill Adventure Base, The 7D **46**
Millbank NG6: Bulw 1B **84**
Millbank Pl. NG6: Bestw V 3K **75**
Mill Baulk Rd. DN10: Walk 6H **11**
Millbeck Av. NG8: Woll 4H **93**
Millbeck Cl. NG2: Gam 3F **109**
Mill Bri. Cl. DN22: Retf 4E **22**
Millbrook Dr. NG4: Carl 6F **87**
Mill Cl. DN10: Mist 3H **11**
  DN22: Nth L 6B **24**
  NG17: Huth .7E **44**
  NG23: Sut T 3D **128**
Mill Close, The NG6: Basf 4F **85**
Mill Cl. NG18: Mans 5E **46**
Mill Cres. NG5: Arn 6G **77**
Mill Cft. NG17: Sut A 2J **51**
Milldale Cl. NG11: Clif 7D **106**
Milldale Ct. NG18: Mans 5C **48**
Milldale Rd. NG22: Farns 5K **57**
Milldale Wlk. NG17: Sut A 6J **45**
Millennium Bus. Pk.
  NG19: Mans 7D **40**
Millennium Ct. NG6: Bulw 2E **84**
  NG19: Mans 7E **40**
Millennium Way NG8: Cin 3B **84**
Millennium Way E. NG8: Cin 3B **84**
Millennium Way W. NG8: Cin 3B **84**
Miller Hives Cl. NG12: Cotg 6D **110**
Millers Bri. NG12: Cotg 7D **110**
Millers Cl. NG12: Shel 6H **89**
Millers Ct. DN22: Clar 7J **17**
  NG7: Basf 2F **95**
Millersdale Av.
  NG18: Mans 6D **46**
Millers Grn. NG2: Nott 4D **96**
Millers La. LE12: Costo 3E **122**
Millers Way DN22: Retf 1C **22**
  NG17: Kirk A 6A **52**
  NG17: Sut A 5D **46**
Mill Fld. Cl. NG14: Bur J 4D **86**
  NG23: Harby 6K **31**
Millfield Cl. DN22: Ord 7E **22**
Millfield Rd. NG16: Kimb 7J **73**
Millfield Vw. S80: Work 3D **20**
Mill Gdns. S80: Work 3D **20**
Mill Ga. NG13: East B 5D **90**
  NG24: New T 2B **136**
Mill Grn. NG24: New T 1E **136**
Mill Heyes NG13: East B 4E **90**
Mill Hill Rd. NG13: Bing 5E **100**
Mill Holme DE55: Sth N 7A **50**
Mill Ho. Pk. S80: Work 3E **20**
Millcent Gro.
  NG2: West Br 1C **108**
Millicent Rd. NG2: West Br 1B **108**
Millidge Cl. NG5: Bestw 2G **85**
Mill Lakes Country Pk. 2K **75**
Mill La. DN10: Bawt, Scro 2J **9**
  DN10: Eve 7B **10**
  DN10: Walk .7H **11**
  DN22: Clay 7J **15**
  DN22: Nth L 7A **24**
  DN22: Sth L 1H **25**
  LE12: East L 4B **122**
  LE12: Will W 5G **143**
  LE14: Hick 5D **142**
  NG4: Lamb .7F **79**
  NG5: Arn 6G **77**
  NG6: Bestw V 3K **75**
  NG10: Sand .3B **104**
  NG11: Rudd 6C **116**
  NG12: Cotg .5D **110**
  NG12: Crop Bi 5B **112**
  NG12: C'ton, Cotg 7C **110**
  NG13: Aslo, Scar 1C **102**
  NG13: Ors 1K **103**
  NG16: Coss .7A **82**
  NG16: Pinx .2B **58**
  NG17: Huth .7E **44**
  NG17: Kirk A 7H **51**
  NG21: Edwin 7E **36**
  NG22: Eakr .3B **126**
  NG22: Egma 3D **124**
  NG22: Wale .5F **27**
  NG23: Caun 5G **127**
  NG23: Norm T 1K **125**
  NG23: Nth C 3D **30**
  NG23: Nth M, Sth M 7J **129**
             (not continuous)
  NG23: Thor .3G **31**
  NG23: Upton 1H **139**
  NG23: Wigs .7F **31**
  NG24: New T 1B **136**
Millman Way DN22: Retf 1C **22**
Mill Mdw. Vw. S81: Blyth 6H **13**
Mill Pk. NG25: Sout 4J **131**
Mill Pk. Ind. Est.
  NG25: Sout 4J **131**
Mill Pond Cl. NG17: Ann W 3J **59**
Millrise Rd. NG18: Mans 5K **47**

Mill Rd.—Moyra Dr.

Mill Rd. DN10: Gri H 3A 16
NG9: Stap 1C 104
NG16: Newth 3E 72
NG23: Elston 2E 140
Mills Bldgs. NG1: Nott 6H 7
Mills Dr. NG24: New T 5K 133
Millside NG18: Mans 2K 47
Millstone Cl. NG18: Mans 5A 48
Mill St. DN22: Retf 4F 23
NG6: Basf 4E 84
NG17: Sut A 1J 51
NG18: Mans 4K 47
S80: Work 1F 21
Mill Vw. NG23: Upton 7B 132
Mill Vw. Cl. NG2: Nott 4C 96
Millview Ct. NG2: Nott 6K 7 (4B 96)
Mill Wlk. NG18: Mans 3H 47
Millway NG19: Mans W 1K 47
Mill Yd. NG15: Huck 6G 67
Milne Av. DN11: Birc 2F 9
Milne Dr. DN11: Birc 2G 9
Milne Gro. DN11: Birc 2F 9
Milnercroft DN22: Retf 1D 22
(not continuous)
Milnercroft Grn. *DN22: Retf 1D 22*
(off Milnercroft)
Milne Rd. DN11: Birc 2F 9
Milner Rd. NG5: Sher 5K 85
Milner St. NG17: Skeg 4A 46
NG24: New T 2D 136
Milnhay Rd. DE75: Hea 5A 72
NG16: Lang M 4A 72
MILTON 1C 147
Milton Cl. NG17: Sut A 6B 46
Milton Ct. NG5: Arn 7K 77
NG5: Sher 4J 85
NG15: Rave 2C 62
Milton Cres. NG9: Atten 7J 105
NG15: Rave 2B 62
Milton Dr. NG15: Rave 2B 62
S81: Work 1J 21
Milton Ho. NG1: Nott 4F 7 (3K 95)
Milton Ri. NG15: Huck 1D 74
Milton St. NG1: Nott 3F 7 (3K 95)
NG17: Kirk A 6B 52
NG18: Mans 3G 47
NG24: New B 3E 136
Milton Wlk. S81: Work 1J 21
Milverton Rd. NG5: Bestw 6E 76
Mimosa Cl. NG11: Clif 1D 114
Minerva Gro. NG15: Huck 5J 67
Minerva St. NG6: Bulw 6H 75
(not continuous)
Minkley Dr. NG16: Lang M 2A 72
Minster Cl. NG15: Huck 5H 67
NG17: Kirk A 5K 51
Minster Ct. NG5: Sher 1J 95
Minster Gdns. NG16: Newth 5F 73
Minster Rd. DN10: Mist 2G 11
Minstrel Av. NG5: Sher 5H 85
Minstrel Cl. NG15: Huck 1G 75
Minton Cl. NG9: Chil 7G 105
Minton Pastures NG19: Mans W 1C 48
Minver Cres. NG8: Aspl 6B 84
Minver Crescent Sports Cen. 6C 84
Mirberry M. NG7: Lent 5F 95
Mire La. DN22: Sut L 6A 14
Miriam Ct. NG2: West Br 2B 108
Misk Hollows NG15: Huck 5F 67
Misk Vw. NG16: Eastw 4F 73
Mission St. NG3: Mapp 5B 86
MISSON 3C 10 (2B 144)
MISTERTON 2H 11 (2C 145)
Misterton Ct. NG19: Mans 1H 47
Misterton Cres. NG15: Rave 3B 62
Mitchell Cl. NG6: Bulw 1B 84
S81: Work 4F 19
Mitford Dr. NG5: Arn 4H 77
Mob La. LE12: Will W 6G 143
Moffat Cl. NG3: Nott 1K 7 (1C 96)
Mollington Sq. NG6: Cin 3C 84
Mona Rd. NG2: West Br 7D 96
Mona St. NG9: Bee 3B 106
Monckton Dr. NG25: Sout 5H 131
Monckton Rd. DN11: Birc 2F 9
DN22: Retf 2C 22
Monks Cl. DE7: Ilk 7A 82
Monk's La. NG11: Goth 7G 115
Monks Mdw. LE12: East L 2B 122
Monks Way S81: Shire 5A 18
Monksway NG11: Wilf 5H 107
Monkton Dr. NG8: Bilb 1K 93
Monkwood Cl. NG23: Coll 1J 129
Monmouth Cl. NG8: Woll 4G 93
Monmouth Rd. S81: Work 6H 19
Monroe Wlk. NG5: Bestw 7C 76
Monsall St. NG7: Basf 6G 85
Monsell Dr. NG5: Redh 5G 77
Montague Rd. NG15: Huck 5G 67
Montague St. NG6: Bulw 7J 75
NG9: Bee 2K 105
NG18: Mans 4A 48
Montford Rd. S81: Gate 4D 18
Montfort Cres. NG5: Sher 3A 86
Montfort St. NG7: Radf 4A 6 (3H 95)
Montgomery Cl. NG9: Chil 7H 105
Montgomery Rd. NG24: New T 4D 136
Montgomery St. NG7: Radf 2B 6 (2H 95)
Montpelier Rd. NG7: Lent 7F 95
Montrose S81: Work 7J 19
Montrose Ct. NG9: Stap 7D 92
Montrose Sq. NG19: Mans W 3H 41
Montys Mdw. S81: Gate 5E 18
Moody Cl. NG9: Chil 7G 105
Moon Cres. NG16: Eastw 5C 72
Moor, The NG9: Trow 2F 93
NG16: Brins 5B 64
Moor Bridge (Park & Ride) 4K 75
Moorbridge Caravan Pk. NG6: Bulw 4K 75
Moorbridge Cotts. NG6: Bulw 4K 75
Moorbridge Ct. NG13: Bing 3F 101
Moorbridge La. NG9: Stap 7C 92
Moorbridge Rd. NG13: Bing 3F 101
Moorbridge Rd. E. NG13: Bing 3F 101
Moor Bridge Stop (NET) 4K 75
Moore Cl. LE12: East L 2B 122
NG2: West Br 7E 96
Moore Ga. NG9: Bee 3A 106
Moore Rd. NG3: Mapp 5D 86
Moores Av. NG10: Sand 2B 104
Moores Pl. NG5: Sher 5H 85
Moore St. NG6: Bulw 2D 84
Moor Farm Holiday & Home Pk. NG14: Calv 7G 71
Moor Farm Inn La. NG9: Bram 6F 93
Moorfield Ct. NG9: Stap 7D 92
NG25: Sout 7G 131
Moorfield Cres. NG10: Sand 4A 104
Moorfield Pl. NG20: Mkt W 3E 34
Moorfields Av. NG16: Eastw 3D 72
Moorgate DN22: Retf 2F 23
Moorgate Pk. DN22: Retf 2F 23
Moorgate St. NG7: Radf 3A 6 (3H 95)
MOORGREEN 3H 73 (1A 148)
Moorgreen NG16: Newth 1G 73
Moorgreen Dr. NG8: Stre 5J 83
Moorgreen Ind. Pk. NG16: Newth 1F 73
Moorhades La. DN22: Ramp 7K 25
MOORHAIGH 6B 40 (2A 146)
Moorhaigh La. NG19: Plea 6A 40
MOORHOUSE 2C 147
Moorhouse La. NG23: Sth M 7H 129
Moorhouse Rd. NG8: Bilb 2K 93
NG22: Lax 6B 124
Moorings, The NG7: Lent 6G 95
Moorland Av. DN10: Walk 6H 11
NG9: Stap 3C 104
Moorland Cl. DN10: Walk 6H 11
NG17: Skeg 4A 46
Moorlands Cl. NG10: Long E 7A 104
NG23: Norw 3H 127
Moorland Wlk. *DN10: Walk 6H 11*
(off Moorland Av.)
Moorland Way NG18: Mans 4C 48
Moor La. DN22: Chu L 2H 29
DN22: Ramp 7K 25
LE12: Norm S 6F 121
NG9: Bram 6G 93
NG11: Bunny 2A 118
NG11: Goth, Rudd 7G 115
NG11: Rudd 4K 115
(Leys Ct.)
NG11: Rudd 1A 118
(Littlemoor La.)
NG13: Bing 3F 101
NG13: Ors 3H 103
NG13: Scar 3A 102
NG14: Calv, Epp 7G 71
NG18: Mans 4F 47
NG23: Caun 4H 127
NG23: Nth C 4E 30
NG23: Sth C 7D 30
NG23: Sth S 7K 125
NG23: Syer 3B 140
NG25: Mort 6F 139
S81: Blyth 7K 13
Moor Rd. NG6: Bestw V 3K 75
NG8: Stre 6J 83
NG14: Calv 6E 70
NG15: Pap 3K 67
NG16: Brins 5C 64
NG23: Coll 1J 129
Moorsholm Dr. NG8: Woll 4H 93
Moor St. NG4: Neth 1J 97
NG18: Mans 4G 47
Moor Top Rd. DN11: Harwo 1C 8
Moor Vw. NG11: Bunny 3B 118
Moray Ct. NG16: Kimb 7K 73
Moray Sq. NG19: Mans 5D 46
Morden Cl. NG8: Bilb 7J 83
Morden Rd. NG16: Gilt 6G 73
Moreland Ct. NG2: Nott 5C 96
NG4: Carl 1F 97
Moreland Pl. NG2: Nott 5C 96
Moreland St. NG2: Nott 5C 96
Morel Ho. *NG7: Lent 3F 95*
(off Faraday Rd.)
Morello Av. NG4: Carl 1J 97
Moreton Rd. NG11: Clif 3F 115
Morgan M. NG11: Clif 7E 106
Morgans Cl. NG24: Codd 6K 135
Morkinshire Cres. NG12: Cotg 5E 110
Morkinshire La. NG12: Cotg 5D 110
Morley Av. DN22: Retf 1C 22
NG3: Mapp 5B 86
Morley Cl. NG18: Mans 5D 48
Morley Ct. NG2: Nott 4J 7 (4B 96)
Morley Gdns. NG5: Sher 6J 85
NG12: Rad T 4F 99
Morley Rd. NG3: Nott 6D 86
Morley's Cl. NG14: Lowd 5E 80
Morley St. NG5: Arn 1A 86
NG17: Kirk A 7B 52
NG17: Stant H 4G 45
NG17: Sut A 7K 45
Mornington Cl. NG10: Sand 3B 104
Mornington Cres. NG16: Nuth 4J 83
Morrell Bank NG5: Bestw 1G 85
Morris Ct. NG4: Colw 3K 97
Morris Rd. NG8: Stre 6J 83
Morris St. NG4: Neth 1K 97
MORTHEN 3A 144
MORTON
Gainsborough 2D 145
Lincoln 2D 147
Southwell 6F 139 (3C 147)
Morton Cl. NG12: Rad T 5H 99
NG18: Mans 4D 48
Morton Gdns. NG12: Rad T 5H 99
Morton Gro. S81: Work 4F 19
Morton St. NG19: Mans 1E 46
Morval Rd. NG8: Bilb 1K 93
Morven Av. NG15: Huck 7H 67
NG17: Sut A 1J 51
NG19: Mans W 7H 41
Morven Ho. S80: Work 4H 21
Morven Rd. NG17: Kirk A 6B 52
Morven Ter. NG20: Mkt W 5D 34
Mosborough Rd. NG17: Huth 2E 50
Moseley Rd. NG15: Ann 4C 60
Moses Vw. S81: Shire 4A 18
Mosgrove Cl. S81: Gate 5D 18
Mosley St. NG7: Basf 7G 85
NG15: Huck 7G 67
Mosscar Cl. NG20: Mkt W 7B 34
Mosscar La. NG20: Mkt W 6A 34
Moss Cl. NG5: Arn 6E 76
NG13: East B 4E 90
Mosscroft Av. NG11: Clif 1E 114
Mossdale S81: Work 4H 19
Mossdale Rd. NG5: Sher 2K 85
NG19: Mans W 2A 48
Moss Dr. NG9: Bram 2G 105
Moss Ri. NG3: Mapp 5E 86
Moss Rd. NG15: Huck 6F 67
Moss Side NG11: Wilf 6H 107
Mosswood Cres. NG5: Bestw 7D 76
Mottram Rd. NG9: Chil 3H 105
Moulton Cres. NG24: New B 6F 137
Mount, The NG3: Mapp 5F 87
NG5: Redh 5F 77
NG6: Bestw V 2A 76
NG8: Stre 6K 83
NG9: Stap 3C 104
NG19: Mans W 6F 43
NG24: New T 7C 134
Mount Av. S81: Work 7F 19
Mountbatten Gro. NG4: Ged 5H 87
Mountbatten Way NG9: Chil 7G 105
Mount Cl. DN11: Harwo 1C 8
Mount Ct. NG24: Bald 5F 137
NG24: New T 7C 134
(off Mount La.)
Mount Cres. NG20: Mkt W 5E 34
Mountfield Av. NG10: Sand 5A 104
Mountfield Dr. NG5: Bestw 7C 76
Mount Hgts. NG7: Basf 6H 85
Mount Hooton NG1: Nott 1B 6 (2H 95)
Mt. Hooton Rd. NG7: Radf 1A 6 (1H 95)
Mount La. NG24: New T 1D 136
Mount Milner NG18: Mans 4K 47
Mountney Pl. NG24: New T 5E 134
MOUNT PLEASANT 5E 34
Mt. Pleasant DN22: Retf 3F 23
NG4: Carl 1H 97
NG6: Basf 5E 84
NG12: Key 7J 117
NG12: Rad T 5D 98
NG14: Lowd 4D 80
NG17: Nunc 3K 59
NG17: Sut A 6K 45
NG18: Mans 3G 47
Mount Prospect DN10: Eve 5B 10
Mount Rd. NG24: Bald 5F 137
Mountsorrel Dr. NG2: West Br 3E 108
Mount St. NG1: Nott 5D 6 (4J 95)
(not continuous)
NG7: Basf 6G 85
NG9: Stap 2D 104
NG19: Mans 1G 47
Mount St. Arc. NG1: Nott 5D 6
Mt. Vernon Pk. DN22: Retf 6G 23
Mount Vw. Cl. NG18: Mans 4K 47
Mowbray Ct. NG3: Nott 3H 7 (3A 96)
Mowbray Gdns. NG2: West Br 4C 108
Mowbray Ri. NG5: Arn 5H 77
Mowcrofts La. NG22: Ragn 1A 30
Mowlands Cl. NG17: Sut A 1B 52
Moyra Dr. NG5: Arn 7E 76

Moyra Ho. NG5: Arn 7G 77
Mozart Cl. NG7: Radf 3F 95
Mr Straw's House 7H 19
Mudpie La. NG2: West Br 7E 96
Muir Av. NG12: Toll 2G 117
Muirfield S81: Work 6J 19
Muirfield Cl. NG17: Kirk A 4J 51
Muirfield Rd. NG5: Arn, Top V 5B 76
Muirfield Way NG19: Mans W 3A 42
Mulberry Cl. NG2: West Br 4J 107
NG18: Mans 5J 47
Mulberry Ct. DN10: Miss 3C 10
Mulberry Cres. S81: Carl L 5C 12
Mulberry Gdns. NG6: Bulw 6G 75
Mulberry Gro. NG15: Huck 2H 75
Mulberry Way DN11: Harwo 2C 8
Mumby Cl. NG24: New T 7D 134
Mundella Rd. NG2: Nott 7A 96
Munford Cir. NG8: Cin 4B 84
Munks Av. NG15: Huck 6F 67
Murby Cres. NG6: Bulw 6H 75
Murden Way NG9: Bee 3C 106
Murdoch Cl. NG22: Farns 4J 57
Muriel Gdns. NG6: Bulw 7H 75
Muriel Rd. NG9: Bee 2A 106
Muriel St. NG6: Bulw 7H 75
Murray Cl. NG5: Bestw 2G 85
Murray St. NG18: Mans 5H 47
Muschamp Ter. NG20: Mkt W 5D 34
Museum of Nottingham Life at Brewhouse Yard 7D 6 (5J 95)
Mushroom Farm Ct. NG16: Eastw 3B 72
Muskham Ct. NG19: Mans 1H 47
Muskham La. NG23: Bath 6F 129
Muskham St. NG2: Nott 7A 96
Muskham Vw. NG24: New T 7C 134
Muspitts La. DN22: Sth W 4H 17
Musters Ct. NG2: West Br 1B 108
NG15: Huck 7J 67
Musters Cres. NG2: West Br 4C 108
Musters Cft. NG4: Colw 5J 97
Musters Rd. NG2: West Br 1B 108
NG11: Rudd 4J 115
NG13: Bing 4E 100
NG13: Lang 7K 113
NG15: News 6D 60
Musters Wlk. NG6: Bulw 7G 75
MUSTON 2D 149
Muston Cl. NG3: Mapp 6C 86
Mutton La. DN10: Beck 6A 16
Muttonshire Hill DN22: Gam 1K 27
Mynd, The NG19: Mans W 4A 42
Myrtle Av. NG7: H Grn 7J 85
NG9: Stap 3D 104
Myrtle Gro. NG9: Bee 2B 106
Myrtle Rd. NG4: Carl 7F 87
Myrtle St. DN22: Retf 4D 22
Myrtus Cl. NG11: Clif 7D 106
Mytholme Cl. NG10: Long E 7B 104

N

Nabarro Ct. NG14: Calv 6C 70
Nabbs La. NG15: Huck 7D 66
Naburn Ct. NG8: Basf 6E 84
Nairn Cl. NG5: Arn 5K 77
NG22: Farns 6K 57
Nairn M. NG4: Carl 1H 97
NANPANTAN 3A 148
Nansen Gdns. NG5: Bestw 1G 85
Nansen St. NG6: Bulw 1D 84
Naomi Ct. NG6: Bulw 5J 75
Naomi Cres. NG6: Bulw 5J 75
Naples Cres. NG19: Plea 4A 40
Naranjan M. NG7: Radf 1B 6 (2H 95)
Narrow La. NG16: Want 5K 73
Naseby Av. NG24: New T 1H 137
Naseby Cl. NG5: Sher 3G 85
Nash Cl. S81: Work 1K 21
Nathans La. NG12: Rad T 2K 109
National Ice Centre, The 5H 7 (4A 96)
National Water Sports Cen. 6H 97
National Water Sports Cen. Holme Pierrepont Caravan & Camping Pk. NG2: West Br 7G 97
Natural History Mus. 5B 94
Naturescape 2C 149
Navdeep Ct. NG2: West Br 2B 108
Navenby Wlk. NG11: Clif 7F 107
Navigation Yd. NG24: New T 1B 136
Naworth Cl. NG6: Bulw 2F 85
Naylor Av. NG11: Goth 7G 115
Naylor Ho. *NG5: Arn* *1D 86*
(off Derwent Cres.)
Nazareth Ct. NG7: Lent 6F 95
Nazareth Rd. NG7: Lent 6F 95
NEAP HOUSE 1D 145
Nearsby Dr. NG2: West Br 3E 108
Neatholme Rd. DN22: Lound 3D 14
Needham Rd. NG5: Arn 6J 77
Needham St. NG13: Bing 4F 101
Needwood Av. NG9: Trow 6C 92
Neeps Cft. NG14: Epp 1A 80
Negus Ct. NG4: Lamb 7F 79
Neighbours La. NG14: Lowd 5E 80
Neighwood Cl. NG9: Toton 7D 104
Nell Gwyn Cres. NG5: Arn 5E 76
Nelson Cl. NG19: Mans 3E 46
Nelson La. NG23: Nth M 6J 129
Nelson Rd. NG5: Arn 7G 77
NG6: Bulw 7J 75
NG9: Bee 5B 106
NG24: New B 5E 136
Nelson St. DN22: Retf 4G 23
NG1: Nott 5H 7 (4A 96)
Nene Cl. NG15: Huck 3E 74
Nene Wlk. S81: Work 5F 19
Nesbitt St. NG17: Sut A 2K 51
Nest Av. NG17: Kirk A 7C 52
Nest Cres. NG17: Kirk A 7C 52
Neston Dr. NG6: Cin 3C 84
NETHER BROUGHTON 3K 143 (3B 148)
Nether Cl. NG3: Nott 2D 96
NG16: Eastw 2D 72
Nethercross Dr. NG20: Mkt W 3E 34
NETHERFIELD 2J 97 (1B 148)
Netherfield Cl. NG20: Mede V 1F 35
Netherfield Grange NG17: Sut A 2H 51
Netherfield La. NG20: Chu W, Mede V 1E 34
Netherfield Rd. NG10: Sand 4A 104
Netherfield Station (Rail) 2J 97
Nethergate NG11: Clif 7D 106
NETHER GREEN 2D 72
Nether Grn. NG16: Eastw 3D 72
NETHER LANGWITH 5B 26 (1A 146)
Nether Pasture NG4: Neth 2K 97
Nether St. NG9: Bee 3B 106
Netherton Pl. S80: Work 4H 21
Netherton Rd. S80: Work 4H 21
Nettlecliff Wlk. NG5: Top V 6A 76
Nevile Dr. NG12: Kin 2C 142
Neville Rd. NG14: Calv 7D 70
Neville Sadler Ct. NG9: Bee 2B 106
New Alexandra Court, The NG3: Nott 7A 86
Newall Dr. DN10: Matt T 1G 15
NG9: Chil 7H 105
Newark Air Mus. 3K 135
Newark Av. NG2: Nott 6K 7 (4B 96)
Newark Bus. Pk. NG24: New T 7E 134
Newark Castle 7C 134
Newark Castle Station (Rail) 7C 134
Newark Cl. NG18: Mans 1B 54
Newark Ct. NG5: Bestw 2G 85
Newark Cres. NG2: Nott 6K 7 (4B 96)
Newark Dr. NG18: Mans 1B 54
Newark Golf Centre (Driving Range) 3H 135
Newark Hall NG8: Woll 4E 94
Newark Ho. NG22: Bils 5C 126
Newark Northgate Station (Rail) 6E 134
NEWARK-ON-TRENT 1C 136 (3C 147)
Newark Rd. NG17: Sut A 2C 52
NG22: Eakr 2D 126
NG22: Kirk 1C 132
NG22: New O, Well 6D 38
NG22: Oll 5A 38
NG22: Tuxf 7C 28
NG23: Aver 3F 133
NG23: Caun 7J 127
NG23: Coll 4G 129
NG24: Barn W 6K 137
NG24: Codd 7J 135
NG24: Haw 6A 136
NG25: Sout 5J 131
Newark Showground 3J 135
Newark St. NG2: Nott 6J 7 (4B 96)
Newark Way NG18: Mans 1C 54
New Art Exchange 1G 95
NEW BAGTHORPE 1F 65
NEW BALDERTON 4F 137 (3D 147)
NEW BASFORD 6G 85
New Basford Bus. Area *NG7: Basf* *6G 85*
(off Palm St.)
Newberry Cl. NG12: Crop Bi 5B 112
Newbery Cl. NG21: Edwin 6E 36
Newbold Way NG12: Kin 2B 142
Newboundmill La. NG19: Plea 6A 40
NEW BRINSLEY 4B 64 (3A 146)
New Brook Ho. NG7: Radf 2G 95
New Bldgs. Dr. NG20: Mans W 2E 42
Newbury Cl. NG3: Mapp 3D 86
Newbury Ct. NG5: Sher 7J 85
Newbury Dr. NG16: Nuth 4J 83
Newbury M. S80: Work 3G 21
Newbury Rd. NG24: New T 7H 135
Newcastle Av. NG4: Ged 6H 87
NG9: Bee 3A 106
NG24: New T 3D 136
S80: Work 3E 20
Newcastle Chambers NG1: Nott 5E 6 (4K 95)
Newcastle Cir. NG7: Nott 6A 6 (4H 95)
Newcastle Ct. NG7: Nott 6A 6 (4H 95)
NG22: Tuxf 7C 28
Newcastle Dr. NG7: Nott 5A 6 (4H 95)
Newcastle Farm Dr. NG8: Aspl 6D 84
Newcastle St. NG6: Bulw 6J 75
NG17: Huth 7D 44
NG18: Mans 3G 47
NG19: Mans W 6H 41
NG20: Mkt W 4D 34
NG22: Tuxf 7B 28
S80: Work 3G 21
Newcastle Ter. NG7: Nott 4B 6 (3H 95)
NG8: Aspl 6E 84
New Cl. NG17: Kirk A 6A 52
NG21: Blid 6J 55
Newcombe Dr. NG5: Arn 7A 78
New Cotts. NG20: Cuck 4B 32
NG20: Nort 2E 32
New Ct. NG1: Nott 5G 7
New Ct. Gdns. DN22: Retf 5G 23
NEW CROSS 7K 45
New Cross St. NG17: Sut A 6K 45
New Derby Rd. NG16: Eastw 3B 72
Newdigate Rd. NG16: Want 7A 74
Newdigate St. NG7: Radf 3A 6 (3H 95)
NG16: Kimb 1E 82
Newdigate Vs. NG7: Radf 3A 6 (3H 95)
NEW EASTWOOD 5D 72
New Eaton Rd. NG9: Stap 3C 104
NEW EDLINGTON 2A 144
Newells Ter. DN10: Mist 4K 11
New England Way NG19: Plea 6C 40
Newfall St. NG17: Huth 7D 44
New Farm La. NG16: Nuth 1H 83
Newfield La. NG23: Sibt 7E 140
Newfield Rd. NG5: Sher 4G 85
Newgate Cl. NG4: Carl 1H 97
Newgate Ct. NG7: Lent 4G 95
Newgate La. NG18: Mans 4J 47
Newgate St. NG13: Bing 3F 101
S80: Work 3G 21
New Hall, The NG18: Mans 7K 47
Newhall Gro. NG2: West Br 7C 96
Newhall La. NG22: Edin 4A 130
Newhaven Av. NG19: Mans W 6H 41
New Hill NG22: Farns 5K 57
NG22: Wale 5G 27
New Holles Ct. S80: Work 3G 21
Newholm Dr. NG11: Wilf 4H 107
NEW HOUGHTON 2A 40 (2A 146)
New Hucknall Waye NG17: Huth 2E 50
Newings La. DN22: Habb 7E 24
NEWINGTON 2B 144
New Inn Wlk. DN22: Retf 6F 23
Newland Cl. NG8: Aspl 3D 94
NG9: Toton 7F 105
NEWLANDS 7F 43
Newlands DN22: Ord 6D 22
Newlands Av. NG22: Bou 3E 38
Newlands Cl. NG12: Edwal 5F 109
Newlands Dr. NG4: Ged 6J 87
NG19: Mans W 7F 43
Newlands Rd. NG19: Mans W 2C 48
(not continuous)
New La. DE55: Hilc 1A 50
NG13: Aslo, Scar 5A 102
NG13: Car C 3H 91
NG17: Stant H 4H 45
NG21: Blid 5F 55
NEW LENTON 5G 95 (2A 148)
New Line Rd. NG17: Kirk A 7J 51
Newlyn Dr. DE55: Sth N 5A 50
NG8: Aspl 7E 84
Newlyn Gdns. NG8: Aspl 7E 84
Newmanleys Rd. NG16: Eastw 6C 72
Newmanleys Rd. Sth. NG16: Eastw 5C 72
Newman Rd. NG14: Calv 5C 70
Newmarket Rd. NG6: Bulw 1C 84
Newmarket St. NG18: Mans 4A 48
Newmarket Way NG9: Toton 7E 104
New Mill La. NG19: Mans W 6K 41
Newnham Rd. NG24: New T 7D 134
NEW NUTHALL 1H 83
NEW OLLERTON 4C 38 (2B 146)
New Pl. DN22: Retf 3G 23
Newport Cres. NG19: Mans 1D 46
Newport Dr. NG8: Basf 6E 84
Newquay Av. NG7: Radf 1F 95
New Ri. NG11: Clif 2D 114
New Rd. DN22: Tres 4G 25
NG7: Radf 2E 94
NG9: Stap 7C 92
NG11: Bart F 7A 114
NG12: Cols B 6G 141
NG12: Rad T 5E 98
NG16: Newth, Want 2H 73
NG21: Blid 6J 55
NG22: Bils 5B 126
NG25: Mort 5F 139
NG25: Oxt 2F 71
NEW ROSSINGTON 2B 144
New Row LE12: Will W 6G 143
NG4: Carl 1G 97
NG13: Aslo 3D 102
NG14: Woodbo 2G 79
New Scott St. NG20: Whal T 5B 26
NEW STAPLEFORD 7D 92
NEWSTEAD 6D 60 (3A 146)
Newstead Abbey & Priory (remains of) 4J 61
Newstead Abbey Pk. 4J 61
Newstead Av. NG3: Mapp 5E 86
NG12: Rad T 4F 99
NG24: New T 7D 134
Newstead Cl. NG16: Sels 5F 59
NG17: Kirk A 6C 52
Newstead Ct. NG5: Woodt 2D 86

Newstead Dr. NG2: West Br	.2E **108**
Newstead Gro. NG1: Nott	.1D **6** (2J **95**)
NG13: Bing	.4D **100**
Newstead Ind. Est. NG5: Arn	.7J **77**
Newstead Rd. NG10: Long E	.6B **104**
NG15: Ann	.5D **60**
Newstead Station (Rail)	.6E **60**
Newstead St. NG5: Sher	.4K **85**
NG19: Mans	.3D **46**
Newstead Ter. NG15: Huck	.5G **67**
Newstead Way NG8: Stre	.5J **83**
New St. DE55: Hilc	.3A **50**
DN22: Retf	.4F **23**
NG5: Redh	.5G **77**
NG5: Sher	.6J **85**
NG17: Huth	.7D **44**
NG17: Kirk A	.7B **52**
NG17: Sut A	.1J **51**
NG24: New T	.1D **136**
New Ter. NG10: Sand	.3A **104**
NG19: Plea	.4A **40**
NEWTHORPE	.5G **73** (1A **148**)
NEWTHORPE COMMON	.6F **73**
Newthorpe Comn. NG16: Newth	.5E **72**
Newthorpe St. NG2: Nott	.6A **96**
NEWTON	
Nottingham	.7C **90** (1B **148**)
Sutton in Ashfield	.3A **146**
Newton Av. NG12: Rad T	.4F **99**
NG13: Bing	.4E **100**
(not continuous)	
Newton Cl. NG5: Arn	.1E **86**
NG14: Lowd	.5E **80**
S81: Gate	.5D **18**
Newtondale Av. NG19: Mans W	.1A **48**
Newtondale Cl. NG8: Aspl	.6E **84**
Newton Dr. NG2: West Br	.5K **107**
NG9: Stap	.3D **104**
Newton Gdns. NG13: Newton	.2D **100**
(not continuous)	
NEWTON ON TRENT	.1D **147**
Newton Rd. LN1: Kett	.1G **31**
NG4: Ged	.4G **87**
Newton's La. NG16: Coss	.4A **82**
(not continuous)	
Newton St. DN22: Retf	.6F **23**
NG7: Lent	.1F **107**
NG9: Bee	.3K **105**
NG18: Mans	.4J **47**
NG24: New T	.2E **136**
NEWTON TOWN	.2F **47**
Newtonwood La. DE55: Newton	.6A **44**
NEWTOWN	.5G **23**
New Vale Rd. NG4: Colw	.3G **97**
NEW VILLAGE	.1A **144**
New Villas NG20: Wars	.4A **34**
NEW WESTWOOD	.1B **64**
New Westwood NG16: Westw	.1B **64**
New Windmill Ct. NG2: Nott	.4C **96**
New Works Cotts. NG14: Stoke B	.7B **88**
ng2 Bus. Pk. NG2: Nott	.6H **95**
Nicholas Pl. NG22: Tuxf	.6D **28**
Nicholas Rd. NG9: Bram	.7J **93**
Nicholson Ct. NG24: New T	.2D **136**
Nicholson St. NG24: New T	.2D **136**
Nicholson's Wharf NG24: New T	.7C **134**
Nicker Hill NG12: Key	.6J **117**
Nicklaus Ct. *NG5: Top V*	.6C **76**
(off Crossfield Dr.)	
Nidderdale NG8: Woll	.4H **93**
Nidderdale Cl. NG8: Woll	.5H **93**
Nightingale Av. NG19: Plea	.5A **40**
Nightingale Cl. NG7: Nott	.7B **94**
NG16: Nuth	.1J **83**
NG24: Bald	.5H **137**
Nightingale Cres. NG16: Sels	.6F **59**
Nightingale Dr. NG19: Mans	.1E **46**
Nightingale Gro. S81: Gate	.5E **18**
Nightingale Ho. NG3: Mapp	.5C **86**
Nightingale Way DN22: Woodbe	.7G **25**
NG13: Bing	.5H **101**
Nile St. NG1: Nott	.4H **7** (3A **96**)
Nilsson Ri. NG9: Chil	.6G **105**
Nimbus Way NG16: Want	.7K **73**
Nine Acre Gdns. NG6: Bulw	.7F **75**
Nine Corners NG16: Kimb	.1E **82**
Ninth Av. NG19: Mans W	.2C **48**
Nixon Ri. NG15: Huck	.1D **74**
Nixon Wlk. LE12: East L	.2A **122**
Nixon Way NG23: Coll	.1H **129**
Nobel Rd. NG11: Clif	.2D **114**
Noble Ho. NG24: New T	.5C **136**
Noble La. NG13: Aslo	.3D **102**
Noel St. NG7: Basf, H Grn	.1A **6** (7G **85**)
(not continuous)	
NG16: Kimb	.1F **83**
NG18: Mans	.3G **47**
Noel Street Stop (NET)	.1G **95**
Nook, The LE12: East L	.3A **122**
NG8: Woll	.4K **93**
NG9: Bee	.2B **106**
NG9: Chil	.5K **105**
NG14: Calv	.6D **70**
NG16: Kimb	.2F **83**
Nookin NG14: East M	.3E **28**
Norbett Cl. NG9: Chil	.6H **105**

Norbett Ct. NG5: Arn	.5J **77**
Norbett Rd. NG5: Arn	.6J **77**
Norbreck Cl. NG8: Cin	.4C **84**
Norburn Cres. NG6: Basf	.4G **85**
Norbury Dr. NG18: Mans	.6A **48**
Norbury Way NG10: Sand	.3A **104**
Nordean Rd. NG5: Woodt	.2D **86**
Norfolk Av. DN11: Birc	.2G **9**
NG9: Toton	.7F **105**
Norfolk Cl. NG15: Huck	.1D **74**
NG20: Mkt W	.4C **34**
Norfolk Ct. NG19: Mans W	.4A **42**
Norfolk Dr. DN11: Birc	.2F **9**
NG19: Mans	.2H **47**
Norfolk Gdns. NG17: Huth	.1E **50**
Norfolk Gro. DN11: Birc	.2F **9**
Norfolk Pk. NG5: Arn	.2E **86**
Norfolk Pl. NG1: Nott	.4E **6** (3K **95**)
Norfolk Rd. DN11: Birc	.2F **9**
Norfolk St. S80: Work	.3F **21**
Norfolk Wlk. NG10: Sand	.4A **104**
Norland Cl. NG3: Nott	.1B **96**
(not continuous)	
Norman Av. NG17: Sut A	.2A **52**
NG24: New T	.4E **134**
Normanby Rd. NG8: Woll	.5H **93**
Norman Cl. NG3: Nott	.1F **7** (2K **95**)
NG9: Chil	.4H **105**
Norman Dr. NG15: Huck	.2E **74**
NG16: Eastw	.4F **73**
Norman Rd. NG3: Nott	.7D **86**
Norman St. NG4: Neth	.2K **97**
NG16: Kimb	.7K **73**
NORMANTON	
Grantham	.1D **149**
Newark-on-Trent	.1D **149**
Southwell	.4J **131** (3C **147**)
Normanton Brook Rd. DE55: Sth N	.4B **50**
Normanton Cl. NG21: Edwin	.5D **36**
Normanton Dr. NG18: Mans	.4A **48**
Normanton La. NG12: Key	.7J **117**
NORMANTON ON SOAR	.7G **121** (3A **148**)
NORMANTON-ON-THE-WOLDS	.4K **117** (2B **148**)
NORMANTON ON TRENT	.1K **125** (2C **147**)
Normanton Rd. NG23: Weston	.1F **125**
NG24: New T	.7G **135**
NG25: Sout	.5J **131**
NORNAY	.5G **13**
Nornay Cl. S81: Blyth	.5G **13**
Norris Homes NG7: H Grn	.7J **85**
Northall Av. NG6: Bulw	.1C **84**
Northampton St. NG3: Nott	.1K **7** (2B **96**)
NORTH ANSTON	.3A **144**
North Av. NG10: Sand	.3A **104**
NG21: Rain	.2J **55**
NORTH CARLTON	
Lincoln	.1D **147**
Worksop	.6D **12**
Nth. Carr Rd. DN10: West S	.1K **11**
Nth. Church St. NG1: Nott	.3E **6** (3K **95**)
Nth. Circus St. NG1: Nott	.4C **6** (4J **95**)
Northcliffe Av. NG3: Mapp	.5D **86**
NORTH CLIFTON	.3D **30** (1D **147**)
Northcote Way NG6: Bulw	.2D **84**
Northcroft La. NG23: Coll	.1F **129**
Northdale Rd. NG3: Nott	.1E **96**
Northdown Dr. NG9: Chil	.5H **105**
Northdown Rd. NG8: Aspl	.2E **94**
North Dr. NG9: Chil	.3K **105**
NG22: Bils	.4C **126**
NG24: Bald	.7H **137**
NORTH ELMSALL	.1A **144**
North End NG24: Farnd	.6G **133**
Northern Bri. Rd. NG17: Sut A	.7K **45**
Northern Ct. NG6: Basf	.3E **84**
Northern Dr. NG6: Bestw V	.2B **76**
NG9: Trow	.5C **92**
Northern Rd. NG24: New T	.6E **134**
Northern Vw. NG17: Sut A	.7K **45**
North Farm NG22: Egma	.1E **124**
Northfield Av. NG12: Rad T	.4H **99**
NG19: Plea	.5F **41**
(not continuous)	
Northfield Cres. NG9: Chil	.5E **104**
Northfield Dr. NG18: Mans	.4A **48**
Northfield Farmstead DN10: Eve	.6B **10**
Northfield La. DN22: Tres	.4F **25**
NG19: Mans W, Plea	.5E **40**
Northfield Leys Rd. DN22: Nth W	.1F **17**
Northfield Rd. DN22: Habb	.6E **24**
DN22: Ramp	.6J **25**
NG9: Chil	.5F **105**
Northfields Cl. NG17: Sut A	.7J **45**
Northfields Way LE12: East L	.1A **122**
Northfield Way DN22: Retf	.2D **22**
North Gate NG7: Basf	.6G **85**
NG24: New T	.7C **134**
(not continuous)	
North Ga. Pl. *NG7: Basf*	.6G **85**
(off High Chu. St.)	
Northgate Retail Pk. NG24: New T	.6D **134**
North Grn. NG14: Calv	.4A **70**
North Hill Av. NG15: Huck	.6F **67**

North Hill Cres. NG15: Huck	.6F **67**
NORTH HYKEHAM	.2D **147**
NORTH LEVERTON	.6B **24** (3C **145**)
North Leverton Windmill	.6A **24**
Nth. Moor Dr. DN10: Walk	.6H **11**
Nth. Moor Rd. DN10: Walk	.6G **11**
NORTH MUSKHAM	.6K **129** (3C **147**)
North Nottinghamshire Community Arena	.1H **21**
Northolme Av. NG6: Bulw	.7J **75**
Northolt Dr. NG16: Nuth	.4J **83**
NORTHORPE	.2D **145**
North Pk. NG18: Mans	.7A **48**
(not continuous)	
North Rd. DN22: Retf	.1B **22**
(not continuous)	
NG2: West Br	.3B **108**
NG5: Sher	.3H **85**
(not continuous)	
NG7: Nott	.6E **94**
(West Rd.)	
NG7: Nott	.5A **6** (4H **95**)
(Western Ter.)	
NG11: Rudd	.2J **115**
Northrowe NG17: Ann W	.4J **59**
NORTH SCARLE	.2D **147**
Nth. Scarle Rd. NG23: Wigs	.7F **31**
Nth. Sherwood St. NG1: Nott	.1D **6** (1J **95**)
Northside La. DN22: Habb	.6D **24**
Northside Way NG5: Arn	.4H **77**
North St. DN22: Stu S	.1C **24**
NG2: Nott	.5J **7** (4B **96**)
NG9: Bee	.3K **105**
NG16: Kimb	.2F **83**
NG16: Lang M	.3A **72**
NG16: Newth	.4G **73**
NG16: Pinx	.1B **58**
NG17: Huth	.6E **44**
NG17: Kirk A	.2B **60**
NG17: Sut A	.7K **45**
NG20: Whal T	.5B **26**
Northumberland Av. S81: Costh	.5B **12**
Northumberland St. NG3: Nott	.2G **7** (2A **96**)
Northumbria Cl. S81: Work	.6H **19**
Northumbria Dr. DN22: Retf	.5D **22**
Northville Ct. NG3: Nott	.1A **96**
North Wlk. DN22: Retf	.2C **22**
Northway S81: Carl L	.5C **12**
NORTH WHEATLEY	.1H **17** (3C **145**)
NORTH WITHAM	.3D **149**
Northwold Av. NG2: West Br	.3A **108**
Northwood S81: Work	.6H **19**
Northwood Av. NG17: Sut A	.6H **45**
Northwood Cres. NG5: Bestw	.1K **85**
Northwood Rd. NG5: Bestw	.1K **85**
Northwood St. NG9: Stap	.1C **104**
NORTON	.2E **32** (1A **146**)
Norton Ct. NG7: Radf	.2F **95**
NORTON DISNEY	.3D **147**
Norton La. NG20: Cuck	.4D **32**
Norton St. NG7: Radf	.2F **95**
(not continuous)	
NORWELL	.2J **127** (2C **147**)
Norwell Ct. NG19: Mans	.1H **47**
Norwell La. NG23: Crom, Norw	.2K **127**
Norwell Rd. NG23: Caun	.6J **127**
NORWELL WOODHOUSE	.2C **147**
Norwich Cl. NG19: Mans W	.4K **41**
Norwich Gdns. NG6: Bulw	.5H **75**
NORWOOD	.3A **144**
Norwood Cl. NG17: Sut A	.7F **45**
Norwood Gdns. NG25: Sout	.4G **131**
Norwood Pk. Golf Course	.4E **130**
Norwood Rd. NG7: Radf	.3F **95**
Noskwith St. DE7: Ilk	.3A **92**
Nostell M. *S80: Work*	.3G **21**
(off Newgate St.)	
Notintone Pl. NG2: Nott	.5K **7** (4B **96**)
Notintone St. NG2: Nott	.6K **7** (4B **96**)
NOTTINGHAM	.5F **7** (1A **148**)
NOTTINGHAM AIRPORT	.4J **109**
Nottingham Arts Theatre	.5G **7** (4A **96**)
Nottingham Bus. Pk. NG2: Nott	.7K **7** (5B **96**)
NG8: Stre	.5H **83**
Nottingham Castle	.7D **6** (4J **95**)
Nottingham Castle Caves	.7D **6**
Nottingham City Golf Course	.4G **75**
Nottingham Climbing Cen.	.7G **85**
Nottingham Contemporary	.6F **7** (4A **96**)
Nottingham Forest FC	.7B **96**
Nottingham Forest Football Academy	.2A **108**
Nottingham Greyhound Stadium	.4E **96**
Nottingham Indoor Bowls Cen.	.1B **94**
Nottingham Industrial Mus.	.5A **94**
Nottingham Intl. Clothing Cen. NG15: Huck	.3E **66**
Nottingham La. LE14: Upp B	.6K **143**
Nottingham Playhouse	.5D **6** (4J **95**)
Nottingham Racecourse	.5F **97**
Nottingham Raceway Karting	.6K **143**
Nottingham RFC	.6B **96**
Nottingham Rd. DE7: Ilk	.2A **92**
LE12: Costo	.3F **123**
NG5: Arn	.1B **86**
NG6: Basf	.4F **85**
(not continuous)	
NG7: Basf	.5G **85**
NG8: Cin	.3A **84**

Nottingham Rd. NG9: Chil, Toton 7G **105**
NG9: Stap 2C **104**
NG9: Trow 4B **92**
NG11: Goth .7G **115**
NG12: Crop Bi 5J **111**
NG12: Key 1H **119**
NG12: Rad T .6C **98**
NG13: Bing .4C **100**
NG14: Bur J 4C **88**
NG14: Lowd 6D **80**
NG14: Thur 1H **81**
NG14: Woodbo 4B **78**
NG15: Huck 1J **75**
NG15: Rave 1A **62**
NG16: Cin, Nuth 2J **83**
NG16: Eastw .4D **72**
NG16: Gilt, Newth 5F **73**
NG16: Kimb 1F **83**
NG16: Sels, Unde 6C **58**
NG17: Kirk A .2B **60**
NG18: Mans 5H **47**
NG25: Oxt 3F **71**
NG25: Sout .7G **131**
Nottingham Rd. E.
NG16: Eastw, Gilt, Newth 5F **73**
Nottingham Sailing Club 6G **97**
Nottingham Science & Technology Pk.
NG7: Nott 7E **94**
Nottinghamshire County Cricket Ground 7B **96**
Nottinghamshire Golf Course, The 2B **110**
Nottingham South & Wilford Ind. Est.
NG11: Wilf 5J **107**
Nottingham Station (Rail) 7G **7** (5A **96**)
Nottingham Tennis Cen. 1E **106**
Nottingham Transport Heritage Cen. 5K **115**
Nottingham Trent University
City Campus 3D **6** (3J **95**)
Clifton Campus 6E **106**
Union Rd. 3K **95**
Waverley St. 2C **6** (2J **95**)
York St. 3F **7** (3K **95**)
Nottingham Trent University Stop (NET) . . .3D **6** (3J **95**)
Nottingham Wildcats Arena 3E **96**
Notts County FC 6B **96**
Notts (Hollinwell) Golf Course 3E **60**
Nuart Rd. NG9: Bee 3A **106**
Nuffield Health Club
Nottingham 3E **96**
Nugent Gdns. NG3: Nott 1J **7** (2B **96**)
Nuncar Ct. NG17: Nunc 3A **60**
NUNCARGATE 3A **60** (3A **146**)
Nuncargate Rd. NG17: Nunc 3K **59**
Nunn Brook Ri. NG17: Huth 2C **50**
Nunn Brook Rd. NG17: Huth 1C **50**
Nunn Cl. NG17: Huth 2C **50**
Nurseries, The NG16: Eastw 4E **72**
Nurseries Caravan Site
NG21: Rain 1H **55**
Nursery Av. NG9: Chil 4H **105**
NG17: Sut A 1G **51**
NG24: Farnd 6H **133**
Nursery Cl. NG12: Rad T 5G **99**
NG15: Huck 2G **75**
NG23: Coll 3H **129**
Nursery Ct. NG18: Mans 2J **47**
NG24: New T 7D **134**
Nursery Covent NG18: Mans 2J **47**
Nursery Dr. NG4: Carl 7G **87**
Nursery End NG25: Sout 5G **131**
Nursery Gdns. DE55: Sth N 7A **50**
DN10: Beck 7D **16**
NG14: Lowd 4D **80**
NG21: Rain 1F **55**
NG24: Bald 6G **137**
S80: Work 3D **20**
Nursery La. NG6: Basf 3F **85**
NG23: Sut T 3D **128**
Nursery Rd. NG5: Arn 7H **77**
NG12: Rad T 5G **99**
NG13: Bing 4J **101**
Nursery St. NG18: Mans 2J **47**
Nutcroft Way DN10: Harwe 5A **10**
NUTHALL 2J **83** (1A **148**)
Nuthall Gdns. NG8: Aspl 7E **84**
Nuthall Rd. NG8: Aspl, Cin 4C **84**
Nuthatch Cres. S81: Gate 3E **18**
NUTWELL .1B **144**

O

Oak Acres NG9: Chil 4F **105**
Oakash Ct. NG16: Nuth 1G **83**
Oak Av. NG10: Sand 2A **104**
NG12: Rad T 4D **98**
NG13: Bing 4H **101**
NG16: Lang M 1A **72**
NG18: Mans 2J **47**
NG21: Blid .7K **55**
NG21: Rain 2A **56**
NG22: New O 4D **38**
NG24: Farnd 6H **133**
Oak Bank Cl. NG18: Mans 2H **47**
Oak Bank Mnr. NG19: Mans 2H **47**
Oak Cl. NG16: Pinx 1A **58**
S80: Work .4F **21**

Oak Cres. LE12: East L 3K **121**
Oakdale Dr. NG9: Chil 5H **105**
Oakdale Rd. DN22: Retf 2E **22**
NG3: Nott .2E **96**
NG4: Carl .2G **97**
NG5: Arn 6K **77**
NG18: Mans 3F **47**
Oak Dr. NG16: Eastw 4C **72**
NG16: Nuth 1G **83**
NG19: Mans W 7K **41**
NG24: New B 4F **137**
Oakenhall Av. NG15: Huck 6J **67**
Oakfield Cl. NG12: Rad T 4F **99**
Oakfield Av. NG17: Kirk A 3H **51**
NG20: Mkt W 5D **34**
Oakfield Cl. NG8: Woll 5H **93**
NG18: Mans 1B **54**
Oakfield Ct. NG12: Rad T 5G **99**
Oakfield Dr. NG10: Sand 6A **104**
Oakfield La. NG20: Mkt W 7C **34**
Oakfield Rd. NG8: Woll 5H **93**
NG9: Stap 2C **104**
NG15: Huck 7H **67**
NG24: Bald 7J **137**
Oakfield Row NG20: Mkt W 5D **34**
Oakfields Rd. NG2: West Br 7D **96**
Oak Flatt NG9: Chil 3F **105**
Oakford Cl. NG8: Brox 5B **84**
Oak Gro. NG15: Huck 2H **75**
Oakham Bus. Pk.
NG18: Mans 7F **47**
Oakham Cl. NG5: Top V 7B **76**
NG18: Mans 6H **47**
Oakham Dr. NG16: Sels 5E **58**
S81: Carl N 6C **12**
Oakham Rd. NG11: Rudd 7A **108**
Oakholme Av. S81: Work 7G **19**
Oakholme Ri. S81: Work 7G **19**
Oakington Cl. NG5: Bestw 2J **85**
Oakland Av. NG17: Huth 1D **50**
Oakland Ct. NG9: Bram 7F **93**
Oakland Cft. NG17: Huth 7D **44**
Oakland Gro. NG14: Calv 6D **70**
Oakland Rd. NG19: Mans W 2A **48**
Oaklands DN10: Beck 6C **16**
NG23: Coll 2H **129**
Oaklands Cl. NG23: Coll 3H **129**
Oaklands Dr. DN11: Sty 4A **8**
Oaklands La. DN22: Retf 5G **23**
Oaklands Track 5G **23**
Oakland St. NG7: H Grn 1F **95**
Oakland Way NG8: Bilb 7J **83**
Oakleaf Cl. NG18: Mans 7E **48**
Oakleaf Cres. NG17: Sut A 2G **51**
Oakleigh Av. NG3: Mapp 5F **87**
NG19: Mans W 5A **42**
Oakleigh St. NG6: Bulw 3E **84**
Oakley M. NG6: Bulw 1A **84**
Oak Lodge NG13: Bing 4H **101**
Oak Lodge Dr. NG16: Kimb 7K **73**
Oakmead Av. NG8: Bilb 7A **84**
Oakmeadows DE55: Sth N 7A **50**
Oakmere Cl. NG12: Edwal 5F **109**
Oakridge Cl.
NG19: Mans W 1B **48**
Oak Ri. NG22: Bils 4B **126**
Oaks, The NG3: Nott 3J **7** (3A **96**)
NG18: Mans 7J **47**
NG24: Bald 5H **137**
NG24: New B 5F **137**
Oaks Cl. DN22: Rans 1J **13**
Oak St. NG5: Sher 6J **85**
NG17: Kirk A 6B **52**
NG17: Skeg 3H **45**
Oak Tree Av. NG12: Rad T 4E **98**
NG21: Edwin 6E **36**
Oak Tree Bus. Pk. NG18: Mans 6D **48**
Oak Tree Cl. NG2: West Br 1D **108**
NG14: Blea 2B **138**
NG15: Huck 2D **74**
NG18: Mans 3D **48**
Oaktree Cl. NG17: Sut A 2B **52**
Oak Tree Cres.
NG19: Mans W 5H **41**
Oak Tree Dr. NG4: Ged 5K **87**
Oaktree Dr. NG22: Bils 7C **126**
Oak Tree La. NG18: Mans 3C **48**
Oak Tree Lane Leisure Cen. 5D **48**
Oak Tree Ri. S81: Carl L 5B **12**
Oak Tree Rd. DE55: Hilc 2A **50**
NG17: Sut A 6A **46**
Oak Vw. NG7: Radf 2G **95**
NG24: New T 1F **137**
Oak Vw. Ri. NG18: Mans 4K **53**
Oakwood Ct. NG15: Ann 6A **60**
Oakwood Dr. NG8: Aspl 1D **94**
NG15: Rave 3C **62**
Oakwood Gdns. NG16: Nuth 4J **83**
Oakwood Gro. NG21: Edwin 7H **37**
Oakwood M. S80: Work 2D **20**
Oakwood Rd. NG18: Mans 6D **48**
Oasis Health Club, The
Mansfield .5H **47**
Oatfield La. NG12: Rad T 1J **99**
Oban Rd. NG9: Chil 3H **105**
Observatory Way NG17: Kirk A 3B **52**

Occupation La. LE12: Will W, Wym 7G **143**
NG13: East B 2F **91**
NG17: Kirk A 5K **51**
NG21: Edwin 7F **37**
NG25: Fis .4H **139**
Occupation Rd. NG6: Bulw 2C **84**
NG13: Elton 4K **103**
NG15: Huck 1G **75**
NG19: New H 2A **40**
Ocean Dr. NG20: Mkt W 3C **34**
Oceans of Fun 6G **67**
Ockbrook Dr. NG3: Mapp 5C **86**
Ockerby St. NG6: Bulw 1D **84**
Oddicroft La. NG17: Sut A 2A **52**
Odeon Cinema
Mansfield .5H **47**
Newark 1C **136**
Odesa Dr. NG6: Bulw 3C **84**
Odin Cl. NG4: Carl 7J **87**
Off the Avenue NG17: Sut A 2H **51**
Ogdon Ct. NG3: Nott 2C **96**
Ogle Dr. NG7: Nott 7C **6** (5J **95**)
Ogle St. NG15: Huck 6G **67**
Okehampton Cres. NG3: Mapp 1F **87**
Oldacres NG14: Woodbo 2H **79**
Old Bakery Way NG18: Mans 1J **47**
Old Bakery Yd. S80: Work 3F **21**
Old Bank Cl. NG6: Basf 5E **84**
Old Bar Cl. NG6: Basf 5D **84**
Old Barn Cl. NG21: K Cli 3K **43**
OLD BASFORD 3F **85** (1A **148**)
Old Bell La. NG23: Carl T 7D **128**
Old Bowling Grn. S80: Rhod 1C **20**
Old Brickyard NG3: Nott 1D **96**
Old Bull Farm Cl. LE12: Sut B 2A **120**
Oldbury Cl. NG11: Clif 3E **114**
Old Chapel Cl. NG17: Kirk A 6J **51**
Old Chapel La. NG16: Unde 3E **64**
NG23: Elston 1E **140**
Old Church St. NG7: Lent 6F **95**
Old Coach Rd. NG8: Bilb, Woll 2K **93**
S80: Work .6K **21**
Old Cobham Orchard
NG24: New B 4E **136**
OLDCOTES 6A **8** (3A **144**)
Old Dairy, The NG14: Lowd 4D **80**
OLD DALBY .3B **148**
Old Derby Rd. NG16: Eastw 3B **72**
Old Dr. NG9: Bee 1J **105**
OLD EDLINGTON 2A **144**
Old Engine Yard, The LE12: Remp 7G **123**
Old England Gdns. NG23: Sut T 3D **128**
Old Epperstone Rd.
NG14: Lowd 2A **80**
Oldershaw Rd. LE12: East L 4B **122**
Old Fall St. NG17: Huth 7D **44**
Old Farm Ct. NG11: Bart F 7A **114**
Old Farm Rd. NG5: Top V 6B **76**
Old Forge Cl. DN10: Mist 2H **11**
Old Forge La. NG13: Gran 1K **141**
Old Forge Rd. DN10: Mist 2G **11**
Old Gainsborough Rd.
DN10: Drake, Eve 7C **10**
Old Gateford Rd. S81: Gate 4D **18**
Old Grantham Rd. NG13: What 4D **102**
Old Great Nth. Rd. NG23: Nth M 5J **129**
NG23: Sut T 2B **128**
(not continuous)
Old Hall Cl. NG14: Calv 6C **70**
NG20: Mkt W 3E **34**
NG24: Farnd 7G **133**
Old Hall Dr. DN22: Retf 4C **22**
NG3: Mapp P 6A **86**
NG12: Widm 6J **119**
Old Hall Gdns. NG24: Codd 7J **135**
Old Hall La. NG22: East M 2C **28**
NG23: Norw 2K **127**
Oldham Ct. NG9: Chil 5H **105**
Old Haxey Rd. DN10: Mist 1H **11**
Old Hill La. NG13: East B 2E **90**
Old Kiln La. NG16: Eastw 5E **72**
Oldknow St. NG7: H Grn 2G **95**
OLD LENTON 5F **95** (2A **148**)
Old Lenton Cl. NG12: Crop Bi 5B **112**
Old Lenton St.
NG1: Nott 4G **7** (3A **96**)
Old Lodge Dr. NG5: Sher 3A **86**
Old London Rd. DN22: Elk 1G **27**
DN22: Gam 2H **27**
DN22: West D 3K **27**
Old Main Rd. LE12: Costo 3F **123**
NG14: Bulc 2F **89**
Old Maltings, The DN10: Mist 3H **11**
Old Manor Cl. NG14: Woodbo 2H **79**
Old Manor Dr. NG24: Codd 7K **135**
Old Manor Rd. NG19: Mans W 6H **41**
Old Market Pl. NG18: Mans 3H **47**
Old Market Square Stop (NET) 5E **6** (4K **95**)
Old Melton Rd. NG12: Plum 3H **117**
Old Mill Cl. NG6: Bestw V 3K **75**
NG7: Radf 3A **6** (3G **95**)
NG9: Toton 7F **105**
NG19: Mans W 1A **48**
Old Mill Ct. NG13: Bing 3F **101**
Old Mill Cres. NG24: New T 1E **136**

Old Mill La. NG18: Mans .7J 41
NG19: Mans W .7J 41
NG20: Cuck .4D 32
Old Mill La. Ind. Est. NG19: Mans W .1J 47
Old Mission Forge Wlk. NG16: Newth .4G 73
Old Moat Ct. NG12: Kin .1C 142
Old Moorgate NG22: East M .2E 28
Oldmoor Wood Nature Reserve .7E 82
Old Newark Rd. NG18: Mans .2K 53
(not continuous)
NG21: Rain .1D 54
Old Nurseries, The NG23: Norw .2H 127
Old Oak Rd. NG11: Clif .7H 107
Old Park, The NG12: Cotg .5E 110
Old Park Cl. NG8: Bilb .1K 93
Old Post Office St. DN10: Eve .6B 10
OLD RADFORD .2E 94
Old Rectory Cl. LE12: East L .3A 122
Old Rectory Ct. NG24: Wint .2F 135
Old Rd. NG2: West Br .6B 108
NG11: Rudd .1A 116
NG17: Skeg .3K 45
Old Rufford Rd. NG14: Calv .1K 69
NG22: Bils, Farns .1F 57 & 7A 126
NG22: Oll, Ruff .7K 37
Old School Cl. NG11: Clif .2F 115
Old School Ct. NG22: Farns .5K 57
Old School Dr. NG21: Edwin .7D 36
Old School Ho. Cl. NG12: Crop Bu .2C 112
Old School La. NG16: Aws .2B 82
NG19: Plea .4A 40
NG23: Best .7H 125
NG24: New T .2E 136
Old Silk Mill, The NG25: Mayt .2G 131
Old Sookholme La.
NG20: Mkt W .4C 34
Old Station Dr. NG11: Rudd .3J 115
Old Station Yd. NG21: Edwin .7F 37
Old Storth La. DE55: Sth N .7A 50
Old St. NG1: Nott .3F 7 (3K 95)
Old Tannery Dr. NG14: Lowd .5E 80
Old Ter. NG19: Plea .5A 40
Old Tollerton Rd. NG2: Gam .2F 109
Old Trent Rd. DN10: Beck .7E 16
Old Water La. NG19: Mans .1D 46
Olga Ct. NG3: Nott .2C 96
Olga Rd. NG3: Nott .2C 96
Olive Ct. NG17: Sut A .6K 45
Olive Gro. NG14: Bur J .2E 88
NG19: Mans W .2B 48
Oliver Cl. NG7: Radf .2B 6 (2H 95)
NG24: New T .1E 136
Oliver St. NG7: Radf .2B 6 (2H 95)
OLLERTON .5A 38 (2B 146)
Ollerton Rd. DN22: Gam .1K 27
DN22: Ord .6E 22
NG5: Arn .2G 77
(not continuous)
NG14: Calv .4H 69
NG21: Edwin, Oll .6F 37
NG22: Kirt .7J 27
NG22: Oll .4A 38
NG22: Tuxf .7A 28
NG23: Caun .4F 127
NG23: Kel .1H 133
NG23: Lit C .1A 134
S80: Work .7H 21
Ollerton Watermill .5A 38
Olton Av. NG9: Lent A .7A 94
Olympus Ct. NG15: Huck .3D 74
Omberley Av. NG17: Skeg .4B 46
Omer Ct. NG16: Want .7A 74
OMPTON .2B 146
Onchan Av. NG4: Carl .2H 97
Onchan Dr. NG4: Carl .2H 97
One Call Stadium .5G 47
Ontario Dr. NG16: Sels .5E 58
Opal Cl. NG18: Mans .6A 48
NG21: Rain .2A 56
Open University, The
Nottingham .7J 85
Orange Gdns. NG2: Nott .6A 96
Orby Cl. NG3: Nott .2K 7 (2C 96)
Orby Wlk. NG3: Nott .3K 7 (3C 96)
Orchard, The DN22: Hay .5H 17
NG17: Sut A .1B 52
NG23: Elston .2E 140
NG24: New T .3E 136
Orchard Av. NG4: Carl .1H 97
NG13: Bing .4E 100
Orchard Cl. LE12: East L .4K 121
LE12: Sut B .6C 120
NG11: Clif .7D 106
NG12: Rad T .5D 98
NG12: Toll .2G 117
NG13: Barns .3G 141
NG13: East B .4E 90
NG14: Blea .2B 138
NG14: Bur J .2E 88
NG14: Gun .2B 90
NG18: Mans .1J 53
NG23: Sth M .1B 134
NG25: Sout .4G 131
Orchard Ct. NG4: Carl .1H 97
NG4: Ged .5G 87
NG8: Basf .7F 85
Orchard Ct. NG15: Huck .7G 67
NG23: Thor .2G 31
NG25: Oxt .1G 71
Orchard Cres. NG9: Chil .4H 105
NG22: Tuxf .7C 28
Orchard Dr. DN22: Ramp .7K 25
NG14: Calv .6E 70
Orchard Gro. DN10: Mist .4J 11
NG5: Arn .1K 85
Orchard La. DN22: Sth L .1G 25
Orchard Leigh DN22: Ord .6D 22
Orchard M. NG16: Pinx .1C 58
Orchard Pk. NG3: Mapp .1F 87
NG24: Codd .6J 135
Orchard Pk. Ind. Est.
NG10: Sand .3B 104
Orchard Pl. NG8: Stre .5H 83
Orchard Ri. DN10: Beck .6C 16
DN22: Tres .5G 25
NG4: Lamb .7G 79
Orchard Rd. NG17: Kirk A .6J 51
Orchards, The NG4: Ged .6K 87
NG14: Lowd .6E 80
NG16: Jack .6A 64
NG25: Oxt .1G 71
Orchard St. NG11: Goth .7G 115
NG15: Huck .7G 67
NG16: Kimb .1E 82
NG16: Lang M .3A 72
NG16: Newth .5E 72
NG19: Mans .1H 47
Orchard Vw. NG14: Thur .5C 138
NG19: Mans W .6H 41
Orchard Wlk. NG17: Kirk A .6J 51
Orchard Way NG10: Sand .6A 104
NG17: Sut A .3G 51
NG24: Bald .6G 137
Orchid Cl. NG2: West Br .5K 107
NG17: Kirk A .4K 51
NG24: New B .4E 136
Orchid Cft. NG15: Huck .2J 75
Orchid Dr. NG17: Sut A .2A 52
NG24: Farnd .5J 133
Orchil St. NG16: Gilt .6F 73
Ordnance Ct. NG9: Chil .6H 105
Ordoyno Gro. NG24: Codd .6J 135
ORDSALL .6E 22 (1C 147)
Ordsall Cl. NG18: Mans .4A 48
Ordsall Pk. Cl. DN22: Retf .4D 22
Ordsall Pk. Dr. DN22: Retf .4D 22
Ordsall Pk. Rd. DN22: Retf .5C 22
Ordsall Rd. DN22: Ord .6D 22
DN22: Retf .4C 22
Orford Av. NG11: Clif .5G 107
NG12: Rad T .6D 98
Orient M. NG16: Want .7A 74
Orion Cl. NG8: Bilb .1K 93
Orion Dr. NG8: Bilb .1K 93
Orlando Dr. NG4: Carl .7J 87
Orlock Wlk. NG5: Bestw .2J 85
Ormonde Ter. NG5: Sher .5K 85
NG16: Lang M .2A 72
Ornsay Cl. NG5: Top V .5A 76
Orpean Way NG9: Toton .7D 104
ORSTON .1J 103 (1C 149)
Orston Av. NG5: Arn .7J 77
NG24: New T .3B 136
Orston Dr. NG8: Woll .4D 94
Orston Grn. NG8: Woll .5E 94
Orston La. NG13: What .5E 102
Orston Rd. E. NG2: West Br .7C 96
Orston Rd. W. NG2: West Br .7B 96
Orton Av. NG9: Bram .3H 105
Orton Flds. NG9: Bram .3G 105
Ortzen Ct. NG7: Radf .2A 6 (2G 95)
Ortzen St. NG7: Radf .2A 6 (2G 95)
Orville Rd. NG5: Bestw .2F 85
Osberne Way NG21: C'tone .7H 43
Osberton Rd. DN22: Retf .4F 23
Osberton Vw. S81: Work .7K 19
Osborne Av. NG5: Sher .4K 85
Osborne Cl. NG10: Sand .5A 104
Osborne Gro. NG5: Sher .4K 85
Osborne St. NG7: Radf .2F 95
Osbourne Cl. NG16: Want .7B 74
Osbourne St. NG17: Ann W .4K 59
Osbourne Yd. NG20: Mkt W .4D 34
Osgood Rd. NG5: Arn .2F 87
Osier Dr. NG15: Ann .5A 60
Osier Flds. LE12: East L .2B 122
Osier Rd. NG2: Nott .7K 95
Osiers, The NG24: New T .5K 133
Osman Cl. NG2: Nott .7J 95
Osmaston St. NG7: Lent .5G 95
NG10: Sand .4B 104
Osmaston Wlk. *NG18: Mans* .5D 48
(off Mayfield Cl.)
Osprey Cl. NG11: Clif .1D 114
NG13: Bing .5G 101
Osprey Gro. NG15: Huck .4K 67
OSSINGTON .2C 147
Ossington Cl. NG1: Nott .2E 6 (2K 95)
NG20: Mede V .7F 33
Ossington La. NG23: Sut T .3A 128
Ossington M. *NG24: New T* .7C 134
(off Bar Gate)
Ossington Rd. NG23: Carl T .6A 128
NG23: Norw .1H 127
Ossington St. NG7: Radf .2G 95
Ossington Way NG24: New T .7C 134
Osterley Gro. NG16: Nuth .4J 83
Otter Bank NG24: New T .6D 134
Otter Way NG19: Mans .1D 46
Oulton Cl. NG5: Arn .1C 86
Oulton Lodge NG5: Top V .5K 75
Oundle Dr. DE7: Ilk .1A 92
NG8: Woll .5D 94
NG19: Mans .1D 46
Ousebridge Cres. NG4: Carl .7K 87
Ousebridge Dr. NG4: Carl .7K 87
Outgang La.
NG19: Mans W .5K 41
(not continuous)
NG19: Plea .3B 40
Outram St. NG17: Sut A .1K 51
Oval, The DN22: Ord .6D 22
NG17: Sut A .6H 45
S81: Work .1H 21
Oval Gdns. NG8: Aspl .7E 84
Overdale Av. NG17: Skeg .3J 45
Overdale Rd. NG6: Basf .5D 84
Overend Rd. S80: Work .1F 21
Overstone Cl. NG17: Skeg .5K 45
Overstrand Cl. NG5: Arn .1C 86
Owday La. S81: Work .3B 18
Owlston Cl. NG16: Eastw .3D 72
Owsthorpe Cl. NG5: Top V .6C 76
OWSTON .1A 144
OWSTON FERRY .1D 145
Owston Rd. NG15: Ann .5D 60
OWTHORPE .2B 148
Owthorpe Gro. NG5: Sher .5J 85
Owthorpe La. NG12: Kin .1B 142
Owthorpe Rd. NG12: Cols B .7F 141
NG12: Cotg .7E 110
Oxborough Rd. NG5: Arn .7E 76
Oxbow Cl. NG2: Nott .7K 95
Oxbury Rd. NG16: Want .6K 73
Oxclose La. NG5: Arn .1J 85
NG19: Mans .6D 40
NG19: Mans W .6G 41
Oxendale Cl. NG2: West Br .3F 109
Oxengate NG5: Arn .1K 85
Oxford Cl. NG21: Rain .3J 55
Oxford Dr. DN11: Harwo .1C 8
Oxford Rd. NG2: West Br .2D 108
S81: Carl L .6C 12
Oxford St. NG1: Nott .5C 6 (4J 95)
NG4: Carl .6H 87
NG16: Eastw .4D 72
NG17: Kirk A .7B 52
NG17: Sut A .1H 51
NG18: Mans .1J 47
OXTON .1G 71 (3B 146)
Oxton Av. NG5: Sher .3K 85
Oxton By-Pass NG25: Oxt .1E 70
Oxton Cl. DN22: Ord .7E 22
NG19: Mans .3E 46
Oxton Hill NG25: Sout .1J 71
Oxton Rd. NG5: Arn .6H 69
NG14: Calv .6H 69
NG14: Epp .3F 71
NG25: Oxt .3F 71
NG25: Sout .7A 130
Oyster Way NG20: Mkt W .3C 34
Ozier Holt NG4: Colw .4H 97

P

Pach Way NG24: Bald .7J 137
Packet Landing, The DN10: Mist .2K 11
Packham Ct. NG6: Basf .3F 85
Packhorse Row NG20: Nort .3E 32
Packman Dr. NG11: Rudd .2A 116
Packman's Rd. NG19: Mans W .5D 42
NG20: Mkt W .2C 42
Paddington M. NG3: Nott .1D 96
Paddock, The DN22: Retf .6G 23
NG9: Atten .7J 105
NG11: Bunny .3B 118
NG13: Bing .4F 101
NG17: Kirk A .7J 51
NG17: Stant H .5G 45
NG19: Plea .4A 40
NG23: Coll .3H 129
Paddock Caravan Site, The S80: Rhod .7C 18
Paddock Cl. NG6: Bulw .2C 84
NG12: Rad T .6D 98
NG14: Calv .6D 70
NG18: Mans .7H 47
NG21: Edwin .5E 36
NG23: Elston .2E 140
Paddock Farm Cotts. NG14: Epp .1A 80
Paddocks, The DN10: Beck .6C 16
DN22: Lound .2D 14
LE12: Sut B .6B 120
NG12: Edwal .6E 108
NG16: Nuth .2G 83
NG17: Huth .1D 50
NG19: Mans W .4A 42
NG23: Elston .2E 140

Paddocks, The—Peary Cl.

Paddocks, The NG24: New T 2E 136
NG25: Hock 1K 131
S81: Work 5J 19
Paddocks Cl. NG16: Pinx 6A 50
Padge Rd. NG9: Bee 3C 106
Padgham Ct. NG5: Top V 6C 76
Padley Ct. NG6: Bulw 1B 84
Padley Hill NG18: Mans 4G 47
Padleys La. NG14: Bur J 2D 88
Padstow Cl. NG18: Mans 1D 54
Padstow Rd. NG5: Bestw 1G 85
Pagdin Dr. DN11: Sty 4A 8
Page Av. NG5: Bestw 2H 85
Paget Cres. NG11: Rudd 2K 115
Pagett Cl. NG15: Huck 7J 67
Paige Gdns. NG10: Sand 4A 104
Paignton Cl. NG8: Aspl 5C 84
Paisley Gro. NG9: Chil 7H 105
Palace Gdns. NG21: C'tone 4H 43
Palace Theatre
Newark-on-Trent 1D 136
Palace Theatre, The
Mansfield 3J 47
Palace Vw. NG25: Sout 6H 131
Palatine St. NG7: Nott 7C 6 (5J 95)
Palin Ct. NG7: H Grn 1G 95
Palin Gdns. NG12: Rad T 5F 99
Paling Cres. NG17: Sut A 7J 45
Palin St. NG7: H Grn 2G 95
Palm Cotts. NG5: Sher 4A 86
Palm Ct. NG7: Basf 6G 85
Palmer Av. NG15: Huck 5G 67
Palmer Cres. NG4: Carl 1G 97
Palmer Dr. NG9: Stap 4C 104
Palmer Rd. DN22: Retf 1F 23
NG23: Sut T 3D 128
Palmers Ct. NG25: Sout 6J 131
Palmerston Gdns.
NG3: Nott 2F 7 (2K 95)
(not continuous)
Palmerston St. NG16: Unde 3D 64
NG16: Westw 7A 58
Palm St. NG7: Basf 6G 85
Palmwood Ct. NG6: Bulw 2D 84
PALTERTON 2A 146
Paper Mill Cotts. *DN22: Retf 4E 22*
(off Albert Rd.)
PAPPLEWICK 2K 67 (3A 146)
Papplewick Grange
NG15: Pap 4K 67
Papplewick La. NG15: Huck 6H 67
Papplewick Pumping Station 7G 63
Parchment M. NG5: Sher 6J 85
Parfitt Cl. NG22: Farns 6K 57
Parfitt Dr. NG22: Farns 6K 57
PARK, THE
Mansfield 1H 47
Nottingham 5C 6 (4J 95)
Park, The NG12: Cotg 5E 110
NG14: Thur 7B 138
NG17: Teve 3E 44
NG18: Mans 2J 47
NG23: Nth M 5K 129
NG24: New T 3D 136
Park & Ride
Hucknall 6J 67
Moor Bridge 4K 75
Phoenix Park 3B 84
Queen's Drive (Nottingham) 2H 107
Racecourse (Nottingham) 5E 96
The Forest (Nottingham) 1H 95
Wilkinson Street 7F 85
Park Av. DN10: Mist 1G 11
NG2: West Br 1C 108
NG3: Mapp P 7K 85
NG4: Carl 7J 87
NG5: Woodt 2B 86
NG12: Key 7G 117
(Croft Rd.)
NG12: Key 6J 117
(Park Rd.)
NG14: Bur J 3E 88
NG14: Woodbo 2F 79
NG15: Huck 6F 67
NG16: Aws 2A 82
NG16: Eastw 3C 72
NG16: Kimb 3F 83
NG17: Ann W 4B 60
NG18: Mans 2J 47
NG19: Mans W 4H 41
NG21: Blid 6K 55
Park Av. E. NG12: Key 7G 117
Park Av. W. NG12: Key 7G 117
Park Chase NG6: Bulw 2C 84
Park Cl. NG3: Mapp 5B 86
NG16: Pinx 2A 58
Park Ct. NG7: Lent 7F 95
NG17: Kirk A 1H 59
NG18: Mans 2J 47
Park Cres. DN22: Retf 2G 23
NG8: Woll 4H 93
NG16: Eastw 2D 72
NG24: New T 5E 134
Parkcroft Rd. NG2: West Br 3C 108
Parkdale Rd. NG3: Nott 2E 96
NG4: Carl 2E 96
Park Dr. NG7: Nott 6B 6 (4H 95)
NG10: Sand 6A 104
NG15: Huck 1G 75
S81: Blyth 6G 13
Parker Cl. NG5: Arn 6A 78
Parker Gdns. NG9: Stap 1E 104
Parker's La. NG19: Mans W 6J 41
Parkers Row NG20: Cuck 4C 32
Parker St. NG15: Huck 6H 67
NG24: New T 1D 136
Parkes Bldg. NG9: Bee 2A 106
Parkes Cl. NG24: Codd 6K 135
Park Farm Cotts. LN1: Kett 1F 31
Park Gdns. NG17: Huth 7E 44
Parkgate NG15: Huck 4H 67
Park Hall Gdns. NG19: Mans W 4J 41
Park Hall Rd. NG19: Mans W 3J 41
Parkham Rd. NG16: Kimb 7K 73
Park Hgts. NG7: Nott 7A 6 (5H 95)
Park Hill NG7: Nott 4B 6 (3H 95)
NG16: Aws 2A 82
Park Ho. Gates NG3: Mapp P 6A 86
Parkin Cl. NG12: Crop Bi 5B 112
Parkins Row NG23: Caun 6H 127
Parkland Cl. NG11: Clif 6D 106
NG18: Mans 1A 54
Parklands Cl. NG5: Top V 5D 76
NG24: Codd 6J 135
Parkland Vw. NG17: Huth 1E 50
Park La. DN22: Elk 3H 27
DN22: Retf 1G 23
LE12: Sut B 6B 120
NG4: Lamb 7G 79
NG6: Basf, Bulw 3F 85
NG14: Epp 1A 80
NG16: Pinx 1A 58
NG16: Sels 4E 58
NG17: Kirk A 4E 58
NG18: Mans 5H 47
NG22: Well 6D 38
NG23: Wigs 6F 31
NG25: Sout 7G 131
S80: Holb 4A 26
Park La. Bus. Cen. NG6: Bulw 2F 85
Park La. Bus. Pk. NG17: Kirk A 1H 59
Park Lodge Rd. NG16: Gilt 7E 72
Park M. DN22: Retf 2G 23
NG3: Mapp P 7K 85
NG17: Skeg 5K 45
NG19: Mans W 5J 41
Park Pl. S80: Work 4G 21
Park Ravine NG7: Nott 7B 6 (5H 95)
Park Rd. DE7: Ilk 7A 82
NG4: Carl 1J 97
NG5: Woodt 2B 86
NG6: Bestw V 2A 76
NG7: Lent 7A 6 (5G 95)
NG9: Bram 1E 104
NG9: Chil 3K 105
NG12: Key 6J 117
NG12: Rad T 4E 98
NG13: Barns 3F 141
NG14: Calv 5B 70
NG15: Huck 6F 67
NG19: Mans W 6H 41
Park Rd. E. NG14: Calv 5D 70
Park Rd. Nth. NG9: Chil 3K 105
Park Rock NG7: Lent 7B 6 (5H 95)
Park Row NG1: Nott 6D 6 (4J 95)
Parkside NG8: Woll 5K 93
NG12: Key 6J 117
NG17: Huth 7E 44
Parkside Gdns. NG8: Woll 5K 93
Parkside Ri. NG8: Woll 6K 93
Parkside Rd. NG21: Edwin 6D 36
Parkstone Av. NG21: Rain 1H 55
Parkstone Cl. NG2: West Br 4K 107
Park St. NG7: Lent 4G 95
NG9: Bee 3K 105
NG9: Stap 3B 104
NG17: Kirk A 6K 51
NG17: Sut A 7K 45
NG19: Mans W 6H 41
S80: Work 3F 21
Park Ter. NG1: Nott 5C 6 (4J 95)
NG12: Key 5J 117
NG25: Sout 6G 131
Park Valley NG7: Nott 6C 6 (4J 95)
Park Vw. NG3: Mapp 5B 86
NG15: Huck 7H 67
NG16: Eastw 5D 72
NG19: Plea 4A 40
NG20: Whal T 5A 26
Park Vw. Ct. NG1: Nott 4H 7 (3A 96)
NG9: Chil 3J 105
Parkview Dr. NG5: Bestw 7C 76
Park Vw. Way NG18: Mans 5H 47
Parkway NG17: Sut A 7F 45
NG19: Mans W 6F 43
NG24: New T 3B 136
Parkway Ct. NG8: Bilb 3J 93
Park West NG7: Nott 4A 6
Park Wharf NG7: Nott 7D 6 (5J 95)
Parkwood Ct. NG6: Bulw 2F 85
Parkwood Cres. NG5: Sher 4B 86
Park Yacht Club 6D 96
Parkyn Rd. NG5: Arn 1A 86
Parkyns Piece LE12: East L 2A 122
Parkyns St. NG11: Rudd 3K 115
Parliament Ct. NG24: New T 1B 136
Parliament Rd. NG19: Mans 2E 46
Parliament St. NG17: Sut A 1K 51
NG24: New T 1B 136
Parliament Ter. NG1: Nott 4D 6 (3J 95)
Parliament Wlk. NG21: C'tone 4H 43
NG24: New T 2B 136
(off Parliament St.)
Parnhams Cl. LE14: Neth B 4K 143
Parr Ct. NG12: Rad T 5E 98
Parr Gate NG9: Chil 4F 105
Parrs, The NG9: Bee 3C 106
Parry Bus. Pk. NG23: Sut T 2C 128
Parry Ct. NG3: Mapp 3D 86
NG3: Nott 2D 96
Parry Way NG5: Arn 6K 77
Parson La. NG22: West M 2A 28
Parsons Cl. NG24: Bald 7H 137
Parsons Mdw. NG4: Colw 4H 97
Parthenon Cl. NG19: Plea 4A 40
Partridge Cl. NG13: Bing 5G 101
NG21: Rain 3K 55
Paschall Rd. NG17: Nunc 3B 60
Pasteur Ho. NG3: Mapp 5C 86
Pasture Av. NG21: Rain 2K 55
Pasture Cl. LE12: Sut B 6A 120
NG2: Colw 4H 97
NG17: Stant H 5G 45
NG22: Kirt 7H 27
S80: Work 3D 20
Pasture La. DE55: Hilc 2A 50
DN10: Harwe 4A 10
LE12: Hath 7F 121
LE12: Sut B 7A 120
NG11: Rudd 4G 115
NG12: Crop Bi 6C 112
Pasture Rd. NG9: Stap 7C 92
Pastures, The DN10: Bawt 1K 9
DN22: Ramp 7K 25
NG8: Bilb 1C 94
NG14: Calv 6B 70
NG16: Gilt 6F 73
NG19: Mans W 4K 41
NG22: Tuxf 7B 28
Pastures Av. NG11: Clif 2E 114
Pasture Vw. NG14: Gun 2B 90
Patchills, The NG18: Mans 3B 48
Patchills Centre, The NG18: Mans 3B 48
Patchings Art Cen. 5K 69
Pateley Rd. NG3: Mapp 3D 86
Paton Ct. NG14: Calv 4C 70
Paton Rd. NG5: Bestw 2F 85
Patricia Dr. NG5: Arn 5J 77
Patrick Rd. NG2: West Br 1B 108
Patriot Cl. NG16: Want 7A 74
Patterdale Cl. NG2: Gam 2F 109
Patterdale Ct. NG9: Chil 4F 105
Patterdale Rd. NG5: Woodt 2C 86
Patterson Pl. NG18: Mans 3K 47
Patterson Rd. NG7: H Grn 1G 95
Paul Av. NG18: Mans 4C 48
Paulson's Dr. NG19: Mans 2H 47
Pavilion, The NG7: H Grn 1H 95
Pavilion Cl. NG2: Nott 7A 96
NG20: Mkt W 4D 34
Pavilion Ct. NG14: Lowd 6E 80
Pavilion Gdns. NG17: Skeg 4A 46
Pavilion Rd. NG2: West Br 7B 96
NG5: Arn 5D 76
NG17: Kirk A 5B 52
Pavior Rd. NG5: Bestw 2G 85
Paxton Gdns. NG3: Nott 3J 7 (3B 96)
(not continuous)
Paxtons Ct. NG24: New T 7C 134
Payne Rd. NG9: Chil 6F 105
Peach Av. NG16: Sels 6D 58
Peache Way NG9: Bram 2G 105
Peachey St. NG1: Nott 3E 6 (3K 95)
Peacock Cl. NG11: Rudd 4J 115
NG14: Gun 3B 90
Peacock Cres. NG11: Clif 7F 107
Peacock Dr. NG16: Eastw 5C 72
Peacock St. NG18: Mans 4H 47
Peafield La. NG19: Mans W 5A 42
NG20: Mkt W 5A 42
Peak Hill Cl. S81: Gate 3E 18
Pearce Dr. NG8: Bilb 1C 94
Pearl Av. NG17: Kirk A 1B 60
Pearl Cl. NG21: Rain 2A 56
Pearl Gdns. NG20: Mkt W 3C 34
Pearmain Dr. NG3: Nott 1C 96
Pearson Av. NG9: Chil 4G 105
Pearson Cl. NG9: Chil 4G 105
Pearson Ct. NG5: Arn 7G 77
NG9: Bram 1G 105
Pearson St. NG4: Neth 2K 97
NG7: Basf 5G 85
Pear Tree Cl. DN22: Clar 7H 17
Pear Tree Ct. NG6: Basf 3F 85
Peartree La. NG17: Teve 1F 45
Peartree Orchard NG11: Rudd 3K 115
Pear Tree Yd. NG10: Sand 3A 104
Peary Cl. NG5: Bestw 1G 85

Peashill La. NG12: Cotg 4B 110
Peas Hill Rd. NG3: Nott 1G 7 (2A 96)
Peatfield Ct. NG9: Stap 7C 92
Peatfield Rd. NG9: Stap 7C 92
Peck La. NG1: Nott 5F 7 (4K 95)
  NG14: Gun 2B 90
Pecks Hill NG18: Mans .3A 48
Pedmore Valley
  NG5: Bestw 7C 76
Peebles Rd. NG24: New T 4A 136
Peel Av. DN22: Retf 7H 23
  NG22: Tuxf 7C 28
Peel Cres. NG19: Mans .7D 40
Peel Rd. NG19: Mans 2E 46
Peel St. NG1: Nott 2D 6 (2J 95)
  NG17: Sut A 7A 46
Peel Vs. NG3: Mapp 5B 86
Peets Dr. NG23: Nth M 6K 129
Pegswood Dr. NG5: Arn 4J 77
Pelham Av. NG5: Sher 7J 85
Pelham Cl. NG24: New T 1B 136
Pelham Cotts. NG7: Nott 6A 6
Pelham Ct. NG5: Sher 7J 85
Pelham Cres.
  NG7: Nott .6A 6 (4G 95)
  NG9: Bee 2C 106
Pelham Gdns. NG24: New T 1C 136
Pelham Rd. DN22: Retf .4D 22
  NG5: Sher 7J 85
  NG17: Kirk A 6A 52
Pelham St. NG1: Nott 5F 7 (4K 95)
  NG17: Sut A 1H 51
  NG18: Mans 3J 47
  NG24: New T 1B 136
  S80: Work 4H 21
Pelham Way NG19: Mans W 6F 43
Pemberley Chase NG17: Sut A 3H 51
Pemberton St. NG1: Nott 6H 7 (4A 96)
Pembleton Dr. NG19: Mans 1D 46
Pembrey Cl. NG9: Trow .6C 92
Pembridge Cl. NG6: Basf 5E 84
Pembroke Cres. NG24: New T 5F 135
Pembroke Dr. NG3: Mapp P 6K 85
  S81: Carl L 6B 12
Pembroke Rd. S81: Shire 5A 18
Pembury Rd. NG8: Woll .3K 93
Penarth Gdns. NG5: Sher 4B 86
Penarth Ri. NG5: Sher 4B 86
Pendean Way NG17: Sut A 2H 51
Pendennis Cl. NG4: Ged 6A 88
Pendine Cl. DE55: Sth N 5A 50
  NG5: Redh 5F 77
Pendle Cres. NG3: Nott .6C 86
Pendock Ct. NG12: Toll .1G 117
Pendock La. NG11: Rudd 1C 118
Penhale Dr. NG15: Huck 1C 74
Penhurst Cl. NG11: Wilf 5H 107
Penllech Cl. NG5: Bestw 7C 76
Penllech Wlk. NG5: Bestw 7C 76
Pennant Rd. NG6: Basf 5E 84
Pennard Wlk. NG11: Clif 2E 114
Penn Av. NG7: Lent 5F 95
Pennhome Almshouses NG5: Sher 5K 85
                          (off Haydn Rd.)
Pennhome Av. NG5: Sher 5K 85
Penniment La. NG19: Mans 6B 40
                      (not continuous)
Pennine Cl. NG5: Arn 5D 76
  NG17: Huth 6C 44
  NG19: Mans W 5J 41
Pennine Dr. NG5: Sels 5D 58
  NG17: Kirk A 7H 51
Pennington Wlk. DN22: Retf 4F 23
Penn La. NG12: Widm 7K 119
Penn St. NG17: Sut A 7K 45
Penny Emma Way NG17: Sut A 3K 51
Pennyfoot St. NG1: Nott 6J 7 (4B 96)
Pennyroyal Way NG17: Kirk A 7A 52
Penrhyn Cl. NG3: Nott 2G 7 (2A 96)
Penrhyn Cres. NG9: Chil 5G 105
Penrith Av. NG12: Rad T 4F 99
Penrith Cres. NG8: Aspl .5D 84
Penrith Pl. NG19: Mans .2D 46
Penrose Ct. NG16: Sels .5E 58
Penryn Cl. DE55: Sth N .5A 50
Penshore Cl. NG11: Clif 1E 114
Pensom Ct. NG22: Oll 5B 38
Penswick Gro. NG24: Codd 6J 135
Pentland Ct. NG19: Mans 5D 46
Pentland Dr. NG5: Arn 4D 76
  S81: Carl L 5B 12
Pentrich Rd. NG16: Gilt .7G 73
Pentrich Wlk. NG18: Mans 5D 48
Pentwood Av. NG5: Arn .4H 77
Penzance Pl. NG18: Mans 3D 48
Peoples Hall Cotts. NG1: Nott 5G 7
PEPPERLY HILL 3F 27
Pepperly Ri. DN22: Elk .2F 27
Pepper Rd. NG14: Calv 5C 70
Pepper St. NG1: Nott 6F 7 (4K 95)
  NG17: Sut A 1A 52
Percival Cl. NG17: Sut A 7J 45
Percival Cres. NG17: Sut A 7J 45
Percival Rd. NG5: Sher 5J 85
Percival St. S81: Work 7F 19

Percy St. NG6: Basf 4E 84
  NG16: Eastw 4E 72
  NG17: Sut A 1H 51
Peregrine Cl. NG7: Lent .4F 95
Peregrine Ct. S81: Gate .5D 18
Peregrine Rd. NG15: Huck 4K 67
Perivale Cl. NG16: Nuth .4J 83
Perkins Way NG9: Chil .6J 105
PERLETHORPE 1B 146
Perlethorpe Av. NG2: Nott 6K 7 (4C 96)
  NG4: Ged 5G 87
  NG19: Mans 1F 47
  NG20: Mede V 1F 35
Perlethorpe Cl. NG4: Ged 5H 87
  S81: Edwin 5D 36
Perlethorpe Cres. NG4: Ged 5H 87
Perlethorpe Dr. NG4: Ged 5H 87
  NG15: Huck 6H 67
Perry Gro. NG13: Bing .4G 101
Perry Rd. NG5: Sher 5G 85
Perth Cl. NG19: Mans W 4J 41
Perth Dr. NG9: Stap 7D 92
Perth St. NG1: Nott 3F 7 (3K 95)
Peterborough Rd. NG23: Coll 1H 129
Peters Cl. NG5: Arn 1F 87
  NG5: Newth 4G 73
Petersfield Cl. NG5: Top V 7B 76
  NG19: Mans 3D 46
Petersgate NG10: Long E 7A 104
Petersgate Cl. NG10: Long E 7A 104
Petersham M. NG7: Lent 5G 95
Petersham Rd. NG10: Long E 7A 104
Petersmith Cres. NG22: New O 2C 38
Petersmiths Cl. NG22: New O 2C 38
Petworth Av. NG9: Toton 6E 104
Petworth Dr. NG5: Sher .3G 85
Peverell Hall NG11: Clif 6E 106
Peveril Ct. NG2: West Br 2B 108
Peveril Dr. NG2: West Br 6B 108
  NG7: Nott .7C 6 (5J 95)
  NG17: Sut A 1G 51
Peveril M. NG7: Nott 6A 6
Peveril Rd. NG9: Bee 1A 106
Peveril St. NG7: Radf 1A 6 (2G 95)
  NG15: Huck 5G 67
Pheasant Hill NG19: Mans 1G 47
Philip Av. NG16: Eastw .5E 72
  NG16: Nuth 1H 83
  NG17: Kirk A 2B 60
Philip Cl. NG21: Rain 3A 56
Philip Gro. NG4: Ged 5H 87
Philip Rd. NG24: New T 4B 136
Phillipott Cl. NG24: New T 1G 137
Phoenix Av. NG4: Ged 5H 87
Phoenix Cen. NG8: Cin 3B 84
Phoenix Cl. NG2: Nott 6J 95
Phoenix Ct. NG7: Lent .1G 107
  NG16: Eastw 4E 72
Phoenix La. NG24: Bald 7J 137
Phoenix Park (Park & Ride) 3B 84
Phoenix Park Stop (NET) 3B 84
Phoenix Pl. NG8: Cin 3C 84
Phoenix Ri. NG19: Plea .4A 40
Phoenix Rd. NG16: Newth 2F 73
Phoenix St. NG17: Sut A 6B 46
Phyllis Cl. NG15: Huck 4F 67
Piccadilly NG6: Bulw 1E 84
Pickard St. NG18: Mans .3A 48
Pickering Av. NG16: Eastw 4D 72
Pickins Row NG22: Bou .2F 39
Pieris Dr. NG11: Clif 1D 114
Pierpoint Pl. NG17: Kirk A 5K 51
Pierrepont Av. NG4: Ged 6H 87
Pierrepont Rd. NG2: West Br 7E 96
Pierrepont Rd. NG2: West Br 1D 108
Pierson St. NG24: New T 4B 136
Pilcher Ga. NG1: Nott 5F 7 (4A 96)
Pilgrim Cl. NG15: Rave 2B 62
Pilgrim Ct. S81: Shire 5A 18
Pilgrim Way S80: Work 3G 21
PILHAM 2D 145
Pilkington Rd. NG3: Mapp 6D 86
Pilkington St. NG6: Bulw 7H 75
Pimlico Av. NG9: Bram 5G 93
Pine Av. NG22: New O 4D 38
Pine Cl. DN10: Eve 6B 10
  LE12: East L 4K 121
  NG17: Kirk A 5K 51
  NG19: Mans W 4J 41
  NG21: Rain 2H 55
  NG24: Bald 7J 137
  NG24: New T 4E 134
Pine Gro. NG15: Huck 2H 75
Pine Hill Cl. NG5: Top V 5B 76
Pinehurst Av. NG15: Huck 1C 74
Pines, The NG9: Bram .1H 105
  S80: Work 4G 21
Pines Ct. NG5: Sher 3A 86
Pines Way NG18: Mans .4K 53
Pine Tree Cl. S80: Work .4F 21
Pine Tree Wlk. NG16: Eastw 4C 72
Pine Vw. NG7: Radf 2G 95
Pineview NG18: Mans 1B 54

Pinewood Av. NG5: Arn .5K 77
  NG21: Edwin 7J 37
Pinewood Cl. NG17: Kirk A 5C 52
  NG25: Sout 5G 131
Pinewood Dr. NG18: Mans 1B 54
Pinewood Gdns. NG11: Clif 2E 114
Pinfold NG13: Bing 4G 101
Pinfold, The DN10: Miss 3C 10
Pinfold Cl. DN22: Lound 3D 14
  NG12: Cotg 5E 110
  NG12: Kin 2B 142
  NG14: Woodbo 2G 79
  NG23: Coll 1H 129
Pinfold Cres. NG14: Woodbo 2G 79
Pinfold Dr. S81: Carl L 5C 12
Pinfold Gdns. NG19: Mans W 7B 42
Pinfold La. DN10: Harwe 5A 10
  DN10: Mist 2G 11
  DN11: Sty 4A 8
                      (not continuous)
  DN22: Welh 2K 23
  NG9: Stap 2C 104
  NG11: Wilf 3J 107
  NG12: Kin 2B 142
  NG12: Plum 3J 117
  NG12: Shel 6H 89
  NG23: Aver 3F 133
  NG23: Elston 1D 140
  NG24: Bald 6G 137
Pinfold Rd. NG16: Gilt 5G 73
Pinfold Trad. Est. NG9: Stap 2D 104
Pinfold Wlk. LE12: East L 3A 122
Pingle Cl. S81: Shire 5A 18
Pingle Cres. NG5: Top V 6B 76
Pings Cl. NG23: Best 7H 125
Pintail Cl. NG4: Neth 2A 98
PINXTON 1B 58 (3A 146)
Pinxton Ct. NG18: Mans .5D 48
Pinxton Grn. NG16: Pinx 1C 58
Pinxton La. DE55: Sth N .6A 50
  NG16: Pinx 7F 51
  NG17: Sut A 5D 50
Pinxton Rd. NG17: Kirk A 1H 59
PINXTON WHARF 2B 58
Pinxton Wharf NG16: Pinx 3A 58
Piper Cl. NG15: Huck 4H 67
  NG19: Mans W 7H 41
Pippin Cl. DN10: Mist 4K 11
  NG3: Nott 1C 96
  NG16: Sels 4E 58
Pippin Ct. NG24: New T 6E 134
Pippistrelle Cl. DN22: Nth L 7C 24
Pitcairn Cl. NG2: Nott 7K 95
Pitch Cl. NG4: Carl 7F 87
  NG16: Gilt 6G 73
Pit Hill NG20: Whal T 5A 26
Pithouse La. LE12: West L 3E 120
Pit La. NG19: Plea 4A 40
Pitt La. DN10: Gri H 2B 16
Plackett Cl. NG9: Stap .1E 104
Plains Farm Cl. NG3: Mapp 2F 87
Plains Gro. NG3: Mapp 3D 86
PLAIN SPOT 3C 64
Plainspot Rd. NG16: Brins, Unde 4C 64
Plains Rd. NG3: Mapp 4C 86
Plane Cl. NG6: Bulw 7F 75
Plane Tree Ct. NG15: Huck 1H 75
Plantagenet Ct. NG3: Nott 2H 7 (3A 96)
Plantagenet St. NG3: Nott 3H 7 (3A 96)
Plantation Av. NG22: East M 2D 28
Plantation Cl. NG5: Arn .5D 76
Plantation Cotts. NG14: Epp 7K 71
Plantation Dr. DN10: Matt T 1F 15
Plantation Hill S81: Work 7J 19
Plantation Rd. NG8: Woll 4H 93
  NG12: Key 7G 117
  NG22: East M 2D 28
Plantation Side NG7: H Grn 1F 95
Plantin Rd. NG5: Sher 6J 85
Plants Yd. S80: Work 3F 21
                      (off Bridge St.)
Platt La. NG12: Key, Norm W 6J 117
Platts, The NG24: New T 3B 136
Platt St. NG16: Pinx 2A 58
Player Cl. NG7: Radf 2F 95
Player St. NG7: Radf 2F 95
Playmania
  Mansfield 1G 47
Plaza Gdns. NG6: Basf 3F 85
Pleasant Ct. NG7: H Grn 1G 95
Pleasant Row NG7: H Grn 1G 95
PLEASLEY .3A 40 (2A 146)
Pleasley Cross NG19: Plea 4A 40
PLEASLEYHILL 5B 40
Pleasley Pit Country Pk. .3A 40
Pleasley Rd. NG17: Skeg .4A 46
  NG17: Teve 3F 45
Pleasley Springs NG19: Plea 4B 40
Pleasley Va. NG19: Plea .3D 40
Pleasley Va. Bus. Pk. NG19: Plea 3D 40
Pleasley Vale Canoe & Activity Cen. 3E 40
Plimsoll St. NG7: H Grn .7F 85
Plough Dr. S81: Carl L 5C 12
Plough La. NG1: Nott 6J 7 (4B 96)
  NG14: Lowd 5D 80
Ploughman Av. NG14: Woodbo 2H 79

Ploughmans Gro. NG17: Huth 2E 50
Plough Yd. NG20: Mkt W 3D 34
Plover Dene S81: Gate 5D 18
Plover Wharf NG7: Lent 6H 95
Plowman Ct. NG9: Stap 3C 104
Plowright Ct. NG3: Nott 1A 96
Plowright St. NG3: Nott 1A 96
Plumb Rd. NG15: Huck 6F 67
Plumptre Cl. NG16: Eastw 5D 72
Plumptre Gdns. NG16: Eastw 4D 72
Plumptre Pl. NG1: Nott 6G 7 (4A 96)
Plumptre Rd. NG16: Lang M 1A 72
Plumptre Sq. NG1: Nott 6H 7 (4A 96)
Plumptre St. NG1: Nott 6G 7 (4A 96)
Plumptre Way NG16: Eastw 5D 72
PLUMTREE 3H 117 (2B 148)
Plumtree DN11: Birc 1F 9
Plum Tree Av. NG19: Mans W 1D 48
Plumtree Caravan Pk. DN11: Birc 1E 8
Plum Tree Cl. DN22: Clar 7H 17
Plumtree Ct. NG12: Plum 3H 117
Plumtree Farm Ind. Est. DN11: Birc 1F 9
Plumtree Gdns. NG14: Calv 6D 70
PLUMTREE PARK 6J 117 (2B 148)
Plumtree Rd. DN11: Birc 1F 9
  NG12: Cotg 7C 110
Plum Way NG24: Bald 7H 137
PLUNGAR 2C 149
Plungar Cl. NG8: Bilb 2C 94
Plungar Rd. NG13: Gran 1K 141
Plymouth Av. NG16: Pinx 2C 58
Pochard Cl. NG19: Mans W 7B 42
Pocklington Cres. NG24: Wint 2G 135
Pocklington Rd. NG23: Coll 1J 129
Podder La. NG3: Mapp 1F 87
Point, The NG1: Nott 6H 7
  NG2: West Br 2B 108
    (off Loughborough Rd.)
  NG3: Mapp P 7A 86
  S81: Shire 5B 18
Pointers Ct. NG3: Nott 1D 96
Pollard Ct. NG9: Bee 2A 106
Pollard Dr. NG18: Mans 3J 47
Pollard's La. NG25: Sout 7J 131
Polperro Way NG15: Huck 1C 74
Pond Cl. NG24: Bald 7J 137
Pond Hills La. NG5: Arn 6H 77
Pond St. NG17: Kirk A 6A 52
Pool Cl. NG16: Pinx 1B 58
Pool Mdw. NG4: Colw 4J 97
Popham Cl. NG1: Nott 6G 7 (4A 96)
Popham St. NG1: Nott 6G 7 (4A 96)
Poplar Av. LE12: East L 4K 121
  NG5: Sher 5H 85
  NG10: Sand 2A 104
  NG17: Kirk A 5C 52
Poplar Cl. NG4: Carl 2G 97
  NG13: Bing 4H 101
  NG23: Sut T 3D 128
  S80: Work 4E 20
Poplar Cres. NG16: Nuth 1F 83
Poplar Dr. NG19: Plea 5B 40
Poplar Gro. NG19: Mans W 1D 48
  NG20: Chu W 2C 34
Poplars, The DN22: Rans 2H 13
  NG2: West Br 2C 108
  NG7: H Grn 7F 85
  NG9: Bee 2A 106
  NG12: Plum 4H 117
  NG17: Sut A 7A 46
Poplars Av. NG14: Bur J 2F 89
Poplars Cl. NG12: Key 6J 117
Poplars Ct. NG7: Lent 6G 95
Poplars Rd. NG7: Lent 6G 95
Poplar St. DN22: Retf 4F 23
  NG1: Nott 6H 7 (4A 96)
    (not continuous)
  NG19: Mans W .6J 41
  NG22: New O 4D 38
Poplars Way NG18: Mans 4K 53
Poplar Ter. NG16: Sels 6C 58
Poppy M. NG15: Huck 2K 75
Poppy Pl. NG24: New T 7G 135
PORCHESTER 5E 86
Porchester Cl. NG15: Huck 6J 67
Porchester Cl. NG3: Nott 7D 86
Porchester Rd. NG3: Mapp, Nott 5C 86
  NG13: Bing 4E 100
Porrit Cl. LE12: East L 1A 122
Portage Cl. NG12: Rad T 6D 98
Port Arthur Rd. NG2: Nott 4C 96
Porter Cl. NG11: Clif 2D 114
Porters Wlk. NG3: Nott 1D 96
Portinscale Cl. NG2: West Br 4F 109
Portland Av. NG17: Ann W 3A 60
Portland Bungs. DN22: Sut L 6B 14
Portland Cl. NG17: Sut A 1K 51
Portland Ct. NG5: Bestw 2J 85
  NG24: New T 1C 136
Portland Ct. M. NG19: Mans W 5J 41
Portland Cres. NG9: Stap 3D 104
  NG19: Mans W .6K 41
  NG20: Mede V .6G 33
Portland Flats DN22: Sut L 6B 14
Portland Gdns. NG15: Huck 6F 67
Portland Grange NG15: Huck 6E 66

Portland Hgts. NG17: Huth 6C 44
Portland Hill NG7: Nott 7D 94
Portland Ind. Est. NG17: Kirk A 4A 52
Portland Leisure Cen. 7A 96
Portland Mdws. DN22: Sut L 6B 14
Portland Pk. NG17: Kirk A 1K 59
Portland Pk. Cl. NG15: Huck 6F 67
Portland Pk. Vis. Cen. 1K 59
Portland Pl. DN22: Sut L 6B 14
  NG18: Mans 4G 47
  S80: Work 1G 21
Portland Retail Pk. NG18: Mans 4G 47
Portland Rd. DN22: Retf 5D 22
  NG2: West Br 3C 108
  NG4: Carl 5F 87
  NG7: Radf 3B 6 (3H 95)
  NG9: Toton 7E 104
  NG15: Huck 6H 67
  NG16: Gilt 6F 73
  NG16: Sels 4E 58
  NG20: Whal T 5B 26
Portland Row NG16: Sels 4E 58
  NG21: Edwin 7J 37
Portland Sq. NG7: Radf 3B 6 (3H 95)
  NG17: Sut A 1K 51
Portland St. NG5: Arn 1A 86
  NG9: Bee 2B 106
  NG17: Kirk A 6A 52
  NG17: Sut A 1K 51
  NG18: Mans 4H 47
  NG19: New H 2A 40
  NG20: Mkt W 4D 34
  NG24: New T 1C 136
  S80: Work 2F 21
Portland Ter. NG20: Whal T 5B 26
Portland Way NG21: C'tone 6H 43
Portree Dr. NG5: Top V 5B 76
Port Said Vs. NG7: Basf 6G 85
Postern St. NG1: Nott 5D 6 (4J 95)
Post Office Rd. NG17: Kirk A 6B 52
Post Office Yd. NG17: Hove 4K 81
Posts, The NG12: Crop Bu 3B 112
Potmakers Gro. NG17: Sut A 6A 46
Pot 'n' Kettle (Ceramic Cafe) 2B 106
    (off High Rd.)
Potomac M. NG7: Nott 6B 6 (4H 95)
POTTER HILL 3C 149
Potter Hill Rd. NG23: Coll 3J 129
Potter La. NG22: Well 7D 24
Potters Cl. NG5: Top V 7C 76
Potters Ct. NG9: Bram 7J 93
Potters Hollow NG6: Bulw 2D 84
Potters La. LE12: East L 3A 122
Potters Nook S81: Shire 5A 18
Potter St. NG17: Sut A 6A 46
  S80: Work 3G 21
Potters Way DE7: Ilk 7A 82
Pottery Ct. NG6: Bulw 7G 75
Pottery Way NG6: Bulw 7G 75
Potwell Cl. NG25: Sout 6J 131
Pot Yard, The NG22: Farns 5K 57
Poulter Cl. NG7: Radf 1E 94
Poulter Country Pk. 5A 26
Poulter St. NG20: Langw 6A 26
Poulter Vw. DN22: Retf 5F 23
Poulton Dr. NG2: Nott 5C 96
Poultry NG1: Nott 5F 7 (4K 95)
Poultry Arc. NG1: Nott 5F 7
Powell Ct. NG22: Farns 6K 57
Powell Gdns. S81: Gate 4E 18
Powerleague
  Nottingham 3F 107
Powis St. NG6: Bulw 7H 75
Powtrell Pl. DE7: Ilk 2A 92
Poynton St. NG1: Nott 4D 6 (3J 95)
Poyser Cl. NG7: Basf 6H 85
Pratt Cl. NG19: Mans 1D 46
Prebble Cl. NG24: New T 5B 136
Prebend Pas. NG25: Sout 6G 131
Prebends Cl. NG24: Farnd 7G 133
Precinct Rd. NG17: Kirk A 6B 52
Premier Rd. NG7: H Grn 7H 85
Prendwick Gdns. NG5: Bestw 6D 76
Prest Av. NG20: Mede V 7G 33
Preston Rd. NG21: Rain 3J 55
Prestwick Cl. NG8: Stre 5J 83
PRESTWOLD 3A 148
Prestwold Av. NG19: Mans W 1D 48
Prestwood Dr. NG8: Aspl 1C 94
Pretoria Vs. NG8: Aspl 5D 84
Previn Gdns. NG3: Nott 2C 96
Priestgate NG22: East M 4A 28
Priestley Ct. NG22: New O 5D 38
Priestsic Rd. NG17: Sut A 7J 45
Primrose Av. NG16: Unde 3D 64
  NG24: Farnd 5J 133
  NG24: New T 4E 134
Primrose Bank NG13: Bing 4E 100
Primrose Cl. NG3: Nott 1H 7 (1A 96)
  NG17: Kirk A 4K 51
Primrose Ct. NG17: Sut A 2B 52
  NG19: Mans W .5B 42
Primrose Cres. NG4: Carl 1J 97
Primrose Gdns. NG15: Huck 2K 75

Primrose La. NG22: Kirt 3H 39
Primrose Ri. NG16: Newth 6E 72
Primrose St. NG4: Carl 1J 97
Primrose Way NG17: Sut A 2G 51
  NG21: C'tone 5H 43
  S81: Work 6H 19
Primula Cl. NG11: Clif 7D 106
Primula Gro. NG17: Kirk A 1A 60
Prince Charles Rd. S81: Work 5E 18
Prince Edward Cres. NG12: Rad T 6C 98
Prince of Wales St. DN22: Retf 4E 22
Princess Anne Rd. S81: Work 6F 19
Princess Av. NG9: Bee 3B 106
  NG19: Mans W .2C 48
  NG20: Mkt W 4E 34
Princess Cl. NG4: Ged 5H 87
Princess Dr. NG10: Sand 5A 104
Princess St. NG17: Kirk A 1H 59
Princes St. NG16: Eastw 3D 72
  NG18: Mans 5G 47
  NG24: New T 2C 136
Princeton Cl. NG22: New O 5C 38
Prior Cl. NG17: Sut A 6B 46
Prioridge NG12: Cotg 7F 111
Prior Rd. NG5: Arn .1A 86
Priors, The NG14: Lowd 4D 80
Priors Cl. NG13: Bing 3H 101
Priorswell Rd. S80: Work 3G 21
Priory Av. NG12: Toll 1F 117
  NG15: Rave 3D 62
  NG17: Ann W 4B 60
Priory Centre, The S80: Work 2F 21
Priory Cir. NG12: Toll 1F 117
Priory Cl. DN10: Matt 2H 15
  NG4: Bald 6G 137
  S81: Blyth 6G 13
Priory Ct. NG3: Mapp 6B 86
  NG4: Ged 6J 87
  NG7: Lent 5F 95
  NG19: Mans W .6H 41
Priory Cres. NG4: Ged 6J 87
Priory Gro. NG17: Kirk A 6D 52
Priory La. NG14: Thur 6C 138
Priory M. NG7: Lent 6F 95
Priory Pk. NG14: Thur 6D 138
Priory Rd. NG2: West Br 1C 108
  NG4: Ged 6J 87
  NG14: Thur 6B 138
  NG15: Huck 6E 66
  NG16: Eastw 5D 72
  NG19: Mans W .6H 41
  NG21: Blid 6J 55
Priory Sq. NG19: Mans W 6H 41
Priory St. NG7: Lent 6F 95
Priory Vw. S80: Work 3H 21
Pritchard Dr. NG9: Stap 3D 104
Private Rd. NG3: Mapp 5K 85
  NG5: Sher 5K 85
  NG14: Woodbo .1F 79
  NG15: Huck 6E 66
  NG25: Sout 5H 131
Private Rd. No. 1 NG4: Colw 2J 97
Private Rd. No. 2 NG4: Colw 3J 97
Private Rd. No. 3 NG4: Colw 3K 97
Private Rd. No. 4 NG4: Colw 3A 98
Private Rd. No. 5 NG4: Colw 3A 98
Private Rd. No. 7 NG4: Colw 2J 97
Private Rd. No. 8 NG4: Colw 3J 97
Private St. NG24: New T 1E 136
Privet Av. NG17: Kirk A 5A 52
Prize Cl. NG11: Clif 1D 114
Procter Dr. NG23: Girt 4G 125
Promenade NG3: Nott 3H 7 (3A 96)
Promenade, The NG17: Kirk A 5D 52
Prospect Cl. NG17: Kirk A 4B 52
Prospect Ct. NG4: Carl 6D 86
  NG17: Huth 2C 50
Prospect Dr. S81: Work 6G 19
Prospect M. DN10: Mist 2H 11
Prospect Pl. NG7: Lent 5G 95
  NG17: Sut A 1J 51
Prospect Pct. S81: Work 6H 19
Prospect Rd. NG4: Carl 6D 86
Prospect St. NG7: Radf 2F 95
  NG18: Mans 4K 47
Prospect Ter. NG7: Radf 2F 95
Prospect Units NG17: Kirk A 4C 52
Prospect Vs. NG14: Lowd 5D 80
Providence Rd. NG16: Jack 6A 64
Provident Works NG7: Radf 3A 6
Prudhoe Ct. NG2: Nott 7A 96
Pudding La. LE14: Hick 7E 142
Pulborough Cl. NG5: Sher 3G 85
Pullman Rd. NG2: Nott 4C 96
Pump Hollow La. NG18: Mans 3C 48
  NG19: Mans W .3C 48
Pump Hollow Rd. NG19: Mans W 2C 48
Pumping Station, The NG22: Halam 6B 130
Pumping Sta. Way S80: Work 2J 21
Pump La. NG22: Wale 5G 27
Purbeck Cl. NG19: Mans W 3J 41
Purbeck Dr. NG2: West Br 4K 107
PureGym
  Mansfield 5H 47
Pure Land Meditation Centre & Japanese Garden
  . . . . .3D 30

Pusto Hill La. DN10: Eve . . . . .7C **10** & 1K **15**
Pyatt St. NG2: Nott 7A **96**
Pye Av. NG19: Mans 3D **46**
PYE HILL 6A **64**
Pye Hill Rd. NG16: Jack 6A **64**
Pygall Av. NG11: Goth .7F **115**
Pym St. NG3: Nott 2K **7** (2C **96**)
Pym Wlk. NG3: Nott 2J **7** (2B **96**)
Python Hill Rd. NG21: Rain 2K **55**

Q

Quadrangle, The NG15: News 6D **60**
  NG19: Mans 2H **47**
  NG21: Blid 6J **55**
Quakefield Rd. NG22: East M 3E **28**
Quaker La. NG18: Mans 3H **47**
  NG22: Farns 6K **57**
Quaker Way NG18: Mans 3H **47**
Quantock Cl. NG5: Arn 4D **76**
Quantock Gro. NG13: Bing 4D **100**
Quantock Rd. NG10: Long E 7A **104**
Quarries Way NG17: Kirk A 7J **51**
Quarry Av. NG6: Bulw .1C **84**
Quarry Bank NG18: Mans 6K **47**
Quarry Cl. NG15: Rave 4C **62**
Quarrydale NG15: Huck 4F **67**
Quarrydale Av. NG17: Sut A 5J **45**
Quarrydale Dr. NG17: Sut A 5J **45**
Quarrydale Rd. NG17: Sut A 6K **45**
Quarry Dale Vw. NG18: Mans 5A **48**
Quarry Dr. NG17: Kirk A 1B **60**
Quarry Gro. S81: Gate 5D **18**
Quarry Hill DE7: Stant D 1A **104**
Quarry La. NG15: Lin .7H **61**
  NG18: Mans 6G **47**
Quarry Rd. NG15: Rave 4C **62**
Quarry Yd. NG17: Sut A 1J **51**
Quartz Av. NG18: Mans 6A **48**
Quasar Elite
  Nottingham 4H **7** (3A **96**)
Quays, The NG7: Lent 7A **6** (5H **95**)
Quayside Cl. NG2: Nott 7B **96**
Queen Elizabeth Cres. S80: Rhod 1B **20**
Queen Elizabeth Rd. NG9: Chil 5F **105**
Queen Mary's Cl. NG12: Rad T 6J **99**
Queens Av. NG4: Ged 5H **87**
Queensberry St. NG6: Basf 3F **85**
Queen's Bower Rd. NG5: Bestw 6D **76**
Queens Bri. Rd. NG2: Nott 5K **95**
Queensbury Av. NG2: West Br 6K **107**
Queens Cl. NG22: East M 2D **28**
Queens Ct. DN22: Retf 4D **22**
  (off Queen St.)
  NG2: Nott 2H **107**
  NG13: Bing 3E **100**
  NG19: Mans W 6F **43**
  NG24: New T 7D **134**
Queens Dr. NG2: Nott 2H **107**
  NG9: Bee 3B **106**
  NG10: Sand 5A **104**
  NG16: Brins 6C **64**
  NG16: Nuth 1H **83**
Queen's Drive (Park & Ride) (Nottingham) 2H **107**
Queens Dr. Ind. Est. NG2: Nott 7H **95**
Queens Farm Gdns. NG24: Bald 6G **137**
Queens Gro. NG2: Nott 5K **95**
Queen's Head Ct. NG24: New T 1C **136**
Queens Rd. NG2: Nott 7G **7** (5K **95**)
  NG9: Bee 4B **106**
  NG12: Rad T 4E **98**
  NG24: New T 7C **134**
  S81: Carl L 5C **12**
Queen's Rd. E. NG9: Bee 2C **106**
Queens Rd. Nth. NG16: Eastw 4D **72**
Queens Rd. Sth. NG16: Eastw 5D **72**
Queen's Rd. W. NG9: Bee, Chil 5J **105**
Queen's Sq. NG16: Eastw 4D **72**
Queen St. DN22: Retf 3D **22**
  NG1: Nott 4E **6** (3K **95**)
  NG5: Arn 5H **77**
  NG15: Huck 5F **67**
  NG16: Lang M 3A **72**
  NG16: Pinx 1A **58**
  NG17: Kirk A 7A **52**
  NG17: Sut A 6K **45**
  NG18: Mans 3H **47**
  NG23: Coll 1H **129**
  NG24: Bald 6H **137**
  NG24: New T 2B **136**
  NG25: Sout 5G **131**
  S80: Work 3G **21**
Queens Wlk. NG2: Nott 7J **95**
  NG18: Mans *3H 47*
  (off Queen St.)
  NG20: Neth L 6B **26**
Queensway NG17: Kirk A 2B **60**
  NG19: Mans W 1C **48**
  S81: Work 1G **21**
Querneby Av. NG3: Mapp 5B **86**
Querneby Rd. NG3: Mapp 5B **86**
Quibell Rd. NG24: New T 4D **136**
Quibell's La. NG24: New T 5D **134**
Quines Hill Rd. NG19: Mans W 7D **42**
Quinton Cl. NG11: Wilf 4H **107**

. . . . .3A **148**
Quorn Cl. NG9: Atten .6K **105**
QUORNDON 3A **148**
Quorn Gro. NG5: Sher 4H **85**
Quorn Rd. NG5: Sher .4H **85**

R

Racecourse (Park & Ride) (Nottingham) 5E **96**
Racecourse Rd. NG2: Colw, Nott 4E **96**
  NG18: Mans 5A **48**
  NG25: Sout 5K **131**
Radbourne Rd. NG2: Nott 5C **96**
Radbourne St. NG19: Mans W 5A **42**
Radburn Ct. NG9: Stap 7D **92**
Radcliffe Gdns. NG4: Carl 7G **87**
Radcliffe Lodge NG12: Rad T 5D **98**
Radcliffe Mt. NG2: West Br 7C **96**
RADCLIFFE ON TRENT 5E **98** (2B **148**)
Radcliffe on Trent Golf Course 6G **99**
Radcliffe Rd. NG2: Gam, West Br 7B **96**
  NG12: Crop Bu 2A **112**
  NG12: Hol P 1G **109**
Radcliffe Station (Rail) 5E **98**
Radcliffe St. NG2: Nott 7A **96**
RADFORD 3G **95** (1A **148**)
Radford Blvd. NG7: Radf 2F **95**
Radford Bri. Rd. NG8: Aspl, Woll 2D **94**
Radford Ct. NG7: Basf 5G **85**
  (off Radford Rd.)
  NG7: Radf 3G **95**
Radford Ct. Ind. Est. NG7: Radf 3G **95**
Radford Cres. NG4: Ged 5H **87**
Radford Gro. La. NG7: Radf 2F **95**
Radford Rd. NG7: Basf, H Grn 1A **6** (5G **85**)
Radford Road Stop (NET) 7G **85**
Radford St. NG18: Mans 4H **47**
  S80: Work 4H **21**
Radham Ct. NG5: Sher 5K **85**
Radley Rd. NG22: Halam 7A **130**
  (not continuous)
Radley Sq. NG6: Bulw 2E **84**
Radley Ter. NG22: Halam 5C **130**
RADMANTHWAITE 6D **40**
Radmanthwaite La. NG19: Plea 4B **40**
Radmanthwaite Rd.
  NG19: Plea 6D **40**
Radmarsh Rd. NG7: Lent 5F **95**
Radnor Gro. NG13: Bing 4D **100**
Radnor Pl. NG19: Plea 5C **40**
Radstock Rd. NG3: Nott 1D **96**
Radway Dr. NG11: Wilf 4H **107**
Raeburn Dr. NG9: Toton 7D **104**
Rafters, The NG7: Basf 5G **85**
RAGDALE 3B **148**
Ragdale Rd. NG6: Bulw 6H **75**
  (not continuous)
Raglan Cl. NG3: Nott .1A **96**
Raglan Ct. NG9: Lent A 7B **94**
Raglan Dr. NG4: Ged .6A **88**
Raglan Gdns. NG24: New T 2D **136**
Raglan Rd. DN22: Retf 3F **23**
Raglan St. NG16: Eastw 4C **72**
RAGNALL .7G **29** (1D **147**)
Raibank Gdns. NG5: Woodt 2B **86**
Railway Cotts. NG16: Kimb 1E **82**
Raines Av. S81: Work .6F **19**
Raines Pk. Rd. S81: Work 5F **19**
Rainham Gdns. NG11: Rudd 4K **115**
RAINWORTH 2H **55** (3A **146**)
Rainworth By-Pass NG21: Rain 7F **49**
Rainworth Leisure Cen. 3H **55**
Rainworth Water Rd. NG21: Rain 2H **55**
Raithby Cl. NG5: Bestw 1H **85**
Raleigh Cl. NG11: Clif 1D **114**
Raleigh Ct. NG7: Radf 2A **6** (2H **95**)
Raleigh Pk. NG7: Lent 3E **94**
Raleigh Rd. NG19: Mans 2D **46**
Raleigh Sq. NG7: Radf 3A **6** (3H **95**)
Raleigh St. NG7: Radf 3A **6** (3H **95**)
Ralf Cl. NG2: West Br .5B **108**
Ralph Way NG5: Sher 2K **85**
Ramblers Cl. NG4: Colw 3H **97**
RAMPTON 7K **25** (1C **147**)
Rampton La. DN22: Sth L 1H **25**
Rampton Rd. DN22: Lane 1G **29**
  DN22: Tres 5J **25**
Ramsdale Av. NG14: Calv 5B **70**
Ramsdale Cres. NG5: Sher 4A **86**
Ramsdale Pk. NG5: Arn 7K **69**
Ramsdale Pk. Golf Cen. 6K **69**
Ramsdale Rd. NG4: Carl 6H **87**
Ramsden Av. S81: Lango 1B **12**
Ramsden Cres. S81: Carl L 5C **12**
Ramsden Cft. NG21: Rain 2J **55**
Ramsey Cl. NG9: Stap 6D **92**
  NG19: Mans W 7C **42**
Ramsey Rd. NG5: Sher 6J **85**
Ramsey Dr. NG5: Arn .1E **86**
RANBY 3B **144**
Ranby Wlk. NG3: Nott 2C **96**
Rancliffe Av. NG12: Key 6G **117**
Randal Gdns. NG7: H Grn 1G **95**
Randall Cl. NG24: New T 1G **137**
Randall Pk. Way DN22: Retf 1C **22**

Randall Way DN22: Retf 1C **22**
Randal St. NG7: H Grn 1F **95**
  (not continuous)
Randol Cl. NG18: Mans 6D **46**
Ranelagh Gro. NG8: Woll 3B **94**
Rani Dr. NG5: Basf 3G **85**
Ranmere Rd. NG8: Bilb 1B **94**
Ranmoor Rd. NG4: Ged 6J **87**
Ranmore Cl. NG9: Bram 6G **93**
Rannerdale Cl. NG2: West Br 3E **108**
Rannoch Dr. NG19: Mans 5D **46**
Rannoch Ri. NG5: Arn 5H **77**
Rannock Gdns. NG12: Key 7J **117**
RANSKILL 2J **13** (3B **144**)
Ranskill Gdns. NG5: Top V 6C **76**
Ranskill Rd. DN10: Matt 3F **15**
  S81: Blyth 7K **13**
Ransom Dr. NG3: Mapp, Nott 6B **86**
Ransome Cl. NG24: New T 1G **137**
Ransom Rd. NG3: Nott 6B **86**
  NG21: Rain 7F **49**
Ransom Wood Bus. Pk.
  NG18: Mans 7D **48**
  NG21: Rain 7F **49**
Ranson Rd. NG9: Chil 7G **105**
Ratcher Way NG19: Mans W 2D **48**
Ratcliffe Ga. NG18: Mans 4J **47**
Ratcliffe La. S80: Hodt 6A **20**
RATCLIFFE ON SOAR 3A **148**
Ratcliffe St. NG16: Eastw 4D **72**
Rathgar Cl. NG8: Woll 4J **93**
Rathmines Cl. NG7: Lent 5F **95**
Rathvale Ct. NG9: Chil 5F **105**
Raven Av. NG5: Sher .3J **85**
Ravencroft La. DN10: Beck 6C **16**
RAVENFIELD 2A **144**
RAVENFIELD COMMON 2A **144**
Ravenhill Cl. NG9: Chil 5G **105**
Ravens Ct. NG5: Bestw 2J **85**
Ravenscourt S81: Work 6H **19**
RAVENSDALE 3B **48**
Ravensdale Av. NG10: Long E 7A **104**
  NG18: Mans 2K **47**
Ravensdale Dr. NG8: Woll 5H **93**
Ravensdale Rd. NG18: Mans 2K **47**
Ravensdene Ct. NG3: Mapp P 7K **85**
RAVENSHEAD 2B **62** (3A **146**)
Ravenshead Leisure Cen. 4C **62**
Ravenshill Cl. DN22: Rans 2J **13**
Ravensmore Rd. NG5: Sher 5J **85**
Ravenstone Ct. NG15: Huck 3E **74**
Ravensworth Rd. NG6: Bulw 6H **75**
Rawlings Ct. NG12: Crop Bu 5C **112**
Rawson St. NG7: Basf 6G **85**
  NG16: Sels 6E **58**
Raylawn St. NG18: Mans 4C **48**
Raymede Cl. NG5: Bestw 1G **85**
Raymede Dr. NG5: Bestw 1F **85**
Raymond Cl. NG17: Kirk A 4H **51**
Raymond Dr. NG13: Bing 4H **101**
Raymond Way NG19: Mans W 1K **47**
Raymoth La. S81: Work 5E **18**
Rayner Ct. NG7: Lent .3G **95**
Raynford Av. NG9: Chil 5J **105**
Raynham Lodge NG5: Top V 5K **75**
Raysmith Av. NG25: Sout 4H **131**
Rayton Ct. DN11: Birc .2D **8**
Rayton La. S81: Work .2J **21**
Rayton Spur S81: Work 2J **21**
Read Av. NG9: Bee 3B **106**
Read Cl. NG24: Bald .7H **137**
Read Lodge NG9: Bee 3B **106**
Readman Rd. NG9: Chil 6F **105**
Rearsby Cl. NG8: Bilb .3J **93**
Rebecca Adlington Swimming Cen. 1H **47**
Recreation Rd. NG10: Sand 3A **104**
  NG15: Ann 4C **60**
  NG19: Ann H 2A **40**
Recreation St. NG16: Sels 6F **59**
  NG18: Mans 3J **47**
Recreation Ter. NG9: Stap 3C **104**
Rectors Ga. DN22: Retf 2E **22**
Rectory Av. NG8: Woll 4K **93**
Rectory Cl. LE12: Sub B 5B **120**
Rectory Ct. NG2: West Br 2C **108**
  NG13: Elton 5J **103**
Rectory Dr. LE14: Upp B 3H **143**
  NG4: Ged 5J **87**
  NG11: Wilf 1J **107**
Rectory Gdns. DN10: Beck 6C **16**
  NG8: Woll 4A **94**
  NG22: Kirt 1H **39**
Rectory La. NG17: Kirk A 7J **51**
Rectory Pl. NG11: Bart F 7A **114**
Rectory Rd. DN22: Retf 3E **22**
  DN22: Tres 5F **25**
  NG2: West Br 2B **108**
  NG4: Colw 3H **97**
  NG12: Cotg 6D **110**
  NG20: Chu W 2E **34**
Red Barn La. DE55: Newton 7A **44**
Redbarn Way NG17: Sut A 2G **51**
Redbourne Dr. NG8: Aspl 2D **94**
Redbrick Ho. Campsite NG20: Mkt W 2D **42**
Redbridge Dr. NG16: Nuth 4J **83**

Redcar Cl. NG4: Ged 5H 87
  NG18: Mans 5A 48
Redcliffe Gdns. NG3: Mapp P 7K 85
Redcliffe Rd. NG3: Mapp P 7J 85
  NG18: Mans 4K 47
Redcliffe St. NG17: Sut A 6K 45
Redcroft Cl. NG21: Edwin 6D 36
Redfield Rd. NG7: Lent 1F 107
Redfield Way NG7: Lent 7F 95
Red Flats La. DN22: Clar 7K 17
Redforde Pk. Av. DN22: Retf 1C 22
Redforde Pk. Dr. DN22: Retf 1C 22
Redforde Pk. Rd. DN22: Retf 1C 22
Redgate Cl. NG19: Mans 2E 46
Redgates Ct. NG14: Calv 6B 70
Redgate St. NG16: Pinx 2B 58
  NG19: Mans 2E 46
REDHILL 5G 77
Redhill La. DN22: Stu S 1A 24
Redhill Leisure Cen. 5G 77
Redhill Lodge Dr. NG5: Redh 5F 77
Redhill Rd. NG5: Arn 5G 77
Redholme Cl. S81: Carl L 5C 12
Red Kite Cl. NG15: Huck 5K 67
  S81: Gate 5D 18
Redland Av. NG4: Carl 7J 87
Redland Cl. NG9: Chil 5H 105
Redland Dr. NG9: Chil 6H 105
Redland Gro. NG4: Carl 7H 87
Redland Rd. NG19: Mans 2E 46
Red La. NG14: Lowd 5D 80
  NG16: Brins 5C 64
  S81: Work 2H 19
Red Lion Yd. NG15: Huck 6G 67
                 (off High St.)
Red Lodge La. NG13: East B 1K 91
Redmays Dr. NG14: Bulc 1G 89
REDMILE 2C 149
Redmile Rd. NG8: Aspl 5D 84
Red Oaks Ct. NG20: Mkt W 4C 34
Redoubt St. NG7: Radf 3F 95
Redruth Cl. NG8: Bilb 2H 93
Redruth Dr. NG18: Mans 1D 54
Redwing Cl. S81: Gate 6D 18
Redwood NG2: West Br 3J 107
Redwood Av. NG8: Woll 5J 93
Redwood Cl. NG8: Bilb 1J 93
Redwood Ct. NG7: Lent 4F 95
              (off Faraday Rd.)
  NG15: Huck 5F 67
  NG18: Mans 6K 47
           (off White Rose Av.)
Redwood Cres. NG9: Bee 4B 106
Reeders Cft. NG9: Chil 6J 105
Reedham Wlk. NG5: Bestw 6D 76
Reef Cl. NG20: Mkt W 3C 34
Rees Gdns. NG5: Top V 5C 76
Rees Row DN22: Woodbe 6G 25
Reform St. NG17: Ann W 4K 59
  NG17: Sut A 1K 51
Reform St. Ind. Est. NG17: Sut A 1K 51
             (off Reform St.)
Regal Ct. S80: Work 3J 21
Regal Dr. NG18: Mans 7J 47
Regan Way NG9: Chil 7G 105
Regatta Way NG2: West Br 1F 109
Regency Ct. NG9: Bee 2B 106
Regency Point NG2: West Br 1C 108
Regent M. NG1: Nott 4C 6 (3J 95)
Regents Cl. NG23: Coll 2J 129
Regents Pk. Cl. NG2: West Br 4K 107
Regents Pl. NG11: Wilf 3J 107
Regent St. NG1: Nott 5C 6 (4J 95)
  NG7: Basf 6H 85
  NG9: Bee 2B 106
  NG10: Sand 4B 104
  NG16: Kimb 1E 82
  NG16: Lang M 3A 72
  NG17: Kirk A 7K 51
  NG17: Sut A 1H 51
  NG18: Mans 3H 47
Regina Cl. NG12: Rad T 6D 98
Regina Cres. NG15: Rave 3B 62
Reid Gdns. NG16: Want 1G 83
Reigate Cl. NG9: Atten 7K 105
Reigate Dr. NG9: Atten 7K 105
Reigate Rd. NG7: Basf 5G 85
Reindeer St. NG18: Mans 4K 47
REMPSTONE 6F 123 (3A 148)
Rempstone Dr. NG6: Bulw 2E 84
Rempstone La. LE12: Remp 5H 123
  NG12: Remp, Wys 5H 123
Rempstone Rd. LE12: East S, Stanf S . . .4K 121
  LE12: Norm S 6H 121
Renals Way NG14: Calv 7D 70
Renfrew Ct. NG19: Mans 5E 46
Renfrew Dr. NG8: Woll 4K 93
RENISHAW .1A 146
Rennie Hogg Rd. NG2: Nott 7G 95
Repton Ct. NG19: Mans W 5A 42
Repton Dr. DE7: Ilk 1A 92
Repton Rd. NG2: West Br 4B 108
  NG6: Bulw 1E 84
Restfil Way NG24: Bald 7J 137
RETFORD 3F 23 (3C 145)
Retford & Worksop Boat Club 7J 15

Retford Ent. Cen. DN22: Retf 1C 22
Retford (Gamston) Airport DN22: Gam . . .1H 27
Retford Ga. DN22: Nth L 7A 24
Retford Golf Course 7D 22
Retford Leisure Cen. 4C 22
Retford Little Theatre 4F 23
Retford Rd. DN10: Matt . . . . . .2J 15 & 1D 14
  DN22: Nth L, Sth L . . . . .7A 24 & 1F 25
  DN22: Nth W 4F 17
            (not continuous)
  DN22: Ramp, Woodbe . . . .6F 25 & 7H 25
  NG5: Sher 4H 85
  NG22: Bou, Wale 4F 27
  NG22: Tuxf 4A 28
  S80: Work 3J 21
  S81: Blyth 6H 13
Retford Station (Rail) 5E 22
Retlaw Ct. NG9: Chil 4J 105
Revelstoke Av. NG5: Top V 5K 75
Revelstoke Way NG5: Top V 5K 75
Revena Cl. NG4: Colw 2H 97
Revesby Gdns. NG8: Aspl 1D 94
Revesby Rd. NG5: Woodt 2C 86
Revill Ct. NG17: Kirk A 4J 51
Revill Cres. NG9: Stap 1E 104
Reydon Dr. NG8: Basf 6E 84
Reynolds Dr. NG8: Woll 3A 94
RHODESIA 7B 18 (3A 144)
Rhodes Wlk. NG18: Mans 4E 46
Rhodes Way NG6: Bestw V 7D 68
Rhyl Cres. NG4: Ged 5J 87
Ribbledale Cl. NG18: Mans 5C 48
Ribblesdale S81: Work 5H 19
Ribblesdale Ct. NG9: Chil 5F 105
Ribblesdale Rd. NG5: Sher 2K 85
Riber Cl. NG17: Nunc 3A 60
Riber Cres. NG5: Bestw 2G 85
Rice Hill NG22: Kirt 7J 27
Richard Herrod Cen. 7F 87
Richards Cl. NG12: Crop Bi 6B 112
Richardson Cl. NG11: Clif 1D 114
Richard St. DN22: Retf 5G 23
Richborough Pl. NG8: Woll 6J 93
Richey Cl. NG5: Arn 7K 77
Richmond Av. NG3: Nott 1C 96
  NG10: Sand 5A 104
  NG14: Calv 5E 70
  NG16: Newth 4F 73
Richmond Cl. NG24: New B 5E 136
Richmond Ct. NG9: Chil 4K 105
Richmond Dr. NG3: Mapp P 5A 86
  NG9: Chil 4K 105
  NG12: Rad T 4E 98
  NG19: Mans W 7K 41
Richmond Gdns. NG5: Redh 5G 77
Richmond Rd. DN22: Retf 1G 23
  NG2: West Br 7C 96
  NG17: Kirk A 6D 52
  S80: Work 4H 21
  S81: Carl L 6C 12
Richmond St. NG18: Mans 4B 48
Richmond Ter. NG12: Rad T 5E 98
Ricket La. NG21: Blid 7A 54
Ricklow Ct. NG5: Top V 6C 76
            (off Gautries Cl.)
Rick St. NG1: Nott 4G 7 (3A 96)
Riddel Av. S81: Lango 1B 12
Riddings, The NG4: Neth 1K 97
            (off Morris St.)
  NG25: Sout 5F 131
Ridding Ter. NG3: Nott 2F 7 (2K 95)
Riddles Cl. NG16: Want 6A 74
Ridge Cl. NG17: Sut A 7H 45
Ridge Hill NG14: Lowd 4D 80
Ridge La. NG12: Rad T 3F 99
Ridgeway NG5: Top V 7A 76
  NG25: Sout 4G 131
  S81: Work 6H 19
Ridgeway, The NG22: Farns 5K 57
Ridgeway Cl. NG22: Farns 5K 57
Ridgeway La. NG20: Mkt W 5D 34
Ridgeway Ter. NG20: Mkt W 4D 34
Ridgeway Wlk. NG5: Top V 6C 76
Ridgewood Dr. NG12: Key 5H 105
Ridgewood Gro. NG15: Rave 2C 62
Ridgmont Wlk. NG11: Clif 2E 114
Ridgway Cl. NG2: West Br 4F 109
Ridgway St.
  NG3: Nott 1K 7 (2B 96)
Ridings, The NG12: Key 7K 117
  NG14: Bulc 2F 89
  NG19: Mans W 1B 48
Ridsdale Rd. NG5: Sher 2K 85
Rifle St. NG7: Radf 3F 95
Rigg La. NG5: Arn 5G 63
  NG15: Rave 5G 63
  NG21: Blid 5G 63
Rigley Dr. NG5: Top V 7A 76
Riley Av. NG17: Sut A 7G 45
Riley Cl. NG17: Sut A 7G 45
RINGING HILL 3A 148
Ring Leas NG12: Cotg 7E 110
Ringrose Cl. NG24: New T 1G 137
Ringstead Cl. NG2: West Br 4K 107
Ringstead Wlk. NG5: Bestw 6D 76
Ringwood S81: Work 6H 19

Ringwood Av. NG18: Mans 6J 47
Ringwood Cres. NG8: Woll 3D 94
Ringwood Rd. NG13: Bing 4D 100
Rio Dr. NG23: Coll 1H 129
Ripon Rd. NG3: Nott 3E 96
Rise, The NG5: Sher 4A 86
Riseborough Wlk. NG6: Bulw 5H 75
            (not continuous)
Rise Ct. NG5: Sher 7J 85
Risegate NG12: Cotg 6E 110
Risegate Gdns. NG12: Cotg 6E 110
RISE HILL 3A 60
Riseholme Av. NG8: Woll 5H 93
RISE PARK .5A 76
Rise Pk. Rd. NG5: Top V 5K 75
Rise Pk. Shop. Cen. NG5: Top V 5A 76
RISLEY 2A 148
Risley Dr. NG2: Nott 6J 95
Riste's Pl. NG1: Nott 5G 7 (4A 96)
Ritchie Cl. NG12: Cotg 7F 111
Ritson Cl. NG3: Nott 2H 7 (2A 96)
Riva Bingo
  Newark-on-Trent 1C 136
       (within Castlegate Cen.)
Riveraine Cl. NG17: Sut A 1B 52
River Cl. DN22: Retf 1F 23
River Cres. NG2: Nott 6D 96
Riverdale Pk. NG4: Gun 3B 90
Riverdale Rd. NG9: Chil 7J 105
Rivergreen NG11: Clif 6F 107
Rivergreen Cl. NG9: Bram 6H 93
Rivergreen Cres. NG9: Bram 6H 93
Riverlands Cl. NG14: Gun 2B 90
River La. DN10: Miss 3D 10
  DN22: Retf 3E 22
River Maun Recreation Cen. 2A 48
Rivermead NG22: West Br 2A 108
  NG12: Cotg 6E 110
  NG24: New T 3B 136
River Rd. NG4: Colw 4H 97
Riverside NG13: What 4E 102
  NG14: Stoke B 7E 88
  NG25: Sout 5J 131
Riverside Caravan Pk.
  S80: Work 2F 21
Riverside Cl. NG9: Bee 6C 106
  NG20: Cuck 4C 32
Riverside Fishery 2H 9
Riverside Golf Course 3G 107
Riverside Pk. NG24: New T 1A 136
Riverside Point NG7: Lent 5F 95
Riverside Retail Pk. NG2: Nott 1H 107
Riverside Rd. NG9: Bee 6B 106
  NG24: New T 4A 136
Riverside Wlk. DN22: Retf 3E 22
Riverside Way NG2: Nott 7J 95
  NG19: Mans W 4K 41
River Vw. DN22: Ord 7E 22
  NG2: Nott 7A 96
  NG20: Mkt W 3D 34
  NG24: New T 6D 134
Riverview DN22: Chu L 1J 29
Riverway Gdns. NG2: Nott 6A 96
Rivington Rd. NG9: Toton 7D 104
Roadways, The S80: Work 2F 21
Roadwood La. NG23: Thor 1F 31
Robbie Burns Rd. NG5: Bestw 6E 76
Robbinetts La. NG8: Stre 6E 82
  NG16: Babb, Coss 6C 82
            (not continuous)
Robert Av. NG18: Mans 5F 47
Robert Dukeson Av. NG24: New T 4D 134
           (not continuous)
Roberts Av. NG17: Huth 1D 50
Roberts Cl. NG22: Ragn 7G 29
Roberts La. NG15: Huck 6F 67
Roberts St. DE7: Ilk 2A 92
  NG2: Nott 5K 7 (4B 96)
Roberts Yd. NG9: Bee 2B 106
Robert Wilkinson Smith Homes
  NG3: Mapp P 1K 95
Robey Cl. NG15: Lin 4H 67
  NG19: Mans W 1D 48
Robey Dr. NG16: Eastw 3D 72
Robey Ter. NG7: H Grn 1G 95
Robina Dr. NG16: Gilt 6G 73
Robin Bailey Way NG15: Huck 7J 67
Robin Down Cl. NG18: Mans 1K 53
Robin Down Ct. NG17: Kirk A 1A 60
Robin Down La. NG18: Mans 1J 53
Robinet Rd. NG9: Bee 4A 106
Robin Gro. NG15: Rave 3C 62
ROBIN HOOD AIRPORT DONCASTER SHEFFIELD
                    .2B 144
Robin Hood Av. NG20: Mkt W 6D 34
  NG21: Edwin 7J 37
Robin Hood Chase NG3: Nott 1H 7 (1A 96)
Robin Hood Cl. NG16: Eastw 5D 72
Robin Hood Dr. NG15: Huck 7J 67
Robin Hood Ind. Est. NG3: Nott 3J 7 (3B 96)
Robin Hood Rd. NG5: Arn 5E 76
  NG17: Ann W 4B 60
  NG21: Blid 6K 55
Robin Hood Statue 6D 6
Robin Hood St. NG3: Nott 4J 7 (3B 96)

Robin Hood Ter.—Rufford St.

Robin Hood Ter. NG3: Nott 3H 7 (3A 96)
NG15: Rave 1D 62
Robin Hood Theatre 4G 133
Robin Hood Wlk. NG24: New T 1C 136
Robin Hood Way NG2: Nott 7J 95
Robinia Ct. NG2: West Br 4D 108
Robins Ct. NG24: New T 1D 136
Robinson Cl. *DN22: Elk* *2G 27*
(off High St.)
NG24: New T 1H 137
Robinson Ct. NG9: Chil 7G 105
Robinson Dr. S80: Work 4F 21
Robinson Gdns. NG11: Clif 1D 114
Robinson Rd. NG3: Mapp 4C 86
Robinsons Hill NG6: Bulw 7H 75
Robin's Row *NG15: Huck* *1E 74*
(off Knoll Av.)
Robins Wood House 1C 94
Robins Wood Rd. NG8: Aspl 2C 94
Rob Roy Av. NG7: Lent 5G 95
Rochdale Ct. NG18: Mans 5C 48
Roche Cl. NG5: Arn 7A 78
Rochester Av. NG4: Neth 1K 97
Rochester Cl. S81: Work 5H 19
Rochester Ct. NG6: Bulw 1A 84
Rochester Rd. NG21: Rain 3J 55
Rochester Wlk. NG11: Clif 1G 115
Rochford Ct. NG12: Edwal 6F 109
Rock City 4D 6
Rock Ct. NG6: Basf 4E 84
NG18: Mans 3J 47
Rock Dr. NG7: Nott 7B 6 (5H 95)
Rocket Cl. NG16: Want 7A 74
Rockfield Dr. S81: Woods 1A 18
Rockford Ct. NG9: Stap 7D 92
Rockford Rd. NG5: Sher 4G 85
Rock Hill NG18: Mans 4K 47
Rock Hill Gdns. NG18: Mans 4K 47
Rockingham Gro. NG13: Bing 4D 100
Rockings Vw. NG21: Blid 6J 55
Rock La. DN10: Eve 7C 10
Rockley Av. NG12: Rad T 4E 98
NG16: Newth 5E 72
Rockley Cl. NG15: Huck 7C 66
NG21: C'tone 5H 43
Rockleys Vw. NG14: Lowd 4A 80
Rocks, The NG20: Wars 3A 34
Rock Side *NG16: Kimb* *1E 82*
(off Edgwood Rd.)
Rockside Gdns. NG15: Huck 6E 66
Rockstone Way NG19: Mans W 7H 41
Rock St. NG6: Bulw 6G 75
NG18: Mans 4K 47
Rock Ter. NG21: Blid 7G 55
Rock Valley NG18: Mans 3J 47
(not continuous)
Rockwell Ct. NG9: Stap 2D 104
Rockwood Cres. NG15: Huck 7D 66
Rockwood Wlk. NG15: Huck 7E 66
Rodel Ct. NG3: Nott 2G 7 (2A 96)
Roden St. NG3: Nott 4J 7 (3B 96)
Roderick Av. NG17: Nunc 3B 60
Roderick St. NG6: Basf 3E 84
Rodery, The NG18: Mans 5A 48
Rodice Ct. NG7: Lent 3F 95
Rodney Rd. NG2: West Br 3D 108
Rodwell Cl. NG8: Aspl 2D 94
Roebuck Cl. NG5: Arn 6D 76
Roebuck Dr. NG18: Mans 7H 47
Roecliffe NG2: West Br 5B 108
Roe Gdns. NG11: Rudd 3J 115
Roehampton Dr. NG9: Trow 6C 92
Roe Hill NG14: Woodbo 7G 71
Roe La. DN10: Eve 6B 10
NG14: Woodbo 2G 79
Roes La. NG14: Calv 6E 70
Roewood Cl. NG17: Kirk A 4K 51
Roger Cl. NG17: Skeg 5K 45
Roker Cl. NG8: Aspl 6B 84
Rolaine Cl. NG19: Mans W 5J 41
Roland Av. NG11: Wilf 2J 107
NG16: Nuth 3K 83
ROLLESTON 3K 139 (3C 147)
Rolleston Cl. NG15: Huck 1D 74
Rolleston Cres. NG16: Want 5K 73
Rolleston Dr. NG5: Arn 7J 77
NG7: Lent 7A 6 (4G 95)
NG16: Newth 6E 72
Rolleston Rd. NG25: Fis 6J 139
Rolleston Station (Rail) 3J 139
Roman Bank NG19: Mans W 6K 41
Roman Bank La. DN10: Serl 7H 9
DN22: Rans 6K 13
S81: Blyth 6K 13
Roman Cres. NG15: Huck 5K 67
Roman Dr. NG6: Basf 3F 85
Roman Rd. S81: Work 5E 18
Romans Ct. NG6: Basf 5F 85
Romilay Cl. NG9: Lent A 7B 94
Romney Av. NG8: Woll 6J 93
Romsey Pl. NG19: Mans 4D 46
Rona Cl. NG19: Mans 5E 46
Rona Ct. NG6: Bulw 2F 85
Ronald St. NG7: Radf 4A 6 (3G 95)
Ronchin Gdns. NG17: Kirk A 7A 52
Roods Cl. NG17: Sut A 3H 51
Rookery, The NG18: Mans 2G 47
NG23: Coll 1H 129
Rookery Farm NG12: Crop Bu 3C 112
Rookery Gdns. NG5: Arn 6H 77
Rookery La. NG17: Sut A 3E 50
Rook's La. DN10: Mist 1G 11
Rookwood Cl. NG9: Bee 3K 105
NG21: Blid 6J 55
Rooley Av. NG17: Sut A 7G 45
Rooley Dr. NG17: Sut A 7G 45
Rooley La. NG17: Huth, Sut A 7E 44
Roosa Cl. NG6: Bulw 2A 84
Roosevelt Rd. NG17: Sut A 6B 46
Rooth St. NG18: Mans 4H 47
Ropewalk LE12: East L 3K 121
Ropewalk, The NG1: Nott 4B 6 (3H 95)
NG24: New T 1E 136
NG25: Sout 5G 131
Ropewalk Ct. NG1: Nott 4C 6 (3J 95)
Ropeway, The NG17: Kirk A 6J 51
Ropsley Cres. NG2: West Br 7D 96
Rosa Ct. NG4: Ged 6K 87
Roscoe Av. NG5: Redh 4G 77
Roseacre NG9: Bee 4B 106
Rose Ash La. NG5: Bestw 6D 76
Rose Av. DN22: Retf 6G 23
Rosebank Dr. NG5: Arn 5K 77
Rosebay Av. NG7: H Grn 7F 85
Roseberry Gdns. NG15: Huck 7J 67
Roseberry St. NG17: Kirk A 7B 52
Rosebery Av. NG2: West Br 7B 96
Rosebery Cl. S80: Work 2F 21
Rosebery Hill NG18: Mans 4J 47
Rosebery St. NG6: Basf 3F 85
Rose Bowl Gdns. DN22: Ord 6E 22
Rose Cl. NG3: Nott 1A 96
Rose Cott. Dr. NG17: Huth 1D 50
Rose Cotts. NG14: Bur J 2D 88
Rosecroft Dr. NG5: Bestw 1K 85
Rosedale S81: Work 4H 19
Rosedale Dr. NG8: Woll 4G 93
Rosedale Gdns. NG17: Sut A 3H 51
Rosedale La. NG15: Rave 1B 62
Rosedale Rd. NG3: Nott 2F 97
Rosedale Way NG19: Mans W 7B 42
Rose Farm Dr. NG23: Sut T 3D 128
Rosefield Cl. NG24: Bald 7J 137
Rosefinch Way
NG19: Mans W 7B 42
Rose Flower Gro. NG15: Huck 2J 75
Rose Gdns. DN22: Retf 2D 22
S80: Work 3F 21
Rosegarth Wlk. NG6: Basf 3E 84
Rose Gro. NG9: Bee 4C 106
NG12: Key 6J 117
Rosegrove Av. NG5: Arn 5H 77
Rose Hill NG12: Key 7H 117
Roseland Cl. NG12: Key 1H 119
Rose La. NG19: Mans W 5J 41
Rose Lea DN22: Ord 6D 22
Roseleigh Av. NG3: Mapp 5E 86
Rosemary Av. NG19: Mans 2G 47
Rosemary Cen. NG18: Mans 3G 47
Rosemary Cl. NG8: Brox 6K 83
ROSEMARYHILL 5D 58
Rosemary St. NG18: Mans 3G 47
NG19: Mans 2G 47
Rose M. NG3: Nott 1A 96
Rosemont Cl. NG17: Skeg 4J 45
Roseneath Av. NG5: Top V 5A 76
Rosetta Rd. NG7: Basf 6G 85
(not continuous)
Rosewall Ct. NG5: Arn 7K 77
Rosewood Cl. NG24: New T 6E 134
S81: Gate 3E 18
Rosewood Dr. NG17: Kirk A 5C 52
Rosewood Gdns. NG2: West Br 6K 107
NG6: Bulw 7F 75
Rosings Ct. NG17: Sut A 2J 51
Roslyn Av. NG4: Ged 5H 87
Roslyn Ct. NG14: Bur J 2E 88
Ross Cl. NG14: Lowd 5E 80
Rossell Dr. NG9: Stap 4D 104
Rossett Cl. NG2: Gam 3G 109
Rossetti Gdns. S81: Work 2K 21
ROSSINGTON 2B 144
Rossington Rd. NG2: Nott 3C 96
Ross La. NG4: Lamb 7G 79
Rosslyn Dr. NG8: Aspl 5B 84
NG15: Huck 5J 67
ROSTHOLME 1A 144
Rosthwaite Cl. NG2: West Br 4F 109
Roston Cl. NG18: Mans 5D 48
Roston Ct. NG18: Mans 5D 48
Rothbury Av. NG9: Trow 6C 92
Rothbury Gro. NG13: Bing 3D 100
ROTHERBY 3B 148
ROTHERHAM 2A 144
Rotherham Baulk S81: Carl L 5A 12
Rotherham Rd. NG19: New H, Stony H 1A 40
Rothesay Av. NG7: Lent 3G 95
Rothley Av. NG3: Nott 3C 96
Rothwell Cl. NG11: Wilf 5H 107
Rotunda, The DN10: Beck 7D 16
Roughs Wood La. NG15: Huck 2D 74
Roulstone Cres. LE12: East L 1A 122
Roundhead Building, The
NG24: New T *6D 134*
(off North Gate)
ROUND HILL 2C 52
Roundhill Cl. NG17: Sut A 2C 52
Roundhouse Cres. S81: Work 5E 18
Roundwood Rd. NG5: Arn 7E 76
Row, The NG13: Elton 6J 103
NG13: Ors 2J 103
Rowan Av. NG9: Stap 6D 92
NG15: Rave 3C 62
Rowan Cl. NG13: Bing 4H 101
NG14: Calv 6B 70
NG17: Kirk A 6J 51
NG19: Mans W 1K 47
Rowan Ct. NG15: Huck 5J 67
NG16: Nuth 1G 83
Rowan Cres. S80: Work 4F 21
Rowan Cft. NG17: Huth 6D 44
Rowan Dr. NG11: Wilf 5H 107
NG12: Key 1K 119
NG16: Sels 5B 58
NG17: Kirk A 5K 51
Rowan Gdns. NG6: Bulw 7F 75
Rowans Cres. NG6: Cin 3C 84
Rowan Wlk. NG3: Nott 7D 86
Rowan Way NG24: New B 4E 136
Rowe Gdns. NG6: Bulw 1E 84
Rowland Av. NG3: Mapp 5D 86
Rowland M. NG3: Nott 1B 96
Rowley Ct. NG5: Sher 5H 85
Rowley Dr. NG5: Sher 5H 85
Rowsley Ct. NG17: Sut A 2F 51
ROWTHORNE 2A 146
Roxburgh Cl. NG5: Arn 6A 78
Roxby Ho. NG5: Arn 1D 86
Roxley Ct. NG9: Bee 2K 105
Roxton Ct. NG16: Kimb 7K 73
Royal Albert Ct. NG7: Radf 2A 6
Royal Av. NG10: Long E 7C 104
Royal Cen. NG1: Nott 4E 6
Royal Centre Stop (NET) 4E 6 (3J 95)
Royal Concert Hall 4E 6 (3K 95)
Royal Ct. *NG5: Sher* *5K 85*
(off Haydn Rd.)
S80: Work *3G 21*
(off Newcastle St.)
Royal Cres. S81: Work 6F 19
Royal Exchange Shop. Cen.
NG24: New T *1C 136*
(off Middle Ga.)
Royal M. NG9: Chil 6H 105
Royal Oak Ct. NG21: Edwin 6F 37
Royal Oak Dr. NG16: Sels 5F 59
Royal Standard Ho. NG1: Nott 6D 6 (4J 95)
Royal Standard Pl. NG1: Nott 6D 6
Royal Victoria Ct. NG7: Radf 2A 6 (2H 95)
Roy Av. NG9: Bee 5C 106
Royce Av. NG15: Huck 2E 74
Royds Cres. S80: Rhod 7B 18
Royston Cl. NG2: Nott 7J 95
Royston Ct. NG4: Carl 7F 87
Ruby Gdns. NG17: Kirk A 7D 52
Ruby Gro. NG21: Rain 2A 56
Ruby Paddocks NG16: Kimb 2E 82
Ruby's Av. NG24: Bald 7H 137
Ruby's Wlk. NG24: Bald 7H 137
Ruby Way NG18: Mans 5K 47
RUDDINGTON 3K 115 (2A 148)
Ruddington Ct. NG18: Mans 1C 54
Ruddington Flds. Bus. Pk. NG11: Rudd 5A 116
Ruddington Framework Knitters Mus. 4K 115
Ruddington Grange Golf Course 7K 107
Ruddington La. NG11: Wilf 3J 107
Ruddington Pl. *NG18: Mans* *1C 54*
(off Bellamy Rd.)
Ruddington Rd. NG18: Mans 1C 54
Ruddington Station
Great Central Railway 5K 115
Ruddington Village Mus. 3K 115
Rudge Cl. NG8: Woll 3A 94
Rue De L'yonne NG23: Coll 1H 129
Ruffles Av. NG5: Arn 2E 86
Rufford Abbey Country Pk. 2B 146
Rufford Abbey (remains of) 2B 146
Rufford Av. DN22: Ord 7D 22
NG4: Ged 5G 87
NG9: Bram 1F 105
NG18: Mans 3J 47
NG20: Mede V 6G 33
NG21: Rain 2K 55
NG22: New O 4C 38
NG24: New T 2C 136
Rufford Cl. NG15: Huck 7J 67
NG17: Skeg 5K 45
NG22: Bils 7D 126
Rufford Colliery La. NG21: Rain 2J 55
Rufford Ct. NG21: Rain 2A 56
Rufford Dr. NG19: Mans W 6A 42
Rufford Gro. NG13: Bing 4E 100
Rufford Hall NG2: Nott 6D 96
Rufford La. NG22: Ruff, Well 7A 38
Rufford Rd. NG5: Sher 4K 85
NG11: Rudd 3A 116
NG21: Edwin 7F 37
Rufford St. S80: Work 5J 21

Rufford Wlk. NG6: Bulw 7H **75**
   NG11: Rudd .3A **116**
Rufford Way NG2: West Br 3E **108**
RUFFS 1E **74**
Ruffs Dr. NG15: Huck 1E **74**
Rugby Cl. NG5: Top V 7A **76**
Rugby Ct. NG2: West Br 4B **108**
Rugby Rd. NG2: West Br 4K **107**
   NG21: Rain 3J **55**
Rugby Ter. NG7: H Grn 1G **95**
Rugged Butts La. DN10: Miss 1B **10**
Ruislip Cl. NG16: Kimb 7J **73**
Runcie Cl. NG12: Cotg 7E **110**
Runnymede Ct. NG7: Radf 3B **6** (3H **95**)
   NG9: Bee 4B **106**
                 (off Grove St.)
Runswick Dr. NG5: Arn 6H **77**
   NG8: Woll 3B **94**
Runton Dr. NG8: Basf 3G **85**
Rupert Cres. NG24: New T 2C **136**
Rupert Rd. NG13: Bing 4E **100**
Ruscombe Pl. NG3: Nott 1H **7** (2A **96**)
Rushcliffe Arena .3A **108**
Rushcliffe Av. NG4: Carl 7G **87**
   NG12: Rad T 5E **98**
Rushcliffe Country Pk. 5K **115**
Rushcliffe Ct. NG6: Bulw 1E **84**
Rushcliffe Golf Course 1K **121**
Rushcliffe Gro. LE12: East L 1A **122**
Rushcliffe Halt Station
   Great Central Railway 1A **122**
Rushcliffe Leisure Cen. 5C **108**
Rushcliffe Ri. NG5: Sher 2A **86**
Rushcliffe Rd. NG15: Huck 1E **74**
Rushes, The NG11: Goth 7G **115**
   NG19: Mans W 4K **41**
Rushes Cl. NG9: Bee 3B **106**
Rushey Cl. S80: Work 3J **21**
Rushford Dr. NG8: Woll 4H **93**
Rushley Vw. NG17: Sut A 2G **51**
Rushmere Wlk. NG5: Woodt 2C **86**
Rushpool Av. NG19: Mans W 5K **41**
Rushpool Cl. NG19: Mans W 7B **42**
Rushton Gdns. NG3: Nott 1K **7** (1B **96**)
Rushworth Av. NG2: West Br 1B **108**
Rushworth Cl. NG3: Nott 1J **7** (1B **96**)
Rushworth Ct. NG2: West Br 1B **108**
Rushy Cl. NG8: Bilb 3J **93**
Ruskin Av. NG9: Chil 5J **105**
Ruskin Cl. NG5: Arn 7F **77**
Ruskin Rd. NG19: Mans 7D **40**
Ruskin St. NG7: Radf 3F **95**
Russell Av. DN11: Harwo 2C **8**
   NG8: Woll 3A **94**
   NG24: New B 5E **136**
Russell Cres. NG8: Woll 3A **94**
Russell Dr. NG8: Woll 3K **93**
Russell Farm Cl. NG12: Toll 1G **117**
Russell Gdns. NG9: Chil 7H **105**
Russell Pl. NG1: Nott 4D **6** (3J **95**)
Russell Rd. NG7: H Grn 7G **85**
Russell St. NG7: Radf 2A **6** (2H **95**)
                (not continuous)
   NG17: Sut A 7K **45**
Russet Av. NG4: Carl 1H **97**
Russet Cl. NG14: Lowd 5E **80**
Russley Rd. NG9: Bram 1F **105**
Ruth Dr. NG5: Arn .5J **77**
Rutherford Av. NG18: Mans 5A **48**
Rutherford Ho. NG7: Nott 7E **94**
Ruthwell Gdns. NG5: Top V 4C **76**
Rutland NG17: Kirk A 5D **52**
Rutland Av. NG9: Toton 7F **105**
   NG24: New T 3D **136**
Rutland Cl. NG20: Mkt W 4C **34**
Rutland Cres. DN11: Harwo 1C **8**
Rutland Dr. DN11: Harwo 1C **8**
Rutland Gro. NG10: Sand 4B **104**
Rutland Rd. DN22: Retf 6H **23**
   NG2: West Br 7C **96**
   NG4: Ged 4G **87**
   NG13: Bing 4G **101**
   NG16: Westw 6A **64**
Rutlands, The NG23: Kel 1H **133**
Rutland St. NG1: Nott 6D **6** (4J **95**)
   NG18: Mans 5H **47**
Rutland Vs. NG2: Nott 4C **96**
Ryan Way NG9: Bee 6B **106**
Rydal Av. NG10: Long E 7A **104**
Rydal Dr. NG9: Bram 1J **105**
   NG15: Huck 5F **67**
   S81: Work .4F **19**
Rydale Rd. NG5: Sher 2K **85**
Rydal Gdns. NG2: West Br 4D **108**
Rydal Gro. NG6: Basf 4F **85**
Ryder St. NG6: Basf 3E **84**
Ryecroft NG19: Mans W 7D **42**
Ryecroft St. NG9: Stap 7D **92**
Ryedale Av. NG18: Mans 5C **48**
Ryehill Cl. NG2: Nott 6A **96**
Ryehill St. NG2: Nott 6A **96**
Ryeholme Cl. LE12: East L 1B **122**
Ryeland Gdns. NG2: Nott 6K **95**
Ryemere Cl. NG16: Eastw 4C **72**
Ryemere Ct. NG16: Eastw 4C **72**
             (off Bailey Gro. Rd.)

Rye St. NG7: Basf .6G **85**
Ryknield Rd. NG15: Huck 5J **67**
RYLANDS 4C **106** (2A **148**)
Rylands Cl. NG9: Bee 5C **106**
Rylands Ct. NG9: Bee 4B **106**
Ryton Cl. S81: Blyth 7H **13**
Ryton Ct. NG2: Nott 7A **96**
Ryton Flds. S81: Blyth 7H **13**
Ryton Pl. S80: Work 2G **21**
Ryton Sq. NG8: Aspl 6C **84**
Ryton St. S80: Work 2G **21**

S

Sacheverall Av. NG16: Pinx 1A **58**
Saco Ho. NG11: Nott 5C **6** (4J **95**)
Saddlers Cl. NG19: Mans W 1B **48**
Saddlers Courtyard DN10: Bawt 1K **9**
               (off South Pde.)
Saddlers Ga. NG12: Rad T 5E **98**
Saddlers Yd. NG12: Plum 3H **117**
Saddleworth Ct. NG3: Nott 1F **7** (1K **95**)
Sadler St. NG19: Mans 2F **47**
Saffron Gdns. NG2: Nott 6J **95**
Saffron St. NG19: Mans W 1B **48**
St Agnes Cl. NG8: Bilb 7J **83**
St Aidans Ct. NG6: Basf 3F **85**
St Albans M. NG6: Bulw 1E **84**
St Albans Rd. NG5: Arn 7F **77**
   NG6: Bestw V 2A **76**
   NG6: Bulw .6J **75**
St Albans St. NG5: Sher 4K **85**
St Andrew Cl. NG11: Goth 7G **115**
St Andrew Cl. NG6: Bulw 7J **75**
   NG15: Huck 5F **67**
St Andrews Ct. NG6: Bulw 7K **75**
St Andrews Cres. NG17: Skeg 4K **45**
St Andrews Ho. NG3: Mapp 4F **87**
St Andrew's Rd. NG3: Mapp P 1J **95**
St Andrews St. NG17: Kirk A 5B **52**
   NG17: Skeg 4J **45**
St Andrew St. NG18: Mans 5J **47**
St Andrews Way DN22: Ord 7E **22**
St Annes Cl. S80: Work 2D **20**
St Annes Dr. S80: Work 3C **20**
St Anne's La. LE12: Sut B 6B **120**
St Annes M. S80: Work 2D **20**
             (off St Annes Way)
St Annes Vw. S80: Work 2D **20**
St Annes Way S80: Work 2D **20**
ST ANN'S 1J **7** (2A **96**)
St Ann's Gdns. NG3: Nott 1B **96**
St Ann's Hill NG3: Nott 1K **95**
St Ann's Hill Rd. NG3: Nott 1E **6** (1K **95**)
St Ann's St. NG1: Nott 3F **7** (3K **95**)
St Ann's Valley NG3: Nott 1J **7** (2B **96**)
St Ann's Way NG3: Nott 1E **6** (2K **95**)
St Ann's Well Rd. NG3: Nott 3G **7** (3A **96**)
St Anthony Ct. NG7: Lent 6F **95**
St Augustines Cl. NG7: Basf 6H **85**
   NG24: New T 2E **136**
             (off Newton St.)
St Austell Dr. NG11: Wilf 4J **107**
St Austins Ct. NG4: Carl 7J **87**
St Austins Dr. NG4: Carl 7J **87**
St Barnabas' RC Cathedral 4C **6** (4J **95**)
St Bartholomews Ct. DN22: Sut L 6B **14**
   NG3: Nott .1C **96**
St Bartholomew's Rd. NG3: Nott 1C **96**
St Catherines Cl. NG24: New T 2B **136**
St Catherines Ct. NG12: Rad T 6D **98**
St Catherine St. NG18: Mans 5J **47**
St Cecilia Gdns. NG3: Nott 1G **7** (2A **96**)
St Chads NG4: Carl 1J **97**
St Chads Ct. NG18: Mans 7J **47**
St Chad's Rd. NG3: Nott 4K **7** (3B **96**)
St Christopher St. NG2: Nott 4C **96**
St Clare's Ga. NG24: New T 3D **136**
St Cuthbert's Rd. NG3: Nott 3K **7** (3B **96**)
St Cuthbert St. S80: Work 3G **21**
St David's Cl. S81: Work 6H **19**
St Edmund's Av. NG19: Mans W 6J **41**
St Edwin's Dr. NG21: Edwin 6E **36**
St Emmanuel Vw. NG5: Arn 5D **76**
St Ervan Rd. NG11: Wilf 3J **107**
St George's Ct. NG24: New T 7D **134**
St Georges Dr. NG2: Nott 6K **95**
   NG9: Toton 7E **104**
St Giles Cl. DN22: Retf 2C **22**
St Giles Way NG12: Crop Bi 5B **112**
   NG24: Bald 5H **137**
St Helens Av. NG16: Pinx 7A **50**
St Helens Cres. NG9: Trow 4B **92**
   NG14: Bur J 3E **88**
St Helen's Dr. NG16: Sels 5B **58**
St Helen's Gro. NG14: Bur J 4D **88**
St Helen's La. NG22: Halam 4B **130**
St Helens Ri. DN22: Sth W 2K **17**
St Helens Rd. DN22: Retf 6H **23**
   NG2: West Br 3C **108**
St Helen's St. NG7: Nott 4B **6** (3H **95**)
St Helier NG12: Toton 6B **6** (4H **95**)
St James Av. DE7: Ilk 1A **92**
St James Ct. NG3: Mapp 5E **86**
   NG10: Sand 6A **104**

St James Dr. NG16: Brins 5B **64**
St James Gdns. NG19: Mans W 3A **42**
St James's St. NG1: Nott 6D **6** (4J **95**)
St James's Ter. NG1: Nott 6D **6** (4J **95**)
St James St. NG9: Stap 3B **104**
St James Ter. NG9: Stap 3B **104**
St John M. DN22: Retf 3F **23**
              (off St John St.)
St Johns S81: Blyth 7H **13**
St John's Av. NG17: Kirk A 7B **52**
St John's Cl. NG16: Brins 4B **64**
St John's Ct. NG4: Carl 1G **97**
   S80: Work .2G **21**
St John's Cres. NG15: Huck 1J **75**
St John's Dr. DN22: Clar 7H **17**
St John's Pl. NG18: Mans 3G **47**
St John's Rd. NG11: Rudd 3K **115**
St John St. DN22: Retf 3F **23**
   NG18: Mans 3G **47**
St John's Vw. NG18: Mans 3G **47**
St Jude's Av. NG3: Mapp 5A **86**
St Judes Way NG21: Rain 2J **55**
St Lawrence Blvd. NG12: Rad T 6C **98**
St Lawrence Cl. NG11: Goth 7G **115**
St Leonard's Ct. NG24: New T 7C **134**
              (off Kirk Ga.)
St Leonard's Dr. NG8: Woll 4A **94**
St Leonards Way NG19: Mans W 1D **48**
St Leven Cl. NG8: Bilb 7J **83**
St Lukes Cl. NG2: West Br 4E **108**
St Luke's St. NG3: Nott 4J **7** (3B **96**)
St Lukes Vw. S81: Shire 5A **18**
St Lukes Way NG15: Woodbe 7F **25**
   NG14: Stoke B 7E **88**
St Margaret's Av. NG8: Aspl 7D **84**
St Margaret's Cl. NG22: Bils 7D **126**
St Margaret St. NG18: Mans 5J **47**
St Mark's Cl. S81: Gate 4E **18**
St Marks Ct. NG17: Sut A 3F **51**
St Mark's La. NG24: New T 1C **136**
             (not continuous)
St Mark's Pl. NG24: New T 1C **136**
St Mark's St. NG3: Nott 3G **7** (3A **96**)
St Martins Cl. DN22: Nth L 6B **24**
   NG8: Stre .7K **83**
   S81: Blyth .7H **13**
St Martins Gdns. NG8: Stre 7J **83**
St Martins Rd. DN22: Nth L 6B **24**
   NG8: Stre .7K **83**
St Mary and St Martin's Priory Church 6G **13**
St Mary's Av. NG4: Ged 5H **87**
St Mary's Church 6G **7** (4A **96**)
St Mary's Cl. NG5: Arn 5H **77**
   NG9: Atten 7J **105**
   NG14: Lowd 4D **80**
St Mary's Ct. NG17: Sut A 6H **45**
   NG24: New T 1D **136**
   S81: Blyth .6G **13**
St Mary's Cres. LE12: East L 1A **122**
   NG11: Rudd 3K **115**
St Mary's Dr. NG21: Edwin 6E **36**
St Mary's Gdns. NG24: New T 1E **136**
St Mary's Ga. NG1: Nott 5G **7** (4A **96**)
   S80: Work .4G **21**
St Marys Pl. NG1: Nott 5G **7** (4A **96**)
St Marys Rd. NG13: Bing 3G **101**
   NG17: Sut A 6H **45**
St Marys Vw. NG15: Huck 6G **67**
              (off Ogle St.)
St Mary's Wlk. NG16: Jack 7A **64**
St Marys Way NG15: Huck 5F **67**
St Matthias Rd. NG3: Nott 2K **7** (2B **96**)
St Mawes Av. NG11: Wilf 3J **107**
St Mellion Way NG17: Kirk A 5J **51**
St Michael's Av. NG4: Ged 5H **87**
   NG8: Bilb 7J **83**
St Michael's Cl. NG22: Halam 5C **130**
St Michaels Ct. NG17: Sut A 7A **46**
St Michael's Grn. DN22: Retf 2D **22**
St Michaels Ho. LE12: Sut B 4B **120**
St Michaels NG9: Bram 1G **105**
St Michaels St. NG17: Sut A 7A **46**
St Michaels Vw. NG15: Huck 4H **67**
   NG16: Sels 7E **58**
St Modwens Ct. NG17: Sut A 1K **51**
St Nicholas Cl. NG5: Arn 7G **77**
St Nicholas St. NG1: Nott 6E **6** (4K **95**)
St Oswalds Pk. NG22: Dun T 5J **29**
St Patrick's Rd. NG15: Huck 6F **67**
   NG16: Nuth 1G **83**
St Paul's Av. NG7: H Grn 1G **95**
St Pauls Ct. NG16: Kimb 1E **82**
St Paul's Rd. S80: Work 4H **21**
St Paul's St. NG8: Radf 3E **94**
St Paul's Ter. NG7: H Grn 1G **95**
St Peters Av. NG20: Chu W 2D **34**
St Peters Chambers NG1: Nott 5F **7**
              (off Bank Pl.)
St Peter's Chu. Wlk. NG1: Nott 5F **7** (4K **95**)
St Peters Cl. DN22: New O 4B **38**
   NG24: Farnd 7G **133**
St Peters Ct. NG7: Radf 3E **94**
St Peters Cres. NG11: Rudd 3K **115**
St Peter's Dr. NG21: Rain 2J **55**
St Peter's Ga. NG1: Nott 5F **7** (4K **95**)
St Peter's La. DN22: Clay 6H **15**

St Peters Retail Pk. NG18: Mans 4H 47
St Peter's Sq. NG1: Nott 5E 6
(off St Peter's Ga.)
St Peter's St. NG7: Radf 3F 95
St Peter's Way NG18: Mans 3H 47
St Saviours Cl. DN22: Retf 2G 23
St Saviours Gdns. NG2: Nott 6A 96
St Stephen's Av. NG2: Nott 7K 7 (4C 96)
St Stephens Rd. DN22: Retf 6H 23
NG2: Nott 6K 7 (4B 96)
NG22: New O 5D 38
St Swithuns Grn. DN22: Retf 3F 23
(off Spital Hill)
St Thomas Av. NG17: Kirk A 7B 52
St Thomas Dr. NG13: Aslo 3D 102
St Wilfreds Cl. NG23: Nth M 6K 129
St Wilfreds Pk. NG17: Kirk A 7H 51
St Wilfrids Chu. Dr. NG11: Wilf 1J 107
St Wilfrids Dr. NG17: Kirk A 6H 51
St Wilfrid's Sq. NG14: Calv 6D 70
St Winifreds Ct. NG11: King 1A 120
Salamander Cl. NG4: Carl 5G 87
Salcey Dr. NG9: Trow 6C 92
Salcombe Cir. NG5: Redh 5F 77
Salcombe Cl. NG16: Newth 5G 73
Salcombe Cres. NG11: Rudd 2A 116
Salcombe Dr. NG5: Redh 5F 77
Salcombe Rd. NG5: Sher 4G 85
Salestune M. NG16: Sels 6D 58
Salford Gdns. NG3: Nott 3H 7 (3A 96)
(not continuous)
Salisbury Av. LE12: East L 3B 122
Salisbury Cl. NG19: Mans W 5K 41
S80: Work 1F 21
Salisbury Ct. NG3: Mapp 5B 86
Salisbury Rd. NG19: Mans 2E 46
NG24: New T 3C 136
Salisbury Sq. NG7: Lent 4F 95
Salisbury St. NG7: Lent 3F 95
NG9: Bee 2B 106
Salisbury Wlk. S81: Carl L 5B 12
Salmon Cl. NG6: Bulw 7F 75
Salmon La. NG17: Ann W 5G 59
Salop St. NG5: Arn 7F 77
Saltburn Rd. NG8: Bilb 2B 94
SALTBY 3D 149
Saltby Grn. NG2: West Br 6J 107
Salterford Av. NG14: Calv 5D 70
Salterford La. NG14: Calv 1B 70
Salterford Rd. NG15: Huck 1E 74
Saltford Cl. NG4: Ged 5J 87
Salthouse Cl. NG9: Bee 1B 106
Salthouse Ct. NG9: Bee 1B 106
Salthouse La. NG9: Bee 1B 106
Saltney Way NG11: Wilf 6H 107
Salvin Cl. NG12: Crop Bi 5B 112
Sam Derry Cl. NG24: New T 1E 136
Samian Cl. S81: Work 5E 18
Sampson's La. NG19: Plea 6B 40
Sampson St. NG17: Ann W 4K 59
Sampsons Yd. NG17: Huth 6D 44
Samson Cl. NG11: Rudd 2J 115
Samuel Brunts Way NG18: Mans 2J 47
Samuel Cl. NG18: Mans 2F 47
Samuel Unwin's Ct. NG17: Sut A 1B 52
Sandale Cl. NG2: Gam 3F 109
Sandalwood Cl. NG18: Mans 6D 48
Sandalwood Dr. NG17: Kirk A 5C 52
Sandays Cl. NG2: Nott 7K 95
Sandby NG1: Nott .3D 6
Sandby Ct. NG9: Chil 4H 105
Sanderling Rd. S81: Gate 6D 18
Sanderling Way NG19: Mans W 7A 42
Sanders Av. NG18: Mans 2A 48
Sanders Cl. NG23: Best 6H 125
Sanderson Dr. NG3: Mapp 1G 87
Sandfield Av. NG15: Rave 4D 62
Sandfield Cl. NG18: Mans 6D 48
Sandfield Ct. NG6: Bulw 1B 84
Sandfield La. NG22: Kirt 2H 39
Sandfield Rd. NG5: Arn 1C 86
NG7: Lent 4G 95
NG9: Toton 7D 104
NG17: Nunc 4K 59
Sandfield Way NG24: New T 4A 136
Sandford Rd. NG3: Mapp 5C 86
Sandgate NG9: Bram 7J 93
Sandgate Av. NG19: Mans W 5K 41
Sandgate Rd. NG19: Mans W 5K 41
Sandham Wlk. NG11: Clif 6F 107
Sandhill Adventure Base 2F 21
Sandhill Ho. S80: Work 2F 21
(off Sandhill St.)
Sandhill La. DN22: Stu S 1C 24
Sandhill Rd. NG16: Unde 2F 65
NG24: Farnd 6H 133
Sandhills Cl. NG24: New T 7B 134
Sandhill Sconce NG24: New T 1A 136
Sandhills Pk. NG24: New T 7B 134
Sandhill St. S80: Work 2F 21
Sandholes, The NG22: Farns 5J 57
Sandhurst Av. NG18: Mans 6J 47
Sandhurst Dr. NG9: Chil 7H 105
NG11: Rudd 4J 115
Sandhurst Rd. NG6: Bulw 5H 75
SANDIACRE 4A 104 (2A 148)

Sandiacre Rd. NG9: Stap 3B 104
Sandlands Way NG19: Mans W 1B 48
Sand La. NG23: Best 6H 125
Sandmartin Cl. NG18: Mans 6K 47
(off White Rose Av.)
Sandmartins S81: Gate 5D 18
Sandon St. NG7: Basf 6H 85
Sandown Rd. NG9: Toton 6E 104
NG17: Sut A 7B 46
NG18: Mans 6D 48
Sandpiper Cl. NG13: Bing 5G 101
Sandpiper Pl. NG20: Wars 3A 34
Sandpiper Way NG7: Lent 4F 95
Sandringham Av. NG2: West Br 1B 108
Sandringham Ct. DN11: Birc 1D 8
NG19: Mans W 3H 41
Sandringham Cres. NG8: Woll 3H 93
S81: Work .5F 19
Sandringham Dr. NG9: Bram 7H 93
NG19: Mans W 3H 41
Sandringham Pl. NG15: Huck 5H 67
Sandringham Rd. DN22: Retf 1D 22
NG2: Nott .4C 96
NG10: Sand 6A 104
NG19: Mans W 4A 42
Sandrock Rd. DN11: Harwo 1C 8
Sands Cl. NG4: Colw 3H 97
Sandside NG12: Cotg 7E 110
Sandstone Ct. NG6: Bulw 6G 75
Sandstone Pl. NG18: Mans 5A 48
SANDTOFT 1C 145
Sandwich Cl. NG17: Kirk A 5J 51
Sandycliffe Cl. NG19: Mans W 1B 48
Sandyford Cl. NG6: Basf 4D 84
Sandy La. DN22: Gam 3K 27
NG9: Bram 6J 93
NG12: Hol P 6A 98
NG15: Huck 6G 67
NG15: Rave 7D 54
NG18: Mans 3K 47
NG20: Cuck 6D 32
NG34: Mkt W 3D 34
(not continuous)
NG21: Edwin 7H 37
NG22: Eakr 1C 126
NG25: Oxt .2G 71
S80: Work .1D 20
Sandy La. Ind. Est. S80: Work 1E 20
Sandy La. Retail Pk. S80: Work 1F 21
Sandymount DN11: Harwo 1D 8
Sandymount E. DN11: Harwo 2D 8
Sandymount W. DN11: Harwo 2D 8
Sanger Cl. NG11: Clif 2D 114
Sanger Gdns. NG11: Clif 2D 114
Sanigar Ct. NG24: New T 6F 135
Sankey Dr. NG6: Bulw 7G 75
Santon Cl. NG19: Mans W 7C 42
Santon Rd. NG19: Mans W 7C 42
Sapele Cl. NG4: Ged 5K 87
Sapling Cl. NG4: New B 4F 137
Sapphire Cl. NG21: Rain 3A 56
Sapphire Dr. NG17: Kirk A 3A 52
Sapphire St. NG18: Mans 6K 47
Saracen's Head Yd. NG24: New T 1C 136
Saracens La. DN10: Scro 4J 9
Sarah Av. NG5: Sher 5H 85
Sargent Gdns. NG3: Nott 2C 96
Sartfield Rd. NG19: Mans W 7D 42
Saskatoon Cl. NG12: Rad T 6D 98
Saucemere Dr. NG24: New T 3C 136
Saucers, The NG13: Scar 1B 102
Saunby Cl. NG5: Arn 7K 77
SAUNDBY 3C 145
Saundby Av. NG19: Mans 1D 46
Saunton Cl. NG12: Edwal 5F 109
Savages Rd. NG11: Rudd 2K 115
Savages Row NG11: Rudd 2K 115
Saversick La. NG25: Sout 5D 130
Savile Ct. NG22: Eakr 2C 126
Savile Rd. NG22: Bils 5C 126
Savile Row NG21: Edwin 6F 37
NG42: New O 4C 38
Saville Cl. NG9: Stap 1D 104
Saville Rd. NG5: Woodt 2C 86
NG17: Skeg 4K 45
Saville St. NG21: Blid 6J 55
Saville Way NG20: Mkt W 4C 34
Savoy Cinema
Nottingham 4G 95
Worksop 3G 21
Savoy Ct. NG24: New T 1C 136
Savoy Workshops NG7: Lent 5G 95
SAWLEY 2A 148
Sawley Dr. NG18: Mans 6D 48
Saw Pit Ind. Est. DE55: Tibs 3A 44
Saw Pit La. DE55: Newton, Tibs 4A 44
Sawyers Cl. NG24: New T 1E 136
SAXBY 3D 149
Saxby Ct. NG11: Rudd 3A 116
Saxby Dr. NG18: Mans 6D 48
SAXELBY 3C 149
SAXELBYE 3C 149
Saxelby Gdns. NG6: Bulw 6H 75
SAXILBY 1D 147
SAXONDALE 4A 100 (1B 148)

Saxondale Ct. NG6: Bulw 5J 75
Saxondale Dr. NG6: Bulw 2E 84
NG12: Rad T 4J 99
Saxon Grn. NG7: Lent 5F 95
Saxon Way DN11: Harwo 2C 8
NG12: Cotg 7E 110
Saxton Cl. NG9: Bee 2C 106
S80: Work .3E 20
Saxton Ct. NG5: Arn 7A 78
Scafell Cl. NG22: West Br 4F 109
Scafell Way NG11: Clif 3E 114
SCAFTWORTH 2B 144
Scalby Cl. NG16: Eastw 4B 72
SCALFORD 3C 149
Scalford Dr. NG8: Woll 4D 94
SCAMPTON 1D 147
Scampton Rd. S81: Gate 4E 18
Scarborough Rd. NG22: Bils 5C 126
Scarborough St. NG3: Nott 3H 7 (3A 96)
SCARCLIFFE 2A 146
Scarcliffe Cl. NG17: Sut A 7K 45
Scarcliffe St. NG18: Mans 4K 47
Scarcliffe Ter. NG20: Whal T 5B 26
Scarf Wlk. NG11: Wilf 2J 107
Scargill Av. NG16: Newth 5F 73
Scargill Cl. NG16: Newth 5F 73
Scargill Wlk. NG16: Eastw 3D 72
SCARRINGTON 1C 102 (1C 149)
Scarrington Ct. NG18: Mans 1C 54
(off Bellamy Rd.)
Scarrington Rd. NG2: West Br 7C 96
SCAWSBY 1A 144
Sceptre St. NG5: Sher 5K 85
Scholars Way NG18: Mans 5K 47
Scholey Av. S81: Woods 1A 18
School Av. NG15: Huck 2D 74
School Cl. NG2: Nott 7A 96
School Gdns. NG25: Oxt 2F 71
School Grn. LE12: East L 3A 122
School Hill NG17: Ann 4B 60
School Ho. La. DN10: Walk 6H 11
School La. LE12: Remp 7F 123
NG9: Chil .5H 105
NG12: Cols B 7H 141
NG13: Aslo 3D 102
NG13: Bing 3F 101
NG13: What 5E 102
NG19: Mans W 6J 41
NG20: Cuck 4C 32
NG22: Eakr 2C 126
NG22: Halam 4C 130
NG22: Kirk 2C 132
NG22: Oll .5B 38
NG23: Caun 7J 127
NG23: Norw 2J 127
NG23: Thor 2K 31
NG24: Farnd 7G 133
School Rd. NG16: Sels 5E 58
NG16: Unde 1E 64
S81: Lango 1B 12
School St. NG17: Kirk A 6B 52
School Wlk. NG6: Bestw V 2A 76
School Way NG2: Nott 7A 96
Schrimshire's Rd. DN22: Nth L 6A 24
Science Rd. NG7: Nott 7E 94
SCOFTON 3B 144
Scofton Cl. S81: Gate 4D 18
Sconce Wlk. NG24: New T 3B 136
Scotholme Av. NG7: H Grn 7G 85
Scotland Bank NG12: Cotg 6E 110
Scotland Rd. NG5: Basf 4G 85
Scotswood Rd. NG19: Mans W 3H 41
Scott Av. NG9: Bee 3A 106
Scott Cl. NG6: Bulw 2A 84
S81: Work .1K 21
SCOTTER 1D 145
Scotter La. DN22: Hay 5G 17
SCOTTERTHORPE 1D 145
SCOTTON 2D 145
Scotton Sq. DN22: Retf 1D 22
Scotts Way NG17: Nunc 3B 60
SCREVETON 1C 149
Screveton Rd. NG13: Car C 5J 91
Scrimshire La. NG12: Cotg 6D 110
Script Dr. NG6: Basf 3F 85
Scrivelsby Gdns. NG9: Chil 5J 105
SCROOBY 4K 9 (2B 144)
Scrooby Cl. DN11: Harwo 2D 8
Scrooby Rd. DN11: Birc, Harwo 2D 8
(not continuous)
Scrooby Row NG5: Top V 6C 76
SCUNTHORPE 1D 145
Seaburn Rd. NG9: Toton 6D 104
Seacroft NG24: New T 1H 137
Seaford Av. NG8: Woll 3C 94
Seaforth Sq. NG19: Mans 5D 46
SEAGRAVE 3B 148
Seagrave Av. NG17: Ann W 3B 60
Seagrave Ct. NG5: Arn 7G 77
NG8: Stre .6J 83
Seagrave Rd. NG8: Stre 6J 83
Seamer Rd. NG16: Kimb 7K 73
Sean Upton Cl. NG9: Chil 6J 105
Searby Rd. NG17: Sut A 2C 52
(not continuous)
Searwood Av. NG17: Kirk A 4J 51

Seatallan Cl. NG2: West Br 3F 109
Seathwaite Cl. NG2: West Br 5F 109
Seatoller Cl. NG2: West Br 4F 109
Seaton Cres. NG8: Aspl 6B 84
Second Av. NG4: Carl 1F 97
  NG4: Ged 6J 87
  NG6: Bulw 7H 75
  NG7: H Grn 7J 85
  NG7: Nott 3D 106
  NG19: Mans W 1C 48
  NG21: C'tone 6J 43
  NG21: Edwin 6E 36
  NG21: Rain 1H 55
SEDGEBROOK CL. 2D 149
Sedgebrook Cl. NG6: Basf 4D 84
Sedgebrook St. NG19: Mans W 6A 42
Sedgemere DN22: Ord 6D 22
Sedgewood Gro. NG11: Clif 6F 107
Sedgley Av. NG2: Nott 3C 96
Sedgley Rd. NG12: Toll 2G 117
Sedgwick Cl. NG16: Pinx 2B 58
Sedgwick St. NG16: Jack 7A 64
Sedley Av. NG16: Nuth 1H 83
Seeley Ho. NG1: Nott 6H 7
  (off Malin Hill)
Seely Av. NG14: Calv 5B 70
Seely Rd. NG7: Lent, Radf 4A 6 (3G 95)
Sefton Av. NG9: Stap 1D 104
Sefton Dr. NG3: Mapp P 6A 86
Selby Cl. NG9: Toton 6D 104
Selby La. NG12: Key 1H 119
Selby Rd. NG2: West Br 3C 108
Selhurst Ct. NG7: H Grn 1G 95
Selhurst St. NG7: H Grn 1G 95
Selkirk Way NG5: Sher 6J 85
Sellars Av. NG11: Rudd 4K 115
Sellers Wood Dr. NG6: Bulw 6F 75
Sellers Wood Dr. W. NG6: Bulw 7E 74
Seller's Wood Nature Reserve 7E 74
Selsey Ct. DN22: Retf 1D 22
Selside Ct. NG9: Chil 5F 105
SELSTON 5D 58 (3A 146)
SELSTON COMMON 6E 58
Selston Dr. NG8: Woll 5D 94
SELSTON GREEN 6B 58
Selston Leisure Cen. 5C 58
Selston (Par 3) Golf Course 6B 58
Selston Rd. NG16: Jack . . . .6A 64 & 7A 58
Selwyn Cl. NG6: Bulw 2F 85
Selwyn St. NG18: Mans 5A 48
Sennen Ct. DN22: Retf 1E 22
Senso Ct. NG4: Ged 6A 88
Sentinel Dr. NG15: Ann 7K 59
Serina Ct. NG2: West Br 2B 108
  NG9: Bee 2C 106
SERLBY 6G 9 (3B 144)
Serlby Pk. Golf Course 7H 9
Serlby Ri. NG3: Nott 2C 96
Serlby Rd. DN11: Sty 4A 8
  NG16: Newth 3E 72
Serpentine Cl. NG12: Rad T 6J 99
Seven Hills NG24: New T 5D 134
Seven Oaks Cres. NG9: Bram 7G 93
Seven Oaks Rd. DE7: Stant D 7A 92
Seventh Av. NG7: Nott 4D 106
  NG19: Mans W 2C 48
  NG21: C'tone 6G 43
Severals NG9: Stap 2E 104
Severn St. NG6: Bulw 7H 75
SEWSTERN 3D 149
Seymour Ct. NG7: Radf 2B 6 (2H 95)
Seymour Pl. NG2: West Br 7E 96
Seymour Rd. NG2: West Br 1E 108
  NG15: Huck 1E 74
  NG16: Eastw 5D 72
Seymour St. NG3: Nott 3K 7 (3B 96)
Shackleton Cl. NG8: Stre 5J 83
Shacklock Cl. NG5: Arn 4C 76
Shadwell Gro. NG12: Rad T 5D 98
Shady La. DN22: Welh 2J 23
  NG9: Atten 7J 105
  NG25: Sout 6J 131
Shaftesbury Av. NG10: Sand 4A 104
  NG12: Rad T 5J 99
  NG14: Bur J 2F 89
  NG19: Mans 1D 46
Shaftesbury St. NG7: Basf 6H 85
Shaftesbury Way NG23: Coll 1H 129
Shakespeare Av. NG19: Mans W 5H 41
Shakespeare Cl. NG4: Colw 3H 97
Shakespeare Ho. NG1: Nott 3F 7 (3K 95)
Shakespeare Rd. NG16: Aws 2B 82
Shakespeare St. NG1: Nott 3D 6 (3J 95)
  NG24: New B 3E 136
  S81: Work 1J 21
Shakespeare Vs. NG1: Nott 3E 6 (3K 95)
Shakir Ct. NG7: Basf 6H 85
Shaldon Cl. NG5: Top V 5B 76
Shale La. NG14: Blea 2B 138
Shandwick Cl. NG5: Arn 5K 77
Shanklin Dr. NG9: Stap 2C 104
Shanwell Cl. NG8: Stre 5J 83
Shardale Gdns. NG6: Basf 3E 84
Shardlow Way NG18: Mans 6D 48
Sharnford Way NG9: Bram 4G 93

Sharpes Way NG6: Bestw V 1D 76
Sharphill Rd. NG12: Edwal 5E 108
Sharpley Dr. LE12: East L 1B 122
Sharrard Cl. NG16: Unde 3E 64
Sharratt Ct. NG18: Mans 1C 54
Shaw Cres. NG15: Huck 2E 74
Shawcroft NG17: Sut A 5K 45
Shaw Gdns. NG4: Ged 7A 88
  NG11: Clif 2D 114
Shaw St. NG11: Rudd 3K 115
  NG18: Mans 3A 48
  S80: Work 2F 21
Shaw St. E. DE7: Ilk 2A 92
Shaw St. W. DE7: Ilk 2A 92
Sheaf Pl. S81: Work 5F 19
Shearing Cl. NG4: Ged 6K 87
Shearing Hill NG4: Ged 6K 87
Shearsby Dr. NG19: Mans W 7B 42
Sheepbridge La. NG18: Mans 5F 47
Sheepfold La. NG11: Rudd 4K 115
Sheep Plank La. LE12: East L 2C 122
Sheepwalk La. NG15: Rave 1B 62
Sheepwash La. NG17: Sut A 7B 46
  (not continuous)
Sheffield Rd. S81: Blyth 6G 13
Shelby Cl. NG7: Lent 4F 95
Sheldon Cl. NG10: Long E 6A 104
  NG17: Sut A 6J 45
Sheldrake Rd. NG24: New T 1G 137
SHELFORD 6H 89 (1B 148)
Shelford Av. NG17: Kirk A 5H 51
Shelford Cl. NG9: Chil 5J 105
  NG12: Rad T 4F 99
Shelford Cres. NG14: Bur J 2F 89
Shelford Dr. NG13: Bing 4E 100
Shelford Hill NG12: Shel 7H 89
  NG19: Mans 4E 46
Shelford Nurseries Caravan Pk.
  NG12: Shel 7H 89
Shelford Ri. NG3: Nott 2D 96
Shelford Rd. NG4: Ged 4F 87
  NG12: Rad T, Shel 5E 98
  NG13: Newton 1J 99
Shellburne Cl. NG5: Top V 4A 76
Shelley Av. NG11: Clif 6F 107
  NG19: Mans W 5H 41
Shelley Cl. NG15: Huck 7D 66
  NG16: Nuth 1G 83
  NG17: Kirk A 4C 52
  NG24: Bald 6G 137
Shelley Rd. NG5: Arn 7F 77
Shelley St. S80: Work 2H 21
Shelt Hill NG14: Woodbo 2H 79
SHELTHORPE 3A 148
SHELTON 1C 149
Shelton Av. NG15: Huck 2J 75
  NG24: New T 4B 136
Shelton Cl. NG19: Mans 1E 46
Shelton Ct. NG18: Mans 1C 54
Shelton Gdns. NG11: Rudd 3J 115
Shelton Rd. NG18: Mans 1C 54
Shelton St. NG3: Nott 2F 7 (2K 95)
Shenfield Gdns. NG5: Top V 5K 75
Shepard Cl. NG6: Bulw 1A 84
Shepherd Ct. NG15: Huck 2D 74
Shepherd Ho. NG5: Bestw 2H 85
Shepherd's Av. S81: Work 7G 19
Shepherds Cl. LE12: Sut B 7C 120
  NG8: Bilb 1B 94
Shepherd's La. NG17: Teve 1C 44
Shepherds Oak NG17: Skeg 4J 45
Shepherds Way NG17: Sut A 1B 52
Shepherds Wood Dr. NG8: Aspl 1D 94
Sheppards Ct. NG24: New B 5F 137
  (off Stafford Av.)
Sheppard's Row NG25: Sout 5H 131
  (off Private Rd.)
SHEPSHED 3A 148
Shepton Cres. NG8: Aspl 5C 84
Sheraton Dr. NG8: Woll 5K 93
Sherborne Rd. NG2: West Br 4C 108
  NG8: Aspl 6B 84
Sherbrook Av. NG15: Ann 1A 86
Sherbrook Bus. Cen. NG5: Arn 1A 86
Sherbrooke Cl. NG14: Calv 5C 70
Sherbrooke Rd. NG5: Sher 6J 85
Sherbrooke Ter. NG5: Sher 6J 85
Sherbrook Rd. NG5: Arn 1K 85
Sherbrook Ter. NG5: Arn 1A 86
Sheridan Cl. NG24: Bald 5G 137
Sheridan Ct. NG1: Nott 2E 6
  NG9: Stap 7E 92
Sheridan Way NG5: Sher 4H 85
  NG15: Huck 1G 75
Sheriffs Lea NG9: Toton 7D 104
Sheriffs Way NG2: Nott 5K 95
Sheringham Cl. NG5: Arn 1C 86
Sheringham Dr. NG18: Mans 5J 47
Sherman Dr. NG9: Chil 7H 105
Sherrington Cl. NG11: Clif 1D 114
Sherview Av. NG18: Mans 3C 48
Sherwin Gro. NG7: Lent 5F 95
Sherwin Rd. NG7: Lent 5F 95
  NG9: Stap 7E 92

Sherwin Wlk. DN22: Retf 1C 22
  NG3: Nott 1E 6 (2K 95)
SHERWOOD 4H 85 (1A 148)
Sherwood Av. NG5: Sher 4A 86
  NG14: Calv 5B 70
  NG18: Mans 1D 54
  NG21: Blid 6A 56
  NG21: Edwin 6E 36
  NG24: New T 2D 136
Sherwood Bus. Pk. NG15: Ann 6K 59
Sherwood Castle Holiday Forest
  NG22: Ruff 7A 38
Sherwood Cl. NG18: Mans 3A 48
Sherwood Ct. NG9: Chil 6H 105
  NG14: Calv 5D 70
  NG17: Kirk A 6B 52
  NG19: Mans W 7H 41
Sherwood Cres. S81: Blyth 7G 13
Sherwood Dene NG17: Ann W 3J 59
Sherwood Dr. DN22: New O 4C 38
Sherwood Energy Village NG22: New O 5C 38
Sherwood Forest Art & Craft Cen. 5E 36
Sherwood Forest Caravan Pk. NG21: K Cli 2J 43
Sherwood Forest Country Pk. 3C 36
Sherwood Forest Crematorium
  NG22: New O 6D 38
Sherwood Forest Golf Course 3F 49
Sherwood Forest Vis. Cen. 4F 37
Sherwood Grange NG18: Mans 2B 48
Sherwood Gro. NG13: Bing 4E 100
  NG14: Calv 5D 70
Sherwood Hall Gdns. NG18: Mans 2B 48
Sherwood Hall Rd. NG18: Mans 3A 48
Sherwood Heath Nature Reserve 4K 37
Sherwood Ho. NG17: Sut A 1H 51
  NG22: Bils 4C 126
Sherwood Lodge Dr. NG5: Arn 3E 68
Sherwood Network Cen. NG22: New O 5D 38
Sherwood Oaks Bus. Pk. NG18: Mans 7D 48
Sherwood Oaks Cl. NG18: Mans 7D 48
Sherwood Pde. NG21: Rain 2K 55
  (off Kirklington Rd.)
SHERWOOD PARK 6K 59
Sherwood Pk. NG22: Wale 6F 27
Sherwood Pines Forest Pk. 2B 146
Sherwood Pines Vis. Cen. 2B 146
Sherwood Pl. NG17: Nunc 3A 60
  NG21: C'tone 6K 43
SHERWOOD RISE 7J 85
Sherwood Ri. NG7: Sher 6H 85
  NG16: Eastw 5D 72
  NG17: Nunc 3A 60
  NG19: Mans, Mans W 6H 41
  (not continuous)
Sherwood Rd. DN11: Harwo 1C 8
  DN22: Ord 7E 22
  NG17: Sut A 2J 51
  NG21: Rain 2K 55
  S80: Work 1G 21
Sherwood St. NG15: Huck 7J 67
  NG17: Ann W 4A 60
  NG17: Huth 7D 44
  NG17: Kirk A 6B 52
  NG18: Mans 4A 48
  NG19: Mans W 6H 41
  NG20: Mkt W 4D 34
Sherwood Va. NG5: Sher 4B 86
Sherwood Vw. NG21: Rain 2K 55
  (off Sherwood Rd.)
Sherwood Wlk. NG15: Lin 3G 67
Sherwood Way NG16: Sels 6F 59
Sherwood Way Sth. NG17: Sut A 7C 46
Shetland Cl. NG19: Mans W 1B 48
Shetlands, The DN22: Retf 1G 23
Shilo Way NG16: Aws 3A 82
SHIPLEY 7A 72 (1A 148)
Shipley Ga. NG16: Eastw 7C 72
Shipley Ri. NG4: Carl 1H 97
Shipley Rd. NG8: Brox 5A 84
Shipstones Bus. Cen. NG7: Basf 6G 85
Shipstone St. NG7: Basf 7G 85
Shipstone Street Stop (NET) 7G 85
Shipstones Yd. NG6: Bulw 6J 75
Shirburn Av. NG18: Mans 2J 47
SHIREBROOK 2A 146
Shirebrooke Cl. NG6: Basf 4D 84
Shire Cl. S81: Carl L 5D 12
Shire Hall & Galleries of Justice Mus. 6G 7 (4A 96)
SHIREOAKS 5A 18 (3A 144)
Shireoaks Bus. Cen. S81: Shire 6B 18
Shireoaks Comn. S81: Shire 6A 18
Shireoaks Ct. NG18: Mans 1C 54
Shireoaks Ent. Cen. NG18: Mans 1C 54
  (off Ruddington Rd.)
Shireoaks Marina S81: Shire 6A 18
Shireoaks Rd. S80: Rhod, Work 7C 18
  S81: Shire 6A 18
Shireoaks Row S81: Shire 5A 18
Shireoaks Station (Rail) 5A 18
Shireoaks Triangle S81: Shire 5B 18
Shires, The NG17: Sut A 2H 51
  NG19: Mans W 1B 48
Shires Dr. NG3: Mapp 5B 86
Shires Way NG23: Sut T 4D 128
Shirland Dr. NG18: Mans 6D 48
Shirley Ct. NG9: Toton 7F 105

Shirley Dr. NG5: Arn .7K 77
Shirley Rd. NG3: Mapp P .7K 85
SHOBY .3B 148
Shorelark Way S81: Gate .5D 18
Shoreswood Cl. NG5: Bestw .6D 76
Shortcross Av. NG3: Mapp .3C 86
Short Hill NG1: Nott .6H 7 (4A 96)
Short Stairs NG1: Nott .6H 7
Short St. NG17: Sut A .7A 46
NG20: Mkt W .4D 34
Shortwood Av. NG15: Huck .1F 75
Shortwood Cl. NG1: Nott .6G 7 (4A 96)
Shortwood La. NG22: Omp .7J 39
Shorwell Rd. NG3: Nott .1F 97
Shotton Dr. NG5: Arn .4J 77
Shoulder of Mutton Hill NG17: Ann W .3B 60
Showcase Cinema
Nottingham .1F 107
Shrewsbury Rd. DN11: Birc .2E 8
NG2: Nott .4D 96
S80: Work .3J 21
Shrewsbury Vw. DN22: Retf .1C 22
Shrimpton Ct. NG11: Rudd .4A 116
Shropshire Av. NG16: Westw .1A 64
Shrubberies, The NG5: Sher .4J 85
SHUTTLEWOOD .1A 146
Sibcy La. NG24: Bald .6G 137
Sibson Wlk. NG5: Arn .4H 77
SIBTHORPE
Newark, NG22 .2A 28
Newark, NG23 .6E 140 (1C 149)
Sibthorpe St. NG18: Mans .5G 47
Siddalls Dr. NG17: Sut A .7F 45
Side La. NG22: Eakr .3C 126
Side Row NG24: New T .1E 136
Sidings, The NG13: Aslo .4D 102
NG14: Lowd .6E 80
NG16: Kimb .1E 82
NG19: Mans W .6G 41
Sidings La. NG9: Bram .5F 93
Sidings Rd. NG17: Kirk A .4C 52
Sidlaw Ri. NG5: Arn .4D 76
Sidmouth Cl. NG12: Key .6H 117
Sidney Rd. NG9: Bee .2K 105
Sidney St. NG16: Kimb .1E 82
Sidsaph Hill DN10: Walk .7J 11
Siena Gdns. NG19: Mans W .7C 42
(not continuous)
Sikey La. NG22: Eakr .2C 126
Sikorski Cl. NG24: New T .7C 134
Silbury Cl. NG11: Clif .3E 114
Silk St. NG17: Sut A .1J 51
Sillitoe Ct. NG7: Lent .3E 94
Sillitoe Way NG7: Lent .4E 94
Silver Birch Cl. NG6: Cin .3C 84
SILVERDALE .5H 107
Silverdale NG9: Stap .4D 104
Silverdale Av. NG19: Mans W .5H 41
Silverdale Cl. DN22: Retf .1C 22
Silverdale Rd. NG7: Basf .5G 85
Silverdale Wlk. NG11: Clif, Wilf .6H 107
Silverhill Cl. NG8: Stre .5J 83
Silverhill Cotts. NG17: Teve .2E 44
Silverhill La. NG17: Teve .1C 44
Silverhow Cl. NG2: West Br .4F 109
Silver St. DN22: Retf .4D 22
NG23: Grass .3K 125
NG23: Nth C .3D 30
Silverwood Av. NG15: Rave .3C 62
Silverwood Rd. NG9: Bee .3K 105
Silvey Av. NG25: Sout .4G 131
Sime St. S80: Work .1F 21
Simkin Av. NG3: Mapp .6D 86
Simon Cl. DN22: Woodbe .6F 25
Simone Gdns. NG11: Clif .7F 107
Simons Ct. NG9: Bram .7J 93
Simpson Cl. NG24: Bald .6H 137
Simpson Rd. NG19: Mans .3D 46
Singleton Av. NG18: Mans .2A 48
Sir John Robinson Way NG5: Arn .7F 77
Siskin Cl. NG9: Bram .3H 105
Siskin Ct. NG18: Mans .6D 48
S81: Gate .5D 18
Sisley Av. NG9: Stap .3D 104
Sitwell Cl. S81: Work .1J 21
Sitwell Rd. S81: Work .1J 21
SIX HILLS .3B 148
Sixth Av. NG7: Nott .4D 106
NG19: Mans W .2C 48
NG21: C'tone .6G 43
NG21: Edwin .7E 36
SKEGBY
East Markham .1C 147
Sutton in Ashfield .4G 45 (2A 146)
Skegby Hall Dr. NG17: Skeg .4J 45
Skegby Hall Gdns. NG17: Skeg .4J 45
Skegby La. NG17: Skeg .4B 46
NG19: Mans .4B 46
Skegby Mt. NG19: Mans .5E 46
Skegby Rd. NG17: Ann W .3J 59
NG17: Huth .7E 44
NG17: Sut A .6A 46
NG23: Norm T .1H 125
SKEGNESS .6F 59
SKELBROOKE .1A 144
SKELLINGTHORPE .1D 147
SKELLOW .1A 144
Skelwith Cl. NG2: West Br .4F 109
Skerry Hill NG18: Mans .3K 47
Sketchley Ct. NG6: Bulw .7G 75
Sketchley St. NG3: Nott .1K 7 (2C 96)
Skiddaw Cl. NG2: West Br .4F 109
SKILLINGTON .3D 149
Skipton Cir. NG3: Nott .2D 96
Skithorne Ri. NG14: Lowd .6D 80
Skylark Cl. NG13: Bing .5G 101
NG15: Rave .4C 62
Skylark Dr. NG6: Basf .3E 84
Skylark Hill NG12: Crop Bi .7K 111
Slack Wlk. S80: Work .4F 21
SLADE HOOTON .3A 144
Slade Rd. NG9: Chil .4G 105
Slaidburn Av. NG11: Wilf .4H 107
Slake La. NG23: Sth M .2B 134
Slalom Run NG4: Carl .6F 87
Slant La. NG19: Mans W .4H 41
Slater St. NG17: Sut A .6K 45
Slaters Way NG5: Bestw .2G 85
Slaughter Ho. La.
NG24: New T .7C 134
Slaynes La. DN10: Miss, Newi .4B 10
Sleaford Rd. NG24: New T .7D 134
Sleath Dr. NG23: Bath .6F 129
Sleights La. NG16: Pinx .2A 58
Sloan Dr. NG9: Bram .5G 93
Sloane Ct. NG2: West Br .6K 107
Sloethorne Gdns. NG5: Arn .6F 77
Sloswicke Dr. DN22: Retf .1C 22
Smalley Cl. NG16: Unde .3E 64
Small Ga. NG19: Mans W .3A 42
Small's Cft. NG14: Woodbo .2G 79
Smeath La. DN22: Clar, Hay .7F 17
Smeath Rd. DN22: Bol .1F 23
NG16: Unde .3D 64
Smedley Av. DE7: Ilk .1A 92
Smedley Cl. NG8: Aspl .5C 84
Smedley's Av. NG10: Sand .4A 104
Smeeton St. DE75: Hea .5A 72
Smite Cl. NG13: What .4C 102
Smite Ct. NG7: Radf .1E 94
Smite La. NG13: Aslo, Ors .1G 103
Smithfield Av. NG9: Trow .4C 92
Smith Ho. NG24: New T .5C 136
Smiths Cl. NG12: Crop Bi .5B 112
Smithson Cl. NG24: New B .5F 137
Smith Sq. DN11: Harwo .1C 8
Smith St. NG18: Mans .4A 48
NG24: New B .4F 137
NG24: New T .2D 136
Smithurst Rd. NG16: Gilt .6E 72
Smithy Cl. NG11: Clif .7E 106
NG14: Woodbo .3G 79
Smithy Cres. NG5: Arn .6H 77
Smithy Row NG1: Nott .5F 7 (4K 95)
NG17: Sut A .1H 51
Smithy Vw. NG6: Bestw V .1D 76
NG14: Calv .6C 70
Smythson Dr. NG8: Woll .4K 93
Snaefell Av. NG19: Mans W .7C 42
Snaith Ct. NG24: New T .7C 134
Snape La. DN11: Harwo .4C 8
Snape Nook Ct. NG6: Bulw .7F 75
Snape Wood Rd. NG6: Bulw .7F 75
Snead Ct. NG5: Top V .5C 76
SNEINTON .5K 7 (4C 96)
Sneinton Blvd. NG2: Nott .4C 96
Sneinton Dale NG2: Nott .6K 7 (4C 96)
NG3: Nott .3D 96
Sneinton Hermitage NG2: Nott .7K 7 (5B 96)
Sneinton Hollows NG2: Nott .6K 7 (4C 96)
Sneinton Mkt. Sq. NG1: Nott .4J 7
Sneinton Rd. NG2: Nott .5J 7 (4B 96)
Snell Cl. NG23: Sut T .2C 128
Snipe Pk. Rd. DN11: Birc .2E 8
Snowdon Cl. NG5: Top V .5D 76
Snowdon Rd. NG23: Coll .2H 129
Snowdrop Av. NG24: New T .7H 135
Snowdrop Cl. NG15: Huck .2J 75
Snowdrop Dr. NG19: Mans W .5B 42
Soarbank Cl. NG16: Kimb .7J 73
Soar La. LE12: Norm S .7G 121
LE12: Sut B .4A 120
Sobers Gdns. NG5: Arn .1E 86
Softwood Cl. NG6: Bulw .7F 75
Soloman Pk. DE7: Ilk .5A 82
Soloman Rd. DE7: Ilk .5A 82
Solway Cl. NG9: Chil .4K 105
Somerby Ct. NG9: Bram .4G 93
Somerleyton Dr. DE7: Ilk .4A 92
Somersall St. NG19: Mans .2E 46
Somersby Ct. NG18: Mans .5D 48
Somersby Rd. NG3: Mapp .2C 86
NG5: Woodt .2C 86
Somerton Av. NG11: Wilf .5H 107
Somerton Rd. S81: Gate .4D 18
Songthrush Av. NG6: Basf .3E 84
SOOKHOLME .6A 34 (2A 146)
Sookholme Dr. NG20: Mkt W .5C 34
Sookholme La. NG19: Sook .6A 34
NG20: Mkt W, Wars .4C 34
Sookholme Rd. NG19: Sook .6A 34
Sophie Rd. NG7: H Grn .1A 6 (2G 95)
Sorrel Dr. NG13: Bing .4D 100
NG17: Kirk A .1A 60
Soss La. DN10: Mist .2J 11
Sotheby Av. NG17: Sut A .2C 52
Soudan Dr. NG2: Nott .7J 95
Soundwave Art of Life Centre, The .2G 21
Southampton St. NG3: Nott .1J 7 (2B 96)
SOUTH ANSTON .3A 144
South Av. NG12: Rad T .4G 99
NG21: Rain .2J 55
S80: Work .4J 21
Southbank La. DN22: Cott .1K 25
Southbreck Ri. S80: Work .4J 21
SOUTH CARLTON
Lincoln .1D 147
Worksop .7C 12 & 1H 19
Southchurch Ct. NG11: Clif .6G 107
Southchurch Dr. NG11: Clif .2F 115
Southcliffe Rd. NG4: Carl .1G 97
SOUTH CLIFTON .7D 30 (1D 147)
South Ct. NG9: Bee .5C 106
South Cres. NG21: C'tone .6J 43
Southdale Dr. NG4: Carl .1G 97
Southdale Rd. NG4: Carl .1G 97
Southdene S81: Work .6H 19
Sth. Devon Av. NG3: Mapp .5E 86
South Dr. NG22: Bils .4C 126
SOUTH ELMSALL .1A 144
South End NG23: Coll .3G 129
Southend Av. NG24: New T .2C 136
Southern Wood S80: Work .5F 21
Southey St. NG7: Radf .1A 6 (2G 95)
Southfall Cl. DN22: Rans .1J 13
Southfield NG24: Bald .6H 137
Southfield Ho. NG24: New T .2B 136
Southfield La. DN10: Beck .7D 16
Southfield Rd. DN22: Tres .5H 25
NG8: Aspl .2E 94
Southfields Av. NG16: Pinx .1B 58
Southfields Cl. NG17: Ann W .3J 59
Southfields Ct. NG9: Chil .3G 105
Southfields Dr. DE55: Sth N .6A 50
Southfields Ri. DN22: Nth L .7B 24
Southfield Ter. NG24: New T .2B 136
South Forest Leisure Cen. .7J 37
Southgate DN22: Ord .7E 22
Southgate Rd. NG20: Mkt W .3E 34
Southglade Food Pk. NG5: Bestw .1F 85
Southglade Leisure Cen. .7B 76
Southglade Rd. NG5: Bestw .1F 85
Southgore La. DN22: Nth L .6C 24
Southgreen Cl. NG18: Mans .1A 54
Southgreen Hill NG18: Mans .1A 54
SOUTH HYKEHAM .2D 147
SOUTH KIRKBY .1A 144
Southlands NG17: Sut A .6J 45
South La. NG23: Norm T .2K 125
Southlea Rd. NG4: Carl .1G 97
SOUTH LEVERTON .1G 25 (3C 145)
Sth. Moor Rd. DN10: Walk .6G 11
Southmoor Rd. S80: Work .4J 21
SOUTH MUSKHAM .1B 134 (3C 147)
South Pde. DN10: Bawt .1K 9
NG1: Nott .5E 6 (4K 95)
S81: Work .1G 21
Southpark Av. NG18: Mans .1B 54
Southport Ter. NG7: H Grn .1F 95
Southreef 1,2,3 & 4 NG1: Nott .7G 7 (5A 96)
SOUTH RETFORD .5E 22
Southridge Dr. NG18: Mans .7K 47
South Rd. DN22: West Bu .1D 24
NG2: West Br .3B 108
NG5: Sher .3J 85
NG7: Nott .6B 6 (5H 95)
(Newcastle Cir.)
NG7: Nott .6E 94
(West Rd.)
NG9: Bee .5B 106
SOUTH SCARLE .2D 147
Sth. Scarle Rd. NG23: Coll .1J 129
Sth. Sherwood St. NG1: Nott .3E 6 (3K 95)
Southside NG5: Arn .6A 78
Sth. Snape Cl. NG6: Bulw .7F 75
South St. DN22: Retf .4F 23
NG15: Huck .6G 67
NG16: Eastw .4C 72
NG16: Gilt .6G 73
NG23: Norm T .1K 125
South Vw. NG24: New B .5F 137
S81: Oldc .6A 8
S81: Work .7G 19
South Vw. Dr. DN22: Clar .7H 17
Southview Gdns. NG15: Rave .2C 62
South Vw. Rd. NG4: Carl .5G 87
Southwark St. NG6: Basf .4F 85
SOUTHWELL .6J 131 (3B 146)
Southwell Cl. LE12: East L .3A 122
NG17: Kirk A .5A 52
S80: Work .3H 21
Southwell Gdns. NG18: Mans .6C 48
Southwell Golf Course .3J 139
Southwell Hall NG8: Woll .4E 94
Southwell La. NG17: Kirk A .6J 51
Southwell La. Ind. Est. NG17: Kirk A .5A 52
Southwell Leisure Cen. .7G 131
Southwell Minster .6H 131

Southwell Racecourse 2H 139
Southwell Ri. NG16: Gilt 7F 73
Southwell Rd. NG1: Nott 5J 7 (4A 96)
  NG14: Gon, Lowd 5E 80
  NG14: Thur 6D 138
  NG22: Farns 6K 57
  NG22: Kirk .2C 132
  NG23: Upton . . . . .1F 139 & 7A 132
  NG25: Oxt, Sout 3G 71
                  (not continuous)
Southwell Rd. E. NG21: Rain 1F 55
Southwell Rd. W. NG18: Mans 4K 47
  NG21: Rain .6C 48
SOUTH WHEATLEY 2J 17 (3C 145)
SOUTH WITHAM 3D 149
Southwold Dr. NG8: Aspl 3D 94
Southwood Av. NG17: Sut A 6H 45
Sovereign Ct. NG9: Bee 4B 106
Sovereign Way NG18: Mans 6D 48
Sowter Av. NG17: Sut A 6J 45
Spa Cl. NG17: Sut A 3K 51
Spa La. DN22: Retf 4F 23
  NG13: Ors 1K 103
  NG19: Mans W 5D 42
Spalding Rd. NG3: Nott 4K 7 (3B 96)
SPALFORD 2D 147
Spang La. NG17: Huth 6C 44
Spaniel Row NG1: Nott 6E 6 (4K 95)
Sparken Cl. S80: Work 5F 21
Sparken Dale S80: Work 5F 21
Sparken Hill S80: Work 4G 21
Sparrow La. NG23: High M 7A 30
Sparrow La. Caravan Pk. NG23: High M . .7A 30
Spean Ct. NG8: Woll 3B 94
Spean Dr. NG8: Aspl 1C 94
Speedwell Cl. NG13: Bing 4D 100
  NG24: New T 7H 135
Speedwell La. NG16: Kimb 1D 82
Speedwell Pl. S80: Work 1F 21
Speight Cl. NG24: Wint 2F 135
Spencer Av. NG3: Mapp 2F 87
  NG10: Sand .2A 104
Spencer Cl. NG11: Rudd 3J 115
Spencer Ct. NG7: H Grn 2J 85
Spencer Cres. NG9: Stap 1E 104
Spencer Dr. NG16: Nuth 1H 83
Spencer St. NG18: Mans 4G 47
Sperry Cl. NG16: Sels 6D 58
Spey Cl. NG15: Huck 3D 74
Spicer Cl. NG9: Chil 7H 105
Spicers Ct. DN22: Retf 4E 22
Spindle Ct. NG19: Mans 5E 46
Spindle Gdns. NG6: Bulw 7G 75
Spindle La. NG14: Calv, Woodbo 1A 78
Spindle Vw. NG14: Calv 7D 70
SPINKHILL 1A 146
Spinners Cl. NG19: Mans 5E 46
Spinney, The NG5: Woodt 3B 86
  NG6: Bestw V 1A 76
  NG14: Bulc .2G 89
  NG16: Nuth .4A 84
                (Harcourt Cres.)
  NG16: Nuth .1G 83
                  (Keats Cl.)
  NG18: Mans .4K 53
  NG22: Farns 5J 57
                (not continuous)
  NG23: Elston 1D 140
  NG24: Wint .3F 135
Spinney Cl. NG2: West Br 5E 108
  NG12: Cotg .7E 110
  NG17: Kirk A 5J 51
  NG19: Mans W 3A 42
  NG24: New T 3B 136
Spinney Cres. NG9: Toton 6E 104
Spinney Dr. NG10: Long E 7B 104
Spinney Hill NG2: West Br 7A 108
Spinney Mede DN22: Rans 1J 13
Spinney Ri. NG9: Toton 6D 104
Spinney Rd. NG10: Long E 7B 104
  NG12: Key 7G 117
  NG13: Bing .4E 100
Spinney Way NG11: Wilf 5H 107
Spinningdale NG5: Arn 5K 77
SPION KOP 7B 34
Spire Cl. NG17: Ann W 4J 59
Spire Gdns. NG24: New T 5E 134
Spitalfields S81: Blyth 7H 13
Spital Hill DN22: Retf 3F 23
Spital Rd. S81: Blyth 7H 13
Spondon St. NG5: Sher 5K 85
Spray Cl. NG4: Colw 3H 97
Spridgeon Cl. NG10: Long E 7A 104
Spring Cl. NG16: Want 7A 74
  NG17: Kirk A 7A 52
Spring Ct. NG2: West Br 1E 108
  NG9: Stap 2D 104
  NG22: Farns 4J 57
Springdale Gdns. NG9: Trow 6C 92
Springdale La. NG13: East B 5E 90
                (not continuous)
Spring Dr. NG24: Bald 7J 137
Springfield Av. NG10: Sand 6A 104
  NG16: Eastw 4E 72
Springfield Cl. NG12: Crop Bi 5C 112
  NG18: Mans .5C 48

Springfield Ct. NG9: Stap 7E 92
Springfield Dr. NG6: Bulw 1A 84
Springfield Mill NG10: Sand 3A 104
SPRINGFIELD PARK 6A 104
Springfield Retail Pk. NG6: Bulw 6J 75
Springfield Rd. DN22: Retf 2F 23
  NG5: Redh 5G 77
  NG15: Huck .7D 66
  NG25: Sout .4G 131
Springfields NG2: West Br 3A 108
Springfield St. NG7: Basf 6G 85
Springfield Way
  NG17: Kirk A 5D 52
Spring Gdns. NG8: Bilb 1H 93
  NG24: New T 2B 136
Spring Grn. NG11: Clif 3F 115
Springhead Ct. NG6: Bulw 1B 84
Spring Hill NG12: Cols B 5H 141
  NG16: Kimb .2E 82
  NG19: Mans W 6H 41
  NG25: Sout .7J 131
Springhill Cl. NG6: Bulw 5H 75
Springland Farm Cotts. NG16: Nuth 1J 83
              (off Watnall Rd.)
Spring La. NG3: Mapp 1F 87
  NG4: Lamb .1F 87
  NG8: Sook 5A 34
  NG22: Farns 5J 57
  NG23: Flin 7A 140
  NG24: Bald .5H 137
                (not continuous)
  S81: Shire 6A 18
Spring Mdw. NG12: Cotg 6F 111
Springmeadow NG17: Kirk A 1H 59
Spring Moor NG2: Colw 3G 97
Spring Rd. NG6: Bulw 7J 75
  NG17: Sut A 1J 51
Springs La. DN22: Stu S 3A 24
Springs Rd. DN10: Miss 1C 10
Spring St. NG15: Huck 5G 67
Spring Ter. NG16: Nuth 2J 83
Spring Ter. Gdns. NG16: Nuth 1J 83
SPRINGTHORPE 3D 145
Spring Wlk. S80: Work 4F 21
Springwater Golf Course 7G 71
Springwell St. NG17: Huth 1D 50
Springwood Cl. NG14: Calv 6E 70
Springwood Dr. NG19: Mans W 7J 41
Springwood Gdns. NG5: Woodt 4C 86
Springwood Ter. NG17: Stant H 4G 45
                (off Wharf Rd.)
Springwood Vw. Cl.
  NG17: Sut A .7G 45
SPROTBROUGH 1A 144
SPROXTON 3D 149
Spruce Av. NG16: Sels 6B 58
Spruce Ct. S80: Work 3C 20
Spruce Dr. DN22: Retf 5G 23
Spruce Gdns. NG6: Bulw 7G 75
Spruce Gro. NG15: Huck 1H 75
  NG17: Kirk A 5C 52
Sprydon Wlk. NG11: Clif 3G 115
Spur Cres. S80: Work 4J 21
Square, The DN22: Retf 3E 22
  LE12: Costo .3E 122
  NG6: Bestw V 2A 76
  NG8: Woll 4K 93
  NG9: Bee 3A 106
  NG11: Goth .7G 115
  NG12: Key 1H 119
  NG21: Rain .2K 55
Squires Av. NG6: Bulw 5H 75
Squires Cl. NG12: Crop Bi 5C 112
Squires Cft. NG21: K Cli 3K 43
Squires Dr. NG6: Bestw V 7D 68
Squires La. NG21: K Cli 3J 43
Squires Way NG2: West Br 3A 108
Stable Cl. NG13: East B 4E 90
  S81: Work 5H 19
Stable Ct. S80: Welb 1C 26
Stables, The NG14: Thur 6C 138
  NG18: Mans .6K 47
              (off Berry Hill La.)
Stacey Av. NG5: Top V 7B 76
Stacey Rd. NG19: Mans 7D 40
Stackyard, The NG13: Aslo 3D 102
  NG22: Farns 5H 57
              (off Chapel La.)
Stadium Cl. S81: Work 6D 18
Stafford Av. NG6: Bulw 1C 84
  NG24: New B 5F 137
Stafford Cl. NG6: Bulw 2A 84
Staffords Cl. NG4: Neth 1K 97
Stafford St. NG18: Mans 2F 47
Stagsden Cres. NG8: Bilb 3H 93
STAINBY 3D 149
Staindale Ct. NG8: Aspl 6D 84
Staindale Dr. NG8: Aspl 6D 84
STAINFORTH 1B 144
Stainforth St. NG19: Mans W 7J 41
Stainmore Gro. NG13: Bing 4D 100
Stainsborough Rd. NG15: Huck 7C 66
Stainsby Av. NG6: Mans 3C 48
Stainsby Gro. NG17: Huth 1D 50
STAINTON 2A 144
Stakeford Ct. NG5: Arn 4H 77

Stambers Cl. S81: Woods 1A 18
Stamford Ct. NG5: Bestw 6D 76
Stamford Rd. NG2: West Br 4C 108
Stamford St. NG16: Aws 3B 82
  NG16: Newth 5G 73
Stamper Cres. NG17: Skeg 4K 45
Stanage Ct. NG18: Mans 5D 48
Stancliffe Av. NG6: Bulw 7J 75
Standard Cl. NG1: Nott 6D 6 (4J 95)
STANDARD HILL 6D 6 (4J 95)
Standard Hill NG1: Nott 6D 6 (4J 95)
Standhill Av. NG4: Carl 7E 86
Standhill Rd. NG4: Carl 6D 86
Standish Ho. NG24: New T 5D 136
Stanesby Ri. NG11: Clif 1F 115
Stanford Gdns. NG12: Rad T 4E 98
Stanford Hall Est. LE12: Stanf S 7C 122
STANFORD ON SOAR 3A 148
Stanford St. NG1: Nott 6E 6 (4K 95)
STANFREE 1A 146
Stanhome Ct. NG2: West Br 5A 108
Stanhome Dr. NG2: West Br 5A 108
Stanhome Sq. NG2: West Br 5A 108
Stanhope Av. NG5: Sher 6J 85
  NG24: New T 4F 135
Stanhope Cl. NG22: Wale 5G 27
Stanhope Cres. NG5: Arn 6G 77
  NG14: Stoke B 1E 98
Stanhope Rd. NG4: Ged 3G 87
  NG5: Arn 6G 77
Stanhope St. DE7: Ilk 2A 92
  NG1: Nott 5H 7 (4A 96)
Stanhope Way NG13: Bing 4F 101
Staniland Ct. NG9: Chil 7H 105
STANLEY 1C 44
Stanley Av. NG7: H Grn 7H 85
Stanley Cl. NG15: Rave 1C 62
Stanley Ct. NG16: Eastw 5D 72
Stanley Dr. NG9: Bram 1F 105
Stanley La. NG17: Teve 1B 44
Stanley M. NG16: Kimb 7H 73
Stanley Pl. NG1: Nott 4D 6 (3J 95)
Stanley Rd. NG2: West Br 3C 108
  NG3: Mapp .5D 86
  NG7: H Grn .7H 85
                (not continuous)
  NG18: Mans .6H 47
  NG19: Mans W 1D 48
Stanley St. DN22: Retf 6G 23
  NG24: New T 7E 134
  S81: Work 1F 21
Stanley Ter. NG24: New T 1E 136
Stanmore Cl. NG16: Nuth 4K 83
Stanmore Gdns. NG5: Arn 1B 86
                (not continuous)
Stannier Way NG16: Want 7A 74
Stansfield St. NG7: Lent 3F 95
Stanstead Av. NG5: Top V 6K 75
  NG12: Toll 2G 117
Stanthorne Cl. NG11: Wilf 5H 107
STANTON BY DALE 2A 148
Stanton Ct. NG17: Stant H 4G 45
               (off High St.)
Stanton Cres. NG17: Sut A 6H 45
STANTON GATE 7B 92
Stanton Ga. DE7: Stant D 7B 92
STANTON HILL 5H 45 (2A 146)
Stanton La. NG12: Stant W 1K 119
STANTON-ON-THE-WOLDS 2B 148
Stanton Pl. NG18: Mans 3F 47
  NG19: New H 2A 40
Stanton Rd. NG10: Sand 2A 104
Stanton St. NG19: New H 2A 40
Stanway Cl. NG3: Nott 2F 97
Stanwick Cl. NG8: Bilb 7K 83
Stanwick Ct. NG22: New O 5D 38
STAPLEFORD
  Melton Mowbray 3D 149
  Newark-on-Trent 3D 147
  Nottingham 2C 104 (2A 148)
Stapleford By-Pass NG10: Sand 5A 104
Stapleford La. NG9: Toton 5E 104
Stapleford Rd. NG9: Trow 4B 92
Staplehurst Dr. NG5: Sher 3H 85
Staple La. NG24: Bald 7E 136
Staples St. NG3: Mapp 5B 86
Starch Cl. LE12: East L 3A 122
Starch La. NG10: Sand 2A 104
Starling Gro. S81: Gate 6D 18
Starnhill Way NG13: Bing 5F 101
Starr Av. NG17: Sut A 7H 45
Starr's Yd. NG24: New T 1C 136
                (off Mill Ga.)
Starth Wood Rd. NG15: Huck 2D 74
Statham St. S81: Work 7J 19
STATHERN 2C 149
Stathern Wlk. NG5: Bestw 7D 76
Station Av. DN22: Rans 1J 13
  NG4: Ged 6K 87
  NG15: News .6F 61
Station Cl. NG23: Coll 3J 129
Station Hill NG19: Mans W 6H 41
Station La. NG21: Edwin 7E 36
  NG22: Farns 4J 57
  NG25: Fis 5G 139

Station Rd.—Sunnyside Rd.

Station Rd. DE7: Ilk 6A 82
DE74: Sut B 2A 120
DN10: Beck 7D 16
DN10: Miss 2C 10
DN10: Mist 2J 11
DN10: Scro 4K 9
DN10: Walk 7J 11
DN22: Barn M, Sut L 7A 14
DN22: Rans 2J 13
DN22: Retf 5E 22
DN22: Sth L 7C 24
DN22: Stu S 1B 24
LE12: East L 3K 121
LE12: Sut B 2A 120
LE14: Upp B 6K 143
(Nottingham La.)
LE14: Upp B 4F 143
(Sulney Cl.)
NG4: Carl 1H 97
NG6: Bulw 1D 84
NG9: Bee 3A 106
(not continuous)
NG10: Sand 4B 104
NG11: King 1A 120
NG12: Key, Plum 4H 117
NG12: Widm 6K 119
NG13: Elton, Ors 6J 103
NG14: Blea 1A 138
NG14: Bur J 4E 88
NG14: Lowd 5E 80
NG14: Thur 7C 138
NG15: Huck 6H 67
NG15: News 6E 60
NG16: Aws 2B 82
NG16: Kimb 1E 82
NG16: Lang M 4A 72
NG16: Sels 3C 58
NG17: Sut A 1K 51
NG18: Mans 4H 47
NG21: C'tone 7G 43
NG21: Rain 3J 55
NG22: Edin, Kirk 2A 130 & 4C 132
NG22: Kirt 4H 39
NG22: Oll 5A 38
NG23: Coll 2H 129
NG23: Harby 6K 31
NG23: Roll 3J 139
NG23: Sut T 3C 128
NG25: Fis, Sout 4F 139
NG25: Sout 5J 131
Station St. DE7: Ilk 5A 82
DN10: Mist 2H 11
NG2: Nott 7F 7 (5K 95)
NG13: Bing 3G 101
NG17: Kirk A 6A 52
NG17: Sut A 1K 51
NG18: Mans 4H 47
NG19: Mans W 6H 41
Station Street Stop (NET) 7F 7 (5A 96)
Station Ter. NG12: Rad T 5E 98
NG15: Huck 6H 67
Station Vs. NG9: Bee 4B 106
Station Yd. NG17: Skeg 3K 45
Staunton Dr. NG5: Sher 3K 85
STAUNTON IN THE VALE 1D 149
Staunton Rd. NG24: New T 4C 136
Staveley Ct. NG24: Farnd 7H 133
Stavely Way NG2: Gam 2F 109
Staverton Rd. NG8: Bilb 2J 93
STAYTHORPE 3C 147
Staythorpe Rd. NG23: Aver 4F 133
NG23: Roll 3K 139
Steadfold Cl. NG6: Bulw 1C 84
Steads Cl. NG4: Carl 1J 97
Steedman Av. NG3: Mapp 3D 86
Steeles Dr. NG24: Bald 5H 137
Steeles Way NG4: Lamb 7F 79
Steeples, The NG17: Ann W 4J 59
Steetley La. S80: Rhod, Work 1A 20
Steinbeck Rd. NG4: Carl 1F 97
Stella Av. NG12: Toll 2G 117
Stella Gro. NG12: Toll 2G 117
Stella St. NG18: Mans 5H 47
Stenton Cl. NG25: Sout 4H 131
STENWITH 2D 149
Stephen Rd. NG24: New T 4E 134
Stephenson Ct. NG24: New T 5F 135
Stephenson Way NG24: New T 5F 135
Stepnall Hgts. NG22: Bou 2E 38
Stepney Ct. NG8: Brox 6A 84
Sternthorpe Cl. NG23: Sut T 2C 128
Steven Cl. NG9: Toton 5E 104
Stevenholme Cres. NG5: Bestw 1H 85
Stevenson Cres. NG17: Sut A 1H 51
Stevenson Gdns. NG11: Rudd 4A 116
Stevenson Rd. S81: Work 1J 21
Stevens Rd. NG10: Sand 4A 104
Stewart Cl. S81: Carl L 6B 12
Stewarton Cl. NG5: Arn 5K 77
Stewart Rd. S81: Carl L 6B 12
Stiles Rd. NG5: Arn 1F 87
Stillwell Gdns. S81: Gate 4F 19
Stinsford Cl. NG5: Bestw 6E 76
Stinting La. NG19: Mans W 7A 42
Stirling Av. NG19: Mans 5E 46
Stirling Cl. S81: Work 4F 19
Stirling Dr. NG24: Codd 6H 135
S81: Carl L 6B 12
Stirling Gdns. NG9: Chil 7G 105
Stirling Gro. NG11: Clif 2G 115
NG16: Kimb 7J 73
Stirling Rd. DN22: Retf 5D 22
Stockdale Cl. NG5: Arn 4C 76
Stockgill Cl. NG2: West Br 3F 109
Stockhill Cir. NG6: Basf 4D 84
Stockhill La. NG6: Basf 4D 84
Stocking La. LE12: East L 1K 121
Stocks Fold NG22: East M 2C 28
Stocks Rd. NG16: Kimb 7J 73
Stockton St. NG6: Bulw 7H 75
Stock Well NG6: Bulw 1C 84
Stockwell Ct. NG18: Mans 4G 47
Stockwell Ga. NG18: Mans 4G 47
(Dallas St.)
NG18: Mans 3H 47
(Four Seasons Shop. Cen.)
Stockwell Ho. *NG18: Mans* *3G 47*
(off The Connexion)
Stockwell La. NG12: Crop Bi 5C 112
Stockwith Rd.
DN10: Mist, Walk 6J 11
Stodman M. NG24: New T 1C 136
Stodman St. NG24: New T 1C 136
Stoke Av. NG24: New T 5B 136
STOKE BARDOLPH 7E 88 (1B 148)
Stoke Ferry La. NG12: Shel 6E 88
STOKEHAM 1C 147
Stoke La. NG4: Ged 6A 88
NG14: Stoke B 7C 88
(not continuous)
STOKE ROCHFORD 3D 149
Stokesay Wlk. NG2: West Br 4C 108
Stokes Trad. Est. NG18: Mans 6E 46
Stolle Cl. NG5: Arn 7A 78
Stoneacre NG5: Bestw 6D 76
Stone Bank NG18: Mans 6K 47
Stone Bank Ct. NG18: Mans 6K 47
Stonebridge City Farm 3K 7 (3B 96)
Stonebridge Ct. NG3: Nott 3J 7 (3B 96)
Stonebridge Dr. LE12: East L 2B 122
Stonebridge La. NG20: Mkt W 4B 34
Stonebridge Rd.
NG3: Nott 3J 7 (3B 96)
NG20: Mkt W 4C 34
Stonechurch Vw. NG15: Ann 4B 60
Stone Cres. NG19: Mans 3D 46
Stone Cross Ct. NG18: Mans 2H 47
Stone Cross La. NG19: Mans 2H 47
Stonehaven Cl. NG5: Arn 5K 77
Stonehill Cl. DN22: Rans 1J 13
Stonehills Way NG17: Sut A 6B 46
Stonehouse Ter. NG15: News 6D 60
Stonehurst La. LE12: Norm S 7G 121
Stone La. DN22: Nth W 2H 17
Stone Leigh Cl. NG18: Mans 5A 48
Stoneleigh Cl. NG9: Chil 4H 105
Stoneleigh St. NG7: Radf 3B 6 (3H 95)
Stonemasons M. NG17: Kirk A 6B 52
Stonepit Cl. NG3: Nott 6C 86
STONESBY 3D 149
Stonesby Va. NG2: West Br 6J 107
Stoney Bank NG14: Lowd 4D 80
Stoneycroft Rd. NG6: Bulw 2F 85
Stoneyford Ct. NG17: Sut A 6K 45
Stoneyford Rd. NG17: Stant H, Sut A 5H 45
Stoney Houghton Gdns. NG6: Bulw 6F 75
Stoney La. NG9: Trow 2A 92
NG16: Brins 1A 72 & 7B 64
NG16: Sels 5C 58
Stoney St. NG1: Nott 5G 7 (4A 96)
NG9: Bee 2A 106
NG17: Sut A 7K 45
Stonish Hill NG22: Eakr 2A 126
Stony Balk NG22: Lax 5C 124
Stony Clouds Local Nature Reserve 1A 104
Stony Fld. La. NG22: Bils 5C 126
STONY HOUGHTON 2A 146
Storcroft Rd. DN22: Retf 5G 23
Storey Av. NG4: Ged 5H 87
Stornoway Ct. NG9: Bee 4B 106
Storth Av. NG15: Huck 7G 67
Storth La. DE55: Sth N 7A 50
Stort Sq. NG19: Mans W 7K 41
Story Gdns. NG15: Huck 1J 75
Stotfield Rd. NG8: Bilb 3G 93
STOW 3D 145
Stow Ct. NG19: Mans W 6A 42
Stowe Av. NG2: West Br 4A 108
STRAGGLETHORPE
Lincoln 3D 147
Nottingham 2F 111 (2B 148)
Stragglethorpe La. NG12: Rad T 7B 98
Straight Mile DN22: Babw 4A 22
Strand, The NG9: Atten 7J 105
Stranraer Cl. NG19: Mans W 3J 41
Stratford Cl. NG4: Colw 3H 97
Stratford Cres. DN22: Retf 4D 22
Stratford Rd. NG2: West Br 2C 108
Strathaven Rd. S81: Carl L 6C 12
Strathglen Cl. NG16: Kimb 7J 73
Strathmore Cl. NG15: Huck 1E 74
Strathmore Ct. DN11: Birc 1D 8
Strathmore Dr. S81: Carl L 6C 12
Strathmore Rd. NG5: Arn 5K 77
Strawberry Bank NG17: Huth 6B 44
Strawberry Hall La. NG24: New T 6E 134
Strawberry Rd. DN22: Retf 5G 23
Strawberry Way NG19: Mans W 2D 48
Straws Cft. NG13: East B 4E 90
Straw's La. NG13: East B 4E 90
Street La. DN22: Habb 7E 24
Street La. Rd. DN22: Habb 6D 24
STRELLEY 7J 83 (1A 148)
Strelley La. NG8: Stre 7G 83
Strelley Rd. NG8: Bilb, Stre 7H 83
Strelley St. NG6: Bulw 7H 75
Stretton, The *NG7: Lent* *6F 95*
(off Leen Ct.)
Stretton St. NG3: Nott 2G 7 (2A 96)
Striding Edge Cl. NG10: Long E 7A 104
Stripes Vw. NG14: Calv 7D 70
Strome Cl. NG2: Nott 6K 95
Strome Ct. NG2: Nott 6K 95
STROXTON 2D 149
Stuart Av. NG19: Mans W 2B 48
NG22: New O 2D 38
Stuart Cl. NG5: Arn 6K 77
Stuart St. NG17: Sut A 2J 51
NG18: Mans 3A 48
Stubbing Ct. S80: Work 2E 20
Stubbing La. S80: Work 1D 20
STUBTON 1D 149
Studio Theatre, The 3E 108
Studland Cl. NG19: Mans W 3K 41
Studland Way NG2: West Br 4K 107
Stukeley Ct. NG24: New T 6E 134
STURGATE 3D 145
Sturgeon Av. NG11: Clif 5G 107
STURTON BY STOW 3D 145
STURTON LE STEEPLE 2C 24 (3C 145)
Sturton Rd. DN22: Nth L 6C 24
DN22: Sth W 2J 17
Sturton St. NG7: H Grn 7H 85
Styring St. NG9: Bee 3A 106
STYRRUP 5A 8 (2B 144)
Styrrup Ct. DN11: Sty 5A 8
Styrrup Hall Golf Course 4A 8
Styrrup La. DN11: Sty 5A 8
Styrrup Rd. DN11: Harwo 4A 8
DN11: Sty 5A 8
S81: Oldc 6B 8
Sudbury Av. DE7: Ilk 1A 92
NG10: Sand 2A 104
Sudbury Ct. NG18: Mans 5D 48
Sudbury Dr. NG17: Huth 1C 50
Sudbury M. NG16: Eastw 5C 72
Suez St. NG7: Basf 6G 85
Suff La. NG16: Pinx 1A 58
Suffolk Av. DN11: Birc 2G 9
NG9: Bee 5D 106
NG15: Huck 1C 74
Suffolk Gro. DN11: Birc 2G 9
Suffolk Rd. DN11: Birc 2F 9
Sulby Cl. NG19: Mans W 7C 42
Sulis Gdns. S81: Work 5F 19
Sullivan Cl. NG3: Nott 1C 96
Sullivan St. NG7: Radf 3F 95
Sulney Cl. LE14: Upp B 3G 143
Sumburgh Rd. NG11: Clif 1H 115
Summercourt Dr. NG15: Rave 1B 62
Summerdowns NG19: Mans W 1C 48
Summerfield Rd. NG17: Kirk A 4J 51
Summerhill Ct. NG17: Huth 7D 44
Summer Leys Rd. NG2: Nott 5A 96
Summers Rd. NG24: New T 6D 134
Summer Way NG12: Rad T 4D 98
Summerwood La. NG11: Clif 2E 114
Summit Cl. NG17: Kirk A 5A 52
Sunbeam St. NG13: What 4E 102
Sunbourne Ct. NG7: Radf 2A 6 (2H 95)
Sunbury Gdns. NG5: Arn 5J 77
Sunderland Gro. NG8: Stre 5J 83
Sundown Adventureland 5J 25
Sundridge Pk. Cl. NG2: West Br 4K 107
Sunfield Av. S81: Work 1H 21
Sunlea Cres. NG9: Stap 4E 104
Sunnindale Dr. NG12: Toll 1G 117
Sunningdale DN22: Ord 7D 22
Sunningdale Cl. NG17: Kirk A 4J 51
Sunningdale Dr. NG14: Woodbo 1G 79
Sunningdale Rd. NG6: Bulw 1E 84
Sunninghill Dr. NG11: Clif 6F 107
Sunninghill Ri. NG5: Arn 5J 77
Sunny Bank NG18: Mans 7J 47
S81: Work 1G 21
Sunnybank Gdns. DN10: Gri H 2B 16
Sunnycroft NG17: Sut A 2G 51
Sunnycroft Ct. NG18: Mans 1J 47
Sunnydale Rd. NG3: Nott 2E 96
Sunnymede S81: Work 6H 19
Sunny Row NG8: Woll 3K 93
SUNNYSIDE
Rotherham 2A 144
Worksop 6H 19
Sunnyside NG22: Farns 6K 57
NG25: Sout 6F 131
S81: Work 6G 19
Sunnyside Rd. NG9: Chil 3H 105

Sunridge Ct.—Thievesdale La.

Sunridge Ct. NG3: Mapp P 7K **85**
Sunrise Av. NG5: Bestw 2G **85**
NG6: Bestw V 1E **76**
Sunstone Gro. NG17: Sut A 3H **51**
Superbowl
Mansfield 4H **47**
Surbiton Ct. NG3: Mapp 6B **86**
Surbiton Sq. NG8: Cin 4C **84**
Surfleet Cl. NG8: Woll 5H **93**
Surgery La. NG21: Blid 7J **55**
Surgey's La. NG5: Arn 5H **77**
Surrey Ct. NG3: Mapp 6B **86**
Surrey Dr. NG19: Mans 2F **47**
Susan Cl. NG15: Huck 4H **67**
Susan Dr. NG6: Bulw 3E **84**
Sussex Cl. NG16: Gilt 6E **72**
Sussex St. NG1: Nott 6F **7** (4K **95**)
Sussex Way NG10: Sand 4A **104**
SUSWORTH 1D **145**
Sutherland Cl. S81: Costh 4B **12**
Sutherland Dr. NG2: West Br 5D **108**
Sutherland Rd. NG3: Nott 1E **96**
SUTTON
Doncaster 1A **144**
Nottingham 7H **103** (2C **149**)
Sutton Av. NG24: New T 5B **136**
SUTTON BONINGTON 6B **120** (3A **148**)
Sutton Cen. NG17: Sut A 1K **51**
Sutton Cen. Leisure Cen. 1K **51**
Sutton Cl. LE12: Sut B 7C **120**
NG17: Skeg 4A **46**
Sutton Ct. NG16: Eastw 4D **72**
SUTTON CUM LOUND 6B **14** (3B **144**)
Suttonfields Dr. LE12: Sut B 2A **120**
SUTTON FOREST SIDE 7A **46**
Sutton Gdns. NG11: Rudd 4K **115**
Sutton Gro. NG9: Chil 3J **105**
SUTTON IN ASHFIELD 1J **51** (3A **146**)
Sutton in Ashfield Sailing Club 7D **46**
Sutton La. DN22: Babw, Retf 1A **22**
DN22: Sut L 7A **14**
NG13: Elton 7H **103**
NG13: Gran 1K **141**
Sutton Middle La. NG17: Kirk A 3K **51**
SUTTON ON TRENT 3D **128** (2C **147**)
Sutton Parkway Station (Rail) 3B **52**
Sutton Passeys Cres. NG8: Woll 4C **94**
Sutton Rd. NG5: Arn 4H **77**
NG17: Huth 7E **44**
NG17: Kirk A 6J **51**
NG18: Mans 6D **46**
Swab's La. NG12: Crop Bi, Owt 7A **112**
Swain's Av. NG3: Nott 2D **96**
Swale Cl. NG6: Bulw 7K **75**
Swaledale S81: Work 5H **19**
Swaledale Cl. NG8: Aspl 6E **84**
Swale Gro. NG13: Bing 5E **100**
Swales Cl. DN22: Retf 2C **22**
SWALLOW BECK 2D **147**
Swallow Cl. NG6: Basf 3E **84**
NG18: Mans 6D **48**
Swallow Ct. DN10: Mist 2J **11**
Swallow Cres. NG15: Rave 4C **62**
Swallow Dr. NG13: Bing 5G **101**
Swallow Gdns. NG4: Carl 6E **86**
Swallow Gro. S81: Gate 5E **18**
SWALLOWNEST 3A **144**
Swan Ct. LE12: Sut B 6B **120**
S81: Gate 5D **18**
Swan La. NG19: Mans W 6H **41**
Swan Mdw. NG4: Colw 4H **97**
Swann Yd. NG17: Huth 7D **44**
SWANPOOL 1D **147**
Swansdowne Dr. NG11: Clif 7G **107**
Swanson Av. NG17: Huth 7D **44**
Swans Quay DN22: Retf 5F **23**
Swanton Cl. DN22: Retf 1C **22**
Sweeney Ct. NG5: Top V 6C **76**
Sweet Leys Dr. LE12: East L 1A **122**
Sweet Leys Rd. NG2: Nott 7K **95**
Swenson Av. NG7: Lent 5F **95**
Swift Ct. NG16: Eastw 4D **72**
Swifts Vw. NG17: Nunc 3K **59**
Swigert Cl. NG6: Bulw 2A **84**
Swildon Wlk. NG5: Top V 6B **76**
Swinburne Cl. NG24: Bald 4G **137**
Swinburne St. NG3: Nott 2C **96**
Swinburne Way NG5: Arn 7E **76**
Swindale Cl. NG2: Gam 2E **108**
Swindell Cl. NG3: Mapp 2E **86**
SWINDERBY 2D **147**
Swinderby Cl. NG24: New T 7G **135**
S81: Gate 4D **18**
Swinderby Rd. NG23: Coll 2H **129**
Swindon Cl. NG16: Gilt 7G **73**
Swinecot Rd. NG21: Edwin 5F **37**
Swiney Way NG9: Chil, Toton 7E **104**
Swinfen Broun NG18: Mans 7J **47**
SWINGATE 2F **83** (1A **148**)
Swingate NG16: Kimb 2F **83**
Swinnow Rd. DN11: Birc 2F **9**
Swinscoe Gdns. NG5: Top V 6B **76**
Swinstead Cl. NG8: Bilb 2A **94**
SWINTON 2A **144**
Swinton Copse NG22: Bou 2E **38**
Swinton Ri. NG15: Rave 2B **62**
Swithland Dr. NG2: West Br 5B **108**
Sycamore Av. NG17: Kirk A 5J **51**
Sycamore Cl. DN22: Retf 5G **23**
NG11: Rudd 3A **116**
NG12: Rad T 6E **98**
NG13: Bing 4H **101**
NG15: Huck 1E **74**
NG16: Pinx 1B **58**
NG16: Sels 5B **58**
NG21: Rain 2K **55**
NG24: Haw 6A **136**
NG24: New T 4C **136**
S80: Work 4F **21**
Sycamore Ct. DN22: Ord 6E **22**
NG9: Bee 2B **106**
Sycamore Cres. NG10: Sand 2A **104**
Sycamore Dr. DE7: Ilk 1A **92**
Sycamore Gro. NG18: Mans 5B **48**
Sycamore La. NG14: Blea 3C **138**
S81: Blyth 7K **13**
Sycamore Pl. NG3: Mapp P 7K **85**
Sycamore Ri. NG6: Cin 3C **84**
Sycamore Rd. LE12: East L 4K **121**
NG16: Aws 2A **82**
NG19: Mans W 4J **41**
NG22: New O 4D **38**
S81: Carl L 5B **12**
Sycamores, The NG16: Eastw 5C **72**
NG17: Sut A 5H **45**
Sycamore St. NG20: Chu W 2B **34**
Syderstone Wlk. NG5: Arn 2C **86**
Sydney Cl. NG19: Mans W 3J **41**
Sydney Gdns. NG24: New T 2D **136**
Sydney Gro. NG12: Rad T 5D **98**
Sydney Rd. NG8: Woll 3C **94**
Sydney St. NG24: New T 7D **134**
Sydney Ter. NG24: New T 2D **136**
SYERSTON 3B **140** (1C **149**)
Syerston Ct. *NG18: Mans* *1C 54*
(off Bellamy Rd.)
Syerston Hall Pk. NG23: Syer 2A **140**
Syerston Rd. NG18: Mans 1C **54**
Syerston Way NG24: New T 7G **135**
Syke Rd. NG5: Top V 6B **76**
Sykes La. NG24: Bald 5G **137**
Sylvan Av. NG17: Kirk A 1A **60**
Sylvan Cres. NG17: Skeg 5A **46**
Sylvester St. NG18: Mans 5F **47**
Synge Cl. NG11: Clif 2D **114**
Syon Pk. Cl. NG2: West Br 4K **107**
SYSTON 1D **149**
Sywell Cl. NG17: Skeg 5K **45**

T

Taft Av. NG10: Sand 3A **104**
Taftleys Rd. LE12: East L 2B **122**
Talbot Ct. NG12: Rad T 5D **98**
Talbot Dr. NG9: Stap 6C **92**
Talbot Rd. DN11: Birc 2E **8**
S80: Work 3H **21**
Talbot St. NG1: Nott 4C **6** (3J **95**)
NG16: Pinx 2A **58**
NG18: Mans 6H **47**
Tall Gables NG22: Dun T 6J **29**
Tall Trees Pk. Homes NG19: Mans W 7A **42**
Tamarix Cl. NG4: Ged 5K **87**
Tambling Cl. NG5: Arn 1E **86**
Tame Cl. NG11: Clif 5F **107**
Tamworth Gro. NG11: Clif 7G **107**
Tangmere Cres. NG8: Stre 6K **83**
Tankard Building, The *NG24: New T* *6D 134*
(off North Gate)
Tanners Wlk. NG1: Nott 6F **7** (4K **95**)
Tannery Rd. NG16: Gilt 7G **73**
Tannery Wharf NG24: New T 1B **136**
Tannin Cres. NG6: Bulw 2D **84**
Tansley Heath NG18: Mans 5E **48**
Tansy Way NG13: Bing 5D **100**
Tanwood Rd. NG9: Toton 7G **105**
Tanyard NG22: Egma 2D **124**
Tapton Pk. NG18: Mans 3D **48**
Tarbert Cl. NG2: Nott 6J **95**
Target St. NG7: Radf 3F **95**
Tatham's Orchard NG25: Sout 5G **131**
Tattershall Dr. NG7: Nott 5A **6** (4H **95**)
NG9: Bee 2C **106**
Tattershall Wlk. NG19: Mans W 5A **42**
Taunton Rd. NG2: West Br 3C **108**
Taunton Way DN22: Ord 6E **22**
Taupo Dr. NG15: Huck 1C **74**
Tavern Av. NG8: Aspl 5D **84**
Tavistock Av. NG3: Mapp P 6K **85**
Tavistock Cl. NG15: Huck 1D **74**
Tavistock Ct. NG5: Sher 6K **85**
Tavistock Dr. NG3: Mapp P 6K **85**
Tavistock Rd. NG2: West Br 3C **108**
Taylor Cl. NG2: Nott 4D **96**
Taylor Cres. NG9: Stap 1E **104**
NG17: Sut A 2K **51**
S81: Woods 1A **18**
Taylor Dr. S81: Woods 1A **18**
Taylor's Cl. NG18: Mans 2A **48**
Taylors Cft. NG14: Woodbo 2F **79**
Teague Pl. S80: Work 2E **20**
Teak Cl. NG3: Nott 1A **96**
Teal Av. NG18: Mans 6D **48**
Tealby Cl. NG6: Bulw 7F **75**
Tealby Wlk. NG19: Mans W 5A **42**
Teal Cl. NG4: Neth 1A **98**
Teal Ct. S81: Gate 5E **18**
Teal Wharf NG7: Lent 6H **95**
Teasels, The NG13: Bing 5E **100**
Technology Dr. NG9: Bee 4B **106**
Tedburn Dr. NG18: Mans 1C **54**
Teesbrook Dr. NG8: Woll 4G **93**
Tees Ct. NG13: Bing 5E **100**
Teesdale Ct. NG9: Chil 5F **105**
Teesdale Rd. NG5: Sher 5H **85**
TEIGH 3D **149**
Teignmouth Av. NG18: Mans 4B **48**
Telford Ct. NG24: New T 5F **135**
Telford Dr. NG16: Newth 3F **73**
NG24: New T 5F **135**
Teme Ct. NG2: West Br 4C **108**
Temperance La. NG23: Coll 2G **129**
Templar Lodge NG9: Bee 3C **106**
Templar Rd. NG9: Bee 3C **106**
Templars Ct. *NG7: Radf* *2E 94*
(off New Rd.)
Temple Cres. NG16: Nuth 3J **83**
Temple Dr. NG16: Nuth 3K **83**
Templeman Cl. NG11: Rudd 2J **115**
Templemans Way NG25: Sout 6J **131**
Templeoak Dr. NG8: Woll 5H **93**
Tenants Hall Cl. NG9: Lent A 7B **94**
Tenbury Cres. NG8: Aspl 6C **84**
Tenby Gro. S80: Work 3H **21**
Tene Cl. NG5: Arn 4H **77**
Tenman La. NG13: Car C 5H **91**
Tennis Ct. Ind. Est. NG2: Nott 5D **96**
Tennis Dr. NG7: Nott 5B **6** (4H **95**)
Tennis M. NG7: Nott 5B **6** (4H **95**)
Tennis Vw. NG7: Nott 5B **6** (4H **95**)
Tennyson Av. NG4: Ged 6J **87**
NG19: Mans W 7J **41**
Tennyson Ct. NG5: Sher 4J **85**
NG15: Huck 7D **66**
Tennyson Dr. NG9: Atten 7J **105**
S81: Work 1J **21**
Tennyson Grange NG4: Ged 6K **87**
Tennyson Rd. NG5: Woodt 3B **86**
NG24: Bald 5G **137**
Tennyson Sq. NG16: Aws 3B **82**
Tennyson St. NG7: Radf 2A **6** (2H **95**)
(not continuous)
NG17: Kirk A 7B **52**
NG18: Mans 3G **47**
Tenpin
Nottingham 7F **95**
Ten Row NG20: Cuck 4C **32**
Tenter Cl. NG5: Top V 6B **76**
NG17: Sut A 7A **46**
Tenter La. NG18: Mans 5G **47**
Tenters La. NG22: Eakr 4B **126**
Tenzing Wlk. NG24: Bald 5H **137**
Teresa Ct. NG25: Sout 5H **131**
Terrace La. NG19: Plea 4A **40**
Terrace Rd. NG18: Mans 3J **47**
Terrace St. NG7: H Grn 1G **95**
Terrian Cres. NG2: West Br 2C **108**
Terry Av. NG24: New T 5E **134**
Terton Rd. NG5: Top V 6B **76**
Tetford Wlk. *NG19: Mans W* *5A 42*
(off Coton Cl.)
Tether Art Gallery 1E **6** (2K **95**)
Tethering La. DN10: Eve 7C **10**
Tetheringrass La. DN10: Beck 5D **16**
Tetney Wlk. NG8: Bilb 1B **94**
Tettenbury Rd. NG5: Sher 4G **85**
TEVERSAL 2G **45** (2A **146**)
Teversal Av. NG7: Lent 4G **95**
NG19: Plea 5B **40**
Teversal Camping & Caravan Site NG17: Teve 2E **44**
Teversal Pastures Nature Reserve 2J **45**
Teversal Trail Vis. Cen. 3F **45**
Tevery Cl. NG9: Stap 1D **104**
Teviot Rd. NG5: Bestw 2G **85**
Tewkesbury Av. NG19: Mans W 5K **41**
Tewkesbury Cl. NG2: West Br 3D **108**
Tewkesbury Dr. NG6: Basf 3F **85**
NG16: Kimb 7J **73**
Thackeray Cl. S81: Work 1J **21**
Thackeray's La. NG5: Woodt 2A **86**
Thackeray St. NG7: Radf 3A **6** (3G **95**)
Thales Dr. NG5: Arn 7A **78**
Thames St. NG6: Bulw 7H **75**
Thane Rd. NG7: Lent, Nott 3E **106**
Thaxted Cl. NG8: Bilb 2J **93**
The . . . .
Names prefixed with 'The' for example 'The Acre'
are indexed under the main name such as 'Acre, The'
Theatre Royal
Nottingham 4E **6** (3K **95**)
Theatre Sq. NG1: Nott 4E **6**
Thelda Av. NG12: Key 7H **117**
Theresa Ct. NG24: Bald 5G **137**
Thetford Cl. NG5: Arn 1D **86**
Thievesdale Av. S81: Work 5G **19**
Thievesdale Cl. S81: Work 5H **19**
Thievesdale La. S81: Work 5G **19**

Thieves' Wood 4K 53
Thieves Wood La. NG18: Mans 3H 53
Thieves Wood Vis. Cen. 3J 53
Third Av. NG4: Carl 7E 86
(not continuous)
NG4: Ged 6J 87
NG6: Bulw 7H 75
NG7: H Grn 7J 85
NG7: Nott 3D 106
NG19: Mans W 2C 48
NG21: C'tone 6H 43
NG21: Edwin 6E 36
NG21: Rain 1H 55
Thirlmere NG2: West Br 4F 109
Thirlmere Cl. NG3: Nott 1C 96
NG10: Long E 7A 104
Thirlmere Rd. NG10: Long E 7A 104
Thirston Cl. NG6: Bulw 7F 75
Thistle Bank LE12: East L 1A 122
NG19: Mans W 5B 42
Thistle Cl. NG16: Newth 6F 73
Thistledown Rd. NG11: Clif 3F 115
THISTLETON 3D 149
Thomas Av. NG12: Rad T 4H 99
Thomas Cl. NG3: Nott 2H 7 (2A 96)
Thomas Forman Ct. NG5: Sher 6J 85
Thomas Parkyn Cl. NG11: Bunny 3B 118
Thomas Pl. NG23: Nth M 7K 129
Thomas Rd. NG24: Bald 7J 137
Thomas St. DN22: Retf 5F 23
Thompson Av. DN11: Harwo 1C 8
Thompson Cl. LE12: East L 2A 122
NG9: Chil 6H 105
NG24: Codd 6H 135
Thompson Ct. NG9: Chil 7G 105
Thompson Cres. NG17: Sut A 2K 51
Thompson Gdns. NG5: Top V 5C 76
Thompson St. NG16: Lang M 3A 72
THORESBY 1B 146
Thoresby Av. NG2: Nott 7K 7 (5C 96)
NG4: Ged 5G 87
NG17: Kirk A 7D 52
NG21: Edwin 6E 36
NG24: New T 3D 136
Thoresby Cl. DN11: Birc 1E 8
NG12: Rad T 4F 99
NG20: Mede V 1F 35
Thoresby Ct. NG3: Mapp P 7A 86
Thoresby Cres. NG17: Stant H 4G 45
Thoresby Dale NG15: Huck 6H 67
Thoresby Dr. NG21: Edwin 6D 36
Thoresby Gallery 1B 146
Thoresby Glade NG22: Bils 6D 126
Thoresby Rd. NG9: Bram 7H 93
NG13: Bing 4D 100
NG19: Mans W 5G 41
NG21: Rain 2H 55
Thoresby St. NG1: Nott 6J 7 (4B 96)
NG17: Sut A 6A 46
NG18: Mans 3G 47
Thoresby Way DN22: Ord 7E 22
Thor Gdns. NG5: Top V 5B 76
Thorlby Dr. S81: Gate 5B 18
Thorn Av. NG19: Mans 1F 47
Thornbury Dr. NG19: Mans 2D 46
Thornbury Way NG5: Top V 7B 76
Thorncliffe Ho. NG5: Top V 6A 76
Thorncliffe Ri. NG3: Mapp P 7K 85
Thorncliffe Rd. NG3: Mapp P 7K 85
Thorndale Rd. NG6: Basf 5D 84
NG14: Calv 6D 70
Thorn Dr. NG16: Newth 6F 73
Thorndyke Cl. NG9: Bee 5C 106
THORNE 1B 144
Thorne Cl. DN11: Harwo 2A 8
Thorner Cl. NG6: Bulw 2F 85
THORNEY 3G 31 (1D 147)
Thorney Abbey Rd. NG21: Blid 6K 55
Thorney Ct. NG18: Mans 1C 54
Thorney Hill NG3: Nott 1C 96
Thorney Rd. NG23: Wigs 7F 31
THORNEYWOOD 7D 86
Thorneywood Av. NG17: Ann W 4J 59
Thorneywood Mt. NG3: Nott 1C 96
Thorneywood Ri. NG3: Nott 1C 96
Thornfield Ind. Est. NG3: Nott 3C 96
Thorn Gro. NG15: Huck 2H 75
Thornham Cres. NG17: Nunc 4K 59
Thornhill Cl. NG9: Bram 6G 93
Thornhill Dr. DE55: Sth N 5A 50
NG22: Bou 3E 38
Thornhill Rd. DN11: Harwo 2A 8
Thornley St. NG7: H Grn 1F 95
Thorn Ter. NG18: Mans 3G 47
Thornthwaite Cl. NG2: West Br 3F 109
Thornton Av. NG5: Redh 5F 77
Thornton Cl. NG8: Woll 4K 93
NG18: Mans 5D 48
NG22: Bils 6D 126
Thornton Dale S81: Work 5J 19
Thornton Rd. NG13: Aslo 1F 103
NG23: Coll 2H 129
Thorntons Cl. NG12: Cotg 6F 111
Thornton's Holt Camping Pk. NG12: Rad T 1C 110
Thornton St. NG17: Sut A 2K 51
Thorn Tree Gdns. NG16: Eastw 2D 72
Thorold Cl. NG11: Clif 7F 107
THOROTON 1C 149
Thoroton Av. NG24: Bald 6G 137
Thoroton Rd. NG2: West Br 7C 96
Thoroton St. NG7: Radf 3A 6 (3H 95)
Thoroughfare La. NG24: Wint 1G 135
THORPE 1C 149
THORPE ACRE 3A 148
THORPE ARNOLD 3C 149
Thorpe Cl. NG5: Top V 6B 76
NG9: Stap 2B 104
NG24: New T 5B 136
Thorpe Cres. NG3: Mapp 5E 86
THORPE IN BALNE 1A 144
THORPE IN THE FALLOWS 3D 145
THORPE IN THE GLEBE 7K 123
Thorpelands Av. NG19: Mans W 1A 48
Thorpe La. NG12: Wys 3K 123
NG24: Farnd 7H 133
Thorpe Lea NG14: Gun 2A 90
THORPE ON THE HILL 2D 147
Thorpe Rd. DN10: Matt, Matt T 1G 15
NG16: Eastw 2D 72
NG18: Mans 1C 54
THORPE SALVIN 3A 144
Thrapston Av. NG5: Arn 4H 77
Thraves Yd. NG12: Rad T 5D 98
Three Leys La. DN22: Fen 4C 24
THREE THORN HOLLOW 1F 55
Three Tuns Rd. NG16: Eastw 4E 72
Threlkeld Cl. NG2: West Br 3F 109
THRUMPTON
Nottingham 2A 148
Retford 5F 23
Thrumpton Cl. DN22: Retf 6F 23
Thrumpton Dr. NG2: Nott 7J 95
Thrumpton La. DN22: Retf 4F 23
THRUSSINGTON 3B 148
THRYBERGH 2A 144
THURCROFT 3A 144
THURGARTON 6D 138 (1B 148)
Thurgarton Av. NG2: Nott 4C 96
Thurgarton La. NG14: Hove 1K 81
Thurgarton Station (Rail) 7D 138
Thurgarton St. NG2: Nott 4C 96
Thurland St. NG1: Nott 5F 7 (4K 95)
Thurlbeck NG12: Cotg 7F 111
THURLBY 2D 147
Thurlby Cl. NG12: Crop Bi 5B 112
Thurlby Ct. NG19: Mans W 5A 42
Thurlestone Dr. NG3: Mapp 1F 87
Thurley Wlk. NG18: Mans 6D 48
Thurloe Ct. NG2: West Br 6K 107
Thurman Dr. NG12: Cotg 6E 110
Thurman St. DE7: Ilk 2A 92
NG7: H Grn 2G 95
THURNSCOE 1A 144
Thursby Rd. NG11: Clif 6F 107
Thurstan Way S80: Work 3H 21
Thymus Wlk. NG11: Clif 1D 114
Thyra Ct. NG3: Nott 6B 86
Thyra Gro. NG3: Nott 6A 86
NG9: Bee 3B 106
Tibshelf Bus. Pk. DE55: Tibs 4A 44
Tibshelf Rd. NG17: Teve 3E 44
TIBSHELF SERVICE AREA 4A 44
TICKHILL 2A 144
Tickhill Rd. DN11: Harwo 1B 8
Tideswell Cl. NG15: Rave 1C 62
Tideswell Ct. NG18: Mans 3K 47
Tidworth Cl. NG8: Bilb 2B 94
Tilberthwaite Cl. NG2: Gam 3F 109
Tilbury Ri. NG8: Cin 4B 84
Tilford Gdns. NG9: Stap 3D 104
Tilford Rd. NG15: News 6D 60
Tiln Ct. DN22: Retf 1F 23
Tiln La. DN22: Bol, Retf 1F 23
Tilstock Ct. NG16: Want 6A 74
Tim La. NG14: Bur J 3E 88
Timothy Rd. NG22: Lax 5B 124
Timson Ct. DN10: Beck 7D 16
Tindall Cl. NG9: Chil 7G 105
Tinker's Hill S81: Carl L 7D 12 & 1J 19
Tinker's La. NG23: Girt 5G 125
Tinkers Way NG7: Lent 5J 95
Tinsley Rd. NG16: Eastw 5C 72
Tintagel Grn. NG11: Clif 1F 115
Tintern Cl. NG17: Kirk A 7C 52
Tintern Dr. NG8: Basf 5E 84
Tippett Ct. NG3: Nott 2C 96
Tippings La. NG22: Farns 6K 57
Tip Tree Cl. NG16: Kimb 7K 73
Tiree Cl. NG9: Trow 6C 92
Tishbite St. NG6: Bulw 7H 75
Tissington Av. NG20: Chu W 1E 34
Tissington Cl. NG7: H Grn 7H 85
Tissington Rd. NG7: H Grn 7H 85
Titchfield Av. NG17: Sut A 1J 51
NG19: Mans W 6K 41
Titchfield Ct. NG15: Huck 7G 67
Titchfield St. NG15: Huck 6H 67
NG19: Mans 2G 47
NG20: Mkt W 5D 34
Titchfield Ter. NG15: Huck 6H 67
TITHBY 3E 112 (2B 148)
Tithby Ct. NG18: Mans 1C 54
Tithby Dr. NG5: Sher 3A 86
Tithby Rd. NG12: Crop Bu 3C 112
NG13: Bing, Lang, Tith 5F 101
(not continuous)
NG13: Tith 3C 112
Tithe Barn Ct. NG24: New T 7D 134
Tithe Gdns. NG5: Top V 5C 76
Tithe La. NG14: Calv 6D 70
Tiverton Cl. NG8: Aspl 5C 84
NG15: Huck 1D 74
TOADHOLE 6A 58
Toad La. NG14: Epp 1A 80
NG22: Lax 6A 124
NG23: Elston 2E 140
Tobias Cl. NG5: Top V 6B 76
Todd Cl. NG11: Clif 2D 114
Todd Ct. NG11: Clif 2D 114
TODWICK 3A 144
Toft Cl. NG12: Cotg 7D 110
Toft Dyke La. DN22: Clay 6J 15
Toft Rd. NG9: Chil 6F 105
Token Ho. Yd. NG1: Nott 5F 7
TOLL BAR 1A 144
TOLLERTON 1G 117 (2B 148)
Tollerton Grn. NG6: Bulw 2E 84
Tollerton La. NG12: Toll 2G 117
Tollerton Pk. Caravan Pk. NG12: Toll 3H 109
Tollerton Rd. NG12: Toll 3G 109
Tollhouse Hill NG1: Nott 4D 6 (3J 95)
Tolney La. NG24: New T 1A 136
Tom Blower Cl. NG8: Woll 3B 94
Tomlinson Av. NG11: Goth 7F 115
Tom Wass Rd. NG17: Sut A 3J 51
Tonbridge Mt. NG8: Woll 6J 93
Ton La. NG14: Lowd 4D 80
Tonnelier Rd. NG7: Lent 7F 95
Toothill La. NG18: Mans 3H 47
Toothill Rd. NG18: Mans 3H 47
Topaz Cres. NG17: Sut A 3H 51
Topaz Gro. NG18: Mans 6K 47
Top Cart Gaps NG22: East M 1D 28
TOP GREEN 7E 140
Top Green LE14: Upp B 3H 143
Top La. NG19: Plea 7A 40
NG22: Egma 1B 124
Topliff Rd. NG9: Chil 7H 105
Top Pasture La. DN22: Nth W 2J 17
Top Rd. DN10: Miss 2C 10
NG11: Rudd 4K 115
NG21: Blid 2J 63
NG23: Thor 4G 31
Top Row NG14: Stoke B 1C 98
NG19: Plea 2F 41
NG22: Oll 6C 38
NG24: New T 1F 137
Top Sandy La. NG20: Mkt W 5E 34
Top St. DN22: Nth W 2H 17
NG21: Rain 2K 55
NG23: Elston 2D 140
TOP VALLEY 6A 76
Top Valley Dr. NG5: Top V 6A 76
Top Valley Way NG5: Top V 7A 76
Topyard La. DN22: Hay 5H 17
Torbay Cres. NG5: Bestw 1J 85
Torkard Ct. NG15: Huck 1G 75
Torkard Dr. NG5: Top V 6B 76
TORKSEY 1D 147
Torksey M. DN22: Ord 7D 22
Torksey St. DN22: Ramp 6K 25
Torksey Wlk. NG19: Mans W 5A 42
Tor La. NG22: Oll 5A 38
Torrington Ct. NG5: Sher 5A 86
Torvill Dr. NG8: Woll 3K 93
Torvill Hgts. NG8: Woll 3K 93
TORWORTH 4J 13 (3B 144)
Toston Dr. NG8: Woll 4D 94
Totland Dr. NG8: Basf 5E 84
Totland Rd. NG9: Bram 6H 93
Totley Cl. NG6: Bulw 4J 75
Totnes Cl. NG15: Huck 7D 66
Totnes Rd. NG3: Nott 3E 96
TOTON 7F 105 (2A 148)
Toton Cl. NG6: Bulw 2E 84
Toton La. NG9: Stap 2C 104
Toton Sidings NG9: Toton 6C 104
Tottle Gdns. NG7: Radf 2E 94
Tottle Rd. NG2: Nott 1H 107
Tourist Info. Cen.
Mansfield 3H 47
Newark-on-Trent 7C 134
Nottingham 5F 7 (4K 95)
Retford 3F 23
Southwell 6H 131
Worksop 3G 21
Tow Ct. NG24: Farnd 7H 133
Tower Cres. NG16: Kimb 3F 83
Towe's Mt. NG4: Carl 1H 97
Towlson Ct. NG9: Chil 6J 105
Towlsons Cft. NG6: Basf 4E 84
Town End NG22: Lax 5A 124
Town End Cotts. NG12: Plum 3H 117
Town End La. NG23: Flin 6B 140
Town Hall Museum & Art Gallery
Newark-on-Trent 1C 136
Town Hall Yd. DN22: Retf 3F 23
Townhill Sq. NG24: Bald 7J 137

Town La. DE55: Newton 7A **44**
  NG23: Grass 3K **125**
Town Mill Cl. NG25: Sout 4H **131**
Townroe Dr. NG19: Mans 2D **46**
Townsend Ct. NG5: Top V 5C **76**
Townside La. DN22: Tres 5H **25**
Townside Rd. DN22: Nth L 6C **24**
Town St. DN22: Clay 6H **15**
  DN22: Lound 5D **14**
  DN22: Sth L 2G **25**
  DN22: Sut L 6A **14**
  DN22: Tres 5F **25**
  NG9: Bram 1G **105**
  NG10: Sand 4A **104**
  NG16: Pinx 7B **50**
  NG23: Grass 3K **125**
Town Vw. NG16: Kimb 7K **73**
Towson Av. NG16: Lang M 4A **72**
Towson Fld. LE12: East L 2A **122**
Towyn Ct. NG5: Bestw 7C **76**
Tracy Cl. NG9: Bram 7K **93**
Trafalgar Cl. NG7: Radf 2G **95**
Trafalgar Rd. NG9: Bee 5B **106**
Trafalgar Sq. NG23: Sut T 3E **128**
Traffic St. NG2: Nott 5K **95**
Trafford Gdns. NG8: Aspl 1E **94**
Tranby Gdns. NG8: Woll 4A **94**
Tranker La. S80: Rhod 6C **18**
  S81: Rhod, Shire 5B **18**
          (not continuous)
Travellers Site DN22: Lound 2A **14**
Travell's Hill LE12: Norm S 5G **121**
Travers Rd. NG10: Sand 3A **104**
Treegarth Sq. NG5: Top V 5D **76**
Tree La. NG18: Mans 5C **48**
Tree Vw. Cl. NG5: Arn 5E **76**
Trefan Gdns. NG5: Bestw 7C **76**
Trefoil Cl. NG13: Bing 5E **100**
Trelawn Cl. NG5: Sher 5A **86**
Tremadoc Ct. NG5: Sher 7J **85**
Tremayne Rd. NG8: Bilb 2H **93**
Trenchard Cl. NG13: Newton 1C **100**
Trent Av. NG11: Rudd 2K **115**
Trent Bank NG23: Sth C 7C **30**
Trent Blvd. NG2: West Br 7C **96**
Trent Bridge .7B **96**
Trent Bri. NG2: Nott, West Br 7B **96**
Trent Bri. Bldgs. NG2: West Br 7B **96**
Trent Bri. Rd. DN22: Ord 6E **22**
Trent Bus. Cen. NG10: Long E 7B **104**
Trent Cl. NG23: Nth M 6K **129**
Trent Cotts. NG23: Kel 1H **133**
Trent Ct. NG2: West Br 7D **96**
Trent Cres. NG9: Atten 6K **105**
Trentdale Rd. NG4: Carl 2G **97**
Trent Dr. NG15: Huck 3D **74**
Trentfield Farm Camping & Caravan Pk.
  DN22: Chu L 1J **29**
Trent Gdns. NG14: Bur J 3F **89**
Trentham Dr. NG8: Aspl 1D **94**
Trentham Gdns. NG8: Aspl 1D **94**
  NG14: Bur J 4C **88**
Trent Ho. NG24: Farnd 7G **133**
Trent La. NG2: Nott 5C **96**
          (not continuous)
  NG13: East B 3B **90**
  NG14: Bur J 3F **89**
  NG14: Gun 3A **90**
  NG23: Kel, Sth M 1H **133**
  NG23: Nth C 3C **30**
  NG23: Sth C 7C **30**
  NG23: Syer 1A **140**
  NG24: New T 6D **134**
  NG25: Fis 7H **139**
TRENTLOCK 2A **148**
Trenton Cl. NG9: Bram 7F **93**
Trent Rd. NG2: Nott 4C **96**
  NG9: Bee 5B **106**
  NG22: Bou 4G **39**
  NG23: Best 7F **125**
Trentside NG2: West Br 1B **108**
  NG9: Bee *6B **106***
          (off Riverside Rd.)
Trentside Bus. Village NG24: New T 5K **133**
Trentside Nth. NG2: West Br 7B **96**
Trent Sth. Ind. Pk. NG2: Nott 5D **96**
Trent St. DN22: Retf 4G **23**
  NG2: Nott 7G 7 (5A **96**)
  S80: Work 1F **21**
Trent Vale Rd. NG9: Bee 5B **106**
Trent Valley Rd. NG4: Ged, Neth 1A **98**
  NG14: Bur J 1A **98**
  NG3: Mapp *6D **86***
Trent Valley Vw. *NG3: Mapp* *6D **86***
          (off Hickling Rd.)
Trentview Ct. NG2: Nott 6C **96**
Trent Vw. Gdns. NG12: Rad T 3F **99**
Trent Vs. NG24: New T 5K **133**
Trent Wlk. NG19: Mans W 5A **42**
Trent Way NG24: New T 6E **134**
TRESWELL 5G 25 (1C **147**)
Treswell Ct. NG18: Mans 1C **54**
Treswell Rd. DN22: Ramp 6J **25**
  DN22: Sth L 4G **25**
Trevelyan Rd. NG2: West Br 1C **108**
Trevino Gdns. NG5: Top V 5C **76**

Trevone Av. NG9: Stap 3D **104**
Trevor Rd. NG2: West Br 3D **108**
  NG9: Bee 4A **106**
Trevose Gdns. NG5: Sher 4A **86**
Treyford Cl. NG11: Wilf 5H **107**
Triangle, The DE7: Ilk 2A **92**
  NG2: Nott 6H **95**
Tricornia Dr. NG6: Cin 3C **84**
Tring Va. NG5: Sher 3H **85**
Trinity Av. NG7: Lent 5F **95**
Trinity Cres. NG4: Lamb 7G **79**
  NG22: East M 2E **28**
          (not continuous)
Trinity Pl. DN22: Retf 3E **22**
  NG25: Sout 6G **131**
Trinity Rd. DN22: Retf 1D **22**
  NG21: Edwin 6D **36**
  NG24: New T 5D **136**
  NG25: Sout 6F **131**
Trinity Row NG1: Nott 4E 6 (3K **95**)
Trinity Sq. NG1: Nott 4E 6 (3K **95**)
Trinity Wlk. NG1: Nott 4F 7 (3K **95**)
Trinstead Way NG5: Bestw 7E **76**
Triumph Cl. NG22: Eakr 3D **126**
Triumph Rd. NG7: Lent 4E **94**
  NG8: Lent 4E **94**
  NG22: Eakr 3C **126**
Trivett Sq. NG1: Nott 6H **7**
Troon Cl. NG16: Kimb 7J **73**
Troon Ct. DN22: Ord 7E **22**
Trough Balk La. DN22: Nth W 1K **17**
Trough La. NG16: Want 6K **73**
  NG16: Want 6K **73**
Troutbeck NG12: Cotg 6F **111**
Troutbeck Cres. NG9: Bram 1H **105**
TROWELL 4B 92 (2A **148**)
Trowell Av. NG8: Woll 3G **93**
Trowell Ct. NG18: Mans 1C **54**
Trowell Gdns. NG8: Bilb 3H **93**
Trowell Gro. NG9: Trow 5C **92**
  NG10: Long E 7A **104**
Trowell La. NG12: Sut B 6E **120**
TROWELL MOOR .3G **93**
Trowell Pk. Dr. NG9: Trow 5C **92**
Trowell Rd. NG8: Woll 4G **93**
  NG9: Stap 6D **92**
TROWELL SERVICE AREA 2D **92**
Trueman Ct. S81: Work 7J **19**
Trueman Gdns. NG5: Arn 1E **86**
Truman Cl. NG3: Nott 2G 7 (2A **96**)
Truman Dr. NG15: Huck 7G **67**
Trumans Rd. NG2: Nott 7A **96**
Truro Cl. LE12: East L 3K **121**
Truro Cres. NG7: Radf 1F **95**
Trusley Wlk. NG19: Mans W 5A **42**
          (Bow St.)
  NG19: Mans W 6A **42**
          (Calver St.)
Tryst, The NG24: New T 6D **134**
Tuckers La. NG19: Mans 2F **47**
Tuckwood Cl. NG21: Rain 6K **123**
Tudor Av. NG19: Mans W 2B **48**
Tudor Cl. NG4: Colw 3H **97**
  NG24: New T 1E **136**
Tudor Ct. NG9: Stap 4C **104**
  NG15: Huck 1C **74**
  NG16: Sels 6B **58**
Tudor Cres. NG21: Rain 3J **55**
Tudor Dr. NG18: Mans 6J **47**
Tudor Gro. NG1: Nott 1D 6 (1J **95**)
Tudor Oaks NG23: Elston 1D **140**
Tudor Rd. NG2: West Br 2C **108**
Tudor Sq. NG2: West Br 2C **108**
Tudor St. NG17: Sut A 2J **51**
Tudsbury Ter. NG17: Sut A 7A **46**
Tudwal Cl. NG5: Bestw 7C **76**
Tudwal Wlk. NG5: Bestw 7C **76**
Tulip Av. NG3: Nott 1H 7 (1A **96**)
Tulip Rd. NG16: Aws 2A **82**
Tumble Town Play Cen. 6G **77**
Tunnel Rd. DN22: Ord 5E **22**
  NG7: Nott 6A 6 (4H **95**)
Tunstall Cres. NG8: Aspl 6B **84**
Tunstall Dr. NG5: Sher 3G **85**
Tunstall Rd. NG5: Woodt 3C **86**
Tupcroft Rd. DN10: Mist 4F **11**
Turnberry S81: Work 7J **19**
Turnberry Av. NG17: Kirk A 4J **51**
Turnberry Cl. NG9: Bram 3H **105**
Turnberry Ct. NG12: Edwal 6F **109**
Turnberry Rd. NG6: Bulw 1E **84**
  NG9: Stap 3D **104**
Turner Cl. NG5: Sher 2J **85**
Turner Dr. NG16: Gilt 7F **73**
  S81: Work 1G **21**
Turner La. NG22: Bou 2E **38**
Turner Rd. S81: Work 1F **21**
Turner Rd. Ind. Est. S81: Work 1F **21**
Turners Cft. DN22: Nth L 7B **24**
Turners Cl. NG15: Huck 6G **67**
Turneys Ct. NG2: Nott 7B **96**
Turney St. NG2: Nott 7A **96**
Turnley Rd. DE55: Sth N 5A **50**
Turnpike, The NG22: Halam 4C **130**
Turnpike La. NG9: Bee 1B **106**

Turnpike Village NG9: Bee 1B **106**
Turnstone Cres. NG18: Mans 6D **48**
Turnstone Wharf NG7: Lent 6G **95**
Turpin Av. NG4: Ged 4G **87**
Turton Ct. NG15: News 6E **60**
Turton Dr. NG5: Arn 7G **77**
Tutlin Ct. LE12: East L 3A **122**
Tutt Cl. NG24: Bald 7J **137**
TUXFORD 7C 28 (1C **147**)
Tuxford Av. NG20: Mede V 7F **33**
Tuxford Cl. NG18: Mans 1C **54**
Tuxford Rd. NG22: Bou, New O 4D **38**
  NG22: East M 3C **28**
  NG22: Egma 1D **124**
  NG22: Kirt, Wale 5H **27**
  NG23: Norm T 1G **125**
Tuxford Wlk. NG3: Nott 2C **96**
Tuxford Windmill 5B **28**
Twells Cl. NG3: Nott 1K 7 (1C **96**)
Twentylands Dr. LE12: East L 3K **121**
Twin Oaks Dr. NG17: Sut A 1G **51**
Twinyards Cl. NG17: Sut A 2G **51**
Twitchell, The NG9: Chil 5K **105**
  NG17: Sut A 1K **51**
  NG24: New T 4B **136**
Twitchell Vw. NG17: Sut A 2K **51**
Two Acres S81: Blyth 7H **13**
Twycross Rd. NG5: Bestw 7D **76**
Twyford Gdns. NG11: Clif 5F **107**
Twyford La. DN22: Elk, West D 2H **27**
Tyburn Cl. NG5: Arn 5C **76**
Tylden Rd. S80: Rhod 7B **18**
Tylden Way S80: Rhod 7B **18**
Tyne Cl. NG8: Aspl 5D **84**
Tynedale Cl. NG8: Aspl 6E **84**
Tyne Gdns. NG15: Huck 3D **74**
Tyrian St. NG16: Gilt 6F **73**

U

UK Superbowl
  Newark-on-Trent 1C **136**
          (within Castlegate Cen.)
Ulldale Ct. NG9: Chil 5G **105**
ULLEY 3A **144**
Ullscarf Cl. NG2: West Br 4F **109**
Ullswater Cl. NG2: Gam 3G **109**
  NG4: Ged 5J **87**
Ullswater Cres. NG9: Bram 7H **93**
Ullswater Dr. NG15: Huck 6F **67**
UNDERWOOD 4E 64 (3A **146**)
Underwood Av. DN22: Torw 3J **13**
Underwood Gdns. S80: Work 2D **20**
UNDERWOOD GREEN 3D **64**
UNDERWOOD HILL .3C **64**
Union Cl. NG15: Lin 3G **67**
Union Rd. NG1: Nott 3F 7 (3K **95**)
  NG3: Nott 3G 7 (3A **96**)
Union St. DN22: Retf 3F **23**
  NG9: Bee 3A **106**
  NG13: Bing 4F **101**
  NG16: Sels 5E **58**
  NG17: Sut A 1K **51**
  NG18: Mans 3G **47**
Unity Cres. NG3: Mapp 5F **87**
Unity Rd. NG17: Kirk A 4B **52**
University Blvd. NG7: Nott 1C **106**
  NG9: Bee 1C **106**
University of Nottingham, The
  Jubilee Campus 4E **94**
  King's Meadow Campus 7G **95**
  Sutton Bonington Campus 3A **120**
  Sutton Bonington Campus Dairy Cen. 1B **120**
  University Pk. Campus 6D **94**
University Pk. NG7: Nott 7C **94**
Unwin Rd. NG17: Sut A 7B **46**
Unwin St. NG17: Huth 7E **44**
Uplands Ct. NG8: Woll 2A **94**
Upminster Dr. NG5: Arn 5H **77**
  NG16: Nuth 3J **83**
UPPER BROUGHTON 3H 143 (3B **148**)
Upper Canaan NG11: Rudd 2A **116**
Up. College St. NG1: Nott 4C 6 (3J **95**)
Up. Cross La. NG20: Mkt W 4E **34**
Up. Eldon St. NG2: Nott 5K 7 (4B **96**)
UPPER LANGWITH .2A **146**
Up. Mexborough Rd. NG16: Sels 5E **58**
Up. Mill St. NG17: Sut A 7B **46**
Up. Orchard St. NG9: Stap 2D **104**
Up. Parliament St.
  NG1: Nott 4D 6 (3J **95**)
UPPER PLEASLEY .4A **40**
Upper Row NG22: Dun T 6H **29**
UPPER SAXONDALE 5K **99**
UPPERTHORPE 1C **145**
Up. Wellington St. NG10: Long E 7B **104**
UPPER WHISTON .3A **144**
Uppingham Cres. NG2: West Br 4A **108**
Uppingham Gdns. NG2: Nott 6A **96**
UPTON
  Gainsborough 3D **145**
  Newark 7C 132 (3C **147**)
  Pontefract 1A **144**
  Retford .1C **147**
Upton Dr. NG5: Sher 2A **86**

Upton Hall Time Mus. 7B **132**
Upton M. NG3: Nott 7E **86**
Upton Mt. NG19: Mans 1E **46**
Upton Rd. NG25: Sout 6J **131**
Urban Rd. NG17: Kirk A 6A **52**
Utile Gdns. NG6: Bulw 7G **75**

V

Vale Av. NG20: Mkt W 4C **34**
Valebrook Rd. NG5: Sher 2K **85**
Vale Cl. NG3: Aslo 4D **102**
  NG16: Eastw 4F **73**
  NG18: Mans 6A **48**
Vale Ct. NG19: Mans W 6H **41**
Vale Cres. Nth. NG8: Aspl 2E **94**
Vale Cres. Sth. NG8: Aspl 2E **94**
Vale Gdns. NG4: Colw 3G **97**
Valentine Av. NG16: Sels 5B **58**
Valerian Way NG13: Bing 4D **100**
Vale Rd. NG4: Colw 3H **97**
  NG19: Mans W 5G **41**
Valeside Gdns. NG4: Colw 3H **97**
Valetta Rd. NG5: Arn 7K **77**
Vale Vw. NG24: New T 4A **136**
Valeview Ho. NG12: Cotg 6E **110**
Vallance St. NG19: Mans W 5H **41**
Valley App. NG22: Bils 5C **126**
Valley Ct. NG4: Carl 6E **86**
  NG5: Sher .2A **86**
Valley Dr. NG16: Newth 4F **73**
Valley Farm Ct. NG5: Top V 6C **76**
Valley Gdns. NG2: West Br 4F **109**
Valley Ho. NG1: Nott 6D **6**
Valley Prospect NG24: New T 3A **136**
Valley Rd. NG2: West Br 4D **108**
  NG4: Carl 6E **86**
  NG5: Basf, Sher 5G **85**
  NG9: Chil 4F **105**
  NG12: Rad T 3F **99**
  NG16: Kimb 7H **73**
  NG22: Bils .4B **126**
  S81: Work .5F **19**
Valley Vw. NG18: Mans 6A **48**
  NG24: Codd 7K **135**
Valmont Av. NG18: Mans 4C **48**
Valmont Rd. NG5: Sher 4H **85**
  NG9: Bram .1F **105**
Vancouver Av. NG12: Rad T 6D **98**
Vantage, The NG7: H Grn 7J **85**
Varden Av. NG9: Lent A 7B **94**
Varney Rd. NG11: Clif 6G **107**
Vaughan Av. NG15: Huck 4J **67**
Vaughan Rd. NG9: Chil 5F **105**
Vedonis Pk. NG15: Huck 1G **75**
Vellus Ct. NG17: Sut A 1B **52**
Venn Ct. NG9: Bee 3A **106**
Ventnor Ri. NG5: Sher 3G **85**
Ventura Ct. NG17: Kirk A 4C **52**
Ventura Dr. NG6: Bulw 5J **75**
Venture Av. NG17: Huth 3D **50**
Venus Cl. NG6: Basf 2F **85**
Vera Cres. NG21: Rain 3K **55**
Verbena Cl. NG3: Nott 1A **96**
Verder Gro. NG5: Top V 6A **76**
Vere Av. NG17: Sut A 6J **45**
Vere St. NG6: Bulw 7H **75**
Verne Cl. NG4: Carl 1F **97**
Verney St. NG19: New H 2A **40**
Verney Way NG19: New H 2A **40**
Vernon Av. DN22: Retf 6G **23**
  NG4: Carl 7J **87**
  NG6: Basf 4F **85**
  NG9: Bee 3A **106**
  NG11: Wilf .1J **107**
  NG15: Rave 3B **62**
  NG24: New T 1E **136**
Vernon Ct. NG12: Rad T 5E **98**
  NG16: Nuth 4A **84**
Vernon Cres. NG15: Rave 3B **62**
Vernon Dr. NG16: Nuth 4A **84**
Vernon Pk. Dr. NG6: Basf 4F **85**
Vernon Pk. Trad. Est.
  NG6: Basf 4F **85**
Vernon Pl. NG6: Basf 3E **84**
Vernon Rd. NG6: Basf 3E **84**
  NG17: Kirk A 6K **51**
Vernon St. NG1: Nott 4C **6** (3J **95**)
  NG24: New T 1E **136**
Vernon Works NG6: Basf 4F **85**
Verona Av. NG4: Colw 2J **97**
Verona Ct. NG18: Mans 7C **48**
Veronica Dr. NG4: Carl 6G **87**
  NG16: Gilt .6G **73**
Veronica Wlk. NG11: Clif 1D **114**
Veronne Dr. NG17: Skeg 4A **46**
Versailles Gdns. NG15: Huck 1G **75**
Vesper Ct. NG19: Mans W 2B **48**
Vessey Cl. NG24: New B 5F **137**
Vessey Rd. S81: Work 5F **19**
Vicarage Cl. NG5: Sher 4G **85**
  NG23: Coll .1H **129**
Vicarage Ct. NG17: Skeg 3J **45**
  NG19: Mans 7E **40**
  NG24: Codd 6K **135**

Vicarage Dr. DN22: Hay 6H **17**
  NG14: Bur J 3D **88**
Vicarage Gdns. NG24: Bald 5H **137**
Vicarage Grn. NG12: Edwal 6E **108**
Vicarage La. DN10: Beck 5D **16**
  DN10: Scro .3H **9**
  NG11: Rudd 3K **115**
  NG12: Rad T 5D **98**
  NG22: Farns 5J **57**
  NG23: Nth M 4H **129**
Vicarage Rd. NG23: Sth C 7D **30**
  NG25: Sout 6F **131**
Vicarage St. NG9: Bee 3K **105**
Vicarage Way NG17: Ann W 4K **59**
Vicar La. DN10: Miss 2D **10**
Vicars Ct. NG21: C'tone 7H **43**
  NG25: Sout 6H **131**
Vicar's Wlk. S80: Work 3G **21**
Vicar Water Cl. NG21: C'tone 7H **43**
Vicar Water Country Pk. 7H **43**
Vicar Water Vis. Cen. 7H **43**
Vicar Way NG19: Mans W 3D **48**
Vickers St. NG3: Mapp P 7A **86**
  NG20: Mkt W 4D **34**
Vickers Way NG22: Bils 4C **126**
Vickery Way NG9: Chil 7G **105**
Victor, The NG7: Lent 6F **95**
                    (off Leen Ct.)
Victor Cres. NG10: Sand 5B **104**
Victoria Av. NG2: Nott 4C **96**
  NG14: Lowd 6E **80**
                (not continuous)
Victoria Bus. Pk. NG4: Neth 2A **98**
Victoria Cen. NG1: Nott 3F **7** (3K **95**)
Victoria Cen. Sth. NG1: Nott 4F **7**
           (within Victoria Cen.)
Victoria Cl. NG5: Arn 4H **77**
  NG22: Bou .3F **39**
Victoria Ct. NG18: Mans 5G **47**
Victoria Cres. NG5: Sher 5A **86**
Victoria Emb. NG2: Nott 7K **95**
Victoria Gdns. NG16: Want 5A **74**
  NG24: New T 1D **136**
Victoria Gro. NG15: Lin 3H **67**
Victoria Hall NG3: Nott 3G **7** (3A **96**)
                (not continuous)
Victoria Leisure Cen. 4H **7** (3A **96**)
Victoria Mkt. NG1: Nott 4F **7** (3K **95**)
Victoria Pk. NG11: Rudd 3K **115**
Victoria Pk. Way NG4: Neth 2A **98**
Victoria Rd. DN22: Retf 5E **22**
  NG2: West Br 2B **108**
  NG4: Neth .1J **97**
  NG5: Sher .4J **85**
  NG10: Sand 4A **104**
  NG11: Bunny 2B **118**
  NG13: Bing .3H **101**
  NG16: Pinx .7B **50**
  NG16: Sels .6D **58**
  NG17: Kirk A 6K **51**
  S80: Work .3G **21**
Victoria Sq. S80: Work 2G **21**
Victoria St. NG1: Nott 5F **7** (4K **95**)
  NG4: Ged 6J **87**
  NG9: Stap .2C **104**
  NG12: Rad T 5E **98**
  NG15: Huck 5F **67**
  NG16: Eastw 3D **72**
  NG16: Kimb 1F **83**
  NG16: Lang M 3A **72**
  NG16: Sels .5E **58**
  NG17: Stant H 4G **45**
  NG17: Sut A 1J **51**
  NG18: Mans 4G **47**
  NG24: New T 2B **136**
Victoria Ter. NG2: Nott 5K **7** (4B **96**)
  NG16: Sels .3C **58**
  NG24: New T 1C **136**
Victor Ter. NG5: Sher 5K **85**
Victory Cl. NG17: Kirk A 5B **52**
  NG19: Mans W 1C **48**
Victory Dr. NG19: Mans W 1B **48**
Victory Rd. NG9: Bee 5B **106**
View, The NG9: Bram 2G **105**
Village Cl. NG12: Edwal 6E **108**
  NG24: Farnd 6J **133**
Village Farm Cl. LE12: West L 2F **121**
Village Rd. LE12: Norm S 7G **121**
  NG11: Goth 7D **106**
Village St. NG12: Edwal 6D **108**
Village Way NG24: Farnd 6H **133**
Villa Rd. NG3: Mapp P 1E **6** (1K **95**)
  NG12: Key .6J **117**
Villas, The NG20: Whal T 4A **26**
Villa St. NG9: Bee 2A **106**
Villiers Rd. NG2: West Br 3D **108**
  NG5: Woodt 3A **86**
  NG18: Mans 3A **48**
Vimy Ridge NG12: Kin 1A **142**
Vina Cooke Museum of Dolls & Bygone Childhood
  . . . . .2C **147**
Vincent Av. NG9: Bee 4A **106**
Vincent Gdns. NG7: H Grn 1F **95**
Vine Cres. NG10: Sand 3A **104**
Vine Farm Cl. NG12: Cotg 6D **110**
Vine Farm Yd. NG23: Coll 1H **129**

Vines, The NG23: Sut T 3D **128**
Vines Cross NG8: Woll 6K **93**
Vine Ter. NG15: Huck 6H **67**
Vincent Av. NG24: New T 1E **136**
Violet Av. NG16: Newth 6F **73**
Violet Cl. NG6: Basf 4E **84**
Violet Gro. NG15: Huck 6J **67**
Violet Hill NG18: Mans 2C **48**
  NG19: Mans W 2C **48**
Violet Rd. NG2: West Br 1D **108**
  NG4: Carl 5G **87**
Virgin Active
  Nottingham 7H **7** (5A **96**)
Vision Bus. Cen. NG6: Bulw 5G **75**
Vista, The NG9: Stap 4D **104**
Vivian Av. NG5: Sher 7J **85**
Vivian Cl. NG5: Sher 7J **85**
Vixen Cl. NG24: New T 5C **136**
Viyella Gdns. NG15: Huck 1G **75**
Viyella M. NG15: Huck 7G **67**
Voce Ct. S81: Work 6J **19**
Voce Gdns. NG15: Huck 7J **67**
              (off Larwood Av.)
Vulcan Cl. NG6: Basf 3F **85**
Vulcan Pl. S80: Work 2G **21**

W

Waddington Dr. NG2: West Br 5A **108**
Waddington La. NG23: Best 7H **125**
Wade Av. DE7: Ilk 1A **92**
Wade Cl. NG18: Mans 7J **47**
Wades Av. NG7: H Grn 7F **85**
Wades Way NG13: Bing 5H **101**
Wadham Rd. NG5: Woodt 2B **86**
Wadhurst Gdns. NG3: Nott 2H **7** (2A **96**)
Wadhurst Gro. NG8: Woll 6J **93**
Wadnall La. NG23: Weston 3F **125**
Wadsworth Rd. NG9: Stap 1E **104**
WADWORTH 2A **144**
Wagstaff La. NG16: Jack 6A **64**
Wain Ct. S81: Work 5J **19**
Wainfleet Ct. NG5: Arn 4J **77**
Waingrove NG11: Wilf 6H **107**
Wainwright Av. NG19: Mans 1D **46**
Wakefield Av. NG12: Rad T 4F **99**
Wakefield Cl. NG11: Wilf 4H **107**
Wakeling Cl. NG25: Sout 7H **131**
Walbrook Cl. NG8: Cin 4B **84**
Walcote Dr. NG2: West Br 5K **107**
Walcott Grn. NG11: Clif 1E **114**
Waldeck Rd. NG5: Sher 6J **85**
Waldemar Gro. NG9: Bee 3B **106**
Waldron Cl. NG2: Nott 6A **96**
WALES 3A **144**
WALESBY 5G **27** (1B **146**)
Walesby Ct. NG18: Mans 7C **48**
Walesby Cres. NG8: Aspl 2D **94**
Walesby Dr. NG17: Kirk A 6D **52**
Walesby La. NG22: New O 4B **38**
Walesby La. Cotts. NG22: New O 4B **38**
Walgrave Wlk. NG5: Bestw 7D **76**
Walk, The NG13: Ors 1J **103**
Walkden St. NG18: Mans 3H **47**
Walker Cl. NG22: New O 3C **38**
  NG24: New T 2D **136**
Walker Gro. NG9: Stap 3D **104**
WALKERINGHAM 6H **11** (2C **145**)
Walkeringham Rd. DN10: Beck 4C **16**
  DN10: Gri H 2C **16**
WALKERITH 2C **145**
Walkers Cl. NG13: Bing 4F **101**
  NG19: Mans W 1D **48**
Walker St. NG2: Nott 4J **7** (3B **96**)
  NG16: Eastw 4E **72**
Walker's Yd. NG12: Rad T 5E **98**
Walk Mill Dr. NG15: Huck 4H **67**
Walks of Life Heritage Cen. 6D **28**
Wallace Av. NG4: Carl 1J **97**
Wallace Gdns. NG9: Toton 7E **104**
Wallace St. NG11: Goth 6G **115**
Wallan St. NG7: Radf 2F **95**
Wallet St. NG2: Nott 6A **96**
  NG4: Neth .1K **97**
Wallett Av. NG9: Bee 1A **106**
Wallingbrook Ri. S80: Work 3C **20**
WALLINGWELLS 7A **12**
Wallingwells La. S81: Wall 7A **12**
Wallis Rd. NG18: Mans 3J **47**
Wallis St. NG6: Basf 3F **85**
Walnut Av. S81: Shire 5A **18**
Walnut Cl. DE7: Ilk 1A **92**
  NG2: West Br 7F **97**
  NG13: Aslo .3C **102**
  NG23: Weston 3G **125**
Walnut Ct. NG12: Rad T 5E **98**
              (off Walnut Gro.)
Walnut Dr. NG9: Bram 1G **105**
Walnut Gdns. LE12: East L 3K **121**
Walnut Gro. NG12: Cotg 6E **110**
  NG12: Rad T 5E **98**
  NG13: East B 5D **90**
  NG14: Calv .5D **70**
Walnut Tree Cres. NG19: Mans W 7F **43**
Walnut Tree Gdns. NG6: Bulw 7F **75**

Walnut Tree La. NG13: East B 5D **90**
Walnut Tree M. *NG24: New T* 5D **134**
(off Winthorpe Rd.)
Walsham Cl. NG9: Chil 7H **105**
Walsingham Rd. NG5: Woodt 2D **86**
Walters Av. NG16: Brins 7C **64**
Walter's Cl. NG24: Farnd 5H **133**
Walters Cres. NG16: Sels 6B **58**
Walter St. NG7: Radf 2B **6** (2H **95**)
Waltham Cl. NG2: West Br 3E **108**
NG24: Bald 6G **137**
WALTHAM ON THE WOLDS 3D **149**
Waltham Rd. NG15: Rave 2C **62**
Walton Av. NG3: Nott 4K **7** (3C **96**)
Walton Cl. NG19: Mans W 2D **48**
Walton Ct. NG4: Carl 1H **97**
NG12: Key 7J **117**
Walton Cres. NG4: Carl 1H **97**
Walton Dr. NG12: Key 7J **117**
Walton M. NG3: Nott 1C **96**
WALTON ON THE WOLDS 3A **148**
Walton Rd. NG5: Arn 5J **77**
Walton's La. NG23: Nth M 5J **129**
Walton St. NG17: Sut A 7A **46**
Wands Cl. NG25: Sout 6G **131**
Wansbeck Cl. NG7: Radf 3A **6** (3H **95**)
Wansford Av. NG5: Arn 4H **77**
Wansley La. NG16: Bagt 2C **64**
Wanstead Way NG5: Top V 5A **76**
Warburton Cl. NG15: Huck 7H **67**
Warburton St. NG24: New T 7D **134**
Ward Av. NG3: Mapp 4E **86**
NG15: Huck 4F **67**
Wardle Gro. NG5: Arn 6J **77**
Ward Pl. NG18: Mans 4E **46**
Ward Rd. NG21: C'tone 5H **43**
Ward St. NG7: Basf 7G **85**
Wareham Cl. NG2: West Br 4K **107**
NG8: Cin 4B **84**
Warehouse, The NG1: Nott 6G **7**
Warkton Cl. NG9: Chil 4H **105**
WARMSWORTH 1A **144**
Warnadene Rd. NG17: Sut A 3J **51**
Warner St. NG7: Radf 3F **95**
Warrands Cl. NG25: Sout 6F **131**
Warren, The NG12: Cotg 7E **110**
Warren Av. NG5: Sher 5H **85**
NG9: Stap 2C **104**
NG15: Ann 4C **60**
Warren Cl. NG17: Huth 1E **50**
Warren Ct. NG9: Stap 2C **104**
Warrender Cl. NG9: Bram 7H **93**
Warrener Gro. NG5: Top V 6A **76**
Warren Hill Cl. NG5: Arn 7E **76**
Warren Rd. NG15: Huck 1D **74**
NG17: Ann W 3B **60**
Warren Way NG19: Mans W 3E **48**
Warrington Rd. NG6: Bulw 7J **75**
Warser Ga. NG1: Nott 5G **7** (4A **96**)
WARSOP 4D **34** (2A **146**)
Warsop Cl. NG8: Stre 5J **83**
Warsop Ent. Cen. NG20: Mkt W 3D **34**
WARSOP HILL .6D **32**
Warsop La. NG21: Blid, Rain 5H **55**
Warsop Rd. NG19: Mans W 6K **41**
WARSOP VALE 3A **34** (2A **146**)
WARTNABY 3C **149**
Warton Av. NG3: Nott 7C **86**
Warwick Av. NG5: Woodt 2B **86**
NG9: Bee 1A **106**
S81: Carl L 6C **12**
Warwick Brewery NG24: New T 6D **134**
Warwick Cl. NG17: Kirk A 6D **52**
Warwick Ct. NG24: Bald 5G **137**
Warwick Dr. NG18: Mans 3A **48**
Warwick Gdns. NG12: Cotg 7E **110**
Warwick Rd. NG3: Mapp P 5A **86**
NG24: Bald 5G **137**
Warwick St. NG7: Lent 6F **95**
Wasdale Cl. NG2: West Br 4F **109**
Washdyke La. NG15: Huck 4E **66**
Washington Cl. NG5: Arn 7H **77**
Washington Dr. NG9: Stap 7E **92**
NG18: Mans 5E **46**
Wash Pit La. LE14: Hick 7E **142**
Washpit La. NG12: Cols B 6H **141**
Wasnidge Cl.
NG3: Nott 3H **7** (3A **96**)
Wasnidge Wlk. NG3: Nott 2H **7**
Watchwood Gro. NG14: Calv 5D **70**
Watcombe Cir. NG5: Sher 5J **85**
Watcombe Rd. NG5: Sher 6K **85**
Watendlath Cl. NG2: West Br 4F **109**
Waterdown Cl. NG19: Mans W 4K **41**
Waterdown Rd. NG11: Clif 1E **114**
Waterfield Av. NG20: Mkt W 3C **34**
Waterfields DN22: Retf 2F **23**
Waterfield Way NG21: C'tone 5H **43**
Water Fir Dr. DN11: Harwo 2C **8**
Waterford St. NG6: Basf 4F **85**
Waterfront, The NG24: New T 2B **136**
Waterfront Plaza
NG2: Nott 7H **7** (5A **96**)
Waterfurrows La. NG12: Shel 6J **89**
Waterhouse La. NG4: Ged 5K **87**

Water La. DE55: Sth N 5A **50**
DN22: Retf 2F **23**
NG12: Rad T 5D **98**
NG12: Shel 6H **89**
NG19: Mans, Plea 5B **40**
NG24: New T 7C **134**
NG25: Oxt 2F **71**
S81: Carl L 6D **12**
Waterloo Cl. DE55: Hilc 3A **50**
Waterloo Cres. NG7: Radf 1A **6** (2H **95**)
Waterloo La. NG9: Trow 2D **92**
Waterloo Prom. NG7: Radf 2A **6** (2H **95**)
(not continuous)
Waterloo Rd. NG7: Radf 1A **6** (2H **95**)
NG9: Bee 4B **106**
NG15: Lin 3G **67**
NG19: Mans W 7H **41**
Watermark Cl. NG5: Sher 5J **85**
Watermark Ho. NG5: Sher 5J **85**
Water Mdws. S80: Work 3E **20**
Water Meadows Swimming and Fitness Complex
. . . . .4H **47**
Water Orton Cl. NG9: Toton 6D **104**
Waters Edge NG11: Wilf 2J **107**
Waters Edge NG24: New T 6D **134**
Waterside Cl. NG2: Gam 3F **109**
NG10: Sand 6A **104**
Waterside Gdns. NG7: Lent 7F **95**
Waterside Orchard DN10: Mist 3G **11**
Waterside Way NG2: Colw, Nott 6D **96**
Waterslack Rd. DN11: Birc 2E **8**
Waterson Av. NG18: Mans 7B **48**
Waterson Oaks NG18: Mans 6B **48**
Waterway, The NG10: Sand 5B **104**
Waterway St. NG2: Nott 6A **96**
(Newthorpe St.)
NG2: Nott 6A **96**
(Wallet St.)
Waterway St. W. NG2: Nott 6K **95**
Waterworks Dr. NG21: K Cli 4K **43**
Watford Rd. NG8: Aspl 5C **84**
Watkins La. DN22: Stu S 1C **24**
Watkin St. NG3: Nott 2F **7** (2K **95**)
WATNALL 6A **74**
WATNALL CANTELUPE 6K **73**
WATNALL CHAWORTH 5A **74**
Watnall Cres. NG15: Mans 3E **46**
Watnall Rd. NG15: Huck 4D **74**
NG16: Nuth 1H **83**
Watnall Rd. Factory Units NG15: Huck 1F **75**
Watson Av. NG3: Nott 2E **96**
NG18: Mans 3J **47**
Watson Cl. NG23: Nth C 3D **30**
Watson Pk. DN10: Beck 7D **16**
Watson Rd. S80: Work 2G **21**
NG20: Mkt W 4D **34**
Wavell Cl. DN10: Matt T 1G **15**
S81: Gate 4F **19**
Wavell Cres. DN10: Matt T 1G **15**
Waveney Cl. NG5: Arn 1D **86**
Waverley Av. NG4: Ged 6K **87**
NG9: Bee 3B **106**
Waverley Cl. NG17: Kirk A 6D **52**
Waverley Mt. NG7: Nott 1B **6** (2H **95**)
Waverley Pl. S80: Work 5H **21**
Waverley Rd. NG18: Mans 6H **47**
Waverley St. NG1: Nott 1B **6** (2H **95**)
NG7: Nott 1B **6** (2H **95**)
Waverley Ter. NG1: Nott 3D **6** (3J **95**)
Waverley Way S80: Work 5H **21**
Wayford Wlk. NG6: Bulw 6H **75**
Wayne Cl. NG11: Clif 1F **115**
Wayte Ct. NG11: Rudd 1B **116**
Weardale Rd. NG5: Sher 5H **85**
Wearmouth Gdns.
NG5: Top V 5C **76**
Weave Cl. NG6: Basf 3F **85**
Weavers, The NG24: New T 5K **133**
Weavers Cl. LE12: East L 1B **122**
Weaver's La. NG15: Ann 3J **65**
Weaverthorpe Rd.
NG5: Woodt 2D **86**
Webb Rd. NG8: Bilb 1C **94**
Webb St. NG15: News 6E **60**
Webster Av. NG16: Eastw 5D **72**
Webster Cl. NG21: Rain 2K **55**
WEECAR 2D **147**
Weedon Cl. NG3: Nott 2E **96**
Weekday Cross NG1: Nott 6F **7** (4K **95**)
Weeland Cl. NG20: Chu W 2D **34**
Weetman Gdns. NG5: Top V 6C **76**
Weighbridge Rd.
NG18: Mans 4J **47**
Weightman Dr. NG16: Gilt 7F **73**
Weirside S81: Oldc 6A **8**
Welbeck Av. NG4: Ged 5G **87**
NG24: New T 7D **134**
Welbeck Cl. NG17: Skeg 5K **45**
NG5: Woodt 3D **86**
Welbeck Dr. NG21: Edwin 6D **36**
Welbeck Gdns. NG5: Woodt 3D **86**
NG9: Toton 6E **104**
Welbeck Gro. NG13: Bing 4D **100**
Welbeck Pl. NG22: Tuxf 6D **28**

Welbeck Rd. DN11: Harwo 1D **8**
DN22: Ord 6D **22**
NG2: West Br 1B **108**
NG10: Long E 6A **104**
NG12: Rad T 4F **99**
NG19: Mans W 6J **41**
Welbeck Sq. NG17: Stant H 4G **45**
Welbeck St. NG17: Kirk A 7B **52**
NG17: Sut A 1K **51**
NG18: Mans 3G **47**
NG20: Mkt W 4D **34**
S80: Work 1G **21**
Welbeck Wlk. NG3: Nott 1F **7** (2K **95**)
Welbeck Workshops NG3: Nott 1F **7**
Welburn Cl. NG19: Mans W 7B **42**
Welby Av. NG7: Lent 4G **95**
Welch Av. NG9: Stap 1E **104**
Weldbank Cl. NG9: Chil 5G **105**
Welfitt Gro. NG20: Neth L 5C **26**
Welford Cl. NG17: Skeg 5B **46**
WELHAM 2K **23** (3C **145**)
Welham Cres. NG5: Arn 7J **77**
Welham Gro. DN22: Retf 2G **23**
Welham Rd. DN22: Retf, Welh 2G **23**
Welland Cl. NG24: New T 6E **134**
S81: Work 5F **19**
Welland Ct. NG3: Nott 2K **7** (2C **96**)
Welland Gdns. NG13: Bing 5E **100**
Wellcroft Cl. NG18: Mans 5F **47**
Wellesley Cl. S81: Gate 4E **18**
Wellesley Ct. DN22: Retf 2F **23**
Wellesley Cres. NG8: Stre 5J **83**
Well Grn. Ho. NG3: Codd 6K **135**
Wellin Cl. NG12: Edwal 6E **108**
Wellin Ct. NG12: Edwal 6E **108**
Wellington Cir. NG1: Nott 5C **6** (4J **95**)
Wellington Cl. NG20: Mkt W 5D **34**
Wellington Ct. NG1: Nott 5D **6**
NG16: Eastw 4D **72**
Wellington Cres. NG2: West Br 2C **108**
Wellington Pl. NG16: Eastw 4D **72**
Wellington Rd. NG14: Bur J 2F **89**
NG24: New T 1D **136**
Wellington Sq. DN22: Retf 3F **23**
NG7: Nott 4A **6** (3H **95**)
Wellington St. DN22: Retf 3F **23**
NG3: Nott 2F **7** (2K **95**)
NG9: Stap 3B **104**
NG10: Long E 6B **104**
NG16: Eastw 3D **72**
Wellington Ter. NG7: Radf 4A **6** (3H **95**)
Wellington Vs. NG7: Lent 4A **6** (3H **95**)
Wellin La. NG12: Edwal 6E **108**
Well La. LE14: Upp B 3H **143**
WELLOW 7D **38** (2B **146**)
Wellow Cl. NG17: Sut A 2C **52**
NG19: Mans 2D **46**
Wellow Grn. NG22: Well 6D **38**
Wellow Rd. NG22: Eakr 1C **126**
NG22: Oll, Well 5B **38**
Wellow Wood Vw. NG22: New O 4C **38**
(off Rufford Av.)
Wells Cl. NG19: Mans W 5K **41**
Wells Gdns. NG3: Nott 7C **86**
Wellspring Dale NG9: Stap 4D **104**
Wells Road, The NG3: Mapp, Nott 5B **86**
Welshcroft Cl. NG17: Kirk A 5A **52**
Welstead Av. NG8: Aspl 5B **84**
Welton Gdns. NG6: Bulw 6G **75**
Welwyn Av. NG19: Mans W 5A **42**
Welwyn Rd. NG8: Woll 3K **93**
Wembley Gdns. NG9: Bram 6G **93**
Wembley Rd. NG5: Arn 1E **86**
S81: Lango 1C **12**
Wemyss Gdns. NG8: Woll 5E **94**
Wendling Gdns. NG5: Bestw 7D **76**
Wendover Dr. NG8: Aspl 5C **84**
Wenham La. NG17: Huth 6D **44**
Wenlock Cl. NG16: Gilt 6G **73**
Wenlock Dr. NG2: West Br 4C **108**
Wensleydale S81: Work 5J **19**
Wensleydale Cl. NG8: Aspl 6E **84**
NG19: Mans W 1A **48**
Wensley Rd. NG5: Woodt 2B **86**
Wensor Av. NG9: Lent A 1A **106**
Wentbridge Dr. NG18: Mans 6C **48**
Wentworth Cl. DN22: Ord 7D **22**
NG19: Mans W 7B **42**
Wentworth Cnr. NG24: New T 4B **136**
Wentworth Ct. NG16: Kimb 1D **82**
Wentworth Rd. NG5: Sher 5J **85**
NG9: Chil 3H **105**
NG17: Kirk A 4J **51**
Wentworth St. DE7: Ilk 5A **82**
Wentworth Way NG12: Edwal 6E **108**
Wesleyan Chapel Wlk. NG9: Stap 2C **104**
Wesley Cl. NG24: Bald 5G **137**
Wesley Ct. *NG5: Sher* 5K **85**
(off Drayton St.)
Wesley Gro. NG5: Sher 6J **85**
Wesley Pl. NG9: Stap 1D **104**
Wesley Rd. DN22: Retf 3F **23**
Wesley St. NG5: Sher 6J **85**
NG16: Lang M 3A **72**
NG17: Ann W 4A **60**
Wesley Way NG11: Rudd 4A **116**

Wessex Cl. S81: Work 6H **19**
Wessex Dr. NG16: Gilt, Newth 6E **72**
Wessex Rd. S81: Work 6H **19**
West Av. NG2: West Br 2B **108**
NG9: Stap 1D **104**
NG10: Sand 3A **104**
W. Bank Av. NG19: Mans 2H **47**
W. Bank Lea NG19: Mans 1H **47**
W. Bank Link NG19: Mans 1H **47**
W. Bank Wynd NG19: Mans 2H **47**
WESTBOROUGH 1D 149
Westbourne Cl. DN22: Retf 4G **23**
NG17: Sut A 7H **45**
NG19: Mans W 5A **42**
Westbourne Ct. NG9: Bram 7E **92**
Westbourne Rd. NG16: Unde 3E **64**
NG17: Sut A 1H **51**
Westbourne Vw. NG17: Sut A 7H **45**
Westbrecks La. DN22: Cott 4K **25**
WEST BRIDGFORD 3B 108 (2A 148)
Westbrook Av. NG15: Rave 1B **62**
Westbrook Dr. NG21: Rain 3K **55**
Westbury Cl. NG9: Chil 5H **105**
Westbury Rd. NG5: Sher 5G **85**
WEST BUTTERWICK 1D 145
Westby La. NG16: Babb, Coss 3B **82**
WEST CARR 1C 145
W. Carr Rd. DN22: Retf 4D **22**
W. Carr Rd. Ind. Est. DN22: Retf 5D **22**
Westcliffe Av. NG4: Ged 4G **87**
NG12: Rad T 4F **99**
Westcliffe Ct. NG12: Rad T 4F **99**
West Cl. NG12: Key 1H **119**
West Ct. DN22: Retf 3D **22**
West Cres. NG9: Bee 5C **106**
West Cft. Cl. DN22: Ramp 6K **25**
W. Cross Av. NG9: Stap 1D **104**
Westdale Av. NG17: Skeg 5A **46**
Westdale Ct. NG4: Carl 5G **87**
Westdale Cres. NG4: Carl 6H **87**
Westdale La. E. NG4: Carl 5F **87**
Westdale La. W. NG3: Mapp 4D **86**
Westdale Rd. NG16: Jack 6A **64**
NG19: Mans 1H **47**
WEST DRAYTON 1C 147
West Dr. NG7: Nott 1C **106**
NG21: Edwin 6E **36**
West End NG9: Bee 4A **106**
NG12: Kin 3A **142**
NG14: Calv 5A **70**
NG16: Pinx 7A **50**
NG17: Sut A 1J **51**
NG24: Farnd 7G **133**
West End Arc. NG1: Nott 5D **6** (4J **95**)
West End Ct. *NG17: Sut A* *1H **51***
(off West End)
West End St. NG9: Stap 3B **104**
West End Vs. *NG12: Rad T* *5D **98***
(off Main Rd.)
NG14: Lowd 3C **80**
Westerdale S81: Work 4H **19**
Westerfield Way NG11: Wilf 5H **107**
Westerham Cl. NG8: Bilb 1J **93**
Westerham Rd. NG11: Rudd 4J **115**
Westerhope Cl. NG12: Edwal 5F **109**
Westerlands NG9: Stap 3D **104**
Western Av. NG13: Bing 3E **100**
NG17: Kirk A 1B **60**
NG18: Mans 5F **47**
Western Blvd. NG8: Aspl, Basf 7E **84**
Western Cl. NG18: Mans 5E **46**
Western Flds. NG11: Rudd 4J **115**
Western Gdns. NG8: Aspl 7E **84**
Western St. NG1: Nott 4G **7** (3A **96**)
Western Ter. NG7: Nott 5A **6** (4H **95**)
WEST FIELD 4E 22
Westfield Cl. *NG17: Sut A* *1J **51***
(off Church La.)
NG19: Mans 2F **47**
Westfield Dr. NG19: Mans 2E **46**
S81: Work 7H **19**
Westfield La. NG14: Woodbo 2E **78**
NG18: Mans 2G **47**
NG19: Mans 1D **46**
NG23: Coll 2F **129**
Westfield M. *NG19: Mans* *2F **47***
(off Westfield La.)
Westfield Rd. DN22: Retf 4D **22**
NG13: Bing 4E **100**
NG17: Nunc 3B **60**
Westfield Way NG24: Farnd 7H **133**
West Furlong DN22: Retf 2D **22**
NG12: Cotg 7F **111**
WESTGATE 1C 145
West Gate NG18: Mans 3H **47**
Westgate NG25: Sout 6F **131**
S80: Work 3F **21**
Westgate Ct. NG9: Chil 4K **105**
Westgate M. NG25: Sout 6G **131**
Westgate St. NG3: Nott 1J **7** (2B **96**)
Westgate Vw. S80: Work 3F **21**
West Gro. Rd. DN22: Retf 5F **23**
Westhay Ct. NG8: Woll 3D **94**
West Hill NG17: Skeg 4H **45**
NG19: Mans 2G **47**
West Hill Av. NG18: Mans 3H **47**
West Hill Dr. NG18: Mans 3H **47**
West Hill Pk. NG19: Mans W 6H **41**
West Hill Rd. DN22: Ord 6D **22**
West Hill Way NG18: Mans 3H **47**
Westholme Gdns. NG8: Aspl 2D **94**
WESTHORPE 6H 131
Westhorpe NG25: Sout 6E **130**
Westhorpe Av. NG3: Nott 4K **7** (3C **96**)
Westland Av. NG15: Huck 2D **74**
Westland Dr. NG16: Pinx 1A **58**
West La. NG21: Edwin 6E **36**
NG23: Girt 4G **125**
W. Lawns, The NG25: Sout 6F **131**
WEST LEAKE 3F 121 (3A 148)
W. Leake La. LE12: West L 1E **120**
W. Leake Rd. LE12: East L 3H **121**
Westleigh NG19: Mans W 3K **41**
Westleigh Rd. NG8: Brox 5K **83**
Westmaner Ct. NG9: Chil 4J **105**
West Mnr. Pk. NG14: Epp 7K **71**
WEST MARKHAM 3A 28 (1C 147)
Westminster Av. NG10: Sand 4B **104**
NG17: Kirk A 6C **52**
Westminster Cl. NG3: Nott 1B **96**
S81: Work 5H **19**
Westminster Ct. NG19: Mans W 6K **41**
Westminster Dr. NG12: Rad T 5J **99**
WEST MOOR 6G 11
West Moor NG2: Colw 4G **97**
Westmoore Cl. NG3: Mapp 4E **86**
Westmoore Ct. NG3: Mapp 4E **86**
W. Moor Rd. DN10: Walk 6G **11**
Westmoreland Ct. *NG5: Sher* *6J **85***
(off Ebury Rd.)
Westmorland Ct. DN11: Birc 2G **9**
Westmorland Dr. S81: Costh 5B **12**
Westmorland Ho. DN11: Birc 2G **9**
Westmorland Way NG16: Jack 7A **64**
WESTON 3G 125 (2C 147)
Weston Av. NG7: Radf 1A **6** (2H **95**)
Weston Cl. NG5: Woodt 3B **86**
NG17: Sut A 3C **52**
Weston Cotts. NG7: Radf 2F **95**
Weston La. NG23: Norm T 2J **125**
Weston Rd. NG22: Egma 2E **124**
Weston Ter. NG5: Sher 4K **85**
West Pk. Pl. DN22: Retf 4D **22**
Westpoint NG2: West Br 2A **108**
Westray Cl. NG9: Bram 5G **93**
WEST RETFORD 2E 22
W. Retford Hall DN22: Retf 3E **22**
West Rd. NG7: Nott 6E **94**
NG23: Thor 2G **31**
WEST STOCKWITH 2C 145
West St. DN10: Miss 3C **10**
DN11: Harwo 1D **8**
DN22: Retf 4E **22**
NG2: Nott 5J **7** (4B **96**)
NG5: Arn 7G **77**
NG12: Shel 6H **89**
NG15: Huck 6G **67**
NG16: Kimb 3F **83**
NG16: Lang M 3A **72**
NG20: Wars 4A **34**
NG20: Whal T 4B **26**
S80: Work 3F **21**
West Ter. NG15: Huck 6G **67**
West Thorpe LE12: Will W 6F **143**
West Vw. NG2: West Br 4A **108**
NG24: Bald 5G **137**
S81: Costh 4C **12**
West Vw. Ct. NG15: Pap 2K **67**
Westview Ct. NG4: Carl 7J **87**
West Vw. Rd. NG4: Carl 7J **87**
WESTVILLE 2D 74 (1A 148)
Westville NG2: West Br 3B **108**
Westville Dr. NG15: Huck 3E **74**
Westville Gdns. NG3: Nott 1G **7** (1A **96**)
West Wlk. DN22: Retf 2C **22**
NG2: Nott 5J **7** (4B **96**)
Westward Av. NG9: Bee 3B **106**
Westway NG12: Cotg 7E **110**
S81: Work 5H **19**
W. Wells La. DN10: Gri H 3A **16**
Westwick Rd. NG8: Bilb 2H **93**
Westwick St. DE7: Ilk 2A **92**
WESTWOOD 1A 64
Westwood Dr. S80: Work 2C **20**
West Wood Est. DN10: Bawt 1H **9**
Westwood Gdns. NG16: Westw 1A **64**
Westwood Rd. DN10: Bawt 1J **9**
NG2: Nott 4C **96**
WESTWOODSIDE 1C 145
Wetherby Cl. NG8: Aspl 6C **84**
NG16: Kimb 7J **73**
Wetherlam Cl. NG2: Nott 6K **95**
Wetlands Animal Pk. 5D **14**
Wetsyke La. NG24: Bald 6H **137**
WHALEY 1A 146
Whaley Bri. Cl. NG18: Mans 5E **48**
Whaley Rd. NG20: Langw 6A **26**
WHALEY THORNS 4B 26 (1A 146)
Whaley Thorns Heritage Cen. 4B **26**
Whaley Thorns Ind. Est. NG20: Whal T 4A **26**
Wharf, The NG24: New T 7C **134**
Wharf Cl. DN10: Mist 2H **11**
Wharf Ct. DN10: Mist 3H **11**
Wharfedale NG8: Woll 5G **93**
S81: Work 4H **19**
Wharfedale Gdns.
NG18: Mans 5C **48**
Wharf Gdns. NG13: Bing 5D **100**
Wharf La. NG12: Rad T 5D **98**
Wharf Rd. DN10: Mist 2H **11**
DN22: Retf 4E **22**
NG7: Nott 7D **6** (5J **95**)
NG16: Pinx 2A **58**
NG17: Stant H 5E **44**
Wharf Rd. Ind. Est. NG16: Pinx 1C **58**
Wharf Yd. NG17: Ann W 3J **59**
Wharmby Av. NG19: Mans 6D **40**
Wharncliffe Rd. DN22: Ord 6D **22**
Wharton Cres. NG9: Bee 5A **106**
Wharton St. DN22: Retf 4G **23**
WHATTON 5D 102 (2C 149)
Whatton Ct. NG18: Mans 7C **48**
Whatton Dr. NG2: West Br 6J **107**
Whatton Ri. NG5: Sher 3J **85**
Wheatacre Rd. NG11: Clif 1G **115**
Wheat Cl. NG8: Bilb 3J **93**
Wheat Cft. S81: Work 5J **19**
Wheatcroft Vw. NG2: West Br 6K **107**
Wheatfield Cres. NG19: Mans W 4A **42**
Wheatfields Rd. NG3: Nott 1D **96**
Wheatfield Way NG17: Skeg 3J **45**
Wheatgrass Rd. NG9: Chil 4G **105**
WHEATLEY 1A 144
Wheatley Av. NG17: Kirk A 6K **51**
Wheatley Cl. NG11: Rudd 5K **115**
NG19: Mans W 1B **48**
Wheatley Dr. NG4: Carl 1F **97**
Wheatley Gro. NG9: Chil 5A **106**
WHEATLEY PARK 1A 144
Wheatley Rd. DN22: Clay 7J **15** & 1A **24**
DN22: Stu S 3K **17**
Wheatsheaf Av. NG24: New T 4E **134**
Wheatsheaf Ct. NG14: Bur J 3E **88**
Wheeldale Cl. NG8: Woll 4G **93**
Wheeldon Ct. NG7: Basf 6G **85**
Wheeler Av. NG16: Eastw 5F **73**
Wheeler Ga. NG1: Nott 5E **6** (4K **95**)
NG16: Unde 3E **64**
Wheelgate Adventure Pk. 4F **57**
Wheelwrights, The NG21: Edwin 6F **37**
Wheldon Av. NG4: Carl 5F **87**
Whernside Rd. NG5: Woodt 2B **86**
Whetstone Cl. NG16: Nuth 5J **83**
Whickham Ct. NG2: Nott 7A **96**
Whilton Cl. NG17: Skeg 5A **46**
Whimsey Pk. NG4: Carl 2J **97**
Whinbush La. NG14: Calv 7K **63**
Whinfell Cl. NG11: Clif 7G **107**
Whinlatter Dr. NG2: West Br 3F **109**
Whinney Bank NG19: Mans W 5K **41**
WHINNEY HILL 5A 42
Whinney Hill NG19: Mans W 5K **41**
Whinney La. NG22: New O 1D **38**
Whinney Moor Cl. DN22: Retf 5F **23**
Whinney Moor La. DN22: Retf 5F **23**
Whinney Moor Way DN22: Retf 5F **23**
Whipling Cl. NG13: What 5E **102**
WHISBY 2D 147
WHISTON 2A 144
Whiston Cl. NG5: Bestw 1H **85**
Whitaker Cl. DN22: Retf 1C **22**
Whitbread St. NG7: Basf 7G **85**
Whitburn Rd. NG9: Toton 6D **104**
Whitby Cl. NG8: Woll 4G **93**
Whitby Cres. NG5: Woodt 2D **86**
Whitby Rd. DN11: Harwo 1D **8**
NG16: Newth 3E **72**
Whitchurch Cl. NG5: Top V 6B **76**
Whitcliffe Gdns. NG2: West Br 4C **108**
Whitcombe Ct. DN22: Ord 6C **22**
Whitcombe Gdns. NG5: Top V 6C **76**
Whiteacre NG14: Bur J 2D **88**
White Av. S81: Lango 1B **12**
Whitebeam Gdns. NG6: Bulw 7F **75**
Whitechapel St. NG6: Basf 5E **84**
White City Trad. Est. NG2: Nott 5D **96**
White Furrows NG12: Cotg 7D **110**
Whitegates Way NG17: Huth 1C **50**
Whitegate Va. NG11: Clif 1E **114**
Whitehall Ct. DN22: Retf 4E **22**
NG12: Rad T 5K **99**
Whitehall Gdns. DN22: Retf 4F **23**
Whitehall Rd. DN22: Retf 4F **23**
White Hart La. NG23: Coll 2G **129**
White Hart St. NG18: Mans 4H **47**
White Hart Yd. *NG24: New T* *1C **136***
(off Market Pl.)
S80: Work *3F **21***
(off Bridge St.)
Whitehead Dr. NG16: Brins 5B **64**
Whitehead La. NG17: Skeg 4K **45**
Whitehouse Ct. DN11: Birc 2F **9**
Whitehouse Dr. DN11: Birc 2F **9**
Whitehouse M. *S81: Blyth* *6H **13***
(off Retford Rd.)
White Ho. Rd. DN11: Birc 2F **9**
WHITE HOUSES 7G 23
Whitehouses Rd. DN22: Retf 6G **23**

White Lady Ct. NG15: Rave 1D **62**
Whitelands NG12: Cotg 7F **111**
White Lion Yd. *NG18: Mans* 3H **47**
                           (off Church St.)
White Lodge Gdns. NG8: Bilb 1J **93**
Whitely Cl. NG9: Stap 1D **104**
WHITEMOOR 7E **84**
Whitemoor Av. NG8: Aspl, Basf 7E **84**
Whitemoor Cl. NG8: Aspl 7E **84**
Whitemoor Ct. Ind. Est. NG8: Aspl 7E **84**
Whitemoor Rd. NG6: Basf 5E **84**
Whitemoss Cl. NG8: Woll 5K **93**
WHITE POST 4F **57**
White Post Bungs. DN22: Nth L 6B **24**
White Post Farm 4F **57**
White Rd. NG5: Basf 4F **85**
White Rose Av. NG18: Mans 6K **47**
White's Av. NG3: Nott 2E **96**
Whites Cft. NG14: Woodbo 2F **79**
Whitestone Cl. NG18: Mans 6C **48**
Whitewater Cl. NG22: New O 3C **38**
Whitewater Rd. NG22: New O 3C **38**
Whiteways Ct. NG11: Clif 1F **115**
Whitfield Cl. NG11: Wilf 3J **107**
Whitfield St. NG24: New T 2D **136**
Whiting Av. NG9: Toton 7E **104**
Whitney Cl. NG19: Mans W 1C **48**
Whitsun Dale S81: Work 5J **19**
Whittaker Rd. NG9: Chil 6F **105**
    NG21: Rain 3J **55**
Whittier Rd. NG2: Nott 5D **96**
Whittingham Ct. NG3: Mapp 4D **86**
Whittingham Rd. NG3: Mapp 4D **86**
Whittle Cl. NG24: New T 6F **135**
Whitton Cl. DN22: Rans 2J **13**
    NG5: Top V 5D **76**
    NG9: Chil 7H **105**
WHITWELL 1A **146**
Whitwell Cl. NG8: Brox 6A **84**
Whitwell Rd. NG8: Brox 6K **83**
Whitworth Dr. NG12: Rad T 6D **98**
    NG14: Bur J 5B **88**
Whitworth Ri. NG5: Top V 6B **76**
Whomsley Cl. NG24: New T 1G **137**
Whyatt Ct. NG5: Arn 1A **86**
Whyburn La. NG15: Huck 6C **66**
Whyburn Pct. NG15: Huck 1E **74**
Whyburn St. NG15: Huck 7J **67**
Whyston Ct. NG15: Huck 1C **74**
Wibberley Dr. NG11: Rudd 3J **115**
Wichal Cl. NG5: Bestw 2K **85**
Wichnor Cl. NG11: Clif 5F **107**
Wickens Wlk.
    NG3: Nott 1K **7** (2B **96**)
Wicker Cl. NG6: Basf 3F **85**
WICKERSLEY 2A **144**
Wickerwood Dr. NG17: Kirk A 5J **51**
Wicket Cl. NG17: Kirk A 1A **60**
Wicket Gro. NG7: Lent 4F **95**
Wickets, The NG2: West Br 7C **96**
    NG20: Mkt W 5D **34**
Wickstead Cl. NG5: Woodt 4C **86**
Widdington Cl. NG5: Arn 4H **77**
Widdowson Cl. NG6: Bulw 6F **75**
Widdowson's Row *NG11: Rudd* 3K **115**
                     (off Easthorpe St.)
Widecombe La. NG11: Clif 2E **114**
WIDMERPOOL 6J **119** (3B **148**)
Widmerpool Hall NG12: Widm 6J **119**
Widmerpool La. LE12: Will W 4G **143**
    NG12: Key, Widm 1K **119**
Widmerpool Rd. NG12: Wys 6K **123**
Widmerpool St. NG16: Pinx 2A **58**
WIGHAY 4F **67**
Wighay Rd. NG15: Huck, Lin 4F **67**
Wigley Cl. NG3: Nott 1K **7** (2B **96**)
Wigman Ct. NG15: Huck 7K **67**
Wigman Rd. NG8: Bilb 7J **83**
WIGSLEY 7G **31** (1D **147**)
Wigsley Rd. NG23: Harby 6J **31**
    NG23: Thor 4F **31**
WIGTHORPE 1H **19**
Wigthorpe La. S81: Wigt 1H **19**
Wigwam Gro. NG15: Huck 6J **67**
Wigwam La. NG15: Huck 6J **67**
Wilberforce Rd. NG11: Wilf 4H **107**
    NG19: Mans 7D **40**
Wilcocksons Yd. *NG15: Huck* 6G **67**
                        (off Baker St.)
Wilcox Av. NG19: Mans W 4H **41**
Wilcox Dr. NG16: Unde 4E **64**
Wilde Cres. NG16: Sels 6E **58**
Wilden Cres. NG11: Clif 6F **107**
Wildflower Gro. NG17: Sut A 2H **51**
Wild Hill NG17: Teve 3B **44**
Wildman St. NG7: Radf 2A **6** (2H **95**)
WILDSWORTH 2D **145**
WILFORD 3J **107** (2A **148**)
Wilford Cl. NG24: New T 1E **136**
Wilford Cres. NG11: Rudd 2K **115**
Wilford Cres. E. NG2: Nott 7A **96**
Wilford Cres. W. NG2: Nott 6K **95**
Wilford Gro. NG2: Nott 6K **95**
                   (not continuous)
WILFORD HILL 5B **108**
Wilford Hill Crematorium NG2: West Br 6A **108**

Wilford La. NG2: West Br 3J **107**
    NG11: West Br, Wilf 3J **107**
Wilford Rd. NG2: Nott 7E **6** (6J **95**)
                   (not continuous)
    NG11: Rudd 6J **107**
    NG18: Mans 7C **48**
Wilford St. NG2: Nott 7E **6** (5K **95**)
Wilfred Av. NG2: New B 5F **137**
Wilfrid Gro. NG2: West Br 6B **108**
Wilhallow La. NG16: Westw 2C **64**
Wilkins Gdns. NG11: Clif 1D **114**
Wilkinson Av. NG9: Bee 3A **106**
Wilkinson Cl. NG9: Chil 7G **105**
    NG19: Plea 4A **40**
Wilkinson St. NG7: Basf 6E **84**
    NG8: Basf 6E **84**
Wilkinson Street (Park & Ride) 7F **85**
Wilkinson Street Stop (NET) 7F **85**
Willand Ct. DN22: Retf 1E **22**
Willaston Cl. NG4: Ged 3D **84**
Willbert Rd. NG5: Arn 6J **77**
Willerby Rd. NG5: Woodt 2D **86**
Willersley Dr. NG2: Nott 6K **95**
Willesden Grn. NG16: Nuth 4J **83**
Willetts Ct. NG17: Sut A 2K **51**
Willey La. NG16: Newth, Unde 4E **64**
William Av. NG16: Eastw 4D **72**
William Bailey Ho. NG23: Coll 2H **129**
William Bancroft Bldg. NG3: Nott 3J **7**
William Booth Birthplace Mus. 5K **7** (4B **96**)
William Booth Rd. NG2: Nott 4D **96**
William Cl. NG4: Ged 7A **88**
William Hall Way NG24: Bald 7H **137**
William Lee Bldgs.
    NG7: Nott 1E **106**
William Olds Ct. NG8: Woll 3B **94**
William Rd. NG2: West Br 1B **108**
    NG9: Stap 2C **104**
Williams Dr. NG14: Calv 4C **70**
Williams La. NG24: Bald 7H **137**
Williamson Row *NG5: Bestw* 2H **85**
                     (off Arnold Rd.)
Williamson St. NG19: Mans 3F **47**
Williams Rd. NG9: Chil 6F **105**
Williams St. S81: Lango 1B **12**
William Straw Gdns. S80: Work 4G **21**
William St. NG10: Long E 7B **104**
    NG15: Huck 6G **67**
    NG24: New T 2D **136**
WILLINGHAM BY STOW 3D **145**
Willingham Cl. NG18: Mans 5C **48**
Willis Rd. NG24: New T 4C **136**
Willoughby Av. NG7: Lent 4G **95**
    NG10: Long E 7B **104**
Willoughby Cl. NG7: Nott 1C **106**
    NG18: Mans 1C **54**
Willoughby Ct. NG7: Lent 5G **95**
    NG23: Norw 2J **127**
Willoughby La. NG12: Widm 7K **119**
WILLOUGHBY-ON-THE-WOLDS 6G **143** (3B **148**)
Willoughby Rd. NG2: West Br 3C **108**
Willoughby St. NG7: Lent 5G **95**
    NG9: Bee 2A **106**
Willoughby Way NG22: Wale 5H **27**
WILLOUGHTON 2D **145**
Willow Av. DN10: Mist 2G **11**
    DN22: Rans 2K **13**
    NG4: Carl 7K **87**
    NG9: Stap 3C **104**
    NG10: Long E 7C **104**
    NG15: Huck 2D **74**
    NG17: Kirk A 5J **51**
    NG19: Mans W 1C **48**
    S81: Carl L 5B **12**
Willowbridge Cl. DN22: Retf 4E **22**
Willowbridge Ct. *NG17: Sut A* 1H **51**
                   (off Grosvenor Av.)
Willowbridge La. NG17: Sut A 2G **51**
Willow Brook NG12: Key 1K **119**
Willowbrook Ct. NG2: Nott 7K **95**
Willow Cl. LE12: East L 4K **121**
    NG2: West Br 7G **97**
    NG12: Rad T 6E **98**
    NG14: Bur J 2E **88**
    NG16: Sels 5F **59**
    S80: Work 4F **21**
Willow Cotts. NG8: Bilb 1B **94**
    NG24: New T 5K **133**
Willow Ct. NG2: West Br 4A **108**
    NG16: Unde 4E **64**
Willow Cres. NG4: Ged 5K **87**
    NG4: Lamb 7F **79**
    NG17: Sut A 7H **45**
Willowdene NG12: Cotg 6F **111**
Willow Dr. NG15: Ann 6K **59**
    NG23: Nth M 6J **129**
Willow Gdns. NG17: Sut A 1B **52**
Willow Gro. DN11: Harwo 2C **8**
Willow Hill Cl. NG6: Bulw 1B **84**
Willow Holt DN22: Ord 7E **22**
    NG14: Lowd 5E **80**
    NG23: Sut T 3D **128**
    NG17: Sut A 5D **46**
Willow La. NG4: Ged 5J **87**
    NG13: Lang 7K **113**
Willow M. DN10: Beck 7D **16**

Willow Poole La. LE12: Sut B 7C **120**
Willow Ri. NG10: Sand 4A **104**
Willow Rd. NG2: West Br 5B **108**
    NG4: Carl 7K **87**
    NG7: Lent 7F **95**
    NG13: Bing 4H **101**
    NG24: New B 4F **137**
Willows, The DN10: Eve 6B **10**
    NG8: Bilb 1B **94**
    NG9: Bee 3A **106**
    NG19: New H 3A **40**
    NG20: Mkt W 3D **34**
    NG24: Farnd 7H **133**
    S80: Work 3F **21**
Willow Tree Cl. NG19: Mans W 7F **43**
Willow Vw. NG7: Radf 2G **95**
Willow Wong NG14: Bur J 2E **88**
Willow Wong Cotts. NG14: Bur J 2E **88**
Will Scarlet Cl. NG21: Blid 7H **55**
Willwell Dr. NG2: West Br 6K **107**
Wilmington Gdns. NG5: Arn 1A **86**
Wilmore Cl. NG9: Chil 5J **105**
Wilmore Way NG17: Huth 5D **46**
    NG18: Mans 5D **46**
Wilmot Cl. NG13: Car C 4J **91**
Wilmot La. NG9: Bee .4A **106**
Wilson Av. NG17: Kirk A 6K **51**
Wilson Cl. DN10: Matt T 1G **15**
    NG5: Arn 1E **86**
Wilson Ho. NG24: New T 5C **136**
Wilson Rd. NG16: Eastw 5D **72**
Wilsons Ct. NG11: Rudd 3K **115**
Wilson's La. NG25: Mort 6G **139**
Wilson St. NG16: Pinx 1B **58**
    NG19: Mans 6D **40**
    NG24: New T 7C **134**
Wilton Rd. NG7: Radf 2F **95**
Wilton St. NG6: Basf .3F **85**
Wilton Ter. NG6: Basf 3F **85**
Wiltshire Av. NG16: Jack 6A **64**
Wimbledon Dr. NG16: Nuth 4K **83**
Wimbledon Rd. NG5: Sher 4H **85**
Wimborne Cl. NG2: West Br 4K **107**
Wimbourne Rd. NG7: Radf 2G **95**
Wimpole Rd. NG9: Bram 7J **93**
Winborne Cl. NG19: Mans 4D **46**
Winchester Av. NG9: Bee 1K **105**
Winchester Cl. LE12: East L 3A **122**
    NG18: Mans 7C **48**
    S81: Work 5H **19**
Winchester Ct. NG5: Sher 4B **86**
Winchester Dr. NG19: Mans W 5K **41**
Winchester M. DN11: Birc 2F **9**
Winchester St. NG5: Sher 4K **85**
Winchester Ter. NG5: Sher 4K **85**
Winchilsea Av. NG24: New T 2D **136**
Wincobank Way DE55: Sth N 4A **50**
Windermere Rd. DN11: Harwo 2C **8**
Windermere Cl. NG2: Gam 2G **109**
    NG4: Ged 5J **87**
    NG19: Mans W 6A **42**
    S81: Work 4F **19**
Windermere Gdns. NG10: Long E 7A **104**
Windermere Rd. NG7: H Grn 7H **85**
    NG9: Bram 7J **93**
    NG10: Long E 7A **104**
    NG15: Huck 6F **67**
Windings, The *NG4: Carl* 1G **97**
                  (off Chesterfield St.)
Windles Sq. NG14: Calv 6E **70**
Windmill Av. NG15: Huck 7D **67**
Windmill Cl. NG3: Nott 4K **7** (3C **96**)
    NG11: Goth 7G **115**
    NG22: Kirt 2H **39**
Windmill Ct. NG12: Key 1J **119**
Windmill Gro. NG15: Huck 6G **67**
Windmill Hill NG25: Oxt 1G **71**
Windmill La. NG2: Nott 5K **7** (4B **96**)
    NG3: Nott 5K **7** (4B **96**)
    NG18: Mans 2J **47**
    S80: Work 5H **21**
Windmill Vw. NG2: Nott 4D **96**
Windmill Way NG17: Huth 1E **50**
    NG21: Blid 7H **55**
                    (off Main St.)
Windrush Cl. NG9: Bram 7J **93**
    NG17: Sut A 1J **51**
Windsmoor Rd. NG16: Brins 4B **64**
Windsor Av. NG17: Sut A 7F **45**
    NG24: New T 3B **136**
Windsor Cl. *DN10: Gri H* 3A **16**
                   (off W. Wells La.)
    NG9: Trow 3A **92**
    NG15: Huck 5H **67**
    NG23: Coll 2H **129**
    S81: Carl L 6C **12**
Windsor Ct. DN11: Birc 1E **8**
    NG10: Sand 5A **104**
    NG13: Bing 4D **101**
    NG19: Mans W 4H **41**
Windsor Cres. NG5: Woodt 1D **86**
    NG9: Stap 2D **104**
Windsor Dr. NG20: Mkt W 4C **34**
Windsor Gdns. NG18: Mans 5K **47**
    S81: Carl L 6B **12**
Windsor Ho. NG3: Mapp P 7K **85**

Windsor Rd. DN22: Retf 1C 22
NG16: Sels 4E 58
NG18: Mans 5K 47
NG19: Mans W 6F 43
NG24: New T 2C 136
S81: Carl L 6B 12
S81: Work 5E 18
Windsor Rd. Bungs. DN22: Retf 1C 22
Windsor St. NG9: Bee 3B 106
NG9: Stap 2D 104
Windy Ridge NG20: Mkt W 5E 34
Windyridge DN10: Eve 6B 10
Wing All. NG1: Nott 5G 7 (4A 96)
Wingate Cl. NG8: Bilb 2A 94
Wingbourne Wlk. NG6: Bulw 5J 75
(not continuous)
Wingfield Av. S81: Work 6G 19
Wingfield Dr. NG9: Lent A 7B 94
Wingfield Rd. NG18: Mans 6C 48
Wings Dr. NG15: Huck 2D 74
Winifred Cl. NG11: Wilf 3H 107
Winifred Cres. NG14: Bur J 3E 88
Winifred St. NG15: Huck 7H 67
S80: Rhod 1B 20
WINKBURN 3C 147
Winkburn Rd. NG19: Mans 2F 47
Winnings, The S80: Welb 2C 26
Winrow Gdns. NG6: Basf 4D 84
Winscale Av. NG5: Top V 6C 76
Winscale Gdns. NG5: Top V 6C 76
Winscombe Mt. NG11: Clif 2E 114
Winsford Cl. NG8: Aspl 5C 84
Winstanley Dr. NG24: New T 1H 137
Winster Av. NG4: Carl 6G 87
NG15: Rave 1D 62
Winster Cl. NG9: Lent A 7A 94
Winster Gro. S81: Work 4G 19
Winster Pk. DE7: Ilk 3A 92
Winster Way NG18: Mans 5D 48
Winston Cl. NG3: Mapp 2F 87
NG9: Stap 1D 104
Winston Ct. DN10: Matt T 1F 15
NG24: New T 4B 136
Winston Dr. NG23: Elston 2E 140
Winston Grn. DN10: Matt T 1F 15
Winston Gro. DN22: Retf 1G 23
Winterbank Cl. NG24: Sut A 2G 51
Winterbourne Dr. NG9: Stap 7D 92
Winter Closes NG16: Unde 4D 64
Winterdale Cl. NG24: New T 7G 135
Winterton Cl. NG5: Arn 1C 86
Winterton Ri. NG5: Bestw 7D 76
WINTHORPE 1G 135 (3D 147)
Winthorpe Rd. NG5: Arn 7J 77
NG24: New T 5E 134
(not continuous)
S81: Gate 4D 18
Winthorpe St. NG19: Mans W 4D 46
Wintringham Cres. NG5: Woodt 2D 86
Wisa Ter. NG5: Sher 4A 86
Wisdom Cl. NG24: Bald 7J 137
WISETON 3C 145
Wiseton Rd.
DN10: Clay, Wise 4F 15
DN22: Clay 4F 15
Wishford Av. NG7: Lent 5F 95
Wisley Cl. NG2: West Br 6K 107
Wistow Cl. NG8: Basf 7F 85
Witch La. NG23: Sut T 3D 128
Witham Cl. NG24: New T 6E 134
WITHAM ST HUGHS 2D 147
Withern Rd. NG8: Brox 6A 84
Withorn M. NG18: Mans 3E 46
Witney Cl. NG5: Top V 6A 76
Wiverton Rd. NG7: H Grn 7H 85
NG13: Bing 4F 101
Woburn Av. NG17: Kirk A 6C 52
Woburn Cl. NG12: Edwal 5F 109
Woburn Cft. NG10: Sand 5A 104
Woburn Gro. DN22: Ord 7E 22
Woburn La. NG19: Plea 4B 40
Woburn Pl. NG19: Plea 5C 40
Woburn Ri. NG5: Woodt 2E 86
Woburn Rd. NG19: Plea 5C 40
Wodehouse Av. NG11: Goth 6G 115
Wolds Cl. LE12: Remp 7G 123
Wolds Dr. NG12: Key 1J 119
Wolds La. NG12: Key 3H 119
NG12: Norm W 3K 117
Wolds Ri. NG12: Key 7J 117
Woldsview Ho. NG12: Cotg 6E 110
Wolfit Av. NG24: Bald 5H 137
WOLLATON 5J 93 (1A 148)
Wollaton Av. NG4: Ged 4G 87
Wollaton Ct. NG18: Mans 3D 48
Wollaton Ct. NG6: Bulw 1F 85
Wollaton Cres. NG9: Bee 1K 105
Wollaton Hall 5B 94
Wollaton Hall Dr. NG8: Woll 5E 94
Wollaton Paddocks NG8: Woll 4H 93
Wollaton Pk. Golf Course 5C 94
Wollaton Ri. DN22: Ord 7E 22
NG8: Woll 6K 93
Wollaton Rd. NG8: Radf, Woll 4K 93
NG9: Bee 7K 93
NG17: Kirk A 6C 52

Wollaton St. NG1: Nott 4C 6 (3J 95)
NG15: Huck 6H 67
Wollaton Va. NG8: Woll 4G 93
Wolseley Ct. NG17: Sut A 7K 45
Wolsey Av. NG7: Radf 3G 95
Wolsey Cl. NG25: Sout 6G 131
Wolsey Dr. NG17: Kirk A 4B 52
Wolsey Rd. NG24: New T 5D 134
WOODALL 3A 144
Wood Av. NG10: Sand 3A 104
Woodbank Cl. NG22: Bils 5D 126
Woodbank Dr. NG8: Woll 6J 93
WOODBECK 7G 25 (1C 147)
Woodbeck Ri. DN22: Retf 1E 22
WOODBOROUGH 2G 79 (1B 148)
Woodborough La. NG3: Mapp 3K 77
NG5: Arn 3K 77
Woodborough Rd. NG1: Nott 2F 7 (2K 95)
NG3: Mapp, Nott 2F 7 (7A 86)
NG19: Mans 1E 46
Woodbridge Av. NG11: Clif 6F 107
Woodbridge Cl. DE75: Hea 5A 72
Woodbridge Ct. NG7: H Grn 1G 95
(off St Paul's Av.)
Woodchurch Rd. NG5: Arn 5D 76
Wood Cl. NG19: Mans W 2B 48
Woodcock Ter. NG24: Bald 7H 137
(off Goldstraw La.)
Wooden Beck Hill DN10: Walk 1E 16
Woodend S80: Rhod 7C 18
Woodend Dr. NG15: Rave 2C 62
Woodfield Gdns. S81: Work 6F 19
Woodfield Rd. NG8: Brox 6K 83
NG16: Pinx 7B 50
Woodford Cl. NG5: Top V 5A 76
Woodford Cotts. NG18: Mans 5J 47
(off Littleworth)
Woodford Rd. NG5: Woodt 2D 86
NG15: Huck 7H 67
Woodgate Cl. NG12: Cotg 6D 110
Woodgate Ct. NG7: Radf 4A 6 (3H 95)
Woodgate La. NG12: Cotg 5C 110
Woodgate Rd. LE12: East L 5H 121
Wood Gro. NG14: Calv 5D 70
Woodhall Cl. NG17: Kirk A 4J 51
NG18: Mans 2B 48
Woodhall Gdns. NG18: Mans 2B 48
Woodhall Grn. DN22: Ord 7D 22
Woodhall Rd. NG8: Woll 3C 94
Woodhead Cl. NG21: Edwin 7F 37
Woodhedge Dr. NG3: Nott 7D 86
Woodhill Rd. NG23: Coll 1H 129
WOODHOUSE 7C 18
Woodhouse Cl. S80: Rhod 7C 18
Woodhouse Ct. NG19: Mans W 7J 41
Woodhouse Gdns. NG11: Rudd 2J 115
Woodhouse La. NG17: Skeg 3K 45
S81: Carl L, Hods 4D 12
Woodhouse Pl. DN22: Tuxf 7D 28
Woodhouse Rd. NG18: Mans 2H 47
NG23: Norw, Norw W 1F 127
Woodhouse Sta. Ent. Cen. NG19: Mans W 6H 41
Woodhouse St. NG3: Nott 3K 7 (3C 96)
NG16: Nuth 6J 83
Woodhouse Way NG8: Stre 6J 83
Woodkirk Rd. NG11: Clif 7G 107
Woodland Av. NG6: Bulw 2D 84
NG17: Huth 6C 44
S80: Work 4J 21
Woodland Cl. NG12: Cotg 7E 110
NG12: Rad T 5G 99
NG16: Want 7A 74
NG21: C'tone 5K 43
Woodland Ct. NG9: Bee 2B 106
S81: Work 6G 19
Woodland Cres. NG18: Mans 6B 48
Woodland Dr. NG3: Mapp P 6A 86
NG16: Nuth 3A 84
NG18: Mans 6B 48
NG25: Sout 5G 131
S81: Work 6F 19
Woodland Gro. NG4: Colw 2J 97
NG5: Sher 3A 86
NG9: Chil 4J 105
NG19: Mans W 5J 41
NG20: Mkt W 4D 34
Woodland Ri. NG15: Rave 2C 62
Woodland Rd. NG2: West Br 7C 96
NG19: Mans W 1B 48
WOODLANDS 1A 144
Woodlands DN22: Retf 5F 23
NG24: Wint 1G 135
Woodlands, The NG12: Rad T 5D 98
NG19: Mans 1H 47
NG20: Whal T 4B 26
NG24: New T 1H 137
S81: Blyth 7E 8
Woodlands Cl. NG24: New T 3B 136
Woodlands Farm Cl. NG15: Huck 2D 74
Woodlands Gro. NG15: Huck 2D 74
Woodlands Pk. Homes NG21: Rain 1H 55
Woodlands Vw. DN22: Retf 5G 23
Woodlands Way NG17: Sut A 2G 51
NG20: Mkt W 7B 34
Woodland Vw. NG20: Whal T 4B 26
NG25: Sout 5G 131

Woodland Wlk. NG17: Kirk A 6D 52
Woodland Way NG16: Eastw 4C 72
Wood La. DN10: Beck 7A 16
DN10: Drake 7E 10
DN10: Gri H 1A 16
DN22: Nth W 1H 17
DN22: Stu S 3A 24
NG4: Ged 6K 87
NG15: Huck 6E 66
NG19: Plea 1C 40
NG20: Chu W 1A 34
NG22: Egma 2E 124
Woodlane Gdns. NG3: Nott 7D 86
Woodlark Cl. S81: Gate 6D 18
Woodlark Ho. NG3: Nott 1C 96
Woodleigh NG12: Key 1H 119
Woodleigh Gdns. NG3: Mapp 5E 86
Wood Leys NG3: Nott 1D 96
Woodley Sq. NG6: Bulw 4J 75
Woodley St. NG11: Rudd 3K 115
Wood Link NG6: Bulw 7E 74
Woodlot Cotts. NG17: Kirk A 7J 51
(off Rectory La.)
WOODNOOK
Grantham 2D 149
Nottingham 6E 58
Woodnook Cl. NG16: Sels 6D 58
Woodpecker Cl. NG13: Bing 5G 101
S81: Gate 3E 18
Woodpecker Dr. NG21: Rain 3K 55
Woodroffe Way LE12: East L 1A 122
Woodrow Av. NG8: Bilb 7B 84
Woodruff La. NG22: Bils 6D 126
Woods Ct. NG24: New T 2D 136
Woodsend Cl. NG14: Bur J 3E 88
WOODSETTS 1A 18 (3A 144)
Woodsford Gro. NG11: Clif 7F 107
Woods Hill NG17: Sut A 1J 51
Woodside DN22: Retf 4C 22
NG16: Eastw 4C 72
NG17: Skeg 3J 45
NG22: Farns 5A 57
Woodside Av. NG12: Rad T 5G 99
NG16: Nuth 1G 83
NG18: Mans 7K 47
Woodside Dr. NG5: Arn 6F 77
Woodside Gdns. NG15: Rave 1C 62
Woodside Rd. NG9: Bee, Lent A 7A 94
NG9: Chil 5F 105
NG10: Sand 4A 104
NG12: Rad T 5G 99
NG14: Bur J 4C 88
NG15: Rave 1B 62
S81: Shire 5A 18
Woodside Vw. DN11: Birc 2E 8
Woods La. NG14: Calv 6C 70
NG23: Flin 5A 140
Woodstock Av. NG7: Radf 2F 95
Woodstock Cl. NG24: New T 1F 137
Woodstock Rd. NG9: Toton 6D 104
Woodstock St. NG15: Huck 7H 67
Woodstock St. W. NG15: Huck 6H 67
Woodston Wlk. NG5: Arn 4J 77
Wood St. NG5: Arn 6H 77
NG7: Radf 4B 6 (3H 95)
NG16: Eastw 4D 72
NG18: Mans 3G 47
NG20: Mkt W 3D 34
NG24: New T 1E 136
WOODTHORPE
Chesterfield 1A 146
Loughborough 3A 148
Nottingham 2C 86
Woodthorpe Av. NG5: Woodt 3B 86
Woodthorpe Ct. NG5: Sher 4B 86
Woodthorpe Dr. NG3: Mapp 3A 86
NG5: Woodt 3A 86
Woodthorpe Gdns. NG5: Sher 3A 86
Woodthorpe Grange NG5: Woodt 4B 86
Woodthorpe M. NG5: Woodt 3A 86
Woodthorpe Rd. NG3: Mapp 4C 86
Woodvale NG8: Woll 4G 93
Woodview NG12: Cotg 6F 111
NG12: Edwal 6E 108
Woodview Bus. Cen. NG5: Top V 5C 76
Woodview Ct. NG3: Nott 3F 97
Woodview Gdns. NG19: Mans W 7E 42
Woodville Cl. NG9: Chil 3H 105
Woodville Dr. NG5: Sher 4K 85
Woodville Rd. NG5: Sher 5K 85
Woodward Av. NG9: Chil 7G 105
Woodwards, The NG24: New B 3F 137
Woodward St. NG2: Nott 7A 96
Woodyard La. NG8: Woll 3B 94
(Coachmans Cft.)
NG8: Woll 3B 94
(Tom Blower Cl.)
Woolacombe Cl. NG3: Mapp 2G 87
Woolmer Rd. NG2: Nott 7K 95
Woolpack La. NG1: Nott 5G 7 (4A 96)
Woolpack St. DN22: Retf 3F 23
(off Spital Hill)
Woolsington Cl. NG8: Stre 5J 83
WOOLSTHORPE BY BELVOIR 2D 149
WOOLSTHORPE-BY-COLSTERWORTH 3D 149

Woolsthorpe Cl. NG8: Bilb 2A **94**
Wootton Cl. LE12: East L 2A **122**
  NG8: Bilb 1J **93**
Worcester Av. NG19: Mans W 4J **41**
Worcester Cl. NG14: Lowd 5E **80**
  S81: Work 5H **19**
Worcester Gdns. NG5: Woodt 1B **86**
Worcester M. NG19: Mans W 3J **41**
Worcester Rd. NG5: Woodt 2B **86**
Wordsworth Av. NG15: Huck 7D **66**
  NG17: Sut A 7F **45**
  NG19: Mans W .5H **41**
Wordsworth Dr. NG24: Bald 4G **137**
Wordsworth Rd. NG2: West Br 3B **108**
  NG5: Arn 7F **77**
  NG7: Radf 2F **95**
  NG16: Aws 2B **82**
Workhouse, The
  Southwell 5K **131**
Workhouse La. NG25: Sout 5K **131**
Workshop Rd. DN22: Elk 1F **27**
Works La. NG13: Barns 3F **141**
WORKSOP 3F **21** (1A **146**)
Worksop Golf Course 5J **21**
Worksop Leisure Cen. 7F **19**
Worksop Mnr. S80: Work 4C **20**
Worksop Priory Church 3H **21**
Worksop Rd. NG3: Nott 3C **96**
  NG20: Cuck 3C **32**
  NG22: Bud, Oll .1E **36**
  S81: Blyth 7G **13**
  S81: Woods 1A **18**
  S81: Work 2A **18**
Worksop Station (Rail) 1G **21**
Worksop Town FC
  Windsor Food Service Stadium 1E **20**
Works Row NG13: Barns 3F **141**
Worktown Ind. Units NG24: New T 6E **134**
Worrall Av. NG5: Arn 7H **77**
  NG10: Long E .7D **104**
Worsbrough Cl. NG18: Mans 5F **47**
Worthington Rd. NG24: Bald 6H **137**
Worth St. NG4: Carl 7H **87**
Worthy Row *NG5: Bestw* 2H **85**
                         (off Arnold Rd.)
Wortley Av. NG9: Trow 5C **92**
Wortley Cl. DE7: Ilk 7A **82**
Wortley Hall Cl. NG7: Nott 6D **94**
Worwood Dr. NG2: West Br 5K **107**
Wossock La. LE12: West L 1F **121**
Woulds Fld. NG12: Cotg 7E **110**
Wragby Rd. NG7: Lent 3F **95**
WRANGBROOK 1A **144**
Wray Cl. NG3: Nott 3K **7** (3B **96**)
Wren Ct. S81: Gate .5D **18**
Wren Dr. NG6: Bestw V 3A **76**
Wrenthorpe Va. NG11: Clif 1F **115**
Wright Gdns. DN10: Walk 7J **11**
Wrightson Cl. NG17: Sut A 7A **46**
Wrights Orchard NG12: Key 1H **119**
Wright St. NG4: Neth 1K **97**
  NG24: New T .1E **136**

Wright Wilson St. DN22: Retf 4F **23**
WROOT 1C **145**
Wroughton Ct. NG16: Eastw 4E **72**
Wroxham Dr. NG8: Woll 5J **93**
Wycar Rd. NG22: Bils 7D **126**
Wychwood Dr. NG9: Trow 6C **92**
Wychwood Rd. NG13: Bing 4D **100**
Wycliffe Gro. NG3: Mapp 5B **86**
Wycliffe St. NG7: Basf 6G **85**
Wycombe Cl. NG11: Clif 2E **114**
Wycombe Grange
  NG19: Mans W .7B **42**
Wye Gdns. NG7: Radf 2E **94**
WYFORDBY 3C **149**
Wykeham Rd. NG5: Woodt 2D **86**
Wyke La. NG24: Farnd 7G **133**
Wykes Av. NG4: Ged 5J **87**
WYMESWOLD 3B **148**
Wymeswold Rd.
  LE12: Remp 7G **123**
  NG12: Wys 6J **123**
WYMONDHAM 3D **149**
Wymondham Cl. NG5: Arn 1D **86**
Wynbreck Dr. NG12: Key 7J **117**
Wyndham Ct. NG9: Chil 5G **105**
Wyndham M. NG3: Mapp P 1J **95**
Wyndings, The NG5: Woodt 3C **86**
Wynhill Ct. NG13: Bing 3D **100**
Wynlea Dr. S81: Oldc 6A **8**
Wynndale Dr. NG5: Sher 4H **85**
  NG18: Mans 5C **48**
Wynwood Cl. NG9: Toton 7G **105**
Wynwood Rd. NG9: Toton 7G **105**
Wyrale Dr. NG8: Stre 6K **83**
WYSALL 6J **123** (3B **148**)
Wysall Cl. NG19: Mans 1E **46**
Wysall La. LE12: Remp 7G **123**
  NG11: Bunny .2E **118**
  NG12: Key 4G **119**
  NG12: Widm 7J **119**
Wysall Rd. LE12: Costo 3F **123**
Wyton Cl. NG5: Bestw 2H **85**
Wyvern Cl. NG16: Newth 6E **72**
WYVILLE 3D **149**
Wyville Cl. NG7: Radf 3F **95**

Y

YADDLETHORPE .1D **145**
Yalding Dr. NG8: Woll 4H **93**
Yalding Gdns. NG8: Woll 4H **93**
Yale Ct. NG22: New O 5D **38**
Yard, The NG7: H Grn 1A **6**
Yard Gallery, The 5B **94**
Yarwell Cl. NG3: Nott 1F **97**
Yatesbury Cres. NG8: Stre 7K **83**
Yates Gdns. NG5: Top V 6C **76**
Yellowhammer Dr. S81: Gate 5D **18**
Ye Olde Trip To Jerusalem Inn 7E **6**
                         (off Castle Rd.)
Yeoman Av. NG6: Bestw V 2B **76**

Yeoman Cl. S80: Work 4H **21**
Yeomans Pde. NG4: Carl 1J **97**
Yeovil Ct. NG18: Mans 1C **54**
Yewbarrow Cl. NG2: West Br 4F **109**
Yew Cl. LE12: East L 4K **121**
  NG5: Sher 5A **86**
Yewdale Cl. NG2: West Br 4F **109**
  NG11: Clif 2E **114**
Yews Farm Ct. DN11: Sty 5A **8**
Yew Tree Av. NG5: Sher 6K **85**
  NG17: Kirk A 5K **51**
  NG19: Mans W .7F **43**
Yew Tree Cl. NG12: Rad T 5C **98**
  NG22: New O 3C **38**
Yew Tree Ct. NG5: Sher 6K **85**
  NG9: Bee 3B **106**
Yew Tree Dr. NG17: Huth 1D **50**
Yew Tree La. NG4: Ged 5K **87**
  NG11: Clif 7D **106**
Yew Tree Ri. DN22: Nth L 6C **24**
Yew Tree Rd. DN22: Elk 2F **27**
  NG15: Huck 1H **75**
  NG22: New O 4C **38**
Yew Tree Way NG24: Codd 6J **135**
Yonge Cl. NG12: Rad T 6D **98**
York Av. NG9: Bee 5A **106**
  NG10: Sand 4A **104**
  NG16: Jack 6A **64**
York Cl. LE12: East L 3K **121**
  NG4: Ged 5J **87**
York Dr. NG8: Stre .5J **83**
Yorke Dr. NG24: New T 6E **134**
Yorke St. NG15: Huck 6G **67**
  NG19: Mans W .7H **41**
York Gro. NG17: Kirk A 6D **52**
York Paddock
  NG22: East M 2C **28**
York Pl. S81: Shire .5A **18**
York Rd. DN11: Harwo 2D **8**
  NG10: Long E 7B **104**
York St. NG1: Nott 2F **7** (2K **95**)
  NG4: Neth 1K **97**
  NG17: Sut A 7J **45**
  NG18: Mans 5G **47**
  NG22: East M 2C **28**
York Ter. DN10: Mist 2K **11**
  NG16: Pinx 3A **58**
  NG20: Mkt W 4D **34**
Youldholes La. DN10: Eve . . . . .7A **10** & 1H **15**
Young Cl. NG6: Bulw 2A **84**
Young Cres. NG17: Sut A 1B **52**
Youngs Av. NG24: Bald 7H **137**
Youngs Cl. NG24: Codd 6H **135**
Yvonne Cres. NG4: Carl 1J **97**

Z

Zone, The NG1: Nott 4G **7**
ZOUCH 3A **148**
Zulla Rd. NG3: Mapp P 7K **85**
Zulu Rd. NG7: Basf 5G **85**

HOSPITALS, HOSPICES and selected HEALTHCARE FACILITIES covered by this atlas.

N.B. Where it is not possible to name these facilities on the map,
the reference given is for the road in which they are situated.

ASHFIELD HEALTH VILLAGE 6A **52**
Portland Street
Kirkby-in-Ashfield
NOTTINGHAM
NG17 7AE
Tel: 01623 784723

BASSETLAW HOSPICE 3D **22**
Cedar House
North Road
RETFORD
DN22 7XF
Tel: 01777 863270

BASSETLAW HOSPITAL .7H **19**
Kilton Hill
WORKSOP
S81 0BD
Tel: 01909 500990

BEAUMOND HOUSE COMMUNITY HOSPICE 2C **136**
32 London Road
Newark
NEWARK
NG24 1TW
Tel: 01636 610556

CITY HOSPITAL (NOTTINGHAM UNIVERSITY) 2J **85**
Hucknall Road
NOTTINGHAM
NG5 1PB
Tel: 0115 969 1169

HAYWOOD HOUSE HOSPICE 3J **85**
Nottingham City Hospital
Hucknall Road
NOTTINGHAM
NG5 1PB
Tel: 0115 962 7619

HIGHBURY HOSPITAL .2D **84**
Highbury Road
Bulwell
NOTTINGHAM
NG6 9DR
Tel: 0115 9770000

JOHN EASTWOOD HOSPICE 6C **46**
John Eastwood House
Mansfield Road
SUTTON-IN-ASHFIELD
NG17 4HJ
Tel: 01623 622626

KING'S MILL HOSPITAL
. . . . .5C **46**
Mansfield Road
SUTTON-IN-ASHFIELD
NG17 4JL
Tel: 01623 622515

KING'S TREATMENT CENTRE 6C **46**
Mansfield Road
SUTTON-IN-ASHFIELD
NG17 4JL
Tel: 01623 622515

LINGS BAR HOSPITAL 3G **109**
Beckside
Gamston
NOTTINGHAM
NG2 6PE
Tel: 0115 945 5577

MANSFIELD COMMUNITY HOSPITAL
. . . . .4G **47**
Stockwell Gate
MANSFIELD
NG18 5QJ
Tel: 01623 785050

NEWARK HOSPITAL .3D **136**
Boundary Road
NEWARK
NG24 4DE
Tel: 01636 681681

NHS WALK-IN CENTRE
(CITY LINK) NOTTINGHAM 7H **7** (5A **96**)
City Link
NOTTINGHAM
NG2 4LA
Tel: 0115 883 8500

NHS WALK-IN CENTRE
(UPPER PARLIAMENT STREET) NOTTINGHAM
. . . . .4E **6**
79a Upper Parliament Street
NOTTINGHAM
NG1 6LD
Tel: 0115 883 1960

NOTTINGHAM NHS TREATMENT CENTRE
. . . . .6F **95**
QMC Campus
Lister Road
NOTTINGHAM
NG7 2FT
Tel: 0115 705800

NOTTINGHAMSHIRE HOSPICE 7A **86**
384 Woodborough Road
NOTTINGHAM
NG3 4JF
Tel: 0115 910 1008

NOTTINGHAM WOODTHORPE HOSPITAL
. . . . .2A **86**
748 Mansfield Road
Woodthorpe
NOTTINGHAM
NG5 3FZ
Tel: 0115 9209209

PARK BMI HOSPITAL, THE 3F **69**
Sherwood Lodge Drive
Burntstump Country Park
Arnold
NOTTINGHAM
NG5 8RX
Tel: 0115 9662000

QUEEN'S MEDICAL CENTRE UNIVERSITY HOSPITAL
. . . . .6E **94**
Derby Road
NOTTINGHAM
NG7 2UH
Tel: 0115 9249924

RAMPTON HOSPITAL .7G **25**
Rampton Hospital
RETFORD
DN22 0PD
Tel: 01777 248 321

RETFORD HOSPITAL .2D **22**
North Road
RETFORD
DN22 7XF
Tel: 01777 274 400

The representation on the maps of a road, track or footpath is no evidence of the existence of a right of way.

The Grid on this map is the National Grid taken from Ordnance Survey® mapping with the permission of the
Controller of Her Majesty's Stationery Office.

Copyright of Geographers' A-Z Map Company Ltd.

No reproduction by any method whatsoever of any part of this publication is permitted without the prior consent of
the copyright owners.

SAFETY CAMERA INFORMATION

PocketGPSWorld.com's CamerAlert is a self-contained speed and red light camera warning system for
SatNavs and Android or Apple iOS smartphones/tablets. Visit www.cameralert.co.uk to download.

Safety camera locations are publicised by the Safer Roads Partnership which operates them in order to encourage drivers to comply
with speed limits at these sites. It is the driver's absolute responsibility to be aware of and to adhere to speed limits at all times.

By showing this safety camera information it is the intention of Geographers' A-Z Map Company Ltd., to encourage
safe driving and greater awareness of speed limits and vehicle speed. Data accurate at time of printing.